Th .... Europe ..... o—1500

This major survey of political life in late medieval Europe – the first for more than thirty years – provides a new framework for understanding the developments that shaped this turbulent period. Rather than emphasising crisis, decline, disorder or the birth of the modern state, this account centres on the mixed results of political and governmental growth across the continent. The age of the Hundred Years War, schism and revolt was also a time of rapid growth in jurisdiction, taxation and representation, of spreading literacy and evolving political technique. This mixture of state formation and political convulsion lay at the heart of the 'making of polities'. Offering a full introduction to political events and processes from the fourteenth century to the sixteenth, this book combines a broad, comparative account with discussion of individual regions and states, including eastern and northern Europe alongside the more familiar west and south.

JOHN WATTS is Fellow and Tutor in History, Corpus Christi College, Oxford. His previous publications include *Henry VI and the Politics of Kingship* (1996) and, as co-editor, *Power and Identity in the Middle Ages* (2007).

Cambridge Medieval Textbooks

This is a series of introductions to important topics in medieval history aimed primarily at advanced students and faculty, and is designed to complement the monograph series *Cambridge Studies in Medieval Life and Thought*. It includes both chronological and thematic approaches and addresses both British and European topics.

For a list of titles in the series, see end of book.

THE MAKING OF POLITIES
EUROPE, 1300–1500

JOHN WATTS

Corpus Christi College, Oxford

CAMBRIDGE UNIVERSITY PRESS
Cambridge, New York, Melbourne, Madrid, Cape Town, Singapore,
São Paulo, Delhi

Cambridge University Press
The Edinburgh Building, Cambridge CB2 8RU, UK

Published in the United States of America by Cambridge University Press,
New York

www.cambridge.org
Information on this title: www.cambridge.org/9780521796644

First published 2009

Printed in the United Kingdom at the University Press, Cambridge

A catalogue record for this publication is available from the British Library

Library of Congress Cataloguing in Publication data
Watts, John, 1964–
The making of polities : Europe, 1300-1500 / John Watts.
p. cm. – (Cambridge medieval textbooks)
Includes bibliographical references.
ISBN 978-0-521-79232-5 – ISBN 978-0-521-79664-4 (pbk.)
1. Europe – Politics and government – 476–1492. 2. Political culture –
Europe – History – To 1500. 3. State, The – History – To 1500.
4. Middle Ages. I. Title. II. Series.
JN7.W38 2009
320.9409′023–dc22
2009007358

ISBN 978-0-521-79232-5 hardback
ISBN 978-0-521-79664-4 paperback

For Adrian

CONTENTS

———————— • ————————

MAPS

———— • ————

ACKNOWLEDGEMENTS

———————— • ————————

Three things prompted me to set about researching and writing this book. The first was a desire to know more about the politics of fourteenth- and fifteenth-century Europe and about how they fitted together. In Oxford, pre-modern historians, regardless of specialism, routinely teach large amounts of British and European history, and I wanted to have a sounder grasp of what it was I was discussing in tutorials and lectures. A second factor was a dissatisfaction with what appeared to be the prevailing narratives of the period: not only did they not seem to explain very much about political life, they also set out from questionable assumptions; it seemed to me that the big picture might be understood and reconstructed differently, and what follows is an attempt to do that. One reason why these narratives appeared unconvincing is that they are rather different from the ways in which most British historians think about later medieval English political and constitutional history: I found that, when reading or teaching European material, I was required to accept perspectives that I would instantly reject if I encountered them in an English context. This was my third motivation: to think about the political life of the whole continent with the conceptual tools derived from a couple of decades spent studying English history – and equally, of course, to look again at what I thought I knew of England from a wider, European field of vision. As a historian of English politics, with a research experience that has not strayed much beyond the Public Record Office and the British Library, I have often felt anxious about attempting to write about Europe, even in the synthetic and introductory manner of this book, which draws on the first-hand research of others. (On that note, indeed, I would like, at this moment, to express hearty thanks to those proper continental historians who forbore to say, 'What, *you*?', when I told them of my plans.) But of course, the kingdom of England is a historic political unit readily comparable to others in Europe: it may have been distinctive in certain ways, but it was not at all detached or unique; its affairs, as we all know, overlapped with those of every part of the continent. The English historiography of the later middle ages, for all its insularity, is rich and subtle; it engages with many of the same themes, problems and past realities as the historiographies of continental states; and, given that most European historians are really experts in one place or another, familiarity with the affairs of this small, outward-looking, but highly governed, lowland realm began to seem a reasonable qualification for embarking on a wider comparative study.

That said, I am very conscious of the gap between what I would like to have achieved and what I have been able to do. I have read as much as I can, but I have not read as extensively as I would have wished, especially in foreign languages. My strategy has been to try to read enough continental writing, whether in the original or in translation, to understand how the historians of other countries think, and then to fill the gaps in English or translated material from what I could get at in French, or – on a more restricted scale – in Spanish, Italian and German. No doubt the limitations of my linguistic knowledge have skewed my understanding, and better-informed readers will see how. I am also well aware that the treatment of some parts of Europe is better and thicker than that of other parts. There are some justifications for this. The west, south-west and centre of the continent have long dominated treatments of Europe, so an introductory and interpretative text like this one needs above all to engage with these areas. Equally, it can be argued that the relatively urbanised regions of west-central and Mediterranean Europe experienced a particular kind of political complexity which demands space to discuss and which, for various reasons, it has been a principal aim of this book to untangle. Finally, it is simply much easier to find out about these regions than many others (and easier, in English, to study east-central Europe than Scandinavia, Russia, the Balkans and the Byzantine/Ottoman world). Even so, I regret that I have not managed to learn more about the east and north, and it is clear to me that comparisons between 'west' and 'east', and 'north' and 'south' (acknowledging the crudity of these terms) would teach us a great deal. It would be very good to look in depth at the Holy Roman Empire alongside Byzantium, or to compare the expansion of Muscovy and the Ottomans, or to place a kingdom like Scotland alongside Denmark or Sweden, but this is beyond what I could do. At any rate, I hope that I have learned and considered enough to provide some sort of introduction, and to support a broad interpretation which others, if they find it worthwhile, can challenge, refine or develop.

I have benefited from the help of many people in working on this book. First of all, I am most grateful to those who encouraged me at the outset – to the late Rees Davies, and Barrie Dobson, Michael Jones and Steven Gunn, who read my initial proposal and made valuable comments. To Steve, I owe several other debts: he was kind enough to read and comment on Chapter 4, and has been a consistent source of support and advice throughout my time in Oxford. It was also his idea to start a seminar in later medieval European history, which he and Malcolm Vale and I – latterly with Natalia Nowakowska – have run for the last decade. I have learned a huge amount from my co-conveners, and also from the eighty-plus people who have given papers at our seminar; I have tried not to pinch their ideas, and to credit their published work wherever possible, but I would like to acknowledge here, with his permission, the influence of a brilliant and unpublished overview paper presented by Henry Cohn on 'The Empire in the Fifteenth Century: Decline or Renewal?'. I would also like to thank Jean-Philippe Genet for involving me in a number of collaborative projects and conferences: while I differ in some ways from his interpretation of the developments of this period, I have gained enormously from his conversation and his work, from the connections he has opened up for me with other scholars in France and elsewhere, and from his generosity of spirit. Two other debts are to David Abulafia and David D'Avray. Both of them have kindly supported me through a series of AHRC applications, only the last of which was successful, and I thank them for their help and patience. To the former, I owe even more. I first learned about medieval Europe from David Abulafia in the autumn of 1983, and his inspiration, advice and criticism have been absolutely invaluable throughout the six years I have been working on this book. In a very busy schedule, he has somehow found the time to read the whole typescript, some of it twice, and has given both generous encouragement and face-saving correction: I am extremely grateful. A number of other colleagues and friends have also made time to read sections of the book for me: to Catherine Holmes, Natalia Nowakowska, Jay Sexton, Serena Ferente, Jan Dumolyn, Jenny Wormald, David Rundle and Len Scales, I am very grateful indeed for the trouble they took with my work, often at highly inconvenient moments. Finally, I would like to thank Robert Evans, Jeremy Catto and Craig Taylor for various bits of reading advice, and Magnus Ryan for many inspiring discussions about later medieval Europe: Magnus and I once thought of writing a book like this together, and I'm sure it would have been a more distinguished effort if we had done so. While all these people have tried to save me from error, and I have done what I can to save myself, I naturally take full responsibility for any and all mistakes.

I have also been helped by a number of institutions. I feel that I owe a great debt to the History Faculty at Oxford, and also to my college, Corpus Christi. For one thing, I would never have dared attempt a book like this without the encouragement and stimulation of Oxford colleagues. For another, University, Faculty and College have helped in tangible ways: I am very grateful for two terms' special paid leave from the University, and for a further term from the Faculty; Corpus too has given me two terms' leave, and I am grateful to the President and Fellows, and especially to my excellent History colleague, Jay Sexton, who has held the fort during two lengthy absences. I also thankfully acknowledge a term's paid leave from the AHRC under its (now threatened) 'Research Leave' scheme: I can't imagine when I would have been able to finish the book, had I not received this grant. Finally, I would like to thank Michael Watson, Helen Waterhouse and other members of the History team at Cambridge University Press: apart from the beautiful job they have done with this book, I am grateful for their helpfulness and patience.

And lastly I thank my partner, Adrian. This book has been a great trial for him – not least because he thinks the only interesting thing about the Middle Ages is the Black Death, which gets barely a mention (see p. 14) – but I promise that I won't write another one. Well, not for a bit, anyway.

—— I ——

INTRODUCTION

—— • ——

This book has two main aims. The first is to write about the later middle ages in language other than the prevailing currencies of 'waning', 'transition', 'crisis' and 'disorder'. That, perhaps, is pushing at an open door – few of today's late medievalists really see their period in these terms – but, for reasons to be explored below, they continue to be the terms in which textbook literature is written. The second aim, which may be more ambitious, is to provide an analytical account of the politics of the period, explaining what those politics were about, where they came from, and how they developed over time. When we turn to the fourteenth and fifteenth centuries, we enter a period with no meaningful political and constitutional narrative. True, there is a general sense that the nascent kingdoms of the thirteenth century plunged into 'crisis' in the fourteenth and entered 'recovery' in the later fifteenth. There is also the familiar story of the decline of the universal Church from its zenith under Innocent III to the disaster of 1517. More recently, there is an account of the 'origins of the modern state', in which the expanding fiscality of our period plays a central role. And there is Bernard Guenée's perceptive summary, which proposes that the development of royal bureaucracies was thwarted from the 1340s onwards by war, chivalry and democracy, to be resumed in the later fifteenth century when these volatile forces had burned themselves out.[1] But these narratives do not explain or even,

[1] B. Guenée, *States and Rulers in Later Medieval Europe*, trans. J. Vale (Oxford, 1985), pp. 207–8.

for the most part, deal with the general course of politics across the continent. 'Crisis' and 'recovery' are too big and vague to account for what was going on: these terms have become substitutes for analysis rather than ways of framing it. The history of the Church benefits from a rich historiography, but the tendency to treat it as a specific kind of institution, in dialectical tension with 'the state', has placed unnecessary limits on what it can tell us about politics in general. Narratives of state growth, meanwhile, have little to say about the course of events; they tend to neglect the frequent and dramatic collapse of central authority in this period, to give undue solidity to the pretentious, diverse and halting efforts of rulers, to understate the complexity of the world in which institutions operated, and to ignore the less state-like power structures that also held sway across Europe. Even Guenée's rather brilliant sketch shares some of these flaws, and its three phases are set out in little more than a page.

Against this background, the politics of the continent remain opaque: they were 'a mass of undignified petty conflicts' according to one historian.[2] Another writes perceptively that 'the actors in this European drama were seldom in possession of the plot', indeed that 'there was not one plot but many', but although select details of the plot(s) are duly recounted in these and other works, their inner dynamics go largely unexplored.[3] To Jacques Heers, writing vividly about the political life of medieval Italian cities, it almost seemed that a political history could not be written. His words could stand just as well for the politics of later medieval Europe as a whole:

To establish a simple chronology…would seem to be a terribly tedious and futile exercise. To disentangle the astonishing confusion, the skein of multiple relationships, bound together with flexibility and striking fragility, of alliances between political groups and individuals, between towns or even between sovereign powers would be a monumental enterprise. The analyst moved at the outset by the noblest of motives feels himself in the long run seized by an irresistible desire to abridge and simplify…Every remotely clear presentation of events, ordered, selected, tied to well-defined causes, provoked by a logical chain of events, thus seems to be in some degree an artificial construction.[4]

---

[2] G. Holmes, *Europe: Hierarchy and Revolt, 1320–1450* (London, 1975), p. 12.
[3] D. Hay, *Europe in the Fourteenth and Fifteenth Centuries*, 2nd edn (Harlow, 1989), pp. 25–6.
[4] J. Heers, *Parties and Political Life in the Medieval West*, trans. D. Nicholas (Amsterdam, 1977), pp. 1–2.

Small wonder, thought Heers, that historians had taken refuge in recounting the more manageable history of institutions, even if this made it impossible 'to grasp the realities of political life from the social point of view'. Like many of the writers of his time, and since, Heers thought that the answers might lie in prosopography – detailed collective biography of the political actors of the age and their myriad interconnections. This book proposes another approach, one that notes the consonances and shared patterns – the structures – of European political life and aims to trace their interactions and developments. Let us begin with some examples of structured political behaviour.

On 12 July 1469, the duke of Clarence, the archbishop of York and the earl of Warwick rose up against the government of King Edward IV of England (1461–83), indicating in an open letter that, for 'the honour and profit of our said sovereign lord and the common weal of all this his realm', they proposed to join together with other lords to put before the king a series of protests and petitions delivered to them by his 'true subjects of divers parts of this his realm of England'.[5] These protests recited the way in which certain earlier kings had been drawn away from the counsel of great lords by men interested only in 'singular lucre and enriching of themselves and their blood'. By this means, these kings had been impoverished and so they had gone on to lay unaccustomed and inordinate taxes on the people, and especially on the enemies of these 'seducious persons' about them; they had allowed these men to suspend the operation of law and justice; and they had favoured their friends and supporters in disputes. As a result, the realm had been reduced to disorder, division and poverty. It now appeared that Edward IV also was surrounded by a group of such persons, who had robbed the king of his lands, forced him to change the coinage, to impose inordinate taxes and levy forced loans that went unpaid, to misspend papal taxation, to suspend the execution of his laws against their clients, and to estrange the true lords of his blood from his council. Having all this in mind, the 'true and faithful subjects and commons of this land, for the great weal and surety of the king our sovereign lord and the common weal of the land' asked for these men to be punished, and for the king to resume his lost estates by the

---

[5] Printed in J. O. Halliwell, ed., *A Chronicle of the First Thirteen Years of King Edward the Fourth by John Warkworth D.D.*, Camden Society, old series, 10 (London, 1839), pp. 46–51 (spelling modernised).

advice of the lords spiritual and temporal, so as to release his people from unnecessary taxation, as he had promised in his last parliament.

Five years earlier, on 28 September 1464, the marquis of Villena, the archbishop of Toledo, the admiral of Castile and other lords had similarly risen up against the government of King Henry IV of Castile (1454–74), expressing their concern for 'the *cosa pública* [the republic, or public business] of your realms and lordships' and claiming to speak 'with the voice and in the name of the three estates'.[6] In a long letter, these lords recited the good advice the king had been given by the magnates at the beginning of his reign, urging him to rule himself and his people according to law and custom and in the manner of his glorious ancestors, as he was obliged to do. The king, they alleged, had not taken this advice, but had instead surrounded himself with enemies of the Catholic faith and men of suspect faith, whom he had heavily rewarded and whose counsel he had preferred to that of the great lords. As a result, Church and people had been burdened with taxes and extortions. Papal crusade taxation had been misapplied and the coinage had been changed and devalued. Because the law only worked in favour of the men around the king, his subjects did not dare to sue in his court of audience and large parts of the realm were destroyed for lack of justice. The king would not receive petitions put up to him for his own good, but responded to them violently, as if they were from his enemies. And there was plenty more to be said when the king was in a mood to listen to his people's complaints, but for now the important thing was to strike at the root cause of all these problems: 'the oppression of your royal person by the power of the count of Ledesma, so that your lordship is unable to act as natural reason teaches you'. Stressing their loyalty to the king, their concern for his honour and his soul, and their desire to respond to the grievances of the people, the confederates asked for Ledesma and his '*parciales*' (supporters) to be taken and imprisoned, and for the king to summon his *Cortes* to ordain for the good government of his realms.

When historians have discussed these two rather similar episodes, they have done so in relation to the national political situation in each case: the emerging tensions between Warwick the Kingmaker and the Yorkist usurper, on the one hand, and the factional discords that surrounded the 'impotent' King Henry IV, on the other. They have

---

[6] *Memorias de Don Enrique IV de Castilla*, ed. F. Fita and A. Bonilla, Real Academia de la Historia (Madrid, 1913), vol. II, pp. 328ff.

also tended to regard the public claims of these protesters as spurious, and have assigned them personal motives – in fact, essentially the *same* personal motives: both Warwick and Villena had formerly been the close advisers and allies of their respective kings; once each reign was underway, however, they found themselves displaced by rising men, and they are supposed to have resented the fact. Certain patterns have been noted – after all, what Warwick was doing in 1469, Richard of York had done in 1450, while the manoeuvres of Villena and his allies more or less duplicated the words and actions of those noble leagues that had dogged the rule of John II of Castile earlier in the century – but this perception has generally been taken to undermine the credibility of these protests still further, even when it is recognised that in mid-fifteenth-century England or Castile there was much to protest about. These historiographical parallels are rather interesting, and we shall return to them, but first of all there is a *historical* parallel to deal with, and one that has been largely missed. As is plain from the extracts quoted, the formats of these two rebellions were strikingly similar. In both cases, magnates claimed to act for the people – and not only for the people, but for the people as a political community: the 'commons' or 'three estates'. These magnates produced, or circulated, vernacular manifestoes; and they made a roughly similar litany of protests about the king's wicked advisers, who had come up from nothing, and were now distorting, by their self-interested control of the royal person, the judicial, conciliar and fiscal transactions of the polity. Almost exactly the same complaints were made against Louis XI by the duke of Burgundy and the other princes of the so-called League of the '*Bien Public*' in 1465, and they too were made in the same way – with public letters written in the vernacular, professions of loyalty and calls for a meeting of the traditional representative assembly, the 'Estates General'. And meanwhile in Florence, the leading families who rebelled against the Medici in 1466 also advertised their claims in public letters, which called for the city to be ruled by its traditional magistrates and not by the will of a few men whose avarice had brought ruination through excessive taxes, and whose corruptions had produced disorder by destroying confidence in the laws.

It is clear, then, that there were certain common forms for the expression of political opposition in the 1460s, and this fact should raise questions about the rather isolated way in which these episodes have been treated. There were certainly variations in the rhetoric from country to country: English evil councillors were not usually regarded as religious deviants, for instance, whereas Spanish ones were routinely linked with Jews and Muslims. There are also many local differences in the causation of these various risings, though it is striking that the causes emphasised by historians – personal relationships within the court, and the shaping of these by a competition for patronage and influence – should be so similar. All the same, the structural parallels between the demonstrations of the 1460s are surely important, and must deserve more attention. Historians have tended to dismiss the historical significance of these common patterns, seeing them, for example, as the conventional repertoires of 'overmighty' behaviour, or as the product of direct connections – such that Warwick, for example, may have adopted the postures of 1469 as a result of his frequent visits to France in the period of the '*Guerre du Bien Public*'. Priority has been given to tracing the specific causes and motivations behind these events, as if those are the unique and significant element, while the modalities of political action are comparatively timeless and incidental. We might reasonably wonder, however, if the real situation is the reverse – that there are always interpersonal and competitive tensions driving political events, but that what changes, and thus requires discussion, are the structures and processes through which those tensions are formed and expressed. Any political conflict can be explained in the way that later medieval political conflicts are customarily explained, but the structuring of conflict manifestly changes across time and space, its changing forms are rarely unique, and such common patterns as exist in these changes must be worth measuring. A look at an earlier set of late medieval confrontations may help to illustrate this point.

On the death of the powerful King Erik Menved of Denmark (1286–1319), the magnates of his realm, meeting as the *Danehof*, or high court of the realm, demanded a thirty-seven-point charter, or *håndfaestning*, from his brother Christopher, as the price for his coronation.[7] Beginning with the Church, and moving on to knights, merchants, burgesses and finally to the people and the general concerns of the realm, this charter of January 1320 bestowed liberties that are readily familiar from such documents as *Magna Carta* (1215) and the Provisions of Oxford and Westminster (1258–9), Philip IV's reforming *ordonnance* of 1303, and the charters granted in response

---

[7] Printed in *Diplomatarium Danicum 2.raekke, 8.bind, 1318–1322*, ed. A. Afzelius *et al.* (Copenhagen, 1953), no. 176.

to the French Leagues of 1314–15. As a national statement of rights, it also had much in common with the contemporary 'charter of liberties' granted by Magnus Eriksson of Sweden in 1319 and, less closely, with the Scottish Declaration of Arbroath (1320). The Danish charter addressed particular problems typical of the early fourteenth century, so that, for example, clause 12 provided that knights could not be compelled to serve outside the realm, a concession which was also made by the incoming king of Bohemia in 1310 and sought from Edward I of England in 1297. Clause 13 declared that the king should not begin wars without the counsel and consent of the prelates and more powerful men of the realm, just as in the Aragonese *Privilegio General* of 1283, and the English 'Ordinances' of 1311. Clause 20 forbade interference in, or impositions on, the free passage of merchandise 'unless by reasonable cause, and urgent necessity, the king, by common consent of the better sort, has thought to make such restrictions'. Here too were echoes of the English crisis of 1297, couched in the new pan-European language of communal taxation. The provision of clause 28 that people should have justice first in their own district (or '*haerraeth*') and not immediately in the king's court, and that of clause 35, that people should be tried according to the custom of their land ('*terra*'), closely parallel the terms of the *ordonnance* given by Louis X of France to the inhabitants of the *bailliage* of Amiens in 1315.[8] This ordered that men should be tried first in their own local jurisdictions ('*chastellenies*'), and only cited before the king's high court of *Parlement* on appeal; almost every clause of the document upheld local custom and local justice, and limited the grounds on which royal judges could hear cases. Finally, where Christopher II was made to swear to uphold in all things the laws of King Valdemar, who had reigned eighty years before, Philip IV and his son Louis X swore to preserve liberties, franchises and customs as they had been in the time of St Louis, while Edward I of England was obliged to reissue *Magna Carta*, though it was recognised, with varying degrees of explicitness, that these kings may need to amend their laws with due consultation and consent.[9]

[8] *Les ordonnances des rois de France de troisième race*, ed. E. de Laurière *et al.*, 22 vols. (Paris, 1723–1849), vol. I, pp. 562–3.
[9] *Ordonnances*, vol. I, pp. 354, 562; *English Historical Documents*, vol. III, ed. H. Rothwell (London, 1969), pp. 485–6.

If we compare these confrontations from the early fourteenth century with those of the 1460s, a series of meaningful contrasts emerge. There is a change, first of all, in the languages used. The charters and ordinances of the earlier period were written mainly in a Latin informed substantially by the vocabulary of Roman and canon law; the documents of the later period were written in the vernacular, informed by the practice of royal chanceries, and shaped by the common political, religious and ethical language of their times. There is a continuity in the principle of action for the realm in these episodes, but changes in the way that realm is represented. Notwithstanding some repeated terminology – 'estates', 'common(s)' – the realm is seen less, by the 1460s, as a set of particular groups, constituted by their individual liberties and privileges, and more as a socially diverse, but nationally united, community, with a set of common concerns, ventilated by and before a wide public. There are changes, moreover, in the points at issue. By the 1460s, there is less concern with the defence of rights and liberties against intrusive royal jurisdiction, or with the definition of what the king and his officers should or should not be allowed to do. Instead, there is more of a sense that the king's government is accepted, indeed, that the wellbeing of Church and people depend on it at every point and in every detail, and that the problems requiring attention concern the perversion of this government, its improper exclusiveness, and its failure to deliver what is expected, not its intrusions into the lives of subjects. There are changes, finally, in the nature and affiliations of these documents themselves: not, by the 1460s, charters and ordinances, but petitions and manifestoes, seeking to say something public, and on behalf of the public. Much as legislation of some kind was surely anticipated from the assemblies envisaged by the rebels in Castile and France, if not also in England, their immediate aim was to counsel the king, rather than to make law: to wield a kind of common, or national, opinion, rather than to advance a set of sectional interests.

It is hard to deny that this evidence points to some significant developments over the hundred-and-fifty-year period that separates the two sets of events. A substantial degree of political integration has taken place, as well as what appears to be a politicisation of social and legal relationships: that is, a more self-conscious sense on the part of status groups that they have responsibilities to the political whole, together with a reconsideration of their roles in relation to that whole and in relation to its political interests and requirements. It is not that the wholeness of society went unrecognised in the early fourteenth century – references to the good old laws of long-dead kings, to all the realm and to the common consent of the better sort make that plain – but it is clear that, earlier on, the liberties of estates and districts were a more pressing and real concern than the common good, whatever that might have been. By the 1460s, on the other hand, the tentacles of central government were everywhere, and participation in high politics had spread, in one way or another, very widely across most European societies. The political community was thus, in every country, a much more extensive, complex and ever-present phenomenon, and politicians of all kinds were forced to engage with it in real, as well as verbal, terms. These, then, are changes not just in the vocabulary of politics, but also in its formats, its aims, its nature. What we are seeing here is evidence of structural change, and structural change in what historians have commonly seen as a creative and positive direction – towards the making of coherent and extensive polities, or political societies. A history which took more account of the importance of political structures and of the presence of political evolution within our period would thus capture something about the political life of Europe in the later middle ages. More than this, it would be a new departure in the historiography, at least at the level of the continent as a whole.

HISTORIOGRAPHY

Although a great deal of specialised writing has been published in the last few decades, together with the multi-volume *New Cambridge Medieval History* (henceforth *NCMH*) and a number of important country-level studies, the main introductory surveys of later medieval politics available to English readers are now about thirty or forty years old. Daniel Waley's *Later Medieval Europe from St Louis to Luther* was first published in 1964. Denys Hay's *Europe in the Fourteenth and Fifteenth Centuries* followed in 1966. George Holmes' book *Europe: Hierarchy and Revolt, 1320–1450* came along in 1975, and, while *States and Rulers in Later Medieval Europe*, by Bernard Guenée, came out in English as recently as 1985, it was a translation of a work first published in France in 1971. These books have been revised and republished, in some cases several times, but, inevitably, and for all their virtues, they have not altogether escaped the state of research and understanding that prevailed when they were created. The volumes of the *NCMH*, on the other hand, contain many fundamental challenges to older views, as well as a wealth of important new material, but as a series of multi-authored works, they do not offer a new synthesis, and the editors' introductions typically take a cautious line on the big picture of each century. A few new survey works have emerged, such as David Nicholas' *Transformation of Medieval Europe, 1300–1600* (1999), or Robin W. Winks and Lee Palmer-Wandel's *Europe in a Wider World, 1350–1650* (2003), but their novelty principally lies in their placing of the fourteenth and fifteenth centuries alongside the six-teenth; they do not offer reinterpretations of politics in the later middle ages. But a reinterpretation is precisely what is needed. Before we go any further, it will be helpful to explore how the historiography of this period has developed, and to consider what may be wrong with some of its guiding assumptions.

Perhaps the most fundamental influences on our understanding of the fourteenth and fifteenth centuries lie in the very term, 'later middle ages', and the narratives of 'decline' and 'transition' with which it is associated. The invention of the middle ages, and the subdivision of that epoch into three broad phases – 'early', 'high' and 'late' – have had an enduring effect on the way in which our period has been approached. A series of institutions and cultural forms that grew or flourished between the tenth and thirteenth centuries have been regarded as characteristic of medieval civilisation – above all, the Latin Church, united under papal headship and the Holy Roman Empire of the Salians and Hohenstaufen; but also the crusade and chivalry, 'scholasticism' and Roman and canon law, Gothic art and architecture, 'feudalism', monasteries and communes. While the coming of these things is often regarded as sudden and revolutionary, their disintegration in the later middle ages was slow, and it has formed one of the twin poles of later medieval historiography. 'The Decline of Empire and Papacy' was the title of the penultimate volume of the pre-war series of the *Cambridge Medieval History*; *The Waning of the Middle Ages* was the title chosen for the first English translation of Johan Huizinga's famous study of fourteenth- and fifteenth-century culture. No modern work is quite so infused with an atmosphere of decay, but the sense of old rules not working, or of old ways becoming corrupted, remains widespread. In part, this is because of the mixed fortunes enjoyed by what is supposed to have been the main agency and beneficiary of papal and imperial decline: the nation state. The juridical kingdoms, which had seemed so powerful and promising at the end of the thirteenth century, succumbed to war and internal division over the course of the next few decades, while the Empire sank into anarchy and the contests over Italy grew ever more bitter and complex. As a result, and taking their cue from the plangent criticisms of contemporary observers, many political historians have seen the period as a time of declining order, expanding warfare and sharply increasing violence. Besides the decadence and corruption of the old order, therefore, disorder and chaos are prominent motifs in the representation of the later middle ages. But it is not only as what R. W. Southern called 'the age of unrest' and David Nicholas calls 'the old age of a civilisation' that the fourteenth and fifteenth centuries are known.[10] As 'the end of the middle ages', they are also on the cusp of 'modernity', and the second pole in later medieval historiography is a search for the origins of the new.[11] For many historians, therefore, this period has been one of 'transition', though the 'transition' in question takes on various forms. For some, like George Holmes, it is the 'Renaissance' that provides the key motif.[12] More commonly, especially in British works, transition has a political focus: the long-delayed emergence of new monarchies and nation states, or of national churches in the age of Hus and Luther. In a lot of continental writing, on the other hand, the underlying transition is a socioeconomic one, from 'feudalism', in a Marxian sense, to 'capitalism': this slow revolution, as we shall see, is used both to explain the convulsions of later medieval polities and to foreshadow the emergence of stronger states in the later fifteenth century.

These grand narratives of 'decline' and 'transition' raise many problems for the political historian. For one thing, very few of them explore, or even trace, the processes of change that they purport to identify. In W. K. Ferguson's 1962 study of *Europe in Transition*, for example, the rise of commerce and the money economy, coupled with the decline of the manor, is supposed to have disrupted the old order, facilitating the rise of the centralised state and undermining the particularist tendencies of nobility and clergy. It is an attractive and

---

[10] R. W. Southern, *Western Society and the Church in the Middle Ages* (London, 1970), ch. 2.II; D. Nicholas, *The Evolution of the Medieval World, 312–1500* (London, 1992).

[11] Quotations from J. L. Watts, ed., *The End of the Middle Ages?* (Stroud, 1998) and D. Nicholas, *The Transformation of Europe, 1300–1600* (London, 1999), p. 1.

[12] Holmes, *Hierarchy and Revolt*, 11: 'Very roughly, this book is about the transition from "medieval" to "Renaissance" Europe'.

comprehensible thesis, if not one acceptable to modern research, but it soon emerges that many of the alleged changes are highly localised, and that economic and political developments are generally out of phase with each other. The commercial advances in Italy, Flanders and northern Germany did not, for example, produce centralised states in those areas; and, while the later Capetian kingdom looks like a classic product of thirteenth-century political economy, there is nothing in this work to explain its double disintegration in the succeeding two centuries, and no real reason given for its subsequent revival. In the preface, it is conceded that the period's transitional character is really established not by any movement or development, but by 'the co-existence of medieval and modern elements in a constant state of flux' – an admission that the book offers no real account of change.[13]

Ferguson's book is typical in this respect. Many textbooks make use of a period of 'crisis' to explain the gap between the strong states of the thirteenth century and those of the later fifteenth, but this does not rescue them from selectiveness in the choice of examples, nor does it challenge the tendency for 'transition' accounts to substitute symbolic description for overall explanation. Survey literature typically moves from a thirteenth century of 'expansion and hegemony' captured in 'the triumph of the French monarchy'; through a fourteenth century of war, famine and plague, in which 'French defeats and chivalric ideals', 'Fragmentation in Germany' and 'a Europe of violence' set the tone; to a fifteenth century framed by cultural flowerings in Italy and Burgundy, 'recovery' in France, new monarchy in England and unification in Spain.[14] Textbooks have to simplify, of course, but should the politics of the continent really be captured in this way? 'Decline' makes only a superficial kind of sense for the western Church, and less than that, perhaps, for the Empire. Meanwhile, if 'crisis' and 'recovery' roughly describe what happened to the Valois kingdom of France, or – more roughly still – capture the progress of the crown of Castile from the deposition and death of Alfonso X in 1284 to the successes of Ferdinand and Isabella two centuries later, these narratives do not fit very well with the trajectories of many other

---

[13] W. K. Ferguson, *Europe in Transition, 1300–1520* (London, 1962), vii.

[14] Chapter headings and subheadings taken from D. Waley and P. Denley, *Later Medieval Europe, 1250–1550*, 3rd edn (London, 2001) and J. Le Goff, *The Birth of Europe*, trans. J. Lloyd (Oxford, 2005).

European polities, whether these are kingdoms, such as England, Poland and Hungary, principalities like Brittany, Flanders or Saxony, or city states like Florence, Nuremberg or Novgorod. The obvious survival and adaptation of such older institutions as Roman law and feudal tenure, or crusading, or monasteries, or even the Empire and Papacy, and the flourishing of institutions which have only a limited existence in most parts of Europe outside our period – such as 'leagues' and representative 'estates' – suggest that 'decline' and 'rebirth', or 'medievalism' and 'modernity', are not very helpful terms for approaching this period. Connecting the fourteenth and fifteenth centuries to the better-known eras either side of them must remain an important aim for historians of this period, but there may be better ways of achieving it.

THREE GRAND NARRATIVES

The stability of these old motifs of decline and transition is in some ways surprising, since three relatively complex and ambitious accounts of the dynamics of the later middle ages have been produced in the last half-century or so. While none of these accounts is primarily political in nature, they all offer some explanation of the course of politics and they locate the period within a longer account of historical development. Given their structural and sometimes rigorous quality, these three grand narratives might have been expected to offer a corrective to older approaches, but the tendency instead has been for them to be assimilated to the older, vaguer interpretations we have just been considering. There are many points at which the three accounts overlap and reinforce each other, but it might make sense to take them in turn, considering the strengths and weaknesses of each, before moving to the reasons for their failure to disturb the traditional picture.

Social and economic crisis

The first narrative centres on the perception that the later middle ages witnessed a profound social and economic crisis. In some accounts, this is a crisis of feudalism – the breakdown of a sociopolitical order essentially based on the extraction of peasant surpluses by lay and clerical lords, and its gradual replacement (at least, in the West) by economic and social conditions more congenial to capitalism. In other accounts, it is a less precisely focused set of convulsions sparked off by a mixture of overpopulation, warfare, climatic change and epidemic disease. The famines which struck most of the northern half of Europe between 1315 and 1322 are said to have ushered in a period of economic recession and stagnation, which was worsened and prolonged by the fiscal burdens, monetary instability and bankruptcies of the 1320s, 1330s and 1340s. The impact of the Black Death (1347–52) and succeeding plagues on this weakened population and its wobbling economy is supposed to have produced another century of depression, much of it marked by the additionally damaging effects of warfare, taxation and bullion shortage. Although there were signs of economic recovery in individual sectors or places at various points in this period, it was generally short-lived or localised, and a substantial return to prosperity is only discernible in the second half of the fifteenth century.

This mixture of transition and depression is taken to have had both general and specific relevance for the politics of the period. For Marxist historians like Robert Brenner, Rodney Hilton and Guy Bois, this is axiomatic – for them, the movement of the economy is driven by the social and political order, whatever that order owes in turn to prevailing modes of production – but the main foundations for a socioeconomic approach to later medieval politics were laid by a group of post-war French historians with looser and more variable ideological affiliations: Edouard Perroy, Robert Boutruche, Jacques Heers, Michel Mollat and Philippe Wolff, among others.[15] Work in this tradition proposes that the hardships of fourteenth-century society created a general atmosphere of dislocation that underlay the revolts, feuds and wars of the period. More specifically, socioeconomic conditions provoked the popular uprisings and pogroms that broke out in both urban and rural areas in and around the 1320s, 1350s and 1380s, while, at the same time, a *crise nobiliaire*, resulting from falling seigneurial incomes, is supposed to have stimulated aristocratic

[15] The key works are R. Brenner, 'Agrarian Class Structure and Economic Development in Pre-Industrial Europe', *Past and Present*, 70 (Feb. 1976) (and see also *The Brenner Debate*, ed. T. H. Aston and C. H. E. Philpin (Cambridge, 1985)); R. Hilton, *Bond Men Made Free* (London, 1973); G. Bois, *The Crisis of Feudalism* (Cambridge, 1984); E. Perroy, 'Les crises du XIVe siècle', *Annales ESC*, 4 (1949), 167–82; R. Boutruche, *La crise d'une société* (Paris, 1947); J. Heers, *L'occident aux XIVe et XVe siècles: aspects économiques et sociaux* (Paris, 1963); M. Mollat and P. Wolff, *The Popular Revolutions of the Late Middle Ages* (London, 1973).

violence and troublemaking across the continent. In the West, impoverished nobles are said to have pushed their rulers into war, in order to benefit from 'budgets of noble assistance' – whether these came in the form of military wages paid to themselves as captains, or as the right to control the collection and spending of royal taxes raised from the local population.[16] The resulting dependence of the nobility on royal wages, offices and pensions is then supposed to have underlain the various civil wars and conflicts of the period, especially those of the fifteenth century: the 'distribution of patronage', to use the characteristic phrase of English historiography, would have been a matter of acute economic and social significance to landowners who were no longer able to maintain themselves from landed incomes alone; this, it has been suggested, was the underlying reality behind the political struggles of 'ins' and 'outs' that dominated the politics of emerging states. Meanwhile, in areas where central power was less effective, notably in east-central Europe, but also in Spain, lords succeeded in limiting the freedoms of the peasantry, imposing a 'second serfdom' and vigorously defending their control of peasant surpluses from royal intrusions. At the same time, outright 'land–wars' were fought by the likes of *Raubritter* (robber-knights) and *routiers* (roving mercenaries), who sought to replace their lost manorial revenues by the more old-fashioned arts of plunder. In these ways, then, a dramatic series of demographic, economic and social disturbances has been taken to explain much about the culture and the politics of the later middle ages, and the economy has thus been allotted a central role in most, if not quite all, the textbook literature mentioned above.

There are, however, big problems with interpretations of politics which invoke this generalised socioeconomic context. First of all, there is, and always has been, substantial disagreement among social and economic historians about what was actually going on in this period. As Perroy himself pointed out in 1949, 'crisis' is an ambiguous word – it can mean turning point, as well as depression, and historians have disagreed profoundly about the condition of the later medieval economy, let alone the nature of its relationship with social and political life.[17] While there is a rough consensus on stagnation in the first half of the fourteenth century and slump in the mid-fifteenth,

---

[16] The phrase is Philippe Contamine's: 'The French Nobility and the War', in K. Fowler, ed., *The Hundred Years War* (London, 1971), 135–62, p. 151.

[17] Perroy, 'Crises', p. 168.

assessments of the later fourteenth and later fifteenth centuries vary widely, with some emphasising vibrancy and expansion (notably in manufacturing), others recession and decline. It may seem obvious that the generally falling population of the later fourteenth and early fifteenth centuries produced contraction in the economy, but, of course, the same falling population produced a more positive balance of population and resources, created new markets for goods, and, as Marxist historians especially have emphasised, coincided with some sharply divergent socioeconomic developments in East and West. Even some of the most basic assumptions of the historiography have come to be questioned, with one leading historian challenging the once-universal belief that Europe had reached the limit of sustainable population in 1300, while another suggests that the population of France in 1328 was perhaps only half what we used to think it was.[18] At the same time, French and German historians are increasingly sceptical about the supposed impoverishment of the later medieval nobility: while strictly agrarian revenues may have declined, these families had always drawn income from a range of resources – mills, markets, tolls, tallages, tithes, jurisdiction – and they went on doing so; certainly, they could benefit from new governmental media, such as royal taxation, but they had benefited from older ones as well.[19] Not surprisingly, the notion of 'crisis' is itself under attack: the late Stephan Epstein refashioned it as an 'integration crisis' – a process of adjustment in the commercial frameworks of the continent – but many Italian historians have abandoned the term altogether, preferring to talk of 'reconversion' or 'transformation'.[20] It is, of course, difficult for economic historians working from fragmentary and localised data to distinguish cyclical shocks from long-term trends, and it is difficult to decide where to place emphasis when every demographic or social change produces a mixture of positive and negative results. If a

---

[18] S. R. Epstein, *Freedom and Growth. The Rise of States and Markets in Europe, 1300–1750* (London, 2000), pp. 38, 41–6; J. Goldsmith, 'The Crisis of the Late Middle Ages: The Case of France', *French History*, 9 (1995), 417–50.

[19] See, for instance, P. Charbonnier, 'La crise de la seigneurie à la fin du moyen-âge, vue de l'autre France', in *Seigneurs et seigneuries au moyen-âge*, Actes du 117e Congrès Nationale des Sociétés Savantes (Paris, 1995), 99–110; T. Scott, *Society and Economy in Germany, 1300–1600* (Basingstoke, 2002), pp. 153–66.

[20] Epstein, *Freedom and Growth*, ch. 3; F. Franceschi, 'The Economy: Work and Wealth', in J. M. Najemy, ed., *Italy in the Age of the Renaissance* (Oxford, 2004), ch. 6, p. 125.

measure of consensus was once possible, or if there were once manageable debates between those who emphasised the depressed aspects of the economy and those who focused on areas of growth, the picture is now so complicated as to defy generalisation. Under these circumstances, the claims of the economy to serve as a central means of explaining and interpreting medieval political life seem weak.

In fact, however, there has always been some slipperiness in attempts to relate economic causes and political outcomes. For one thing, the major models of political economy tend to focus on the fourteenth century, leaving the fifteenth century a relatively un-theorised and under-explored mixture of stagnation and recovery.[21] It is true that there is a well-established emphasis on the role of monetary factors in the problems of mid-century, and there has been some interest in the 'Renaissance economy', but economistic explanations do not dominate accounts of fifteenth-century politics as they do those of the fourteenth.[22] Meanwhile, it has become clear from more detailed research that neither economic hardship nor economic wellbeing take us very far in explaining the political revolts of the period, whether popular or aristocratic. The view of Mollat and Wolff that 'immiseration' produced the risings of the 1350s, 1370s and 1380s has been shown to be wrong in enough cases for it to be unhelpful as a general cause, while the alternative explanation – the mounting prosperity of the lower orders – only half works for the English Peasants' Revolt, and does not fit such well-known insurrections as the Flemish revolt of 1323–4, the Ciompi of 1378, the Spanish pogroms of 1391 or the Caux rising of 1435. When we note that many popular demonstrations involved other groups, including those with opposed economic interests, it seems likely that other factors may be more important in shaping these episodes, and Samuel Cohn has recently noted the prominence of feelings of injustice and other political values among the motives advanced by rebels for their own behaviour.[23]

---

[21] J. Hatcher and M. Bailey make a somewhat similar point in *Modelling the Middle Ages. The History and Theory of England's Economic Development* (Oxford, 2001), p. 175.

[22] For the role of silver shortages in the mid-century slump, and some attention to the political results, see P. Spufford, *Money and its Use in Medieval Europe* (Cambridge, 1988), ch. 15. For the 'Renaissance Economy', see e.g. H. A. Miskimin, *The Economy of Early Renaissance Europe, 1300–1460* (Cambridge, 1975).

[23] S. K. Cohn, *Lust for Liberty. The Politics of Social Revolt in Medieval Europe, 1200–1425* (Cambridge, MA, 2006), esp. chs. 9–10.

In their accounts, Mollat, Wolff and others give some attention to political causes, including general ones like taxation and the growth of the state, but these are invariably regarded as secondary. Today's economic history, on the other hand, puts greater emphasis on the interaction of economic, social and political factors, and this has at last allowed the third of these to be an influence over the other two. Epstein's bold reinterpretation of the later medieval economy allows a major, even central, role in shaping economic change to an essentially politically driven process of state formation: in the short term, he argues, growing states were a factor in the burgeoning warfare of the period and thus contributed to the distribution crises and underinvestment of the early fourteenth century; in the longer term, they fostered enhanced growth, by breaking down the obstacles to specialisation and exchange that had been imposed by once-independent towns and feudal lords. More localised studies equally emphasise the role of government policy and political culture in producing economic outcomes, so that the oppression of the Catalan peasantry has been shown to derive mainly from the legal and political order developed in the thirteenth century, while the fortunes of the wool and cloth industries in fifteenth-century Castile were conditioned by the balance of power between kings, magnates and towns.[24]

It is not hard to see why the master-notion of a socioeconomic crisis has done so little to disturb conventional narratives of decline and transition. Indeed, if anything, it has strengthened them, by lending the historiographical weight of Marxist theory to more traditional accounts and by acknowledging the historical importance of the striking mortality of the period. While political history has unquestionably been enriched by a recognition of its social and economic circumstances, however, it seems likely that the overwhelming dominance of this approach in accounts of our period – and especially of the fourteenth century – lies in the attractions of a large-scale explanation and in the absence of any alternative thesis from the political and constitutional historians of the mid-twentieth century. The famines, the Black Death, the prolonged demographic downturn, the shortages of silver around 1400 and in the mid-fifteenth century, the fluctuations in urban and rural production and the changing patterns

---

[24] P. Freedman, *The Origins of Peasant Servitude in Medieval Catalonia* (Cambridge, 1991); J. Vicens Vives, *An Economic History of Spain*, trans. F. M. López-Morillas (Princeton, 1969), pp. 257, 259–60.

of economic exploitation must have affected politics, and it is not at all the intention of this book to deny that, but it should be clear from the foregoing that the processes of the economy are too complex and various to provide the sort of general explanation of later medieval politics that they have been pressed to do. Now that it is recognised that political factors help to shape social and economic behaviour, it seems all the more important to consider the part that developments in political and governmental culture might themselves have played in causing the rash of political crises in this period.

War and disorder

A second broad approach to explaining fourteenth- and fifteenth-century political conditions focuses on the prominence of war and disorder in the period. Once again, it is not hard to see how this could readily be subsumed within traditional views on later medieval decadence, and in part, perhaps, it may derive from Huizinga's classic description of 'the violent tenor of life' at the time.[25] As we have seen, war and its attendant miseries – taxation, monetary fluctuations, the destructiveness of campaigns, and the ungovernable behaviour of militarised populations – have long been an integral component of French accounts of the fourteenth-century *crise*. Thanks partly to the wide influence of French historiography, these effects have been generalised to the continent as a whole. For Philippe Contamine, for instance, 'war imposed its formidable weight on a Latin Christendom that was in other ways disorientated, anxious, even split and torn apart by profound political and social rivalries, economically weakened, unbalanced and demographically bled white'.[26] For Richard Kaeuper, meanwhile, 'it seems likely that nearly continuous, destructive and highly costly warfare helped to create the late medieval depression', and it also helped to produce 'the late medieval crisis of order'.[27] By the 1280s and 1290s, it is argued, rulers were able to raise larger armies and to keep them in being for longer, and this, in turn, permitted warfare on a larger scale. As a result, the fourteenth

---

[25] J. Huizinga, *The Waning of the Middle Ages*, trans. F. Hopman (Harmondsworth, 1955), title of ch. 1.

[26] P. Contamine, *War in the Middle Ages*, trans. M. C. E. Jones (Oxford, 1984), p. 123.

[27] R. W. Kaeuper, *War, Justice and Public Order: England and France in the Later Middle Ages* (Oxford, 1988), p. 390 and ch. 2.4.

and fifteenth centuries suffered a series of long wars, often of unparallelled intensity, and touching large parts of the continent. The fighting was bloodier, because infantry contingents were not interested in the niceties of ransom, while the practice of paying wages meant the creation of a large pool of mercenaries who remained in arms during periods of peace, living off the land and stimulating further conflicts by hiring themselves out to regional disputants. Meanwhile, the ubiquity of warfare in this period fed off and fomented a culture of chivalry which attracted much of the attention and most of the resources of Europe's ruling classes, halting or thwarting bureaucratic and legal development, and diverting finance into unproductive uses. Against this background, order deteriorated and feuding increased, while royal governments and other regimes oscillated between fleeting triumphs purchased through victory and the divisions wrought by strain and defeat. For many historians, then, big wars are a new and mainly negative feature of the later middle ages, contributing significantly to the political chaos of the period.[28]

Once again, however, this damning view of the period deserves scrutiny. War, no doubt, is always dreadful, but were the wars of the fourteenth and fifteenth centuries so much worse than those before? Most of them do not appear to have been as enormous, frequent and destructive as those of the sixteenth and seventeenth centuries, yet war has not shaped the interpretation of those later periods in the same despairing way. Sorokin's statistics on the frequency of wars record 311 for the fifteenth century, as against 732 in the sixteenth and 5,193 in the seventeenth: however questionable these data may be, the differences in scale are striking, especially when the tenfold increase in the total number of soldiers in Europe between 1500 and 1800 is set alongside them.[29] While the armies of the later thirteenth century were certainly sizeable – Edward I took over 30,000 men to Scotland in 1298, while Philip III took 19,000 to Aragon in 1285, the Florentines had 16,000 at Montaperti in 1260 and the armies at Courtrai in 1302 were probably 10,500 each – the highly mobile

---

[28] Those who have noted the role of war in promoting the more positive project of state formation will be considered below.

[29] W. Reinhard, ed., *Power Elites and State Building* (Oxford, 1996), p. 9. There are other suggestive statistics on the growth of armies from the later fifteenth century in P. Contamine, ed., *War and the Competition Between States* (Oxford, 2000), p. 131.

forces of the fourteenth century were mostly a good deal smaller.[30] Edward III took fewer than 5,000 men to France in 1338, while the Black Prince had perhaps 8,500 men at Nájera in 1367 and John of Gaunt led 6,000 on his chevauchée of 1373; the so-called *Grandes Compagnies* that are said to have terrorised southern France in the 1360s numbered no more than 4,500 at the height of their extent, while the largest mercenary companies in mid-fourteenth-century Italy did not exceed 10,000 combatants.[31] The later middle ages certainly experienced long wars and intense ones, but were these so different from the conflicts in Normandy between around 1100 and the 1150s (or 1193–1204), or the sequence of wars in Italy stretching from the first invasion of Barbarossa in 1154 almost uninterrupted into the 1260s? Eleventh-and twelfth-century conflicts typically involved plenty of raiding, burning and slaughter, and we might question whether the destructiveness of Edward III's chevauchées, or of the Hussite wars, was really any greater than that of the anti-Cathar crusades of the 1210s and 1220s, or the Mongol invasions of the 1240s, the wars in Iberia between 1229 and 1265, or, for that matter, the Italian wars of the decades following 1494. As for brutality, Malcolm Vale suggests that – civil wars apart – it is most discernible from the very end of our period: from the last few decades of the fifteenth century, which is also the time that army sizes were increasing again and a renewed role for infantry was being developed.[32]

We may question, then, whether the fourteenth and fifteenth centuries really witnessed a significant expansion in warfare. One

---

[30] M. C. Prestwich, *Edward I* (London, 1988), p. 479; Contamine, *War in the Middle Ages*, p. 116; C. J. Rogers, 'The Age of the Hundred Years War', in M. H. Keen, ed., *Medieval Warfare, A History* (Oxford, 1999), p. 137 (and see also p. 273); Najemy, *Italy in the Age of the Renaissance*, p. 199; J. F. Verbruggen, *The Art of Warfare in Western Europe During the Middle Ages*, trans. S. Willard and S. C. M. Southern (Amsterdam and Oxford, 1977), p. 143.

[31] Contamine, *War in the Middle Ages*, pp. 129, 152; K. Fowler, *Medieval Mercenaries. I. The Great Companies* (Oxford, 2001), pp. 6, 331–2. M. Mallett, *Mercenaries and their Masters. Warfare in Renaissance Italy* (London, 1974), pp. 29–36, discusses the size of four companies, three of them numbering 3,000, 3,500 and 6,000, respectively, and that of Fra Moriale, said to be at 10,000 in 1353–4. If this is a chronicler's estimate, the real figure may have been rather smaller. Note that French royal armies were still apparently very large in the 1340s – more than 40,000 men under arms in 1340, and 20,000–25,000 with Philip VI at Crécy: Holmes, *Hierarchy and Revolt*, pp. 25–6; J. Sumption, *Trial by Battle: The Hundred Years War I*, (London, 1990), p. 526.

[32] M. G. A. Vale, *War and Chivalry* (London, 1981), pp. 156–7 and ch. 5.

reason why the preceding period is taken to be relatively peaceful is that many of its conflicts took place outside France, or were resolved in favour of the Capetian crown, and have therefore had a less negative impact on the Francocentric historiography. Moving forward in time, it is important to remember that even a conflict like the Hundred Years War involved long periods of truce, and left large areas of France (to say nothing of England, Scotland and Spain) untouched. Even in the fourteenth century, war remained a localised phenomenon, and the culture of feuding and skirmishing which is commonly invoked by historians to generalise its application had, as Howard Kaminsky has recently pointed out, been more or less endemic across much of the continent anyway.[33] There is something very revealing about the insistence of the French crown that 'private' war must be abandoned during periods of 'public', or royal, war: it suggests that the problems with *routiers* and *écorcheurs* were closer to business-as-usual for the fragmented and militarised societies of the French periphery than we might think.[34] Equally, the various exactions levied from the French peasantry by armed lords, freebooters and garrison commanders are hard to separate from traditional seigneurial *tailles*, on the one hand, and from new royal taxes, on the other.[35] It is certainly the case that martial violence was coming to be organised differently in the later middle ages – that gangs and armies were held together by different media, and that some of these organisations acquired new kinds of power or permanence – and it is no surprise that contemporaries sometimes reacted to these changes with bitter protests. But these patterns may tell us more about changes in political technology, in public opinion and in prevailing discourse than they do about the actual level of violence in society.

This leads on to an important point about the source material. Contamine begins his discussion of the expansive warfare of the

---

[33] H. Kaminsky, 'The Noble Feud in the Later Middle Ages', *Past and Present*, 177 (Nov. 2002), 55–83.

[34] R. Cazelles, 'La réglementation royale de la guerre privée de Saint Louis à Charles V, et la précarité des ordonnances', *Revue Historique de Droit Français et Étranger*, 4th series, 38 (1960), 530–48.

[35] N. Wright, *Knights and Peasants: The Hundred Years War in the French Countryside* (Woodbridge, 1998), chs. 2–3, and note p. 126: 'There was, no doubt, more fighting to be done against the public enemy than in more orderly times, and the insecurities of life were more pronounced, but the familiar patterns of lordship were everywhere apparent'.

fourteenth and fifteenth centuries by noting the explosion of evidence, but this important factor does not simply reflect a growth of conflict: more than anything else, it is testimony to the increased literacy, expanded governance and raised expectations of the period. The same is surely true of the expanded evidence for disorder: the more judicial intrusiveness and record-keeping, the more evidence for violence and criminality, and the greater the apparent horror of society, whose pundits rapidly adjust their expectations to reflect the pretensions of royal legislation. English historians are familiar with the ways in which the resorts provided by the judicial system stimulated particular kinds of allegation: if an accusation that one had been wronged 'with force and arms' enabled one to get justice in a higher and more powerful court, there were good reasons to make that accusation, whatever the realities of the situation.[36] As K. B. McFarlane pointed out long ago, 'it is the very richness of their sources which has given the later middle ages a bad name'.[37] When we can look more closely at the pre-1300 world, we often find it just as brutal and just as disorderly as the period that followed: it was mostly kinder to the upper classes, but that may tell us more about the relative concentration of power in aristocratic hands than it does about relative civility. The Europe of the high middle ages may have differed more from the succeeding era in the evidence it left behind and in the limited media through which it was governed than in general political morality.

The rise of the state

Perhaps the largest problem with allowing too much causal power to war is the simple one that it is also an outcome. The wars of the fourteenth and fifteenth centuries were the product not only of violence, but also of conceptual and governmental development – of the growth of centralised jurisdictions, governmental intrusiveness and administrative capacity. To explain the politics of the later middle ages in terms of war, then, is, in a sense, to explain them in terms of

[36] A. Harding, *The Law Courts of Medieval England* (London, 1973), pp. 76–7; C. Carpenter, 'Law, Justice and Landowners in Late Medieval England', *Law and History Review*, 1 (1983), 205–37, pp. 207–9.

[37] K. B. McFarlane, *The Nobility of Later Medieval England* (Oxford, 1973), p. 114.

state growth. This leads neatly on to the third grand narrative of the later middle ages: their role as the birthplace of the 'modern state'.

Until quite recently, accounts of state formation mostly neglected the later middle ages. Milestone works like Perry Anderson's *Lineages of the Absolutist State* (1974) and Charles Tilly's collection on *The Formation of National States in Western Europe* (1975) focused on the period from the end of the fifteenth century onwards, and when medievalists argued for earlier origins, it was the period before 1300 on which they generally focused.[38] In the classic formulation of the American historian J. R. Strayer, for instance, the judicial, administrative and financial achievements of the high medieval kingdoms were fundamental in the making of modern states, but they were brought to a halt by the troubles of the fourteenth and fifteenth centuries: for almost two hundred years, governmental innovation ceased, and 'the sovereign state' made no progress until the relative prosperity and social peace of the later fifteenth century permitted recovery.[39] Whether they engaged with the middle ages or not, therefore, older histories of the state dovetailed neatly with the traditional narrative of late medieval stagnation and Renaissance recovery, but two alternative ways of thinking – one an offshoot from the concern with war, the other a deliberately revisionist move by Bernard Guenée – began to produce a different emphasis in the writing of some medievalists from the 1970s onwards.

Tilly's pithy observation, 'War made the state, and the state made war', echoes a point made by Strayer, and the first half of it, in particular, is reflected in the work of a number of historians who have explored the role of war in shaping political and governmental development in the later middle ages.[40] In some accounts, such as those of Gerald Harriss, looking at England, the dynamic is a positive one: the strains of thirteenth- and fourteenth-century warfare

---

[38] The discussion that follows focuses on general and comparative works on the later medieval state. It does not consider the mountain of work that explores the growth of states within individual countries. Examples of the latter, many of which have helped to form the critical perspectives expressed in the text, are featured in the bibliography.

[39] J. R. Strayer, *On the Medieval Origins of the Modern State* (Princeton, 1970). For a continental approach, which also focuses on the period between 900 and 1300, see H. Mitteis, *The State in the Middle Ages: A Comparative Constitutional History of Feudal Europe*, trans. H. F. Orton (Amsterdam, 1975; 1st edn 1940).

[40] C. Tilly, *The Formation of National States in Western Europe* (Princeton, 1975), p. 42.

produced fiscal and representative developments that forged a cohesive political community.[41] More commonly, the picture is neutral or negative: R. W. Kaeuper's 'law state', closely modelled on Strayer and advancing nicely by 1300, is distracted and partly overturned by the wars of the fourteenth century, even if the 'war state' that emerged from the period possessed certain strengths, especially in France.[42] Either way, these approaches tend to reaffirm the view that war is the great motor of later medieval political life, and this is echoed in the more synthetic literature, which tends to narrate the major developments in taxation and representation, presenting them largely as by-products of the pressure of war. While most textbooks document the undeniable growth of fiscal and political institutions in the fourteenth century, therefore, they do so in a manner essentially detached from domestic politics. This, in turn, has serious consequences for both institutional and political history, with the former driven almost purely by the exigencies of military activity and the latter reduced to a narrative of good kings, bad kings, faction and patronage.

A rather different path was taken by Bernard Guenée. In a number of essays published in the 1960s, and in his 1971 book on '*Les États*', Guenée launched a powerful and multifaceted critique of the older literature on state growth. A central part of his concern was to get away from the emphasis on 'transition' in accounts of the period. He thought that the state forms of the later middle ages should be seen in their own terms, as something distinctive to the fourteenth and fifteenth centuries. What in his view characterised the states of this period was a kind of duality: the equal prominence in contemporary ideas and structures of, on the one hand, the ruler, and, on the other, the country, nation or community. The former was typically a prince; the latter was partially represented through estates organisations, but also capable of acting through aristocratic networks or popular revolts. Political culture prescribed 'dialogue' as the best way to make this dual structure work, and the developing governmental institutions and political practices of the period combined to ensure that this was indeed the keynote of its politics. One consequence of Guenée's attempt to rescue the period from its position in larger developmental narratives was that he paid more attention to describing the structures

---

[41] G. L. Harriss, *King, Parliament and Public Finance in Medieval England to 1369* (Oxford, 1975) and *Shaping the Nation: England, 1360–1461* (Oxford, 2005).

[42] Kaeuper, *War, Justice and Public Order*. See also above, p. 19.

of later medieval states than to explaining them or considering how they changed over time. Even so, his work is not devoid of a narrative element, and, as mentioned above, he offered, in sketch form, a three-phase model of the period. From the later thirteenth century to the mid-fourteenth, Guenée proposed, there was a long period of bureaucratic growth, including the crystallisation of government departments and the multiplication of officers. This favoured kingly states and stimulated national consciousness, but it was not to last. The crises of the 1340s and 1350s, centring on plague, war and bullion shortage, brought governmental development to a halt and ushered in a second period of fifty to seventy-five years, which was characterised by orders of chivalry, representative institutions, popular revolts and grants of privilege to nobles, towns and provinces. These decentral-ising tendencies produced a democratic trend that reached a kind of zenith in the decades around 1400, but the chaos that attended such contemporary developments as the 'Conciliar movement', the Hussite revolution in Bohemia and the struggles of Burgundians and Armagnacs in France led to a third period of monarchical reassertion, gaining strength from around 1425. In many ways, the later middle ages ended with a return to the situation of the later thirteenth century – strong kings, ruling through national bureaucracies – but some permanent gains from the experience of these two centuries are implied: a stronger sense of the nation state, perhaps, and a more organised and stratified society.

These ideas came too late to make much impact on British text-book literature, most of which was created at around the same time; and in any case, for all the fresh thinking behind it, Guenée's three-phase model relies on some of the usual explanations for constitutional change and resembles older narratives of crisis and recovery. In its emphasis on dialogue, however, and in its serious attempt to engage with political society and political culture (if not actual politics), Guenée's work somewhat anticipates the European projects for studying state growth inaugurated by Jean-Philippe Genet and Wim Blockmans during the 1980s. Thanks to this initiative, a richer and more reasoned comparative account of the formation of European states in the later middle ages is beginning to emerge. While the thematically organised volumes published by the European Science Foundation range between 1200 and 1800 and give variable attention to our period, Genet's own 'working model' of the 'genesis' of the modern state deals directly and sensitively with the fourteenth and fifteenth centuries and has been widely influential, especially in France and Spain.[43] In this account, the birth of the modern state took place between about 1280 and 1360; its midwife, once again, was the pressure of war and its associated fiscal and representative expedients. Its growth was facilitated by socioeconomic changes which – alongside the development of state fiscality – eroded the political independence of feudal lords, and ensured that informal social hierarchies refashioned themselves around the expanding state structures, seeking to control them, rather than to reject them. This pattern, known as 'bastard feudalism' to English readers, may have involved some disruption of state power, but Genet points out that it also helped to confirm that power and to spread its influence through society; the ambivalent relationship of government and political society helps to structure and explain both the convulsive politics of the later middle ages and their outcome in the less contested and more centralised states of the 1500s. In a similar way, the early development of the secular state tended to produce conflict with the Church, but, over the longer term, clerical techniques and personnel, and finally the institution itself, were successfully absorbed. Finally, it was not just social and political factors that determined the progress of the state, but also cultural ones. Genet places particular emphasis on three developments: the creation of a national political community in dialogue with the prince, which he locates in the 1290s; the gradual evaporation of the ecclesiastical monopoly over the languages of power, in favour of a diversity of discursive fields; and the creeping dominance of a specifically 'political' language in the later fifteenth century. The state certainly faced vicissitudes in this period, and later, but it was now irreversibly present in the politics of Europe.

Wim Blockmans, meanwhile, pays more attention to the role of cities in the development of states.[44] While an early wave of state formation in the eleventh and twelfth centuries created feudal kingdoms and principalities, he argues, a second wave, associated with the commercialisation of the thirteenth century, produced a more

---

[43] J.-Ph. Genet, 'L'État moderne: un modèle opératoire', in Genet, ed., *L'État moderne: genèse* (Paris, 1990), 261–81; also 'Which State Rises?', *Historical Research*, 65 (1992), 119–33.

[44] W. P. Blockmans, 'Voracious States and Obstructing Cities: An Aspect of State Formation in Pre-Industrial Europe', in C. Tilly and Blockmans, eds., *Cities and the Rise of States in Europe, A.D. 1000 to 1800* (Boulder, 1994), ch. 11; also *A History of Power in Europe: Peoples, Markets, States* (Antwerp, 1997).

complex picture, in which rulers were often able to create more powerful governments, while newly wealthy towns exploited their concentrations of capital and population to acquire political rights. The fourteenth and fifteenth centuries were thus characterised by a spectrum of political forms, ranging from autonomous cities, wherever rulers were notably weak, through to aristocratic kingdoms, wherever towns were underdeveloped. Between these two extremes lay a more typical situation in which reasonably effective kings and princes confronted towns whose power was substantial, but not overwhelming. Commonly, these towns joined together with others in leagues or representative estates, and this made for a politics of negotiation with the surrounding rulers. By the later fifteenth century, however, the exigencies of the developing 'states system' pressed the more powerful rulers to raise larger armies and heavier taxes, while economic stagnation reduced the relative wealth and bargaining power of most towns. Under these circumstances, towns were subordinated, representative institutions lost much of their vigour, and 'consolidated monarchical states' emerged.

It is clear that these approaches involve some very important gains over the older literature on state formation. Not only do they recognise the expansion of governmental institutions and give some attention to the political dynamics of our period, but also, as in Guenée's work, they tentatively acknowledge that the growth of state forms could contribute to political complexity and conflict – and that, perhaps, is the most important theme neglected in other historical writing on this period. Both models go far beyond a narrowly institutional focus to recognise not only the importance of ideas – after all, nineteenth-century historiography managed that – but also the role of social structures, social behaviour, patterns of communication, and so on; they thus provide a much more rounded and realistic account of state growth. They also abandon the intentionalist assumptions that characterised older writing on the state. For a writer like J. R. Strayer, the French state was built by the deliberate and determined action of kings like Philip IV and their educated ministers, while in Genet's model, it is a '*machine folle*', an unreasoning bundle of structures and notions, driven forward by a mixture of social use and its own inherent tendencies.[45] This too seems much more plausible and avoids an old

---

[45] J. R. Strayer, 'Philip the Fair – A "Constitutional" King?', *American Historical Review*, 62 (1956), 18–32; Genet, 'L'État moderne', p. 278.

problem with accommodating the many values and practices of contemporaries that did not seem to have the interests of the state at heart. The actions of Charles V, who laid the foundations for permanent taxation and a national army, but also fostered the semi-independent principalities of Burgundy, Berry and Anjou, are much more comprehensible from this perspective, and Charles V's behaviour, as we shall see, was absolutely characteristic of the political leaders of his time.

In this book, many of these ideas will be taken up and pursued, but it would be as well to note some of their limitations at the outset. One immediate problem is the causal importance bestowed on war, when – as we have just noted – the wars of the period were the products, as well as the causes, of political and constitutional development. The role of legal and judicial concepts and institutions, which developed in many parts of Europe rather earlier than 1280–1360, and surely drove many of its conflicts, deserves more attention in explaining the progress of states: indeed, it was a particular regret of Tilly's that judicial institutions had not been considered by his team of researchers in the 1970s.[46] Equally, it cannot be enough to say that later fifteenth-century rulers were obliged to raise higher taxes and larger armies by the pressure of the wars they were expected to fight; we need to know why the scale of warfare was expanding, and how rulers were able to increase their claims on the resources under their jurisdiction. War may be one of the most dramatic ways in which human political resources are harnessed and co-ordinated, but it is far from being the only one, and a war-centred account of politics is as much a distortion of political causation as any that focuses on class struggle.

Other problems arise from the concern of this literature with the birth of the modern state. This has been a preoccupation of academic history since its origins in the nationalistic culture of the nineteenth century, when political and constitutional history centred on the evolution of the nation states that then existed. That enterprise involved a whole series of biases and distortions: the imposition of modern frontiers on a world that was divided up differently (if at all); an emphasis on national uniqueness, at the cost of neglecting the

---

[46] Tilly, *Formation of National States*, p. 6. These issues are addressed by one of the European Science Foundation volumes, however: A. Padoa-Schioppa, ed., *Legislation and Justice* (Oxford, 1997).

extensive common heritage of European peoples; an account of historical development that focused on the forging of national political unity. This last, in particular, meant that actors who seemed to be working towards the ends of the nineteenth-century state (typically, but not exclusively, kings and their ministers) were extensively studied and celebrated, while actors, forces and groups that appeared to work against these ends – particularistic towns and magnates, universal empires and churches, rebels and factionaries and courtiers – were neglected and depreciated. The latest writing on the rise of states escapes much of the old nationalistic inevitability: it pays much more attention to some of the polities which did not make it to the nineteenth century, such as the Valois duchy of Burgundy, the Hanseatic League, or the cities and territorial states of Italy; it is ready to talk of 'transformation' rather than 'formation'; it is as likely to examine ideology, local government or the relationship between regimes and 'repertoires' of protest, as it is to focus on war and fiscality.[47] A similarly revisionist spirit prevails in the treatment of political and governmental developments in individual countries: these too have generally shaken off nineteenth-century paradigms, and there are now a large number of highly sophisticated and persuasive accounts on offer that embed the growth of institutions in the workings of political society. But comparative work in the Genet-Blockmans tradition sometimes betrays older assumptions. Because its central story is the emergence of nation-sized ethnic states, this kind of writing tends to see every other power formation – the universal Church and empire, other churches, towns, principalities, rural communes, leagues and estates – largely in their relation to these emerging Leviathans. Even Guenée, who was emphatically not concerned with the path to modernity, reflects this tendency to privilege the national – or, in Susan Reynolds' term, 'regnal' – level.[48] The problem with this

---

[47] See, for example, H. Spruyt, *The Sovereign State and its Competitors. An Analysis of System Change* (Princeton, 1994); C. Tilly, 'Entanglements of European Cities and States', in Tilly and Blockmans, eds., *Cities and the Rise of States*, ch. 1 (p. 6 for 'transformation'); G. Chittolini, 'The "Private", the "Public", the State', in J. Kirshner, ed., *The Origins of the State in Italy, 1300–1600* (Chicago, 1995); T. Ertman, *Birth of the Leviathan: Building States and Regimes in Medieval and Early Modern Europe* (Cambridge, 1997); C. Tilly, *Regimes and Repertoires* (Chicago, 2006).

[48] S. Reynolds, *Kingdoms and Communities in Western Europe, 900–1300*, 2nd edn (Oxford, 1997), p. 254.

approach is that Europe's various power forms were undergoing many of the same processes of state formation as the kingdom-sized jurisdictions that existed above and below them. They interacted with each other directly, and not only through 'regnal' media, so that 'dialogue' can be a drastic oversimplification of the multiplicity of political relations that existed in any given territory. For much of the time, moreover, these other power forms possessed objective legitimacy and credibility to much the same extent as the 'regnal' authorities that were ultimately to triumph. Blockmans himself, as one might expect from a historian based in the Low Countries, is highly sensitive to these issues, but even in his work, it is difficult to trace a developmental path between the first emergence of bargaining between princely and urban authorities in the early fourteenth century and the triumph of 'consolidated states' in the later fifteenth; yet we need to know why it was that regnal frameworks were, in the end, able to prevail over other statal structures. The rise of the nation states certainly provides one route through the complex politics of the later middle ages, but it needs to be worked out in relation to the politics of the period, and counterbalanced by recognition of the other kinds of states – and kinds of state growth – that shaped that politics. At the very least, institutional developments at other political levels must be a major explanation of the conflicts of the period: Genet's '*états intermédiaires*' did not only spread familiarity with the royal state, they also facilitated resistance to its pretensions and iniquities.[49]

There are other problems too. Genet, like most modern commentators on the state, notes how much secular powers borrowed from the Church in the evolution of their own regimes; yet, in his model, the Church is presented as a different kind of institution, an 'other' alongside which the secular state inevitably exists in tension, until it effectively absorbs it at the end of our period. Does 'the Church' deserve this distinctiveness among the many other power structures which existed alongside the royal state? It seems doubtful. Much as there were legitimations and practices that were peculiar to clerical power structures, there were plenty that were shared with the other polities of the period. Following Maitland, Sir Richard Southern famously presented the universal Church of the middle ages as a 'state'; while, on the other hand, many historians have been equally

---

[49] Genet, 'L'État moderne', p. 268.

concerned with the spiritual, even thaumaturgic, claims of kings and other supposedly secular authorities.[50] Southern went on to point out that ecclesiastical structures and mentalities changed with the rest of society, and in fact the politics of the papal Church – indeed of all churches – in the fourteenth and fifteenth centuries resemble those of lay polities, even as they interacted with them. Once again, we need to detach ourselves from any undue emphasis on the regnal/national state and recognise it as one form among many in this period: state-like structures were not necessarily derived from it, nor were they peculiar to it. In fact, pursuing that point, we might emphasise that state-like practices were not the only, or even the normative, ways in which kings and other powers ruled. Grace was the characteristic medium through which personal authority was expressed, at least in the face-to-face context in which a great deal of later medieval political activity was still conducted: flexible justice, mercy and anger, gifts, bribes and compromises, tacit understandings, rewards – sometimes very vaguely defined – in expectation of future service, or present advantage. This kind of power had often – perhaps increasingly – to be exercised, and sometimes justified, in public contexts, but it was a different kind of power from that of 'the state', and it frequently relied on different legitimations, venues and media. When exercised successfully by kings, as it frequently was, it is all too readily confused with the advance of the state, but the freedom that characterised this mode of rule was frequently at odds with the expectations and formalities that went with state power, and its inevitable impermanence helps to explain the fluctuating efficacy of government in all its forms, during this period and beyond. Genet recognises the presence of informal authority in the later middle ages, but tends to see it as characteristic of lords, not kings. He also sees it as hierarchical and vertical, and juxtaposes it with the horizontal associations of the state, but peer-group associations – factions, parties, guilds, leagues – could be quite as formal or informal as affinities, households and other stratified organisations. Once again, rather than giving priority to one power form – the rising modern state – and looking at everything else through its lens, we need, in this period above all, to recognise the

---

[50] R. W. Southern, *Western Society and the Church*, ch. 1. Classic treatments of the spiritual and magical aspects of monarchy are, respectively, E. H. Kantorowicz, *The King's Two Bodies* (Princeton, 1957) and M. Bloch, *The Royal Touch*, trans. J. E. Anderson (London, 1973).

interaction of a multiplicity of valid and effective power forms and power types.

We have now strayed some way from the grand narratives that shaped the present generation of textbooks, but it should be clear that the larger-scale analytical accounts bearing on later medieval politics have not disturbed older approaches as much as one might expect. The crisis of feudal society – whether perceived essentially in economic, social or military terms – provides an attractive general explanation of fourteenth-century political disorders; the growth of state forms is mainly treated as a product of these disorders and offers a reason for their long-term resolution in the more stable polities of the 1500s. We are entitled to wonder whether these accounts have drawn as much sustenance from the older stories of decline and recovery as they have contributed to them. For all their potential, they rest on problematic assumptions and, whatever they may offer at the broadest level of change from 'medieval' to 'modern', most of them do surprisingly little to explain the course of political events and developments over the span of the fourteenth and fifteenth centuries themselves. As a result, pan-European political history remains essentially meaningless: a random succession of strong and weak rulers, produced by the vagaries of heredity; the ceaseless play of factions, rising and falling as wealth and power are redistributed and networks form and re-form; a series of wars and squabbles driven along by the acquisitive and aggressive instincts of dynasties, merchant companies and urban elites. I hope that enough has been said to suggest that a different approach to the politics of the period may be justified – indeed, it is already present in most writing at a national, or regional, level. Before we leave the historiography, however, let me just mention one last problem with most of the existing literature. It is a very familiar one: the restricted scope of the 'Europe' that is described.

Medieval European history has generally been most concerned with the area now occupied by France, Germany and Italy, with Britain (or rather England), the Low Countries and the Iberian peninsula admitted to a secondary place, and everywhere else very much third in coverage and importance. Updated versions of Hay and Waley include specially commissioned chapters on the kingdoms east of the Elbe (though very little on Scandinavia), but Holmes' book is mainly restricted to the Carolingian heartlands and the Mediterranean; being a work for a British market, it excludes

England and ignores the rest of our archipelago.[51] There have, of course, been serious obstacles to incorporating the history of northern and eastern Europe in works written in the West: the limited knowledge of Nordic and Slavonic languages among westerners; the imposition of official Marxist-Leninist ideology on the historians of the Eastern bloc; the difficulty of accessing archives and the relative underdevelopment of medieval political history in some of these regions. Many of these obstacles have begun to be overcome since the 1960s and 1970s, when the present generation of textbooks was written, and the *NCMH* volumes, for instance, contain valuable, up-to-date treatments in English of all the polities in the European orbit. Properly comparative and integrative studies have begun in certain areas, generally those in which engagement with the rest of Europe is almost unavoidable – trade and the circulation of money, for instance; the divergent fate of the peasantry in East and West – while the European Science Foundation volumes on the origins of the modern state have also made serious efforts to incorporate a wider Europe in their exploration. Even so, there remain many challenges to any historian wishing to engage in this kind of work. Naturally enough, the historiography of northern and eastern Europe is also full of nationalistic myths, some parallelling those of the West, some the obverse of them, and – in some fields – these nationalisms have been revivified by recent history. Equally, the moves made by western historians to recover these subaltern histories for western readerships can actually tend to reinforce the division of the continent by focusing attention exclusively on 'east-central Europe', the 'Balkans' or 'Scandinavia', and ignoring, or simplifying, the interactions between these regions and the polities to the west or south of them. It is certainly not easy for a textbook writer to identify parallels and address distinctions in ways that break free from discredited narratives and that avoid the overstatement, or underestimation, of difference, but to make the attempt itself seems inescapable.

STRUCTURES

It was suggested above that historians might pay more attention to the changing political structures and processes of later medieval Europe. This, of course, is what the newer histories of state formation have

[51] Byzantium and the Ottomans are treated in all three works, however.

attempted, but it is not necessary to frame – one might almost say burden – the structural history of politics with the notion of the state.[52] As we have seen, there were many political forms, practices and processes besides those that fostered the state or are commonly associated in historians' minds with its operations. Nor were structures of authority, or of power, or even of government, necessarily or consistently co-ordinated in the way that a term like 'state' implies. Even if states emerged during the period, as some historians would wish to argue, it is not clear that that process is a helpful centre for a political history; indeed, organising an account that way may make the task of explaining the emergence of states harder, rather than easier. A more open-ended perspective on the changing political structures of the period is more likely to deliver not only a new and plausible narrative, but also a better explanation of the period's developments.

This word 'structure' is a heavily freighted one, and maybe needs some elucidation. I am using it to mean the frames and forms and patterns in which politics took place; frames, forms and patterns which conditioned those politics, and which also – because they supplied politicians with tools, solutions, ideas, possibilities – had some role to play in causing, as well as explaining, political action. Among the most familiar of these structures are the political and social institutions on which historical attention has already been lavished: kingdoms, empires, churches, communes, principalities, leagues, guilds, companies, 'estates', courts, lordships, dynasties, affinities, parties and so on. Within them, and not infrequently cutting across them, were other institutional structures, or substructures: networks of taxation, representation, administration and military organisation; hierarchies both formal and informal; agencies of communication, exploitation or regulation. It is worth stressing, perhaps, that informal arrangements can also be seen in structural, even institutional, terms: relationships and practices of grace or service, lordship or fellowship, equally rested on codes and expectations, reflected models and possessed all kinds of typical features; we may stress the interpersonal and flexible aspects of these structures in order to differentiate them from more standardised routines and procedures, such as those associated with bureaucracies, but we can recognise their common forms without doing too much

---

[52] For further scepticism about states, see Rees Davies, 'The Medieval State: The Tyranny of a Concept', *Journal of Historical Sociology*, 16 (2003), 280–300.

violence to their variations – one affinity, *alliance* or *bando* is as much like another as one chancery, or law–code or king.

Political history cannot restrict itself to the organisations of power that physically existed, however; it must also deal with languages and ideas, and structures can be identified in these areas too. There were, for example, large bodies of interconnected terminology and reasoning, such as Roman and canon law, or the works of Aristotle or Augustine. These were some of the major frameworks of contemporary political thinking – its 'languages', as Antony Black has called them.[53] But if we are concerned with ideas in political and social use, we must also consider some of the familiar formats of expression, such as the sermon, the romance, the letter or the manifesto. These influenced the presentation and linkage of ideas, channelling them towards particular kinds of audience, creating particular kinds of impact: Heiko Oberman once commented on the 'fraternal' quality of fourteenth-century religion, but the preaching of the friars had effects far beyond the religious sphere, as we shall see; the fraternal sermon helped to shape the way power was explained to the emerging publics of this period, and also to posterity, in chronicles and other moralising records.[54] Beyond these are other structures: oft-recycled images, narratives and topoi that simplify and shape the presentation of reality, such as the conventional formulae of saints' lives, for instance, the presumptive rights and virtues (or vices) of kings, the repertoire of wicked counsellors with which this introduction began. Taken all together, these forms and patterns, physical, mental and linguistic, can be regarded as the basic currencies in which later medieval politics were conducted: they help to explain why the politics of these centuries followed the courses they did, and why and how they changed over time.

Structural approaches have attracted many criticisms. For one thing, it is not clear that the parallels between similar things – the courts of the kings of England and France, for example – are such that these can be helpfully treated as variations on a theme: perhaps the differences are more important than the similarities, and these differences are not only spatial, of course, but also temporal; with structures dissolving, merging and re-forming over time, perceived continuities

---

[53] See below, p. 131.
[54] H. A. Oberman, 'Fourteenth-Century Religious Thought: A Premature Profile', *Speculum*, 53 (1978), 80–93, and below, pp. 150–1ff.

may be the distortions of the viewer. Or perhaps contingency is so important in determining what happens that any attempt to model the development of similar institutions is doomed to be inaccurate and over-schematic. These are old problems.[55] The contention of this book will be that more can be gained than lost through the application of this approach to this particular period, and some reasons for that position are advanced below, but first it might make sense to consider some of the more familiar objections to structural accounts.

Works that focus on particular structures have drawn criticism for placing them at the centre, and unduly reifying or essentialising them – rather along the lines of the critique levelled above at histories of state formation. The influential work of Otto Brunner has faced this objection, critics doubting that the '*Land*-community' he identified in later medieval Austria had any real existence, and noting that the '*Herrschaft*' (lordship) that supplied another major structure in his work was not a term used by contemporaries.[56] Similar criticisms have been made of Georges Duby's account of the '*mallus publicus*' – the public court whose putative alterations in the eleventh-century Mâconnais lay at the heart of Duby's identification of the *mutation féodale*, or 'feudal revolution'.[57] But the aim of the book before you is to consider lots of different structures, or rather to propose that there were a significant number of common forms across Europe that interacted in various ways to produce particular patterns in the continent's politics. The structures that we are concerned with, moreover, will be those that received contemporary recognition, a condition that somewhat reduces the charge of concretising, or inventing, what did not properly exist. Nor is there any need for us to assume that the structures of the period cohered into a 'system', as many structuralist traditions have implied: in fact, much later medieval evidence points in the other direction – towards a world in which

---

[55] P. Burke, *History and Social Theory*, 2nd edn (Cambridge, 2005), pp. 127–40, provides an introduction.

[56] See Land *and Lordship: Structures of Governance in Medieval Austria*, trans. with an introduction by H. Kaminsky and J. van Horn Melton (Philadelphia, 1992), introduction; and B. Arnold, 'Structures of Medieval Governance and the Thought-World of Otto Brunner', *Reading Medieval Studies*, 20 (1994), 3–12.

[57] S. D. White, 'Tenth-Century Courts at Mâcon and the Perils of Structuralist History: Re-reading Burgundian Judicial Institutions', in W. C. Brown and P. Górecki, eds., *Conflict in Medieval Europe: Changing Perspectives on Society and Culture* (Aldershot, 2003), 37–68.

there were areas of structural coherence, certainly, but also copious divergence and incompatibility. Structural approaches can actually help to challenge essentialising interpretations of other kinds. If we recognise a kingdom, or an ethnicity, as a 'structure' rather than a unity, for example, we make it into something different and perhaps more plausible – the object, or tool, of action, on the part of individuals, rather than the uncomplicated subject; we may find that these forms possessed or generated what Susan Reynolds calls 'affective solidarity', but we should not take its presence for granted.[58] Equally, we can avoid some of the intentionalism that frequently makes historical accounts of political motivation unconvincing: instead of speculating about the sincere beliefs or cynical posturings of politicians, we might give more emphasis to the range of structures through which they were able to act. The behaviour of men of the Villena/Warwick generation with whom we began this chapter is condemned as ambitious and self-interested because they rose up in support of public programmes which they failed to pursue, but this is greatly to underestimate and misrepresent their dilemma. These programmes were what the rhetorics and political frameworks of the period fostered; they were pushed along by many power groups, and not only (perhaps not even principally) by the magnates that led them; they clashed with other structures, such as the crown, and all those powers, networks and interests that it represented; and they typically undermined aristocratic security, rather than promoting it. Small wonder that the initiatives of the 1460s had such mixed results: the unknowable aims of their supposed leaders play only a tiny part in accounting for these episodes.

Another facet of structural approaches that has drawn criticism is that the structural level has sometimes been regarded as a fundamental level – typically economic – which changed slowly, or not at all, and shaped the supposedly more superficial activities of culture and politics in broad and basic ways. This has produced the criticism that such approaches are aprioristic and unfalsifiable: they precede the reading of the evidence and are untestable by anyone but their self-satisfied creators. But it is not clear that structures have to be fundamental in order to be recognisable or to affect behaviour. The forms and patterns to be discussed in this book will be, as far as possible, empirically demonstrable, and open to empirical challenge.

---

[58] Reynolds, *Kingdoms and Communities*, p. 248.

Significantly, too, they will be political structures, not economic ones. For most of the last century, structural history has assumed the primacy of socioeconomic pressures and frameworks over politics, but as the *Annales*-influenced historians – who have been, with the Marxists, the main exponents of this kind of history – came to admit, 'politics and institutions can themselves contribute to the understanding of politics and institutions'.[59] It is not, of course, that politics is a wholly independent process, but that its own patterns of causation and interaction need to be apprehended and given prominence alongside others. Interestingly, a model of political causation has been developed by Wolfgang Reinhard to parallel the three-layer model in Braudel's *Mediterranean*. There is a '*base*' or 'macro-level', composed of the broadest social influences; a '*structure*' or 'meso-level' of 'autonomous processes', determined by prevailing institutions and paradigms; and a 'superstructure' or 'micro-level', constituted by the short-termist operations of individuals and interest groups.[60]

Finally, structural approaches have typically had problems in accommodating change: if action is influenced by structure, why does change happen? But if we accept that there are many structures in play, and that they are incomplete and overlapping, it will not be hard to see how the structures themselves must be subject to processes of adaptation and manipulation. A man wishing to bring a legal case in our period would know that he had to engage with the structures of the law and those of the courts, but he would also seek lordship, friendship and professional help. These different structures developed partly in relation to one another: the law changing to cover a changing range of complaints and/or to encourage or forestall the extra-legal and semi-legal activities of lords, friends and lawyers; courts changing in status or procedure as they faced competition from other courts or felt the influence of new legislation or executive direction; networks of friendship and lordship changing with the social, legal and judicial

---

[59] F. Braudel, *The Mediterranean and the Mediterranean World in the Age of Philip II*, trans. S. Reynolds, 2 vols. (London, 1972–3), vol. II, p. 678. For the growing concern among the Annalistes of the 1960s and 1970s that they had neglected political history, see T. Stoianovich, *French Historical Method: The Annales Paradigm* (Ithaca, NY, 1976), pp. 91–5.

[60] Reinhard, *Power Elites*, pp. 4–18. Jacques Le Goff made a similar suggestion in his 1967 essay on political history: 'Is Politics still the Backbone of History?', trans. B. Bray, in F. Gilbert and S. Graubard, eds., *Historical Studies Today* (New York, 1971), 337–55, p. 347.

climate. These processes of interaction and adaptation were not infinite – if they had been, structures would have little meaning – but they are sufficient to account for changes, such as the growth of centrally administered equitable jurisdiction (and its tendency to become formalised, so that further provision became necessary), or the gradual centralisation of political interference in justice, and its refocusing on legal chicanery rather than threat and bribery.

Whatever the overall strengths and weaknesses of structural approaches, there would seem to be particular advantages in them for the historian of later medieval politics. One we have already noted: that the politics of this period are under-conceptualised and under-explained; a structural approach could lend it some shape, some rigour. But there are also some reasons rooted firmly in past realities. As we have seen, the men and women of the later middle ages were clearly confronted by a variety of frameworks and agencies, many of which were actually or potentially in conflict. Our man seeking justice, for example, could probably choose from several different bodies of law and custom; with a bit of ingenuity and some helpful connections, he could have access to a wide array of different courts, courts which were not for the most part arranged in clear hierarchies; he would also have sought extra-legal help, as we have seen, and that from a number of different possible agencies – kin, friends, lords or patrons, neighbours, business associates and so on. This multiplicity of structures, available in many spheres of social and political life, not only the judicial, must help to explain such familiar features of the period as the tendency for larger collectivities to wax and wane, even to fragment, and for loyalties to be flexible and limited. It might provide some reasons for the attachment to informal associations and methods of peacekeeping, even as it also hints at some of the grounds for conflict and for the escalation of disputes upwards through conflicting jurisdictional structures.

Other reasons why structural approaches could be helpful relate to contemporary habits of thought and diction. These will be explored further below, but such well-known features of later medieval culture as the common desire to ground action in suitable authority, the systematic tendency in scholarly thinking, the celebration and circulation of a fairly limited number of major texts, the particular biases of late medieval schooling, the 'restricted literacy' that characterised the political society of the period – all these conspired to encourage the recognition, preservation and transferability of structures between different areas and different groups. This did not prevent mutation – quite the contrary – but it did mean the reproduction of recognisably common forms across the continent. Consideration of these structures helps to disclose the dynamics driving politics. It also, of course, helps us to read the evidence. When we learn that both Philip IV of France (1285–1314) and John II of Castile (1406–54) are described by contemporary chroniclers as indolent and fond of hunting, we might perceive a topos at work, rather than a straightforward presentation of reality; going further, we might recognise such observations as (among other things) ways of capturing the emergence of more bureaucratic frameworks of government, which, in some polities, could appear to rescue the ruler from full-time activity or dilute the element of personal discretion and energy in ruling. The lamenting and frequently critical tone of much of the more 'medieval' writing of the period, and the prurience, cynicism and pseudo-realism associated with its 'renaissance' voices have had a powerful influence on the way the later middle ages are envisioned and described by historians. But, as all the specialist work suggests, these writings need to be read deconstructively: unless we know the rhetorical routines and textual inheritance of the period's writers, we cannot make much sense of what they wrote.

Finally, the positioning of our period in the wake of the great movements of the eleventh, twelfth and thirteenth centuries helps to explain why attention to structures, and to common structures, could be useful. The internationalising trends of the period – the spread of a Christendom co-ordinated by the Papacy, the enterprise of crusading, the commercial and credit networks established by Italians and Catalans – helped, however superficially and incompletely, to create a common political and social space. The legal and theological scholarship of Bologna, Paris, Oxford, the notarial and rhetorical schools and other centres where the administrative elites of Europe received their education, the chanceries of popes and kings and the preaching of friars spread a particular set of notions and technologies around this space. 'The making of Europe' in this period of 'the making of the middle ages' sets the stage for the centuries we are concerned with, both historiographically and historically.[61]

---

[61] R. Bartlett, *The Making of Europe: Conquest, Colonization and Cultural Change, 950–1350* (London, 1993); R. W. Southern, *The Making of the Middle Ages* (London, 1953).

Historiographically, as we have seen, 'growth' and 'making' more or less have to be followed by crisis, decline and recovery or rebirth: indeed, it is only possible to construct narratives of making by ending them somewhere between 1250 and 1350, when the limitations, divergences, deviations and failures of 'high medieval' processes were still unclear. Historically, of course, 'growth' and 'making' simply continued: the contraction of the continent's population did not mean the contraction of everything else. A study of the politics of the later middle ages must begin, therefore, with a survey of the forms and structures inherited from the 'age of growth', and that is the subject of the following chapter.[62]

---

[62] R. W. Southern's phrase: *Western Society and the Church*, p. 34.

2

EUROPE IN 1300: THE POLITICAL INHERITANCE

The thirteenth century has commonly been seen as an age of culmination, even 'completion', or 'perfection'.[1] It is not hard to see why. It was in this century that the principal developments of the expanding society of the high middle ages gained a kind of cohesion, or fruition, or maximum extent. In population, and more or less in territory, Latin Christendom arrived at the limits of its medieval expansion, while the papal monarchy was at the height of its powers, and the basic framework of the pre-Tridentine church was laid down in the decrees of the Fourth Lateran Council (1215). The *Summa Theologiae* (1266–72) of Thomas Aquinas brought scholastic research to a point of coherence by synthesising Aristotelian philosophy with Christian theology; Accursius produced the essential guide to Roman law in the work that came to be known as the *Glossa Ordinaria* (1220×40); and the codification of canon law, the law of the Church, approached conclusion in two classic collections: the *Liber Extra* of 1234 and the *Liber Sextus* of 1298. In the world of secular politics, meanwhile, kings like Edward I of England (1272–1307), Philip IV of France (1285–1314), James II of Aragon (1291–1327) and Alfonso X of Castile (1252–84) appeared to preside over embryonic nation states, bound together by overarching royal jurisdiction, networks of officers, notions of community and ethnicity, and experimental media of consultation and taxation.

[1] These words are taken from the preface to the *Cambridge Medieval History* VI, ed. J. R. Tanner, C. W. Prévité-Orton and Z. N. Brooke (Cambridge, 1929), p. vii.

At the same time, there has also been a sense that many of these achievements were short-lived. The thirteenth century is classically the scene of a series of turning points. First among these is the papal deposition (1245) and subsequent death of Frederick II (1250), which was once thought to have spelt the end of the Holy Roman Empire as an effective force, not only in Italy but even in the German lands. Another is the uprising in Sicily, in 1282, known as the 'Sicilian Vespers', which has been granted even wider significance. Not only did it dash papal hopes of controlling southern Italy, with its powerful monarchy, rich resources and suitability as a base for crusading, it is also supposed to have begun the 'ruin of the Hildebrandine papacy', as Pope Martin IV (1281–5) invoked Holy War against Christian oppo-nents for all-too-obviously secular ends.[2] Apart from the reputational damage they brought to the Papacy, the Vespers and the wars that followed are also credited with helping to cause the lasting political and economic eclipse of southern Italy and with setting up a contest between Anjou/France and Catalonia/Spain which embraced much of the Mediterranean and lasted through to 1559. A third turning point came around the end of the century: the epic confrontation between Pope Boniface VIII (1294–1303) and Philip IV of France, in which the Papacy made some of its grandest-ever claims to authority in the bull *Unam Sanctam* (1302), only to be humiliated the following year, when the king's agents besieged the Pope in his palace at Anagni and pressed for his trial and deposition. This, it seemed, was the moment at which the rising power of the kingdoms surpassed the failing spiritual and legal jurisdiction of the Papacy, and the path to Avignon, the Great Schism and the emergence of national churches lay clear ahead.

In the last few decades, these views have come to be questioned. While thirteenth-century achievements are still recognised as consid-erable, few would now wish to see them as 'complete'. As we shall see throughout this book, the institutions which had reached a kind of coherence in this period went on developing in the years that fol-lowed, and often in ways that revealed their contradictions or com-plexities. Growing ranks of theologians got to grips with the Thomist synthesis and opened out its variant possibilities. The Church gradually learned the ambivalent consequences of the decisions of Lateran IV,

---

[2] Quotation from S. Runciman, *The Sicilian Vespers: A History of the Mediterranean World in the Later Thirteenth Century* (London, 1958), p. 286.

finding that new rules and new religious orders meant new crimes and new problems. Meanwhile, further research and reflection has raised doubts about the fullness of royal authority in the thirteenth century. The reign of Alfonso X ended, after all, in a civil war which the king was losing when he died. Edward I expired with Scotland unconquered, Flanders abandoned and a host of mounting political difficulties which helped to cause the civil disorders of his son's reign. And was Philip IV really a stronger king than the less intrusive Louis IX (1228–70)? Was his fleecing of the Lombards, the Jews and ultimately the Templars a sign that his experiments with universal taxation were substantially unsuccessful? He too died with conquests incomplete, and with much of France on the point of revolt. It is only by closing one eye that we can see some sort of perfection in the kingdoms of the later thirteenth century.

Nor have the various turning points fared much better. The end of Frederick II was not the end of the Empire. In the German lands, the decline of Hohenstaufen influence preceded 1250 and was, in any case, part of a series of adjustments in the distribution of power. In its most immediate sense, it was not brought about by papal action, but by the break-up of alliances around the ruling house; more distantly, it can be seen as one among many responses to the growth of political co-ordination in the territories of princes, lords and towns. If it meant the redistribution of the remaining imperial assets and ushered in a period of so-called 'little kings', it did not prevent the formation of new imperial dynasties, among whom the Luxemburgs (temporarily) and the Habsburgs (more lastingly) recreated something like the 'hegemonic kingship' of old.[3] Nor did the fall of the Hohenstaufen mean an end to imperial influence in Italy. Not only did the dynasty's network in the peninsula hold up well for more than fifteen years after 1250, the claims of the Emperor remained an important factor in the legal, political and intellectual culture of northern Italy well into the fourteenth century and beyond. Intervention south of the Alps remained a central ideal in German political culture, and five more Emperors entered Italy before 1500, three of them at the head of armies. These invasions may not have been quite the same as the campaigns of Frederick II, but they ought to make us pause before pronouncing the death of the imperial programme in 1250.

---

[3] For these terms, see P. Moraw, *Von Offener Verfassung zu Gestalteter Verdichtung. Das Reich im Späten Mittelalter, 1250 bis 1450* (Berlin, 1985).

A similarly sceptical line could be taken with the Sicilian Vespers, or the clashes between Philip IV and Boniface VIII: however important and far-reaching were the conflicts in Rome and across the Mediterranean which stemmed from these episodes, there was no transformation of political powers and alignments, but rather a series of continuities and gradual developments.

These perspectives are important, because they have implications both for how we formulate our notion of the later middle ages and for our sense of what it was that drove the period's politics. If there are no meaningful turning points between the 'age of growth' and the 'age of crisis' then we ought to question whether it is really helpful to see either period in such terms, or indeed to identify the 'later middle ages' as a specific period at all. Equally, if the kinds of politics which supposedly characterise the later middle ages are already apparent before 1300 – in the unscrupulous use of crusades to pursue secular ends, for example, or in the power-struggles of the Roman families of Caetani and Colonna that shaped the downfall of Boniface VIII – then it is clear that those politics bear no intrinsic relation to the demographic crises of the fourteenth century, nor to such specific sources of conflict as the Plantagenet–Valois contest for the throne of France. Rather, it seems more likely that later medieval politics were essentially born in the political developments – broadly conceived – of the high middle ages.

This, indeed, is what newer approaches to the thirteenth century tend to suggest. 'Expansion', not 'completion', is the keynote of the relevant *New Cambridge Medieval History* volume, and of several other works besides.[4] This emphasis does not assume an end point: specifically, governmental and political expansion does not have to stop when demographic pressure drops, nor with the commercial contraction of the first half of the fourteenth century (indeed, a significant cause of that contraction was the redirection of mercantile credit into the hands of more ambitious and assertive rulers). In a similar way, Susan Reynolds has noted that the accumulating complexity of the political environment over the course of the thirteenth century created new tensions and placed more challenging obstacles in the path of consensus: the political values of the ensuing period may not have been significantly different from those of 900–1300, she suggests, nor any less shared between rulers and subjects, but the swelling range of

---

[4] *NCMH* V, ed. D. Abulafia (Cambridge, 1999), pp. xvii, 1.

media at the disposal of political consumers, the spread of writing and
of more substantially articulated bodies of authoritative ideas, meant a
changed – and in various ways more contradictory – politics.[5] For
Rees Davies, meanwhile, the arrival of new media of rule in the
twelfth and thirteenth centuries enabled an 'intensification of lordship': new strategies of administration, domination and conquest, and
new expectations of uniformity, on the part of kings and lords.[6] In a
parallel way, R.I. Moore has written of 'the formation of a persecuting society', a process intrinsically connected to the growth of
jurisdiction, both in the church and in secular authorities, and one
which gathered pace with the extensive legislation of the Fourth
Lateran Council of 1215 and the development of the papal inquisition from the 1230s.[7] Thirteenth-century dynamics, then, had continuing impact, just like those of the eleventh, twelfth and any other
century.

   This impact was an ambivalent one. 'Intensification' and 'persecution' have both divisive and unifying results, and that duality can
already be perceived in thirteenth-century political developments.
Governmental pressure of a more standardised and articulate kind
created media of resistance cast in its own image, as, for example,
the bureaucratised common law of England's Angevin kings helped to
produce Magna Carta (1215), a document written in the language
of royal justice, enforceable in the king's courts and yet capable of
challenging aspects of the exercise of royal power. The forms of
thirteenth-century government were thus an incitement and an
inspiration to all power-holders, which is to say to almost everyone
who came into contact with them, since – as we shall see – many
institutions could be operated from below as well as from above.
Moreover, as Robert Bartlett's *The Making of Europe* particularly
emphasises, the corollary of expanding Christendom was the spread of
its replicable techniques and frameworks across an enlarged European
space – 'German law', diocesan structures, commercial media, aristocratic customs and rituals, linguistic nationalisms are among his main
examples, but we might add other juridical, intellectual and political

[5] S. Reynolds, *Kingdoms and Communities in Western Europe, 900–1300*, 2nd edn
(Oxford, 1997), pp. 337–9.
[6] R.R. Davies, *Domination and Conquest: The Experience of Ireland, Scotland and Wales,
1100–1300* (Cambridge, 1990), ch. 5.
[7] R.I. Moore, *The Formation of a Persecuting Society* (Oxford, 1987).

structures to this list, and some of them are discussed below.[8] While these brought a higher measure of cultural and political homogeneity to the affairs of the continent, they also spread abroad copious means of contest, division, assertion and complication, and they forced, in time, a more self-conscious search for new means of accommodation and order. The aim of this chapter is to introduce some of the major forms and entities available to the politicians of Europe as they were in 1300. We shall begin with the larger structures of politics and government, before moving on to some of the more influential bodies and patterns of ideas, the major means of communication and, finally, the most typical forms of social network.

FORMS OF GOVERNMENT AND RESISTANCE

Empires

For all the diversity of political systems at work in Europe in 1300, it is nonetheless possible to identify a series of types. The first of these is the Roman Empire, which was both an idea – perhaps the most fundamental political idea – and a concrete reality. The Rome of the Caesars was, of course, long gone, but it had suited almost every succeeding regime across the Mediterranean and beyond to adopt some at least of what it understood to be the rights, rituals and accoutrements of imperial power, and to insist on some kind of continuity with the Roman imperial tradition. This means that Rome lay, in some sense, behind virtually every formal political entity in later medieval Europe, but its legacy had descended more particularly on three powers above all: the Emperor and king of the Romans, whose Roman associations went back to the ninth and tenth centuries, and who claimed to rule over much of central Europe; the 'Eastern' Roman emperor, based at the city of 'New Rome' founded by Constantine in the fourth century, and later known as Constantinople; and the Papacy, whose claims to rule extended over the Christian world and beyond. As a spiritual leader, the Pope's claims to anything as worldly as empire may seem a little strained, but sacred and secular power were easily intermingled at the imperial level, and of these three powers it was actually the Pope who

---

[8] R. Bartlett, *The Making of Europe: Conquest, Colonization and Cultural Change, 950–1350* (London, 1993), esp. ch. 11.

possessed the highest, most extensive and consistently meaningful authority over Europe. At home in the Lateran Palace, clad in imperial crown and purple, and issuing decretals, the Pope of 1300 was every inch an emperor, and it is his empire that we shall discuss first.

The Papacy

The collapse of the Roman Empire in the west and the success of early popes in wielding its memory were central to the subsequent history of the Papacy, but it was not, of course, to the Caesars alone that the Pope owed his high authority. Nor was that authority simply due to the city of Rome's important spiritual associations, as the site of St Peter's diocese and martyrdom, the home of his relics, and the world capital in the time of Christ. Most fundamentally, perhaps, papal hegemony derived from particular interpretations of Scripture and Christian tradition, developed over generations by successive popes and their supporters. First among these was the doctrine of the Petrine supremacy: that Christ had founded his Church on Peter, and that the Pope, as bishop of Rome, was Peter's heir. As Christ had given the Church to Peter and not, it was argued, to all the apostles, so the Pope enjoyed primacy over all other churchmen. This primacy was gradually puffed up to full sovereignty, with Innocent III (1198–1216), for example, arguing that, while 'the others were called to a part of the care…Peter alone assumed the plenitude of power', so that the Pope himself, 'successor of Peter' and 'Vicar of Jesus Christ' was 'set between God and man, lower than God, but higher than man, who judges all and is judged by no one'.[9] Christian dogma was thus central to the Pope's position, but we should not see that position as any the less political for that. After all, more simply secular authorities also found a basis in Scriptural precept and Christian tradition, and the spiritual arguments that underpinned the Papacy were devised by men with political, as well as spiritual, aims; these arguments were, as R. W. Southern pointed out, shot through with the legal and political assumptions of their times.[10]

Equally, the papal headship of the Church was readily extended to be a kind of headship of the world. This was essentially because 'church' and 'world' were not clearly distinguishable. For one thing,

[9] B. Tierney, *The Crisis of Church and State 1050–1300* (Toronto, 1988), p. 132.

[10] R. W. Southern, *Western Society and the Church in the Middle Ages* (London, 1970), pp. 15–16.

churchmen typically possessed extensive properties and other forms of secular power. For another, the Church itself could be defined in several ways. If there was a visible church of ordained priests and prelates claiming possession of the keys of Heaven and a mediating role between man and God, there was also an invisible church of unknown identity – the inhabitants of Augustine's Heavenly City, who were destined to live with Christ when their earthly sojourn came to an end – and, beyond that, there was a sense of the Church as the *congregatio fidelium* ('congregation of the faithful'), that is, all baptised Christians – most of the inhabitants of Christendom, in other words, though not the Jews, Muslims and remaining pagans who lived among them. Headship of the Church was thus far-reaching in its implications, and *ratione peccati* ('by reason of sin'), Innocent III claimed jurisdiction over all Christians in all of their affairs, so as to recall the sinner from error to truth. It is true that he and other popes recognised a distinction between secular and spiritual authority, often invoking the scriptural metaphor of two swords, or citing Christ's injunction to 'render unto Caesar the things that are Caesar's', but they were also in no doubt that their own authority was higher than that of any secular lord. Boniface VIII, for example, declared that 'one sword ought to be under the other and the temporal authority subject to the secular power'. For Innocent III, a century earlier, meanwhile, the position was even more extreme – using the metaphor of the sun and the moon, he argued that 'the royal power derives the splendour of its dignity from the pontifical authority'.[11] These assertions arose not only from the general papal jurisdiction over Christians, but also from more specific agreements made when the Roman Empire was re-established in 800 and 962, and from particular interpretations of past imperial grants, from the fabricated 'Donation' of the first Christian Emperor, Constantine (306–37), which supposedly bestowed the Western Empire upon the Papacy, to the subsequent gifts and concessions of Ottonian and Salian Emperors. It was partly on the basis of these acquired rights that the Papacy felt able to bestow crowns on secular rulers within its dominion, and – from the mid-thirteenth century – to announce the deposition of those kings who offended.

Such, then, were the imperial claims of the Papacy: by what means, and in what ways, were they made real at the beginning of

---

[11] Tierney, *Crisis of Church and State*, pp. 189, 132.

our period? Like all other monarchs, the Pope possessed a court, or
Curia, which combined his household, his chief administrators,
advisers and officers, and the wellsprings of his jurisdiction, or
judicial authority. It was in this central core that papal policy and
claims to authority were devised, and from it, through the publication of letters and laws (encyclicals and bulls), the despatch of
legates and other officers, and the attendance of appellants and
petitioners, that papal rule was carried out. Well-established traditions of hierarchy and law within the Church helped to make the
exercise of authority by the Papacy relatively straightforward and
readily generalised – at least over the Church itself. There were, as
we shall see, all kinds of tensions in this massive and complex
organisation, but papal instructions still had general efficacy: they
were usually guided by sound legal and theological advice; they
were rapidly assimilated to the body of Church law in collections of
papal 'decretals'; and they tended to satisfy powerful interests. Three
other trends had helped to build up the papal monarchy during
the eleventh, twelfth and thirteenth centuries. One was the close
association of papal rule with the reform movement that began
in the 1040s and 1050s. This movement, which had focused on
re-spiritualising the Church, removing it from lay control and co-
ordinating its operations, had immense ideological and legal authority within Christian society, and, up to the later thirteenth century,
at least, it delivered much of that authority to the Papacy, which
was regarded as the key means through which reform would be
achieved. Not only did the Pope typically affirm and defend the
hierarchy of ecclesiastical powers which enabled clerics to protect
their estate from secular lords, but he was also the direct sponsor
and protector of several agencies that were central to the reforming
mission: the crusades, which had a metaphorical and liturgical as
well as military importance; the leading universities, which were
developing and defining the doctrine and law of the Church; the
friars, whose main roles lay in preaching to the laity and hearing
their confessions; and the inquisition, which set out to identify and
correct deviance within the Christian flock. By the second half of
the thirteenth century, it is true, the relationship between the
Papacy and reform had become vexed and complicated – indeed,
the Papacy has often been seen as the principal object of later
medieval reform, rather than its exponent – but that relationship
had played a major part in building the papal empire.

Two other key trends lay in the fields of jurisdiction and patronage. During the twelfth century, the Papacy built up a remarkably accessible system of appeals: disputants could so readily appeal to the Pope against decisions made in lesser ecclesiastical courts that the Papacy was able to present itself as 'ordinary judge' of the whole Church. By 1200, this ease of access had generated an unmanageable amount of business at the Curia and various restrictions were introduced, but it had generalised papal authority throughout the Church, and broken the potential independence of intervening layers by making their authority effectively conditional upon repeated papal endorsement. It was perhaps in relation to the growth of its appellate jurisdiction, which focused so many clerical interests on itself, that the Papacy began to extend its rights over ecclesiastical appointments ('provisions'). Instead of merely intervening in disputed elections or making recommendations, it began to grant 'expectatives' (or titles to office) to petitioners on a significant scale from the mid-twelfth century, and was making the first general reservations of particular categories of post by 1265. This development too was problematic and came to be much resented by those who gradually lost their power of appointment to the ever-growing Papacy, but it had a similar effect on the distribution of power within the Church as the development of appellate jurisdiction, and it attracted support not only from the individual petitioners who benefited from it, but also from those groups best placed to exploit papal patronage: the bureaucrats and placemen of the Curia; university men; and, as we shall see, the clerical servants of kings and lords.

The near-complete dominion which the Papacy had established over the Church by the early thirteenth century was full of consequences for its relations with lay powers. The development of a partly separate clerical estate[12] under papal jurisdiction had been one of the great political and constitutional traumas of the high middle ages: prior to the 'reform', the Church had been, at every level, under lay control, and energetic attempts to defend lay interests were made along virtually every front. As both clerical and secular powers grew in scope and complexity, there were copious conflicts, typically focusing on whatever means of power was most important at the time – from investiture and homage around 1100, to jurisdiction in the twelfth and thirteenth centuries, and on, in succeeding years, to taxation,

---

[12] An estate, in this sense, is a group of people sharing the same status or identity.

patronage and national allegiance. But, throughout the period, accommodation, even resolution, was generally possible: 'Church' and 'State' were not continually, or even frequently, at odds; participants in either structure were usually participants in both, and had many interests, both individual and collective, in common. This means that the main areas of potential conflict were also areas of compromise, and were developed over time in ways that tended to protect – for better and worse – the relationship between the Papacy and the leading secular authorities.

This is clear when we look at what were perhaps the three most important front lines between the papal Church and lay powers: jurisdiction, appointment and – from the thirteenth century – taxation. In all three cases, the Papacy was generally willing to resolve questions in favour of secular rulers. For all the high statements mentioned above, the Papacy rarely interfered in secular jurisdiction and was usually prepared to compromise along uncertain boundaries. The assumed powers of kingmaking and deposition were very rarely used after the early thirteenth century: apart from the imperial cases of 1245, 1301 (swiftly reversed) and 1324, the deposition of Sancho of Portugal, in 1245, in the midst of a civil war in that country, and in response to pleas from one Portuguese faction, is a lone example.[13] When, in 1298, an embassy from the county of Flanders brought up the papal supremacy over lay rulers and invited Boniface VIII to intervene in its struggle with its overlord, Philip IV of France, the Pope refused to get involved, despite his own disagreements with Philip over other matters; he was not, he said on another occasion, so foolish as to confuse spiritual and temporal power, when both had been ordained by God. As far as appointments were concerned, meanwhile, the provisions system, as it developed, was well tailored to the interests of rulers: generally speaking, it was chapters and other clerical electors and patrons who lost out, while kings and princes, in frequent contact with the Papacy, tended to increase their influence

---

[13] The papal grants of the throne of Hungary to Charles II of Anjou in 1290 and to Charles-Robert in 1301, both made on the basis that Hungary was a papal fief, are roughly parallel to the Portuguese example, though the Angevins already had a dynastic claim to the kingdom and papal interventions were fairly peripheral to Charles-Robert's success. See *NCMH* VI, ed. Michael Jones (Cambridge, 2000), p. 736; P. Engel, *The Realm of St Stephen: A History of Medieval Hungary*, trans. I. Pálosfalvi and ed. A. Ayton (London, 2005), pp. 110–11, 128–30; and below, p. 175.

over benefices. Similarly, in the sphere of taxation, while the Papacy moved to protect the Church from the first extractive experiments on the part of lay rulers, its decree of 1179 allowed the consensual taxation of clergy in circumstances of necessity. As it began to develop a tax system of its own to fund crusades, from 1199, it allowed lay rulers to collect and spend the resulting dividends. When, after a long period of agreed papal taxation for a nominal crusade (1285–91), the French king pushed at the convention by taxing the Church on his own authority and for a war against his defaulting vassals, the Papacy reacted sharply with the bull *Clericis laicos* of 1296. But, in general, Popes conceded taxative rights over the Church pretty freely and, as they moved to establish a taxation-based revenue system for themselves in the fourteenth century, they took care to ensure that it did not cut across the fiscal interests of secular rulers.

The great exception to all this flexibility in dealings with lay powers was where papal territorial interests were concerned. This is important, because it means that the papal empire was rather a different beast in its universal form from what it was on a more local basis. In the region of Rome, where Innocent III had decided to create what was effectively a secular state, the Pope was, quite straightforwardly, a lay ruler. In the rest of Italy and Sicily (and, to a lesser extent, in Provence, the Languedoc, the German lands and Hungary), the Papacy controlled little territory directly, but was generally aggressive in the promotion of its rights, and those of the Church, against secular powers. This is a central explanation for the frequently bitter relations with the Emperors, since the latter also possessed a network of territories, rights and interests in Italy, including the papal client state of Sicily between 1194 and 1254. It also explains tensions in the relations between the Papacy and Charles of Anjou and his descendants, who were otherwise its most favoured lieutenants from the 1250s until the 1330s. They had been brought into the peninsula to regain Sicily from the Hohenstaufen, but once they had achieved control of the kingdom, in 1266, they began to pose a similar threat to papal dominance. There was also a territorial factor in the confrontations between Boniface VIII and Philip IV, since these blew up along what truly was a frontier between papal and French spheres of influence: in the conflicts of the turn of the century, it was among the bishops of southern France – a region where royal and episcopal jurisdictions were often shared, papal networks prominent and the inquisition active – that the French king faced the strongest resistance.

That the Pope had a territorial dimension to his rule has often been treated as a corruption of the Petrine ideal, but the real-world confusion of secular and spiritual power made it inevitable. Even at the height of the reform period, the Papacy was centrally concerned with the restoration of its rights and properties. But it is also worth remembering that the territorial activities of the popes were prompted from below, as well as from above. Papal overlordship in Sicily had been revived in 1190 because Empress Constance wanted the backing of Pope Clement III to establish herself and her husband as rulers of the kingdom. The Papal State of Innocent III was established partly through the desire of various parties in the duchy of Spoleto and the march of Ancona to throw off imperial lordship in favour of the supposedly lighter yoke of the Papacy. Equally, the French crown had been quite keen to encourage papal activity in the counties of Toulouse and Provence in the twelfth century, when these territories were held by stubbornly independent feudatories with heretical tastes. Even in Germany, papal interventions against the Emperor were almost always made in response to entreaties from his opponents. The uses to which papal power could typically be put are thus an important thing to know, if we want to understand the impact of this particular imperial structure on the politics of Europe. Besides the defence of rights and territory within its immediate sphere of influence, what else was the Papacy for, as far as contemporary politicians were concerned?

We have already seen that the Pope was an important means of jurisdiction and appointment. These functions could have a general as well as individual utility: it could suit all kinds of powers to support papal claims, if the Papacy was willing to exercise its rights in ways compatible with their interests. The papal interest in crusading, and the associated willingness to grant privileges and powers related to it, were additional attractions to lay powers: the honour and spiritual redemption that crusading brought were powerful currencies, and papal crusade taxation was a valuable asset in this early period when other means of taxation had not yet been developed. Crusading was especially compatible with the interests of younger sons and cadet lines, such as the house of Anjou – power groups with rather limited resources of their own, but also with limited responsibilities for territorial government, especially by comparison to the kings who had sometimes led crusades (and who might additionally favour the removal of powerful relatives to a sphere where they could expand their status and resources unproblematically). A general expectation that the Papacy would defend the clerical estate – or anything that could plausibly be represented as part of it – animated a lot of appeals for its support: even if most popes were unwilling to push things too far against most secular rulers, some papal backing could be antici-pated and could alter the terms on which any such dispute was conducted. Even papal responsibilities towards the faith – the defi-nition of doctrine, the repression of heresy, or sin – could attract politicians with essentially secular aims. For example, the early thirteenth-century crusades against the Cathars were famously a means by which the French crown could impose its authority on the Languedoc and counter the influence of the rulers of Aragon, Gascony and Toulouse. Nor was it only secular rulers who mixed politics with matters of faith: a later bishop of Albi turned a blind eye to the Catharism of the leading burgesses of his city while these men accepted his jurisdiction; when they advanced the interests of the king's court, in 1299–1300, he unleashed the inquisition against them.

There were a variety of routes through which the Papacy could be invoked and manoeuvred, besides the obvious ones of appealing to its jurisdiction or its interests. One was through the conclave that elected each pope. The ancient ecclesiastical principle of consensual rule had combined with the Roman inheritance to produce an electoral mon-archy, with the right of election concentrated, from 1059, in the hands of the cardinals, an increasingly defined group of high prelates with parishes in Rome and positions in the Curia. Papal elections were predictably open to political pressure – most notably from the great baronial families of Rome, from whose ranks many of the cardinals were drawn, but also from other secular interests, like the house of Anjou, whose influence across Italy enabled it to secure a number of extremely compliant popes in the 1270s and 1280s. The trends of ecclesiastical politics could also be powerful factors, leading to the election of popes who were known for their legal learning, or for their spirituality, or for their support of bishops, friars or other orders of the Church. But these two kinds of pressure were not really so distinct. As we shall see, ecclesiastical divisions and interest groups were fre-quently intertwined with secular ones, so that the election of a decrepit hermit, Celestine V, in 1294, for example, was brought about by the conjunction of Angevin pressure with the belief of certain cardinals that an angelic pope was required to silence criticism of papal worldliness and to calm apocalyptic fears. Celestine proved incompetent, and his swift replacement with a more traditional Roman lawyer-pope, in the form of Boniface VIII, not only created new political possibilities through the constitutional innovation of a papal abdication, but helped to determine the pattern of allegiances inherited by the new Pope – enmity from other Roman families, unease from Charles II of Anjou, and a conviction on the part of the more spiritual Franciscan friars that the rule of Antichrist was, after all, beginning.

Other means of influence over the Papacy were more directly challenging. The ecclesiastical empire was a complex one, with many constituent organisations and layers, whose power could – in both theory and practice – be arranged differently in ways that could threaten papal sovereignty. There were also, as we shall see, numerous ambivalences within canon law concerning the proper relationship between corporations and their heads, while the bits of Scripture that underlay the Petrine supremacy could be read in other ways, or countered by other texts more friendly to the sharing of apostolic authority among churchmen. Since the Papacy was by no means alone in these kinds of predicaments, they will be discussed in more detail below, as a general legacy of the political and legal theory of the thirteenth century and as a general problem faced by all rulers. But there was one kind of assault to which the Papacy and other prelates were uniquely vulnerable on account of their spiritual status. Because this played such a major role in the politics of the Church from the mid-thirteenth century to the early 1500s, it makes sense to introduce it here. It was what has often been called the 'apostolic ideal'.

Apostolic visions of the Church expected the clergy to resemble Christ and the apostles: to be, in effect, poor preachers, lacking temporal authority and worldly goods. These visions spread across Europe with knowledge of the gospels, and were helped along by the various dualistic heresies of the twelfth century, which tended to sharpen existing distinctions in people's minds between complexes of ideas linking goodness, asceticism and the spirit, on the one hand, and evil, worldliness and the flesh on the other. Most powerfully, they were taken up by two movements at the end of that century: the 'poor men of Lyons', or Waldensians, who were ultimately left outside the Church because they would not accept the distinctive authority of the ordained clergy; and the followers of St Francis of Assisi, who were allowed into the Church because, on the whole, they, or their leaders, would do so. The Franciscans' emphasis on preaching and poverty made them ideally fitted to some of the Papacy's major concerns in the early thirteenth century: the conversion of the dualists who seemed so alarmingly numerous in the heartlands of Latin Christendom; the ministry in the towns, where the established parochial network could not cope with the rising population, and where the poor were gathered together in large numbers; and finally what has been called the 'pastoral revolution' – the beginning of serious efforts to spread Christian knowledge and liturgical practice more widely abroad within the laity. Between papal recognition in 1209 and the middle of the thirteenth century, the Franciscans thus became a massively influential and numerous group, especially prominent in universities, towns and the entourages of great men. From this position, they canvassed an idea of the Church which was profoundly at odds with the possession of secular authority and worldly goods.

These ideas were causing very serious problems at the very heart of the Church by the end of the thirteenth century, but they began to be mobilised against the Papacy earlier than this. It was already common for representations of papal power on the part of the Emperor to present clerical authority as purely spiritual and thus intrinsically different from lay authority, so that, in 1232, for instance, Frederick II could make reference to 'the ointment of the priestly office' in contrast to 'the might of the imperial sword'.[14] But Frederick's later conflict with Popes Gregory IX (1227–41) and Innocent IV (1243–54) led him into two postures which were to be formative. In 1239, he appealed to the cardinals as Senators of Rome, calling on them to convoke a general council of the Church at which the issues in play between himself and the Pope could be judged. This manoeuvre, of course, accepted the existence of a papal church-state, even as it asserted the existence of an imperial one; it also restricted the Emperor's attack to the person of the current Pope, even if it laid down precedents which would be highly undesirable for the Papacy if accepted. In 1245, however, after six years of gruelling conflict culminating in his deposition, Frederick took a different tack, launching a general critique of the worldliness of the Church and calling for a return to apostolic poverty: the perverse confusion of priestly and temporal roles should end, and the Church should give up its property. The letters he wrote on this theme to the crowned heads of

---

[14]　E. Kantoworicz, *Frederick the Second, 1194–1250*, trans. E.O. Lorimer (London, 1931), p. 392.

Europe seem to have had little effect, and of course Frederick himself had too much invested in the worldly Church really to push for its destruction, but this adoption of an apostolic/Franciscan perspective by a lay ruler was a harbinger of things to come, and later experiments with the same cocktail were to have more profound effects. Ideas that directly assaulted the legitimacy of the Church as it was currently ordered were being openly canvassed, and – for the first time – a powerful figure had used them for political ends. It is true that a lack of legitimacy does not, in itself, prevent structures from working, and those of the Church continued to harness and organise large amounts of power, but the prominence of this potentially devastating critique of clerical dominion, and its intersection with the kinds of constitutional conflict to which all later medieval political forms were subject, meant that the Papacy entered our period in a strangely ambivalent position.

The Holy Roman Empire

For western Europeans, the term 'emperor' generally meant the ruler of the conjoined central European kingdoms of the Germans (*regnum Teutonicorum* or *Teutonicum*), of Lombardy (or Italy) and of Burgundy (or Arles). He was the recreated heir of the Roman Empire in the West, descendant of Charlemagne, who had been crowned Emperor at Rome in 800, and more specifically of the East Frankish king, Otto I, whose coronation at Rome was in 962. Although his empire was divinely appointed, although he was conventionally a crusader, and although he could enjoy, or assert, spiritual prerogatives, especially in periods of papal schism or vacancy, the Emperor's holiness was less a result of more generalised spiritual claims than of a particular responsibility for the defence of the Roman Church. But even if the imperial role was essentially different from the papal one – the one primarily temporal, the other primarily spiritual – the claims of Pope and Emperor copiously overlapped. In periods of conflict with the Papacy, the Emperor could express his rights in the fullest possible terms: he too might wield the metaphor of the two swords, or of the sun and the moon (usually accepting his lunar role, but often insisting that he shone independently); he might call himself *dominus mundi* ('lord of the world'). Even so, it is important to realise that these claims were advanced mainly for the benefit of a papal audience – or, more broadly, for an Italian one. The Emperor's high assertions were mainly restricted to the territorial space of his own kingdoms. Even in the wake of the Roncaglia decrees of 1158, in which the rights bestowed on the Emperor by Roman law were first canvassed to his Italian subjects, and in the elevated circumstances of summoning a council to resolve the schism of 1160, Frederick Barbarossa (1157–90) acknowledged the existence of 'other kingdoms' beyond his empire – those of England, France, Hungary and Denmark were named in the summons.[15] To the north and east, it is true, the scope of the Empire was less clear-cut, with the Emperors and their vassals claiming jurisdiction over fluctuating areas of Poland, Silesia and the Baltic littoral from the tenth century, until the rising Polish crown was able to contain and repel them from the fourteenth century onwards. But it remains the case that, in most respects, the 'Empire' was essentially a territorial monarchy, albeit a very large one that comprehended other monarchies within it.

This means that many of the characteristics of the Empire can be discussed below, alongside those of other kingdoms (and it is an argument of this book that the kingdom of the Germans, at least, is less untypical than historical tradition has tended to suggest). Most of the Empire's peculiarities stem not from its designation as an 'empire': those 'kings of the Romans', as German kings were called, who did not obtain a Roman coronation or affect imperial titles ruled in the same ways, and over the same spaces, as those who did. Rather, it was the vast extent of the Empire and the unavoidable interaction of its ruler with that other western emperor, the Pope, that account for most of its differences. There are perhaps only two or three ways in which the imperial, as distinct from royal, identity of the Emperors was determinative for their history and that of their lands and dependants.

The first relates to Roman law, which was recovered and redeveloped from the later eleventh century, particularly at the city of Bologna, where its study was directly encouraged and protected by the Hohenstaufen Emperors. The *Corpus Iuris Civilis*, as the main collection of Roman law texts came to be known, assigned particular roles and prerogatives to the Roman Emperor, and thus to any ruler who could claim to be his heir. The Holy Roman Emperors were among the earliest – and in an Italian context, the most obvious – claimants to this status. From the 1150s, Barbarossa and his heirs employed Roman law terminology and claimed the sovereign, and

---

[15] I.S. Robinson, *The Papacy 1073–1198* (Cambridge, 1990), p. 474.

remarkably complete, legislative and judicial rights which the Roman people were thought to have handed over to their ruler. In making these claims, the Emperors were not, as we shall see, particularly distinctive: by 1200, and in some cases much earlier, a number of other kings had asserted a similar status in their own realms. Even so, the Emperor's claim to this juridical sovereignty was extremely important for his operations in Italy, where Roman law exercised particular dominance and where another plausible emperor resided, in the shape of the Pope. In some ways, the main importance of the Emperor's status was a negative one: the power-holders of Italy feared his legal rights and expended a great deal of energy resisting him – diplomatically, militarily and, indeed, conceptually, through the attempts to find legal justification for limitations to his power. Among the reasons for papal animosity towards the emperors was the anxiety that what these men had gained (or given) as mere kings might be held (or resumed) as possessions of the Emperor, whose absolute rights, according to Roman law, could not be alienated. Rome, the Papal States and the kingdom of Sicily, all of them under papal (over)lordship, could be seen as the inalienable possessions of the Emperor, and, while the Papacy had a barrage of defences against that view, its own authority in these areas was thus rendered challengeable by anyone with the desire and the capacity to make that challenge. A similar state of affairs existed throughout northern and central Italy, where a host of city states, lordships and principalities had emerged, usurping the authority of bishops, counts and other representatives of the Italian/Lombard king. Once that king was recast as the Roman Emperor, he manifestly regained, at least in law, all that he had once lost. On the other hand, vulnerable cities might also see in the Emperor a source of aid against enemies closer at hand. It is interesting that it was the city of Pisa and not the German princes that first elected Alfonso X of Castile as Emperor in 1256, citing an ancient historical right to do so; Pisa was seeking imperial help against its pro-papal Tuscan neighbours, but its act reflected and affirmed a lasting strand of Italian enthusiasm for imperial intervention and even sovereignty which was developed and articulated in the early fourteenth-century works of Dante and Marsiglio of Padua. It does not matter that the Emperor was only intermittently able to pursue his claims: as in the case of the Papacy, imperial claims were there for others to invoke on his behalf, or against more immediately pressing authorities. The solvent power of the rights bestowed on the Emperor by the law and history of Rome was thus a powerful force wherever Roman law was influential and wherever the Emperors, their 'vicars'[16] or their putative allies (such as the so-called ' Ghibellines') were active. Above all, this meant Italy, from the mid-twelfth century onwards, but all the rulers in and around the Empire experienced something of the same problem: Roman law had the potential to destabilise almost all pre-existing claims to authority, and its potential was greatest where the claims of the Emperor were most closely involved.

A second way in which the imperial title made the Emperor more than a mere king of the domains under his sway lay in its other ideological associations. For the ever-expanding and multi-ethnic 'German' lands of the high middle ages, the notions of emperor and empire seem to have been more real than any idea of a German kingdom, and this meant that Rome provided much of the focus for such 'regnal' or 'national' politics as then existed. By the thirteenth century, in fact, this was changing. The accretion of bits of constitutional kit which only applied to the German lands – the *Reichslandfrieden* (imperial land-peace associations), a more regularised election proce- dure, laws governing the exercise of jurisdiction and so on – helped to create the sense of a specifically German *regnum*, with its own com- mon interest and its own customs to apply alongside those of the *Länder* (provinces), towns, princes and royal/imperial courts. Even so, this does not seem to have reduced the consciousness of empire within the German space. The role of the ruler – called 'king of the Romans', let us remember – was still understood to be an imperial one, which meant, inter alia, that he was expected to take action in Italy, and to defend the interests of Christendom more generally. Although inter- nal political issues – peacekeeping and the like – acquired ever-greater weight in German politics, rather as they did everywhere else, it is important to realise that the domestic agenda remained, in certain respects, a secondary concern for the king-Emperor: he should be winning glory beyond the Alps, and bestowing grand titles on his vassals: he should be just and keep order, certainly, but he should not get bogged down in local disputes, for which other media of reso- lution existed, and still less should he attempt to reform the institu- tions of government. That the German peoples were less inclined to see their king in domestic, or governmental, terms has been consid- ered one of the peculiarities of German history – part of the *Sonderweg*

---

[16] I.e. lieutenants, officers.

(special path) taken by the Germans, and celebrated or execrated according to whatever view is taken of the German past. It can easily be exaggerated: the Plantagenet kings of England, for example, aimed at an empire scarcely less dazzling than that of the Hohenstaufen, and we might suggest that they became ensnared in domestic government against their will, and largely as an unplanned result of the fiscal and juridical structures they had built to milk their kingdom. The crusading ideal was probably as important to the kings of France and Castile as the imperial ideal was to the king of the Romans, and Castilian rulers, at least, were no more active than German ones in the direct rule of their kingdom. But the issue may have some significance in determining the pattern of governmental development in the German lands: it could help to explain why the emperors were mostly relaxed about the independent authority claimed and exercised by their underlings, and why they ruled the Empire with such a light administrative touch. The king's imperial status was not only a domestic influence, moreover. The proximity of the Emperor was also a conditioning factor in the political history of all the adjoining and overlapping territories, from those of the Dutch, Flemish and French in the West, to those of the Poles, Bohemians and Austrians in the East and South. It was also an issue for the Church, as we have seen. In the politics of ecclesiastical reform, which were tending to take an antipapal direction from the middle of the thirteenth century, the Emperor was a significant focus of appeal and, at times, an active player. In parts of Germany and Italy, indeed, it was not just the Emperor's claims to jurisdiction that made him a force to conjure with, but his implication in theories and prophecies of reform – not only those of popular zealots like Brother Arnold of Swabia (*fl. c.*1250) or Fra Dolcino of Novara (d.1307), but also the later, theologically informed ideas of William of Ockham and Marsiglio of Padua. This theme contributed a powerful sacral aura to imperial assertions, and it was to resurface dramatically in later fifteenth-century Germany, where the reforming Councils of Constance and Basle had stimulated a process of 'imperial reform' and helped to set the stage for the emergence of Martin Luther. This merging of German and ecclesiastical politics was a direct consequence of the imperial nature of the region's king.

A third feature of the Empire which was becoming more prominent in the later middle ages and which influenced German political development is its elective kingship. It is not very clear what this development owes to the kingdom's imperial dimension, however, even if the action of the Pisans, described above, suggests a link. If we go back far enough, all monarchies turn out to have had an elective aspect (though most, including those of Germany and Rome, also had a dynastic one). In the eleventh and twelfth centuries, as rules for the inheritance of property became more formalised, most secular dignities, including kingships, became substantially heritable, though politically inconvenient accidents of heredity still needed to be addressed, and the support of others for the exercise of power remained as important as ever, so election remained in play in many countries. Between 936 and 1254, the German crown mainly descended, sequentially, in the Ottonian, Salian and then Hohenstaufen/Staufer families, switching to a new dynasty only when the previous one had died out, fallen apart or lost credibility. Election played a part in these descents, but it was not a very different part from that played by ceremonies of homage, acclamation and coronation in other countries. By the later twelfth century, however, election was becoming an issue in Germany, as its procedures were increasingly defined, and the kings and other leading men began to take positions on the electoral and hereditary aspects of the monarchy. The resulting affirmation of election was partly for reasons of contingency and practical politics: the long antagonism between the Saxon Welfs and the ruling dynasty in the eleventh and twelfth centuries; the collapse of the Hohenstaufen network in the mid-thirteenth century; the absence of a clear successor family, which helped to create the so-called interregnum of 1254–73; the rough equality of the major dynasties that emerged towards the end of the century – the Wittelsbachs, Habsburgs and Luxemburgs; and, finally, the desirability of establishing a satisfactory system which could be proof against papal interference in disputed successions. At the same time, as that last point suggests, it seems likely that interactions and comparisons with the ecclesiastical empire played an important role. If one of the twin heads of the world was to be an elected figure, so surely must the other be. It is certainly worth noting that, in the fourteenth and fifteenth centuries, the rights of the electoral colleges, the cardinals on the one hand, and the seven Electors of the Empire, on the other, were developed and expanded in very similar ways. On the other hand, elective kingship was also to become normative in the kingdoms of Bohemia, Hungary and Poland, and if German influences played a part in that development, so did local contingencies and constitutional conditions.

It remains, then, to comment on the nature and scope of the Emperor's power at the beginning of our period. Apart from a blip at the beginning of Albert I's reign (1298–1308), the late thirteenth century and the first decade or so of the fourteenth saw an unusual degree of papal-imperial rapprochement, as a sequence of rulers from new families focused on establishing themselves in the German lands, while the Papacy intermittently looked to the post-Hohenstaufen Empire as a possible counterbalance to the overweening power of the Angevins. This general state of affairs meant that the Emperor was still a politically significant figure over much of the territory where he had traditionally held sway. Only southern Italy had moved fully out of the imperial orbit by the end of the thirteenth century: even though Rudolf I (1273–91) had surrendered imperial claims over the main provinces of the Papal States (duchy of Spoleto, march of Ancona, Romagna), imperial interventions as far south as Rome continued into the mid-fourteenth century, and imperialist rebellions by areas subject to the Papacy lasted even longer. In the Low Countries, it was still worth Edward III's while to seek an imperial vicariate to facilitate his actions in the late 1330s, while the struggle of King Ludwig the Bavarian for dominance over Germany attracted the attention of all the neighbouring polities. In the historic kingdom of Burgundy/Arles, where the Angevins of Provence were the major power, imperial rule had become more or less irrelevant, but even here it could be invoked against the pretensions of the crown of France, whose territories and claims in the region expanded throughout the thirteenth and fourteenth centuries.

Nonetheless, it is important to realise that, much as individual Emperors had the potential to project power in almost any part of their large domains, their means of doing so had shrunk from the heights of the Hohenstaufen period (1138–1254). The growth of urban and princely government, the end of Staufer hegemony and the twenty years of rather ineffective kingship between 1254 and 1273 meant the dispersal of many of the imperial estates north of the Alps, and further reduced the frequency of intervention in northern Italy. While Wittelsbach, Habsburg and Luxemburg Emperors were able – like the Staufer before them – to place major new private resources (*Erblände*) at the disposal of the crown, these resources were mostly located at the edges of the Empire and, as lordships or kingdoms in their own right, could rarely be employed freely in support of imperial projects. Even so, these changes should not be overstated: imperial rule had always been a matter of persuasion, assertion and selective intervention; the old fisc had probably done more to sustain the emperor's vassals and officers – the *ministeriales* – than the ruler himself, and, as we shall see, Rudolf I had some success in reasserting imperial rights over it. Throughout the fourteenth and fifteenth centuries, the Emperor's authority was widely sought within the area we have been discussing, and – usually in coalition with others – he could often make it work to help his allies and petitioners. It remained an important factor in the political history of central Europe, both north and south of the Alps.

The Eastern Empire

The third of our empires will be dealt with more briefly, and with an emphasis on comparison. It is generally known by the curious name of 'Byzantium', a Latinised version of the original name of the Greek city which later became Constantinople, but its real significance is as the remnant of the eastern half of the Roman Empire. It was, if one accepts the stress on continuity in its history, the most ancient of the three empires considered here, but it was also the least influential – and certainly in the affairs of the West. Where the western half of the Roman Empire had fallen apart in the fifth century and was thus rebuilt afresh by the popes and emperors we have been discussing, the ancient centre of the eastern half survived, lending great prestige to its secular and religious leaders, the 'Emperor of the Romans' himself and the patriarchs of the (Orthodox) Church, among whom the greatest was the Ecumenical Patriarch of Constantinople. The relationship between spiritual and temporal powers was quite different from that in the West, however. While emperor and patriarch drew strength from each other, and the emperor felt that he could intervene in matters of religion, the ecumenical patriarch had few, if any, of the worldly pretensions of the Papacy, and presided over the Eastern Church, which had been separated from its western counterpart in 1054, in a remarkably collegial fashion. Orthodox Christianity was a powerful force across a vast area of south-eastern Europe and Russia, typically commanding greater allegiance than the emperor himself, but it was sensitive to regional ethnicities and did not require an overall governmental unity in order to function. Separate Orthodox churches were established in Serbia in 1219 and Bulgaria in 1235, and the metropolitan see of Rus' at Kiev almost broke away in the 1240s. While these developments owe something to the disintegration of the secular structures of the Byzantine Empire in this period, they also reflect some significant differences in the nature of eastern and western Christianity.

Rather as in the West, the ideological, material and ritual trappings of the Eastern Empire exerted considerable influence over the various powers that succeeded to its territories in the course of the middle ages. The doges of Venice, the kings of Sicily and the grand princes, later tsars, of Muscovy all drew on Byzantine imperial forms and ideas; in some respects, the same might be said of the Ottomans. But, in contrast to its western counterparts, the Eastern Empire was, by 1300, little more than a model, an inspiration; it had very little concrete existence, even within its shrunken domains, let alone outside them. The conquest of Constantinople in 1204 by the Flemish, French and Venetian participants in the Fourth Crusade had driven both emperor and patriarch out of their capital, had broken the remaining Byzantine territory into three parts, and had established a Latin version of the Empire in Greece and Thrace which lasted, in a state of high anarchy, until 1261. While émigrés from Constantinople re-established both Empire and Patriarchate at Nicaea, and regained control over the Byzantine territories in western Anatolia, the other Byzantine lands, centred on Epirus and Trebizond, remained aloof. The new Lascarid dynasty at Nicaea was overthrown by the military leader Michael Palaeologus, who seized the throne in 1258, and conquered Constantinople in 1261. Although he and his heirs managed to regain much of what we would call Greece during the following century, western Anatolia was rapidly lost: its allegiances were shaken by disputes arising from the usurpation, and, by a mixture of conquest and coalescence, it fell to the Ottoman Turks during the first half of the fourteenth century. Within the Empire, the public powers of the emperor had proved hard to reconstruct, and rule had mainly devolved to towns and magnates; the Roman and international identity of the old state was giving way to a distinctly Greek ethnicity that fused Hellenistic and Orthodox Christian elements. At the beginning of our period, therefore, the Eastern Empire was little more than a congeries of independent territories grouped around Constantinople and Thrace, and sharing a strong, but localised, culture. If this development anticipated the descent of the Papacy to the status of Italian prince and head of a sectional and segmented Church, or that of the king of the Romans to a similar position in Germany, it is worth noting that it happened much earlier. In the West, by contrast, empires were meaningful political structures for the whole of the two centuries covered by this book.

Kings and kingdoms, lords and principalities

Kings and lords

Wherever imperial rights, titles and attributes were known about, they were claimed by other rulers. English, French and Spanish kings were using imperial language in the tenth century, while the Norman adventurers who became kings of Sicily were crowned in imperial robes from 1130 and claimed some of the powers bestowed by Roman law as early as the 1120s, in advance even of the western Emperors. Almost any ruler with a chancery might claim to be a kind of emperor in his own domains, and, if it was only from around 1200 that kings started brandishing such tags as *imperator in regno suo* ('emperor in his realm') or *non recognoscit superiorem* ('he does not recognise a superior'), this was not because they were newly liberated, but because the spread of Roman and canon law required them to express their high authority in new currency. If the endowments of empire were so widely claimed, does it make sense to discuss kings as a separate category? What did kingship distinctively amount to?

In a way, of course, the question is rather contrived. There were large numbers of kings in the later middle ages, and most of them were content, most of the time, to call themselves by that name. Kingship was itself an idea, with powerful scriptural and historical legitimations; if it drew on the resources of empire, it was not assimilated by them. At the same time, this is a useful question to ask, because it reminds us that kingship was a structure, a contrivance, and not something that naturally belonged to a limited number of individuals; nor, for all its implications, did it automatically deliver effective rule over a kingdom or a people. The distribution of kingly power was ever-changing, and – perhaps more remarkably – so was the distribution of kingly titles. The eleventh, twelfth and thirteenth centuries had seen the number of formally recognised kings increase, as the Pope bestowed crowns on the rulers of Portugal and Sicily, Serbia, Bulgaria and, more briefly, Lithuania, while the Emperor did the same in Cyprus, Poland, Hungary and Bohemia, and contemplated it for Austria and Styria. At the same time, the mere title of king – or even a distinguished tradition of kingship – did not necessarily have any political force. The ancient crown of Scotland, for example, could be dismissed by

Edward I with the observation that, 'though the land of Scotland be called a "kingdom", the land itself is only a lordship, like Wales, the earldom of Chester, or the bishopric of Durham', and it is clear that some of the kingdom's leading subjects were prepared to go along with this perspective.[17] The twelfth- and thirteenth-century kings of Bohemia, it has been argued, gained nothing but short-term advantage from their crown: their power as dukes was just as great, and this helps to explain why one or two of them agreed to resume their former title. Meanwhile, as Duke Władisław Łokietek began to overcome the other dukes of a long-divided Poland at the beginning of the fourteenth century, the acquisition of the ancient crown was an important political goal for him; but what it gave him over Poland's other leaders, beyond a vague pre-eminence, is not entirely clear – he had to crush them in order to rule them. In discussing kingship, therefore, we should be wary of overstating its completeness and its fixity, especially at the beginning of our period. Kings made large claims, and these were only to increase, but they also lived among other potentates, and in times of great political creativity. For both reasons, the future shapes of kingly regimes were variable and uncertain.

There were, perhaps, two main aspects to medieval kingship. On the one hand, kings were seen in terms of their social and political function: they were axiomatically the rulers of peoples and lands. 'Peoples' were essentially political groupings, defined, as much as anything, by the shared customs and routines in which the rule of their king was a significant shaping factor; 'lands' came about through the reach of these activities and by association with the peoples that inhabited them. The *rex* (king) and the *regnum* (realm, sometimes kingship) thus helped to define and affirm each other, and we might usefully borrow Susan Reynolds' helpful term 'regnal' to capture this side of kingship.[18] As part of their regnal authority, kings anciently possessed bodies of presumptive rights over their lands and peoples, many of which had an implicitly public and governmental nature. They were typically said to own large amounts of the territory, and especially the uncultivated swathes of forest and highland. They were entitled to head-taxes, or taxes on plough-teams, hearths or areas of tilled land. They imposed obligations of upkeep on those in the

---

[17] R.R. Davies, *The First English Empire* (Oxford, 2000), p. 27, n. 64.
[18] See *Kingdoms and Communities*, pp. 253–6, for a valuable discussion.

vicinity of roads, bridges and castles (and often claimed a general authority over the last). They asserted jurisdiction over the highest crimes and issued law-codes. Their subjects were generally obliged to offer them hospitality as they toured the realm, and usually owed military service in times of war. They claimed a unique right to unusual resources – salt and precious metals, wrecks and wild animals; often, they asserted a special control over the Jews and their property. In most kingdoms, in practice, these *regalia* (royal things) were exercised by many others besides the king, but the fact, or fiction, of their kingly nature was widely upheld. Meanwhile, texts and rituals reinforced the association of kings with ruling. An influential axiom of the seventh-century dictionary-writer, Isidore of Seville, explained that the title *rex* was derived *a regendo, a recte agendo* (from ruling, from right doing), so that kings were linked to moral leadership, and rule acquired a high moral status: something which was multiplied by the part-sacralisation of monarchy in rituals of anointing, the singing of *Laudes Regiae* (royal praises), the curing of scrofula and other elements of what the French call *la religion royale*. All these factors combined to link conceptions of kingship not just with high authority, but also with expectations of the governance and common welfare of the people who lived together under the king's authority. Out of these expectations came notions of the kingdom and the kingship against which the king might be measured.

At the same time, kings were also great lords. '*Dominus rex*', 'the lord king', was the usual title of the king of England, and if this was a simple courtesy it also captured an essential aspect of his nature. Lordship was the exercise of possession over territory and something close to possession over men. Whatever the more general powers kings claimed or exercised over their kingdoms, there were also things that they regarded as peculiarly their property: lands, often known as 'demesnes', from the Latin word for lordship; palaces and castles; servants and ministers; tenants, vassals and commended men, who had accepted royal lordship – some through elaborate ceremonies of homage and fealty, some prescriptively, by paying dues, or simply by submitting. The king's possessive instinct often extended beyond his demesnes, his *familia* (household, entourage) and his tenantry, to the rest of his *regalia* – for all their connotations of public right and duty, these too were for the king to deploy and administer, sell and bargain (or even expand), as he saw fit. Over time, as we shall see, the resources of royal government came to be more clearly distinguished from the ruler's private possessions, and to be seen as a kind of public property, but kings retained a basic freedom of action with the resources at their disposal, and they continued to regard their authority in lordly terms. Royal lordship, after all, did not only benefit the king. Although relationships of lord and man were typically forceful and contestable, and either party would be likely to exploit the weakness of the other, lordship was not just force: it was shaped by conventions and traditions, and it involved reciprocities; people might want the lord's protection, or the fiefs (grants of land or money), favours and privileges he could bestow. Kings and lords were fighting men, doughty, masterful and violent, but they were also required by the mores of aristocratic society to be hospitable, generous, just, courteous, flexible and gracious, as the occasion demanded. As these qualities suggest, lordship was a highly personal form of rule, which does not mean that it was simply dependent on individual character, but rather that it involved the direct interactions of individuals, the management of individual relationships, and attention to individual needs and misdemeanours. Through the successful management of his resources – both his property and his men – the king could maintain his power over other lords of his realm, binding them and their men to his service and thereby substantiating a more general authority. Lordship was thus as integral to the task of kingship as the more familiar ideal of regnal authority discussed above.

Both of these aspects of kingship were, to a greater or lesser extent, reproduced throughout society. Other lordships, or seignories, worked in much the same way as the king's, albeit usually on a smaller scale and in ways that were affected by the greater lordships around and above them. Equally, every lay holder of a dignity or office or fief typically presided over some kind of community towards which he had global responsibilities, as the king did to the kingdom. Either aspect might be much less elaborate or articulate when wielded by a castellan, or bailiff, a baron or a burgrave, and the balance between what we might call ownership and office could vary from role to role, but it is important to remember that the distinctiveness of kingship should not be overstated, especially before about 1200. The counts and dukes of northern France, the Low Countries and the German lands, several of whom controlled as much territory as their putative overlords, exercised many of the same rights as the kings in their domains, received the full allegiance of their subjects and adopted many of the cultural affectations of monarchy, including ceremonies of investiture, even if they stopped short of calling themselves kings. Further south, there was little to choose between the kings of León, Castile and Aragon and the counts of Barcelona, Toulouse and Provence – indeed, when Aragon and Barcelona were joined, in 1137, the county did not become subordinate to the kingdom, but remained a completely separate (and much more powerful) unit. Even on a smaller scale, such local princes as the earls of Chester, the bishops of Durham and the lords of the March of Wales exercised quasi-regal and mainly autonomous power in their border lordships, notwithstanding their general allegiance to the powerful king of England. It is true that kings had many political advantages: they were richly endowed with mythic and historical legitimations; their rituals of installation were often especially elaborate, typically featuring anointment with holy oil, which enabled them to claim a sacred status; they usually had superior means of attracting service, storing records and generating publicity; they always had a claim to *regalia* and typically disposed of large resources scattered across broad realms; they generally enjoyed the support of churchmen and were able to exploit new technologies of rule in advance of other lords. These things gave them a kind of power and authority that could enable them to supervise, or even perforate, the smaller authorities they claimed as their subjects. A lot of the time, they could obtain the compliance of others with little effort, as kingly authority was frequently useful to other power-holders besides the king himself. If anything usefully differentiates the status of king from that of lord, it is that the former generally acknowledged no superior, while the latter – however reluctantly, pragmatically or variably – generally did. This difference was a lot more meaningful in some periods than in others, and we should not draw from it a sense that royal rule automatically possessed normative force or overwhelming legitimacy for the inhabitants of a kingdom. Royal records, royalist apologetics and nationalistic historiography typically conceal the limitations of royal authority, painting its frequent failures as unnatural or fortuitous, and reading the interested and conditional support of other powers as evidence of loyalty or submission. Kings were frequently ineffective and their interventions were often resented and resisted; other power-holders could command allegiance too; other communities and their leaders could often be more meaningful than the 'regnal' one. A balanced perspective on kingship, that acknowledges its powers without assuming a natural pre-eminence, is an essential basis for understanding the politics of our period. Over time, a process of differentiation was to raise the status of kings and depress, or contain, that of lords; but that process was not a straightforward or linear one. Its first important stage occurred with the transformations of jurisdiction that began in the twelfth and thirteenth centuries.

The revolution in law and justice

In the two hundred years between *c.*1100 and *c.*1300, the spread of literacy and record-keeping, the development of notions of office associated with ecclesiastical reform, the emergence of *studia* (schools of higher education) and universities at which high officials could be trained, and the impact of the learned law – canon and Roman – had profound effects on rulers. Techniques of accounting and supervision were developed that increased the oppressiveness of lordship and strengthened the ambitions of government. It became possible, at least in principle, to separate the exercise of official functions from the possession of property. Writing enabled decisions to be easily communicated and this permitted more decision-making and more innovation in centres of authority (as well as more conflict when the results of these activities became known in the provinces). Very crudely, it might be said that, in the twelfth century, the main effect of these developments was to enable first kings and then other great lords to administer their demesnes and regulate their dependants more effectively. This was, conventionally, the great age of the 'feudal monarchy', but what that really means is that this was the first period in which the laws and customs of fief-holding were committed to writing and developed into media of government and exploitation. Not surprisingly, these processes were full of conflict, as lords and vassals sought to define their once-negotiable relationships and customs in ways that suited themselves. In these conflicts, kings, as the only lords who were not also tenants, often had the edge. Louis VII (1137–80) and Philip II Augustus (1180–1223) of France, for example, policed their feudal jurisdiction so efficiently that they were able to revise the terms of homage, entertaining appeals from subtenants and corroding the authority of princes. In England, where centralised media of rule had survived alongside feudal networks, twelfth-century kings were able more or less to eradicate the judicial powers of their inferiors, establishing a common legal system under royal direction which had driven out most competitors by 1250. But this was a rare outcome. It was often possible for greater vassals to strengthen their hold over lesser ones, sometimes because lords applied the same refinements – more effective courts, more precise demands for service – to their own tenants, or because they challenged royal interference and bargained for concessions. Frederick Barbarossa's moves to extend and define his feudal rights over the leading magnates of the Empire, for example, resulted in the emergence of a privileged estate of princes, each with a more complete control of his dependants.

In the thirteenth century, again crudely, the tendency of developments in jurisdiction was slightly different. The supervision of demesnes and dependants was just as tight, and feudal law remained a powerful influence at every level, but the accent of royal policy-makers came to fall much more heavily on the restoration of the public authority of the prince. This was primarily a result of the reception of Roman law in the chanceries of western Europe, a process which had been going on since the early twelfth century but approached a kind of dominance by the mid-thirteenth. Roman law dramatically reinvigorated older conceptions of the king and the kingdom. Concentrating legislative and judicial authority in a king-emperor and depicting a polity in which this figure was the sole source of legitimate secular authority, it distinguished the king from other lords and ignored the rough-and-ready power-sharing that actually characterised a lot of European politics. Because of the way it portrayed royal power, it was a huge stimulus to legislative and judicial activity on the part of rulers, clearly lying behind the legislative programmes that characterised the reigns of Emperor Frederick II, Louis IX of France, Edward I of England and Alfonso X of Castile, but also shaping the widespread codification of customary law and the formalisation of high courts with appellate and corrective jurisdiction. Together with canon law, which itself was full of Roman influences, it made available a whole range of concepts and models which were eagerly taken up throughout society, partly because the systematic quality of Romano-canonical writing encouraged the progressive implementation of its content, and partly because these things seemed to map on to the powers and predicaments of the continent at the time. The absorption of Roman and canon law was a central cause of both political development and political conflict in the high and late middle ages, and it consequently deserves to be introduced at some length. Four notions, perhaps, were particularly important for kingdoms.

The first was the idea of the fisc, diadem or crown: the body of rights and powers required for the rule of the realm. Where the royal demesne and *regalia* had been simply the inheritance of the king, they could now be regarded as public goods, which it was the responsibility of the king and everyone else to preserve, because they were required for the rule of the realm. Although this idea could potentially restrain the king's freedom of action – for example, by making his estates and rights inalienable – it mainly served to enhance his authority, by making him the sole rightful owner of everything necessary for the good government of the realm, especially jurisdiction, but also, by implication, such goods and services as may be required for the common defence, and, by association, anything which had once belonged to the royal patrimony. Since no king was, in reality, the owner of everything, even everything pertaining to justice, principles like these were a licence for him to increase his estate at the expense of other holders of property and authority, or at least to challenge, through his courts and officers, their possession and exercise of these things. A powerful king in a manageable realm like Edward I promptly set about demanding to know *quo warranto* ('by what warrant, title, or right?') landowners held judicial franchises when these were, in principle, his. Other kings would later do the same, the Angevin kings of Hungary and the restored kings of Poland even extending the principle from jurisdiction to property from the 1320s onwards.

A second group of ideas related to these concerned the king-emperor's role as *tutor*, or guardian, of the realm, and his consequent rights in circumstances of emergency, or 'necessity' – the defence of the realm, in other words. These ideas provided a powerful new rationale for taxation, and – in principle at least – re-centred the control of taxation in the hands of the king. Taxation was not, of course, invented in the thirteenth century, but it would be fair to say that it was transformed towards the end of that century and in the succeeding one. Older regnal taxes had drifted into the hands of other lords – perhaps they had always been in those hands – but the new Romano-canonical taxes were part and parcel of the king's sovereignty. While he might be forced to alienate their collection, or bargain over them in other ways, he possessed a superior legal right to them, and that was no mean asset in an age of lawmaking. The crowns of Aragon and England were experimenting with this kind of taxation in the years around 1200, and the latter kingdom was making consistent use of it by the 1290s; similar taxes were developed in Sicily from 1223, and in Castile from the 1270s, while Philip IV of France imposed levies for the defence of the realm on half a dozen occasions between 1295 and 1304. And it was not just kings who deployed these ideas: the Papacy sought the general taxation of the Church on the grounds of common defence and common welfare on a number of occasions between 1199 and 1311; in the following century, as we shall see, the same principles would come to be invoked by princes, lords and urban governments.

English royal taxation drew on another Romano-canonical idea which was to have wide application: the principle that what touches all should be approved by all, commonly shortened in history books to its first three Latin words, '*Quod omnes tangit*'. This principle was central to the developing canon law of corporations, which set out a legal framework for the relationship between defined groups – *universitates, communitates* (wholes, communities) – and their leaders. While the canonical model was often the cathedral chapter and the bishop, the idea could be applied more broadly: to monks and the abbot; to the whole Church, or the college of cardinals, and the Pope; or to any plausible lay *communitas* – vill, town, realm – and its head. Together with canonical ideas of procuration (representation by proxy), this tag and its related net of legal principles refashioned and affirmed older practices of consent and counsel-giving with newer models of representation. The rash of representative assemblies that grew up across Europe, mainly from the thirteenth century, were stimulated and defined by this powerful and widespread principle. Once again, counsel and consent were not new phenomena, but canon law had given them a new means of justification and the potential for different ordering, as, for instance, the men called to counsel might now be expected to come as plenipotentiaries for their region or social group, able to bind, by their representative advice, those on whose behalf they came. Although this principle, so powerful in the making of the English parliament, was generally thwarted in regnal assemblies on the continent, it typically worked on a more localised basis and exerted a more general influence over the negotiations of rulers and subjects. The coming of *quod omnes tangit* meant new legitimations for consulting rulers, for their consultees and for anyone else who might claim to represent a *communitas* of some kind.

The last cluster of particularly formative Romano-canonical ideas is perhaps even more fundamental, and underpins all of those that we have been discussing. It stems from the so-called *Lex Regia* (royal law, law of the king), by which the authority of the king-emperor was first legally established; namely by a grant from the Roman people, having in mind their common safety. On the one hand, this provided the basis for the sovereignty of kings, but – at the same time – it indicated that that sovereignty was derived from the people and given by them for their own collective good. This bestowed on the *Lex Regia*, and on Roman and canon law more generally, a certain ambivalence. If these laws have appeared so far as the friends of kings, they were also, potentially, the friends of peoples, and in elevating royal power they consistently canvassed its responsibilities and emphasised the notions of *utilitas publica, salus populi, bonum commune* (public utility/good, safety of the people, common good) and so on, for which it had been created. There were inevitable questions about the basis on which the king-emperor held his powers: was he merely the *procurator* (proxy) of the people? If he failed to protect their good, or utility, or safety, could they take back what they had given? Could they do this anyway, as an exercise of sovereign right? And which 'people' are referred to – did 'the Roman people' mean any people, or all people, or the people of the city of Rome, or the better people among them? Most juristic opinion argued that the people had exhausted their power once and for all in making their gift, and that no other people could have back what the Romans had given. Indeed, because the imperial power was created for *salus populi*, its defence was a matter of the greatest importance: the *majestas* (majesty, public power) of the king-emperor was a public property and any individual or group who acted against it was acting against the whole people. This was the basis of the Roman law *crimen majestatis* (crime of majesty) or *crimen laesae majestatis* (crime of *lèse-majesté*, harm to the public power), which underpinned the new concepts of treason with which monarchies were beginning to protect themselves. Actions against the king were now qualitatively different from the mere betrayal of a lord; they were crimes against the whole people and the *majestas*, or public power, by which it was justly ruled; such crimes thus deserved the most far-reaching punishment – death, mutilation, the confiscation of all property, the disinheritance of heirs: enough to make action against the king, even by or for 'the people', a distinctly dangerous prospect. Even so, Romano-canonical ideas were available for uses not sanctioned by the best juristic opinion, and the general idea that authority was bestowed for the good of the people became a commonplace of later medieval political thought and action, frequently justifying moves to correct the king.

   Together with the developments mentioned at the beginning of this section, and some other ideological innovations discussed below, the learned law had a tremendous impact on the kings and kingdoms of Europe. It distinguished the ruler more sharply, and in new ways, from other power holders; it made his authority a matter of public concern, in ways which strengthened, but also re-framed, it; and it created, or recreated, a series of connected institutions and practices which became a model for monarchies. Where once the typical king had had a court and household, a *familia*, a series of dependants, some demesnes and some *regalia*, he now came to have – alongside these older elements – legislative and jurisdictional structures and routines, archives and a codifying instinct, rights to taxation and military service that extended in principle over his whole realm, representative assemblies, and the administrative means necessary to manage at least some of these public powers – a secretariat, an exchequer and treasury, a network of officers with responsibilities beyond the demesne. Elements of this kit were borrowed closely from Romano-canonical principles. Other elements represented compromises between indigenous customs and traditions and the perspectives created by the new learning. Still others were copied, or adapted, from kingdom to kingdom, rather than flowing directly from the wellsprings of Bologna, or Orleans, or other centres of Romanic learning. Older conceptions of kingship, as sacred, heroic, chivalrous or gracious, remained in play; but they were supplemented by a powerful new emphasis on jurisdiction and its associated powers and forms. How, then, was the ideal type of juridical kingship realised in practice?

Juridical kingdoms
Although by the middle of the fourteenth century most European polities conformed in some way to the identikit kingdom we have just described, it is important to note three things. First, by no means all of these polities were kingdoms properly so called: the model was usable by other powers too, as we shall see below. Second, they did not all get there at the same time. If governmental literacy spread at a roughly uniform rate, the penetration of Romano-canonical ideas depended on the extent to which ruling elites and their advisers were exposed to them, whether through education in the relatively small number of universities and *studia* that existed before 1300, or through density of

contact with such Romanising forces as the Papal Church, the Italian cities and the chanceries of the Empire, Sicily, France, England and the Spanish kingdoms. It took time for the new notions and practices to spread, and, as we shall see, the polities of western Britain, Scandinavia and east-central Europe were often doing in the four-teenth century what their neighbours to the west and south had done in the thirteenth, and in the thirteenth what had been done in the twelfth. Where, for example, King Magnus introduced the *lex julia majestatis*, or law of *lèse-majesté*, to Sweden in a judgement of the 1280s, King Alfonso I of Aragon was legislating to make assaults on the highway a species of *lèse-majesté* in 1173. While regnal law-codes were promulgated in Castile in the 1250s and 1260s, and earlier than this in Sicily and (in a sense) England, Sweden and Poland had to wait until the middle of the fourteenth century (though Magnus Law-mender of Norway (1263–80) was more advanced, issuing the 'Landlaw' in 1274 and the 'Townlaw' in 1276). It is not, of course, that these distant kingdoms were more primitive, but rather that the different, piecemeal and somewhat delayed way in which they received the Romano-canonical package meant that it tended to confirm a different distribution of power.

A third, and very obvious, point to make about the way in which the kingdom model was realised is that it varied enormously from place to place. While it is hard to disagree that most kingdoms had, or came to have, something like the features listed above, they worked, and fitted together, in different ways in different places. The reasons behind this kind of variation are, of course, manifold. One has just been mentioned – proximity to those centres of Europe in which particular ideologies and technologies were generated – but there are many others. The size of the territory claimed by the kingdom inevitably affected the development of its institutions, as did the presence of internal barriers: the small kingdoms of England, Majorca, Sicily and (for a time) Denmark were rather more integrated than the enormous kingdoms of France, Poland and the Germans, while the presence of mountains or highlands in the similarly small kingdom of Scotland (or for that matter in Bohemia, in Aragon and northern Catalonia, and in Calabria and northern Sicily) enabled areas of resistance which helped to shape the political culture. The degree of urbanisation and, not unrelated, the amount of competition from other powers within the acknowledged, or imagined, bounds of the kingdom also had a significant effect. The presence of the big trading city of Barcelona at the centre of Catalan political society, for instance, did much to underpin the effectiveness and durability of the local representative assembly, the *Corts,* and this, in turn, helps to explain the emphasis on consultation, and the tendency to protect local privilege, on the part of the Aragonese monarchy. Meanwhile, in Scotland, geographically and ethnically driven traditions of provincial lordship, the close association of royal power with the relatively urbanised 'core' of Lothian and Perthshire, together with powerful competition from the kings of England after the 1280s, were to ensure that the Scottish crown developed in a federal direction, with most jurisdiction in the hands of regional magnates and very limited fiscal and administrative pressure from the ruler. Random events must also be taken into account. The kingdom of Hungary, for example, might have developed very differently if its great plains had not been invaded and laid waste by the Mongols in 1241–2. The massacres, and the famine which inevitably followed in 1243, are thought to have destroyed at least 15–20 per cent of the population, making this a catastrophe comparable to the Black Death, though one more sharply targeted at peasants and town-dwellers. In order to prevent further assaults, King Béla IV (1235–70) reversed his policy of restoring royal authority and allowed the unrestricted building of stone castles by the nobles, a move which, like other examples of *incastellamento* (the spread of castles), facilitated localised resistance to the crown and helped to produce the anarchy that followed his death. While, significantly, encastellation did not prevent a return to more centralised modes of rule under the Angevin kings, it ensured a lasting role for great magnates in the shaping of the kingdom.

Continent-wide models interacted with variable situations in time and space, therefore, but that does not make it impossible to trace general patterns of development in Europe. For one thing, even 'random' events have some patterning. The same flatness of the Carpathian Basin that allowed the construction of a large and powerful Hungarian monarchy in the eleventh and twelfth centuries made the same structure vulnerable to invasion, which happened fatally, of course, at the hands of the Ottomans in the 1520s, as well as more briefly in the 1240s. Nor was this vulnerability purely a geographical matter: strong monarchies discouraged encastellation, and that meant an openness to conquest, as was clear in the fate of the Old English kingdom in 1016 and 1066. To take a different example, the failure of the Scottish royal line in 1286/90, or the problem of too many sons, which led to the 'fragmentation' of Poland in 1138, look, at first sight, to be fortuitous events with major results. But these events only possessed the significance they did because of the strengthening of inheritance customs: in other words, they are incomprehensible except in relation to political and constitutional developments which were actually more widespread (and indeed problems of this kind struck every ruling house at one time or another; the timing might have some significance, but intermittent dynastic crises were part and parcel of the workings of monarchy, their impact varying as the institution evolved). Finally, it must be worth noting that neither of these dynastic calamities had any lasting impact, in that the crowns of both Scotland and Poland recovered, and in that one might reasonably wonder whether Poland was just as 'fragmented' before 1138 as afterwards, or whether Scotland would have escaped the imperial designs of Edward I even if its throne had been occupied. There is an iterative quality to the relationship between structures and contingencies, whether the latter are temporal or spatial. The way in which a kingdom had already developed shaped the way it responded to particular challenges, and these challenges, in turn, confirmed certain aspects of its development and closed off others. It is not, to choose a well-worn example, that Castile, with its martial traditions and Romanised ruler, was *inevitably* going to turn 'absolutist', while Aragon-Catalonia was predestined to 'pactism' (contractual monarchy), but it is easy to see how these things came about, and how the developing political traditions of the kingdoms were not simply the result of chance events.

The point to emphasise about the transformation of kingship in the twelfth and thirteenth centuries is that, however much the new structures proposed a new coherence for the kingdom, they actually provoked, and to some extent licensed, conflict within and around it. The results of high medieval political development, therefore, were highly ambivalent, and profoundly formative for the conflicts of the centuries that followed. Because this fact is so little appreciated in a historiography which mainly celebrates the thirteenth-century political achievement, and because the theme is so central to this book, it will be helpful to look at why this was. There are perhaps two major reasons. The first is that the various polities that were undergoing this transformation overlapped. It was not uncommon for the boundaries between kingdoms to be unclear, or for the king of one area to claim hegemony over another. Sometimes this was because he had some sort of personal dynastic claim over it, as had Peter III of Aragon (1276–85) to Sicily, or Otakar II of Bohemia (1253–78) to Austria/ Styria. Sometimes it was because he claimed historic, or juridical, rights over it, as was the case in the wars raised by the kings of Castile, Aragon and Portugal against the Muslim kingdoms of Spain, or those raised by the Papacy against Frederick II and his heirs over Sicily. Sometimes both sets of claims were in play, as in Edward I's intervention in Scotland, which was justified both by the ancient overlordship he pretended and by his son's marriage to the last ruler of the line of Canmore, the Maid of Norway who died in 1290. The examples listed here gave rise to most of the major political and military conflicts of thirteenth-century Europe. Kings had always fought each other over conflicting claims, of course, but there were distinctive features to these wars. They were generated in many different places, because many kingdoms were recording and pursuing their rights, and seeking to exercise a greater degree of authority in marginal areas. And they were often backed by more effective governmental machines, which typically increased their impact and certainly prolonged their length. The notion that Europe was suddenly embroiled in new levels of violence unleashed by major wars in the late thirteenth century has been criticised above, and rightly so: on the whole, these wars were simply a new and different way of organising the violence inherent in an armed society, and they were not a sudden development of the 1290s.[19] But what we particularly need to recognise is that these wars were less a product of later medieval debasement – the taste for blood, the chivalric temperament and so on – than of the pushy administrative and juridical mood of the thirteenth century and its results.

The conflicts in which kingdoms were engaged did not only involve other kingdoms. As has already been suggested, the techniques of literate and legalistic government assisted other powers too: lords of all kinds began to administer their demesnes, dependants and surrounding territories in a more systematic and determined way; this, in turn, produced strains and clashes throughout society, as tenants and vassals resisted new impositions or fought to control their resources against competition from above or below. At times, these processes could result in wars between kingdoms, either because kings might be regarded as vassals of other kings – as the kings of England

---

[19] Above, ch. 1, pp. 20ff.

famously were of the kings of France for their duchy of Aquitaine and county of Ponthieu – or because they might offer protection to more minor powers within their orbits who appealed to them, as Edward I did to the count of Flanders in 1294. But they also produced copious conflict within the space of kingdoms, as those who were normally content to recognise the suzerainty of a king began to contest the terms on which that suzerainty was exercised – sometimes because of kingly innovations, sometimes because of their own innovations, commonly for both reasons, and generally because an age of definition, which is what this was, inevitably produces conflict over the terms in which power relations are defined. This touches on the second major reason why the constitutional developments of the twelfth and thirteenth centuries had such ambivalent results: they created powerful media of resistance as well as powerful media of government.

First of all, the new emphasis on law did not only result in royal lawmaking, it also produced attempts to defend or define custom. 'Custom' enjoyed an ambivalent relationship with Roman and canon law, the former tending to favour it, the latter to regard it with suspicion, but it commanded powerful social support, and, once enacted, of course, it possessed all the authority of the prince's other laws. It covered a multitude of overlapping things: ancient impositions which had been moderated or accepted by the passage of time; flexible relationships which varied according to circumstance; the accumulated (and changing) wisdom of oral societies, which made their decisions through meetings; the 'laws' and conventions of fiefholding, which had not been committed to writing. What it most commonly stood for, in conflicts with innovating rulers, was not so much the old ways of doing things, which were historically variable, but the freedom of lesser powers within the kingdom – especially lords, both secular and ecclesiastical, but also towns – to do things their own way, without royal supervision and interference. It could also, it is true, be invoked by rulers to contest encroachments on what they were coming to regard as their prerogatives, but one of the commonest scenarios of the thirteenth century involves groups of lords rising up to protect their customs, *fueros*, good old laws, ancient rights or whatever, against the new laws, impositions and practices of kings. This was what led to Magna Carta, in the England of 1215, and to the Golden Bull elicited from Andrew II of Hungary in 1222. Both instances are highly revealing, since they show how disingenuous the defence of 'custom' could be. The customs and laws approved in Magna Carta included numerous royal innovations, notably the new legal system, which it suited the barons, knights and churchmen to accept; while the chief beneficiaries of the Golden Bull, which supposedly restated the liberties granted by St Stephen in the early 1000s, were the relatively new nobility of 'royal servants', created by royal grants from the later twelfth century onwards. What was going on in these confrontations, then, was less a resistance to innovation than the wresting of legislative and governmental power away from the monarch alone. We tend to think of charters of liberties as qualitatively different from legislation, but they only differ – if at all – in the extent of input from below, and the distribution of advantage.

Not all of the lawmaking and custom-defending of the thirteenth century was carried out in circumstances of conflict. It could also be achieved through consultation, as in the wave of parliamentary statutes enacted by Edward I in the 1270s and 1280s, or in the convention held at Orleans in 1246 which preceded the reduction to writing of the customs of Anjou. Less publicly, it could also be the work of lawyers, codifying and collecting records of practice and making them into *coûtumiers* (collections of customs), which obtained royal recognition because legal practitioners respected them. The *De Legibus et Consuetudinibus Anglie*, associated with the name of Henry de Bracton (1230s), Eike von Repgow's *Sachsenspiegel* (1220s) and Philippe de Beaumanoir's *Coûtumes de Beauvaisis* (*c.*1280) are among the best-known examples, but similar collections emerged almost everywhere over the ensuing century – the *landskapslagar* (provincial law-codes) of Sweden (*c.*1250–1327), for example, and the 'Rožmberk Book' in Bohemia (1340s). As most customs were collected on a provincial rather than national scale, it was the production and recognition of works like these that helped to shape the patchwork of jurisdictions that characterised much of later medieval Europe. In the tightly governed realm of England, recorded 'custom' was both national and, to a large extent, made and administered by the king and his judges. On the continent, meanwhile, kings establishing regnal jurisdiction found themselves having to engage with bodies of regional and local custom which they were obliged to respect. This custom did not only mean rules, either: it commonly also meant the right to hold courts, do justice and collect any resulting benefits. So it was that, as regnal legal systems began to develop, they typically involved a thin royal crust over a mass of independent jurisdictions. Where these other jurisdictions were conflicting and ill-defined, the king might find copious excuses for intervening, and his own jurisdiction might grow as a result, but there was often a countervailing pressure to keep things customary, or to define limits to the king's rights of intervention. In France, the king's high court, the *Parlement* of Paris, rose rapidly to hegemony in the thirteenth century, though it was less able to intervene in the great fiefs, and as it began to press harder on other jurisdictions in the fourteenth century it provoked criticism and resistance. In the kingdom of Aragon, where, as elsewhere, a sequence of assertive rulers had revised local customs and extended ancient peace legislation to cover the demesnes of lords and bishops, aristocratic resistance went beyond the usual demands for confirmation of *fueros* and *privilegios* to the institution, from 1283, of a high judicial officer – the *Justicia* – whose role it was to protect the liberties of the lords at the heart of the king's government. Meanwhile, over much of eastern and northern Europe, the kings failed to penetrate or supervise the developing jurisdictions below them – those of provinces, urban networks and ecclesiastical and seigneurial immunities. Indeed, in the localities of Poland and Hungary, the nominally royal courts of castellans, *wojewodas* (palatines) and *ispáns* (sheriffs) came to be controlled by the local aristocracy, applying local custom as these men understood it, while in Bohemia, a high 'land-court' (*zemský soud*) emerged in the thirteenth century to protect the customs and freedoms of landowners from royal interference. Not all high courts were agencies of royal power, therefore, and the definition of custom could have variable results.

In a somewhat similar way, many of the maxims, symbols and practices of the new monarchies could be used to challenge, restrict or redirect royal authority and not to advance it. If government was for the *populus,* and if the fisc and the crown were, in a sense, public property, then groups capable of speaking for the people or public could claim to represent the interests of the realm – even against the king, if necessary. So it was that the justification for the league of Rhineland towns in 1254 was the protection of 'all the goods of the empire' during the vacancy of the throne, while the defence of the 'common peace', accompanied by a sense of 'evident utility' and the health of the *res publica*, was invoked in the deposition of the German king, Adolf of Nassau (1292–8).[20]

---

[20] Quotations from F. R. H. du Boulay, *Germany in the Later Middle Ages* (London, 1983), p. 125 and J.-M. Moeglin, 'Chute et mort d'Adolf de Nassau', in F. Foronda et al., eds., *Coups d'état à la fin du moyen âge?* (Madrid, 2005), 153–80, pp. 156–7.

Similarly, rebellions against the English kings Henry III (1216–72) and
Edward II (1307–27) began with royal councillors evoking the oaths
they had sworn to maintain the possessions of the crown. In 1308, the
magnates enunciated the view that their oaths of allegiance were sworn
not to the king in person, but to the crown, and if King Edward were to
act against the crown, or waste its assets, they were obliged to correct
him. Juridically speaking, it was a short step from manoeuvres like these
to the deposition of 1327, in which the king's 'offences against his oath
and his crown' were a central justification; *populi dat iura voluntas* ('the
will of the people bestows rights/laws') was the legend on the medal
struck to celebrate the coronation of Edward's successor.[21] In Hungary,
the notion of the 'crown' was more consistently used as the rallying cry
of noble opposition than it was by the kings themselves, and it is easy to
see how this position arose from a mixture of ritual tradition, governmental practice and juristic concepts. In their insistence that their king
should be crowned with the Holy Crown of St Stephen in 1301, and
not by papal authority, the magnates were not only asserting ethnic
tradition, but arguing for a particular relationship between ruler and
people, in which ideas of elective monarchy and the later notion that the
crown represented an independent corporation of the *regnum* which
should govern alongside the king were already prefigured. Meanwhile,
the coronation oath of Aragon, which offered obedience to the king
'provided that you observe our *fueros* and liberties, and if not, not', may
have been based on a fictional oath of the ancient Aragonese kingdom of
Sobrarbe, but it is a fiction absolutely characteristic of this period, and
one widely echoed. In 1292, for instance, the bishop of Seckau told
Duke Albert of Austria (1291–1308) that the lords would not swear
fealty to him unless he swore 'to preserve the rights and laws of the *Land*
with all the power of his person and wealth', while the Scottish declaration of Arbroath (1320) made it clear that if Robert I (1306–29) did
not defend the 'freedom' of the Scots — a property closely linked to
indigenous laws and to the just succession of a rightful king, endorsed
by popular consent — they would drive him out.[22] If *imperator sit*

---

[21] Quotations from C. Valente, 'The Deposition and Abdication of Edward II',
English Historical Review, 113 (1998), pp. 856, 866.

[22] For the Aragonese coronation oath, see A. Mackay, *Spain in the Middle Ages*
(London, 1977), p. 105. The declaration of the bishop of Seckau is quoted in
O. Brunner, *Land and Lordship: Structures of Governance in Medieval Austria*, ed. and
trans. H. Kaminsky and J. van Horn Melton from 1965 edn (Philadelphia, 1992),
p. 351, n. 223.

Romanorum, non Romani imperatoris (the emperor belongs to the Romans, and not the Romans to the emperor), as a typical reworking of the *Lex Regia* put it, then rulers were obliged to uphold the rights, customs and liberties of their people and could face losing their thrones if they did not.[23]

Nor was this purely a matter of ideological and rhetorical manoeuvring: the institutional developments of the period had also created media of resistance. J.C. Holt has shown how the customs of the king's exchequer and lawcourts in more relaxed times quickly became the custom of the realm when rulers wished to change the rules: it is important to realise that the availability of records indicating what used to be done was a great help to the opponents of change.[24] Similarly, legal, consultative and representative institutions created media which could be used to restrain, as well as to advance, royal interests. Royal inquests to check on the behaviour of officers, for example, were a basic stimulus to local representation in thirteenth-century England, France and Sicily. The great national assemblies summoned by Philip IV of France to lend their support in his struggle against the Pope also provided a forum for the expression of discontent, as was clear in the ecclesiastical demands of 1303 and the more prominent role played by the Estates General in the ensuing few decades. Meanwhile, as the king's council and parliament became more defined institutions under Henry III of England, for example, so they became the major devices through which baronial critics set out, in the 1250s and 1260s, to manage the king's rule in the interests of good government and the community of the realm. However unsuccessful and violent were the results of baronial actions in England, the role of these institutions in enabling them is very important, and elsewhere things could turn out differently: in the Scandinavian kingdoms, for example, regnal councils (the *riksråd*, or *rigsråd*) became permanent agencies of aristocratic power from around the end of the thirteenth century. Similar developments are perceptible in Catalonia, notably in the agreement to an annual meeting of the *Corts*, extorted from Peter III in 1283; while the Angevin habit of

---

[23] Quotation from a letter written by the Senate of Rome to Frederick Barbarossa in 1152: R.L. Benson, 'Political *Renovatio*: Two Models from Roman Antiquity', in Benson and G. Constable, eds., *Renaissance and Renewal in the Twelfth Century* (Oxford, 1982), 339–86, p. 356, n. 81.

[24] J.C. Holt, *Magna Carta*, 2nd edn (Cambridge, 1992).

bestowing powers and responsibilities on Sicilian *universitates* (communities) played a significant role in the capacity of the inhabitants of the island to organise resistance in 1282 and to sustain it thereafter. As these examples suggest, it was in the most tightly administered and centralised polities of the period that these experiments occurred first, but they were to spread all over the continent in the succeeding century.

In all, then, the new governmental devices of the twelfth and thirteenth centuries had mixed and complicated results. They advanced royal power and reinvigorated the notion of kingship as a form of government, and of representative government, rather than simply as a variety of lordship. At the same time, these devices created new media of government and resistance for all the other powers in society, and – through the intrusiveness which is so characteristic of post-twelfth-century regimes – they provoked the use of those media. Ambivalence is thus the major result of the twelfth- and thirteenth-century governmental revolution, and it is a mistake to think of the 'triumph of the French monarchy', or, for that matter, of the failure of the German one. Most polities witnessed periods of royal assertion interspersed with periods of more-or-less successful reaction, containment or modification on the part of other powers: the former often associated with the rule of conquerors in their prime; the latter associated with the succession of minors or women, the failure of royal health or of the royal line of descent, defeat in war or failure to manage its excessive burdens. The pattern of fortunes and misfortunes gradually laid down the political traditions of each realm, and these, in turn, affected how fortunes and misfortunes were received, though few polities were so fixed by 1300 that their shape and nature in 1500 could be safely predicted. At the same time, the way in which structures of jurisdiction developed in this period was formative. Kingdoms like England and Sicily – where the law was king-made, the courts were arranged in a pretty neat hierarchy and supervision of the localities was well organised and uniform – were highly centralised and homogeneous. In England, this was reflected in other emergent institutions, such as Parliament and the tax system, and it also determined the shape of political resistance, which typically sought to improve the working of central institutions and thus tended to reaffirm the legitimacy of the crown and the cohesion of the *regnum*. In Sicily, meanwhile, the same factors help to explain the relatively high degree of unity and organisation shown in the revolt of 1282. The long wars that followed that event, and the separation of the island from the rest of the kingdom, were to cause the fragmentation of Sicily's remarkable government, but it is interesting to note that power continued to focus on the administrative districts and officers created in the Norman, Hohenstaufen and Angevin periods, even if these fell under aristocratic control, rather than being co-ordinated by the king. In most other kingdoms, as we have seen, law and court-holding were often highly localised, and the king's legislation and his officers jostled with those of others. His high court might exert a general supervision, as in France, or it might be supervised by aristocratic defenders of local liberties, as in Aragon-Catalonia, or countered by a land-court, representing aristocratic interests, as in Bohemia. It might barely exist, as in Castile before 1374, or it might exempt the territories of princes from its cognisance, as in Germany after 1232. In these kingdoms, each of them of course different from the others, structures of representation and taxation developed in alternative ways, and resistance often took on less centralising forms. These political and constitutional developments will be considered in succeeding chapters: jurisdiction was far from being the only factor shaping them, but it was arguably fundamental, and the great age of jurisdictional definition that unfolded from the later eleventh century onwards bears heavily on the politics of the later middle ages.

Princes and lords
We have been concerned for some pages with kings and kingdoms; what were the consequences of the developments discussed above for lords and lordship? It might make sense to begin with the lordship of the king. This, we have seen, was both assisted and problematised by the governmental changes of the twelfth and thirteenth centuries. Kings, like other lords, were given new means for the exploitation of their demesnes, but the development of notions of public authority raised questions about their private properties, and somewhat re-contextualised the exercise of personal will and the pursuit of family interests. The relationship between government and older relation-ships of power, such as lordship, or kinship, will be explored at more length in a later chapter – it is one of the central themes of this age of 'state feudalism' (usually called 'bastard feudalism' in England) – but it is important to note here that 'lordship' remained a crucially impor-tant aspect of kingship even as other, more formal, or more systematic,

or more obviously 'public', modes of rule grew up alongside it. Kings continued to exercise the flexible quality of 'grace', for instance, which covered reward, both tangible benefits and general goodwill, as well as dispensation and mercy (indeed, it has been argued by Claude Gauvard that one particular grace of the French king – the grant of pardons – was a more powerful means of spreading his jurisdiction across France than direct assertions of judicial prerogative).[25] They maintained grand courts, which, as we shall see below, were an important means of projecting authority, particularly over those outside their jurisdiction. They cultivated the qualities of magnificence and magnanimity, which entailed copious generosity and delegation: whatever the attitude of their lawyers and clerks, they might be more content with the possession of grand titles and the loosely defined fidelity of great men than with the minute government of space that was beginning to seem technically possible. Indeed, it is clear that some of the more absolute or hardnosed statements of royal prerogative were produced by wounded rulers whose more vaguely expressed authority had been rejected, usurped or threatened by their underlings; there is an air of betrayal about them. Philip IV of France, for example, was most aggressive where his lordship was most overtly challenged – namely in Gascony, Flanders, the Languedoc and in relation to the universal Church; over the dukes of Burgundy and Brittany he exercised a much lighter touch, and these men repaid their relative independence with a much greater degree of complaisance.

If many of the structures of the time made them into judges and rulers of kingdoms, kings also clearly regarded themselves as knights, and were seen in that light by their subjects. They pursued claims of right and honour, particularly when these would shed lustre on their houses, and they did so often without regard to other aspects of the regnal interest. As this suggests, kings were very much the heads of families, households and followings as well as those of states, and it is hardly too much to say that the births, marriages and deaths of Europe's ruling houses set the agenda of international politics, even as the polities in the sway of these families became more complex. It is true that a rather unprepossessing king like Henry III of England might struggle to persuade the community of the realm to fund and serve in his campaigns in Poitou and Gascony (let alone his more

---

[25] 'La justice pénale du roi de France à la fin du moyen âge', in X. Rousseaux and R. Levy, eds., *Le pénal dans tous ses états* (Brussels, 1997), 81–112.

ambitious plans in Sicily and Jerusalem), but greater rulers – such as his contemporaries Louis IX and Frederick II, or his son Edward I – were able to deploy regnal resources in far-flung places with remarkable freedom. As late as the thirteenth century, kings could still break up their holdings to provide for their children, as James I (1276–85) divided Majorca and Peter III Sicily from the crown of Aragon, or (in a sense) as did Louis VIII of France (1223–8) in sharing out the lands conquered from the Angevins among three of his sons. Even so, it is striking that they distinguished the acquisitions of their reigns from the patrimony which must be transmitted intact: it was one of the few clear differences between kings and princes that the latter did not, at this time, observe such distinctions, though they would do so later. Of course, the interests of the royal family were central to the interests of the realm: a wealthy royal house, endowed with foreign allies, would be better able to defend its assets, and would thus relieve the burdens on its subjects; royal princes with great endowments might be less inclined to contest the throne and more able to offer effective lordship to the provinces under them. So it was that thirteenth-century English kings married themselves and their off-spring into families that would assist them in the defence of their continental (or more occasionally, their insular) interests – the well-connected house of Savoy, the crowns of Castile, Scotland and Germany, and various lordships of France and the Low Countries. They bestowed outlying provinces – Ireland, Chester, Wales, Cornwall, the North, Gascony – on brothers and children, albeit with a growing emphasis on the tenure of these territories from the crown itself. But dynastic plans were not only constructed with the family interest at the centre; they could be laid with the concerns of subjects more prominently in mind. Aragonese marital and military adventures in the Mediterranean were, for instance, conducted partly in support of Barcelona and its merchants, which, in turn, provided the crown with money, ships and political support. The conclusion to draw, perhaps, is that although lordly and regnal interests could be opposed, they were more often in harmony, and that kings conducted their lordship with the same qualities of prudence that they showed in the more official aspects of royal government.

And what of lords who did not call themselves kings? For them, a certain amount depended on the powers and inclinations of those who ruled over them. Where overlordship was non-existent, neglectful or benign, lords might turn the opportunities of the period to their advantage in much the same way, and, in a few cases – Charles of Anjou (1226–85), the margraves of Brandenburg, Henry IV of Silesia (d.1290) – on much the same scale, as kings. Most lordly activity was, of course, rather more localised than these examples, but it was not necessarily different in kind. Lords of all sorts responded to the jurisdictional (and economic) conditions of the thirteenth century by attempting to create a more complete and stable territorial authority in the area of their main demesnes. This typically involved a mixture of initiatives, from making marriages, purchases and/or exchanges that rounded out their territorial holdings, to improving the exploitation of lands, tolls and rights; acquiring titles and dignities, offices and local jurisdiction; and seeking means of preventing excessive division of their holdings among heirs and kin-groups. Among the greatest lords, this meant the emergence of principalities, modelled on, and somewhat drawing on, the emerging kingdoms of the period. Over the course of the thirteenth century, the dukes of Brittany, for example, asserted feudal authority over the other barons of their dukedom, acquired a general right to license their castles and established a right of lordship over ecclesiastical temporalities; they addressed the material base of their authority by building up their demesnes; and they extended its political base by expanding administrative capacity, establishing a high court, or '*parlement*', on the model of Paris, and even issuing a general charter to their vassals – the Assize of Rachat (1276), which stood as a kind of basic law for the aristocracy of their province. German princes operated in a somewhat similar way, their pre-eminence over the men around them recognised in a series of late twelfth- and early thirteenth-century royal edicts, while their jurisdiction was territorialised by a mixture of media, from royal *Landfrieden* to the 'advocacy' of ecclesiastical lands,[26] and by a habit of obliging defeated political opponents to surrender their lands for regranting as fiefs. Feudal authority could be helpful to lords in Italy too, though in the later thirteenth century the wealthy counts of Savoy took a more 'public' path, extending their authority in Piedmont by sending in vicars to impose laws and regulate conflicts in the politically underdeveloped communities of the region. Meanwhile the Este family, who had

---

[26] I.e. stewardship, a compromise arrangement in which Church estates were protected by local lords to mutual advantage.

gained the upper hand in Ferrara by the 1230s, established a *signoria* (lordship) in the region by taking over the jurisdiction of the commune and the bishopric, assuming the advocacy of the abbey of Vangadizza whose lands dominated Polesine, and buying off opposition with grants of fiefs confiscated from their defeated enemies. Revealingly, they sold family lands that were too distant and scattered to serve as a basis for authority and used the resources to purchase locally. In Hungary, meanwhile, the thirteenth and fourteenth centuries saw a retreat from traditional kin-based landholding, in favour of substantial individual lordships, which were defended by the newly permitted stone castles and rounded out by a mixture of royal office, naked extortion and the gradual colonisation by magnates of the king's county courts. There, as in thirteenth-century Bohemia and Poland, once-free peasants were brought under seigneurial control as secular lords claimed the same immunity from royal jurisdiction for their estates that had been granted to the major religious houses. Where these immunities were supposed to extend only to 'low justice', the more powerful lords typically sought to extend them to cover the 'high justice' that was supposed to belong to the king alone. With Poland divided into several warring dukedoms until the 1300s, there was no-one to defend the royal prerogative, while the silver-rich and warlike kings of Bohemia, like the Emperors above them, may have been broadly content to allow their barons to exercise local jurisdiction freely. By these means, however, the greater magnates in these kingdoms created such exclusive jurisdictions that the crown was unable to pierce them except by violence, and the task of kingship came to focus on the management of more-or-less autonomous cells of noble power.

In all these cases, mainly drawn from areas of remote or inert royal power, we can see lords both aping and appropriating the jurisdictional tools that the advances of the period were making available to emperors and kings. In areas where royal authority was generally more effective – much of France and Castile, England, Sicily before the 1280s, at times Denmark, Hungary and Aragon-Catalonia – some of the same features of lordly state-making are found. Almost everywhere, lords sought territorial influence, control over peasants and uncultivated land, office or dignity and at least a stake in the changing media of jurisdiction. In some places, they had to fight for these things: the *mals usos* (bad customs), which enserfed the once-free Catalan peasantry, arose from the successful resistance of the barons to the judicial and legislative assertions of the count-king; the liberties granted to the Neapolitan nobility in 1283, which included the right to tax their tenants and to receive pay for military service, followed decades of tussling with royal agents and were probably only conceded at all because of the revolt of Sicily in the previous year. Elsewhere, things might progress more smoothly: after all, kings were not necessarily hostile to lordly power, provided that it was contained within broad frameworks of authority and allegiance. While the developing English legal system eroded most aspects of feudal jurisdiction, for instance, it allowed lords a relatively free hand over certain wastes and certain categories of peasants; most kings – though Edward I less than others – were willing to maintain the numbers of earldoms, and to entrust the leading lords with major military commands and grants of conquered territory. Similarly, the kings of Castile, with vast terrains to rule, allowed lords to entail their estates so as to keep them together (*mayorazgos*), to control peasant tenants and, from about 1300, to transmit fiefs (*tenancias*) by inheritance and to exercise royal jurisdiction in the countryside. There is a general relationship in these cases between periods of royal weakness and the strengthening of lordship, but the one is not the simple or exclusive cause of the other: just like kingdoms, lordships were pre-existing structures extending their political and governmental claims in this age of growth.

Clearly, lordship and kingship could develop in step with one another, and a common way in which tensions between them could be ironed out in polities like this was through the formation of 'estates' organisations – co-ordination and representation for the aristocracy in its dealings with the king. As we have seen, these emerged in many European kingdoms and several principalities in the later thirteenth century, with the aristocracy typically representing either itself or some broader conception of the realm, depending on the socioeconomic and political make-up of the polity in question. For the lords of Aragon-Catalonia, Bohemia, Hungary and some German *Länder* (thirteenth-century Austria is a well-studied example), these organisations were an important means of protecting noble privilege and jurisdiction; in England and Denmark, and in France in 1314–15, movements of lords typically represented, or came to involve, a wider cross-section of social interests. Perhaps the most significant implication of noble participation in 'estates' for the questions we are considering here, however, is the affirmation of a political role for lords within the sphere of the kingdom; lords who attended meetings of 'estates' were less proto-kings in a shapeless political space than counsellors, servants, representatives in someone else's *regnum*. There is, of course, no reason to suggest that this situation was unwelcome to them. Interaction with other power-holders was inescapable – no lordship was an island – and estates organisations facilitated relationships with peers as well as superiors. There are also signs that, even in more cellular polities – that is, those places where lordships and other immunities were more complete – lords favoured an effective authority over them, even as they also sought to protect their own freedoms. This is a reflex that we shall see time and again, but a striking example is the settlement reached at Buda in 1290, when, after two decades of mounting anarchy, representatives of the nobility and clergy of Hungary agreed with the new king, Andrew III (1290–1301), a recipe for the effective rule of the realm. In return for recognition of his authority, the king ordained that castles created without royal permission would be destroyed; estates seized unjustly would be returned; an annual diet of nobles would punish the misdemeanours of lords; and a number of noblemen would be taken on to the king's council. In practice, the king had to keep fighting to get his authority accepted in many parts of the realm, and the various representative measures envisaged in 1290 proved hard to effect, but this programme reflects an impulse towards central co-ordination and may help to explain something of the Angevin kings' success in delivering it from the 1310s onward.

How different, then, were lords from kings? The 'prince' was, after all, a recognised – if somewhat indistinct – grade of society, captured in the emergence of a *Reichsfürstenstand* ('estate of imperial princes') in early thirteenth-century Germany, or in Philip IV's re-creation of the twelve 'peers' of France in the 1290s; nobility too was coming to be a defined and privileged estate in most places by *c.*1300, even if its social boundaries were blurred and its liberties unfixed. There were perhaps two broad differences between kings and lords that stand out. First of all, as we have seen, most princes and lords accepted some sort of overlordship; they even welcomed it when it offered the prospect of further acquisitions, or when their holdings were scattered or precarious, as in Castile before the later thirteenth century, or in England. Kings, too, might accept overlordship, of course – notably that of the Pope – but they generally had more success in limiting its impact, and typically emphasised their freedom from any mediating power below the Almighty. While some overlords weighed much more heavily on their vassals than others, their existence had a number of results. One was that it generally inclined lords to exercise power more by colonising royal structures than by creating their own: their tendency was to absorb, with varying degrees of openness, networks of officers, courts and fiscal systems which were formally royal. They might seek to limit or obstruct royal initiatives, as, for example, the duke of Brittany used his influence, both locally and through his agents and lawyers in Paris, to intercept royal mandates to the inhabitants of the duchy and frustrate appeals against his justice to the king's *Parlement*. Lords certainly developed their own administrative and consultative institutions, the grandest ones often copying royal models; but, in some of the most controversial areas of government – particularly taxation, as it developed, but sometimes also justice – they typically relied on taking over royal systems, whether by force, or influence, or quite commonly, with royal approbation. Although these royal systems were a lot more nominally royal in some areas than in others, this pattern was to have a significant influence on the relations between lords and kings and on the ways in which more coherent and stable kingdoms were gradually formed.

Beyond this, the availability of an overlord tended to modify behaviour and allegiances within the lordship. An overlord could provide the lord with powerful backing, provided that the two were on good terms, and that backing could be important, given that lordships were mostly on a rather smaller scale than kingdoms, and were correspondingly more vulnerable to external attack and, in practice, internal division. The peerage bestowed on the duke of Brittany in 1297, for instance, placed him clearly above the other nobles of his duchy, even if it also extended his obligations to the king. This was the reasoning that prompted lords to accept ambivalent arrangements of this kind, rather as the lords of Gwynedd sought recognition as princes of Wales from the kings of England, but then paid a heavy price when Llywelyn ap Gruffudd got squeezed between the refusal of the other lords of Wales to accept subjection and the devious response of Edward I to his new vassal's predicaments. As this example demonstrates, an overlord could undermine a lordship, as the lord's enemies and neighbours sought help from on high. The struggles that broke out in Flanders in the 1290s are another illustration of this tendency. Against the background of a century of French royal pressure, the count of Flanders and his subjects were highly conscious of the interest of the king of France in their affairs. Faced with tensions in the cities and a need to restore comital authority after several decades of inept rule and French interference, Count Guy of Dampierre (1278–1305) intervened against the patriciates of Ghent and Bruges, who promptly appealed to the king for aid. The result of this was division throughout the county, and, from the mid-1290s, outright war and social revolt, in which the counts several times changed sides, and the French overlord was ultimately forced to withdraw. A delicate balance of interests re-emerged in the 1330s, but that was soon disturbed by the coming of the Anglo-French war. In this case, then, aggressive royal lordship combined with internal tensions to produce a conflict which threatened to destroy the principality altogether.

This leads on to a second general difference between kings and lords: the holdings of the latter generally had less permanence and solidity than the former. Wim Blockmans has remarked that the monarchies created in the tenth and eleventh centuries have generally survived, in some form, to the present day, while the same cannot be said of the principalities and lordships that lay within them and in between them.[27] Kingdoms were historic dignities, sustained by a variable mixture of myth, authority and political infrastructure: they tended to survive dynastic crises, albeit not without considerable disturbance, and it was unusual for them to be swallowed up in wars or treaties. Many lordships, on the other hand, were little more than private estates, with odd scraps of jurisdiction attached – often insecurely. They were much more likely to be reshaped, extended or even removed by the vagaries of events – by the ineptitude of a single generation, by a marriage alliance or a minority, by conflict with a larger or smaller power. Lords were correspondingly more willing than kings to accept a subordinate role in larger power structures, even if their acceptance was often pragmatic and might be withdrawn. Even so, it makes sense to think in terms of a spectrum here. The greatest lordships were like kingdoms, and possessed many of the same attributes, including the sense of a relationship between a historic people and its common authority. Even those that did not enjoy ancient roots – such as the *signorie* developing in northern Italy from the later thirteenth century – could acquire juridical and institutional solidity and mythic legitimacy over time, even if, like the Visconti

---

[27] W. Blockmans, *A History of Power in Europe* (Antwerp, 1997), pp. 66–8.

lordship of Milan between 1350 and 1450, their boundaries continually changed. Lordships were notably flexible, but so – in this age of juridical exuberance – were kingdoms, and it would be a mistake to draw too sharp a distinction between two types that differed most of all in scale, not in form.

Communes and leagues

Communes

Alongside the monarchical structures we have considered so far, there were also collective ones, and these were shaped, from about the twelfth century onwards, by the notion, or model, of the commune: that is, a sworn association with common interests and some form of self-regulation. It used to be thought that the development of this semi-legal means for expressing the solidarity of peer groups was the underlying cause of both collective and popular political action, as if a 'communal movement' swept through Europe, liberating townsmen and peasants from the rule of kings and lords and laying the foundations for future democracy. This picture has now been attacked from every angle. On the one hand, thanks, above all, to the work of Susan Reynolds, we now recognise that peer-group associations are just as natural and historic as the vertical relationships of lords and men: groups of nobles, knights, townsmen or peasants did not need a 'communal movement' in order to join together for political purposes, nor did the existence of media of collective rule depend on the juridical and philosophical developments traditionally associated with the recovery of Roman law and the works of Aristotle.[28] On the other hand, it is understood that communes, like other forms of urban and rural government, were headed by the leading men of the community in question: what differentiated them from lordly regimes was less the status of the participants than the formalised sharing of power among a group of such men. Communes were not intrinsically revolutionary, therefore – still less popular – and they could be compatible with the supervision of kings and lords: indeed, these high powers often played a role in their creation.

To accept all this is not, however, to deny the significance of the development and circulation of the communal model, which was being widely and self-consciously reproduced by the mid-twelfth

---

[28] Reynolds, *Kingdoms and Communities*, esp. ch. 6.

century, and remained in play for a long time afterwards. 'Commune' was only one of its names – *societas, universitas, compagna,* 'consulate' were among other terms used in Italy and Provence alone – but this diversity of terminology does not alter the fact that a newly recognised and reproducible form of power was emerging. In the kind of legalistic, literate and synthesising society we have been discussing, the availability of this form helped to legitimise certain kinds of institutions and practices, to influence the ways in which power was exercised and to inspire the spread of copies and adaptations: it was thus one of the essential structures of high and late medieval political life. While the commune itself is conventionally treated by historians as an urban phenomenon, notwithstanding the copious evidence for rural communes in many parts of Europe, its various cognate forms – leagues, unions, fraternities, guilds, parties, estates, commun(iti)es of the realm, or of the province, or of the vill, and so on – are found practically everywhere. It certainly makes sense to introduce in this section some of the features of urban politics, but we shall need to remember that the impact of the communal format was felt much more widely.

In Italy, urban communes seem to have emerged as a distinct form of authority between about 1080 and 1120, assuming power in the cities of the *regnum italicum* as the bishops lost control of them in the conflicts over ecclesiastical reform. Generally under noble leadership, groups of citizens swore common oaths, set up consuls to govern themselves, and – over the following century – developed most of the familiar elements of communal government. They established general assemblies for consultation, and smaller councils for government; they compiled books of privileges, laws and customs (often developed into statutes, especially after the 1183 Peace of Constance conceded this right); they asserted dominance over the surrounding *contado*;[29] and, initially under imperial pressure, but in the long run as a peacekeeping device, many of them appointed a *podestà* (power, potentate) – a supreme magistrate, with power over justice, finance and defence for a finite period. These developments soon provoked conflict, as surrounding jurisdictions began to feel threatened. Most prominently, the Emperor Frederick Barbarossa, with his Roman law-inspired theme of *renovatio imperii* (renewal of the empire), sought, from 1158, to regain the lost *regalia* which the citizens of northern and

---

[29] I.e. county, but typically, in fact, the diocese of the city's bishop.

central Italy had usurped. The two decades of war that followed helped to cast the communes in a controversial light, and, to some extent, this image stuck. Communes, or *conjurationes* (common oaths, conspiracies) as they were also called, were quite commonly seen as a species of rebellion; equally, looking at it from the other perspective, those who wished to act together to oppose a king, prince or lord had a ready-made form which they could adopt. In practice, Barbarossa was not systematically hostile to urban power. He granted rights of self-government to German cities in return for recognition of his overlordship, and heaped privileges on Genoa and Pisa in order to secure naval assistance against his opponents in Sicily. Having failed to crush the Lombard cities, he ended by allowing them a status parallel to that of imperial princes, and the Peace of Constance thus strengthened the communal form by giving it the seal of imperial recognition.

The discussion of communes tends to be dominated by Italian examples, and it was indeed in Italy that cities acquired the most substantial and enduring powers of self-rule. But the communal form was not only Italian, nor did it necessarily spread from there. Self-governing guilds of landowners, or even merchants, are attested in English towns as early as the ninth and tenth centuries, while the bishop of Cambrai faced demands from a *conjuratio* of his secular officers in the town as early as 958. Communes, or bodies like them, emerged in various parts of France, Germany and northern Spain in roughly the same period as they did in Italy, and they were quickly copied by neighbouring centres. The consular regimes that appeared in the Languedoc and Provence in the 1130s may have been direct imports from Italy, but other communes, *conjurationes* and *hermandades* (brotherhoods, fraternities) seem to have been home-grown. The general growth of government, population and commerce in the twelfth century was everywhere a stimulus to urban political expression: revolutionary events in Italy (or in Cambrai, or Laon, or even Cologne) may have supplied vocabulary and technique, but they were not the underlying cause of action elsewhere. Communes often did emerge in circumstances of conflict, but the interests of kings and princes were not inevitably opposed to those of communities, and just as lords founded free towns and religious houses in the expanding margins of Europe, so rulers were attracted by the economic and cultural potential of self-governing cities, provided that such communities were reasonably orderly and obedient. Lords of all kinds thus conceded or accepted communes in forms compatible with their authority – sometimes under the name 'commune', sometimes not, sometimes as a result of conflict, sometimes as a gracious response to petitions. And yet, the sense of the commune as a self-governing collectivity which could be created, without further authorisation, by people who were otherwise subject, never receded. It did not matter that many communes were either short-lived or quickly tamed, the idea and its associated formats and potentialities remained widely known, and was, as we shall see, recurrently invoked in succeeding centuries. The same package of ideas and forms was, moreover, readily transferred to other contexts. It was but a series of short steps from the 'communes' established, and briefly conceded, in London during the troubled periods of 1141 and 1190–1, to the communes of shires, towns and vills which King John ordered to organise militias in 1205; to the 'commune of all the land' that would help the barons distress that king if he broke the terms of Magna Carta; and thence to the commune, or community, of the realm that rose up against Henry III between 1258 and 1265.

Leagues

Communes claimed to be wholes, *universitates*, but there were other closely related forms of association that more readily acknowledged their federal nature. A prominent example would be what historians have called 'leagues' (sometimes subdivided into 'town leagues' or 'noble leagues'). These too first emerged into some kind of formality in the twelfth century, most famously, perhaps, with the Lombard League of 1167, a sworn association of north Italian towns, with its own college of rectors and enough of a recognisable existence to feature in the Peace of Constance, where it was called a *societas* ('fellowship'). Once again, however, there are older precedents. The *Landfrieden* ('peace associations', often called 'public peaces' in history books) of the German kingdom, prescribed by royal authority from 1103, but assembled on local initiative before and after this date, are a highly formative example.[30] While, in many kingdoms, 'the peace' or 'the king's peace' came to be seen as a simple product of authority, in the German lands it retained its close association with group action: the many *Landfrieden* of the twelfth to fifteenth

---

[30] B. Arnold, *Princes and Territories in Medieval Germany* (Cambridge, 1991), p. 44, defines them as 'contractual sworn unions of the parties who undertook to enforce the peace'.

centuries were, in effect, leagues of the powerful lords, and later also towns, who were sworn to maintain them. This pattern, re-inscribed time and again, created a public role for leagues in the government of the *Reich* and must explain something of the feuding culture of that country – mere alliances of disputants may have lacked imperial recognition (though they sometimes received it), but they were not formally different from the *Landfrieden* through which peace was nominally upheld. Nor was this the only legacy of the *Landfrieden*. As they became linked to princely jurisdiction from the end of the twelfth century, they helped to expand that jurisdiction and give it territorial scope, while their role as networks must have helped to create associations of the *Land*, which were typically the forerunners of estates in the German principalities. *Landfrieden* may also have provided the framework for the development of German town leagues – first, the seven towns that united against the archbishop of Mainz in 1226–7, and later, on a grander scale, the 'Rhenish League' of 1254–7, which comprised over a hundred members, including towns, churches and, for a time, princes. The north German Hansa, which centred on Lübeck and Hamburg, and began to take shape between the 1240s and 1280s, tends to be treated separately from other leagues, perhaps because it was initially a league of merchants, not of towns, and because its aims have been regarded as commercial rather than governmental, but it is not clear that these distinctions are so important if our interest lies in the creation and reproduction of structures. The formation of the Hansa was clearly influenced by the development of other urban associations in northern Germany, and the network of merchants had become a network of towns before 1300. Equally, the prosecution of economic interests inevitably involved the Hansards in military, fiscal, judicial activities, and it is not surprising that, by the fourteenth century, it had made of them a political and governmental union.

Leagues could thus be permanent, formative or recurring institutions. Once again, while the most familiar examples are German or Italian, leagues were not only the products of areas of decadent jurisdiction, but can be found wherever it was desirable for groups of peers to bond together for mutual protection or assertion. The *hermandades* of Castile and León, for example, played a very similar part in Spanish political development to that of the *Landfrieden* in the German lands. These organisations first acquired political prominence in the urban disorders of the reign of Queen Urraca of Castile and

León (1109–26), but the model was adaptable for other purposes, and a nationwide *Hermandad General* was formed by the opponents of Alfonso X of Castile in 1282, as a more-or-less legitimate structure for opposition to the king. This must itself have been an inspiration to the *Unión* of towns and nobles formed in Aragon in 1283 to challenge Peter III (1276–85) over his war on Sicily and to extract the grant of a *privilegio general* guaranteeing local liberties. The *Unión* and its associated *privilegio* (extended in 1287) was to be a prominent feature of the politics of Aragon-Catalonia until 1348, when King Peter the Ceremonious (1336–87) brought it to an end, tearing up the *privilegio* and pouring the molten metal of the unionists' bell down the throats of the more determined members. The Castilian *hermandades* revived in the 1280s were similarly eradicated under Alfonso XI (1312–50), but these associations remained a usable political device in both Spanish kingdoms. For one thing, the crown was not consistently hostile to them: an *hermandad* of León and Galicia made a grant of taxation to Alfonso X in 1283, for example, while, in Burgos, a *Real Hermandad* (royal brotherhood) was established in 1338 with Alfonso XI's backing; its aim was to corral the leading knights and officers and so ensure the orderly compliance of this most important city. Later on, the defensive *hermandades* which quickly grew up in the civil war of Henry IV's reign (1454–74) formed the basis for the famous *Santa Hermandad* of the Catholic Kings, Ferdinand and Isabella, which harnessed these semi-independent bodies as a royal peacekeeping device and, in time, extended their functions to include consultation, taxation and military recruitment.

Leagues, then, no less than communes, might be accommodated within larger polities, becoming part of regnal political tradition or even agencies of royal government. They might be purely temporary emanations, related to crisis, or – in critical circumstances – they might develop from the representative or consultative activities of kings, as the French provincial 'Leagues' of 1314–15 were in part a by-product of the attempts of Louis IX, and more recently Philip IV, to mobilise lay opinion in opposition to papal policy (and, in the latter case, to seek consent for taxation).[31] There is a sense in which leagues merge

---

[31] Although these 'Leagues' are a staple of the historiography, it is worth noting that contemporaries did not use this term, or anything like it. Philippe Contamine's choice of *alliances* probably comes closest to the contemporary record: P. Contamine, 'De la puissance aux privilèges: doléances de la noblesse française

seamlessly into 'estates', bodies representing particular communities or status groups. We have seen that these sometimes arose as part and parcel of the development of the kingdom, and could be driven from above by royal policy or the pressure of royal government. But they could also be a development from below: the result of the desire of smaller units to league together, for common protection or in pursuit of common advantage; or a product of the willingness of towns, lords and churches to accept some kind of overlordship, so long as they and their peers were able to negotiate the exercise of authority. Quite commonly, as this last point suggests, it was a development steered from both above and below, its terms the result of compromises between the desire of overlords to tax, administer and legislate, and the shared interest of inferiors in protecting their liberties, advancing their interests and co-ordinating their dealings with one another. In areas where higher jurisdiction was weaker, or more distracted, meanwhile, leagues might acquire a kind of permanence, as in the Hanseatic example mentioned above, or in the case of the Swiss Confederation, which grew from a peace union formed in 1291 by the lords and peasants of three alpine *Waldstätten* ('Forest Cantons') to assert local control of justice against the claims of the nearby Habsburgs. In all these respects, they were rather like communes: indeed the commune granted to Valenciennes by Count Baldwin of Flanders in 1114 was even called a 'peace association', just like a *Landfriede*, while the Swiss oath was sworn by the *universitates* or *communitates* – communes, in other words – of the three cantons.

Communes and leagues in practice
From the twelfth and thirteenth centuries onwards, communal structures and leagues thus provided widespread means of co-ordinating groups of peers for the purposes of self-government, resistance or representation. This mixture of roles hints at the fluidity of these organisations: although they could find a considerable degree of stability, whether independent or not, communes and leagues never lost the possibility of being more or less than what they were. Temporary coalitions might easily become permanent – as Switzerland or the Hansa did – or they might re-form whenever circumstances encouraged that – as the Rhenish League of the 1250s

envers la monarchie aux XIVe et XVe siècles', in Contamine, ed., *La noblesse au moyen âge, XIe–XVe siècles* (Paris, 1976), 235–57.

provided an important precedent for the primarily urban leagues that formed in Swabia, and sometimes the Rhineland, in 1376–89, 1441–c.1453 and 1488–1533/4, or as the Bohemian noble leagues of the 1310s prefigured those of the 1390s, 1400s and 1410s. In a like way, urban communes might agree to accept limited rights of self-rule under an umbrella of imperial, or royal, or lordly authority, or they might seek to negotiate that authority downwards, buy it out or throw it off. Commonly, they moved back and forth through varying degrees of freedom and dependency; their relations with other powers, internal and external, proved highly changeable. This was true of all later medieval power structures, of course – none of them were set in stone, even if kingdoms generally had more durability than lordships, and greater lordships more than lesser ones – but associational forms were especially protean. Before we discuss the position of these forms in the decades around 1300, it might make sense to ask why it was that communal regimes had this fluctuating quality – why they were so often convulsive and temporary, and why they nonetheless kept recurring.

Part of the answer is that they were often temporary alliances of interests, arising in response to decadent or deviant government on the part of a king or lord, or, in less charged circumstances, created to negotiate with such a figure. It was, after all, the failure of Hohenstaufen kingship that provided the occasion, or perhaps the excuse, for the Rhenish League of the 1250s, and many other leagues can be seen in similar terms. But we should avoid the common trap of assuming that kingship and lordship were more natural forms of social and political organisation than peer groups – as we have seen, monarchies enjoyed powerful sanction in political culture, and they possessed valuable political resources, but they were not the only way of doing things, and their command of the behaviour and imagination of medieval people was far from complete. Communes and leagues were not simply reactions, therefore, and where they were successful in their dealings with kings and lords, the outcomes typically featured written grants of rights and liberties which gave them some kind of permanence, and encouraged them to develop structures of internal rule. The commune, in particular, was not only a frequent rallying cry for dissenting coalitions, but, as we have seen, a means of government too.

Communes and leagues also suffered from the kinds of problems typically faced by the monarchies and lordships of the period. Their rights and boundaries were rarely clear – either territorially, where they hit up against other powers, or in terms of authority over those under them. Like other rulers, they were forever having to vindicate their authority with force and bribery, and, like other rulers, they tended to fail as often as they succeeded. The Hansa, for example, initially failed to draw in the coastal towns of Prussia, despite the semi-dependent position of Elbing and Königsberg, which were governed according to the law of Lübeck. Worse than this, the League was almost broken up in the first two decades of the fourteenth century when the count of Holstein decided to reassert his authority over Lübeck, and the resurgent king of Denmark, Erik Menved (1286–1319), occupied Rostock and much of the rest of Mecklenburg. In a similar way, smaller organisations such as city communes tended to wax and wane in their influence over their hinterlands, losing and gaining independence, and sometimes even struggling to absorb populations within the walls. In her immediate locality, for example, Florence subdued the neighbouring commune of Prato in 1300, lost it to the superior power of the Angevins in 1312, and ended up buying it back in 1351; a successful siege brought her the nearby town of Pistoia in 1306, but its leading family handed it to the lord of nearby Lucca in 1325, and it changed hands twice more before finally succumbing to Florentine sovereignty in 1329. Meanwhile, the community of German merchants given land and authority at Cracow in 1257 quickly absorbed the older Polish settlement; but at Danzig the Polish town remained separate from the German one; while Königsberg was a congeries of three independent townships, one under the bishop, one under the merchants and a third under the Teutonic Order.

But there was a distinctive feature of communal organisations that may explain a lot about their history, and had particular bearing on their circumstances in the period around 1300. This was the ready reproducibility of the communal form, which, combined with its capacity to create some usable legitimacy for whoever adopted it, meant that communes and leagues were frequently challenged by similar organisations in the same places. While emperors, kings and lords could disagree violently about their respective rights and allegiances, there were limits, at any time, to the numbers who could claim their particular kinds of authority; but the situation of leagues and communes was quite different. The north German Hansa co-existed with a host of more localised leagues, for example – those of the Westphalian, Wendish, Prussian or Pomeranian towns, to say nothing of the other peace associations, principalities and kingdoms of the region – and any one of these organisations could prevail in determining the adherence of individual towns to specific projects or agreements. That leagues faced this kind of problem may be obvious, but the position was very similar for communes, and it is worth discussing their predicament in some detail.

If, in the urban context, the commune, consulate or dominant guild could often claim a kind of priority over the town, as the first, or largest, or most important association of inhabitants, it was frequently accompanied by a host of other associations modelled along similar lines: those of craft or trade; parish, ward or neighbourhood; those of family and friends; or those united by more abstract interests that could provide a rallying point for linked interest groups. From the twelfth and thirteenth centuries, these other associations grew and developed in a manner very similar to the communes themselves. In Italian cities, for example, *vicinanze* (neighbourhood organisations) acquired their own representatives, bye-laws and militias. These might be linked to the structures of the commune as a whole – the neighbourhoods might elect officers in the governing council, for instance – but the fact remains that these organisations were essentially communes in themselves and could, under certain circumstances, act independently: the Genoese commune, for example, was effectively an amalgamation of these local units (there known as *compagne*) and they kept much of their old autonomy, especially before 1300. Guild organisations developed in a similar way, each with its own rules, rights and officers. These might be nominally religious, mercantile or craft-based, but their structure and purposes were very similar. Guilds representing elites might already be wired into the government of the commune, as the *Richerzeche* ('Rich Club') of Cologne was entitled to appoint one of the two burgomasters and half the magistrates from 1179. Alternatively, they might exist in tension with it, as the '*hanse*' (association) of long-distance traders, founded in St Omer in about 1215, sought to cream off the richest members of the established merchant guild and negotiate its own privileges. Guilds representing other crafts and businesses also developed. These typically existed in large numbers by the end of the thirteenth century – 73 at Florence, for example, 100 at Marseilles, 150 at Milan. Although they sometimes attracted hostility from urban governments, and were quite often banned in the thirteenth century – especially when they represented demotic and disruptive interests such as weavers – they too could be drawn into the pan-urban structure of the commune, as the rather respectable guilds of moneylenders and drapers were each allowed to choose a member of the consulate of Montpellier after 1204. Family clans, or *consorterie*, were another kind of organisation that was acquiring some institutional solidity in this period. These rarely enjoyed a formalised authority (though membership of family associations might well be formal in itself, since these clans typically extended far beyond the ties of progeny), but their informal influence was widely acknowledged. The ruling patriciates of German cities were revealingly known as the *Geschlechter* (families); that of Genoa was known as the *Alberghi* (inns, dynastic houses); and when Alfonso XI of Castile wanted to provide for the government of Segovia in 1345, he bestowed the right to appoint ten of the fifteen *regidores* of the city on the various *linajes* (families) that had dominated since the 1250s.

From the 1230s, and the height of the papal-imperial conflict, many Italian towns also included party organisations – the *pars imperii* and *pars ecclesiae*, often the forerunners of the better-known Ghibellines and Guelfs.[32] These parties were not the straightforward satellites of papal or imperial power that they might appear; rather, they existed, in the first place, as a means through which alliances of leading interests in each town could secure power from their opponents by invoking the aid of the contending overlords. As the papal-imperial struggle subsided in the 1250s and 1260s, the parties tended to survive as media of local political organisation, sometimes maintaining a loosely pro-papal or pro-imperial stance, but typically concerned as much, or more, with the distribution of power within the commune and *contado*. The Florentine *Parte Guelfa*, for instance, was another mini-commune: it possessed rectors and a captain, councils, statutes and its own army. One telling indication of its function in the domestic government of the city is shown by the fact that, once any realistic danger of imperial intervention had subsided, and the Florentine Ghibellines were correspondingly denied any hope of external support or legitimation, the *Parte Guelfa* split into 'Black' and 'White' Guelfs. As Jacques Heers has pointed out, most towns

---

[32] These names come from Waiblingen, a royal town belonging to the Hohenstaufen, and Welf, the family name of the dukes of Saxony, who had been the Staufer's most consistent opponents.

seem to have required a division into two parties so as to channel disputes and conflicts into routes which were broadly containable and even beneficial.[33] Guelfs and Ghibellines were a common Italian version of this phenomenon, but it is clear that a similar dialectic underlay the competition of *Hoeks* (hooks) and *Kabeljauwen* (codfish) in the towns of Holland, or of the so-called victuallers and non-victuallers in London, or even *Leliaarts* (supporters of the French lily) and *Klauwaarts* (supporters of the Flemish lion's claw) in the wars of Flanders from the 1290s onwards.

The popolo *and the troubles of the later thirteenth century*

The profusion of subgroups within urban communes was an impor-tant context for the emergence of the *popolo* (people), a collectivity which pressed for inclusion in the government of many Italian towns in the mid-thirteenth century. Similar groups, under different names, appeared in most other parts of Europe before the century's end. In much of the historiography, the *popolo* and its equivalents are regarded as a grouping of interests excluded from the rule of noble-dominated communes: typically merchants and manufacturers – whose rise to political prominence in the thirteenth century is presented as a result of urban demographic and economic expansion – but also lesser guildsmen, even workers. Elements of this picture are certainly cor-rect. *Popolo* groups usually were coalitions of the excluded, though for many of their leaders this state of exclusion was only temporary. In Italy, they had often originated as organisations of the parish or ward (called *populus* in Florence and Genoa) or of the *pedites* (non-nobles). Cities were indeed expanding, and, in many places, there certainly were growing tensions over the direction of the commune. At the same time, this is another area where materialist explanations for political action have been preferred over political ones, and the political and constitutional context for these developments has been somewhat understated. While it is clear that new wealth and produc-tivity allowed new political coalitions, in which craft organisations typically played a central role, it is also true that many of those who co-ordinated the action of the *popolo* were indistinguishable from the so-called 'nobles' or 'magnates' who ran the commune. The com-munal 'nobility' was full of merchants and industrialists, and 'popular'

[33] J. Heers, *Parties and Political Life in the Medieval West*, trans. D. Nicholas (Amsterdam, 1977), p. 15.

leaders were often landowners of high blood; intermarriage, investment and land-purchase had made the wealthy into what was effectively a single class. In one sense, therefore, the struggle over the
inclusion of the *popolo* and/or guilds that spread across many European
cities in the later thirteenth and early fourteenth centuries was simply a
continuation of the ceaseless contest for power among urban leaders.
It is true that that contest was increasing in intensity and social reach in
this period, but that is, in part, because urban governments were
themselves growing in intensity and social reach. They sought to
regulate the guild organisations that had developed in their midst;
they extended cavalry service beyond the ranks of the nobility and
asserted a more meaningful jurisdiction over the surrounding countryside; and they developed more complex structures of internal rule.
They also began to experiment with taxation, and this was a major
stimulus to reaction and intervention from power-holders who hitherto had lacked influence over the direction of the commune. The
continual growth in urban political complexity and the increasing
sophistication of political technique were thus central factors in the
rise of the *popolo*. The Florentine version, for example, first organised
in the 1240s, was at that time based on urban companies of arms,
themselves a communal innovation of a few decades previously; later
it drew organisational strength from the *arti* (guilds) and political
support from the *Parte Guelfa*, which brought it to power in the
1250s and again from the 1280s. Finally, the very name *popolo* suggests
a growth in urban political consciousness. Invoking the *popolo* was a
way of calling the commune's bluff, a way of saying that the commune was not itself the *universitas*, or *populus*, but just a sect – a group
of 'magnates', or whichever bogey was most appropriate – while the
real *populus*, or *popolo*, was now claiming its due right. These manoeuvres suggest an acquaintance with Roman history, and with
Ciceronian and Romano-canonical theory, all of which invested
some sort of authority in the *populus*, even if the nature and identity
of that *populus*, and the scope of its rights, remained open to
negotiation.

   The urban struggles of the later thirteenth century were thus at least
as much about the growth of government and political technique as
they were about the socioeconomic pressures on traditional elites.
They were not, of course, restricted to Italy. Even the terminology of
the *popolo/populus* was not peculiar to the peninsula: the *caballeros
villanos* (urban knights) who ran the Castilian municipalities faced

risings of groups variously calling themselves *pueblo*, *gente menuda*, *peones* and *común* from *c*.1275. The *populus* of Montpellier that rose up in 1323 was an alliance of the rich men who were currently excluded from the commune. Barcelona experienced a rising of the *poble menut* under Berenguer Oller in 1285, but it seems likely that the genuine irritations of artisans and lesser merchants in the city were mobilised and manipulated by a faction within the patriciate, just as the banking family of the Tolomei stood behind a rising of black-smiths and butchers in Siena in 1311. Away from the Mediterranean, it was often the 'commons' or '*communes*', or coalitions of crafts or guilds, that jostled with the urban authorities for power, but the root causes were just the same: acculturation to governmental and political norms and greater intrusion on the part of urban rulers and overlords. Elisabeth Lalou has assembled more than forty examples of risings of this kind, concentrated in the period *c*.1270–1325, from around France, Flanders and Provence.[34] In the mostly smaller and less com-plex towns of east-central Europe troubles of this kind generally broke out later, though the conflicts of the 1310s between the German burgher elite of Cracow and the Polish elements in the city who were allied to Władisław Łokietek suggest that similar patterns of confrontation existed there too: certainly, the reunification of Poland was likely to shake up the politics of every part of that king-dom, but the struggles in Cracow may also have been generated by internal tensions and the common pressure for urban regimes to incorporate more of the population.

A consequence of the frequency of conflicts in these fifty-odd years between older elites and 'popular' representatives is that the period has been seen as one of distinctive change, in which urban govern-ments adapted to new social and political realities, typically by com-bining the authority of established patriciates with some kind of representation for other wealthy and even middling interests.[35] This kind of accommodation was certainly not uncommon. In parts of northern Italy, England, the Low Countries and Germany, in partic-ular, city governments were broadened and elaborated so as to include representation for the *popolo*, commons or guilds, whether through

[34] E. Lalou, 'Les révoltes contre le pouvoir à la fin du XIIIe et au début du XIVe siècle', in *Violence et contestation au moyen âge*, Actes du 114e Congrès National des Sociétés Savantes (Paris, 1990), 159–83.

[35] See e.g. D. Nicholas, *The Growth of the Medieval City* (Harlow, 1997), p. 275.

extra councils, or officers, or revised election arrangements. But there are two important things to realise about these changes. The first is that they did not necessarily transform the direction of urban affairs. Institutional broadening typically created a wider elite, rather than extending significant power to lower social groups, although it is true that the façade of extensive representation, or the creation of occasional mass assemblies, laid down political traditions which enabled demotic action whenever elites were seriously divided or regimes seriously overstretched. The second point follows on from this: it is that the broader governments established in the late thirteenth and early fourteenth centuries were not necessarily fixed in form. Towns did not adopt power-sharing everywhere, or once and for all; rather, contests over the organisation of urban government persisted throughout the ensuing century and beyond. For example, F.R.H. du Boulay counted at least 200 risings in German towns between 1300 and 1550, most of them involving some sort of challenge to the structure of rule; English towns witnessed several waves of constitutional change, including some convulsive ones in the later fourteenth century; and the terms on which office was distributed in such institutionally pluralistic towns as Ghent and Florence were turned over on several occasions. This lack of settlement in the organisation of urban government was the result of many factors we have already considered – the profusion of effective corporations in urban environments, the comparable power and legitimacy of many of these organisations, and the sheer difficulty of devising a governmental form that provided a stable mixture of authority and accommodation – but they were also the product of something that we shall consider in later chapters: the continuing growth of urban government and political culture. Just as the political growth of the thirteenth century underlay the urban troubles of the period *c.*1275–1325, so the continuing growth of the fourteenth century lay behind the revolts of the 1370s and 1380s.

Communes, lords and kings
The instability that accompanied pressure for broader-based urban government could have other results. Florence was unusual in having the freedom to cycle through so many different configurations of power, as its leaders tried to make the power-sharing introduced in the 1290s work over the long term. In other Italian cities, clashes between the *popolo* and commune were a major stimulus to the emergence of signorial regimes. Occasionally, these too were

temporary – Lucca, for example, experienced the rule of a series of lords, only to return to a communal format in the later fourteenth century – but the rise of the Visconti of Milan is, in some ways, an object lesson in how durable town-based *signorie* could emerge from the struggles of this period. The war between the powerful Milanese *popolo* and the local nobility linked to the city's archbishop had provided a power base for the della Torre family, who filled the office of *anziano* (captain) four times between 1240 and 1277 and consequently dominated city government. Having been appointed 'permanent *anziano*', Martino della Torre sought recognition for his pre-eminence from Rudolf I, king of the Romans, but his enemies among the noble party and within the Church were too many, and he was overthrown in a coup which brought the Visconti archbishop and his allies back to Milan. Now more accustomed to the ways of lordship, the Milanese commune appointed Visconti *signore* of the city, and he embarked upon a series of manoeuvres to secure himself – revising the list of nobles who were entitled to take part in the cathedral chapter (and thus to direct the commune), establishing a society of nobles to defend both him and the city, and ensuring that his great-nephew Matteo was elected captain of the *popolo*. This combination of actions ensured privileged positions for Visconti's noble supporters and tied them to the continuance of Visconti hegemony, but it also helped to draw the powers represented by the *popolo* into the Viscontean orbit and to secure the city against external threats. The acquisition of an imperial vicariate in 1294 made Visconti lordship more distinctive and permanent, while the gradual erosion of the independence of communal and popular councils and the creation of new signorial institutions, such as a chancery and a 'secret council' for government and high justice, ensured that both the direction of affairs and the means of satisfying interests were concentrated in the hands of the lords. By the early fourteenth century, then, Milan had moved from popular-communal strife to popular 'tyranny' under the della Torre and, finally, to stable lordship under the Visconti. Milan, of course, was bigger and richer than most other cities, and was unusual in generating a stable lordship, sustained, in the first place, from the resources of the city itself, though the situation in Ferrara was similar. For other Italian towns, the outcome of conflict between commune and *popolo*, or other internal strife, was all too often subjection to external lordship, whether this came from another town, a consortium of towns or some kind of amalgam of urban and rural power.

Authority could be secured without submerging communal structures, however. For one thing, most of the emerging *signorie* of later thirteenth-century Italy found it prudent to preserve elements of representation and consultation, even formal ones. But self-governing cities could also devise means of maintaining authority without abandoning the traditions of collective rule. This, of course, is what the guild-regimes established in the decades around 1300 were aiming at, and, while their details remained open to adjustment, and their politics could be convulsive, they also helped to produce order. By creating a more plural institutional structure, they complicated and somewhat tempered the play of factions, and, as they gradually generated traditions of civic liberty, they created a reservoir of moral authority on which their leaders could draw (as long as they ruled in keeping with those traditions). At the same time, almost all late thirteenth-century towns were more concerned to define their constitutions and to fix the classes or groups entitled to take part in the government of the city. While this, as in the kingdoms of the period, was a factor encouraging short-term conflict, and helps to explain some of the troubles of 1275–1325, it could also have a stabilising effect in the longer term, breeding civic self-consciousness and encouraging the politically assertive to express themselves within an agreed political framework rather than against it. The Venetian *Serrata* of 1297–1323, which determined the nobility of the city and excluded all others from participation in the commune, was one famous measure of this kind. It worked by balancing the creation of a more defined elite with a significant expansion of the ranks of those deemed noble and continuing absorption of rising wealth, through intermarriage and exceptional ennoblement. In its way, it was not so very different from the tighter definition of the political class in Florence in the 1290s: in the Tuscan city, '*magnati*' were the ones excluded from power, but many of these so-called nobles were actually urban merchants, and – more strikingly still – a 1343 amendment to the Ordinances of Justice allowed certain '*magnati*' to be accepted as '*popolani*' and thereby eligible for participation in the commune. Venice's snobbery and Florence's inverted snobbery were thus parallel means of stabilising the political class: both systems enabled the representation of the main power elites; and both were flexible enough to accommodate rising families.

These examples, however, are drawn from areas where there was relatively little external authority. In most parts of Europe, urban

convulsions attracted the attention of rulers. Kings and lords intervened with varying degrees of effectiveness and tenacity. Alfonso X
introduced a national law-code – the *Fuero Real* (*c.*1255) – in response
to the beginnings of trouble in Castilian municipalities, but this
attempt to override local customs was a failure, and the crown
achieved more success by establishing new councils – *regimientos* –
and distributing their membership among the major oligarchical
factions and other interests. In France, the communes that had been
established in the eleventh and twelfth centuries were mainly wound
up between about 1270 and 1325, and the era of the *bonnes villes* was
born, in which urban elites were able to rule their municipalities
principally because of their capacity to act as brokers with an increasingly insistent (but also flexible) crown. Even so, in these kingdoms
and in others, royal authority could be compatible with high levels of
urban liberty. The king retained the power to intervene in times of
trouble, but provided that urban authorities could keep order and
comply with ever-rising royal demands, he was mostly unconcerned
about the ways in which individual towns organised their affairs.
Meanwhile, in Castile and Aragon from the twelfth century, in
England, Sicily and other places from the thirteenth, towns were
represented in regnal assemblies and could use these institutions
both to negotiate matters of common concern and to gain access to
the ruler for the transaction of their own particular interests.

On the whole, therefore, it was in areas of weaker or more diffuse
authority that urban politics were most volatile and complicated. In
Flanders, as we have seen, the troubles of the later thirteenth century
attracted the attention of both the count and the king of France, with
complex and violent results. The struggle for power of the guilds
became deeply confused with the larger politics of the region. As a
result, the distribution of power in Flemish cities remained unusually
open to renegotiation, and representatives of craft interests, such as the
van Arteveldes of Ghent, who led rebellions in the 1340s and 1380s,
also stood for alignment with the king of England, which meant in
turn that their political fortunes were shaped, for better and worse, by
an unusually wide array of powers. In the German lands, meanwhile,
as in Italy, the towns were for the most part left to arrange their
relations, both internally and with neighbouring lords and other
powers, free of royal interference. In response to princely protests,
Frederick II and his son and regent Henry banned town leagues and
communes in the Empire in 1220 and 1231–2, though neither

intended to enforce this concession. The status of 'imperial city' or
'free city', widely bestowed by charter in the thirteenth century, gave
many towns a degree of juridical privilege against neighbouring lords,
usually in return for a more direct relationship with the king, but it did
not rescue them from the general struggle of members of the Empire
to secure and extend territory, rights and jurisdiction.[36] Here, as in
Flanders and Italy, infra-urban conflicts interacted with regional ones,
and it was correspondingly in areas like this, as we have seen, that
leagues and alliances particularly flourished. Heers mentions a 1270
pact of *societas* which joined together the commune of Pavia with the
'internal' party at Lodi, the 'external' party at Cremona and the *Land*
of Bavaria.[37] It is a striking example, which captures many of the
features we have been discussing. It demonstrates the strength of the
associational habit in territories where communes and leagues proliferated, but it also shows how these associations could cut across the
boundaries of cities and regions, contributing to the general confusion
and contestation of jurisdictions. Not only did communes and leagues
complicate the politics of empires, kingdoms and principalities, then,
they also brought complexity and flexibility to the politics of towns,
provinces and other communities.

Churches

It will be clear from everything we have said so far that the Church
also needs to be considered as a political form, indeed as a network of
political forms — parishes, dioceses, provinces and the regional or
regnal churches of metropolitans and primates; religious houses and
religious orders; universities and the organs of the Papacy. Some of
these forms have been considered above, and not all of the rest can be
considered here, but it is possible to survey some of the main ways in
which ecclesiastical organisations functioned as political bodies. Both
as a universal organisation and in its more local manifestations, the
Church was profoundly influenced by the changes of the period, and
it was influenced in ways that closely paralleled the experience of
secular powers.

---

[36] For a helpful definition of these terms, see T. Scott, *Society and Economy in Germany,*
1300–1600 (Basingstoke, 2002), p. 20.
[37] Heers, *Parties and Political Life*, pp. 144–5.

The universal Church

We have already seen that the Church as a whole could be seen as an empire or monarchy – indeed, to James of Viterbo (d.1308), it was the only perfect kingdom. Two factors made this conception real. One was the enormous growth in papal government, discussed above: through its burgeoning stake in appointment, justice, the licensing of taxation and the determination of doctrine, the Papacy increasingly affected the lives of individual clergy and, by the thirteenth century, if not before, their lay charges. The other factor was the canonistic tradition of consultation and corporatism: every ecclesiastical unit, including the Church as a whole, could be considered as a body, or corporation, in which the head – be he parish priest, abbot, bishop or pope – was obliged to deal with the members, or limbs – whether these were parishioners, monks, diocesan clergy or larger bodies of Christians stretching up to the whole estate of ordained clergy or the whole body of Christendom. The right relationship of head and members was an endlessly fascinating topic of learned speculation, and it will be discussed at more length below, but it was also a highly practical question, because it affected the management of the huge reservoir of property, jurisdiction and personnel controlled by ecclesiastical institutions. Much of this business was a matter for local negotiation, but the rising influence of the Papacy meant that 'head-and-members' questions were beginning to involve a growing cross-section of the clergy, and a fully international ecclesiastical politics – one going beyond the dealings of Pope and cardinals, or even Curia and metropolitans – had thus begun to develop by the early thirteenth century. The Fourth Lateran Council, with its massive attendance and its volley of legislation, was a major stimulus to this development: not only did it reaffirm the consultative traditions of the Church at an international level, sparking off three more general councils in the ensuing century, it also strengthened other media of representation, above all the synods of local and national churches, which archbishops were now obliged to convene. Not surprisingly, the next few Church councils involved criticism, checks and challenges for the Papacy, as more extensive representation combined with the growth of papal and secular government to provoke reaction. The Council of Bourges (1225) sharply rejected papal plans for general taxation of the Church, while the first Council of Lyon (1245) heard complaints about papal provisions from the barons of England. These complaints were amplified over the next two years to include taxation and jurisdiction, in letters to the Curia from the French and English kings, and from delegations representing the king, barons and clergy of France. As tensions developed among the episcopate over the privileges of the friars, in the 1270s and 1280s, the bishops saw provincial and general councils as the natural forum in which their grievances might be aired and settled. This was an important background to the conciliarist strand in the crises around 1300: especially in France, there was lively support for a council to reform the Church in head and members, and some theorists, at Paris and elsewhere, were beginning to develop plans for full-time conciliar government in the Church. Despite the assembly of a council at Vienne in 1311–12, discussed in the next chapter, these plans would be thwarted. This was partly because the Papacy found more emollient ways of ruling its flock, retreating from representative exercises and developing a system of rule based on individual grievances and individual interests. It was also, no doubt, because most men of influence within the Church wished to wield influence over subordinate corporations themselves and thus regarded conciliar schemes with ambivalence. But the vision of conciliar reform remained available to opponents of papal policy, and it acquired new resonance in the decades around 1400, when the Church was plunged into a collective crisis.

Churches and kingdoms

Besides participating in the evolving polity of the Church, clerical leaders also had to deal with developments in the secular power structures that surrounded them, and in which they played a part. In kingdoms, the experiences of bishops and abbots resembled those of other lords. On the one hand, they could profit from association with the king, as counsellors and officers. On the other, where royal government was growing, as in France and England, prelates felt its pressure on their jurisdiction, just as they also felt pressure on appointments, taxation and the control of ecclesiastical property. If they lashed out with ecclesiastical sanctions to protect their temporal interests, they typically found themselves involved in escalating conflict with royal jurisdiction, in which the Papacy and fellow bishops usually proved unreliable allies: Louis IX, for example, so assiduous in defending French ecclesiastical interests from Innocent IV, did not hesitate to invoke the popes of the 1260s against the bishops who opposed taxation for the royal and Angevin crusades of that decade.

By the end of the thirteenth century, most French prelates regarded litigation and judgement in the royal *Parlement* a surer basis for defending their temporalities than the invocation of ecclesiastical sanctions. Equally, the new regnal assemblies of the period, whether ecclesiastical synods or meetings of estates, provided an effective means for the clergy to negotiate areas of difficulty with the crown. In France, this laid one of the foundations for the later notion of the 'liberties of the Gallican Church' – the ideal of a free French church, with its independence from papal provision and taxation protected by a French king. Similar formations are apparent in England, Castile and other kingdoms. While the *communitas cleri*, as Edward I called it in 1307, could certainly find itself at odds with the crown, and would sometimes drive a hard bargain for its agreement to royal policy, the interest of kings in ruling and protecting the churches of their realms, and the preoccupation of the Papacy with matters often unhelpful or irrelevant to the provincial hierarchies, meant that the regnal church was already becoming a recognisable way of organising ecclesiastical power in the West by 1300.

In much of the centre and east of the continent, where royal governmental pressure was generally less insistent at this stage, the dynamics were somewhat different. Here too there was a trend towards national churches: indeed, as dioceses in the region were fewer and larger, this development was all the more straightforward. The metropolitan see of Gniezno, for instance, readily spoke for the interests of the church and realm of Poland, because that helped to establish its hegemony over Poznán, Cracow and the other half-dozen Polish sees; the bishops of Prague and Olomouc, meanwhile, were the only diocesans for the kingdom of Bohemia and mark of Moravia, and the see of Prague must have pushed for the freedom from Mainz which it gained in 1344. On the other hand, these emergent national churches did not necessarily march closely in step with royal (or indeed any other) authority. Over much of the north, centre and east of Europe, prelates were able to acquire immunities from royal jurisdiction, though their capacity to avoid the more nakedly militaristic pressure of neighbouring lay lordships varied from area to area. Some prince-bishops, like the archbishop of Ravenna or the bishop of Liège, fared better against the princes around them than the bishops of Speyer, Worms and Utrecht did against the Counts Palatine and the counts of Holland and Guelders respectively. Where western prelates typically gained the protection of their estates by royal, as well as ecclesiastical, authority, those of the Empire were often dependent on noble advocates whose stewardship was typically predatory and could become hereditary. They also faced dangers from below. In the German lands (and also elsewhere), cathedral chapters often possessed their own lands and jurisdictions, independently of the bishop, while in both Italy and Germany, prelates had to deal with powerful municipalities. The archbishopric of Milan proved to be the centrepiece of the lordship which triumphed in that city, but the experience of the archbishops of Cologne and the bishop of Adria was probably more typical: the former was locked in near-continual conflict with the commune of his cathedral city, which even allied with the duke of Brabant to defeat him in 1288; the latter entered a series of Faustian bargains with Azzo d'Este of Ferrara, finally surrendering all of the tithes and fiefs of the see to him by the mid-thirteenth century. In this atmosphere of limited central authority, united action in response to either royal or papal policy was less common among the prelates of eastern and central Europe, and although national agreements were possible – as in Frederick II's *Confoederatio* with the ecclesiastical princes in 1220 – their tendency was to confirm local independence, not to defend the common interests of the regnal church. Even so, we shall see that, in the fourteenth and fifteenth centuries, as the assertiveness of kings and metropolitans, the interventionism of the papacy and the consciousness of pan-European political forms all increased, the regnal frame of reference acquired more significance in the Empire and the northern and eastern kingdoms.

Religious and military orders
The Church was not only a collection of provinces and dioceses under the bishop of Rome, of course; it also contained a host of religious orders, devoted to the prosecution of a regular life in buildings and territories granted by the laity. Among these were orders of Christian knighthood, and some of these were well placed to take advantage of the new governmental opportunities provided by the thirteenth century. Their possession of wealth, arms, land, internal structures of authority and, through papal concession, freedom from episcopal supervision, meant that they were essentially autonomous political formations. While the most prominent of these – the Knights Hospitaller and the Knights Templar – lacked the territorial concentration to be effective as rulers, some of the more minor orders enjoyed

greater success, and none more so than the order of Teutonic Knights, which was formed in 1198 and had established a fully-fledged state along the Baltic coast by the late 1280s. The Knights were initially located in the Holy Land, and their first significant incursion into European territory was not in Prussia, but in Transylvania, at the invitation of King Andrew II of Hungary, in 1211. To secure themselves in this territory of the pagan Cumans, the Knights encouraged colonists and granted their territories to the Papacy, a move which threatened to make them independent of temporal as well as spiritual jurisdiction and thus incurred the wrath of the king, who drove them out in 1225. This was the background to their expansion in another frontier zone with heathendom: Prussia, where the fragmented state of Poland and the Emperor's interest in furthering projects that extended his jurisdiction combined to give them a much freer hand. Arriving at Thorn in 1231, the Knights rapidly gained territory at the expense of pagan Prussians and Polish Christians alike, and brought in German settlers to populate their new domains. This manner of operation was by no means unusual on the North European Plain: the missionary bishop of Riga, aided by his own order, the Brethren of the Sword, gained control of pagan Livonia in a similar way between 1202 and about 1230 (he lost it to the Knights in 1237), while the king of Denmark seized Estonia in 1219. The Templars and Hospitallers, meanwhile, built up substantial territories in the impeccably Christian, but jurisdictionally confused, space of Brandenburg and Pomerania. The Templars saw their German estates eroded by the superior power of the Ascanian margraves of Brandenburg, and were, in any case, destroyed in 1307, but the Hospitallers remained a major presence, participating more or less independently in the region's feuding culture for the rest of the middle ages.

Military orders, then, could form states where overlordship was weak and where opportunities for expansion existed. Their resources made them inherently attractive to the jostling rulers in such areas, even if – as the king of Hungary discovered – they might turn out to be 'a viper in the bosom'.[38] This recognition casts a somewhat different light on the military orders of southern Spain, one of which – Calatrava – actually established a brief presence in the Prussian land of opportunity before being elbowed out by the Teutonic Knights. The kings of the Spanish peninsula were active leaders in the wars against

---

[38] Quoted by M. Burleigh, 'The Military Orders in the Baltic', in *NCMH* V, p. 744.

the Muslims, and this helped to ensure that the orders of Calatrava, Santiago and Alcántara, which emerged in the 1160s and 1170s, did so more or less under royal supervision. Even so, the fact that they originated – variously – from the activities of Templars, Cistercians and an *hermandad* of the 'knights of Cáceres' reminds us that they testify to the capacities of non-royal associational forms. The vast terrains acquired by the Spanish military orders in the 1230s and 1240s, as the underpopulated kingdom of Castile suddenly found itself master of Andalusia and La Mancha, gave these organisations, and the noble families linked to them, a role in the politics of Castile not so very different from that held by the Teutonic Order in the politics of Poland and the Baltic littoral. In the course of the fourteenth and fifteenth centuries, the kings of Castile strove to acquire control of the military orders, and their disproportionate power was a significant factor in the turbulent politics of the period . By this time, the Church had long ceased to found new crusading orders, and it is striking that the new orders of chivalry, which fourteenth-century kings and princes created to harness the enthusiasm of the secular aristocracy, were kept firmly under royal control and denied the capacity to acquire property and autonomy which ecclesiastical status and papal favour had permitted their predecessors.

Ambivalence, then, is the keynote of the ecclesiastical experience in the thirteenth century. On the one hand, there were factors encouraging ecclesiastical independence and/or the absorption of clerical leaders in the affairs of the universal Church. On the other hand, like many towns and lords, prelates could generally gain from operating within the frameworks of kings and princes. Regnal churches were just one of the structures of ecclesiastical political life, and participation in the assemblies, councils and administrations of lay rulers just one of the roles played by bishops and university men, but both of these lent texture and reality to the territorial states that were coming into being in this period.

Conclusion

It is clear that thirteenth-century Europe was the scene of two contradictory developments. One is the trend we are all familiar with: the gradual emergence of more powerful and plural 'regnal' polities, which – through a mixture of legal and institutional growth, consultation and effective lordship – were better able to embrace and exploit the lesser powers of the sizeable spaces beneath and around them. The other development, equally pronounced, and all the more important to recognise if we wish to understand the politics of the later middle ages, is the proliferation of overlapping, and at some level autonomous, political and governmental structures. These structures came in all shapes and sizes; they were growing simultaneously; and they compromised or contended with one another as circumstances dictated. This second development greatly complicated the first.

The reasons for this double-sided pattern of evolution have been surveyed. Top-layer jurisdictions, notably kings, were able to benefit from the new ideological and institutional technologies of the twelfth and thirteenth centuries to assert themselves over their putative realms. Lesser powers within these spaces – lords, churches, towns – might favour these developments: sometimes because they were too incoherent or weak to prevent them; sometimes because they could see the advantages of greater co-ordination or protection; sometimes because their own interests were peculiarly bound up with those of the suzerain, his status or his dynasty. There was thus a measure of support for central authority, even among those possessing authority themselves. Beyond these lesser powers, meanwhile, lay much larger numbers of people, who have been little discussed above because their claims to political independence were generally limited or localised. Because such people, who ranged in power and wealth from lesser noblemen, or 'gentry', through minor guildsmen, to workers and peasants, could not hope to obtain a real freedom of action by themselves, they were particularly drawn to collective means of self-protection and advancement. They too provided a reservoir of potential support for high-level jurisdictions, because they could see in the progress of regnal authority, with its laws, offices and assemblies, promising media for the defence, and even the representation, of their concerns.

These trends worked in favour of the development of more integrated, complex and stable polities, but before we start talking about the rise of kingdoms, we should take account of other features of the period. First of all, it was not just kingdoms that could form plausible 'regnal' polities. By 1300, as we have seen, a host of other forms were attaining comparable coherence, whether city states like Florence, Milan or Lübeck; lordships like the duchies of Brittany and Austria, the counties of Flanders and Ferrara and the see of Liège; or indeed other associations, such as the *Ordensstaat* of the Teutonic Knights.

Some of these had greater territorial and political coherence than others, and some comparable forms – the Hanseatic League, the Swiss Confederation, not to mention many other towns, lordships and principalities – would grow considerably in scope and integration in the coming century. Even so, it is important to remember that the meaningfulness of kingdoms also varied, over both time and space. We have seen that the political tools of the twelfth and thirteenth centuries were available to all political units, not only those topped off by a crown or a tiara. Like kings, churches, towns and lords strengthened their jurisdiction and experimented with taxation and representation, and, as they did so, they drew the lesser powers of their *mouvances* more closely into their grip: gentlemen, shopkeepers and peasants were no more the allies of kingdoms than they were the partisans of more provincial or local authorities. Kings, it is true, were becoming able to dispose of large amounts of money and armed force, and this gave them a particular capacity to engulf and disrupt smaller powers. But this should not be exaggerated: royal taxes and armies were typically temporary, while the jurisdiction and authority possessed by more localised powers was often much more enduring. Smaller powers too could exert temporary agglomerations of power: by leaguing together, they could match the resources of even the most powerful kings. After all, a group of northern French crusaders defeated the combined forces of Aragon, Toulouse and Foix at Muret in 1213, while William Wallace and his supporters triumphed over Edward I at Stirling Bridge in 1297, the Flemish destroyed Philip IV's army at Courtrai in 1302, and a mainly peasant army from the Swiss cantons trounced the mighty duke of Austria at Morgarten in 1315.

We have also seen that the progress made in government was accompanied by the creation of new media of resistance – laws, customs, immunities, assemblies, leagues and so on. Some of these forms of resistance could certainly have an integrative effect, as the risings of English aristocrats in the name of the *communitas regni* helped to affirm the scope of the kingdom and to strengthen the role of the crown as its common authority. But others did not. The risings of the French *noblesse* in 1314–15 resulted in charters affirming provincial liberties and licensing private war, for instance: they are often thought to have opened the way for the princely assertions and civil wars of the succeeding century. Meanwhile, the *Cortes*, *hermandades* and noble leagues that flourished in Castile between the 1270s and the 1320s may have been devoted to the defence of the crown and the wellbeing of the kingdom, but the effect of their operations was to advance municipal jurisdiction and to foster the expansion of seigneurial immunities. The governmental rights willingly conceded to the princes of the Empire by Frederick II and his son secured noble support in the short term, and were eminently in line with imperial political values, but they also confirmed the process through which several of these princes – Bohemia, Austria, the territories of the kingdom of Burgundy/Arles – would ultimately break from the Empire altogether. While the regnal framework undeniably had attractions for the powers within it, its demands were frequently unwelcome, and – as the uber-kingdoms of Pope and emperor were already demonstrating – large and plural polities could be too large and too plural to deliver the political services that their members desired. There was a warning here for the kingdoms, principalities and territorial states, as they, in turn, sought to incorporate the diverse powers beneath them.

This, then, was the constitutional basis for the kinds of later medieval politics that have been so often deplored by historians. Kings, lords, towns and prelates behaved disloyally, or broke agreements, because they were subject to multiple allegiances that cut across each other. They fought so much because fighting was the ultimate vindication of right, and rights were everywhere in conflict. Kings could at times mobilise their subjects and create the sensation of a kingdom – even, as we shall see, a nation – but other powers within or overlapping the royal orbit also had the capacity intermittently to mobilise and organise, and they might do so against the king, or against each other, with potentially violent and disintegrative results. Because almost every political form was perforated by others, hierarchies were uncertain, and the balance of power was ever-changing. Moreover, three basic factors helped to keep all these powers in play in a manner which distinguishes the later middle ages from other periods. One is writing and record-keeping, which helped to keep the memory of defunct or failed structures available for re-creation if and when circumstances changed. A second is the legal and ideological atmosphere which enabled every power-holder to regard itself as some kind of potential government, and thus to accept subjection only on the most conditional and temporary terms. A third is the actual inability of any of the various permutations of power convincingly to expunge any of the others, so that even as kingdoms grew in power and potential in the thirteenth century, few other authorities altogether lost their footing. By the end of the fifteenth century, all three of these factors had been altered or eroded, but it should be clear that this was the situation at the beginning of our period, in the decades around 1300.

Even then, however, some political units were more consistently effective than others, and the balance of power consequently varied across the continent. It is a theme and conviction of this book that the parallels between European polities in this period are more compelling and enlightening than the differences, but it would of course be wrong to suggest that the power of emperors, kings, lords, towns and churches was everywhere the same. The permeating authority of the English monarchy, for example, with its common law and centralised structures of justice, and its close control of local office, was very unusual – at least for a territory the size of England. Only the Papacy possessed this kind of jurisdiction – over a much larger area, of course, though it was beginning to experience some diseconomies of scale by the end of the thirteenth century. Among secular regimes, the kingdom of Sicily and the lowland half of Scotland were initially comparable, but the momentum of Scottish jurisdictional development was slowing by the end of the twelfth century, and a mixture of minorities and wars assisted the development of local immunities in both kingdoms over the course of the thirteenth. Royal authority could be very striking in all three kingdoms, and the extractive capacity of the monarchy in the pre-1282 kingdom of Sicily was probably unrivalled across Europe, but there is no question that England was a more integrated polity, even before Sicily was assailed by the traumas of the 1250s, 1260s and 1280s. This in turn influenced the aims and capacities of other authorities in the English space, broadly inclining them towards participation in the regnal structure, rather than resistance to it, and shaping their political resources accordingly: English magnates, churches and towns could be very powerful, but they derived much of their power from association with the projects and structures of the crown.

This kind of authority, and its associated form of polity, was becoming possible elsewhere in Europe on a smaller scale – in the so-called *Kleinstaaten* (little states), both urban and seigneurial, of central Europe and the French periphery. We have seen how the dukes of Brittany, the Visconti lords of Milan and even communal organisations like the priorate of Florence were becoming able to penetrate and manage the other authorities within their domains. Some, like Venice, developed a very complete control, but most of them faced significant obstructions, even when their territorial reach was small: ecclesiastical institutions, vassals, parties, royal enclaves, allodial[39] land belonging to client lords – all these were potential sources of resistance, limiting the grip of the small state and forcing it into jurisdictional compromises. In this way, *Kleinstaaten* in fact resembled the commonest pattern of territorial power in Europe: the patchwork of jurisdictions, operating under a (sometimes very light) co-ordinating authority. This was what the kingdoms of France, Iberia and Germany were really like. At the tidier end of the spectrum, in thirteenth-century Castile, for example, there were (at least on paper) reasonably clear divisions between the ordinary jurisdiction of royal officers such as *merinos* and *adelantados*, dispensing royal justice over reserved cases, and that of municipal *alcaldes*, applying the local *fueros*. It was also understood that jurisdictional confusions – involving, for example, the boundaries of the municipalities, the competence over particular cases or the relationship between these courts and those of lords and churches – should be resolved by the crown, but what happened in practice was doubtless much more variable and locally determined. In France, meanwhile, even in royal France, even as close to Paris as the *bailliage* of Senlis, so brilliantly analysed by Bernard Guenée, jurisdiction was rather more dispersed and uncertain.[40] Although the crown's general right to resolve confusions was accepted, its obligation to uphold local custom created copious grounds for challenge and complexity, while ordinary justice was divided not only into dozens of tiny territorial blocs – distributed between the royal bailiff and local castellans, lords and churches – but also thematically, with vaguely defined 'high', 'medium' and 'low' justice often belonging to different agencies in the same locale. In the German lands, the situation was still more complicated, with the simultaneous availability of different kinds of secular law – the law set down in the *Landfrieden*, the partly codified and partly customary laws of fiefs and *Länder*, the laws of towns, the quasi-laws of feuding – and a host of competing and overlapping agencies providing justice. While the king had certain feudal rights, and a capacity to arbitrate and

---

[39] I.e. free of feudal jurisdiction.

[40] B. Guenée, *Tribunaux et gens de justice dans le bailliage de Senlis à la fin du moyen âge* (Paris, 1963).

intervene in disputes among his vassals, he was unable to do much to regularise justice at lower levels. This did not altogether liberate the towns and princes, however, as their efforts to defend or expand their jurisdiction brought them into conflict with each other, while their advances were eroded by the opportunistic efforts of other powers in their spheres of influence. Beyond the German lands, the position was similar, but – apart from the networks of towns and villages operating under some species of 'German law' – the jurisdictional map was generally simpler and the immunities enjoyed by magnates a stage more complete. In Hungary, the association of lesser nobles with county-based royal jurisdiction, and the general readiness of the crown to challenge magnate agglomerations, meant a rough balance between royal and lordly influence, while in Bohemia, as we have seen, the king possessed jurisdiction in some areas and the great lords in others, though they could face competition from towns and lesser nobles. In Scandinavia, parts of Sweden were still ruled by magnate clans in any case, but the castle-based net of royal justice in the rest of the kingdom, as in Denmark, was typically absorbed into the immunised estates of major magnates during the thirteenth and early fourteenth centuries, creating a series of tiny principalities not unlike the Scottish earldoms and 'provincial' lordships (even Norway, where royal justice had advanced more strongly, went this way after about 1350). This situation, also found in Poland, was echoed in the solidification of law at a provincial, rather than regnal, level in many of these countries, though legal zones were generally much larger than the immunities of individual magnates and, in many areas, enforced traditions of co-operation among them. Juridical immunity did not, of course, mean political immunity, but it did help to influence the terms of regnal co-ordination and the degree to which it was achievable.

This distribution of jurisdiction, which provided a kind of axis for the development of other political and governmental structures, was not, however, set in stone. If justice and law were the great breakthroughs of the twelfth and thirteenth centuries, other political technologies were to have an equally profound effect on the fourteenth and fifteenth – perhaps especially taxation, the potential of which had barely begun to be tapped in 1300, but also consultation, representation and what French historians have called 'dialogue' between rulers and people, all of which would develop significantly in the ensuing centuries. New technologies and new contingencies could combine to alter the balances between different powers in the various regions of Europe. Angevin Hungary (1301–87), for example, and Poland under the restored Piast monarchy (1320–70), began to look a lot more like western kingdoms than they did in either the thirteenth or the fifteenth century. Castile, Naples and Sicily, on the other hand, began to take on a more cellular format, as municipal independence was reduced and the expanding jurisdictions of magnates came to resemble territorial principalities. Sizeable territorial states, combining strings of cities and the countryside between them, gradually became possible in Italy and parts of Germany, while the powerful kingdoms of England (in 1403) and France (in the 1360s and 1420s) were threatened – perhaps not implausibly – with division into three and two parts respectively. Not only were the outcomes of the thirteenth century ambivalent, then, they were also not fixed for all time.

FORMS OF POLITICAL CULTURE

So far, my treatment of political forms has been essentially institutional. There are good reasons for this: the development of institutions of government was a central element in the political history of the high and late middle ages, and the contemporary fascination with law and jurisdiction meant that the institutions, models and types we have been discussing commanded the imagination of contemporaries and shaped their activities to a significant degree. However, the sorts of things explored above were not the only structures that influenced politics. There were, first of all, several fields of ideas – ranging from the systematic thought of jurists and schoolmen, through the histories, myths and stories of the educated, to the moral and religious beliefs spread more widely across society – that helped to constitute what Paul Strohm has called the 'imaginative structures' through which people conceived the world around them.[41] Equally, there were also other means of communication besides the more-or-less governmental agencies on which attention was focused in the previous chapter. People certainly did learn about politics by being governed, but they also learned through media which were not intrinsically governmental – education, art and architecture, preaching, books, conversation and so on. In addition, their political behaviour was influenced by a

---

[41] P. Strohm, *Hochon's Arrow. The Social Imagination of Fourteenth-Century Texts* (Princeton, 1992), p. 4.

range of social pressures beyond those produced by the governments of the period. The men and women of the later middle ages were, like us, participants in groups and networks whose primary purposes were not, in any straightforward sense, political, from families and kin groups, to trade and craft organisations, criminal gangs, aristocratic retinues, parochial and manorial organisations, and even the sense of community that linked the living with the dead. Taken together, these three non-governmental kinds of structure – in basic terms, ideology (and language), media and social networks – form the main content of what historians have come to call 'political culture'.[42] It has become axiomatic that an understanding of political culture is integral to an understanding of politics, and if we want to know what was going on in later medieval Europe, and why it was going on, we will need to pay some attention to these other structural influences.

Clearly enough, the political culture of the later middle ages is a vast topic, and the treatment here will be necessarily brief, and somewhat schematic. It will also be quite precisely focused on the impact of these three groups of forms on the action of politics, and indeed on the theme of developing political community which is a central concern of the book. 'Politics' was not normally a discrete category for medieval thinkers (nor indeed for other kinds of people). Considered formally, it was, at the beginning of our period, and to some extent throughout, a subdivision of moral philosophy: to be political, or politic, was to live well in human society. Political ideas, political language or rhetoric and political behaviour were consequently interwoven with many other kinds of ideas, language and behaviour, including a great deal of what we would today regard as religious, social or personal. On one level, this underlines the enormous breadth of the issues under consideration in this chapter. On another, it somewhat challenges a tendency, especially marked among English historians, to regard political ideas as somehow cut off from, or tangential to, politics. In the last few decades, there has been a growing recognition that the ideas of 'men of action', the prevailing political *mentalités* (attitudes, assumptions) and the discourses of political society could have an important role to play in shaping behaviour, but it is not often appreciated how many points of contact there were

---

[42] See C. Carpenter's introduction to *The Fifteenth Century IV: Political Culture in Late Medieval Britain*, ed. Carpenter and L. Clark (Woodbridge, 2004), for a useful overview.

between the ideas and terms circulating in society, and those generated in the centres of learning that have been studied by historians of political thought.[43] While our touchstone in what follows, therefore, will be the shaping of political action, and we shall concentrate on the forms that possessed most political resonance, we shall need to remember that universities and law schools were part of the political society of this period, and closely connected to some of its most important centres of power. Equally, the contacts within the still-small fraternity of the learned, their employment in ecclesiastical and secular government, their shared use of a particular kind of scholarly Latin and their mutual elevation of a relatively small body of authoritative texts meant that the political applications of ideas were readily explored and rapidly circulated. Once again, this argues for approaching political structures − cultural, as well as institutional − at a European level: much was shared and local variations were often variations on a theme.

Ideas and discourses

It has become fashionable in the history of ideas to emphasise the linguistic qualities of bodies of thought. Much as ideas can be explored and exchanged through processes of reasoning, they are also held together in bundles of repeated terms, assumptions and linkages which have the quality of languages or discourses. In his recent survey of political thought between 1250 and 1450, for example, Antony Black identified four or five master languages in which most political thought was written, each with its own vocabulary, rhetoric, standard texts and modes of argument and proof. In his view, these were the languages of theology and learned law (Roman law and canon law), of Aristotle and Cicero, and finally those of local custom, much of it associated with fiefs, vassalage, fidelity, lordship and so on.[44] In practice, these languages tended to overlap, merge and interact, many Aristotelian themes and terms becoming assimilated into the language of theology, for example, while the links between the languages and traditions of theology and canon law, Roman law and local custom, or even the theories of Aristotle and Cicero, are so extensive that it can

---

[43] Quotation from J.C. Holt, *Magna Carta and Medieval Government* (London, 1985), preface, p. vii.
[44] A. Black, *Political Thought in Europe, 1250–1450* (Cambridge, 1992), pp. 2, 7–10.

sometimes seem artificial to draw distinctions between them. In fact, almost all historians of political thought, Black included, now emphasise the synthesising tendency of medieval political thinking. The preference of writers for eradicating contradictions wherever possible, their practice of transferring arguments and terms from one context to another, their shared Latinity and shared methodology, such as the tradition of glossing authoritative texts, or the practice of syllogistic reasoning, all combined to make the ideas and terms used in each branch of learning available to those at work in other branches. Much language-use remained specialised, certainly – a Parisian theologian would have used a different set of terms and styles from the jurists around the emperor or the *dictatores* (teachers of rhetoric) of an Italian city – but there are a number of themes and concerns that were common to different kinds of practitioner and whose impact on the minds and words of European politicians was reinforced by their appearance in other texts and debates. On the whole, it may be more helpful to the political historian to organise a discussion of political ideas around these themes than it is to identify and explore the traditions from which they came. In what follows, therefore, we shall first of all be concerned with establishing the major topics of political thinking and discussion as they were *c.*1300.

Common to almost every variety of contemporary thought by this time was a sense of the political community. It was recognised that people lived in groups under some kind of government, and it was assumed, or positively argued, that it was good for them to do so. There were plenty of historical, or pseudo-historical, models of political community, in which, as suggested above, the Roman Empire was particularly prominent, though there were plenty of others, including the Roman Republic, the empires of Cyrus, Alexander, Charlemagne and Arthur, the fellowship of peers that were thought to have founded Britain or Hungary, and even the kingdom of God, whether this was understood to be a kingdom over Israel, or over the world, or – in the person of Christ – over the rest of the apostles. Several powerful traditions correspondingly argued that the political community was not only a historical (and present) reality, but a product of nature. While Augustine's foundational work, *The City of God* (AD 413–27) located human government in the defective world of time that began with original sin, it nonetheless promoted an idea of the earthly city as a community founded on the pursuit of the common interests of its inhabitants and devoted to keeping an imperfect kind of justice and order among them. Aristotelian and Ciceronian writing, meanwhile, took a more positive line, proposing that political life was natural to man, and drawing attention to the practices of virtue, reasoning and rhetoric that would advance the statesman and help to maintain the health of the polity. From the sources available to them, the more educated men and women of the later middle ages would thus have regarded the political community as a normative feature of human society. It is important to realise that this kind of thinking did not prescribe a single size and shape for this kind of community: it could exist as readily in a church or town or province as in a principality, a kingdom or an empire.

As we have seen, later medieval politicians would also have been made aware of a range of associated features and practices that might be expected to advance political life: reason, virtue and eloquence on the part of the rulers and/or citizens; law and justice (on which more below); and usually some form of counsel, consultation or even consent on the part of the members of the community. Different political discourses certainly emphasised different parts of this picture – the virtue of citizens is not a prominent theme in Romano-canonical writing, for instance, while the corporateness of the members is a central assumption of canon law, but an ideal requiring action in the works of Cicero – yet it seems likely that these basic notions would have formed a sort of composite in most informed minds. If there was agreement over these fundamentals, however, there was enormous scope for disagreement over how these things should be fitted together and realised in practice. The classical distinction between the rule of one (monarchy/tyranny), the rule of the few (aristocracy/oligarchy) and the rule of the many (polity/democracy) helped to structure some of these debates, reminding readers that there were positive and deviant forms of all these basic types, and drawing attention to the advantages and disadvantages of each form. Giles of Rome, writing his *De Regimine Principum* (concerning the rule of princes) for Philip IV of France *c.*1280, argued that monarchy was the best form, on the grounds that it was uniquely fitted to promote the unity of the state, but just a few decades later it was possible for Ptolemy of Lucca to argue the superiority of collective forms of rule – and this in a treatise with exactly the same name, and a similar range of sources.

Meanwhile, if classical political theory enabled the differentiation of regimes, it also tended to recommend some mixing of their features. Thinking about the polity thus often involved some distribution of political rights between the monarch, the few and the many, with the mixture varying from model to model. A common resolution was to recommend some kind of monarchy, but to argue that the monarch should be guided or restrained by devices which provided for the common good of the political community. Among these, two particularly dominated. One of them was law, which was supposed to protect the community, both by tying the king to the dictates of reason and by reflecting the common will of the people, since law was commonly thought to be made with their assent or at their wish. The other was counsel, which enabled the direct representation of the people's interests through the wise and good men who advised the ruler. So it was that, in his influential gloss on Aristotle's *Politics* (*c.*1340–5), Walter Burley was able to note how, in a typical kingdom, 'the many govern as much as, or more than, the king alone, and on account of this, the king calls parliament for the expedition of difficult business'.[45] Thomas Aquinas, on the other hand, fused the many with the monarch by recommending the ruler's election, and urging the king to subject himself to the just laws of his kingdom. In the first part of his *Defensor Pacis* (Defender of Peace, 1324), Marsiglio of Padua echoed these precepts and took them further, emphasising the collective role in lawmaking and allowing the correction of the ruler by the community on whose behalf he ruled. Giles of Rome, meanwhile, had taken a different tack, insisting that the rule of one was better for the community than the rule of many, and placing the monarch in a mediatory position between divine and natural law, to which he should defer, and human, or positive, law, which required his amendment through legislation and judgement. As is clear from these four examples, the terms of power-sharing were a frequent preoccupation of political writers and thinkers, and the relative rights of rulers and communities were a common subject of debate, in both politics and theory. It is also clear that many of the same arguments were applied to different political forms: urban thinkers dealt in theories of monarchy, simply transferring them to a civic context, while those at work in a royal or ecclesiastical setting typically promoted elements of aristocracy or polity alongside the rule of the

---

[45] S. Harrison Thomson, 'Walter Burley's Commentary on the Politics of Aristotle', in *Mélanges Auguste Pelzer* (Louvain, 1947), *Recueil de Travaux d'Histoire et de Philologie*, 3rd series, 26, 557–78, p. 577.

monarch. The notions of mixed government discussed above reflect the influence of Aristotle, but it is worth noting that there were broadly parallel ideas in other intellectual traditions. Roman law, as we have seen, tended to bestow full legislative power on the emperor, but it acknowledged that this power had popular origins, wavered over the relative authority of law and custom, and proposed, through the influential doctrine of the *digna vox*, that the emperor should choose to rule within the law, even though he was free of its binding force. Canon lawyers, meanwhile, were much concerned with the relationship between corporations and their heads, reaching a variety of conclusions which were to be pitched against each other in the various conciliar crises of the fourteenth and fifteenth centuries. While almost all thinking promoted a notion of political community, therefore, this did not mean widespread agreement over what that meant, in either principle or practice.

A second major theme of contemporary political discourse concerned law, right and justice. This has already been extensively discussed in the previous chapter, and, as we have just seen, it was often woven into discussion of the political community. However, it is worth noting the prominence of legal thinking on its own terms, because the relationships between different kinds of law, between law, right and custom, or between law, legislator, judge and people, were also explored independently of broader political questions. Jurisdiction, for example, was probably a much more robust, coherent and immediate concept to medieval lawyers and their clients than the political community, and this must help to explain why certain kinds of politically inconsiderate behaviour could be readily accepted as legitimate. From a juridical perspective, it was entirely proper to pursue one's rights, regardless of the social and political damage inflicted – indeed, since the whole order of the universe was rooted in law and justice, it could be improper not to. Equally, acculturation in the values and assumptions of law and justice helps to explain the persisting complexity of the map of power. To modern eyes, it might make sense for each state to possess a monopoly of jurisdiction within its bounds, but the people of the later middle ages lived, as we have seen, in a world of overlapping and conflicting jurisdictions, many of them developed by prescription in long ages of royal and imperial weakness, and most of them strengthened by principle and practice in the new age of learned law that opened up from around 1100. Whatever value people may have placed on political community, and whatever interest they had in aligning themselves with such communities, they also expected to be able to use whatever laws and sources of judgement were open to them.

Much as law could be one of the things that helped to build a sense of political community, therefore, acceptance (or rejection) of a jurisdiction – say, that of the emperor in Italy, or of the king of England in North Wales – did not necessarily disclose wider allegiances, identities or assumptions. The Poitevins and Gascons who appealed to the king of France against their English lord, and thereby undermined his lordship, were not traitorous, or disingenuous; nor were they responding to the pull of Frenchness; nor were they short-sightedly dismantling the means of their own relative freedom; nor were they deliberately helping the French king to extend his jurisdiction. Rather, they were thinking juridically and using justice. In fact, it is possible to suggest that this mode of thought was at high tide in the late thirteenth and early fourteenth centuries, and that it helps to explain some of the more culturally insensitive enterprises of the period. The more-or-less unrealistic assertions of Boniface VIII over the king of France, of John XXII over the king of the Romans, of Edward I over Scotland or of Philip IV over Flanders, Brittany and Gascony all made perfect sense in juridical terms. These assertions could certainly be contested in juridical terms as well – pitting the laws and customs of the Scots and Welsh against the jurisdiction of the English king, for instance, or questioning the right of the Pope to declare matters of faith outside a General Council – and they could be contested in other ways as well, but it is striking that a juridical argument was considered necessary by all the parties, and important to recognise that law and justice provided a major sphere of political inspiration in this period.

The papal examples just mentioned remind us that a third important theme in political thought was the relationship between temporal and spiritual powers. We have seen that papal claims to represent the spiritual order could be brought into question (and so could those of other ecclesiastical hierarchies). To proponents of an apostolic vision of the Church, the worldliness of the Papacy and other prelates could make them seem more like secular lords than the vessels of the Holy Spirit, more like Caesar than Christ and his disciples. While this inclined many Christians to call for reform, it encouraged some in more radical directions, towards the outright rejection of papal or prelatical authority, or towards millenarian beliefs which presented

the whole ecclesiastical structure as the work of Antichrist, and anticipated its demise in the coming end of the world. In his commentary on
the apocalypse, the Franciscan intellectual Peter John Olivi (d.1298)
represented the Papacy as setting the standard of Christian practice, but
also described the coming of a Third Age, which would be ushered in
by a short period of persecution by the forces of darkness, prior to the
transfer of control from the existing clerical hierarchy to the elect, or
true Christians. This ostensibly papalist work was thus extremely
dangerous: if papal behaviour fell below the high standards envisaged
by Olivi, it would be a sign to his readers that the rule of Antichrist was
beginning and the ecclesiastical hierarchy was no longer to be obeyed
or trusted; indeed, the beginnings of papal moves against the more
extreme Franciscans were to have precisely this effect in the first few
decades of the fourteenth century. Not all Franciscans shared Olivi's
views, and his work was officially condemned by the Pope in 1326, but
the influence of the friars spread the ideal of a spiritual church far and
wide, and the more radical development of that ideal helped to set the
tone for both the politics and the political theory of spiritual and
temporal relations in our period. Once the capacity of the Papacy to
speak for and control the rest of the Church was brought into question,
and once, in turn, the identity of 'the Church' became uncertain, the
relationship between ecclesiastical agencies and lay powers was much
more complicated.

To a certain extent, the internal politics of the Church were
conducted with reference to ideas of political community parallel to
those encountered in the secular sphere. The view that the Pope
ought to govern with a council, which acquired a new prominence
from around 1300, and the flirtations of the cardinals with claims to a
princely, or aristocratic, or conciliar status within the Church, which
soon followed, were part and parcel of a series of political questions
which were as much secular as spiritual. In his treatise 'On Royal and
Papal Power' (*c.*1302/3), the Dominican canonist John of Paris argued
that the Papacy should rule the Church as a bishop does his diocese:
that is, with the advice of a chapter, which John thought should
include elected representatives from all the provinces of Europe; he
also argued that the Pope was ultimately subject to a general council,
and that – like a secular ruler – he could be deposed if he went against
the common good of the Church. A few years later, in 1311, William
Durand the younger devised an elaborate scheme for an essentially
republican church, in which the Papacy, publicly funded from surplus

ecclesiastical revenues, would govern according to the counsel of the cardinals and under the laws made by a general council. At the same time, the emergence of a more strident kind of papalism, apparent in the condemnations of certain teachings at the University of Paris in the 1270s and 1280s, or in Boniface VIII's bull *Unam Sanctam* (1302), can be seen as an essentially political recognition that order and unity depended on obedience to a single authority; it was paralleled by the recommendations made in a secular context by the sometime papalist Giles of Rome in his *De Regimine Principum*, and by the fiercely antipapal Dante and Marsiglio, in *Monarchia* (1314 or later) and *Defensor Pacis*, respectively. Other prominent themes in Church politics were more peculiarly ecclesiological, though that certainly did not stop them being carried over into the lay sphere. Perhaps the most important example is 'reform', which acquired a different orientation around the beginning of our period. As we have seen, reform was more or less the rallying cry of the high medieval Papacy and its monastic allies; it tended to mean the return to a purer spirituality, coupled with the assertion of papal authority and ecclesiastical independence. Already enriched by neoclassical ideas of *renovatio*, and now enhanced by Roman conceptions of legislation, it became an important feature of secular rule as well, notably in France, where the king's readiness to reform the realm was an important means of legitimising the extension of royal power. 'Reform', however, was a two-edged sword, and it is not surprising that the quest for purity frequently turned on the monarch himself. While Philip IV was pressed to reform his government in 1303, the Council of Vienne (1311–12) heard the first calls for reform of the Church 'in head and members', an ideal of wholesale restructuring from the Papacy downwards which was to reverberate for the next two hundred years and more. Not only did this oft-repeated theme press upon the clergy, adding greatly to the tensions within the ecclesiastical structure, it also had profound effects on the relationships between lay rulers, the churchmen in and around their realms, and the Papacy, as we shall see.

Another worrying aspect of reformism, and one more directly relevant to the theme of temporal and spiritual power, was the tendency of critics to begin to look to lay authorities to reform the Church. Whatever this owed to the reformist pretensions of rulers, whether king-emperors or city councils, it mainly derived from three overlapping traditions. The first has been discussed above: the conflict of Pope and Emperor, which made each the inevitable means of correcting the other. By the mid-thirteenth century, a connection was already beginning to be forged between imperial assertions and the desire for a more spiritual church; it was to intensify considerably in the conflict between Emperor Ludwig of Bavaria (1314–47) and Pope John XXII (1316–34), though it is also visible in the activities of a king-emperor like Philip IV of France, who pressed for councils to judge the Papacy and suppressed the order of Knights Templar with the thinnest tissue of papal authorisation. A second strand has also been mentioned: the Franciscan emphasis on apostolic poverty, which challenged ecclesiastical claims to wealth and power while leaving those of the lay order more or less intact. The third strand requires separate discussion: a series of interconnected and overlapping ideas that brought into question the link between the earthly church and its heavenly counterpart.

We have already seen that the epic conflict between Frederick II and the Papacy unleashed a wave of prophetic activity that threatened the Church by canvassing the idea that it was the work of Antichrist, and that these ideas – based on the prophecies of Joachim of Fiore (d.1202) – were revived in the late thirteenth century. This was by no means the only stimulus to prophecy in the period, however. The fall of Acre (1291), for example, gave rise to the very popular 'Tripoli prophecy', which *ex post facto* 'predicted' that event and looked forward to the destruction of the mendicant orders, while secular myths were another powerful source of inspiration, with Merlin's prophecy in Geoffrey of Monmouth's twelfth-century *Historia Regum Britanniae*, for instance, spawning countless later medieval imitations in the British Isles. It seems to have been during the thirteenth and fourteenth centuries that prophecy became an especially powerful and widespread source of political ideas and languages, and the conflicts of Pope and Emperor were certainly a significant spur to this development. As we have seen, the prophecies of this period added to the common stock of political ideas by emphasising the notion of the millennium, or end of the world, which many of them described and anticipated. Such an emphasis could certainly be challenged – whether by the authoritative condemnations of Augustine against those who sought to know such divine secrets, or more simply by the stubborn failure of the world to end – but, even so, it articulated the possibility of radical social and political change, and this created an important resource for mass political action whenever circumstances were sufficiently disturbed.

Meanwhile, by offering another means of cosmological knowledge, prophecy contributed to a range of forms and ideas that challenged clerical control of access to the supernatural world. It used to be argued that the fourteenth century saw a significant weakening of the clerical hold over the imagination of the laity. In an article entitled 'Mysticism, Nominalism and Dissent', Steven Ozment memorably identified two of the major causes of this weakening.[46] 'Mysticism' was a spiritual movement which sought a more direct apprehension of God through meditation and other devotional exercises. The product of attempts to raise the temperature of piety among monks and nuns, and canvassed through preaching and in vernacular devotional works, it spread quite widely in lay society – especially along the Rhine, in the Low Countries, England and Italy – from the later thirteenth century onwards. While the more responsible mystical preachers and writers urged their followers to obey clerical authority and distrust visions, the possibility that ordinary people might come into direct contact with divine wisdom was effectively opened up and canvassed, and the fourteenth-century religious scene correspondingly included a significant number of vocal divines, many of them women, who claimed authority from their visions, and not from the structures of the Church.

'Nominalism', meanwhile, was a kind of reasoning that emphasised the distinction between words and things. Following the work of John Duns Scotus (d.1308) and William of Ockham (d.1347), it was a flourishing approach among the theologians of the late thirteenth and the fourteenth century, an outgrowth from the achievements of thirteenth-century theology, and potentially a sceptical one, since it tended to emphasise the gap between human understanding and the world of the divine which theology professed to illuminate. In this way, it fed into a contemporary emphasis on God's omnipotence and unknowableness which threatened to undermine confidence in the ministrations of the earthly Church. Not only was it no longer plausible that churchmen possessed the keys of Heaven, there was now a real question about whether the church to which they belonged truly was the Church founded by Christ, or just a temporal organisation based on a corruption of the Christian tradition. In practice, nominalist thought was generally a lot less alarming than this: Ockham, for example, established that there

[46] S. Ozment, 'Mysticism, Nominalism and Dissent', in C. Trinkaus and H. A. Oberman, eds., *The Pursuit of Holiness in Late Medieval and Renaissance Religion* (Leiden, 1974), 67–92.

was no reason to suppose that God would refuse to uphold the 'ordained power' represented by the Church's ministry, which was supported by revelation and sustained by the evidence of history. Equally, it has become clear that the fourteenth-century Church was actually extremely successful in catering to the laity: whatever existential doubts may have lain behind the profusion of cults, offerings and rituals in which the laity engaged, ecclesiastical provision was, if anything, more deeply woven into secular life than in any earlier period. Even so, the profusion of ideas and themes that emphasised the gap between the visible Church and the divine order surely affected the reasoning of educated people and made the environment of theological debate somewhat more unstable than it had been. The relationship between spiritual and temporal was a rather more complicated problem than simply the relationship between 'Church' and 'State', and its ramifications were felt throughout political society in the later middle ages.

The topics discussed so far are, in most cases, widely recognised as themes of political thought. There are several others, however, which deserve recognition in these terms, even if they were not the products of academic speculation and did not often receive the same analytical attention. Three of them concern divisions of humanity: the *gens* (people) or *natio* (nation); the orders and estates into which society could be divided; and sects or minorities. Let us consider them in turn.

It is now widely accepted that medieval people had a concept of the nation, though whether or not that concept resembles our own remains a lively – if rather tangential – question. The hallmarks of nationhood were conventionally the ties of blood and language, though a common name, shared laws and customs, government and territory (present or historic) were also often important. People of the same nation were, it was believed, anciently related to each other; this was signalled by their common tongue, and captured in their common institutions. Recognising that the cultural roots of conceptions of nationhood are ancient and manifold, lying in the Bible and the classics, and in the foundation-myths of kingdoms and cities alike, Susan Reynolds has argued that what really prompted the identification of peoples, or nations, was the establishment of effective rule over them: 'national' identities were more properly 'regnal' identities, deriving their solidarity from common government.[47] This persuasive

---

[47] S. Reynolds, 'Medieval *Origines Gentium* and the Community of the Realm', *History*, 68 (1983), 375–90.

view does not, however, mean that the idea of the nation was inseparable from the idea of the political community, even if the two phenomena might frequently overlap in reality. Some nations and peoples lacked political co-ordination, but retained a strong sense of their own ethnicity – the Welsh, thanks to Rees Davies, are one well-studied example, the Jews another.[48] In the reproduction of Welsh identity, territory, law, genealogy, language and myth were centrally important, while, for Jews, these factors and others, including religious ritual, rules governing intermarriage and the privileges and restrictions imposed by Christian society, helped to create definition. Equally, it remained possible for a single ruler to govern many peoples or nations – though where this had been perceived as a source of strength before 1200, when the kingdom of Hungary, for example, was praised for its mixture of different races, it was coming to be a matter of perplexity and conflict by the fifteenth century.

In fact, the relative coalescence of political, ethnic and juridical identities was one of the most significant developments in later medieval political culture, and it therefore seems important not to predate this process. However much a sense of nationhood may have been stimulated by the perception (more occasionally the reality) of common law and common government, political association and ethnicity were still distinguishable at the beginning of our period. To take one example, the 'aliens' who fell foul of the 'community' in the conflicts of Henry III's England were a political, not an ethnic grouping: they were not alien because they were from Poitou, but because they disregarded the laws and customs of the kingdom (indeed, the Clare earl of Gloucester was among them, though, like many aristocratic 'Englishmen', he was made up of English, French, Norman, Welsh and Irish blood). Meanwhile, Simon de Montfort, earl of Leicester, leader of the 'community' and hero of *The Song of Lewes*, was recognised to be French by birth and language, but his political identity is clearly one of fidelity to the laws, customs and people of the realm of England. Here, then, there is already a sense that ethnic and political identities ought to coincide, but also a recognition that they do not. The view of Ptolemy of Lucca that Romans and other Italians should be ruled by political and not despotic means, because astrological and climatic influences make

---

[48] E.g. R. Davies, 'The Peoples of Britain and Ireland, 1100–1400, Identities', *Transactions of the Royal Historical Society*, 6th series, 4 (1994), 1–20.

them too fierce and vocal, tends in a rather similar direction. Whatever the nation owed to past and present governance, and whatever it was coming to demand, in terms of the fitting of political arrangements to national attributes, it was an idea composed from different associations and mainly developed, at this time, in different texts – romances, histories, poems, rather than academic treatises and laws or other products of government. Nor did it possess the primacy over other identities – political, regional or social – that it was later to acquire: people very conscious of their nationality might nonetheless line up with foreign lords, international organisations, local solidarities and so on.

Just as prominent as the idea of the nation or *gens* was the view that society was divided into types of people – *status* (estates), *gradus* (ranks) or *ordines* (orders). Some social typologies were essentially functionalist. This was true, for example, of one of the oldest and most fundamental, the doctrine of the 'three orders' or 'three estates', which was formed in the early eleventh century and divided society into those who pray, those who fight and those who work. The emphasis of this kind of model was on the reciprocity of different kinds of people: in return for the ploughman's work, the priest would defend him spiritually, while the knight defended him physically. At the same time, the fact that these three estates were commonly numbered – clergy first, knights second and labourers third – demonstrates that even models that proclaimed the mutual interest of society could also involve hierarchy. Other typologies might be more emphatically vertical, placing kings above princes or dukes, earls and counts above barons, bailiffs above sergeants, cardinals above primates and archbishops above bishops and so on. The tendency in the fourteenth and fifteenth centuries was for social typologies to become both more complex and more elaborately stratified, the sumptuary legislation that became common in the midfourteenth century, for example, typically listing upwards of a dozen different classes of people, and prescribing dress and foodstuffs fitting for each (except in Venice and much of northern Italy, interestingly, where the emphasis was on inducing everyone to dress alike). The vices and virtues of different estates were a prominent theme of fraternal preaching, and this in turn formed the basis for sophisticated experiments in estates satire and communal representation in the fourteenth-century vernacular works of writers such as Dante, Boccaccio, Chaucer and Philippe de Mézières.

We have seen that estates thinking promoted ideal-types. The apostolic priest is one we have already discussed. The peasant labourer, whether noble and self-sacrificing, like Langland's Piers Plowman, or lazy, debauched, gossipy and uppity, as s/he was in most social satire, was to come to prominence in the fourteenth and fifteenth centuries. But perhaps the first, most politically significant and fully articulated ideal-type was the knight, who was celebrated in the literature and rituals of chivalry. Born of a fusion of military, social and political developments in the second half of the eleventh century, chivalry is perhaps best understood as the cult of aristocratic knighthood. Its ideas and values centred on the celebration of knightly combat, and its associated practices and paraphernalia: the mounted charge of heavy cavalry, armed with lances, and the dismounted mêlée with sword, shield and mace; the virtues of prowess, honour, right, fidelity and service; the carrying of arms, banners and livery; the activities of the court – feasting, tourneying, hunting; and the accoutrements of gracious living, from castles and parks, to plate, books, furs and jewels. Generally said to have originated in France, it had spread across Europe long before 1300, and – besides the Christian religion, with which it was extensively interwoven – it was probably the most powerful cultural force shaping the lives of aristocratic landowners. During the later twelfth and thirteenth centuries, it is often said, chivalry and the status of knighthood became more courtly, more ritualised and more socially elevated. This may be so, and chivalry certainly contributed much to the emerging court style and to the idealisation of the princely court and household which was such a feature of the period, but it should not be thought that the chivalry of this period had nothing to do with warfare. On the contrary, the main vindications of chivalrous status continued to lie in military activity: according to Sir Geoffrey de Charny's fourteenth-century taxonomy, for instance, the winner of the tournament was praiseworthy, but the knight who served in his lord's war was better, while the knight who fought for Christ – that is, in a crusade – was best of all. By the time Charny wrote, not every chivalrous writer placed the same value on crusading, but all of them would have agreed with his emphasis on military activity, and, as a consequence, several historians have seen in chivalry an underlying cause for the copious feuding and warfare of the later middle ages. It is true, of course, that the chivalrous lifestyle involved an ambivalent attitude to violence – honour required vindication by action; *chansons de geste*, romances, chronicles, tournaments all celebrated fighting – but it should be clear from the rest of this chapter that there were many stimuli to conflict in the Europe of the high and late middle ages, and it is clear that feuding was a well-established method of dispute settlement in all the less tightly governed parts of the continent. We also need to remember that chivalry was not new in 1300, even if it grew and developed in various ways during our period; it cannot be an explanation of the supposedly increased scale of warfare in the fourteenth and fifteenth centuries.

How did chivalry fit with the other politically influential ideas discussed above? It was certainly affected by the legal and bureaucratic developments characteristic of the twelfth and thirteenth centuries, as knights internalised the developing laws of war, adopted written contracts of service and negotiated their way around hardening customs for feuding, duelling and 'private war'. At the beginning of our period, and throughout the fourteenth century and beyond, it bore an international character, with knights travelling far and wide in pursuit of honour, and willingly attaching themselves to foreign lords – even enemies of their own juridical sovereigns – if these men provided better opportunities for rewarding service. But if chivalry reflects the relative freedom and independence of the great landowners, it also registers the influence of political developments. The fourteenth century was to be the great age of the royal (or princely) chivalric order, and rulers who were seeking to control the other powers of their territories by judicial, fiscal and bureaucratic means also sought to engage them via military cults focused on themselves. There were many reasons why these 'regnal' orders developed and why a 'nationalised' form of chivalry often flourished, but one ideological factor deserves particular attention here: the widely recycled treatise of the fourth- or fifth-century pundit Vegetius, *De Re Militari* (Concerning Military Affairs). This coolly rational text, surviving in 260 Latin manuscripts from the middle ages (most of them from after 1200) and translated into Anglo-Norman, French and Tuscan as early as the 1270s and 1280s, was probably the most influential military manual of the period, and its emphasis was, in many ways, rather unchivalrous. While Vegetius wanted his soldiers to be brave and hardy, he also wanted them trained, organised and deployed as a disciplined army in defence of the *res publica*. In certain respects, the Vegetian tradition was antichivalric – it deplored individual heroics except as part of the common effort, and it even advised the ruler to avoid the battlefield itself, thus cutting very much against the tradition of royal knight-hood. It would be wrong to see the popularity of Vegetius as the main reason for the standing armies that began to develop in the thirteenth and fourteenth centuries, but it seems likely that it helped princes and lords to conceptualise the military world in this way, and that this was one more route by which Roman conceptions of the polity were conveyed to medieval readers.

A final element in social thinking in the decades around 1300 was a heightened concern with subgroups and sects. Established minorities, such as Jews or lepers, came to be treated with greater suspicion by Christian authorities and differentiated more sharply from mainstream society. In 1215, for instance, the Fourth Lateran Council prescribed the wearing of signs by Jews; around mid-century, they became vulnerable to missionary programmes on the part of the friars; by the later thirteenth century, they were more likely to live in ghettos; while around 1290, the first large-scale expulsions took place and the first versions of the blood-libel – the belief that Jews killed and sacrificed Christian children – began to circulate. Lepers too were obliged to dress differently, and were increasingly segregated from mainstream society. In south-western France in 1321–2, it came to be believed that the Jews and the lepers had leagued together to poison the wells: forged letters revealed that the Jews were acting in the service of the king of Granada and other Muslim leaders, and had used their wealth to purchase the services of the unfortunate lepers; a series of bloody pogroms ensued, culminating in a second expulsion of the Jews of France (1323) and an order to imprison the remaining lepers. Partly because of a growing ecclesiastical conviction that the works of the devil were timeless and universal, these far-fetched beliefs were readily transferred to other groups, both real and imagined. As Norman Cohn has demonstrated, the Knights Templar were accused in 1312 of essentially the same repertoire of devilish rites and sexual depravities that had been ascribed to the Cathars of the twelfth century, and the heretics detected in the Rhineland in the 1230s.[49] Similar allegations were made against the Jews throughout our period, and many of them were levelled posthumously at Boniface VIII by his detractors, or were hinted at in denunciations of King Edward II of England (1307–27) and his closest counsellors. While the circulation of these notions owed much to the preaching of the friars,

[49] N. Cohn, *Europe's Inner Demons* (London, 1975), chs. 3–5.

discussed below, it is clear that governmental growth, and the legal-istic mania for definition, so characteristic of the thirteenth century, were also factors. The institutionalisation of the papal inquisition around mid-century meant the detection of more religious deviance and this stoked fears of heresy and witchcraft: it is very revealing that the rather miscellaneous pious and mystical movements of the early fourteenth-century Rhineland were perceived by the authorities as an organised 'Heresy of the Free Spirit', for example. Meanwhile, a rising concern with conspiracy, seen, for example, in the statutes of the Cistercian Order in 1237 and 1257, and in English royal legislation in 1293 and 1305, contributed to an atmosphere in which any small group could be imagined as criminal, sexually licentious or downright demonic. So it was that, in the decades to come, the clerks and courtiers of kings and lords were easily cast as 'evil councillors', linked in 'covens' and using witchcraft and guile to deceive both innocent rulers and the general public; religious women, such as the 'beguines' of the Rhineland, were imagined to be witches, heretics or prosti-tutes; aristocratic retinues were caught up in scares about criminal gangs. These neatly transferable stereotypes were more extensively used at some periods than others, of course – and there are reasons why the 1290s, 1310s and 1320s were so full of this kind of conflict – but they were endemic in both the psyche and the language of Europeans by the end of the thirteenth century, and helped to shape the expression of political tensions in the two centuries to come.

Even from this rather brief *tour d'horizon* of political thinking as it was in the decades around 1300, it should be clear that, despite a great deal of sharing of terms, concepts, sources and modes of argumenta-tion, the inhabitants of Europe possessed an intellectual inheritance which was incoherent and flexible in its political implications. Prevailing ideas of authority and community could be used to legit-imise – or equally to denounce – lots of different forms of power. If a political body like the kingdom enjoyed a certain amount of ideo-logical weight, so too did cities, churches and empires, and many of the ideas that supported kings could be applied equally to lords, prelates and citizen-statesmen. On the other hand, all of these forms – and their rulers – were open to challenge. Were they functioning correctly – as history, or right reason, or custom, or written law ordained? What were the proper boundaries of their authority? Who commanded the first allegiance of the people under the sway of each ruler? Various answers to these questions could be derived from authoritative works, and that was a situation full of significance, given the parallel variety of political forms to which contemporaries could lend their attachment.

Communication

We have seen that a common range of politically significant ideas was spread far and wide across the continent of Europe. One major reason for this was the prestige attached to the key texts of Scripture, Roman and canon law, patristics and the classics, and the acceptance of common methods for exploring and reworking them. But it was also the result of particular structures of education, diffusion and communication which helped to determine how ideological and textual materials were moved about, which audiences they reached and in what forms. In this section, we shall be concerned with these structures as they were in the decades around 1300, and with the effects they had on the political culture of the continent.

There were around fifteen universities in 1300, scattered across France, Italy, England and Spain, and headed by the great centres of theology at Paris and Oxford, and the law schools at Bologna and Orleans. This relatively small scholarly network was itself an important medium for the creation, stabilisation and circulation of authoritative knowledge. The ethos of the universities was, to a large extent, utilitarian: they were intended to provide the administrators of Europe with training in such basic skills as rhetoric, grammar, logic and dialectic, as well as higher training in the arcana of law, medicine and theology. The flow of scholars between the universities and the great lay and ecclesiastical households was thus one of the most basic reasons for the spread of common texts, forms and ideas across the continent. An early thirteenth-century Danish archbishop, for instance, Anders Sunesen, had taught at Oxford; in office at Lund (1202–23), he wrote a Latin paraphrase of the laws of the province, combining formal learning with customary law in a manner that was to be characteristic across the continent in the ensuing decades. At the other end of the century, when King Wenceslas II of Bohemia wanted to introduce a Roman law-code in his domains, in 1294, it was natural for him to hire an Italian jurisconsult to come and write it; Alfonso X also drew on Bologna-trained expertise to produce his *Siete Partidas* in the 1250s and 1260s. Meanwhile, a high proportion of Castilian prelates in the eleventh and twelfth centuries had come from

France, and this, in turn, had affirmed canonical norms in the Castilian Church and helped to shape the language of episcopal and royal chanceries, as the entourages of these men found local employment as clerks. As this suggests, the international Church – its network of schools, its mobile legates and proctors, the growing practice of translating benefice-holders from one place to another, and (for particular reasons, as we shall see) the growth of the friars – was a parallel means through which authoritative knowledge and established styles of thought and writing were conveyed around thirteenth-century Europe.

This knowledge, let us remember, was intended to be useful, and it was widely used. We have already explored some of the ways in which the norms of Roman and canon law were put into practice by governments, both secular and clerical, in the form of legislation and judicial and constitutional procedures. These same norms were also spread by notaries and other legal advisers, wherever the learned law had a reasonably direct bearing on legal practice. The notaries of Spain, for instance, were typically educated first in French cathedral schools and then at Bologna: not only does this emphasise the internationally exchangeable quality of contemporary learning, it provides an insight into both how the principles of learned law were made familiar to litigants and how they came to be accepted as *ius commune* – the common bedrock of European law. Indeed, it is now recognised how much the learned law was shaped by the influence of practice. The employment of Roman lawyers in the production of *consilia* (legal advice in specific cases) for Italian clients is thought to have played a significant role in changing the formal techniques of legal study, turning legal academics away from the dialectical analysis of Justinianic legal principle and towards the exploration of contemporary legal problems. This famous shift from the glossatorial tradition to that of the 'commentators' also owed something to the influence of Aristotelian techniques and concepts, which entered legal study at Orleans and were taken to Italy by Cinus of Pistoia (*c.*1270–1336), but it is worth pointing out that both older and newer traditions were equally concerned with the utility of the law: the glosses that circulated in thirteenth- and fourteenth-century Europe were not academic exercises, but attempts to circulate correct and usable opinion.

Nor was it just legal knowledge that was handled in this consumer-conscious way. It is becoming clear that, by the later thirteenth century, the arts faculties of the universities were alert to the question of how to communicate their learning to those outside the lecture halls. While dialectic and learned Latin were regarded as ideal media for the transaction of hard topics among the educated, it was recognised that rhetoric (learned at this stage mainly from Aristotle and bits of Cicero) and the use of the vernacular would be necessary for their transmission outside the academy. The turn towards pastoral questions which Jeremy Catto has identified in the theologians of the fourteenth century was clearly anticipated by a concern with extramural communication among the academics of the thirteenth century.[50] Teaching materials, from the great *summae* of figures like Thomas Aquinas, to the less sophisticated glosses, *florilegia* and *compendia* that covered major extracts or themes, served as models for the handbooks designed for wider use within thirteenth-century society. Collections of model sermons and manuals for confessors seem to have been among the first to emerge – indeed, the preface to a bound version of the Aristotelian *Parvi flores*, written about 1300, notes the particular utility of this arts curriculum staple for those wishing to construct thematic introductions to their 'sermons to the people' – but works of more general moral and political edification, like Giles of Rome's *De Regimine Principum*, soon followed, and rapidly merged with a stream of less academic instructional handbooks written for the laity on such topics as knighthood, nurture, practical medicine, grammar, astrology and estate management.[51]

Perhaps the single most important intermediaries between the thirteenth-century academy and the wider public, however, were the orders of preaching friars – the Dominicans and the Franciscans. These organisations quickly established a presence in the university towns, and they rapidly embraced new learning – so that the Dominicans, for example, made a basic education in Aristotle's teachings an established part of their training from 1314. The centralised structures of the two orders encouraged the standardisation of knowledge and procedure among their members, and the friars' particular concern with preaching and confession meant that both a 'pastoral edifice' of comprehensible Christian lore and 'a vulgate moral philosophy' were communicated directly to clergy and laity

---

[50] J. Catto, 'Currents of Religious Thought and Expression', *NCMH* VI, ch. 3.
[51] C.F. Briggs, 'Teaching Philosophy at School and Court: Vulgarisation and Translation', in F. Somerset and N. Watson, eds., *The Vulgar Tongue. Medieval and Postmedieval Vernacularity* (Philadelphia, 2003), 99–111, pp. 103–4.

alike.[52] Because so much of this kind of preaching was concerned with relating fundamental principles of ethics and religion to day-to-day situations, it helped not only to circulate a particular set of authoritative values, but to establish them as the natural framework for reading the complex world around. Preaching was also, of course, an important medium through which high-status knowledge, stored in Latin, was translated into the vernacular and shared with the many who could not read. This incidentally meant a particular interest in the processes and problems of translation among the friars, an interest which they shared with the inhabitants of royal chanceries and with a handful of poets, notably Dante, who were also beginning to explore the vernacular presentation of material derived from Latin. This same interest helped to determine the character of these emerging languages as public and authoritative, and to shape the contexts in which they might be used. If fourteenth-century English or Czech, for example, were readily characterised as languages of truth, if the capacity for moral criticism of the social and political order was particularly well developed in them, that may owe something to their deployment by the friars.

The emergence of literary and public vernaculars, which we have just touched upon, is one of the most important cultural developments of the later medieval period and deserves further discussion. These qualifying terms, 'literary' and 'public', are important: vernacular speech, of course, had always existed, and vernacular writing, employing a Latin alphabet, was a creation of the early middle ages. What was new (or revived) in our period was the stabilisation of the written vernacular and its regular use for what might be considered high, or public, purposes – the communication of religious truth and other kinds of authoritative knowledge, the circulation of instructions from rulers and officers, the production of modern equivalents of Latin and Greek literature (whether translations or not). Once again there are qualifications to be made to this statement. One vernacular – the French of the Île-de-France – was already an internationally established language, used across western Europe for a range of literary, devotional and even civic purposes (Brunetto Latini's Florentine encyclopaedia of civic life, *Li Livres dou Trésor*, was written in French, for instance, in the 1260s, though it was soon translated into

[52] Quotations from M. Rubin, *Corpus Christi. The Eucharist in Late Medieval Culture* (Cambridge, 1991), p. 34, and Briggs, 'Teaching Philosophy', p. 103.

Tuscan). Meanwhile, several areas more remote from the Carolingian core of Europe had shown resistance to the spread of Latin, and retained the use of the vernacular for some formal purposes, such as royal letters and writs and the recording of customary laws: this was especially the case in Romance-speaking areas, such as Spain, but it is also true of Scotland and Scandinavia. Nonetheless, the increasing range and volume of vernacular writing by educated churchmen and government clerks, the corresponding standardisation and expansion of the major languages, and the acceptance of these partly artificial creations as common to each nation were developments of enormous significance, and they got underway in the later thirteenth century.

What caused the development of vernaculars? One obvious factor was the growth of literacy. Even if the great expansion of writing in the twelfth and thirteenth centuries was mainly in Latin, and most functional literacy was therefore Latinate, familiarity with reading and writing seems to have been transferable to a vernacular context, and certain kinds of writer, such as merchants, seem to have operated in their native languages from the start. Another factor must have been the increasing need to communicate with a wider cross-section of the laity, as both governments and pastoral activities intruded more systematically on people's lives. Up to about 1300, it was mainly literary, historical and pious works that were produced in, or translated into, the leading vernaculars, but in places as various as France, Spain, Norway and Germany, this extended to works of moral, political and even legal resonance, such as Joinville's *Life of Saint Louis* (*c.*1270); the *Grandes Chroniques* of St-Denis (first translated in 1274); the vast legal and political treatise of the *Siete Partidas* (1265) produced at the behest of Alfonso X of Castile and his circle; the Norwegian *King's Mirror* (1250s) or the *Sachsenspiegel* of Eike von Repgow (1220s). Translations and vernacular digests of Giles of Rome's *De Regimine Principum*, so useful as a guide to Aristotle and Vegetius, were made into French and Italian as early as the 1280s, while Vegetius himself, as we have seen, was translated into a number of languages by the 1270s. Political manifestoes in the vernacular also seem to go back to around the end of the thirteenth century: the *Monstraunces* of 1297 which confronted Edward I of England are one example; the 'Ordinances' and *Privilegio* of 1283, presented to James II by the Aragonese, are another. These are a reminder that, of course, the languages of power could be used by subjects and critics as well as authorities.

By 1300, then, there were a number of routes through which a common (if sprawling) body of legal, political and theological understanding was spread around Europe. Part of that understanding was coming to be formatted for the edification of a wider public, potentially including all those who could read, or even hear, the works of such mediators as poets, preachers and the writers of handbooks. At this stage, vernacularisation does not seem to have meant the creation of nationally specific discourses, though it may have helped to affirm the sense of differentiated ethnic and/or political communities: much of the content of vernacular writing seems to have been shared between different places. These features combine to help explain the openness of the European political environment. First of all, it was relatively easy to cross borders and boundaries when there was so much cultural sharing between different jurisdictions. Second, a world in which subaltern groups had access to the same set of ideas and principles as their rulers, and where traditions of public speech and public writing were coming to be well established, was a world where authorities could expect to face articulate resistance, and in which they would need to be prepared to negotiate their power. In the fourteenth century, the growth in literacy and the expansion of written material continued to increase; vernaculars became more widely and deeply established and recognition of the implications of spreading communication dawned on political and religious elites. The rich vocality of later medieval public life was to be a major source of anxiety for contemporary commentators, but it was a fruitful means of political association for those who could get their message across. It is important to recognise that, like so much else, it was a straightforward development from the achievements of the twelfth and thirteenth centuries: it was the lawyers, friars and government clerks of the high middle ages that gave the rebels and heretics of the later middle ages their voices.

Networks

One last feature of the contemporary political environment, which straddles the uneasy division between the political and the social, is the existence of non-governmental relationships and formats of power: lordship and service, patronage and clientage, families, dynasties and clans. We have touched upon these in several places above, but it will be helpful to look at them together here, because they had much in common, and were a cultural and intellectual influence on political behaviour as well as a practical one. Associations of a broadly informal kind enjoyed recognition in contemporary culture and discourse, and so did some of their key means and features, such as the household, or court; the taking of homage or vows, or the giving of livery; the holding of feasts and other ceremonial occasions that brought the network together. To some historians, these associations have seemed a lot more influential than those created by formal institutions of government. Others have placed them at the centre of the supposedly increased corruption and disorder of the later middle ages; but, as we have seen, this nineteenth-century approach, now widely rejected, misunderstands and over-rates the status of centralised bureaucratic authority in pre-modern political life. Now that the antiquity, legitimacy and constitutional importance of social networks is widely acknowledged among later medievalists, it seems less necessary to rate either their power or their rightfulness against those of other forms of political organisation. In fact, it has become clear that networks and governmental institutions typically influenced and fed off, even depended on, each other. The informality and flexibility of interpersonal ties meant that networks waxed and waned as their participants continually changed, but we have seen that the same fluctuating qualities are apparent in more formal political organisations: however firm and consistent the structures, their capacity to move people and to create solidarities varied over time and space. The essential point to grasp is not that institutions were underpinned by more realistic frameworks of private association, but that people had a mixture of claims on their allegiances, and that these claims, which frequently overlapped, could mesh together or produce tension depending on the circumstances.

Informal associations typically had two basic components: first, a household, court or hall, which acted as a kind of home and place of assembly; and second, a *familia* – a group of people tied together in mutual loyalty, on the model of a family. The former was as much an idea and a way of being as an actual place: kings and lords certainly had favoured castles, manors and lodges in which they entertained their friends and followers; guilds had their halls; family clans and *consorterie* or *consorzi* their inns (*alberghi*) and towers; but some networks, such as the followings of Irish lords, were highly mobile – they might return to sacred centres for important business, but the household could often be a travelling camp, defined by its activities of feasting, raiding, counsel and communal living, rather than by any fixed locale. The key political functions of the household – or court, to use a term which captures its more public or ceremonious form – were twofold. First, it established and celebrated the identity of the network. In monarchical networks, it captured the grandeur of the lord or ruler, flanked as he was in it both by his immediate servants – domestics and councillors – and by his more occasional satellites – vassals, officers, fee'd men, neighbours – who came to see him at great feasts or on request. In peer groups, such as guilds or parties, it was the seat of fellowship, the scene of feasts and councils which brought the collectivity together. Second, courts provided a means of communication and exchange between the great and the less great, and among the members or followers themselves: they were thus major social centres and an important means of generating political solidarities. These functions and activities were, in one sense, timeless, but their modalities changed with changing political and cultural conditions. The rise of governmental institutions in the twelfth and thirteenth centuries meant that the informal ways of the court were no longer the only means of power, and in administratively complex polities there were moves to differentiate domestic budgets and activities from public or regnal ones. This tendency, which typically emerged from the later thirteenth century onwards and was full of tension, is discussed in the next chapter, but it is worth noting here that its effect was not to reduce the importance of the household or court. The place where the ruler physically was, or where the key groups physically met, remained central to every political organisation, and whatever the advance of bureaucracy, there was a persisting interest in preserving some flexibility and informality within these places.

The other typical element of these associations – the *familia* – also varied in form, but its central purposes of mutual assistance and defence were similar across different types. Some networks were more communal than others, but all of them possessed some kind of authority structure and, even in royal and seigneurial affinities or extended families, the will of the lord or patriarch had to be exercised with sensitivity to the interests, both general and particular, of the members. Most networks had some formal element to seal them, especially as political society became more literate and legalistic – indentures of retinue,[53] *lettres d'alliance*, liveries of cloth, grants of

---

[53] An indenture was a contract, so called because the two copies were separated by a serrated edge.

office or fees, oaths of loyalty to lords or guild ordinances, marriages and ceremonies of *affrairamentum* (the making of brotherhood). Some were highly mobile, and/or more concerned with co-ordinating manpower than with controlling territory; others were focused on a particular district – a county, a city, a province, even a principality or kingdom – and provided a flexible means of asserting control over its jurisdiction and resources. Many networks involved the sharing, or transfer, of property, but it would be a mistake to draw too sharp a distinction between relations of tenure and common ownership, on the one hand, and those of more general political and social co-operation on the other: while the former kind of relationship could be purely formal, even exploitative, it was unlikely to work well for either party without the maintenance of other kinds of interaction.

It may seem slightly contrived to treat all these different kinds of networks under a single heading, but the parallels between them are clear. The pioneering work of Jacques Heers has pointed up the links between urban family associations and the clan structures characteristic of Ireland, Scotland and the Borders, Brittany, Naples, northern Spain and Poland.[54] In these areas, groups who shared a name, arms or colours, often a device, and acknowledged a blood relationship and common ancestors, operated as political alliances, sharing territory or movable property such as cattle, and feuding or allying with other similar organisations. These structures are often juxtaposed with those of lordship, and conceptually they are indeed different, but in practice there may have been little to choose between them. The blood ties affected by clans and families were often highly artificial: Scottish clans certainly accepted newcomers, for example, and blood-links were quickly developed by intermarriage or even by ceremony; the van den Colveren and the van den Blankarden clans who shared out power in Louvain included many members who were not technically related to either family; Castilian traditions of *deudo* created family networks by oath. Meanwhile, clan structures often concealed a pattern of vertical authority which was very similar to that of the lord and his retinue: the lineages of the fifteenth-century Basque Country, for example, were headed by *parentes mayores*, who inhabited castles, founded religious houses and policed the integrity of the extended family; they were served in turn by the *parentes*

---

[54] J. Heers, *Family Clans in the Middle Ages*, trans. B. Herbert (Amsterdam, 1977).

minores, who ranged from soldiers to peasants, and shared little with their relatives but ties of dependency and the family arms and motto.

As this example suggests, the clan remained a common social structure throughout our period – indeed, there is some evidence to suggest that it was on the increase: in the Highlands and Borders of Scotland, for example, or indeed in the rather different situation of the republican city of Florence, where the hegemony of the Medici clan was more or less formalised by the 1460s. As the institutional complexity of political society increased, clans and networks were interwoven with more official structures. The Medici, for instance, drew on the support of the *Parte Guelfa*, and on their capacity to manage the Priorate through their various placemen; the Medici bank, and its extensive financial and diplomatic networks also played a crucial role in establishing the family's dominant position. In Castile, meanwhile, the 'lineage-*bando*' came to be a common political structure, merging partly artificial family ties with contemporary media of military or political association, such as vassalage, service and clientage. The interaction of networks and institutions brought the former into the records, making them seem like new phenomena, rather than newly adapted ones. It also began to stimulate public concern about affinities, cliques, covens and the like, a concern which is first perceptible around 1300, as we have seen, but which tended to grow throughout the fourteenth century and beyond, even as other discourses accepted and promoted the values of lordship and fellowship on which these networks drew. These developments are discussed more fully in the next chapter, but, once again, it is worth noting that informal ties remained just as central to political life as they had ever been. Some of the tension of fourteenth-century political life derives from the fact that, while these ties and networks were increasingly at odds with the values of government, they remained pragmatically necessary and retained cultural and social support.

3

THE FOURTEENTH CENTURY

•

Whatever its eschatological significance, 1300 did not bring major changes to the politics of Europe; nor, for that matter, did 1400, so it will be clear at once that there is something arbitrary and artificial about the organisation of this chapter and the next one. The political forms and themes of the fourteenth century typically began in the thirteenth century or earlier, and ended, or lost their clarity or their importance, in the fifteenth century or later. A positive argument for dividing things this way would be that a division at 1300 cannot have any causal implications, unlike most of the other divisions of time typically adopted by historians of this period. If the story of 'the fourteenth century' begins with the famine of the 1310s, for instance, then the economy of north-western Europe is placed centre stage in the explanation of events; if it begins with the attack on Boniface VIII at Anagni, in 1303, then the decline of the universal Church is established as the key process, together with the rise of the nation state, characterised, as it usually is, by Capetian France. In either version, the political history of the previous period comes to a natural stop, and the politics of the new period enjoy a natural start, but everything we have seen so far points, not surprisingly, to an absence of natural breaks in the course of politics: the politics of the early fourteenth century emerge seamlessly from those of the late thirteenth century. That is not, of course, the same thing as saying that things did not change. One of the major themes of this book is that the wider deployment and combination of forms and structures that generally began life in the twelfth and thirteenth centuries was a central factor in shaping the politics of the later middle ages. What historians call 'continuity' is thus usually a process of gradual adaptation, development, familiarisation. In this sense, it is apparent across 1300, 1400 and 1500, but that does not prevent us from recognising the ways in which the culture, forms and dynamics of politics changed over the period.

For convenience, then, the discussion and characterisation of politics have been arranged in two century-long chapters, each of them aimed at drawing out what seems distinctive or typical about the patterns and events of these two periods. We begin with a survey of the political events of the fourteenth century, presenting a broad narrative of what happened as a preface to the more analytical examination of the texture of politics. This narrative is necessarily selective – in fact, it is biased towards the internal and external affairs of the larger political formations – but even where it does capture the detail of events, it has a certain falsifying tendency, almost unavoidably implying that what happened was what was supposed to happen, when the course of events was really a complicated dialogue between structure and contingency. In most of the chapter, we will be concerned with what was common to the polities of Europe in the period, and that is, in many ways, more important than the particular succession of revolts and depositions, wars and minorities, dynastic fortunes and misfortunes that affected particular places. On the other hand, the politics of the continent were influenced in one direction or another by specific sequences of events that, however similar they were, only happened one way. There was nothing inevitable about the ascendancy of the kingdom of France up to the 1330s, or the establishment of the 'Avignon Papacy', or the hegemony of Milan over Lombardy in the 1390s, but they are historical facts, and they have meaning not only because they can be explained (to a point) in structural terms, but also because they shaped the options of countless political actors and thus helped to condition the course of politics.

THE COURSE OF EVENTS

c.1300–c.1340

The Papacy and Italy

The decades around 1300 were an ambivalent period for the Papacy, which, at this time, was still head of the most extensive power structure in Europe. On the one hand, this was an era of high

1 Europe in 1300

assertiveness, in which a number of popes sought to regain the direction of spiritual and political affairs that had been damaged by the long struggle for control of Italy and threatened by the rising complexity of the international Church state. On the other hand, the disaster of Anagni is conventionally supposed to have ushered in a period of compromise with lay powers, and especially with France.

Following a series of rather weak popes, many of them dominated by the house of Anjou, Boniface VIII (1294–1303), a distinguished canonist, was determined to restore papal authority in the tradition of Innocent III and Innocent IV. While he backed the Angevins in Hungary (1301) and helped to broker peace in Sicily (1302), this was more in defence of papal prerogatives than French interests; his brief deposition of the Emperor (1301) demonstrates the kinds of claims Boniface meant to uphold. He also tried to promote order among the clergy, vigorously pursuing the pro-Angevin Colonna cardinals who challenged his election, and attempting a resolution of the swelling conflict between the friars and the episcopate in his bull *Super Cathedram* (1300). Most famously, Boniface attempted to preserve the independence of the clerical estate, and the power of the Papacy over it, in two set-piece confrontations with the crown of France: the first, in 1296–7, concerned the right of the Pope to authorise the taxation of the Church; the second, in 1301, concerned the freedom of the clergy from lay jurisdiction. In both confrontations, Boniface was unsuccessful. His bull *Etsi de Statu* (1297) conceded the right to tax the Church to the kings of France and England, and opened the way to increased control of clerical resources on the part of lay powers. The second conflict, over the right of Philip IV to try the bishop of Pamiers for treason, rapidly escalated, as the king's apologists demanded a general council of the Church to judge a pope who seemed to think he had full authority in temporal matters, while the Pope moved towards the excommunication and deposition of the French king. In 1303, Boniface's enemies among the cardinals captured him at the papal palace of Anagni with the aid of French troops, and he died shortly afterwards, with a series of undesirable precedents hanging over him. Far from reasserting papal authority, he had endangered it, as learned opinion focused on the problem of how to manage an erring pope, while pressure mounted for a council – even a heresy trial – and Franciscan suspicions of the Curia deepened.

Boniface was to be followed in many respects by his later successor John XXII (1316–34). He too was prepared to assert authority over the Emperor, claiming the right to rule the Empire during a schism (*Si fratrum*, 1317) and deposing Ludwig of Bavaria in 1324. He too attempted to resolve the problem with the friars, declaring trenchantly in bulls of 1322 and 1323 that there was no difference between using property and owning it,[1] and condemning the notion of apostolic poverty into the bargain; as a result, he spent much of the rest of his pontificate fighting against accusations of heresy made by outraged 'Spirituals' among the Franciscans. Like Boniface, who had headed a delegation to demand obedience to papal instruction from the masters of the University of Paris in 1290, John was also concerned to restore control of doctrine, establishing a panel of theologians (indeed, a curial university) at Avignon, condemning dozens of dubious academic teachings, and publishing his own rather controversial views on the 'Beatific Vision' in 1331–2. From this perspective, John's canonisation of Thomas Aquinas was a telling move, emphasising the rightfulness of Dominican traditions of order and obedience, and establishing the celestial unities of Thomist thought as official dogma in a time of uncertainty. Yet John's policy also unfolded in another direction which was to be more characteristic of the fourteenth-century papacy. In his bull *Ex Debito* of 1316, he made what is usually regarded as the most important step in expanding papal provisions. This both increased the direct control exercised by the Papacy over the Church and created the basis for a new means of funding to replace the taxes which had fallen under lay control in the wake of the Bonifacian crisis – a system sometimes known as 'beneficial taxation', in which the Papacy made a series of VAT-like levies on the expanding range of appointments in which it played a part. In this way, the fourteenth-century western Church was more centralised than before, but in ways that pressed more directly on the clergy than on secular authorities.

This was the keynote of what has come to be known as the Avignon Papacy, so called because of the residence of the Papacy at that (initially) Angevin town between 1309 and 1376, and then again, during the Schism, between 1378 and 1403. The popes did not positively decide to settle permanently in Avignon at any stage, though the administrative developments of the 1310s meant a

---

[1] This decree, which was intended to press the Franciscans to moderate their attacks on clerical property, undermined a convenient fiction that had enabled members of the order to support themselves without technically owning anything.

substantial increase in the personnel of the Curia, and the building of a suitable palace, begun in 1336, set the seal on what had been a series of ad hoc developments. A southern French location made sense in the first place because Rome was too disorderly in the wake of the Bonifacian crisis and the open warfare that had developed between the Gaetani, Orsini and Colonna factions among the Roman nobility. Another factor was that the first substantial pope of the Avignon era, the Gascon Clement V (1305–14), spent much of his reign dealing with schemes emanating from the king of France: first, the suppression of the Templars (1307–12) and then the holding of a Church council, which took place at nearby Vienne in 1311–12. Finally, Avignon, next to papal land in the Comtat Venaissin, and situated near the mouth of the Rhône for relatively easy communication with France, Germany, England, Spain and northern Italy, was a convenient place from which to run the papal operation. Although great efforts were made to regain control of Rome and the Papal States, notably under John XXII and in the 1350s, and the project of returning to the relics and see of St Peter bulked larger and larger in papal consciousness later in the century, the residence at Avignon reflects the fact that the administration and exploitation of the international Church and the management of its jurisdiction had become the major functions of the Papacy and the central sources of its power.

Nonetheless, the papal role in Italian politics continued, even intensified, despite the physical absence of the Papacy. In the decades following the death of Frederick II, the struggle between the popes and the Hohenstaufen had broadened into a conflict of massive alliances which stretched across the whole of Italy. The Papacy and the house of Anjou headed the Guelf alliance, whose most consistent supporter, both military and financial, was Florence. Among the more determined Ghibellines, who were sympathetic to the Empire and, after 1282, to the Aragonese of Sicily, were the Visconti lords of Milan, the della Scala of Verona, the county of Savoy and the city of Pisa. These alliances comprised dynasties, military companies, networks and factions as well as whole cities – in Siena, for example, a Guelf *popolo* opposed the Ghibelline nobility – and part of the underlying dynamic of the conflict was the interaction of the papal/Angevin-imperial struggle with the increasing complication of urban politics, as communal regimes developed wider governmental functions and faced the twin challenges of 'popular' movements and signorial assertion. The 1270s had seen the high tide of Guelf success, with Charles of Anjou dominant in both the *Regno* and much of the north, but the Sicilian revolt of 1282, the rising tensions between the Papacy and the Angevins, the spread of *signori* across the Romagna and the conflicts which arose from Boniface VIII's reign left Rome itself, and much of the centre and the north, in disarray. One papal solution was to seek to broker an alliance between the post-Hohenstaufen emperors and the Angevins, but the arrival of Henry VII in Italy in 1310 prompted Florence to protect its liberty by raising the Guelf network against him, and this novel configuration of Pope, Emperor and king of Sicily rapidly broke up. John XXII opted for a more conventional approach of all-out war on the numerous opponents of papal authority, appointing Robert 'the Wise', the Angevin king of Naples[2] (1309–43), to a clutch of northern vicariates and sending cardinal legates with large armies to the Papal States. But fifteen years of fighting produced nothing more than temporary success, and by the beginning of the 1330s the Guelf alliance was seriously fraying, even Florence joining the Ghibellines for a time in 1332. By this time, city governments had somewhat stabilised and party allegiances had rather changed. Guelf identity was increasingly linked either to the ideology of the emerging popular communes, or to hostility to Visconti Milan, a power formally established by Henry VII in 1311, and beginning to exert extensive influence in Lombardy by the 1330s. If Ghibelline allegiance to the Emperor was refreshed by the presence in Italy of Ludwig of Bavaria between 1327 and 1330, it centred on the acquisition of vicarial powers and was most marked among northern *signori*. In the South, meanwhile, the Angevin/papal position remained bleak. War between the kings of Naples and the Aragonese regime in Sicily, halted for a time by the 1302 Treaty of Caltabellotta, resumed in 1314, and was conducted with great intensity and massive expense for three more decades from the 1330s. The *Regno* was correspondingly exhausted, and its leading magnates were allowed extensive local freedoms, both to maintain control of the territory and to enable the raising of forces. The signs are that Robert himself was able to manage his kingdom under these conditions, retaining noble support through a mixture of charismatic leadership, grace and the defence of his rights over the succession of fiefs. Even so, fiscal pressure and the rise of a more cellular political

---

[2] His title was actually king of Sicily, but it was only the mainland part of the old *Regno* that the Angevins ruled between the 1280s and the 1440s.

structure help to explain the civil war which broke out in the second half of the century.

France and Britain

Perhaps the most striking and sustained dynamic in thirteenth-century western Europe, lasting into the 1320s and beyond, was the expanding influence of the crown of France. From the turning-point reign of Philip II Augustus (1180–1223), the Capetian kings had begun to exert an effective feudal suzerainty, and latterly a more complete and Romanised form of jurisdiction, over most of the great fiefs and principalities of western *Francia*. The great dissenting power bloc of the Plantagenet domains – Normandy, Brittany, Anjou, Maine, Touraine and Poitou, all linked to the kingdom of England – was directly conquered between 1202 and 1224, while Aquitaine was reduced to feudal inferiority in 1259. The Albigensian crusades of the 1210s and 1220s brought in the county of Toulouse and much of the rest of the Languedoc; Provence joined the lands of the king's brother, Charles of Anjou in 1246; and the reigns of Philip III and IV saw a series of further acquisitions along the Scheldt, Meuse, Saône and Rhône, including Toul and Valenciennes, the county of Bar, the Franche-Comté (or county of Burgundy) and the city of Lyon. To be sure, a lot of these spoils had swiftly to be granted out to royal cadets and other magnates; others were held lightly or on terms of *parage* with indigenous rulers, bishops in particular; but the thirteenth-century crown proved tenacious in defending and extending its rights over the territories under its sway, and a mixture of legal advantage and dynastic good fortune protected royal control of the hugely expanded *domaine*. With the more-or-less loyal dukes of Burgundy and Brittany accepting the status of peers under the king, the royal house of Anjou high in papal favour, and that of Valois (descended from Philip IV's younger brother Charles) rising in the same direction, the French crown of the early 1290s was the dominant power in Latin Europe. Small wonder that a clutch of French academics and some of the more francophilic popes seem to have considered a further translation of the Empire from the German lands to France: French candidates were put forward for imperial elections on six occasions from 1273 to 1333, and several schemes were hatched to transfer the (rather notional) kingdom of Arles to the Angevins or the Valois; Rudolf of Habsburg (Emperor 1273–91) may even have lent support to these ventures.

But the Empire remained German and, in fact, by the 1290s, Capetian expansion was beginning to awaken resistance, both internal and external. Philip IV may have emerged victorious from his conflict with the Papacy, but two other conflicts begun in the 1290s were to have less harmonious outcomes. In 1294, Philip responded to a series of piracies and border disputes by confiscating and occupying the duchy of Gascony. In 1297, he invaded Flanders and proceeded to treat it as part of the royal *domaine*, redistributing fiefs and presiding directly over the Flemish towns. These conflicts were linked by the participation in each of the duke of Aquitaine and king of England, Edward I. The crown of England had also spent the thirteenth century engaged in Capetian-style expansion: the loser in France, it was very much the winner in the British Isles, and the king and his leading barons had exploited a bundle of historic, papal and feudal rights to secure control of Wales (by 1282) and much of Ireland. The acquisition of the county of Ponthieu, in northern France, in 1279, and the development of a reciprocal relationship between English wool producers and the Flemish textile industry, had revived English royal interests in Flanders and the Pas-de-Calais. The expiry of the Scottish royal line in 1286–90, meanwhile, presented Edward I with an opportunity to assert his contested overlordship of Scotland. In the mid-1290s, these conflicts became fused, as Edward I entered an alliance with the count of Flanders and also with Emperor Adolf of Nassau (1292–8) against France, while Philip IV joined the resisting king of Scotland, John Balliol (1292–6), in an alliance against England (Treaty of Corbeil, 1295). While the Anglo-French war of 1294–8 was rather a damp squib, with the principals coming rapidly to terms and the Emperor failing to appear, despite the anxiety of many of his western vassals at the encroachments of the French, several of its features set the tone for the coming decades. First of all, the kings of England and France remained bogged down in hot and cold wars in Scotland and Flanders respectively until well into the 1330s. The success of the new Scottish dynasty of Robert Bruce (Robert I, 1306–29) in gaining control of the Highlands in 1307–9 paved the way for a famous victory at Bannockburn in 1314 and English recognition in the Treaty of Edinburgh of 1328. While these gains were almost reversed in the 1330s and 1340s, the English could never secure control of more than the Scottish Lowlands, and that only briefly. Meanwhile, if the French crown secured the compliance of three successive counts of Flanders between 1297 and 1348, it was defeated

horribly at Courtrai in 1302, obliged to concede the effective independence of the county in the Treaty of Athis in 1305, and drawn into
further wars in 1314–16, 1319, 1325–8 and 1338–41, for which the
victory at Cassel in 1328 was scant compensation.

These big wars and their associated strains – taxation, military
obligation, raids and loss of life – created political problems which
affected English and French political life in the first few decades of the
new century. Edward I faced a series of demonstrations in 1297–1301,
and the unresolved questions raised by these, combined with the
incompetence shown by his heir, meant that Edward II's reign
(1307–27) was dominated by political division and downright civil
war. Philip IV, meanwhile, faced serious protests in 1303, and came to
rely on pillaging the Jews, the Lombard bankers and finally the
disgraced order of the Templars in order to finance his wars. Even
these expedients did not rescue him from the need to impose unpopular taxes, and his reign ended with a mass uprising of most of France,
in the so-called Leagues of 1314–15.[3] While this anger was appeased,
royal jurisdictional and fiscal assertions continued and tensions were
introduced into French political culture over the central question of
how much, and on what terms, the increasingly powerful king could
override the customs and rights of his various subjects. These tensions
re-emerged in tussles over taxation under Philip V (1316–22), but
they were to be significantly exploited and sharpened in the more
serious conflicts of the so-called Hundred Years War (1337–1453).

A third legacy of the brief Anglo-French war of 1294–8 was a
return to the relationship of mistrust that had characterised the relationship between the Plantagenets and the French crown prior to
1259. Despite the marriage arranged between Edward II and Isabel,
daughter of Philip IV, in 1308, a further conflict over Gascony broke
out in 1323–4, resulting in a grant of the Agenais to its conqueror,
Charles of Valois, and a rankling sore in relations with England when
he refused to return it. Together with the Franco-Scottish alliance,
this was an important factor in the movement of Edward III (1327–77)
towards all-out war with Philip VI (1328–50) in 1337, but one other
element, perhaps, was decisive. The Capetian bloodline had finally
faltered in the early fourteenth century, failing twice in the direct male
line: once in 1316, when the succession of Philip IV's second son was

---

[3] Almost every part of the kingdom was involved, apart from the Île-de-France and
Aquitaine.

preferred over that of his granddaughter Joan of Navarre, and her son
Charles; and a second time in 1328, when the succession of Philip's
nephew Philip of Valois was preferred over that of his daughter's son,
and closest male relative of the previous king, Edward III of England.
How seriously Edward took his claim to the crown of France we do
not know – he was certainly willing to do homage to Philip VI for
Aquitaine in 1329 and 1331 – but the important point is that it was
there for critics and opponents of the French king to exploit, and that
is exactly what they did. By 1338, when Edward went to war in
northern France, he did so in the name of the good old laws of St
Louis, a light-touch version of French kingship far away from the
governmental styles of the last few decades. He had also acquired
the backing of the dissident count of Artois, the towns of Flanders,
Emperor Ludwig of Bavaria, the count of Hainault and the dukes of
Guelders and Brabant. Reaction to French royal expansion appeared
to be in full spate.

France's other neighbours: the Empire and Spain

As we shall see, it was the smaller powers around and within the
French realm that did most to exploit the difficulties of the Valois
crown. England apart, no other kingdom moved against France:
the sabre-rattling of Emperor Ludwig was swiftly followed by
rapprochement with the French king, in 1340, while the crown
of Aragon, invaded by France as recently as 1285, and principal
victim of Capetian expansion in the Languedoc and along the
Mediterranean littoral, was, for the time being, more concerned to
pursue its claims in Spain and Sardinia, though its reconquest of
Majorca in the 1340s involved a reassertion of its claims in
Roussillon and Cerdagne.

The Empire, first of all, was engaged in a significant process of
restructuring. The so-called interregnum of 1257–73, in which the
imperial title devolved upon an opposing pair of absentee rulers, had
had three significant effects. The first was to entrench the rights and
traditions of the Electors as a small, defined group, with particular
responsibilities for the continuity and wellbeing of the Empire: after
the damaging schisms of 1246 and 1257, the personnel of the electoral
college was fixed roughly along the lines set out in the *Sachsenspiegel*,
and from the deposition of Adolf of Nassau (1298) onwards, the
Electors began to act on their own initiative as collective rulers of
the Empire (though that did not prevent further schisms, in 1314 and

1346).[4] A second effect was to confirm the disintegration of the Hohenstaufen royal estates, and thus to make future Emperors particularly dependent on their private estates, or *Erblände*. A third effect was to strengthen the idea of the Empire as a legal entity, distinct from the Emperor and his family, but capable of bestowing legitimacy on the holders of formal office and on those who could claim to be direct vassals. 'Princes', 'imperial knights', 'imperial' or 'free' cities and the like were thus increasingly inclined to insist on their right to be subject to no-one but the Emperor, and to him only as prescribed in the laws and customs of the Empire.

None of this prevented the re-establishment of effective imperial rule, once local potentates came again to be elected, as they were from 1273 onwards. Rudolf of Habsburg, a former ally of the Hohenstaufen, with estates tellingly concentrated in the old royal heartland of Swabia, summoned diets, took action in the spheres of law and justice, and even enjoyed some success with a programme of regaining the royal fisc. He and several of his successors were able to extract taxes from the imperial towns, and it is striking how many fourteenth-century Emperors were able to exploit imperial prerogatives to transform the territory of their families and allies, Rudolf himself securing the duchy of Austria for his sons in 1282, not only as victor over its conqueror, Otakar of Bohemia, but also as feudal overlord disposing of a defunct fief. In a like way, Henry VII (1308–13) acquired Bohemia for his son in 1310, while Ludwig of Bavaria and Charles IV (1346–78) obtained the valuable mark of Brandenburg for their cadets in 1323 and 1373, respectively.[5] It is true that tensions could develop between the interests of the kings and those of the Electors: the former interested in the fortunes of their family, and keen to secure the succession; the latter variously concerned with their own local rivalries, with regional questions such as the defence of the Rhineland against French encroachment (a common preoccupation of the four western Electors, though the three archbishops were not infrequently French stooges in this period) and with their

---

[4] The electors were the archbishops of Cologne, Trier and Mainz, the (Wittelsbach) Count Palatine of the Rhine, the king of Bohemia (Luxemburg, after 1310), the margrave of Brandenburg (Wittelsbach, 1323–73, Luxemburg 1373–1415, Hohenzollern thereafter) and the duke of Saxony (Ascanian to 1422, Wettin thereafter).

[5] Brandenburg was held by Charles' son Wenceslas until his accession to the throne in 1378, whereupon it passed to his younger brother Sigismund.

collective interest in preventing any one family from securing the throne in perpetuity and undermining the traditions of the Empire. Even so, there was plenty of scope for co-operation, whether over individual interests or the common good of the Empire. The new imperial dynasties of the period relied on holdings located at the periphery – the Habsburgs (1273–91, 1298–1308, 1437 onwards) on their gradually expanded duchy of Austria, the Luxemburgs (1308–13, 1346–1400, 1410–37) on Bohemia and their estates and networks on the middle Rhine, and the Wittelsbachs (1314–47, 1401–10) on Bavaria and the Palatinate, rarely united – but they were nonetheless able to build support among the Electors and in the heart of Germany, and their itineraries continued to focus on the old imperial centres of Swabia and Franconia.

Under these circumstances, it is not surprising that imperial politics continued to feature some traditional themes. Henry VII and Ludwig retained interests in Italy, and the latter put up a particularly robust defence in the resulting conflict with Pope John XXII. Having lent support to papal opponents in Ferrara and Milan in 1323, he was suddenly condemned for governing without papal approval, following a disputed election which the Papacy had ignored in 1314. In keeping with the tradition of Frederick II and now Philip IV, Ludwig appealed to the judgement of a general council of the Church, and was consequently excommunicated and suspended from the imperial throne in 1324. Ludwig had already cited the Pope's dispute with the Franciscans as evidence of papal heresy, and now offered protection to a group of Franciscan intellectuals led by Marsiglio of Padua and William of Ockham, who produced a series of authoritative works denying papal claims to authority in the temporal sphere. Having defeated his main imperial opponent Frederick of Habsburg at Mühldorf in 1322, Ludwig was strong enough to launch an invasion of Italy in 1327, securing coronation in Milan and Rome, declaring John XXII deposed for heresy and violence, and electing a new Pope, Nicholas V, in 1328. The impact of these dramatic events was short-lived in Italy: the war of Guelfs and Ghibellines continued, and Ludwig returned to Germany in 1330 with nothing resolved. Sustained papal hostility led to the cultivation of a Luxemburg candidate for the throne, but it also brought Ludwig extensive support in the Empire – from bishops at war with new papal appointees, from cities which associated their freedom with the rights of the Empire, and from the Electors who were now ready to replace the Papacy as final arbiters of the Empire's fortunes. In their first-ever assembly for something other than an election, the Electors met at Rhens in 1338 and issued a declaration that the Pope had no role in the appointment of the Emperor: election alone conferred on him the right to rule the kingdom and the Empire (which by now were indistinguishable, except in name). Ludwig's brief flirtation with Edward III, to whom he was allied between 1338 and 1340, encouraged French support for the papal-Luxemburg bloc, and, as the Emperor alienated electoral opinion with unduly aggressive moves to secure Holland, Hainault and the Tyrol for his children, Charles of Luxemburg, regent of Bohemia since the 1330s, was elected emperor by all but the Wittelsbach Electors in 1346. Following Ludwig's sudden death in 1347, Charles IV's succession was more or less undisputed, and imperial allegiances and interests were gradually realigned. Henceforth, Emperors were less active in Italy (Charles sought coronation there in 1355, and helped to reinstall the Pope in Rome in 1367, but he took no other action in the peninsula, and it is significant that he sold his rights in Tuscany to Florence and Siena in 1368–9). Popes, in turn, acquiesced in the independence of the Empire in its German heartlands.

The first half of the fourteenth century also witnessed a withdrawal from Italian affairs on the part of the crown of Aragon. As part of a deal with the Papacy, in which James II (1291–1327) was compensated with the novel kingdom of Sardinia and Corsica in 1297, royal claims in Sicily were officially abandoned, though the Aragonese cadet line which actually ruled the island remained at war with the Angevins until 1302. The next few decades were characterised by attempts to make good Aragonese claims in Murcia (1304), Sardinia (1323–4) and the vassal kingdom of Majorca (1343–4). The Privilege of Union, of 1319, preserved the constitutional distinctness of Valencia, Aragon and Catalonia, but it pronounced that they would always share the same ruler, and the introduction of a common financial authority and a network of lieutenants helped to move the disparate elements of the Aragonese crown closer to unity. In neighbouring Castile, meanwhile, a common regnal authority was more accepted at a formal level, but for much of this period it was more completely neutralised. Troubles began in the 1270s with the reaction of magnates and towns against Alfonso X's experiments with jurisdiction and taxation. From 1284 until the 1320s, a succession of weak kings – two of them minors, one a bastard and all three opposed by an alternative royal dynasty, the de la Cerdas – struggled to negotiate authority with noble factions and the town-based *hermandades* that dominated meetings of the *Cortes*. It was not until the fifteen-year-old Alfonso XI (1311–50) seized power in 1325, cancelling the supposedly loyalist *hermandad* in 1326 and pressing his claims to usurped royal estates, that order returned to the kingdom. Alfonso went on to revive the *Reconquista*, defeating the Granadans at the battle of Rio Salado in 1340, and capturing the stronghold of Algeciras in 1342. Famous for introducing the *alcabala* tax, for publishing a common law for Castile in the *Ordenamiento de Alcalá* of 1348, and for reforming the government of the cities, he was a classic example of the 'strong king' of the period, combining martial power with the exercise of judicial and governmental authority.

East-central Europe

Other strong kings were to be found further east. The fourteenth century witnessed two significant processes in the kingdoms of east-central Europe. One was a growth in political co-ordination, most marked perhaps in Hungary and the newly reunited kingdom of Poland, but noticeable also in Bohemia. The other was a closer integration for these kingdoms in the politics of the West. Hungary (from 1309) and Bohemia (1310) acquired French, or Frankish, ruling dynasties with interests in Italy and the Empire, and the kingdom of Poland became a more effective counter-weight to the Teutonic Knights, who were steadily expanding their rule in Prussia and Livonia. Visegrád, Prague and Cracow became splendid capitals, the last two gaining universities in 1347–8 and 1364, respectively.

Bohemia had waxed very powerful indeed in the late thirteenth century under the last of the great Přemysl kings, Otakar II (1253–78), who came close to bringing Austria and parts of Hungary into the Bohemian orbit, and Wenceslas II (1278–1305) and III (1305–6), who extended Bohemian rule across Silesia and into southern Poland. The succession crisis of 1306–10, and the mounting resistance of the eastern German princes, somewhat checked these gains, and the victories of Władisław Łokietek (king of Poland, 1320–33) drove the Bohemians back from Cracow and Sandomierz. Under its new Luxemburg rulers, John (1310–46) and Charles (1346–78), Bohemia acquired relatively fixed boundaries and a somewhat conflicted political identity. On the one hand, the crown and the Church worked for centralisation, much aided by Benedict XII's establishment of a metropolitan see for the kingdom at Prague, by the royal stake in Bohemia's silver mines, and by the amount of territory in the hands of a co-ordinated network of German-speaking, royalist and papalist Cistercian monasteries. Charles bought back lost royal lands and regranted some estates as fiefs, thus gaining feudal jurisdiction over certain noblemen. He even went so far as to impose annual taxation, and to attempt to realise Wenceslas II's plans for a national Roman-style law-code, with his *Majestas Carolina* of 1355. On the other hand, traditions of noble independence remained strong. The magnates leagued together from 1315 and drove out John's German councillors; they imposed a settlement at Domažlice in 1318, which left the king in possession of the incomes from the silver mines and placed the nobility in charge of the rule of the realm. King John's near-complete absence from the kingdom following this settlement confirmed the new distribution of authority, and created obstacles to Charles' attempts to extend the power of the crown from the beginning of his regency in 1340. Although Charles was able to manage the nobility, who joined him, for example, in his Italian campaigns of 1355 and 1368–9, it is telling that his taxes were confined to the royal estates and that the *Majestas* was rejected by the diet and remained a dead letter.

The Bohemian intervention in Poland was arguably central to the reconstruction of that kingdom. This was partly because of the challenge it presented to the honour of the Polish nobility and to the interests of the national Church, but the Bohemians also left a more positive legacy of co-ordination in the south, which included the office of *starosta*, or provincial governor, much exploited by Władisław's successor, Casimir III 'the Great' (1333–70), and attractive to lesser nobles because it undercut the regional hegemonies of the baronial *wojewodas*. Both Władisław and his son were more powerful in the southern territory of Lesser Poland than in Greater Poland to the north, though Casimir's astute diplomacy with Bohemia and the Teutonic Knights left him master of a contiguous kingdom by the Treaty of Kalisz in 1343; and the addition of Kuiavia in 1335 and the gradual assertion of sovereignty over Masovia meant that, by the mid-1350s, Casimir had reassembled all of the ancient realm except for Pomerania.[6] Campaigns in Galicia, Ruthenia and Lithuania during the 1340s and 1350s expanded Polish territory to the

---

[6] The two core duchies of fragmented Poland were Wielkopolska (Greater Poland), focused on Gniezno, to the north, and Małopolska (Lesser Poland), focused on

south-east and gained the kingdom a new archbishopric, at Halyč (later moved to L'wow) in 1365. While the Teutonic Knights had seized Gdánsk/Danzig and Eastern Pomerania in the troubles of 1308, and moved their headquarters to Marienburg, in western Prussia, in 1309, their expansion to the south was checked by this Polish recovery, and it was in eastern Prussia, the see of Riga and Estonia (bought from Denmark in 1346) that the *Ordensstaat* made its most noticeable territorial gains in the fourteenth century.

Turning to Hungary, the Angevin claimant, Charles-Robert (1309–42), foisted on the kingdom by Boniface VIII in 1301, had secured acceptance by 1309–10 and 'full possession', as he put it, by 1323.[7] In its last few decades, under the child-king Ladislaus IV (1272–90) and his successor Andrew III (1290–1301), the Árpád kingdom had partly dissolved into a series of magnate fiefdoms: the crown was too weak to protect its interests and a number of powerful lords took over royal castles and counties, corralling the local nobility into their own service and claiming palatine authority. The failure of the royal line and the ensuing competition for the throne with Wenceslas II of Bohemia only worsened the situation, but the interest of the Church, the towns and many lesser nobles in restoring central authority encouraged the new king to reassert his rights to offices, lands and castles. Divisions among the magnates, together with a policy of proceeding against them individually, and redistributing their assets in a less concentrated fashion among his followers, enabled Charles to make good his claims in a decade of campaigning. Once established, and strengthened by the revenues from clerical tenths and from the new gold mines at Kremnica, he embarked on an ambitious pursuit of Hungarian claims in the Balkans and his own Angevin interests in Naples. The former project produced few lasting results apart from the capture of Belgrade, but the latter ended in the marriage of his second son Andrew to Joanna, heiress of King Robert, in 1333. Improved relations with the neighbouring kingdoms of Bohemia and Poland were sealed with an alliance of the three kings, hatched at the new royal centre of Visegrád in 1335. In this meeting lay the

---

Cracow, to the south. Kuiavia lay between them at this time, and the large duchy of Masovia was to its west.
[7] P. Engel, *The Realm of St Stephen: A History of Medieval Hungary*, trans. T. Pálosfalvi and ed. A. Ayton (London, 2005), p. 144.

origin of the Hungarian succession to the Polish crown, first promised by Casimir III in 1339.

Scandinavia

In the Baltic and northwards, the most dynamic and organised power in this period was probably the Hanseatic League, which grew steadily in political consolidation, its first diet meeting at Lübeck in 1356. Even so, the century began with a series of assaults by the princes of the Baltic littoral on the increasingly wealthy, assertive and co-ordinated towns of the region. For much of the 1310s, Lübeck, Rostock and Wismar were subjugated by an alliance between Erik Menved, king of Denmark (1286–1319) and the counts of Holstein and Mecklenburg. Further east, the cities generally fared better, Stralsund defending its privileges from the duke of Pomerania, and the cities of Brandenburg joining together to force concessions from the margraves; but the emerging unity of the Hanseatic network, and Lübeck's leadership of it, were both suspended for a time. Rescue arrived only when the costs of Erik's wars began to produce reaction from his Danish subjects. As Denmark plunged into civil war in the 1320s, and then fell under the wardship of the German count of Holstein (1326–30, 1332–40), the Hansa joined the princes and lords of northern Germany in a general infiltration of the Danish space. While the resulting atmosphere of disorder and anti-German feeling created some problems for the Hansards, and drove them to work for the re-establishment of effective Danish kingship under Valdemar IV in 1340, these two decades saw the restoration of Hanseatic influence in the Scandinavian seas, and significant economic advance for the League in England and Flanders.

The Hansards were not the only beneficiaries of Danish discomfiture. The kingdom of Sweden, which had suffered two long minorities (1290–1302, 1319–31) and had been formally divided into three blocs for most of the 1310s, gradually drew together under King Magnus Eriksson (1319–63), who seized Skåne and the other Danish possessions on the Swedish mainland in 1332. Magnus was also king of Norway from 1319, as a result of a marriage alliance in 1302, but maintained the separateness of the two kingdoms by appointing his younger son to rule there in 1343. Following almost a century of legal and administrative consolidation between *c.*1240 and 1319, Norway experienced a long period of minority rule under Magnus and his son, Håkon VI (1343–80), in which a council of magnates and prelates established itself as the real ruler of the realm. Magnus' rule in Sweden was soon to falter, though this less-united realm was less easily brought under the control of a council: instead, a historic tension re-emerged between the crown, based in Götaland and the new capital at Stockholm, and the magnates who dominated Svealland and Finland.

Scandinavian historians with their eyes on the Union of Kalmar, which linked the crowns of the three kingdoms in 1397, emphasise the increasing interactions of Swedish, Norwegian and Danish political groupings from the second half of the thirteenth century. It is certainly true that the often-fragile rulers and frequently dissenting magnates of these three kingdoms exploited links with one another, and that they had some overlapping interests – not least the brokerage of the Baltic–North Sea trade, which they negotiated and contested with the Hansards – but this interpretation deserves two qualifications. One is that such cross-border interactions were typical of the whole continent in the period, and those in Scandinavia were by no means restricted to the three Nordic countries, but drew in other powers as well – the king of Scotland, for instance, whose eventual heiress was married to King Eric of Norway (1280–89) in 1281, the princes of northern Germany and even the Emperor himself. The other qualification is that it was only in the later thirteenth century that the royal element in Sweden, in particular, really began to mean more than the provincial structures and their magnate leaders. Under these circumstances, cross-border groupings of magnates are precisely what we would expect, and do not foreshadow future unity. Conversely, the conflicts that enveloped Denmark in the 1310s and 1320s, or Sweden in the 1350s and 1360s, arose from the efforts of more effective kings and the responses of more co-ordinated communities. The Scandinavian kingdoms may have been moving towards a common crown in the fourteenth century, but they were also growing in definition – like everywhere else – as distinct regnal polities.

Russia and the Balkans

It remains to comment on the areas to the east and south of the regions we have considered so far. In the east, the fourteenth century saw the rise of the two major successor states to the vast empire of Kievan Rus', which had been destroyed by the Mongols in the mid-thirteenth century. To the north the aggressive principality of Moscow, initially favoured by the Mongol khans of the Golden

Horde because it was less powerful than the neighbouring powers based on the trading cities of Tver' and Novgorod. Granted the extensive principality of Vladimir by the Mongols in 1331, the city rose to hegemony over the upper Volga and was best placed to exploit the disintegration of the Khanate when succession troubles began in 1359. Although Novgorod was able to preserve its independence in the second half of the century, Moscow, seat of the Orthodox metropolitan of 'Kiev and all-Rus'' from the 1320s, and victor in the Mongol wars of the 1380s and 1390s, was emerging as the dominant power in the region. To the west, the Grand Duchy of Lithuania steadily expanded from its thirteenth-century heartlands around Vilnius across what is now Belarus and Ukraine. It was a loose consortium of chieftains, ruled from around 1290 by the pagan dynasty known as the Gediminds (or, later, Jagiellonians), and one reason for its expansion was its appeal to the Livonians and Rus'ians as a buffer-state against the expansionist powers around them – Orthodox Moscow, Catholic Poland and also the Teutonic Knights, who organised massive international crusades against its northern territories from the 1330s. Its rulers adopted an urbane approach to both Catholic and Orthodox Christianity, tolerating evangelists as they took over the trade routes between the Dnieper and the Dniester and Vistula, and seeking an Orthodox primate to set against Moscow. Finally, one of them, Jogaila/Jagiełło (1377–1434), converted to Catholicism in the interests of securing the throne of Poland, where he became King Władisław II in 1386. The union of Poland-Lithuania, stabilised by the early fifteenth century, created a massive power bloc which radically altered the situation of the *Ordenstaat*, even if, in practice, Lithuania was ruled separately between 1392 and 1430 by the king's cousin Vytautas,[8] who had rebelled against him in the 1380s.

In the Byzantine sphere of Asia Minor and the Balkans, meanwhile, there were three main developments. The first was the recovery of Constantinople from the Latins by the Byzantine warlord and usurper Michael VIII Palaeologus (1258–82) in 1261. This led to almost a century of sporadic warfare with the Angevins, Venetians and Catalans, in which much of modern Greece and the Bulgarian littoral was successfully regained. But the corollary of military investment in the west of the Empire was a loss of control in Asia Minor, while a

---

[8] Called Witold in some books.

long civil war during the minority of Emperor John V (1341–91) in the 1340s and 1350s meant the loss of Macedonia to the rulers of Serbia, and the intervention of the Ottoman Turks on the European mainland as allies of one of the contending parties. In the second half of the century, the Empire effectively fragmented into a series of small principalities and city states, only a few of which – parts of Thrace, Thessalonica, the northern Aegean islands and Morea – remained loyal to Constantinople. These events provide the context for the other two developments of the period: the brief flourishing of the Balkan kingdoms of Serbia and Bulgaria, and the first great expansion of the Ottomans. From being a Byzantine vassal state, perilously placed on the borders of Hungarian influence, Serbia had become a papally recognised kingdom in 1217, in the wake of the Latin take-over of the Empire. The continuing troubles of Byzantium and the development of silver mines enabled the Serbian kings to expand their sway across parts of Albania, Bulgaria and Greece between *c.*1275 and *c.*1350; the greatest of them, Stefan Dušan (1331–55), even claimed the title of tsar (Caesar) in 1345, and clearly regarded himself as the successor of the eastern emperors. Divided after Dušan's death, the Serbs nonetheless organised a Christian alliance against the Ottomans, and the military elite of the kingdom was consequently slaughtered at the battle of Marica in 1371. This was the prelude to the disintegration of Serbia and the absorption of most of its territories by the Ottomans following the bloodbath at Kosovo in 1389. Bulgaria, which had also obtained western recognition in the period of the Fourth Crusade, was a rather less successful power, frequently menaced by Tatar raids in the later thirteenth century and only just able to hold the line against the Byzantines; it was overrun by the Ottomans between 1363 and 1376.

And what, finally, of the Ottomans themselves? Osman Bey (d.1324), the founder of the ruling dynasty, was emir (leader) of one of a number of Islamic Turkish statelets that had developed in the later thirteenth century in the frontier zone between the decaying Seljuk polity, centred on Konya, and the enfeebled Byzantine Empire along the Anatolian coast. From its position in the north-west of Anatolia, the Osmanli emirate was well placed to lead raids into the Byzantine zone; it thus attracted other Turkish adventurers. Quickly securing a series of major Byzantine cities in the 1320s and 1330s, the Osmanlis acquired the wealth and imperial prestige that enabled them to rise to hegemony over the other Turkish emirates by the 1350s, gaining

Ankara by about 1370, and reaching the south coast *c.*1380. Involvement in the Byzantine civil war brought the foothold of Gallipoli, on the European side of the Bosphorus, in 1354, and led to a series of raids and conquests in the Balkans, until Bulgaria, Albania, Serbia and Macedonia were under Ottoman control. By the 1390s, the Ottomans were raiding in Wallachia, and, following a victory at Nicopolis over Hungarian and Burgundian crusaders in 1396, they began to attack Hungary itself. This was to be the height of the fourteenth-century achievement, however. The defeated emirs of Anatolia joined forces with the rising empire of the Asian-Turkish leader Timur/Tamerlane to inflict a terrible defeat on the first Ottoman sultan, Bayezid (1389–1402) at Ankara in 1402. The Ottoman state was driven back to its heartland in Bithynia, but most of the conquests made under its aegis remained in the hands of Ottoman officers and agents, and the gradual recomposition of the Empire in the fifteenth century is consequently no surprise.

c.1340–c.1400

The Hundred Years War in western Europe
The central political phenomenon of the middle of the fourteenth century, at least in the West, was the near-disintegration of the French kingdom in the first two decades of the Hundred Years War. Edward III's early campaigns in Artois and Flanders were inconclusive, but Philip VI's avoidance of battle did him no favours with his subjects, and, as Edward's intervention in the succession dispute in Brittany in 1342 won him support in various parts of northern France, Valois power began to unravel. Landing in Normandy in 1346, Edward marched close to Paris before defeating Philip and killing a host of French magnates at the battle of Crécy; he then went on to besiege and capture the strategically important town of Calais (1347). The prolonged fighting in Aquitaine, combined with the destructive raids into Poitou, Normandy, the north and the Île-de-France, seems to have encouraged the spread of feuding across large parts of France, including areas like the Auvergne and southern Burgundy, which were not directly affected by English action. Although loyalist towns, provinces and aristocratic networks rallied to the Valois regime, and a series of meetings of the Estates General in the north during the 1340s began to organise taxes and troops, an atmosphere of crisis prevailed, as central authority proved ineffective and the future organisation of

power looked uncertain. Following the succession of John II (1350–64), a third potential claimant to the French throne, Charles 'the Bad', king of Navarre (1349–87), broke with the Valois, joining in alliance with Edward III and Louis de Male, count of Flanders (1348–84), and raising a cry of reform which proved attractive to public opinion. When a series of massive Anglo-Navarrese campaigns brought the king to battle, defeat and capture, at Poitiers (1356), it seemed that the kingdom of France was on the point of collapse: Edward was demanding the return of the Plantagenet domains as the price of peace; the Estates General of Languedoïl,[9] in almost continuous session in 1357–8, were trying to wrest control of the government from the dauphin; Paris was in revolt under the merchant leader Étienne Marcel (1356–8); and the common people of the Île-de-France rose up against the local nobility in an episode known as the *Jacquerie* (1358). In the event, John's eldest son, the future Charles V (1364–80), managed to rally Charles of Navarre, and to crush both the revolts and the Estates, while Edward III failed to capture either Paris or Rheims in his expedition of 1359–60. Valois France was saved, but the nine years of uneasy truce that followed the Treaty of Brétigny saw a hugely enlarged Aquitaine transferred to the English, while conflict between princes, towns and 'free companies' of soldiers raged across much of the centre and south.

Charles V reaped the rewards of conflict, in that the defenders of Valois France had seen the need for an effective system of taxation and were willing to tolerate military reforms that placed the defence of the realm more fully under royal direction. But he also had to bow to a major source of pressure which had helped to cause the war, and had certainly been strengthened by it: namely the ambivalent attitude of princes and provinces to the ever-intrusive government in Paris. Not only had two decades of war allowed extensive usurpation of royal rights and territories in the localities, they had also made these necessary, as more disorderly conditions required tougher local powers. Perhaps to keep the royal family together, perhaps to regain control, John II had given large *apanages*[10] to his younger sons: Louis was given the duchy of Anjou and John the duchy of Berry in 1361; Philip received the duchy and county of Burgundy in 1363. Charles

---

[9] I.e. royal France north of the Massif Central.
[10] An *apanage* was an area of delegated royal jurisdiction, accompanied by sections of the *domaine* and an appropriate title.

continued and extended this policy, giving Anjou a powerful regional lieutenancy over the Languedoc in 1364 and, doubtless more reluctantly, conceding extensive power in Normandy to Charles of Navarre. When the war with England resumed in 1369, both the strengths and the weaknesses of the royal position were made clear. On the one hand, the crown's new fiscal and military powers enabled the rapid reconquest, by bribery and warfare, of almost all of Aquitaine and Normandy; the royal princes acted as valuable allies and leaders. On the other hand, Brittany had been lost in 1364 and the other fiefs and principalities gained in definition, their leaders much assisted by extensive shares of the new taxation. When Charles V was succeeded by an infant son in 1380 (Charles VI, 1380–1422), his uncles maintained high levels of taxation, and used the proceeds to fund their own dynastic projects in Flanders (Burgundy), Naples (Anjou) and the south (Berry). Not only did the continuing fiscal burden unleash a serious wave of popular revolts in Paris and Rouen and other northern towns (1380–2), and also across the Languedoc (the so-called *Tuchins*, 1381–4), it set a pattern for the politics that ensued when Charles VI went mad in 1392: the royal uncles fought to direct the royal machine in pursuit of their territorial interests, while other magnates and provinces sought to scale down, or reappropriate, royal powers and exactions. In the meantime, English raiding subsided after about 1380 and, apart from a brief flirtation with a Burgundian scheme to cross the Channel in 1385–6, the French government moved towards peace negotiations which were pursued throughout the 1390s. Even though the war with England had petered out, France was heading back towards civil war by the end of the century, her royal structure significantly expanded, but local and provincial solidarities also greatly strengthened.

There is a tendency in the historical literature to make the Hundred Years War central to accounts of politics in all the territories surrounding France. This makes most sense, perhaps, for the British Isles: developments in the Low Countries, Iberia, the Empire and the soon-to-be-divided Church were less closely related to the Anglo-French conflict than tradition suggests. Britain and Ireland, however, were affected by the Hundred Years War in two fairly fundamental ways. First of all, the redirection of English military and fiscal resources towards the conquest of France reduced pressure on Scotland and almost certainly contributed to the decay of English lordship in Ireland. Much as the English captured King David II (1329–71) during an ill-advised Scottish invasion in 1346, and much as this led to twenty years of ransom payments and occupation of the border fortresses (1357–77), the independence and integrity of Scottish territory was effectively accepted by the middle years of the century. David was rather an effective ruler following his return in 1357, but after 1371, Scottish politics were frequently turbulent, as a succession of com-promised kings and regents attempted to build support for themselves, while the major magnate families developed strong regional hegem-onies, especially in the Highlands and along the border. In Ireland, meanwhile, English power was eroded by a mixture of Gaelic recon-quest in Ulster (c.1318–33) and the gradual withdrawal of anything more than tacit obedience by the great magnates of the south, the earls of Kildare, Ormond and Desmond. Numerous schemes were hatched to restore royal authority, and a couple of royal expeditions during lulls in the French war achieved temporary success (Lionel of Clarence in the 1360s; Richard II in the 1390s), but money and sustained attention were lacking, and Ireland drifted away, with even the loyalist Pale around Dublin substantially dependent on its own resources.

The second major consequence of the war was its effect on English political and governmental arrangements. The extensive campaigning of the 1340s, 1350s and 1370s strengthened the institution of Parliament and accustomed the English to regular taxation. As in France, however, the military, fiscal and administrative developments of the period had both integrative and disruptive effects. While Edward III was an active leader, the English realm was united and its resources tapped as never before, but the king's decline into dotage from about 1370 combined with defeat in France to produce serious political conflicts between the representatives of the political com-munity and the nobles, courtiers and officers around the king. From 1371, and onwards into the long minority of Richard II (1377–99), a succession of difficult parliaments, not dissimilar from the French Estates General of the 1350s, sought limits to taxation and controls over royal government. As Richard was not prepared to accept these restraints, the political situation worsened, reaching the point of civil war in 1387, and placing the king under a sort of regency for much of the 1380s and 1390s. Richard's brief success in turning the tables on his opponents in 1397 led rapidly to his deposition and the usurpation of his cousin, Henry, duke of Lancaster as Henry IV, in 1399. Despite the prominence of magnates in these struggles, they were truly collective:

the community of taxpayers may not have wanted civil war, but it did want economic government, order and effective defence. Nor were these just the concerns of the better-off. In 1381, in a rising parallel to the French *Jacquerie*, the common people of the south-east rose up and occupied London, their complaints a mixture of agrarian grievances and protests about misgovernment which were very similar to those expressed in Parliament.

Two other regions were drawn closely into the diplomatic and military manoeuvres of the English and French crowns – Iberia and the Low Countries – but that is not at all to say that the conflicts that broke out in these regions were merely by-products of the Hundred Years War. Although Castile was moving towards the English from the 1340s, and Aragon was linked to France from 1356, the wars which consumed the former kingdom in the late 1360s, and to a lesser extent in the 1380s, were essentially produced by factors internal to the peninsula: a damaging succession dispute in Castile, and the interaction of networks and claims across the four kingdoms of Portugal, Castile, Aragon and Navarre. Peter 'the Cruel' of Castile (1350–69) was the fifteen-year-old legitimate heir of Alfonso XI, but his position was compromised from the very start of his reign by an illness and by the presence of eight illegitimate half-brothers whom his father had favoured. The eldest of these, Henry, count of Trastámara (Henry II, 1369–79), was, in many ways, a more convincing successor to Alfonso. For one thing, he was the first-born son; also, unlike Peter, he had been at his father's side at the siege of Gibraltar (1350) and was married to the heiress of the de la Cerda claim to the throne within weeks of Alfonso's death. While Peter was able to exercise authority and attract support, and successfully faced down a major rebellion of towns and nobles willing to exploit the Trastámara claim in 1354–6, he was unable to command the unconditional allegiance of his subjects, or to prevent the formation of alliances with foreign powers on the part of his enemies. His decision to go to war against the king of Aragon between 1357 and 1364 weakened his position by draining his revenues and drawing the Aragonese, the French, the Papacy and Henry of Trastámara into an alliance against him; but it is important to recognise that this conflict – in defence or pursuit of Castilian claims in Murcia, or perhaps of a more vaguely conceived notion of pan-Hispanic empire – would have made perfect sense to contemporaries, and was the kind of honourable and collective project likely to stimulate loyalty. In fact, Peter successfully overran Aragon-proper in 1363 and reached the gates of Valencia before an Aragonese counter-attack drove him off. But two French-backed invasions by Trastámara, in 1366 and 1368, secured the allegiance of most of Castile, and the successful counter-attack of Peter's English ally, the Black Prince, at Nájera in 1367, brought only temporary respite for the king: he was defeated and murdered by the usurper at Montiel in 1369. French investment in Henry II was soon repaid by the assistance of the Castilian fleet in manoeuvres against the English, including a decisive naval engagement off La Rochelle in 1372 which ended the English occupation of Poitou.

The position of Peter IV 'the Ceremonious' (1336–87) of Aragon was not so very different from that of his Castilian namesake. He too came to the throne as a teenager, and faced potential difficulties from the highly favoured sons of his father's second marriage, the *infantes* Ferdinand and John. While these two were children in 1336, Ferdinand later emerged as leader of the *Uniones* that sprang up in Aragon and Valencia in 1347–8. These leagues were formed partly in reaction to Peter's plans for the succession, but, more fundamentally, they were a provincial response to increasing fiscal pressure, administrative co-ordination and the assertion of legislative supremacy by the king. Peter defeated the *Uniones*, though he had to confirm the powers of the *Justicia* of Aragon, but he did not prevent the flight of his half-brothers to the Castilian court, and this, together with Castilian friendship towards the Genoese – principal competitors to Catalan merchants and a threat to the royal possessions in the Mediterranean – may explain his enthusiasm for war with Castile in the 1350s. The pressure of funding the wars in Majorca, Castile and, later, Sardinia obliged the king to assemble the *Corts/Cortes* of his three realms far more frequently than hitherto. As in other countries, taxation provoked resistance, and royal demands were argued down in the 1360s and 1370s, but it could also assist integration, and the development, in 1359, of the *diputació* in Catalonia – a permanent delegation from the *Corts* with authority for the management of public finance – helped to secure the commitment of Catalan taxpayers as well as to restrain and influence the king. Peter's influence over ecclesiastical appointments, his control of the military orders in his kingdom and the improvements he made to record-keeping and financial administration helped to draw his three Spanish realms together. A similar aim of co-ordination is apparent in his approach to the Mediterranean territories, and especially in his attempts to bring grain-rich Sicily back under the rule of the house of Barcelona – attempts which led finally to a full-scale invasion in 1392.

Although Aragon escaped further entanglement in peninsular affairs until after 1400, Castile spent the rest of the century dealing with the consequences of the civil war. Henry II was given the opportunity and challenge of refounding the nobility after the blood-bath of the 1360s, and his reign is often – and not altogether fairly, as we shall see – regarded as the point of origin for the princely lordships which were to be such a feature of fifteenth-century Castilian politics. Henry began by fighting off a Portuguese claim to the throne, and his successor, John I (1379–90), attempted to turn the tables by claiming the Portuguese throne when it fell vacant in 1383. This attempt was rebuffed at the battle of Aljubarrota (1385), where an alliance between the local claimant, John of Avis (John I 1385–1433), and the English produced a decisive victory and led to the brief and unsuccessful invasion of John of Gaunt, claimant to the Castilian throne, in 1386–8. All this warfare, coming hard on the exhaustion of the treasury during the civil war, meant a practically annual resort to the *Cortes* during the 1370s and 1380s, with its inevitable consequence of high taxation and demands for administrative reform. When John was followed by the child Henry III (1390–1406), the combination of a weak crown, factional divisions and high fiscal pressure produced a wave of violently anti-Jewish pogroms, spreading outwards from Seville across the whole peninsula in 1391. While rabble-rousing preaching played a part in this event, and so did the example set by Henry of Trastámara, who had cast Peter the Cruel as a Judaiser and allowed the sacking of several Jewish quarters during the civil war, it was the role of Jewish financiers in the royal financial and adminis-trative network, and the strains to which that network had been subjected, that lay at the heart of the troubles (as they had in the smaller-scale anti-Jewish agitation of the '*Pastoureaux*' (shepherd boys) in southern France in 1320–1). Peace with England and Portugal enabled Henry III to restore order, however, and after 1396 the *Cortes* scarcely met, while the king set about reimposing royal author-ity on the municipalities. The stage was set for a reintroduction of the Alfonsine mode of rule, until it became clear that the king was dying and a long minority lay in prospect.

The other region whose politics were most deeply entwined with the Plantagenet-Valois conflict was the Low Countries. As we have seen, the tensions between the cloth-producing Flemish towns and the counts of Flanders had already pulled in the neighbouring rulers of France and England in the 1290s, and both kingdoms were to be active in the region throughout the century. The English harnessed all the leading local powers except Liège in alliance against France (1336–45), but their success was short-lived. The French, meanwhile, made a series of unsuccessful attempts to conquer Flanders during the first three decades of the century, only to be triumphant later, with the entry of the Burgundian dukes in the 1380s. Even so, it would be a mistake to overemphasise the role of external forces in shaping the politics of the Low Countries (or to single out these two kingdoms: the archbishops of Cologne, the Wittelsbachs and the Luxemburgs were also active in the region). Not only were foreign princes drawn in by local conflicts, but the counts and cities of the region sought alliances with them to advance their claims over one another: the alliance with Edward III, for example, enabled Brabant to acquire the city of Malines, and helped the rebellious cities of Ghent, Bruges and Ypres to control Flanders in the absence of its pro-French count. In fact, two dynamics internal to the Low Countries played the largest shaping role in the politics of the region during the century. The first, rather as in Italy, was the negotiation of governmental power between the towns and the princes. This could be volatile and violent, as it often was in Flanders, where very wealthy, sizeable and rather disunited cities confronted a princely structure which was both well established and frequently undermined by French interference. Alternatively, it could be pretty peaceful, as in Brabant, where a succession of ducal minorities opened the way to power-sharing between the ruler and the larger towns. On the whole, the trend of the century was towards more settled and effective relations between princes and municipalities, though the advance of the Burgundians and the rising wealth of the towns of Holland shook things up in the 1370s and 1380s. The other dynamic was towards consolidation of the provinces of the region. This was partly stimulated by dynastic accident, as in the union of Hainault, Holland and Zealand in 1299. It was also the product of commercial interest, as in the coinage union agreed by Brabant and Flanders in 1299–1300, joined by Hainault in 1337. But it owed a certain amount to the designs which most Low Countries rulers had on one another's territory. Among various dynastic initiatives, the key development in the second half of the century was the marriage of Margaret, daughter of Louis de Male, count of Flanders (1348–84), to Philip the Bold, duke of Burgundy

(1363–1404), in 1369. Louis was among the most successful rulers of the region, managing the kings of England and France and the difficult towns of Flanders with remarkable skill for more than three decades. Besides inheriting a county enlarged by Louis' diplomacy and by his successful wars against Brabant and Hainault, Philip and Margaret went on to gain Artois, Franche-Comté, Réthel and Nevers in 1384. A marriage alliance of 1385 brought Duke Philip the friendship of Hainault-Holland, and opened the way to its acquisition in 1419, while an agreement of 1390 placed Brabant under a Burgundian cadet from 1406. The great consortium of the Valois dukes was thus taking shape by the end of the century, though as Philip and his successor began to adopt the close relations with England that were characteristic of the provinces they had acquired, the closeness of the ducal dynasty to the French crown began to wane.

The German lands of the Empire

The alliance of interests which had grown up in the 1330s and 1340s between the French crown, the Papacy and the Luxemburgs continued rather loosely into the 1350s and beyond. As we have noted, relations between the Empire and the Papacy thawed very considerably after Charles IV's election: the Emperors more or less withdrew from an assertive role in Italian politics and the Popes more or less acquiesced in the movement of the Empire towards juridical independence. Charles and his successor Wenceslas (1376–1400) also avoided entanglement in the Anglo-French conflict, even though Charles had been present in the Valois camp at Crécy where his father had died. The internal affairs of Germany were becoming a more central concern for the Emperor, the Electors and other imperial powers, even if the Hansards and the principalities of the northern littoral – notably the counties of Holstein and Mecklenburg – looked towards the Baltic, and even though the royal family tried, with some success, to establish a foothold in Hungary, with the accession of Wenceslas' younger brother Sigismund (king of Hungary, 1387–1437; king of the Romans, 1410/11–37; Emperor, 1433–7) to the throne of St Stephen after a five-year war.

Charles IV's reign had rather mixed results for the imperial office. In his lifetime, he was an influential, even powerful, Emperor. Although he built a splendid capital at Prague in his kingdom of Bohemia, and spent nine or ten years of his reign there, he was an indefatigable traveller within his imperial domains, the only late-medieval Emperor to visit Lübeck, for instance, and a frequent resident of the major imperial cities in the south and centre, especially Nuremberg. What Moraw calls his *hegemoniale Königtum* was based as much on this activity as on his territories in Bohemia, and also on Charles' cultivation of a wide network of support, his exploitation of fiscal rights, his development of the imperial secretariat and his sponsorship of judicial resorts that did not challenge the jurisdictional sensitivities of his subjects, such as the arbitrative Vehmic courts of Westphalia and his own cameral court, or *Reichshofgericht*.[11] The ambivalence in Charles' reign lay in his mortgaging of imperial resources, which he carried out on a greater scale than any other emperor, and in the consequences of some of his other fiscal expedients.

Charles' most famous act was the 'Golden Bull' of 1356, which set down, in grandiose terms, the by-now established electoral procedures of the Empire, and extended high political rights to the Electors, who were to enjoy the protection of *lèse-majesté* over themselves and their dependants, and whose lands were to be maintained intact from holder to holder. In a move commonly presented as setting a seal on the traditional alliance of king and princes, the document also banned urban leagues and forbade towns from offering citizenship to the Electors' subjects. The rights accorded to the Electors were rapidly claimed by other princes, and the Golden Bull has thus been presented as the source of many of the troubles that were to come. By seeking to consolidate princely authority, it is suggested, the Bull almost inevitably drove the excluded interests – imperial cities and those minor barons or vassals of the Emperor who were later to be known as 'imperial knights' – into joining forces to preserve their independence; it can thus be seen as the point of origin for the urban and knightly leagues that broke out in Hesse, Swabia and the Rhineland in the later 1370s. But this may claim too much for imperial legislation. The leagues developed for three reasons. The first was that princely consolidation was happening anyway: Austria, Hesse, Württemberg, Meissen, the Palatinate and the see of Trier are all examples of principalities that grew in size and co-ordination during the fourteenth century. The second is that, as we have seen, leagues were already an established medium through which towns and lesser lords could preserve their freedom, and the fourteenth-century growth in

[11] P. Moraw, *Von Offener Verfassung zu Gestaltete Verdichtung* (Berlin, 1985), ch. 2.6.

size and integrity of the north German Hansa and the Swiss Confederation in the south must have inspired imitation: the former expanded to include Cologne, the Teutonic Knights and the towns of Holland in the 'Cologne Confederation' of 1367–85; the latter had grown to eight members by 1353, including the city states of Lucerne, Zurich and Bern, alongside the rural cantons. The third, more specific, was that Charles spent his last years raising heavy taxes and pawning revenues, offices and other rights in imperial cities as a means of bribing the Electors to choose his son as his successor, which they did in 1376.

Charles' action was so offensive and problematic because it threatened urban independence. The lords of urban *Pfände* (pledges, pawned resources) would gain authority within the cities, and could use it to incorporate them in their domains. More abstractly, the Emperor's actions implied that the goods of the Empire were at his disposal, a notion that contradicted the developing theory that the immediate vassals and cities of the Empire were free. So it was that, in 1376, the heavily taxed city of Ulm formed the Swabian League with Constance and twelve other imperial cities, to challenge further taxation and prevent themselves from being placed in pledge. The League was soon at war with the leading princes of Swabia, whose interests were most directly affected, and it defeated the son of the count of Württemberg at Reutlingen in 1377. Over the next few years, its membership grew, and it joined with a group of Rhenish cities in 1381, and eventually with a number of Swiss communities in 1385; princely and knightly leagues developed across the region in response. The last years of Charles' reign and the first decade of Wenceslas' consequently witnessed disorder and conflict in the heart of the Empire on a scale greater than anything seen since the disputed succession of the 1310s. Wenceslas struggled to broker peace in 1384, tacitly recognising the urban leagues so recently forbidden in the Golden Bull, but it was only after a succession of military confrontations – Sempach (1386) in which the Swiss defeated the Habsburgs; Döffingen (1388), in which the count of Württemberg defeated the Swabian towns; and Worms (1388), in which the Count Palatine defeated the Rhenish ones – that the emperor was able to reunite the exhausted parties in a vast *Landfriede* covering southern Germany made at Eger/Cheb in 1389. This settlement, which involved the establishment of arbitrative panels, combining urban leaders and local princes under imperially appointed presidents, was to have a formative influence over imperial politics in the fifteenth century and was perhaps Wenceslas' greatest achievement. Unfortunately, however, the disastrous start to his reign, combined with the troubles he faced in Bohemia during the 1390s (themselves, in many ways, a legacy of his father's reign there), left the Emperor disabled and surrounded by enemies. He was deposed by a cabal of the Rhenish Electors in 1400, and one of them, Rupert, Count Palatine, became king in his place. The stage was set for the paradoxical situation that obtained for much of the fifteenth century, in which the increasing concern of the Electors with the order and integrity of the Empire confronted the diminished resources of the Emperors.

The Papacy and the Great Schism

The experience of the Papacy in the second half of the fourteenth century was, in certain respects, remarkably similar to that of its imperial counterpart. The popes of mid-century, especially Clement VI (1342–52), were rich, and well able to exercise extensive authority over the Church. The scope of papal providing-power reached its height, with a massive extension to include the large majority of dioceses and significant monasteries, in 1363; the threat from the spiritual Franciscans was more or less contained (though a stream of dissenting opinion survived in the universities to animate the powerful heresies of Wyclif and Hus from the 1370s onwards); the crusading ideal was reanimated with the successful capture of the Turkish port of Smyrna in 1344; and the Papal States were brought back under effective control through the campaigns of the papal legate Cardinal Albornoz between 1353 and 1357. A return to Rome began to be canvassed, so that the Papacy could foster further crusades from an Italian base, and complement its administrative power over the Church with the particular spiritual and imperial aura conferred by the city (the neoclassical revolt of Cola di Rienzo, self-styled tribune and restorer of the Roman Empire, which seized Rome for a few months in 1347, may also have played a part in provoking this policy). In various ways, therefore, the papal monarchy was flourishing in the 1350s and 1360s.

At the same time, however, there were some less positive developments. The bureaucratic and fiscal quality of the Avignon Papacy and its centralisation of rights of appointment was beginning to provoke resistance within the Church: while individuals benefited from the papal structure, with its openness to petition and persuasion, enough collective interests were threatened to provide fuel for the reform demands that were to burst out so trenchantly later in the century. Meanwhile, by strengthening the organisation of the Curia and the administrative responsibilities of the cardinals, the reforms of the Avignon period created a counter-weight at the heart of the papal monarchy. Like the imperial Electors, the College of Cardinals began to see itself as the guardian of ecclesiastical fortunes, and its members attempted, in 1352, to secure papal agreement that major acts of government and appointments to the College would require their agreement. The initiative was thwarted in that year, and the cardinals could generally be managed by a mixture of nepotism and selective favour, but the events of the last quarter of the century were to show what they could do. In 1377, the saintly Gregory XI (1371–8) returned to Rome, with part of the Curia, and died there a year later. His successor, Urban VI (1378–89), cash-strapped after the disastrous war of the Eight Saints against Florence (1375–8), and apparently responsive to complaints about the worldliness of the Curia, imposed unwelcome reforms on the cardinals, overrode their advice and began to engage in Roman faction – an alternative means of political support which had been denied to the Papacy since the time of Boniface VIII. The immediate response of the cardinals was to propose a return to Avignon, where most of the machinery of ecclesiastical government still resided. When Urban refused, the majority, fleeing to Anagni, declared his election invalid and proceeded to elect one of their number as Pope Clement VII (1378–94). While Urban remained in Rome and created twenty-eight new cardinals to help him run the Church, Clement's supporters returned to Avignon and resumed control of the bureaucracy there.

So began the Great Schism of 1378–1417. It has long been regarded as the decisive moment in the decline of the papal monarchy: 'the obvious deduction is the true one', writes George Holmes: 'the Great Schism began the destruction of the medieval papacy'.[12] More recent writing tends in another direction, however. In many ways, at least until the 1390s, the Schism meant business as usual for the government of the Church. Those parts of Europe closest to the papal centres – France, Spain, much of Italy (though not the queen of Naples, who soon switched her support to Clement) – fell rapidly into the camp of the nearest pope; relatively distant powers, such as

[12] G. Holmes, *Europe: Hierarchy and Revolt, 1320–1450* (London, 1975), p. 174.

England and the Emperor, made what look like more calculated choices. Meanwhile, areas of political fragmentation, such as the Rhineland, where localised ecclesiastical schisms were common, experienced further schism, now along Urbanist/Clementist lines. French endorsement of Clement VII meant a prolongation of patterns established since 1309: the Papacy offered substantial (but not unqualified) fiscal and diplomatic support for the Valois crown, in return for making extensive provisions and levying huge tax revenues from the French Church; French princes, just as earlier in the century, pursued papally backed adventures in Italy, with the duke of Anjou awarded Naples in 1379 and the duke of Orleans married to the Visconti heiress in 1387 and made king of 'Adria' (the Papal States) in 1393–4. In Italy, meanwhile, Urban struggled to assert himself in both the centre and the south, but his successor, Boniface IX (1389–1404), was among the most powerful popes of the century, at least in Italian terms: he played Milan off against Florence, used *signori* and mercenaries to regain most of the papal patrimony and reaped the benefits of supporting Ladislas of Durazzo (1390–1414), titular king of Naples from 1390 and effective ruler there by 1399.

As far as authority over the divided Church was concerned, initially, it held up rather well: both popes easily batted off a conciliar solution to their predicament in 1378, and proceeded to rule their obediences with, if anything, greater intensity than before. This, in fact, was to be the major cause of papal difficulties in the longer term. By the 1390s, the French Church was ready to throw off the heavy burden of the schismatic Papacy, not least because there was no consistently effective king to protect its interests after 1392. While the duke of Orleans, one of the three royal princes leading the government, was a direct beneficiary of pontifical taxation, the dukes of Berry and Burgundy, with territorial interests in the Urbanist/Clementist borderlands of Poitou and the Low Countries respectively, wanted the Schism settled. They joined forces with the University of Paris, prompting the French Church to renounce its obedience to Benedict XIII (1394–1423) in 1398 and forcing him to flee to Genoa in 1405. Shorn of the apparatus of Avignon, the Clementist Papacy began to look implausible, while the conquest of Rome by Ladislas of Naples after Boniface's death edged the Roman cardinals towards the conciliar solution that Paris and the 'Gallican' clergy of France were now promoting. Fifteen cardinals from the two obediences met in Pisa in 1408 and summoned a general council to resolve the Schism and address the need for reform. The era of the Councils was about to begin, and – in the Church as in the Empire – its central problem was to be the question of how to promote unity and reform when the powers and resources of the imperial monarchy were both resented and inadequate.

Italy

It is hard to feel that the politics of Italy were significantly affected by the ecclesiastical Schism. In the south, the war between the Angevins and Aragonese of Sicily continued up to 1373, complicated by the decision of the young Queen Joanna I (1343–82) to rule independently of her husband, Andrew, son of King Charles-Robert of Hungary, who was murdered in 1345. These moves provoked Hungarian invasions in 1347–8 and 1350, and then a decade of civil war between two other contending branches of the house of Anjou: that of Louis of Taranto, who married the queen in 1346 and became co-ruler in 1352; and Louis of Durazzo, who was backed by his cousin of Hungary. In these chaotic conditions, the crown lost control of its structures in the localities and the magnates built up local fiefdoms, dealing with the different parties in the dynastic conflict as their interests and circumstances dictated. Although the 1370s brought an end to the wars between Naples and Sicily, the internal situation in both kingdoms remained more or less anarchic, and the arrival in Naples of competing Urbanist and Clementist claimants in 1381–4 and 1390 (as Joanna recognised the French duke of Anjou as her heir) simply inflamed a war with the Hungary/Durazzo interest which was already endemic. Not until the end of the 1390s did Ladislas of Durazzo succeed in crushing his opponents and restoring some kind of royal authority over the effectively independent barons of Naples. In Sicily, meanwhile, order returned at roughly the same time, as the invasion of 1392 brought the son of the Aragonese king to the throne (Martin I, 1392–1409), backed by a Catalan establishment to whom the major noble estates were rapidly redistributed. After this, Sicily was drawn more tightly into the Aragonese network, and the antagonism with Naples subsided for several decades.

Further north, meanwhile, the tendency of the Papacy to focus its military attention more closely on control of the Papal States, already noticeable in the 1350s, was broadly confirmed in the rest of the century. This did not preclude frequent conflicts with the Visconti between the 1340s and the 1370s – most notably over the city of

Bologna – nor did it prevent a short war with Florence, whose leaders feared that the return of the Papacy could mean the renewal of interference in Tuscany (1375–8); nor, finally, did it mean the lasting restoration of control over the Papal States, which – Boniface's reign apart – remained largely unco-ordinated, or disobedient, until the 1420s. On the whole, however, the political interactions of the northern half of the peninsula were much less shaped by papal-Guelf initiatives than they had been, and the second half of the fourteenth century saw the beginnings of a different configuration of power, in which a series of relatively stable regional hegemonies, most of them based on the largest cities, began to emerge.[13] Of these, the most substantial were the county of Savoy, which took over much of Piedmont during the reign of Amadeus VI (1343–83), and the Visconti network, which was centred on Milan and extended over most of Lombardy by *c*.1350. Though dynamic and aggressive, the Visconti principate fluctuated in power. This was partly because, like many lordships, it did not expand in a particularly systematic way, but acquired distant and temporary assets, such as Genoa in 1353–4 and Bologna in 1349–64, as well as more local and durable ones. Like any imperial principality, moreover, it was vulnerable to division among heirs (as happened between 1354 and 1387, and again after 1402); and its expansion tended to provoke alliances of surrounding powers, both large and small, against it. Even so, the Visconti could draw on the traditional hegemony, and great wealth, of Milan and the habits of association that had grown up in the Lombard plain, where few natural obstacles prevented the spread of power between Piedmont in the west and the Adriatic in the east. Under Giangaleazzo (1387–1402), there seems to have been a more determined attempt to establish a lasting state – aided in part by the purchase of a 'duchy of Milan' from the Emperor in 1395, which enabled the duke to exert a legally sound feudal lordship over the Empire's vassals in the region. While this state disintegrated anew in the squabbles following his death, it was quite rapidly reassembled in the 1410s by his son, Filippo Maria, and was clearly the foundation for the durable duchy of the fifteenth century and beyond. Meanwhile, the threat from the Visconti helped to turn the other leading powers of the north, notably Florence and Venice, towards the construction of similar

[13] Venice, Rome, Milan and Florence, to be joined by Naples in the fifteenth century, were far larger than any other Italian cities.

regional states. Florence had already engaged in some conquests in Tuscany, but her efforts increased markedly between the 1380s and the 1420s. Venice, meanwhile, had focused more determinedly on the preservation of her trading empire. This had involved her in wars against Genoa in 1350–5 and 1376–81 (the so-called War of Chioggia) and also with Hungary (1346–8, 1357–8, 1378–81, 1408–9), over her possessions on the Dalmatian coast. These experiences, from which she emerged battered but more or less victorious, may have convinced Venice that the protection of the trade routes on which the city's wealth depended entailed the expansion of territorial control. The Carrara lordship of Padua, which had supported Genoa in the War of Chioggia, was to be the *Serenissima*'s first sizeable victim: wounded by Venice in 1388–90, it was swallowed up in 1405, and the Carrara themselves destroyed.

Eastern and northern Europe

In the great monarchies of east-central and northern Europe, there was a general pattern of territorial expansion and co-ordination – even a kind of unification, between Poland and Hungary (1370–82), Poland and Lithuania (1386 onwards) and Norway, Sweden and Denmark (1397) – but not only did these developments tend to preserve the constitutional distinctness of the kingdoms involved, they were also typically accompanied by the solidification of mechanisms that protected the collective privileges and individual immunities of magnates, and sometimes of the whole noble class in each kingdom. This meant that while there were processes of political integration in this area quite as much as in the West, they took a different form, though perhaps less different in Hungary than elsewhere in the region.

In mid-century, all three central European kingdoms had strong rulers – Emperor Charles IV in Bohemia (discussed above), Casimir III in Poland and Louis I 'the Great' in Hungary (1342–82). Casimir, as we have seen, established a network of effective royal officers – *starostas* – and embarked on an impressive programme of reclaiming lost royal estates, which were then settled with peasants under German law, and building fifty new royal castles. While these policies provoked a serious revolt by the *wojewoda* and other magnates of Greater Poland in 1352, the combination of repression and resettlement enabled the introduction of a new land tax and the extension of military service obligations to the new peasant communities, both of which strengthened the king's hand and enabled him to reassert control by 1360. Casimir gave law-codes to Greater and Lesser Poland in 1347 and 1354, and celebrated the unification of his kingdom with a great international congress and the foundation of a university at Cracow in 1364. His ally and contemporary, Louis the Great, ruled in a rather similar way, albeit in a kingdom with a firmer tradition of royal co-ordination. His father had already rebuilt the royal network of estates and castles, and placed them in loyal hands; Louis took this further by establishing the legal principle that all property was held from the crown and reorganising both central government and local jurisdiction, pulling more business into the royal centre and weakening the old county structures. He was happy to bestow privileges on loyal magnates, who might acquire palatine powers in the region of their estates, judicial rights over peasant tenants, or preferential inheritance arrangements (in return for acknowledging the king as ultimate lord of their lands). In 1351–2, this led to some tensions with Hungary's lesser noblemen, whose independent standing was linked to the counties – they even obtained a confirmation of the Golden Bull of 1222, which included the concession that all liberties held by the magnates would be held equally by lesser nobles – but, in Louis' lifetime, his policies assured him a reservoir of devoted and effective military servants. Supported by them, he was able to regain control of Croatia and to conduct wars in Dalmatia, the Balkans and Naples (in descending order of success). Huge revenues from the gold mines paid for these activities until the later 1370s, but the end of the reign saw the beginning of fiscal and political strain, as the elderly king began to lose his grip.

Royal advances were to be checked in each of these kingdoms in the last few decades of the century. In Poland and Hungary, the main reason lay in the failure of the succession in the male line. On Casimir's death in 1370, the Polish throne passed, as pre-arranged, to Louis the Great, albeit with various guarantees protecting (and modestly extending) the liberties of the Polish nobility. Backed by the Piast establishment in Lesser Poland, Louis was able to rule surprisingly effectively: the real problem he faced was that he was an old man whose sons had both died, and whose three daughters were his only direct heirs. In Poland, this meant another round of negotiations with the magnates, which resulted in the statute of Koszyce of 1374, often regarded as the foundation of Polish constitutionalism because it confirmed the involvement of the magnates in determining the succession and made such far-reaching concessions to the prelates and nobles, both great and small. The nobility were released from almost all their fiscal obligations; they were not to have to serve beyond the frontiers of the kingdom; provincial officers would only be appointed from the nobility of the same province; *starostas* were to be Polish noblemen and not members of the royal family. At the same time, Louis began to return many of the royal lands and towns regained by Casimir to leading magnates. This did not prevent a succession dispute on his death in 1382, and although Louis' younger daughter, Jadwiga (1384–99), was eventually crowned 'king', the union with Hungary was ended. In 1385, she was married off to Jogaila of Lithuania (Władisław II, 1386–1434), who promised in the treaty of Krewo to join his vast empire to the kingdom of Poland and undertook to make war on the Teutonic Knights, which duly followed in 1410.

In Hungary, meanwhile, things went less smoothly. Louis' elder daughter Maria and her husband Sigismund of Luxemburg (1387–1437) had to spend twelve years fighting Charles of Durazzo (Charles I, 1385–6) and his heirs and supporters for the throne. In the resulting chaos, Sigismund was forced to part with over half the royal castles inherited from his father-in-law and a third of royal towns, in order to win support. Following meetings of the diet in 1385 and 1386, the magnates had formed a league of *regnicolae* ('inhabitants of the kingdom'), and assumed royal authority with their own seal and officers; Sigismund was obliged to become a member at his coronation, to swear to uphold custom and to rule with noble advisers. In the event, the league did little to control the king as he set about winning his kingdom, and although he was obliged to reconfirm the Golden Bull in 1397, and was briefly displaced by a noble council in 1401–3, Sigismund secured control and began to claw back royal authority in the manner of his Angevin predecessors. The war of succession had perhaps upset the balance between the crown, the magnates and the rest of the nobles, but less lastingly, perhaps, than an older generation of constitutional historians proposed: Sigismund's confirmation of the Golden Bull, for example, was accompanied by articles that insisted on (and extended) the military obligation of the nobles, and it is clear that he had devoted supporters as well as opponents among the magnates. A more serious turning point for Hungary came at Nicopolis, where its loose hegemony over Serbia, Wallachia and Bosnia was for a time destroyed. From the 1390s, the kingdom began to experience Ottoman raids, and the new pressure from the south was to colour its development in the ensuing century.

In Bohemia, there was no succession crisis, but the reign of Wenceslas IV (king of the Romans 1378–1400, king of Bohemia, 1378–1419) produced what was perhaps the most dramatic collapse of royal power in the region. Like his father, but more aggressively, Wenceslas seems to have sought to extend royal power in Bohemia beyond the royal and ecclesiastical domains and into the rest of the kingdom, which was under the authority of the *zemský soud* (land-court) and its officers. In 1381, the king used his power to appoint provincial justices to create seven new judicial districts in addition to the existing twelve; eight of the nineteen districts, including all the new ones, were headed by officials from the royal towns in a move which was apparently intended to break up the provincial hegem-onies of the magnates; he also seems to have made other appoint-ments in the land-court which increased royal control of its proceedings. Meanwhile, Wenceslas began to exploit the feudal suzerainty that he and his predecessors had painstakingly acquired over many of the Bohemian nobles: lands were seized on default of heirs and farmed out to nobles close to the king; disputes were resolved in the royal courts or the now less independent land-court, and fines and confiscations ensued. Not surprisingly, this produced both feuding and the spread of alliances among the more powerful and established magnates who were less closely linked to the king. A league sprang up under the leadership of Wenceslas' cousin, Jošt, margrave of Moravia, in 1394, capturing the king and forcing him to accept an arbitrated settlement which, in 1396, placed him under the rule of a noble council and restored the nobility to control of the land-court. The king resisted and faced a further league and renewed imprisonment in 1401–3. This time aided by Sigismund of Hungary, the king's brother, the nobles imposed a committee to manage the royal estates and revenues and to remove and replace all those officers found to be unsatisfactory. Although Wenceslas regained power in 1404, he was forced to restore the land-court to its former independence in 1405, curtailing the jurisdiction accorded to the cities at the same time. The king was restricted to his own lands, and the four great officers of the land-court – even the chief justice of the king's own court – were all drawn from the nobles who had leagued against him. Bohemia had rejected integra-tion under royal authority; instead it had opted for a powerful institution which protected the local operation of justice under the influence of the major provincial magnates.

In the Scandinavian monarchies, these trends were still more marked. Valdemar IV of Denmark (1340–75) was able to rebuild the resources of the Danish monarchy following the civil wars of the 1320s and 1330s, regaining parts of the demesne by a mixture of legal proceeding and purchase, the latter made possible by the sale of Estonia, which also helped to pay for the islands of Funen and Sjaelland, where the port city of Copenhagen provided a new capital. Historians differ on whether Valdemar's agreement to assemble prelates and magnates annually in the *Danehof*, in his *landefred* of 1360, represented a check to the king or a sign of his success in drawing the Danish polity around him: he was to regain Skåne that year and Gotland the next one, and he had some success in imposing taxation, but he was facing rebellion from the magnates by the later 1360s – notably over his attempts to prevent the extension of their fortifications and immunities – and a disastrous war with the Hansards and his opponents in 1367–8 led to a humiliating peace in 1370. By 1375, when Valdemar died, all three Nordic kingdoms were in disarray. Magnus Eriksson of Sweden had been driven off the throne in 1363 after a decade of civil war sparked off by an expensive war against Novgorod and by the king's attempts to secure Finland and to contain the spreading immunities of the nobility. The league of nobles who opposed Magnus placed the German prince Albert of Mecklenburg on the throne, but he agreed to accept the rule of a magnate council in 1371, and the bulk of royal castles and lands were in noble hands throughout his reign. In Norway, meanwhile, Håkon VI's long reign was dominated by an unsuccessful war against the Hansards, and was followed by yet another minority in 1380.

The new king of Norway, Olaf (1380–7), was also the titular king of Denmark from 1376, though the real ruler in both realms was his mother, the regent Margaret (d.1412), widow of Håkon VI and daughter of Valdemar IV. Facing resistance based in both Denmark and Sweden, she began to move against Albert of Mecklenburg in alliance with a powerful faction of Swedish magnates, trustees of the lands of Bo Jonsson Grip, the leader of the council and greatest magnate of the realm, who had died in 1386. In three crowded years, Margaret succeeded in maintaining her regency in Denmark (1387) and Norway (1388), while ejecting Albert of Mecklenburg (1389) and securing the right of her young nephew, Eric of Pomerania, to rule in all three countries.[14] The key to Margaret's success in Norway and Denmark may have lain in the negotiations she was conducting with the Hansards on behalf of both countries; in Sweden, it seems to have been the backing of the magnates that was essential. Although Margaret had initially agreed to leave Swedish nobles in possession of royal castles, however, she was able to negotiate – and later to enforce – resumption schemes in both Sweden and Denmark in 1396. While the Union of Kalmar, sealed in 1397, placed the three kingdoms under a single king, it also acknowledged the reality of the situation, which was a high degree of delegation to the regnal council of each kingdom – the *riksråd* in Norway and Sweden, the *rigsråd* in Denmark – and the mortgaging of a lot of royal property and office to local magnates. But this did not mean fragmentation: not only was Margaret able to regain enough assets to reward supporters and create a network of loyalists, but also the magnates of each kingdom seem to have recognised and accepted their common stake in working together for the defence of the interests, as well as the laws and customs, of their respective realms.

Conclusion

What, then, were the main trends and patterns in the political events of the fourteenth century? At one level, this is not an easy question to answer. Almost every political unit experienced significant fluctuations in its power and integrity over the century, and more were to come; to stop the clock in 1400 and make judgements seems inappropriate. But some familiar views can certainly be discarded. This was not simply a period of declining authority, for example: the discussion in the preceding pages reveals many examples of successful and powerful rulers, most of them projecting authority in ways beyond the reach of their predecessors. There were periods of chaos in most regions, certainly, but there were also periods of order, and the warfare of the century brought both political problems and political dividends to its participants. It is often said that the fourteenth century witnessed the beginning of the end for universal authorities – the Papacy increasingly preoccupied with the affairs of France and Italy; the Empire increasingly confined to the German lands; and such

---

[14] He was king of Norway, 1389–1442; king of Denmark and Sweden, 1396–1439; d.1459.

organs of international co-operation as the crusades in serious decline –
but that seems questionable. Papal concentration on France and Italy
goes back to the eleventh century: it had not prevented the construction of a universal jurisdiction and an international network, and
the persisting significance of these was demonstrated in the Schism of
1378–1417 and also in the period of the Councils which followed. It is
true that few Emperors invaded Italy after the 1320s (though Charles
IV was crowned there in 1355, and Rupert of the Palatinate crossed
the Alps in 1401–2), and it is certainly significant that Charles and
Wenceslas seemed more interested in selling their rights in the country than in exercising them, but the ideal of a universal secular prince
certainly persisted, its jurisdictional claims could not easily be ignored,
and, in the following century, Emperors Sigismund (1411–37) and
Maximilian (1493–1519) went on to exercise power and influence
over many parts of Europe, Italy among them. As for the crusades and
other international institutions, it is hard to feel that these had lost
their vigour: the *reisen* in Prussia and Lithuania attracted large numbers
of knights from across Europe between the 1330s and the 1400s; the
Christian army at Nicopolis in 1396 contained French and
Burgundians besides more local men; the *Reconquista* continued to
exert a power over the Spanish imagination, and its completion by
Ferdinand of Aragon (1479–1516) and Isabella of Castile (1474–1504)
was prefigured in the campaigns of Alfonso XI and then of Ferdinand
of Antequera. In all, the politics of the fourteenth century seem to
provide little evidence for the decline of 'medieval' institutions.

The great wars of the fourteenth century – Anglo-Scottish, Anglo-
French, Franco-Flemish, Angevin-Aragonese, inter-Italian – are
often supposed to have given the fourteenth century its defining
character, but perhaps they were not so very different, in location,
participants, or even character, from the conflicts of the twelfth and
thirteenth centuries. True, these conflicts were connected differently –
cross-Channel alliances complicated the wars in Britain, France and
the Low Countries; the Ghibelline network in northern Italy became
relatively detached from affairs in Sicily and Germany; Provençaux
and Aragonese replaced Germans in Sicily – but the Spanish were
hardly a new factor in Tyrrhenian politics, and warfare had long been
endemic in the region and was sustained as much, or more, by the
indigenous population as by outsiders. The wars in France, Flanders
and Scotland are often seen in nationalistic terms, and that too is
presented as a novelty of the fourteenth century. Certainly, they

involved appeals to ethnic and regnal solidarities, and were increasingly financed through national taxation and manned by subjects recruited on the principle of defending the realm, but it is as well to remember that Scots and French fought alongside Edward I and Edward III, and Flemings for the kings of France, that these wars were fought over the rights of princes and other powers, and that they merged into a host of other conflicts, from civil wars to localised feuding. It has been said that the menace of the mercenary companies, which affected Italy and southern France, and more briefly Spain, added a new ingredient to fourteenth-century war, but this should not be overdone either – the companies lent the incessant feuding of these areas a more organised character, and they elicited a more organised response from surrounding rulers, but they were not the inaugurators of a new age of violence.

To perceive the real dynamics of fourteenth-century politics we need to look beyond the headline news of the major wars and schisms to consider common forms and patterns. We also need to remember that the participants, even the drivers, in fourteenth-century politics, were not only the handful of kings, prelates and great lords whose names appear in the foregoing pages, but hundreds and thousands of other powers, both large collectivities, such as municipal authorities, churches, estates and popular movements, and the smaller groups that made them up – guilds, families, retinues, *hermandades*, the representatives of parish, vill or *vicinanza*, and so on. One common feature in the political activities of all these different groups and powers was the articulation and defence of rights – rights bestowed by higher authorities, rights implicit in history, rights prescribed or imagined in learned books. This way of thinking and operating is not peculiar to the fourteenth century, but it does seem particularly widespread in that period, and it also seems clear that the rights to which appeal could be made were sufficiently diverse as to enable the contestation of any authority or power structure. In many ways, as we have seen, the lead in defining rights and challenging custom was taken by the highest authorities – popes, kings and emperors – but other powers were not far behind, either in articulating the same rights for themselves, or in developing counter-rights, as subjects, satellites or neighbours. Frequently, they did both: there was no real contradiction for a lord, a city, a church, even a king, acquiring both the paraphernalia of autonomy – rights to tax and judge, to levy men and appoint officers – and the rights and benefits that went with acceptance of a higher authority, such as justice in someone else's court, backing in one's disputes, dialogue with others over the common good of a larger space. Circumstances would dictate whether it made more sense to play the subject or play the ruler, and in an era of copious conflict, fluctuating power and multiple allegiances, these circumstances were highly changeable. They were also made changeable by another factor: the development of new items of political and constitutional kit, which empowered both rulers and subjects in new ways, even if that empowerment was often temporary or full of unexpected consequences. Here, then, are some of the causes of the volatile politics of the century, and we shall explore them further in the other sections of this chapter, but the point to note here is that the articulation and defence of right, by varying collectivities, in rapidly changing circumstances, was one clear pattern in fourteenth-century politics.

Were there trends as well as patterns? The general political situation, as we have described it here, suggests not: almost any political unit could expect to rise and fall, to grow and shrink, to move through phases of relative harmony or relative disharmony. Because this period was literate and legalistic, as well as characterised by fluctuation, it was difficult for any power to destroy another – the historic rights of vanquished territories or authorities left residues which, in changing conditions, heirs, peoples, even conquerors might choose to revive and exploit. This, in turn, meant that no new order was ever completely established: the successes and the failures of fourteenth-century regimes were always qualified, and were frequently short-lived. So it was that such relics of the old order as papal sanction for the election of the emperor proved to be still important in the first decade of the fifteenth century, Rhens and the Schism notwithstanding; and so it was also that the triumphant France of Charles V had shrunk to a third of its size forty years after his death, its fiscal system in ruins and its chief princes contemplating independence or accommodation with the English king at Paris. Even so, there are signs of a trajectory in fourteenth-century politics, as well as fluidity and repetition. Many places experienced greater co-ordination: Sweden, Poland, Lithuania, Muscovy, Aragon-Catalonia would be obvious examples, areas where meaningful kingdoms developed or advanced, even if there remained scope for disagreement over their boundaries, or over the range and distribution of rights and powers within each realm. Perhaps one could make a similar case for some of the notorious war zones of the continent: northern and central Italy, southern France, southern Germany, Ireland. These areas were as full of conflict in the last decades of the fourteenth century as they had been at the beginning, but they now featured some larger units whose power and coherence enjoyed some stability – the lordships of the Visconti and Este, for example; the duchy of Bourbon, the lieutenancy and the estates of Languedoc; the Swiss Confederation; and the earldoms of Ormond, Desmond and Kildare. By the end of the century, it was becoming implausible for towns to expect to maintain their independence without the resources of a sizeable territory, and even the largest and richest urban centres were beginning to assert control over the communes and lordships around them. What this shows is that the media of territorial power – taxes, troop-raising, jurisdiction – were becoming substantial and workable enough not only to compete with the concentrations of capital and population in towns, but even to surpass them. A hundred years earlier, only a handful of regimes could exercise sufficient leverage to control large towns – and only a handful probably wanted to; there were larger numbers of more-or-less independent communes, and they controlled less space around themselves. By 1400, relatively few towns approached real independence, and they were increasingly the centres of territorial states; other cities certainly retained room for manoeuvre – through estates organisations, by bargaining over taxation, by playing off contending overlords – but they were coming to be more obviously subjects than rulers. Even in the supposedly chaotic fourteenth century, then, there were some moves towards the simplification of the political map.

And there was one other important development: a process of constitutional thickening. By the end of the fourteenth century, most areas had developed a more complex and extensive range of political assumptions and repertoires, based on recognised rules, principles and institutions. These were not always firmly fixed, though they were less unfixed than they had been a hundred years earlier, but they did begin to channel political activity down a more limited number of routes, and, as these became familiar, they made politics a more civil affair. Because this is, in a sense, the theme of the whole book, this development will be illustrated and discussed in more detail in the sections that follow.

THE GROWTH OF GOVERNMENT

Now that we have established what was happening, we need to consider what was going on: that is, what norms and patterns – and, in particular, what causes – shaped and guided the bewildering course of events. In the previous chapter, two main things were emphasised. One was the incomplete and contested nature of the political forms that emerged from the thirteenth century. Instead of thinking of Europe as a series of hard-edged juridical kingdoms in which the imperial core of warring *Kleinstaaten* was exceptional, we need to recognise the presence of overlapping and potentially contending political structures in every part of the continent: the legacy of the 'high middle ages' was not order, but complexity and volatility. The other main theme, in the last chapter and the present one, has been to stress the continuity of European political development between the twelfth and thirteenth centuries, on the one hand, and the fourteenth and fifteenth, on the other. Not only did the 'age of growth' have mixed results, it also went on beyond 1300. This perspective will be developed in the pages that follow, as we look at the ways in which one particular feature of the thirteenth century – the growth of government – continued into the fourteenth century and determined some of the most distinctive features of its political life.

If 'decline' is a rather questionable concept among historians, perhaps 'growth' should be too. It is not clear that an organic metaphor can adequately capture the various processes and phenomena which we are about to explore, but as long as we do not equate 'growth' with 'order', and provided we recognise that it requires explanation, and is not simply an autogenous process, it may not be an inappropriate term to use. In this period, there was a continuing increase in the range, the volume and often the penetration of the media of authority. In the fourteenth century, most of the regimes of Europe became more governmental in nature, or they tried to. They set out to strengthen their jurisdiction and multiplied their legislation; they maintained or extended rights to military service and created more effective armies; they contrived new taxes and raised them on a greater and more consistent scale; they entered into more frequent and systematic dialogue with representative groups of subjects; they overhauled the cadres of officers both central and local, keeping better records and creating more complex bureaucracies and more solid networks of authority connecting centre and locality. They also maintained and developed less formal media of power – they kept grander, more complex and more self-conscious courts, and they developed new mechanisms for sealing the allegiance of other power-holders in their spheres of interest. Emperors, kings, princes and lords, municipalities and other communes, leagues and churches all engaged in this activity and deployed many of the same methods; but they varied greatly, of course, in the resources they already possessed in 1300 and in the contexts in which they operated. The growth of government was correspondingly full of common trends and local variations, both of which will need to be taken into account.

Justice and law

Jurisdiction is often regarded as the most basic ingredient in government, and the dramatic advances in this sphere during the twelfth and thirteenth centuries make it the natural place to start. Those jurisdictions that were already relatively organised and powerful when the fourteenth century began made further assertions, and they did so partly in response to consumer pressure, as litigants flocked to the most relevant and effective courts. Although the Papacy was already 'universal ordinary' in the twelfth century, for instance, the huge expansion in its direct role in appointments meant a significant increase in judicial business, for which a special court – the *Rota* – was created in the 1330s. Similarly, the great pastoral programme of the thirteenth century meant ever-increasing calls on the Pope's spiritual jurisdiction, and another office, the penitentiary, was developed to deal with the flood of requests, from lay people of all classes, for the various kinds of dispensation and absolution that the Pope reserved to himself. Through a mixture of assertion and responsiveness to demand, therefore, papal jurisdiction expanded in both reach and volume, and more of the inhabitants of the Church, lay and clerical, came into contact with the Curia and its growing band of officers.

A similar pattern of increased provision in dialogue with increased demand is apparent in secular kingdoms. In England, for example, royal justice grew in both quantity and effectiveness during the fourteenth century. Commissions of oyer and terminer were created to deal with specific outbreaks of violence (from *c.*1305), while commissions of the peace covered the more permanent supervision of the counties (fixed in 1394, after sixty years of experiment). Serious crimes were increasingly called into the centre to be dealt with by the court of King's Bench, while the major central court for civil litigation, Common Pleas, became much more accessible, and was increasingly used by litigants of all social classes. In the second half of the century, equity courts, based in the king's council and chancery, evolved to dispense royal justice in areas where law was ineffective or absent. New writs were created for the enforcement of debts and contracts, and new legislation on prices and labour arrangements – common across Europe in the wake of the Black Death, but perhaps rarely implemented outside England – was entrusted to specially appointed judges. By these means and others, royal justice was extended further into areas which previously had been managed by lords, either directly, through manors, or indirectly, through the 'popular' courts of hundred and county. While many of these commissions involved independent landowners alongside royal justices, and were once seen as a surrender of royal judicial prerogatives, it is now recognised that they represent a considerable expansion of the crown's judicial estate, in which some sharing of power was inevitable and in which the balance of judicial authority remained with the king and his officers. By 1400, the English people were much more exposed to royal justice than they had been at the beginning of the century, and the system of justice itself was more elaborately organised and centrally managed.

The English judicial system was a marvel of its time, and probably represents the most that could be achieved on a regnal scale, but the instincts of the French crown, especially before the war, were not so very different. The Paris *Parlement* had already emerged as an authoritative high court in the thirteenth century, and one which many notables were keen to use in order to secure legal titles guaranteed by royal jurisdiction. In the first half of the fourteenth century, its personnel expanded significantly, and so did its attempts both to revise local customs, by insisting on conformity with royal practice and royal legislation, and to attract appeals – even from the domains of friendly princes and lords, such as the dukes of Burgundy. Since the crown was also legislating more extensively and on a regnal scale, reining in ecclesiastical justice and attempting to assert control over a wider range of *cas royaux*,[15] there was a possibility that, as in England, more localised jurisdictions would be destroyed or subordinated. It was this danger that the Leagues of 1314–15, with their restatement of local customs and local justice, were aiming to evade, and the enormous size of France, together with the fact that so much ordinary jurisdiction was in private hands, meant that the realities of the situation were on their side. But, despite the concessions of 1315–16, the crown's

---

[15] Cases which only the king's courts were competent to judge.

lawyers and agents maintained their pressure, and jurisdictional tensions remained high, helping to provoke the various movements for
local liberty that fed into the Hundred Years War. After about 1350,
royal judicial aggression was much reduced: *lettres de rémission* (pardons) and *lettres de justice*, in response to individual petitions, became
the dominant ways in which the crown maintained its juridical
hegemony, though Charles V was able to restore much of the traditional authority of those *bailliages* whose powers had been absorbed by
local princes. While these relaxations in part reflect the difficult
circumstances of Philip VI, John II and Charles VI, they may also
point to a positive acceptance of compromise as a more effective way
of building support for the crown within France.

A combination of royal legislation, privately or locally controlled
jurisdiction, and central interventions based on petitions for redress
was, in fact, a common model for justice in the kingdoms of the
period. In Castile, for instance, although the ordinance of Alcalá
(1348) stipulated a royal law-code throughout the realm, the king
left the jurisdictions of municipalities, lords and royal officers essentially alone, dispensing justice mainly in response to individual appeals
and petitions. While the *Cortes* tended to demand that the king be
guided in his decisions by experts in local *fueros*, the tendency was for
these judgements, which gradually created a body of royal case law, to
be shaped instead by *letrados* (jurists) with a training in Roman law. In
1371, Henry II made the royal *audiencia* into a permanent high court,
which formalised this development, though he and later kings continued to dispense justice, mercy and grace in person, and, rather
contrarily, he also conceded full jurisdiction, including freedom from
appeals, to many leading lords. It is interesting to note that, at around
the same time, a similar court of audience emerged in Hungary (1377),
perhaps with rather similar powers. The Angevin kings of Hungary
had been more assertive than their Castilian counterparts, withdrawing property cases from semi-independent local courts to the central
court and exempting many of the more substantial nobles from
county jurisdiction, but this provoked reaction from the lesser nobility
in 1351, and the county courts (*sedriae*), which they dominated,
remained the major agency of justice in the kingdom. In the crown
of Aragon, meanwhile, the king possessed his own court, located in
his chancery, but in at least two of his kingdoms practical judicial
supremacy lay with his subjects. In Aragon proper, the *Justicia*
remained the defender of the kingdom's jurisdiction against royal

interference, even after the royal victory over the *Unión* in 1348, while in Catalonia, supreme jurisdiction over the principality was conceded to the *diputació* of the *Corts* in 1359. Here, then, the judicial situation was somewhat clarified and regularised, as it was everywhere else, but in ways that excluded, rather than enabled, royal control; Peter IV's plans to translate and impose the Castilian *Siete Partidas* remained a fantasy. The Emperor was arguably in a stronger position, at least in his German lands. He had surrendered appellate jurisdiction over the subjects of princes as early as the 1230s, but nonetheless continued to offer a high court for the resolution of disputes among the vassals of the Empire: besides the *Hofgericht*, which travelled with the court, Rudolf I founded a new *Landgericht* at Rottweil in the Hohenstaufen heartland of Swabia (he may also have encouraged the production of the *Schwabenspiegel*, *c.*1275, which purported to declare imperial law), while the Luxemburg emperors encouraged the use of the Vehmic courts of Westphalia, Wenceslas extending their influence across the kingdom in 1385. These resorts were arbitrative, rather than final, but that was in keeping with German tradition and did not prevent them from being authoritative sources of jurisdiction associated with the king (indeed, the introduction of Roman law inquisitorial forms in the royal court of the mid-fourteenth century had the counterproductive effect of encouraging suitors to resort to feud instead of justice). All the Emperors of the period policed their feudal and municipal rights with great care, even if they were also willing to trade these, and improvements to the royal chancery under Charles IV enabled them to handle a growing volume of petitions, especially from their German subjects. In fourteenth-century Germany, then, as in other kingdoms, royal justice remained a factor – generally a growing factor – in a complex net of local jurisdictions.

In the looser kingdoms of central, eastern and northern Europe, royal judicial authority was a stage more confined and contested, existing alongside large ecclesiastical immunities and more-or-less independent land-courts that typically dispensed local custom under local control. Commonly, these land-courts were arranged on a regional basis, though in relatively centralised Bohemia, the *zemský soud* covered all freehold land in the kingdom; meanwhile, most towns formed judicial enclaves, sometimes in networks under the appellate jurisdiction of cities in Germany, though under royal protection in Bohemia, and increasingly in Poland. The relative weakness of royal jurisdiction in these countries did not forestall the production of regnal law-codes, even so. Sometimes these were royal assertions, like *Majestas Carolina* in Bohemia (1355) or the Austrian *Privilegium Maius* (1358), or the Egidian Constitutions, imposed on the Papal States by Cardinal Albornoz in 1357. Sometimes they were statements of custom, imposed from below, such as the Swedish *Eriksgata* (coronation charter, 1335) or the law of the Bavarian *Land* (1346). Sometimes, no doubt, they were a combination of the two, as in the imperial Golden Bull of 1356, the 'Landlaw' of Sweden published *c.*1350, or the law-codes created by Casimir III for Greater and Lesser Poland in 1347. Underneath these grand carapaces, however, the actions of both kings and associations of magnates or prelates were often a lot cruder, and concerned with such fundamentals of power as control of castles – nominally a royal prerogative – or the terms on which noble land was held. The fact that in 1352, and on several other occasions, Polish lords sought guarantees against imprisonment and confiscation without trial suggests that Casimir III, for example, used his *starostas* in a pretty arbitrary fashion, though his law-codes show that he also sought to extend royal justice in formal ways, and he attempted to limit ecclesiastical jurisdiction to purely clerical matters in 1359. A number of other fourteenth-century kings sought to extend their jurisdiction by trying to induce noble subjects to convert allodial land into fiefs or other types of property which could be regarded as held of the king and capable of escheating to him in default of heirs. In Bohemia, this produced a vigorous reaction once the king tried to exercise the feudal rights he had acquired, though the Angevins of Hungary were more successful in exploiting the quasi-feudal interest in land they acquired from *novae donationes* (charters granted from the 1320s, enabling landowners to convey all their holdings to a single heir, in return for accepting royal overlordship). But feudalism, of course, worked both ways, and there was a marked tendency for royal castles and offices and their appurtenant rights and lands to become like fiefs in the fourteenth century, as did the *len* of Norway, the *län* of Sweden, the *honores* granted by Louis and Sigismund of Hungary, or indeed the sheriffdoms and regalities bestowed on nobles by the kings of Scotland. This development contributed to the increasingly federal, even fragmented, nature of these kingdoms as, over time, their rulers often found it harder to exercise rights of revocation or escheat. Even so, the interest of lesser nobles (in Hungary, especially, but also in Bohemia and Poland) or peasants (in Sweden and Norway) in protecting their stake in local jurisdiction from the dominance of magnates provided a means for the king to play at least a supervisory role over local jurisdiction. It is no surprise that the kingdoms of eastern, northern and central Europe developed federal or 'constitutional' regimes, in which the king protected local liberties under the supervision of councils and diets, but it is equally no surprise that they remained kingdoms rather than assemblages of independent fiefdoms.

The activities of kings were matched, sometimes very directly, by those of other powers. The more co-ordinated principalities, for instance, were not far behind their royal overlords (some, as we have seen, were even in advance). One reason why the king of France was able to entertain appeals from the courts of the dukes of Brittany, Gascony and Burgundy was that during the thirteenth century they had developed their own appeal courts, from which the overlord's court was the natural next resort. On the other hand, these internal judicial hierarchies greatly strengthened the dukes' hold over their territories, and provided them with the means to resist, or restrict, royal appeals, an issue on which the duke of Brittany secured agreement as early as 1231. In less feudalised areas, the construction of princely jurisdiction was a more complex and protracted affair: in the German lands, for example, it typically involved some melding of jurisdictions – feudal lordship (which German princes were extending as busily as their Italian counterparts), the criminal jurisdiction derived from the local *Landfriede*, county court or *Zentgericht*, with (in many areas) the customary jurisdiction of the *Land* – as well as a mixture of assertion and negotiation with neighbouring jurisdictions, such as those of towns and of other lords. The landgraves of Hesse, for instance, whose power in the region initially derived from their estates and their tenure of the county court of Maden, held from the archbishops of Mainz, were able to buy up and conquer the rights and powers of other neighbouring lords, and finally to establish a new high court for their *mouvance* (area of influence) at their town of Kassel by the end of the thirteenth century. Their capacity to impose binding arbitration in the area made this court a popular resort for the aristocracy, but the landgraves sought to strengthen its claims by obtaining, in 1355, an imperial privilege *de non evocando*, forbidding their subjects from transferring cases from it into the *Oberhöfe* (high courts) of neighbouring imperial cities (notably Frankfurt). The municipal courts of Kassel itself were subjected to the landgrave's jurisdiction in 1384, following a rebellion of the city in league with local knights, who also wished to resist the prince's judicial and fiscal assertions. In these ways, a plausible territorial jurisdiction was hammered out from a mixture of informal power and acquired right.

Similar moves were being made across Germany (at least seven other princes acquired privileges over their subjects' appeals between 1315 and 1378) and in Italy, where Milan and Ferrara provide well-known examples. In Castile, meanwhile, princely state-making advanced partly independently and partly in dialogue with royal power. While the main jurisdictions in Castile were the municipalities, which extended far over the countryside, lords were able to secure fairly full jurisdiction over their rural estates by *c.*1300, and they generally sought to buy up neighbouring jurisdictions, urban and rural, in order to create continuous territorial blocs. What really transformed the position of the leading nobles, however, was the grant of powerful royal offices with their own jurisdiction, such as the *adelantado*, and – notably from Henry II's reign onwards – of towns, juridical rights and other portions of the *realengo* (royal patrimony). Henry's *mercedes* (graces), as they are known, were the acts of a usurper, forced to license other usurpations that had occurred during the preceding civil wars, and eager to win friends powerful enough to preserve order and maintain his tenure of the throne. But they also recognised the impossibility of governing the vast expanse of Castile without recourse to the local power structures that had developed there and that typically linked urban and rural networks. While Castilian historiography posits, and deplores, a rise of noble power in the period of this book, it might be better understood as the growth of regional power, as royal, municipal and noble governments simultaneously expanded. Just as in England, where princes and nobles typically co-operated with the extension of royal justice, seeking to influence rather than exclude it, this mixture of formal jurisdiction with partly formal, partly informal local power was not inherently disorderly or counterproductive for the crown.

As these German and Spanish examples suggest, it was not just kings and princes who were increasing the reach of their justice: urban jurisdiction also was expanding in the fourteenth century, both externally and internally. Larger and more prestigious towns exerted jurisdictional gravity over their neighbourhoods, not only in Italy, where the takeover of the *contado* had occurred early, but in many other places too. The jurisdiction of Seville, for instance, grew to 12,000 square kilometres (roughly the size of Yorkshire) during its first century in Christian hands, 1248–1348, while, by the end of the century, Berne governed 9,000 square kilometres and Lübeck controlled a third of the duchy of Saxony-Lauenburg, having rights in 240 villages, together with castles and bailiwicks in Holstein and Mecklenburg. These were veritable city states (though Seville's jurisdiction existed by royal permission and Lübeck's relied heavily on buying up mortgages), but a more common situation was for the courts of major cities to exercise power over the surrounding area because litigants wanted to use them, or because they acted as centres of legal learning, or again because they protected privileged merchants and had been prepared to defend those privileges at the point of the sword. This messier situation was very characteristic of the Low Countries and parts of Germany. Networks of towns recognised the authority of *Oberhöfe* located in key centres like Magdeburg and Nuremberg, but for many this authority was purely arbitrative, and there was scope for copious disagreement over the boundaries of municipal authority and its relationship to the jurisdiction of lords, princes, churches and the Empire – indeed, here was the major cause of the great 'town wars' of the 1370s and 1380s. In the more urbanised parts of the Netherlands, meanwhile, towns often expanded their jurisdictions with princely encouragement, their customs and regulations gradually replacing those of the communal and seigneurial countryside. By the middle of the fourteenth century, Bruges, Ypres and especially Ghent had established judicial hegemony over their respective *kwartieren*:[16] in this process, the extension of burgher status to people living outside the city ('outburghers') played an important role, as the city courts took cognisance of all cases concerning such people. In Flanders, the big cities were strong enough to protect their outburghers, at least until later in the century, when first the counts of Flanders and then the dukes of Burgundy began to try to contain urban influence; in Germany, similar devices, pursued by towns like Nuremberg, provoked stern opposition from other court-holders.

Urban jurisdictional growth was an internal matter as well. To a large extent, it was inseparable from other developments in urban government, most notably the growth of fiscal systems, including taxation, but it is worth singling out two particular developments which helped to make municipalities, or communes, more state-like

---

[16] The four administrative districts into which the county of Flanders was divided. The fourth was the rural 'Franc of Bruges'.

and thus more capable of acting independently. One was the increase in the volume of regulation, which was marked throughout the period, and expanded into detailed provision for moral, religious and social behaviour, as well as the more predictable areas of economic and constitutional regulation and the keeping of the peace. The other was the growth in jurisdiction proper, especially significant in Italy. Italian communes had always possessed structures for peacekeeping and dispute settlement, but the former had the quality of leagues and could lack legitimacy, while the latter enjoyed mainly arbitrative authority, though enemies of the commune could always be expelled. The decay of the royal courts of the *regnum italicum* and the juristic conviction that real authority lay with the emperor robbed the communes of jurisdictional integrity, and that, in turn, meant that their claims to authority over the people of their territories remained conditional and variable. From the later thirteenth century, however, the judicial tribunals of Italian communes began to develop inquisitorial functions, and, alongside the emphasis which communal legislation gave to the principles of *utilitas publica*, notions of (public) crime began to displace those of (private) wrong. This was the situation captured in the writings of the leading jurist, Bartolus of Sassoferrato (1314–57), and especially in his influential formulation, *civitas sibi princeps*, which, in Magnus Ryan's interpretation, was aimed more at establishing the internal authority of the civic authorities than their independence from Empire and Papacy.[17] By the later fourteenth century, many communal cities had policing and judicial structures to compare with regimes whose possession of regalian or imperial rights was less contestable. Among cities, one example was Venice, whose Byzantine traditions, ducal structure and physical apartness had encouraged a more confident development of judicial resorts. In that city, the *Signori di Notte*, or police force, had acquired extensive policing functions in the 1270s and 1280s, and unique powers of termination over felonies in 1321, anticipating English JPs by several decades. In Nuremberg, meanwhile, high jurisdiction was granted by the emperor to the council as early as 1320, and by the fifteenth century the city fathers were referring to the inhabitants of the city and its district by the bald but revealing term of *Untertanen* (subjects). Towns could clearly enjoy the same judicial solidity as other kinds of polity.

---

[17] M. Ryan, 'Bartolus of Sassoferrato and Free Cities', *Transactions of the Royal Historical Society*, 6th series, 10 (2000), 65–89, p. 79.

Drawing this discussion of jurisdiction together, we can detect two contrary trends or patterns which were formative for the period. One is the construction of relatively robust and essentially independent jurisdictions, developed against, or in spite of, or even in the absence of, other authorities, whether superior or inferior. The other is the acceptance of some measure of judicial hierarchy, even if that acceptance is accompanied by informal measures to preserve as much independence or influence for different layers as possible. The former pattern points towards conflict, the latter towards compromise and the articulation of more complex polities, arranged on a more-or-less federal basis. Quite commonly, of course, both patterns were present: effective jurisdictions commanded allegiance, but because they sought to compel obedience, they could also provoke their subjects to look elsewhere – upwards to a putative overlord, or towards the formation of local, or even national, solidarities against such an overlord when his justice was felt to be oppressive or alien. As this suggests, the development of justice was, to a substantial extent, consumer-driven. While the holders of jurisdiction characteristically sought to defend what they had, and even to expand their provision, much of the pace was set by the demands of consumers, for new actions or more effective processes, for better legislation or better order; they used the courts that brought them the results they wanted, and resorted to other devices, such as feud or arbitration, when no jurisdiction could give them what they sought.

It is striking that, while institutions of justice grew everywhere in the fourteenth century, and the mass of the people were correspondingly engaged in their values and procedures, there was relatively little lasting resolution of the conflicts between competing agencies. Just as the power of individual rulers, leagues, princes and towns fluctuated, so did the justice they dispensed. While it may be possible to say that the jurisdictional dominance of the king of England, for example, was affirmed in the course of the century, we would have to recognise that the successful management of that dominance depended on delicate compromises with local power structures (compromises that were not managed successfully by two of England's four fourteenth-century kings). Meanwhile, if it seems that the German kingdom, or Bohemia, or Aragon-Catalonia, was edging towards a more settled kind of 'dualism', in which representatives protected the privileges of regions or estates from the intrusions of the king, then it is clear that this destiny had not been revealed to such rulers as Charles IV or

Peter IV, who sought to rule their kingdoms in a more integrated manner, and it will become clear that much remained to be contested in the fifteenth century. More common, and more persuasive, perhaps, as a general model for fourteenth-century jurisdictional growth, is the pattern of development in Castile or France, Italy or Hungary, in which the jurisdictional authority and independence of kings, princes, lords and towns varied over time, the relationship between them hard to characterise and the final balance hard to predict. Even so, a notable feature of almost all European regions is that the juridical framework of the kingdom remained significant, especially outside the more robust principalities and the small number of free cities. One reason for this we have just mentioned: the kingdom could be a means of protecting everyone's liberties as well as a medium of royal power. Another reason is that, outside the heartlands of papal power, churchmen increasingly looked to regnal institutions to protect ecclesiastical jurisdiction: after the Bonifacian crisis, the Papacy was generally unwilling to get involved in disputes over clerical justice unless its own interests were directly involved. A third reason is that one way of holding the balance among smaller powers – lesser nobles, towns, peasants, magnates – was to uphold royal courts, whether these were ancient and open to local influence or central and able to provide appellate or arbitrative jurisdiction. This state of affairs did not straightforwardly deliver power to the kings of Europe, or even to other representatives of the realm, but it does help to explain the survival of kingdoms and the later emergence of regnal polities. As we shall see, the contemporary public debate over justice, and the beginnings of what might be called constitutional literature, helped to advance the regnal paradigm and to disguise the flexibility of jurisdictional development (also to condition that flexibility), but the ambivalences of this development need to be emphasised if the turbulent politics of the period are to be properly understood.

Before we leave the discussion of justice, it would be helpful to make some concluding remarks about the role of legislation, which, as many of the examples above indicate, was growing in both volume and range. Legislation is often confused with jurisdiction, but it is important to remember that laws were much easier to issue than to enforce, and the impression of orderly authority created by statutes was often wildly at variance with reality. It is not uncommon, even now, for history books to tell the reader that Louis IX abolished private war in France with an *ordonnance* of 1258, whereas, in fact, this kind of warfare not only continued well into the later fifteenth century, but was even condoned in most subsequent royal legislation. Much, perhaps most, legislation represented the hopes, rather than the expectations, of rulers and governments. It was only one element in even the secular law of each region, much of which was customary, albeit that customs were increasingly written and recorded. A lot of what passed for enforcement, meanwhile, was a kind of deal-making in which parties in breach of royal statutes could compound financially, or by other settlements, for their disobedience. Even so, this is not to say that the legislation of the fourteenth century was meaningless. For one thing, the statutes of this period were stored in the centres of government with much greater care than in the previous century. They were consulted, and not uncommonly modified and re-enacted, on a greater scale than before, and thus clearly contributed to the cultures of lawmaking and governmental thinking that had developed around rulers. They also articulated an idea of the *regnum*, which, because they were published and circulated, must have affected the political imagination of inhabitants. This did not prevent legislative competition or resistance from other powers: the *ordonnances* of the king of France, for instance, might pretend authority over the whole kingdom, but they typically faced vetting, and even suppression, by the legal apparatus of the leading princes; and some royal legislation, even in the fourteenth century, was only intended to apply to the *domaine*. But lawmaking always generated a sense of the dimensions of the political community, and the most energetic lawmakers – often (in the secular sphere) emperors and kings, but also the Electors of the Empire, together with some princes and many towns – surely helped to propagate notions of sovereignty attached to their own jurisdictions.

A further sign that legislation had some political meaning is the evident desire for it from subjects, or at least from their representatives. One aim of the representative estates that developed in much of thirteenth- and fourteenth-century Europe was to seek legislation as a means of reform and resolution, and this in turn, of course, meant the affirmation of the ruling power. Representation will be discussed more fully below, but it is worth noting here that the laws petitioned from the rulers of this period helped to delineate their realms and formally to subordinate the other powers within them, even if they also restrained the prince himself. Many of these laws dealt with the problems of society, but even when they were directed at the king

and his officers, they had a unifying effect. The coronation oaths/
charters of Edward II, Christopher II or Eric of Pomerania (in
Sweden) or Władisław of Lithuania-Poland; Philip IV's reforming
ordonnance of 1303 or the charters granted by his son to the Leagues;
the reissue of the Golden Bull demanded from Louis of Hungary, the
statutes imposed on Edward III in 1340–1, or on Charles V as
dauphin in 1355–8; even the depositions of Adolf of Nassau and
Wenceslas, or of Edward II and Richard II: all these public *acta* had
potentially beneficial effects for the monarchies concerned because
they helped to incorporate the kingdom and to emphasise its priority
over other political units. Many of these acts also erected the king as
ultimate guarantor of rights, or asserted the importance of royal
authority and/or articulated an image of good royal rule which
could be exploited by succeeding rulers – after all, anti-royal legislation was no more enforceable than any other kind. These sorts of
confrontation were not the only source of public law, moreover. As
political regimes became more complex, so the need to regulate their
affairs became apparent to rulers, as well as subjects. The fourteenth
century consequently saw a lot of legislation clarifying rules for royal
succession or election – as in France in 1374, or in Sweden in 1335
and 1347, in the Empire in 1356 and in Württemberg in 1361. There
were laws setting rules to be followed in royal minorities (as in France
in 1374 and England in 1377); laws on the inalienability and indivi-
sibility of the ruler's domain (as in France in 1361 and in the
Palatinate of the Rhine in 1357); laws declaring the relationship
between regions and the ruler (such as those in France in 1315–16,
in Austria in 1358–9 and in Aragon-Catalonia in 1319 and 1343); and
sequences of laws declaring the composition of the government in all
the major towns and cities of the period. Political communities were
thus more regulated at every level, and, as laws came to deal in detail
with the political and administrative questions raised by the more
complicated governments of the period, they deepened conceptions
of the political order within society.

Military service

Justice was one fundamental duty of the medieval ruler; defence
was another, and fourteenth-century achievements in this area
were just as striking. Once again, there were continuities from the
twelfth and thirteenth centuries, though, in this area, the pattern of

development involved fewer conflicts. Almost everywhere in high-medieval Europe, a knightly aristocracy had developed. In the kingdoms of the north and east, and also in Castile, it was a privileged caste, enjoying, by the end of the thirteenth century, various kinds of freedom from taxation or jurisdiction, in return for a rather loose (sometimes notional) obligation to serve in royal armies. In the Carolingian core of Europe, and its outliers in eastern Spain, Britain and Sicily, feudal ties imposed more direct service obligations on the aristocracy, especially in kingdoms like France and England, where these ties were closely policed. Together with the prince's personal troops, these aristocrats formed the core of royal armies, but, in many places, a wider, more communal service obligation had survived, or been recreated. This was true in England, for example, where the king was able to levy non-noble troops on a county-by-county basis and where he asserted a more general right to the service of landowners on the grounds of their membership of the community of the realm. It was also true in Catalonia from 1285, and in France, where royal charters establishing communes usually stipulated service quotas, while a royal right to the service of all fief-holders (the *semonce des nobles*) and all other men (the *arrière-ban*) was developed under Philip IV. And it was true in Italy, where communes elicited cavalry service from their knightly members and imposed infantry service on the men of the *contadi*. The great exception to these developments was the kingdom of Germany, where the Emperors tacitly abandoned most of their rights to the service of imperial vassals and *ministeriales* in the course of the thirteenth century: even here, however, obligations continued to exist at the princely level, while the kings used more informal means to attract military allies and followers. By the end of the thirteenth century, then, a number of rulers had established the sense that service was owed to them not only by their direct dependants, but also by a wider cross-section of society. That did not mean that they could simply invoke such service – both feudatories and others were adept at negotiating down their obligations – but it gave them a powerful bargaining counter: indeed, in many areas, a juridically defensible right. By negotiating taxes in lieu of service, and using the money to buy mercenaries, or to pay natives for more flexible service, or to fund new contractual devices such as indentures of retainer, *fiefs-rentes*, *tierras* and *acostamientos*, which bound the holder to serve in return for a fee, rulers were able to raise more effective, and often more sizeable, armies.

In many respects, these trends were continued into the fourteenth century. The notion of the ruler's war as an obligation on all his subjects was emphasised almost everywhere, typically drawing strength from Romano-canonical notions of *utilitas publica*, *necessitas* and the 'tutorial' position of the ruler. On the whole, this obligation was converted into a duty to pay taxes, but it could also be used to stimulate recruitment, and Edward III, in the 1340s, and Alfonso XI, in 1348, both made firm efforts to oblige landholders of a certain income to serve in person, while Casimir III attempted to insist that the privileges of the Polish nobility depended on their active service, and successive kings of Hungary refused to abide by the clause of the Golden Bull that made noble service voluntary. In practice, of course, lords and knights could not be made to serve, and they frequently denied their support to militarily feeble kings, but the pressure maintained by rulers in this area must have helped in the negotiation of taxes and may have reinforced the historic associations between nobility and martial activity. The thirty or forty chivalrous orders founded by kings and princes from the 1320s onwards affirmed this message and, when effective, could help to secure a loyal elite of powerful captains, devoted to the ruler and willing to fight in his wars.

Meanwhile, the use of pay and contracts proliferated, assisted by the legal, bureaucratic and fiscal developments characteristic of the period. Between the 1340s and the 1370s, most armies came to be levied on this basis, with very positive results for recruitment, command and flexibility of deployment (it helped that military technique favoured highly mobile, mounted, smaller armies in this period, with relatively limited need for large numbers of infantry). Where royal governments had begun by entering contracts with individual knights, the tendency from mid-century was to contract instead with a smaller number of magnates who would handle the recruitment of the bulk of the troops themselves. This capitalised on the way in which princes and lords already possessed retinues and networks on their own account. It also interlocked neatly with the developments in taxation, where squabbles over the right to tax in jurisdictionally contested areas could be sidestepped by allowing local noblemen an important share in the revenues in return for their assembly of quotas of troops. This reciprocity was established most clearly, perhaps, in Castile, where lords holding clusters of *tierras* were typically granted *juros* (bonds), or even collection rights, on local taxes. In France, the compromise was more shadowy, the crown never quite explaining why it was parting with proportions of taxes to which it supposedly enjoyed a sovereign right, and princes tending to emphasise their independent claims to summon the nobles of their terrains. In England, the king's right to tax was established by other means, but the recycling of tax incomes to the landed classes must have made the system more palatable to the political elite. The fact that, in all of these kingdoms, the nobles were increasingly exempt from taxes on the grounds of military service, made these arrangements neater still and provided an additional inducement for landowners to take up arms.[18]

These contract armies did not only draw on magnate power, they also tended to affirm it. Paid contractual service gave lords a means to induce service from their own recalcitrant underlings and a way of defining their lordships through networks of followers and through the acquisition of rights, resources and offices in their localities. Magnates granted the *honores* established by the Angevins of Hungary, for instance, received clusters of castles and counties, together with the rents and royal tax revenues from their associated territories. In return, they were expected to serve when summoned, accompanied by a retinue, or *banderia*, sustained by these resources. The king got an effective and easily assembled army, but the *honores* could help to establish princely lordships, in a kingdom where noble domains and networks had normally been counterbalanced by a county-based power structure. Like the English wardenships of the Northern Marches, *honores* were formally revocable, but it could be difficult for weaker kings to revoke them. For Italian lords, meanwhile, communally funded military contracts were a helpful means of reinvigorating decadent lordships, and it is clear that some of the disputes between communes, and even the larger struggles between Guelfs and Ghibellines, were both exploited and fomented by military magnates, who saw in these conflicts a means of attracting wealth and service, and thus expanding their domains (indeed, this was a significant element in the 'rise of the *signori*' that altered the political landscape of the peninsula from the later thirteenth century). Wealthy and war-torn Italy had become such a major market for military service by the 1320s, however, that it was pulling in large numbers of foreign mercenaries, as well as native lords. As we have seen, the governmental devices of the period enabled the 'Great

---

[18] The English nobility and gentry were not tax-exempt, but the tax burden on them was trifling in relation to their incomes.

Companies' that grew up from this time to maintain themselves as permanent bodies, servicing, but also, no doubt, stimulating, the copious conflicts of the period.

These developments have been regarded not as an instance of governmental growth, but as a sign of the decadence and violence of the century. The enlistment of magnates as tax-funded recruiters of armies over which they could expect to exercise a fair measure of informal control has sometimes been seen as a return to feudalism, a retrograde step from the claims of thirteenth-century kings to national service. The rampaging of the Companies through Italy and southern France, especially in the 1360s and 1370s, has been presented as an instance of how completely royal or imperial control had degenerated into anarchy amid the strains of warfare. But there are other ways of looking at these developments. The contract was a device available to all powers at once; it was not the special prerogative of kings, and may even have been more highly developed at lower social levels first. If fourteenth-century modes of troop-raising assisted lordships, they also assisted kingships, and in both cases they reflected governmental developments – in fiscality and in ties of service – which strengthened these structures. The temporary nature of royal contracts, and the tendency of rulers to assert control over the armies gathered under them also ensured that the regnal element in these structures remained important: the French crown, for instance, engaged in a see-saw struggle with the princes over whether men at arms should serve under their lords or under royal officers, and the reassertion of the royal position, even in the dark days of 1351, helped to lay the foundation for the royal *compagnies* of the 1440s. Only rarely did the semi-permanent armies of the period operate freely from the governments that funded them, and then they did so in regions where no settled distribution of authority had normally existed and where their depredations merged into a general culture of feuding, ransom and extortion (a culture which flourished equally, without the attentions of the Companies, in places such as Germany, Ireland, the Scottish Highlands and the Basque Country). Even then, the Companies depended on the large sums which only state fiscality could produce to retain their integrity, and the Papacy and the king of France were consequently able to put them to use for their mutual benefit in the later 1360s.[19] This link with royal fiscality, more marked

[19] Against Peter the Cruel and his English allies: see above, p. 185.

still among the magnate captains who supplied the bulk of Europe's armed forces, was, in the longer run, an important means by which regnal and princely structures were brought into harmony. Even in the short term, it acted as a brake on the free disposal by lords of what were widely understood to be royal, public or communal resources. Lordships and other military networks may have been essential in the conduct of fourteenth-century wars, but they deployed a power shared with superiors; they were components in larger wholes, and that is not without significance.

Taxation

The paid armies which enabled rulers to break through the restraints of customary service, and so to fight longer and more flexible wars, were very expensive. This was surely the main reason for the development of large-scale taxation from the later thirteenth century onwards. It was not the only reason, however. The increasing commercialisation of society, as both trade and the money supply grew in the twelfth and thirteenth centuries, made the fiscalisation of relations of authority a natural development, and one which occurred at every social level, as all sorts of obligations of service and payments in kind were commuted into money. It is also clear that the taxes of our period were made possible by the new governmental claims and techniques that had developed. One important basis of universal fiscal obligation was the notion of universal military obligation, which, as we have seen, a number of rulers had succeeded in imposing by 1300. This notion shaded into others culled from thirteenth-century developments in Roman and canon law: the doctrine of 'necessity', for instance, which imposed obligations on the *communitas*; that of *cessante causa*..., which helped to make French royal taxation palatable by promising that it would end when its cause was removed; the principle of *quod omnes tangit*..., and the related legal theory of procuration and representation, which, in many countries, facilitated the raising of taxes through consent-bearing assemblies. Other governmental enhancements, such as improved literacy, record-keeping and accounting, the establishment of trained officers and the habit of summoning representatives for advice or information, were also ingredients in the emergence of taxation. And so, finally, was the precocious achievement of the Papacy in establishing an effective framework of ecclesiastical taxation for the crusade: since the revenues of this framework were, by the later thirteenth century, generally granted to lay rulers, and especially to the kings of France, Castile, England, Aragon and Angevin Sicily, it accustomed these kings to the benefits of taxation and gave them ideas about how to achieve it. This, as we have seen, was a major reason for the bitter conflict between the kings of France and England and Boniface VIII; defeat in that conflict was what led the Papacy to rely on a more indirect system of taxing clerical appointments to fund its activities.

Taxation of the laity took different forms in different places – here a land tax or a tax on movables, there a tax on sales or the movement of goods, a commuted obligation or a forced loan – and each form had its own particular implications, but the main pattern of development is common to most of western Europe. The first substantial and repeated levies were made in the later thirteenth century – the 1290s in England and France, the 1260s and 1270s in Sicily and Castile, earlier still in Italian communes and other municipalities. In the kingdoms, these taxes were often imposed at punishing rates which were not to be matched for some time, and they quickly aroused resistance, some of which – like the revolt of the Sicilian Vespers (1282), the risings of the Spanish *hermandades* (1282 onwards) or the English demonstrations of 1297–1301 – was explosive. In France, where things were calmer, it was nonetheless necessary for Philip IV to trade privileges for his levies on a localised basis, and after 1304 he abandoned the new taxes for a decade. In the first half of the fourteenth century, however, the kings of England, France, Sicily and Naples, together with the Papacy, the count of Flanders and many northern Italian regimes, found that they continued to need money for war, and set about trying to find more durable means of raising it. A volatile period of experimentation ensued, in which rulers attempted, with intermittent success, to extract large sums, while groups of subjects set out to limit or reject the obligations being placed upon them, arguing variously that tax was only due in periods of actual war; or that it could be substituted by personal service; or that it did not apply to the fiefs or manors of the nobility; or that it applied only in the regions directly affected; or that it was uncustomary and should not be levied at all. While these protests often succeeded in thwarting or reducing taxation, they did not prevent governments from incurring big financial obligations, which they struggled to meet by whatever means remained available to them. The corollary of tax resistance, therefore, was not the scaling down of rulers' commitments, but the contraction of huge loans (typically from Italian merchants) and the use of more arbitrary devices levelled at softer targets, such as the seizure of commercial goods, the sale of justice and levying of fines, the suppression of the Templars, the harrying of Jews and foreign merchants and, above all, the debasement of the coinage. The struggles of this formative period produced many political confrontations – most notably, perhaps, the attacks on Jews in southern France in 1320–1, the Flemish revolt of 1323–8 and the convulsions that accompanied the collapse of the overstretched banks of Florence in the early 1340s – but they also began to habituate the political communities of much of Europe to taxation, and to open the way to compromises that could make it more acceptable.

So it was that, between about the 1340s and the 1370s, the rulers of England, France, Castile, Venice, Genoa and Florence and the Papacy all succeeded in establishing workable fiscal regimes, involving high but realistic levels of taxation and a reasonable degree of political consensus. Other governments, including the kingdom of Aragon, the Hanseatic League and many of the *Kleinstaaten* of the Low Countries, Germany and Italy, also began to raise taxation, on an increasing, though comparatively modest scale. There were perhaps three main ways in which these levies were made acceptable to subjects and satellites. The earliest and most common method was to share both the raising and the proceeds of taxation with princes, lords and/or towns. As in the case of military service, this avoided potentially difficult questions of jurisdiction and sidestepped local resistance, enabling kings to raise large sums, while lesser authorities benefited from new means to define their authority and to exploit the resources of their underlings. This was already a technique adopted by the Papacy – kings, as we have seen, had been its major beneficiaries – and it was adopted, with varying patterns and degrees of formality by many other rulers. In Castile, for example, *servicios* began to be granted to nobles from the 1370s, and noble possession of *juros* on these and other taxes became very widespread in the fifteenth century. The main royal tax of the fourteenth and fifteenth centuries, the *alcabala*, remained under crown control for longer, but, being a sales tax, it was farmed to networks of financiers, often Jews, who – royal agents as they were – were also influential figures in the municipalities. It was surely this extensive involvement of Castilian noble and urban elites in the royal tax system that enabled both its expansion in the 1370s and 1380s, and its normalisation, as the *alcabala* became collectable without the consent of the *Cortes* around 1400. In France, meanwhile, a number of pre-1350 taxes were either formally shared with local lords or imposed only on those who were not tenants of nobles. When the tax burden increased, after the mid-1350s, nobles and their tenants were formally liable, but the forms of taxation in much of the kingdom were indirect – *aides* and *gabelles* – and thus fell more heavily on peasants and town-dwellers anyway. Towns were bought off by the concession of jurisdictional privileges, the repayment of urban loans and/or grants to improve local defences; the communes of the Midi were rewarded less directly, but just as substantially, by the redirection of tax proceeds to the paying-off of local *routiers*. The great feudatories were able to raise taxes in parallel with those of the king, while the holders of royal *apanages*, lieutenancies and other offices were allowed to collect wages for themselves and their men from their own districts, either directly, or through pensions charged on these revenues. Between *c.*1355 and *c.*1390, this balanced approach meant huge increases in royal incomes – from around 40 tonnes of silver a year *c.*1340 to more than 70 tonnes in Charles V's reign[20] – but its maintenance depended on effective kingship, and the era of Charles VI's madness, beginning in 1392, saw first the direct and unsupervised absorption of tax revenues by the leading princes, and latterly the collapse of the system outside the more co-ordinated principalities, as taxpayers withdrew co-operation. These outcomes, parallelled in fifteenth-century Castile, and discussed in the next chapter, reveal that however much these shared systems depended on local muscle, they also rested on the legitimising force of an overall ruler, convincingly concerned for the common welfare. It is striking that fiscal discipline held up much more strongly in the southern parts of royal France, where a mixture of royal lieutenants, local unions and patriotic rebels like the *Tuchins* maintained the links between taxation and the defence of the region right up to the beginnings of Valois recovery in the 1420s.

A second way of obtaining consent to taxation was to raise it through negotiation with representative assemblies of powerful subjects. This might be attempted on a regnal level, as it had been in many kingdoms and principalities during the first half of the fourteenth

---

[20] Figures from W. M. Ormrod, 'The West European Monarchies in the Later Middle Ages', in R. Bonney, ed., *Economic Systems and State Finance* (Oxford, 1995), ch. 5, pp. 144, 148.

century, or on a more localised basis, or sometimes both – as in France, where the great meetings of the estates of Languedoïl and Languedoc in the 1340s and 1350s were usually followed by provincial, or even *bailliage*, assemblies. Assemblies offered the chance for formal, legally binding consent; they also, more flexibly, enabled the presentation of grievances and demands for redress in return for grants. Even so, they were not straightforwardly effective: they could only bind the tax-payers if adequate juridical structures existed to compel payment (or at least to threaten sanctions), or if they truly represented the social and political structures through which populations could be persuaded or corralled. In England, the national assembly, Parliament, was rela-tively successful as a means of raising taxation for both these reasons: first, the jurisdictional unity of England both permitted and invited a regnal assembly, and the judicial supremacy of the king enabled him to make its consent legally binding on the communities; second, Parliament contained the effective leaders of urban and rural society and provided them with an effective forum for the negotiation of their collective and individual interests. Although there were periods of difficulty and adjustment, notably in 1340–1 and during the 1370s and 1380s, the king and the representatives were generally able to com-promise over adequate levels of funding for the defence of the realm, including the more extensive royal interests in France and Scotland. In areas with less consolidated jurisdiction, however, regnal assemblies could be a lot less effective. In the much larger kingdom of France, for example, national assemblies were recognised to have an advisory function, and were thus able to devise schemes for a new tax structure and for the reform of royal government between 1345 and 1358, but (despite the efforts of Philip V) they had no procuratorial powers, and it was only at a provincial or municipal level that binding negotiations could take place. In the crown of Aragon, the king could derive benefit from assembling the *Cortes/Corts* of his three mainland king-doms simultaneously – this helped to underline the case for a national necessity – but, in practice, his agents had to negotiate with each assembly separately, and not only that, but with each part – or *brazo* – of each assembly: the nobles, the prelates and the *brazo real* (royal part), typically dominated by the towns. Generally speaking, the smaller the political unit, the more effective its assembly: in towns and in many provinces, the balance of authority and benefit, both common and individual, was such as to permit taxation. Strikingly, this was true even in Germany, where the structure of jurisdiction and the framework of political values did so much to make every unit independent of every other unit. Intermittently, but increasingly, from the later thirteenth century onwards – as early as 1249 in Wrocław – a number of *Länder* were able to raise extraordinary taxation through meetings of estates. The resulting *Landsteuer* were very far from being at the disposal of princes – specially appointed treasurers typically administered the resulting monies (a practice also common in the crown of Aragon, and occasionally demanded, even employed, in Castile, France and England), and lengthy *Bedeverträge* (tax treaties) set out terms for exemptions and for the prevention of future levies – but they do show that fourteenth-century communities could be constituted and mobilised through assemblies of the right kind.

A third means by which higher levels of taxation were made politically acceptable was through the use of loans. Once again, these were an attractive and potentially effective device because they created an interest in tax revenues on the part of potential opponents: in order to see a return on their investments, lenders would want the ruler's levies to work. All rulers raised loans, whether direct levies of liquid cash from merchants and prelates, or through financial systems in which payment followed after service: Europe's paid armies were often, in effect, a forced loan, even a tax, on the magnate captains. After the Tuscan bank crashes of the 1340s, creditors were largely drawn from each ruler's own political community, and while that could produce all sorts of tensions in periods of fiscal strain, it also helped to bind wealthy inhabitants to maintaining government revenue. In some fourteenth-century polities, loans became the major vehicle of public finance. This was the case with the cities of Venice and Florence, which had begun to move away from traditional urban taxes like the *estimo* (property tax) in the thirteenth century, because they were politically difficult to adjust and ill-suited to capturing the wealth of mercantile communities. Indirect taxes made more sense, and the cities levied them, but they did so mainly to pay interest on debts which, by the early decades of the fourteenth century had become effectively unrepayable. In the mid-fourteenth century, this situation was acknowledged – in Florence, in 1343–5, with the establishment of the *Monte*, in Venice and Genoa rather earlier: shares in the public debt became tradeable, repayments were abandoned, interest rates were paid at a level sufficient to ensure continuing investment, and further taxation took the form of compulsory loans or changes to the interest rate. While the cost of servicing these debts was often massive – costing Venice 250,000 ducats a year in the 1380s, more than ten times the level of the 1340s – they were an advanced and socially effective way of finding the revenue for these rich, but high-spending cities. Other towns moved in the same direction, notably several of the larger cities of Germany, but cruder systems based on bonds and debts, employed by monarchs, could also be effective. One of the most important financial media at the disposal of the fourteenth-century Emperors, for instance, was the pledge, or *Pfand*, a device by which imperial rights and resources were pawned to princes, lords and towns in return for service, support or cash. Between 1300 and 1500, upwards of a thousand units of right, revenue or land were pledged by the Emperors, 70 per cent of them in the fourteenth century, and half of that in the reign of Charles IV. In return for substantial sums of money and (notably) the support of the Electors in accepting his son's succession, Charles granted away the bulk of the remaining royal fisc, on terms which made redemption very unlikely. In a sense, therefore, this was a once-and-for-all manoeuvre, obliging future Emperors to rely almost wholly on the resources of their *Erblände* and such public or feudal rights which they could still enforce. But before we condemn Charles for apparent fiscal irresponsibility, we should recognise how difficult it was to exploit imperial assets by any other means and how much short-term influence he was able to gain by this strategy. It is also important to realise that *Pfandschaft* was a powerful medium in the hands of fifteenth-century princes, who seem to have been able to exploit pledges of the rights and revenues that were plausibly at their disposal to construct territorial authorities, staffed by networks of supporters and vassals.

The upshot of these various methods was a much higher level of taxation across much of western Europe in the second half of the fourteenth century. The political consequences were very considerable. First of all, taxes significantly increased the military agency of the major fiscal powers, and they did so not only on a short-term basis, but over the medium to long term, because political and social groups became habituated to them, especially within the Church and in countries like Castile, France, Italy and the Low Countries, where they were levied more or less continuously. Even where taxation had to be negotiated, as in England or the crown of Aragon, it could still enable extensive and long-term military operations, provided these were in keeping with the interests represented in assemblies. It is often argued that the English were withdrawing from war in the last decades of the fourteenth century, but Henry V's expensive and dazzling conquests in the 1410s make this argument hard to sustain, and it seems likely that rulers less politically compromised than John of Gaunt and Richard II could have assembled fiscal and military support for campaigns in France, Scotland, Ireland and the Low Countries on an even grander scale than they actually managed in the 1370s, 1380s and 1390s. But we have seen that taxation was not only a political asset for the kings and princes of Europe, it also strengthened various structures lower down: the lords and towns who shared in the system; the networks of officers who did the collecting; the assemblies involved in granting; and last, but very significant, the groups who bore the brunt of payments. It is clear, then, that taxation strengthened the fabric of governments, including subsidiary ones, but, because of its wide and comparatively standardised incidence, and perhaps because of its association with ideas of collective necessity, defence or wellbeing, it also helped to shape and develop political communities. Taxation mobilised more of the population than military service, and, because it was comparatively centralised, in both theory and practice, it did much to co-ordinate that population and bring it into a more direct relationship with the ruler and his representatives. It stimulated feeling and debate at both local and national levels. In France, for example, the crown's necessary respect for the customary taxes of the various regions – the *fouages* of the South, the *équivalents* of Normandy and so on – and its willingness to negotiate with the notables of individual towns and provinces helped to reinforce regional solidarities and thus to assist the tendency of the kingdom to break up into principalities and *pays*. On the other hand, the readiness with which large parts of the kingdom paid heavily for John II's ransom, the sense of the Tuchins that they were defending the realm, and the claims of the participants in the Jacquerie of 1358 that, in attacking the nobility of northern France, they were punishing the traitors responsible for French defeat and advancing the reformist cause of Charles of Navarre and the estates, all suggest that taxation raised national issues and enlisted ordinary people behind them.

Equally, it is clear that different kinds of taxes prompted different kinds of public political reaction. The sharing of non-consensual taxation with noblemen, as in France, does seem to have produced particular hostility to the nobles when wars went badly (and, in a rather similar way, the evident appeal of financed debt to the *ottimati* (elites) of Italian towns meant that popular movements called for a return to the *estimo*, or other property-based taxes). Papal taxation of appointments, meanwhile, avoided conflict with lay rulers, who were usually able to tax regnal churches through papal tenths or ecclesiastical assemblies, and it was more palatable to the Church than the schemes for universal taxation devised in 1225 and 1311, but it looked perilously close to simony and thus became a favourite target of clerical reformers. Farmed sales taxes created popular hostility towards the farmers, who were rightly assumed to be gaining all kinds of political benefits at the taxpayers' expense. When war and debasement increased the impact of these taxes, and when the tax-farmers were an identifiable religious or ethnic group, as in the Spain of the 1370s and 1380s, the results could be bloody: these were the essential causes of the anti-Jewish pogroms of 1391. In kingdoms where taxes were consensual and publicly negotiated, meanwhile, dissatisfaction was funnelled towards the central government itself, with representatives seeking tighter controls over spending (as in Catalonia, where the upshot of Peter IV's taxation was the takeover of public finance by a permanent *diputació* of the *Corts*), and popular rebels seeking the heads of the traitors around the king (as in the English Rising of 1381). In these ways, the roughly similar trajectory of taxation across the states of the West produced divergent results – results, indeed, which helped to differentiate polities from one another.

It will be clear from the above that fourteenth-century taxation was much more a phenomenon of the West and the Italian peninsula than elsewhere in Europe. We need briefly to consider what was happening instead in the kingdoms of the North and East. Here, within a common picture of limited taxation, there are significant differences between Scotland, Scandinavia and Poland on the one hand, and Bohemia and Hungary on the other. The kings of Denmark, Sweden and Norway had established an entitlement to the military service of most of their subjects, which, by the thirteenth century, was the basis of a commutation tax (the *leding*, *laeding* or *ledung*, respectively); using the castle-based *len/län* that developed over the thirteenth century, they also attempted sporadic general taxation at roughly the same time as in the West – from the 1230s and 1240s in Denmark and from the 1310s in Sweden. The essentially feudal nature of these castle-lordships, however, combined with pressure for ecclesiastical and noble immunity, tax resistance and chaos in Denmark, plus the relative freedom of the Swedish magnates and a tendency to pledge the *len/län* to German lords, meant that by the mid-fourteenth century, taxation was limited and mainly in the hands of nobles. While rulers like Valdemar IV, and later Queen Margaret and her nephew Eric of Pomerania, were sometimes able to resume control of the *len* and revive taxation for a time, their efforts provoked strong opposition, and the kings of Scandinavia, like those of Scotland, were thus generally dependent on their own landed resources and whatever levies on trade they could manage to impose. A similar situation obtained in Poland, where magnates and prelates were mostly exempt from the basic land tax (*poradlne*), and the kings were expected to fund themselves and their wars from what was left of it, together with their domain incomes and such regalities as coinage rights and tolls; a brief, and dramatic, increase in the rate and incidence of the *poradlne* under Casimir III provoked resistance and was firmly reversed in the Koszyce statute of 1374. In these kingdoms, then, taxation remained counter-cultural: kings were generally prevented from collecting it by nobles and peasants alike, and the resistance of the latter – typically enabled by strong provincial and communal structures – meant that lordly taxation was limited too. This was also the position in Bohemia and Hungary, but there the situation was transformed by the kings' success in retaining and exploiting their rights over precious-metal mines. Although the Angevin kings of Hungary created a new market tax, the traditional farms of regalities, the exploitation of papal taxation, and, above all, the revenue from the gold mines at Kremnica, seem to have been the basis of royal incomes – even the drive to regain lost crown lands (parallelled in Casimir III's Poland and in the feudal experiments of the Luxemburg kings of Bohemia) seems to have been more about jurisdiction and political control than about revenue. So it was that, across these vast areas of eastern and northern Europe, as also in the kingdom of Germany, centralised taxation did not develop in the fourteenth century. Although that did not at all mean that central power was impossible – in Hungary, especially, that was very far from being the case – it did mean that the kinds of political integration and communal mobilisation characteristic of the West were much less marked at this stage.

Representation

Taxation was perhaps the major reason for the more systematic con-sultation of subjects in representative assemblies that is so characteristic of the later thirteenth and fourteenth centuries. But it was not the only reason, and not necessarily the first in point of time: a series of factors encouraged rulers and regimes to consult more widely and frequently, even regularly, in this period. Rulers had always consulted their servants, of course; communes rested on recurrent assemblies of their members; and the various corporations of the Church possessed a long and developing tradition of counsel and representation. What was different about this period was that, in many places, some forms of consultation acquired an institutional and representative character, involving greater formality and the participation of those who were less directly connected to the ruling power. The making and recording of laws was one early reason for this kind of assembly, as we have seen. The making of difficult decisions, such as whether or not to go to war, or how to settle the succession, was another; and shading into it was the trial of the highest crimes (though this might be reserved to the peers of the ruler's court). More generally, assemblies were desirable for the acquisition of consent and legitimation: the acclamation of a new ruler of uncertain title (as in the annual diets of Angevin Hungary in 1309–20 or the assembly at Paris in 1328); public support for a controversial stand (as in the national assemblies of laymen and prelates backing Philip IV against Boniface VIII in 1302–3, or the assembly of imperial Electors that produced the declaration of Rhens in 1338, or the meetings of the estates of Skåne to declare their loyalty to the king of Sweden in the 1330s and 1340s); or the gathering of the community of the realm in circumstances of crisis (such as the failure of the Scottish succession in 1286–92, the troubles in France in the wake of Crécy and Poitiers, the risings of the *Uniones* in the crown of Aragon in 1347–8 or the troubles in Hungary after 1382). In other words, assemblies were becoming more common because governments were trying to do more, and they were becoming larger and more representative because the reach of government extended more widely and deeply. The changing legal and political climate also threw up new problems and demanded that old ones be settled in new – typically more communitarian – ways: universal taxation and potentially enforceable legislation were more or less novelties in later thirteenth-century Europe; succession crises, of course, were not, but succession rules had typically become more complicated and confining, and these crises unquestionably affected more of the population by the fourteenth century than they had in the tenth and eleventh.

Although some representative assemblies with multiple roles date back to the late twelfth century – most notably in León-Castile, and a little later in Aragon-Catalonia – it was in the last decades of the thirteenth century and the first decades of the fourteenth that they first became common on a regional or regnal scale: from the 1270s in England and Hungary; the 1280s in Sicily and Brandenburg and other eastern German *Länder*; the 1290s in Scotland and Flanders; and the 1300s in France and its regions. At about the same time, as we have seen, many towns adjusted their governments to incorporate a wider cross-section of the inhabitants.[21] Although some of these assemblies lost vigour in the course of the fourteenth century – notably in Sicily, or in Hungary, where the diet met only twice between 1320 and 1385 – the tendency was for them to meet more frequently, and to become more institutionalised, gathering records, procedural rules, a comparatively fixed membership and a recognised place in the political and governmental life of the polity. This was particularly a consequence of periods of high taxation, which produced more-or-less annual assemblies of the English Parliament in the 1340s, 1350s, 1370s and 1380s, or of the several *Cortes* of Aragon-Catalonia in the 1350s and 1360s, or of the *Cortes* of Castile between 1295 and 1312 or in the 1370s and 1380s, and even of the Estates General of Languedöil in the 1340s and 1350s. In these cases and others, frequent assembly meant innovations in procedure – such as the development of the committee system and the emergence of a speaker to represent the English commons in 1376 – and the devising of schemes for improved financial management which representatives sought to impose in return for grants of taxation. The efficacy of these schemes depended very greatly on the extent to which the assembly concerned truly controlled royal access to money. Even where it did, as in England, compromise with the crown was necessary, and this meant that restrictions on royal control were usually short-lived (though the Catalan *diputació* did become the pre-eminent fiscal agency in the crown of Aragon from the 1360s). Where assemblies did not control taxation, as in France or, from the 1390s increasingly, Castile, councils and restraints imposed by representatives were easily evaded. Certainly, the capacity to tax without formal consultation at a national level was an important reason for what Peter Lewis called 'the failure of the French medieval estates', but (as Lewis noted) more localised

[21] Above, pp. 111ff.

consultation remained essential, and even national estates retained their legitimising function, continuing to meet into the 1360s and in the early 1380s and later enabling Charles VII to rebuild the tax system in the 1420s and 1430s.[22] Meanwhile, we should note that it was not only taxation that could require frequent assemblies: it was the need to co-ordinate war and to exert control over the distant *Kontore*, for example, that provoked the first diets of the Hansa in 1356 and 1358; while the more frequent assembly of the estates of Upper and Lower Bavaria in the 1390s, and of Austria around 1400, related to a mixture of internal and external pressures, including the threat of partition facing the princedoms on which these *Länder* centred. As these last examples suggest, the impetus for assemblies could come from below as much as from above. It was to oppose Gaston de Fébus' sale of their county that the estates of Béarn formed an *union* in 1391, for instance, and their regular meetings over the next few years enabled them to supervise the succession and the rule of the new count. In a similar way, the estates of Brabant, which met more than 1,600 times between 1356 and 1430, established their dominance of affairs during the long wars between the 'duke' Joan (1356–1406) and her sisters, who had married the counts of Flanders and Guelders: the wealth and sophistication of the cities, and the armed force which they and the lords could mobilise meant that their representatives held the ring in the defence of the duchy and in negotiations with neighbouring powers.

The varying forms of representative assemblies reflected the power structures, jurisdictional and social, of the areas being represented. The French model of intermittent national assemblies (themselves divided into two large blocs by language and territory), backed by more frequent local negotiations with individual towns and provincial or princely estates, captures the loosely federal structure of the kingdom perfectly; the ever-changing pattern of representation, with estates more important at some times than others, both locally and nationally, reflects the contested nature of this loose federation. On the other hand, the fact that the representative assembly of Flanders was, for a long time, known as the *drie steden* (three cities) accurately indicates the location of real power and wealth in the county, and the pre-occupation of this body, which met very frequently, with questions of

---

[22] P. S. Lewis, 'The Failure of the French Medieval Estates', *Past and Present*, 23 (Nov. 1962), 3–24.

trade and jurisdiction reminds us that princes and their taxes were by no means the only reason for holding assemblies. Equally, that Denmark, Norway, Sweden and the German kingdom could be represented by small regnal councils of prelates and barons (the Electors, in the German lands) demonstrates how much royal authority had been decentralised by the mid-fourteenth century, and how light the burden of that authority was: provincial assemblies could be vigorous in protecting custom and challenging taxation; but only rarely, and in rebellion, did that bring them into contact with the crown. Similarly, there was little need for representative institutions in the low-tax kingdoms of east-central Europe, but local assemblies of lesser landowners are apparent in Poland by the 1380s, and these formed the basis for negotiations over tax and other matters by the turn of the century, while the occasional meetings of magnates and others for the transaction of important business – such as the charters agreed in Poland in 1374 and 1386, or the diets that met in Hungary in the crisis years of the 1380s and 1390s – laid down precedents for more regular consultation in the future. Finally, that the English Parliament lumped together the rural landowners of the shires with urban leaders as representatives of the 'commons' shows the comprehensiveness of royal jurisdiction in that country; that the lords were also summoned, even though their role in granting taxation was minimal, demonstrates that, even in England, there were subjects whose status and power demanded special treatment. The tendency for continental assemblies to be organised on the basis of 'estates' – typically nobles, prelates and towns, but sometimes also rural communes – helps us to recognise how little most royal governments had really penetrated ecclesiastical, seigneurial and municipal jurisdictions. Even so, the very fact that regnal assemblies existed in so many kingdoms (in particular) is significant, both for what it reveals about the impact of royal government and for what it suggests about the ways in which authority was imagined.

For representative institutions did not only reflect the power structure, they also helped to constitute it. They helped to convey an idea of the kingdom and of the scope of its territory, so that the exclusion from French estates of representatives of several of the great fiefs – Brittany, Burgundy, Aquitaine and Flanders – as well as smaller and more marginal territories like Béarn and Dauphiné, was almost certainly damaging to the pretensions of French kings to authority over these areas. Equally, the emergence of estates in a number of French *pays* and German *Länder* helped to solidify emerging principalities, linking the offices, networks and estates of the prince with the corporate, if constructed, authority of the other powers of his region. We need to remember that estates were not the only, or even the most effective, structures in the polities they were found in: however frequently they gathered, they competed for allegiance with other networks and structures – courts, retinues, lordships, kin groups – and with the attractions of particularism and the pursuit of individual advantage through side-deals with greater powers. But they certainly canvassed an idea of the polity, and they provided an important means through which the potentially conflicting interests and rights of greater and lesser powers could be brought into alignment. It is very telling that, in 1405, a French commentator thought the reformist duke of Burgundy 'wanted the kingdom to be governed by the three estates as it used to be'.[23] This is a travesty of the modes of fourteenth-century royal government in France, but a potent, and widely representative, account of contemporary expectations.

Administration and office

The expansion of governmental functions across Europe, and the spread of governmental will, tended to mean the multiplication of officers and the development of more elaborate official hierarchies, both central and local. This was a phenomenon affecting power structures of every kind and level, and it is copiously reflected in the political comment, and many of the political confrontations, of the period: the agents and councillors of the king, or pope, or lord or town, were very frequently the targets of fourteenth-century public complaint.

The bureaucratisation of centres of authority in the thirteenth and fourteenth centuries is a well-worn theme of historical analysis, albeit one much more fully developed in a kingly context than in any other, and it had several facets in this period, besides a net increase in personnel. As judicial, secretarial and financial business became more extensive, it required both more space – for the storage of records and for increased interaction with other officers and subjects – and more expert supervision. Law courts were perhaps the first to be fixed and professionalised, but chanceries too became more complex: their

---

[23] Lewis, 'Failure of French Estates', p. 110.

record-keeping increased; they found they needed to use their records more; they began to receive and process ever-increasing numbers of written petitions from subjects, and this in turn led to judicial and/or legislative activity. In many kingdoms, these developments were well underway by the mid-thirteenth century, but there was further growth to come. In France, for example, the number of central officers grew sharply in the first half of the fourteenth century: where four councillors handled the *requêtes du palais* (judicial petitions to the king) in 1314, for instance, twenty-nine did so by 1343; in the same period, the number of councillors in the *Parlement* tripled, and the number of notaries in the chancery almost doubled.[24] In a similar way, the papal Curia roughly doubled in size during the years at Avignon, from around three hundred under Boniface VIII to five or even six hundred by the 1370s. Part of this growth was due to the administrative demands of the system of beneficial taxation on which papal revenues were coming to depend. Other regimes too found that the growth of taxation meant the adaptation of what had once been domanial treasuries and counting offices, to cope with increased flows of income and – in the new era of paid armies – of expenditure. This prompted three waves of exchequer reforms in England, for example, in the 1290s, the 1320s and the 1350s, while the duke of Brittany adapted his *chambre des comptes* for the same reason in the 1360s. The price of introducing a system of forced loans in Florence from the 1320s, meanwhile, was a vastly complex structure of assessment committees, to say nothing of the additional accountants the commune must have required to manage the resulting public debt. A further administrative challenge, evaded by cities and by the Avignon Curia, but faced by most other regimes, was that while the enlarged departments of government increasingly settled down, in fixed and accessible quarters, kings and lords remained relatively mobile. This meant some elaboration of the personal secretarial and financial staff attached to princes; it also meant that other institutions – secretaries, lesser seals – had to be developed to convey instructions to the static parts of the government, and to manage the relationship between the free-wheeling financial and political operations of the itinerant ruler and the bodies that maintained overall supervision of his records, resources and policy.

---

[24] Figures collected by A. Rigaudière, *NCMH* VI, ed. Michael Jones (Cambridge, 2000), p. 35.

Broadly speaking, the wider the reach of the regime in question, the more elaboration was necessary, though the intensity of government was also a factor, so that the governmental machine of the king of England, for example, was probably comparable in size to that of the king of France, and much larger than those of the emperor, the king of Poland or the king of Castile. Some regimes were also more precocious than others: the English crown kept systematic records of its letters and judgements from the first decade of the thirteenth century, for example, with the Aragonese crown doing the same from the 1250s, but the crown of France only began to register royal acts consistently from the first decade of the fourteenth century, and the Angevins of Hungary only from about 1330. Administrative growth in Italian cities seems to have occurred most sharply in the thirteenth century, though this perception may reflect the biases of Italian historiography as much as the reality; and in Siena, for example, it is clear both that the business before the city council and the ruling *Consistoro* continued to grow in the fourteenth century, and that the first four decades of the century were a major period of revision and consolidation in the official structures of the city. The growth of central administration was also influenced by the degree to which territories were integrated, even if, in turn, it also affected that process: the count-kings of Catalonia-Aragon, for instance, were more or less obliged to treat their subject territories as separate units, so that it was not until the 1280s that they possessed a central treasurer for their domains, and only from the reign of James II that the accounts of the three mainland provinces were centrally audited. When substantial taxes began to be collected under Peter IV, meanwhile, they were controlled not by the king but by committees of the three *Corts/Cortes* of his realm: it was thus the *diputació* of Catalonia that proved the focus of administrative development, not the royal treasury. In these respects, the crown of Aragon was more like a principality or lordship, and these too – gradually composed as they were from family lands and public offices – acquired more systematic administration in the later fourteenth century. While the counts of Flanders had a receiver general from the 1290s, a central accounting body by 1328 and chancery registers from 1329–30, for instance, the dukes of Bourbon established a central treasury for their domains only in 1372, and set up a *chambre des comptes* on the same basis in 1374; meanwhile, Count Rupert I of the Palatinate (1329–90) overhauled his chancery after 1375, and established the university of Heidelberg in 1386 to provide himself with educated administrators. The burden of all these examples is that administrative development happened more or less everywhere in the fourteenth century: centres became more complex and the personnel involved in central government expanded.

A corollary of this was the development of councils. In certain respects, these were nothing new: rulers had always taken advice, and communal government, in particular, had always been carried out on a collective basis. During the thirteenth and fourteenth centuries, however, it seems to have become necessary, in many different kinds of regimes, for panels of administrators to meet more or less daily in order to manage the increasingly challenging and extensive activity of government. Much remained informal, especially in monarchies both large and small, but the idea that rulers should have councillors became entrenched in the public imagination, and there was recurrent pressure in the more organised polities for the king's or prince's councillors to be openly named, for their duties to be publicly defined and/or for their personnel to be amended. Often, this pressure was a response to fiscal demands: it seemed to overstretched taxpayers that unless the ruler were advised by noblemen, or other suitable representatives of the estates, he would be more likely to run up debts at his subjects' expense, or to fritter away the resources at his disposal on projects which benefited his friends more than the realm as a whole. These were the concerns of the French estates between 1355 and 1358, for instance, or of English MPs in 1340–1 and 1376–88. Sometimes, criticism of royal councillors was a response to governmental incompetence: rulers who seemed weak or foolish or heavy-handed – like Edward II of England, John I of Castile and several of the counts of Holland – might face demands for more substantial advisers, though fiscal pressure was usually a factor in these cases too. Such demands almost always produced conflict. While kings readily sought out competent administrators, were happy to work with councillors of their own choosing, and were willing to consult great men and other representative figures on an occasional basis, they were reluctant to accept the councils or other supervisors that their subjects were inclined to impose on them. The resulting confrontations will be discussed at more length in the next section, but the point to note here is that conflicts of this kind combined with general administrative development to establish expectations of conciliar governance in almost all kinds of regime by the later decades of the century. This was reflected, for instance, in the arrangements made in the 1370s for royal minorities in England, France and Denmark; in the plans of the cardinals prior to the election of Pope Clement VI in 1352; and in the council set up by the counts of Ferrara as they brought the communal administration under their direct control between the 1360s and 1390s. The growth of central administration was thus full of political and constitutional significance.

It was not only at the centre that offices proliferated. Many fourteenth-century regimes increased the range of local agents under their control, either because the functions of central government had expanded, or as part of the assertion (more rarely, *re*assertion) of central authority in the localities. This kind of expansion was marked even in places where government was already highly developed, such as England. The fourteenth century brought a host of new officers to the kingdom: justices of the peace and justices of labour, customs collectors, officers for coastal defence, wardens of the Northern Marches, lieutenants in Ireland and Calais and expanded staffs for many of the more traditional officers; meanwhile, temporary commissioners – for arraying troops, for inquiries and for justice, for collecting taxes – were used more frequently and extensively than before. In France, where there was a similar expansion in judges-delegate, receiverships, military captaincies and lieutenancies, a new tier of financial officers appeared, in the shape of the *élus*, originally appointed by the estates in the 1340s, but soon subsumed into the royal administration and given general responsibility for extraordinary revenues. In Castile, at the same time, the reforming regime of Alfonso XI replaced the large *concejos* of the cities with new, smaller *regimientos*, accompanied by salaried *alcaldes* and *merinos* to preserve royal jurisdiction. Alfonso also began to appoint the masters of the military orders that dominated the south of his kingdom; he licensed new *hermandades*, with policing functions; and he introduced *corregi-dores* – temporary supervisors, not unlike the *enquêteurs* of France, who could resume control of aberrant municipalities. These last were used more extensively by Henry III and his fifteenth-century successors, possibly in response to the disturbance to urban governments that arose from the pogroms of 1391 and the forced conversions that followed. With these examples, we are moving from the expansion of roles to the assertion of firmer control, something that was also witnessed in the imposition of *starostas* in Poland under Łokietek and Casimir III, or in the *honores* set up by the Angevins in Hungary, or in the nine vicariates, or *podestarie*, established by the Carrara lord over the expanded territory of Padua in the 1370s: in the first two cases, kings were supplanting ancient officers – *wojewodas, voivodes* (palatines) – whose titles had become assimilated to aristocratic estates, and whose authority had become fully independent of the crown; in the third, a prince was appointing magistrates whom subject communes would once have chosen themselves.

Partly as a result of these measures, a number of mid-century kings have been seen as nation-builders or -restorers, more fully and completely in control of their realms than any since the thirteenth century or before. There is much to justify that view. Extensive networks of officers were certainly noticed by contemporaries, and helped to create or reinforce the sense of living in a realm. Many of those created in the fourteenth century – notably the *élus* and the *starostas* – were given authority outside the royal domains, and thus promoted the public and comprehensive authority of the king; it is striking, in this respect, that the king's officers were identified by Philippe de Mézières as a fourth estate in his *Songe du Vieil Pèlerin* (1389), to set alongside the prelates, warriors and labourers of France. The ubiquity of royal officers and their increased range of roles brought the inhabitants of kingdoms more directly and consistently into contact with royal government than ever before, and consequently gave particular emphasis to that layer of jurisdiction. Even so, there are some important qualifications to this familiar account of state formation. First of all, other power-holders besides kings increased their own networks of officers. Many town councils grew larger, and where municipalities expanded their jurisdiction in the countryside, they sent out officers to exercise it, as Metz, for instance, established garrisons throughout its substantial 'country' in 1347, and began to collect hearth taxes from it by the 1390s. Lords too, both secular and ecclesiastical, presided over extensive networks of receivers, stewards and, where they possessed regalities, other judicial, fiscal and military officers. Meanwhile, royal officers were often drawn from local communities, and then their political allegiances were compromised, to say the least. In France, *baillis* were supposed to hold office away from their home territories, but this principle was increasingly ignored as the century went by, and even outsiders usually married into local families and became enmeshed in networks of power and lordship quite distinct from that of the king. Nor was it just older offices that were subject to this absorption into local power structures: the royal *élus* of Beaujolais and Bourbonnais were usually agents of the duke of

Bourbon from the later fourteenth century, for instance; while the *regimientos* of Alfonso XI were made up of just the same dominant families and interests that had composed the old *concejos* – in many ways, the new arrangements helped to protect and solidify the power of Castilian urban oligarchies rather than to strengthen the hand of the king. Royal officers might be resisted when they did not suit the locals – Casimir III was at first obliged to make local chieftains his *starostas* in Greater Poland, and faced a decade of rebellion when he reversed this decision in 1352; one feature of the agreement at Koszyce in 1374 was the suspension of the equivalent office (*justitiarius*) in Little Poland, and the *starosta* of Greater Poland was faced down by a noble league in 1383. Equally, some new-seeming offices were really just royal attempts to license power that already existed in magnate hands, as was the lieutenancy that Peter IV gave to his brother James, count of Urgel, in the north of Catalonia, or, perhaps, the lieutenancy that the dukes of Anjou and Berry enjoyed in the south of France in the last few decades of the century. Quite clearly, then, local officers were not only, and sometimes not at all, the king's men; they were also the holders, or agents, of principalities, lordships and towns. Whenever the crown was in disarray, they were free to act as, or with, local, provincial and even foreign powers; and when the crown was strong, officers would generally be balancing its demands with their own interests and those that dominated their localities. Nonetheless, the development, or redevelopment, of networks of local office typically strengthened the contacts between the kings and the other powers of their realms, and, in a manner similar to the developments in military service, created hybrid powers which were neither purely central nor purely local. They did not consistently increase royal agency within the realm, but they did increase the density of government, and they tended to affirm the identity of the realm and its constituent provinces and districts.

Informal structures

Much of the foregoing deals with the formal and institutional expansion of fourteenth-century regimes, but there were also other ways in which they developed: in the evolution of courts; in the maintenance, often the adaptation, of unofficial ties with satellites and subjects; and in what has been called 'patronage' – the distribution of property, titles and other assets to friends and clients. In all three of these areas, a central difficulty lies in determining what was changing. A lot more evidence for these institutions and activities survives from the later thirteenth century onwards, but even in this period there are lots of gaps, which means that patterns can be hard to discern, and, in any case, we need to remember that what is newly recorded is not necessarily new. Meanwhile, forms and practices which, of their very nature, were personal, flexible and adaptable, are less amenable to comparative analysis than more formulaic structures: courts and households expanded or shrank with changing circumstances; some kings and lords possessed extensive networks – or felt the need to put them down in writing – while others did not; some appear to have made more lavish grants than others, and, again, contingencies seem the central factors in explaining why. Even so, some generalisations are possible. Once again, there are signs of growth and development in these different forms of fourteenth-century political expression, and once again the same broad trends are visible at different political levels.

The growth of central administration in the thirteenth and four-teenth centuries seems to be mirrored by a growth in the size, com-plexity and grandeur of domestic establishments. Size is perhaps the least certain of these, since numbers attached to the households of kings and princes could vary dramatically even within single reigns, and many of the reasons for expansion or contraction are politically insignificant. Even so, it is not meaningless that the household of Edward III of England, for instance, was usually numbered in the 400s, while those of Richard II and Henry IV (1399–1413) were frequently in the 500s or 600s. It seems to have become more impor-tant over the course of the century for rulers to show themselves off in more splendid and well-furnished surroundings, and according to more elaborate protocols – a trend neatly, if controversially, captured by Clement VI (1342–52), builder of the papal palace at Avignon, who remarked that his predecessors 'did not know how to be popes'.[25] While household ordinances exist for several kingdoms from the later thirteenth century, books of courtly procedure begin to appear in the West from the second quarter of the fourteenth century, with some of the earliest examples coming from the western Mediterranean: the *Ordinatio* of the dauphin of Vienne (1336); the

[25] Quoted by G. Holmes, *Europe: Hierarchy and Revolt, 1320–1450* (London, 1975), p. 85.

Leges Palatinae of the king of Majorca (1337); and the *Ordenacions* which Peter IV of Aragon modelled on these in the 1340s. While we cannot be sure that the procedures that works like these prescribed were followed in practice, the fact that such books were being produced and circulated has implications for the ideals which shaped contemporary thinking about power and its settings. Malcolm Vale has proposed that courts became more stratified during the period *c.*1270–*c.*1400, as an upper household of knights and esquires emerged to join the clerks that had traditionally surrounded great rulers, and as the distribution of livery began to differentiate different classes and groups within the royal establishment.[26] Livery also seems to have been distributed to larger numbers of officers and associates as the century went by, and it became more meaningful, bearing the symbolic colours, or even devices, of rulers, lords, towns and parties, as heraldry (and cloth manufacture) increased in sophistication and definition. At the same time, rulers were taking control of their courts and using them more dynamically: the count of Flanders bought back hereditary court offices from his vassals in the 1320s and 1330s, for instance, so that he could grant these posts, and the privileged access they entailed, more freely; the regents of France introduced the principle of *service à terme* in 1387, obliging courtiers to share offices, spending part of the year at court, and part in the country, so that a larger group of notables could experience the royal presence, and the impact of the court could be spread more widely. There is more evidence of court ceremonial from the early decades of the fourteenth century: of jousts and tournaments; of games and disguisings; of elaborate feasts and oath-swearing ceremonies. It is unlikely that any of these activities was entirely new in this period, but we can occasionally measure their frequency: civic jousts began in Ghent in the 1330s, for example, and increased over the century; in Holland, they were most frequent in the 1360s and 1390s. Meanwhile, there were also some courtly innovations in the fourteenth century: the orders of chivalry, which developed from the 1320s, are one example; grand town entries, with accompanying pageants, are another – these began in London and Paris, in 1377 and 1380, respectively.

In all, courts were becoming more striking institutions, helping to distinguish the richer and more prestigious power-holders from the

---

[26] M. Vale, *The Princely Court* (Oxford, 2001), p. 298 and also chs. 2 and 3.3, more generally.

rest. In some areas, this was particularly important. In the view of Gerard Nijsten, for example, the court of the counts of Guelders was the essential means of the princes' power: ruling over disparate and disconnected territories, built up by dynastic fortune, and surrounded and permeated by other jurisdictions, the counts had few other ways of drawing their territories around them; it was only the gravity exerted by their splendid court, and the network of servants and pensioners attached to it, that singled them out from other powers in the region of their estates.[27] This was surely true of other Low Countries princes, many of whom faced competition from powerful towns (we have already seen how the cities of Ghent, Ypres and Bruges were absorbing the jurisdictional structures of the county of Flanders into their own hands in the fourteenth century, for example). Courtly grandeur, courtly networks and the distinctive forum for interaction and networking which only a leading court could provide were all important means by which dukes and counts might maintain the right to co-ordinate and lead their territories: small wonder that the count of Flanders was willing to spend more than 40 per cent of his income on his court and household in a typical year.[28] The same concerns must have been present for other princes and lords: no-one's jurisdiction was so secure that it could not benefit from this kind of resource. But it was also increasingly natural for great lords to cultivate the kinds of magnificence described above, and as court-consciousness deepened and spread across the continent, styles of gracious living were copied from centre to centre, involving the leading powers of Europe in a sort of cultural arms race, and no doubt helping to differentiate the greatest among them. Courts were both national and international places, allowing kings, lords and other regimes to receive foreign visitors in suitable style and enabling the maintenance of relations with friends, allies and neighbours, as well as with those who might be claimed as subjects.

Another way in which the influence of kings and lords was translated into power was through networks of retainers, pensioners, servants and allies. It used to be thought that these were a distinctive, and mainly negative, feature of the later middle ages: that much of the disorder of the period was due to the private armies of retainers, built

[27] G. Nijsten, *In the Shadow of Burgundy. The Court of Guelders in the Late Middle Ages* (Cambridge, 2004).
[28] 1335–6: Vale, *Princely Court*, p. 93.

up by the martial aristocracy in the prodigious wars of the period, and used by them to feud with their peers and to challenge the authority of kings and princes. It is now understood that the retinue or following was a much more universal phenomenon than this approach suggests. As we have seen, it was not restricted to the aristocracy, and, like any other means of power in this period, it was no more a cause of disorder than a means of order: the binding of people in alliance created areas of trust and peace as well as lines of potential conflict. We need to remember that the evidence for retaining, which begins to survive with such profusion in the fourteenth century – indentures of retinue, *lettres d'alliance, condotte* and contracts of *accomandigia*,[29] records of annuities and pensions, references in narrative sources to *bandos*, parties, societies, brotherhoods and leagues, or for that matter to *consorterie, alberghi*, surnames, *linajes* – testifies more to the literateness of the period, its more substantial judicial and financial records and the new sharpness of its social comment, than it does to changed circumstances.

The characteristic networks of the middle ages have been discussed above, and it will already be clear that they merge seamlessly into structures we have already explored – frameworks of vassalage, structures of jurisdiction and office, and so on. But there are, perhaps, some specific inferences to be drawn from the forms of association that were common in the fourteenth century. First of all, historians have drawn distinctions between purely military contracts, which were usually temporary and frequently involved the simple transfer of money for service, and more wide-ranging contracts which tended to involve a longer term of association and a wider range of duties – protection and goodwill, as well as cash and other benefits from one party, often a lord, and domestic, judicial, administrative or other governmental service from the other party. These contracts, which became common from around the middle of the fourteenth century, do have certain implications. For one thing, they imply a need to record what may once have been understood. In part, no doubt, this is just a by-product of literate-mindedness, but it is also a reminder that the relative civility

---

[29] In fourteenth- and fifteenth-century Italy, a *condotta* was a contract specifying military service. An *accomandigia* was similar, but typically specified a wider range of duties on the part of the retainer, often including the exercise of governmental roles. See T. Dean, *Land and Power in Late Medieval Ferrara* (Cambridge, 1988), pp. 167ff., for a valuable discussion.

of later medieval society required greater men to use agreements if they wished to bind lesser men to their service (or equally that lesser men needed contracts to ensure the protection and support of greater ones). These agreements also show that it had remained important for lords, as for more elevated authorities, to exercise power outside their own estates: once again, this was surely a matter of wider social expectation and utility – lords no doubt wished to dominate, but lesser men also sought their backing. Finally, they testify to the growth of government. In areas of very uncertain jurisdiction, contracts like *accomandigia* or German *Pfandschaft* defined the local framework of justice and fiscality, enabling both to flourish by determining who held what rights, over whom and from whom: matters that could otherwise only be settled by feud might now be resolved by written agreement (though feuding certainly continued). To a point, of course, these agreements simply shifted the boundaries of dispute: the fact that the petty lords of Modena and Reggio began to obey the Este, or that the nobles of Franconia maintained the pledged rights of local princes in return for the profits, did not prevent other lords and their followers from contesting these claims, but we should not miss the fact that these arrangements created solidarities and defined the political and legal environment for their participants; they helped therefore to settle and clarify the distribution of power, and sometimes lastingly.

Meanwhile, in areas where jurisdiction was more fixed, generally worded agreements of support and service, such as English indentures of retainer, or French *lettres d'alliance*, provided litigants with reliable means to secure their interests. Support at law, backing for officers, the securing of posts in royal or municipal, as well as seigneurial, establishments: these were the para-governmental services that lords provided to their followers. In doing this, of course, they advanced themselves, but they also, in certain respects, advanced the cause of government more generally, by providing the social power that could enable it to function. Inevitably, there were tensions and conflicts – between contending networks, for instance, or between the demands of government and the interests of influential groups – but there was also a means here by which a highly fragmented and contested distribution of authority could be made to work effectively. Not all later medieval ties were of this relatively defined type, of course. Lords and other rich men gave fees, *fiefs-rentes*, pensions and annuities, in the hope of maintaining good service or attracting goodwill; they bestowed honours – as the Este gave knighthoods to their leading military servants, and other princes sought to attach military men through new orders of chivalry; or they created sinecures in their courts – honorific posts, sealed by livery, which extended the holder's *familia* and associated the great men of the region with his service. No doubt there was a lot more of this kind of activity than we know about: as the examples given above suggest, its fourteenth-century manifestations have been most extensively studied in England, the Low Countries, and one or two Italian signories, but British historians have led the way in unearthing a sizeable number of French examples of feeing and retaining: by the counts of Foix and Armagnac early in the century, for instance, and by the count of Béarn and the dukes of Brittany and Orleans later on. It is likely that similar forms of association existed wherever the pattern of government was sufficiently complicated for people's loyalties to be in question.

Retaining shaded into a third informal means of power for Europe's regimes: the granting of offices, lands and honours – what British historians often call 'patronage'. This has been regarded by historians in rather different ways, depending on whether it was carried out by princes, lords or towns in areas of weak or contested jurisdiction, or whether it was carried out by kings or popes as a means of obtaining support or political services. Broadly speaking, the former practice is seen in positive terms, as a kind of state formation, and we have discussed several examples already in the pages above: cities and lords expanded their influence over the countryside by acquiring, and then granting out on conditional terms, chunks of territory and jurisdiction, sometimes as fiefs, sometimes as offices, sometimes as the right to hold particular courts, or to collect particular taxes, and so on. These were among the means by which the dominions of the Visconti, the Este, the Carrara, the Papacy and the leading German, Savoyard and Piedmontese princes were created; they were an element in the creation of 'territorial states' by German, Flemish and Italian cities. When fourteenth-century kings engaged in similar behaviour, however, this has often been treated as a retrograde step: a kind of re-feudalisation or 'seigneurialisation', which counteracted the jurisdictional achievements of the thirteenth century and tended towards the break-up of royal authority. The *mercedes* of Henry II of Castile are perhaps the most notorious example of this phenomenon, but there are plenty of others: the lavish grants of Edward II and Richard II of England, and even the earldoms created by the warrior-king

Edward III in 1337; the *apanages* created by John II of France for his sons, which were confirmed and extended by Charles V; the extensive grants made by Charles I of Anjou in Naples, which are often taken to have revived noble power in the region after the supposedly more centralised regime of the Hohenstaufen; the *honores* granted by Charles-Robert and Louis the Great of Hungary; the extensive pledging of the remnants of the imperial fisc by Charles IV. With many of these examples clustering around the major wars of the period, it is not hard to see why this development has been seen as another undesirable consequence of later medieval warfare and its tendency to promote aristocratic interests.

In fact, there are considerable continuities between the granting practices of thirteenth- and fourteenth-century kings. Even the most juridically minded rulers had been willing to endow lords with lands and rights in certain circumstances – following large conquests of new terrain, for instance; or when the requirements of defence demanded the placing of a powerful lieutenant with local muscle; or when the lands in question had long been in noble hands and did not form part of the recognised royal estate. Edward I, Louis IX and Philip IV had all created substantial lordships for cadet lines – most notably the honours of Lancaster, Poitiers and Valois – and it was largely a matter of chance that these found their way back to the royal house in just a few generations. Equally, fourteenth-century kings were by no means abandoning control of their realms: we have already discussed the various ways in which their governments were expanding, and the grants they made were part of that process. Edward III and Henry Trastámara were both faced with the task of rebuilding the aristocracy after a period of civil war, and so, in a sense, was John II of France, as he returned to a kingdom transformed by the 1350s and the Brétigny settlement: these three kings had to create strong lords where many of their predecessors had simply inherited them. It is now clear that Edward III's endowments were intended to create a body of men capable of defending the British Isles and of helping the king to raise troops for his war in France, and signs of the same policy are visible in the grants made by Edward II (founder, inter alia, of the great earldoms of Kildare, Desmond and Ormond, through which some kind of royal power was preserved in southern Ireland) and in the grants of Richard II. The Valois king needed powerful lieutenants around the edge of the swollen Anglo-Gascon sphere; he also needed an effective power in the north and east, which explains the re-creation of the duchy of Burgundy and the sponsorship of its ties with Flanders. As we have seen, Henry II's grants did little more than acknowledge the steady growth of magnate power in the Castilian localities, a development which he could do nothing to prevent, and which offered him more effective means of co-ordinating rural and urban power than any other available to him. It is interesting to note that, in 1379, he declared all his grants to be heritable only by the legitimate issue of the previous holder, a stipulation that – legally, at least – ensured they would escheat to the crown with much greater regularity. These terms were very similar to the *novae donationes* created by Louis of Hungary, and to the conditions on which the later French *apanages* were granted: while bestowing the means of service on loyal supporters, therefore, these fourteenth-century kings were preserving the long-term interests of their crowns. In most cases, moreover, the lordships of the fourteenth century co-existed with other networks of authority over which the king retained some control – structures of office, which might be infiltrated by lords but were rarely handed over to them; enclaves, such as churches or towns which remained more or less under royal protection (or retained the option of appealing to the king over the heads of local lords). It was only where these alternatives failed that the lordships of this period began to resemble the feudal empires of earlier times. Ireland after about 1370 is one example, as it steadily became clear that no king or royal lieutenant would come for long enough, or with sufficient independent resources, to counteract the influence of the great earls and their Gaelic counterparts. Naples and Hungary in the later fourteenth century are other examples: in both these Angevin realms, a partly independent network of counts and counties had initially kept the magnates in check, but from the 1340s and 1380s respectively, weak kingship, combined with internal and external war, eroded the latter structure and produced a mess of feuding powers, each more solidly in control of its own territory. Even in these kingdoms, however, all was not lost: Ladislas of Durazzo, temporarily, and Alfonso V, Sigismund and Matthias Corvinus, more lastingly, were able to restore royal authority.

What these kinds of royal grants permitted, therefore, was the harmonising of regnal structures with local power. It is now more widely recognised that this was not inherently damaging to royal interests. Like the other informal means of power surveyed above, 'patronage' was a flexible and interpersonal way of achieving rule: it worked most straightforwardly in the shared lifetime of grantor and grantee – men who were friends already and had cause to be grateful to each other. In succeeding generations, it was more complicated: new rulers faced the lieutenants of their predecessors, who were uncertain of their footing in the new dispensation; or they faced their heirs, who regarded their endowments not as gifts, but as property. Not only kings, princes and lords, but popes, bishops and the changing personnel of municipal governments took up the reins of power in environments shaped by the actions of their predecessors and the dynamics of heredity. Even so, the interests of regional power-holders were normally sufficiently entwined with those of more metropolitan authorities for co-operation to be possible, even likely. Rulers retained all kinds of discretionary power, and, as we have seen, they usually possessed other networks and associations besides the great lords; equally, the workings of office and inheritance, and the interactions between them, were familiar to everyone, and codes of behaviour and expectation existed to assist kings and lords in managing their common affairs.

Drawing this together, then, it seems clear that the more flexible, informal and interpersonal resources of power were just as important in this period of jurisdictional and institutional development as they had been before. They were not necessarily *more* important: that impression is mainly the result of enhanced evidence and of the increasing ceremony and splendour of royal and aristocratic lifestyles in an era of cultural accumulation and specialisation. Over the course of the fourteenth century, moreover, places with more developed government began to experience tensions between these informal and discretionary dimensions of rule and the more public and official frameworks of authority. Courtly extravagance and other forms of ungoverned princely spending came under attack from taxpayers and their representatives: in England, in the 1370s and 1380s, for example; in Aragon-Catalonia in 1388–9 and in France in the 1350s and 1380s; and similar pressures may have contributed to denunciations of papal extravagance and nepotism within the Church – notably from the ascetic Pope Benedict XII as early as the 1330s. Concern about the divisive effects of livery distribution and retaining, whether by lords or kings, is apparent in several places by the last couple of decades of the century. The king of England was beginning to regulate retaining by

1390 (if not also in moves against 'conspiracy' around 1300), while Philippe de Mézières had denounced '*alliances publiques*' and their part in corrupting French royal officers in 1389.[30] Royal or princely grants, meanwhile, could be presented as wastage of the fisc or the goods of the crown – these were the accusations made against Edward II and Richard II of England, and against King Wenceslas of the Romans, in each case as a justification for deposition. While the principles of reward and endowment were accepted by the public critics of these rulers, there was already a strong sense that rulers should exercise their lordship in ways compatible with the common interests, fiscal and legal, of their subjects.

Political thinking and writing

One final way in which the growth of government was manifested in the fourteenth century was in the writing and thinking about political questions that went on in Europe's universities, courts and chanceries, and in its emerging public spaces. By 1300, as we have seen, there existed a rich profusion of political ideas and perspectives, and a range of terms and techniques for discussing them. One of the central developments of the fourteenth century lay in the application of learning to contemporary political problems and scenarios. In a sense, of course, there was nothing new in this: the academic study of Roman and canon law, of scripture and patristic thought, of Aristotle, Cicero and other ancient thinkers, had always addressed contemporary concerns, including the rights of political authorities. In the fourteenth century, however, this kind of learning came to be applied to a wider range of political predicaments, by a wider range of writers and for a wider range of readers. Where twelfth- and thirteenth-century thinkers had often been concerned with under-standing and synthesising authoritative materials and thus with laying out the boundaries of human knowledge, fourteenth-century thinkers were more concerned with using that knowledge to solve specific political and administrative problems and/or to improve the understanding of political institutions and activities.

This was already clear in the large volume of writing that accom-panied the conflicts between the Papacy, the crown of France and the Empire in the first few decades of the fourteenth century. The

---

[30] P. S. Lewis, *Essays in Later Medieval French History* (London, 1985), pp. 69–70.

relationship between temporal and spiritual powers was scarcely a new topic, but the way it was being tackled by the writers of this period shows their essentially political conception of the Church and the Christian community. As we have seen, one concern that united many of the thinkers and activists of this period was the restoration of order in the world. Boniface VIII, Giles of Rome, John of Paris and William Durand had different proposals for how to achieve this, and they were certainly defending different frameworks of right and interest; they were also Christians, we must remember, concerned with the whole cosmos, and not only the earthly part of it; but, influenced as they were by the works of Aristotle, Aquinas and Augustine, they were all agreed on the political nature of the Christian community and the need for action to restore its wellbeing – a 'healthy regime for the human race', as Durand put it.[31] Central to this action was the establishment of clear and incontrovertible jurisdiction over temporal affairs: that is why this claim lay at the centre of *Unam Sanctam* and why the period is notable for such extreme statements of papal, imperial and royal authority. The papalists argued that the Church was the only perfect community, with Giles of Rome advancing the quasi-Augustinian view that only those in a state of grace – that is, blessed and accepted by the Church – possessed just title to authority and property. This idea was to redound horribly against the clerical hierarchy in the course of the century, as we shall see, but at this point its aim was to establish the absolute priority of ecclesiastical authorities over lay rulers. The supporters of Philip IV and other critics of the Papacy, on the other hand, went beyond the traditional claim that temporal things should be under temporal jurisdiction to argue for an alternative view of human society. John of Paris argued that temporal authority and property had a popular basis and belonged exclusively to the secular order; these things were appointed by God, but indirectly: through men's natural inclination towards society. The Church did not possess temporal authority, as such: what it had was a 'right of preaching' and its property was merely held in trust, for the fulfilment of its ministry, under the supervision of the secular power. While churchmen could properly attempt to exercise influence over a king and his subjects, they could not judge them; equally, kings were quite entitled to try to influence clerical

---

[31] C. Fasolt, *Council and Hierarchy: The Political Thought of William Durant the Younger* (Cambridge, 1991), p. 177.

opinion, and specifically Philip IV was entitled to cite Boniface VIII before a general council of the Church. John's populist theory made councils a natural way in which any community might resolve its difficulties, and this idea was also central to the theories of William Durand, albeit on the basis of canonistic doctrine laced with Cicero, rather than Aristotle. Both writers called for mixed government in the Church, and allowed the council the power to reform the Pope and to depose him if the common welfare of Christendom required it. Neither writer extended these constitutional views to the lay sphere, and Durand argued confusingly for both hierarchy and republicanism, but these clerical and academic thinkers were addressing contemporary problems of government, drawing partly on secular theory and in a context shaped by secular political struggle.

The same might be said of the works produced amid the conflicts of Guelfs and Ghibellines in Italy between the 1300s and the 1330s. Ptolemy of Lucca's completion of Aquinas' *De Regno* transformed the work into a defence of Guelfism and republican government; he also wrote a treatise 'On the Jurisdiction of the Church over the Kingdom of Apulia and Sicily', to defend the rule of Robert of Naples against the claims of the invading Henry VII. Writing in support of the emperor, meanwhile, Dante and Marsiglio were motivated, at least in part, by the need for an effective solution to the disorders in Italy. The prominence given by Marsiglio's treatise to the role of jurisdictional conflict in damaging the health of urban communities is, from one perspective, as striking as its prolonged denunciation of the papal usurpation of temporal power: the conflicting claims of Pope and Emperor to the rule of Italy did indeed fuel the troubled politics of the region's cities, and Marsiglio was not wrong to say that papal assertions could have disorderly effects elsewhere. While it is important to remember that he wrote in Paris, that (much as he mentioned Italy by name) his arguments were pitched at a universal, even apocalyptic level, and that it was mostly academic churchmen who read his treatise and responded to it, we cannot overlook the fact that his book was called *The Defender of Peace*, and that he was addressing one of the greatest causes of political strife in his lifetime. The problems of the international Church-state continued to be a major, perhaps the major, preoccupation of intellectuals, but while those problems merged, in one direction, into a series of spiritual, pastoral and metaphysical questions, in another, they merged into the political predicaments of those territories in which the universal power of Pope and Emperor continued to be legally significant or physically active.

Marsiglio, Dante and, more openly, Ptolemy were not alone in writing about the political concerns of actual territories. The Parisian defenders of Philip IV made copious reference to the French king and kingdom in their case for the temporal order. In this respect, they may have been influenced by a more frankly nationalistic debate over the proper location of the Empire, which had been sparked by the papal flirtation with moving or dismantling it in the 1270s and 1280s. While, in 1281, Alexander of Roes defended German claims to the Empire on both historical and pragmatic grounds, he was willing to concede juridical independence to the French kingdom. Twenty years later, Pierre Dubois was less generous: his treatise 'On the Recovery of the Holy Land' (1305×7) fantasised about a universal empire for the crusading French ruler, in which the Germans would be pushed aside and the Papacy subordinated to a new Capetian Constantine. Over the course of the fourteenth century, the concern of learned men with the political destinies, structures and problems of specific realms became more pronounced. In 1340, for example, the Bologna-trained canon of Bamberg, Lupold of Bebenburg, wrote a tract 'On the Laws of the Kingdom and Empire', which used legal and historical argument to vindicate the actions taken at Rhens in 1338 and to support the claim that the rights of the Emperor and the king of the Romans were the same. In the mid-1370s, the canonist and royal councillor Evrart de Trémaugon produced a great compendium of laws and debates on the relationship of 'Church' and 'State' in France. The *Somnium Viridarii* (dream of the shepherd), published in Latin in 1376 and French in 1378, was a manual of French public law and political principle, combined with a handbook on kingly rule; seven-teen manuscript copies survive, suggesting that it was required reading in the ruling circles of Charles V's France. Meanwhile, in the 1350s, the great jurist Bartolus of Sassoferrato wrote treatises not only 'On the Tyrant' – perhaps a staple topic of political theory, though one developed by Bartolus in a specifically Italian context – but also 'On the Government of the City', 'On Guelfs and Ghibellines' and 'On Insignia and Arms', together with a famous, and much-copied, com-mentary on nobility. The second of these five works, which was circulated widely in Italy, canvassed the argument for municipal sovereignty which Bartolus had already put forward in his commen-taries on the *Code* and the *Digest*: it thus addressed one of the central dilemmas of Italian urban politics. Bartolus also advanced parallel arguments for 'provinciae', permitting the legal recognition of self-governing units larger than a town, but lacking the juridical solidity of a kingdom or empire; a similar case was made by his younger colleague, Baldus de Ubaldis (1327–1400), on behalf of Italian *signori*, notably Giangaleazzo Visconti, whom he served in the 1390s. Bartolus' tract on the Guelfs and Ghibellines, meanwhile, took a remarkably astute approach to the factions which were usually so bitterly condemned in Italian civic writing: to Bartolus, it seemed that the play of parties could be a natural dynamic of urban political life, and a valuable one if it kept tyranny at bay. In writing on contemporary political problems from a perspective informed by juristic learning, Bartolus opened a new chapter in the study of Roman law. As we have seen, the 'commentator' tradition, which he and his teacher Cinus of Pistoia inaugurated, reflected the way in which the *ius commune* had become the basis of actual legal practice in much of Europe; it also built on the increasing tendency for rulers to approach jurists for *consilia* – advice-texts – on particular questions, and confirmed the growing interest of university men in guiding the activities of holders of authority.

By the second half of the century, this approach was common across the continent and in branches of learning besides the law. Rulers commissioned or received treatises on such hot political topics as the rules of succession, the competing claims of electoral and hereditary systems, the proper relationship of 'Church' and 'State', the organisation of justice, the legal position of fiefs, the inalienability of the fisc, the coronation oath, the king's rights to taxation, the impropriety of seizing property and the problem of usury. Many of these works were highly sophisticated. Nicole Oresme (*c.*1323–82), for example, wrote a widely circulated treatise on money for the king of France; he noted the attractions of debasement as a policy option for cash-strapped rulers, but he also explored its political and economic costs, noting, with great sensitivity to social reality, that while strong money appealed to landowners, weak money was more popular with workers, and merchants required something in between that did not fluctuate too much. While Trémaugon was working on the *Somnium Viridarii*, Oresme wrote translations of Aristotle's major works for the court of Charles V, and the critical comments he inserted on the influence of lawyers in French royal government have been seen as part of a developing struggle between theologians and jurists for the direction of royal policy. Oresme's criticisms may have stemmed from Aristotle's musings on the relative benefits of a good ruler and a good law, but it may not be too far-fetched to see in them a response to the negative results of the aggressions of French royal jurisdiction in the first half of the fourteenth century; a practising lawyer in the south of the kingdom made similar observations in a manual of the early fourteenth century, and it is worth noting that Charles V's government took a more conservative line on royal prerogatives and a more tolerant approach to princely jurisdiction. Other theologians were just as active in public service. The notorious heresies of John Wyclif, for example, began in a series of speeches and treatises written at the invitation of the English government in the 1370s, as it sought to find ways of increasing its tax revenues from the Church; a few decades later, Jean Gerson and other doctors of the University of Paris who publicly promoted solutions to the Great Schism found themselves drawn into a wider debate over the conduct of government in the unstable regency of Charles VI.

Rulers sought and received more general works too. The canonist Philip of Leiden was asked to write a work on the 'Care of the *Res Publica*' (public body, common good) for the count of Holland in 1355: his Bartolist argument that 'a duke, count or baron can also be said to be prince within his own jurisdiction and in his territory', and that 'today the Empire has been split and everyone has empire and is emperor in his own lands', was just what a prince in the Low Countries wanted to hear.[32] The Franciscan scholar, Francesc Eiximenis (d.1409) was asked for a treatise on 'the regimen of the *cosa pública*' by the city council of Valencia, while his Christian dictionary, *Lo Crestia*, written in Catalan for the king and the council of Barcelona, contained a view of political society which has been regarded as the first articulation of 'pactism', the notion that just political authority rested on a contract between ruler and subjects for the common good of the latter. Besides these scholarly texts, there was a host of more derivative ones, frequently translated into the vernacular, so that noblemen, townsmen and other leading officers and councillors could read them. Prominent among these were so-called 'mirrors for princes' – handbooks of royal or lordly

---

[32] Quoted in O. Brunner, *Land and Lordship: Structures of Governance in Medieval Austria*, ed. and trans. H. Kaminsky and J. van Horn Melton from the 1965 edn (Philadelphia, 1992), pp. 321–2.

government, typically based on a mixture of Aristotelian, Ciceronian and Senecan advice, and frequently modelled on other recensions – in particular, the pseudo-Aristotelian *Secretum/Secreta Secretorum* (the secret[s] of secrets), an Arabic text of the tenth century; and Giles of Rome's *De Regimine Principum*, which is one of the most widely copied and translated manuscripts of the middle ages, surviving in hundreds of examples, including versions in Flemish, German, Spanish and Swedish by the mid-fourteenth century. Most mirror-type works were at least adapted for local audiences, and some could be highly original. The Norwegian *King's Mirror*, mentioned above, emerged in the 1250s, more than two decades before Giles wrote, and reflected the international impact of conflicts between the Church and lay rulers, as well as a host of scriptural and Nordic influences. The treatise 'On the Nobilities, Wisdoms and Prudences of the King', written by Walter de Milemete for the young Edward III, is quite closely based on the *Secreta* in its structure and themes, but its advice on how best to pacify the aristocracy, and its unusually shrewd advice on how to manage the politics of reward, are an original response to the problems of Edward II's reign. Some texts were even more *engagé*: the *Nová Rada* (new council), a satirical poem written by a Czech nobleman, Smil of Pardubice, in 1384, attacked King Wenceslas' exploitation of feudal rights as well as offering more familiar protests against foreign and low-born councillors. Besides mirrors for princes, meanwhile, there were equivalent works for knights, treatises of chivalry or warfare – many of them modelled on Vegetius' *De Re Militari* (itself copiously translated from the 1270s and 1280s), or the more recent works of Ramon Lull (*Book of the Order of Chivalry*, 1274–6), Geoffrey de Charny (*Book of Chivalry*, c.1350) and John of Legnano (*Treatise on War*, 1360).

This explosion of academically informed political writing found its place in a literary culture which was burgeoning everywhere as literacy spread, as literary vernaculars expanded and multiplied, and as authors of all kinds – divines, poets, civil servants as well as intellectuals – felt a common pressure to engage in the education of an ever-widening range of society. Political life was just one strand in this culture, of course, and political treatises represent a very small proportion of the books and manuscripts which proliferated in this period: works of spiritual guidance and comfort, psalters and bibles, romances, storybooks, histories, books of nurture and basic school-texts – these were the works that dominated. But different genres of writing affected one another more than these classifications imply. Books of chivalrous lore, for instance, such as the chronicles of Jean le Bel (written *c.*1350s–70) or, more popular still, those of Jean Froissart (written 1369–*c.*1400), transmitted large amounts of recent political history. They projected political principles, such as the correct behaviour of the good king, the proper ordering of society, or what was expected of a knight; and, in their references to taxes and meetings of estates, to legislation and rebellions like that of the Jacquerie, they advertised the growth of government and its political consequences. The same might be said of other chronicles popular in the fourteenth century. The *Erikskrönikan* (*c.*1320), for instance, offered a heroic portrait of one of the rebel dukes who were executed by King Birger Magnusson of Sweden in 1318: it did not develop a fully-fledged theory of aristocratic resistance, but it must have provided a powerful model for the dissenting magnates of the rest of the century. In England, meanwhile, the widely copied and locally embellished *Brut* chronicles linked the events of recent times with the deep history of the British people, supplying copious examples of good and bad kingship and drawing attention to their political consequences. Similar chronicles existed in many kingdoms, and also in a number of towns – those of the Villani brothers in Florence, for instance, or Bonvesin's celebratory book *On the Great Works of the City of Milan* (1288); in Cologne (*c.*1270), Lübeck (1347) and Magdeburg (*c.*1360), chronicles were commissioned by the city-fathers, reflecting an awareness of how such works could help to affirm and glorify the civic community. By the end of the century, some princes too were sponsoring such works – in Brittany, for example, a life of Duke John IV and a chronicle, begun in 1394, which collected evidence for the independence of the duchy, supported the Montfort dynasty and laid the foundations for a Breton history distinct from that of France. Besides chronicles, huge portmanteau works of fiction, combining self-consciously fine writing with ethical, spiritual and social comment, such as Dante's *Divine Comedy* (*c.*1308–21), Boccaccio's *Decameron* (*c.*1349–51), Langland's *Piers Plowman* (*c.*1367–*c.*1385), Chaucer's *Canterbury Tales* (*c.*1388–1400) and de Mézières' *Songe du Vieil Pèlerin* (1389), helped to establish a sense of the contours of society, and often of a national, or regnal, society. Works of this kind came to be regarded as the foundations of national literatures; Chaucer, for instance, became a kind of English Dante, just as Dante had been a Tuscan Virgil (the court-poet of the Emperor Augustus), and this notion carried with it the sense of a public dialogue between rulers, poets and the national readership, a dialogue captured neatly in John Gower's identification of his *Confessio Amantis* (1390–3) as 'a book for England's sake'. These idealisations of regnal community, remote as they often were from reality, and some of them certainly more politically conscious than others, must have helped to establish a sense of whom and what government was for in the minds of politicians. They put flesh on the partly academic notions of practically oriented moral philosophy – 'the common good', 'the three estates', 'the people' and so on – and thus they shaped for rulers and subjects alike a sense of the content of public and social life.

By the end of the fourteenth century, then, there was across Europe a net of political and social theory, which combined authoritative understanding with a plausible picture of social and public life as it was actually lived. This net contained a common underlying grammar, as discussed in the previous chapter, and it tended, almost everywhere, to emphasise some familiar ideas and values. One was that, while society was diverse, and, to a point, stratified, it was also a community to which every group or type should make its own particular contribution. Another, equally prominent, was that communities required government, and that the primary objective of government must be the common wellbeing of the people over whom it presided. By the fourteenth century, this government was recognised to have fairly extensive content: it might centre on defence and justice, but it would certainly involve lawmaking, consultation and discussion, fiscality, and the appointment and supervision of officers; it would possess grand locations and the sort of public domesticity captured in the notion of the court; it would have some kind of ritual life, and – especially in kingdoms and cities – it would possess a history which was intertwined with the history of the people over which it presided. In these ways, then, the content of political imagination was enriched, and in ways that registered and affirmed the growth of government we have been describing. At the same time, it is important to recognise that there were blind spots in this writing too. One tendency which has often been noted is the failure of most works of political reflection to allow for subsidiary political units – regions, provinces, churches and towns which were not sovereign, or independent, but formed part of larger wholes. A parallel uncertainty concerned the role of great territorial lords, ecclesiastical princes and the leaders of municipalities in the governments of kings and princes. Many texts acknowledged the presence of different estates in society, and, even more, identified the ruler's need for counsel from good and wise men who were friends both to him and to his realms; but they did not really bring these two images together, to throw light on the real dynamics and problems of governing complex polities or to explain how lesser units might be incorporated within greater ones. Fourteenth-century political and governmental writing might acknowledge clashes of right or jurisdiction, but its characteristic response was to deny that one or other contending party had any right at all: it did not show how different rights, different units, different potential rulers, could be reconciled with each other. While it was easy, therefore, for contemporary power-holders to conceptualise community, and to recognise themselves as responsible to and for their subjects, there was no practical guidance on how different and overlapping communities were to be brought together. Therein lay one of the essential causes of fourteenth-century conflict.

GOVERNMENT AND POLITICAL LIFE

The growth of government had two major consequences which were central to the fourteenth-century political experience. The first of these was a multiplication of jurisdictional conflict, as kings, princes, towns and churches attempted to exercise new rights over those they claimed as their subjects. This, as we shall see, was the basic cause of many of the wars and other confrontations of the period. The second major consequence, which will also be explored below, is a little harder to capture. In one sense, it is the growth of political community: more active governments created more politically engaged and mutually interactive subjects; they attempted to define the political space more precisely and meaningfully than the feudal suzerainties of earlier times, and they characterised that space in distinctive ways, reflecting their different constitutional forms, traditions and circumstances. At the same time, the term 'community' implies a degree of togetherness and harmony which was frequently absent from the more closely governed territories of the period. As they grew and developed, political and governmental institutions not only provoked reaction, they also created more substantial and far-reaching media of criticism and resistance. This was not, in itself, damaging – communities might, in the long term, gain strength from internal conflicts – but the general context of contested jurisdiction meant that these media of resistance could be used to increase the independence or solidity of powers, groups or units whose subjection to the ruler could not be counted on. The growth of government, and the political techniques and technologies to which it gave rise, could thus have decentralising effects for kingdoms and empires, and disintegrative ones for these and other political units; among the advancing communities of the period were not only those of realms, but those of provinces, parishes, towns and lordships, or of individual estates. While the growth of political community could work towards the consolidation of territory, therefore, it could also be a fertile source of conflict, and tended to complicate the developing polities of the fourteenth century rather than increasing their stability.

In this final section of the chapter, the aim will be to explore these twin consequences of governmental growth more fully, explaining why they should be seen as the underlying causes of the copious, large-scale, and often chaotic conflicts of the fourteenth century. We shall then turn attention to the ways in which these conflicts were resolved, and consider why the various compromises devised and operated by fourteenth-century regimes were not more lasting.

Conflicts of jurisdiction

Contests over jurisdiction were perhaps the commonest kind of conflict in fourteenth-century Europe, occurring virtually every-where, and at every political level. Many of them literally concerned the power to do justice, but they also involved contests over other governmental rights and assertions – fiscal, military, regulatory – which could entail other kinds of subordination. At their most extreme, they could involve the resistance of substantially independent powers to novel attempts at subjugation. A famous example is the conflict which arose from the rejection by the Scottish king, John Balliol, of Edward I's attempt to extract military service from him and his tenants in 1295. No previous king of Scotland had been obliged to summon his host in support of the king of England, and especially not for a conflict in France. More commonly, however, these disputes involved assertion and counter-assertion in the uncertain borderlands of established jurisdictions – assertions which reflected the breakdown of older compromises, typically because one power or another was growing in organisation, ambition or coherence. An example is Philip IV's decision to tax the French Church without papal permission in

1296. To the king, it was a logical next step: he had collected papal crusade taxes every year from 1285 to 1291; he was the willing supporter of papal projects, and ally of his cousin of Anjou against the hated Aragonese; he and the French Church were agreed that, as part of Philip's defence of the realm, he was entitled to a share of clerical goods, and the clergy had duly granted him tenths in 1294 and 1295. Even in 1296, the French Church was willing to pay tax to the king, though it sought various concessions in return. To Boniface VIII, however, Philip's act was an unwarranted intrusion on the liberty of the Church, which he was obliged to defend, and it was an unwelcome one when other kings, like Edward I, were taking similar steps, and when they wanted the money to fight each other instead of the enemies of Rome and Christ. Both rulers were acting to defend what seemed rightful in a situation of jurisdictional mobility, and so, in fact, were the French bishops who were caught in the middle. The security provided by the French king and his developing high court; his preference for consultation over matters of taxation (ironically, in line with canonical principle, while the Papacy preferred to proceed by compulsion); his growing influence over ecclesiastical appointments: these were tangible benefits which inclined many French bishops towards the crown instead of their Roman protector.

As this last example clearly shows, jurisdictional disputes were about resources and power, as well as about right and authority: people did not engage in these disputes for the sake of principle. But the principles were important nonetheless: especially in the later thirteenth century and the first half of the fourteenth, jurisdiction was the main currency of power, and it disclosed to rulers and subjects of all kinds what rights and resources could be claimed, and so determined what the battlegrounds would be. Moreover, because it was such a focus of scholarly and political interest, it presented an ever-changing picture: new techniques, new arguments, new possibilities were developed throughout this period, endlessly threatening the redistribution of power and consequently giving rise to disputes. The importance of jurisdiction is shown partly by the fact that it lay at the bottom of most of the major conflicts that have been discussed in this chapter. For instance, the extended complex of wars involving Britain, France and the Low Countries in the twelfth and thirteenth centuries was essentially caused by the clashing and evolving juridical claims of the kings and princes (and, in the Flanders of the 1290s, the towns) of this vast region. This same theme is very clear in the flashpoints of the 1310s, 1320s and 1330s that led to the Hundred Years War: all of them concern disputed jurisdiction – the Leagues of French nobles in 1314–15, protesting against royal interference in provincial customs; the war of St-Sardos in 1323–4, which followed the destruction of a 'French'-built bastide by the 'English' lieutenant of Gascony and led to the royal/Valois confiscation of the Agenais; the uprising in Flanders, which began in 1323 with a rising of Bruges against a high-handed comital grant that threatened its control of the Zwin waterway (and continued with a universal rejection of the tax levied by the count to satisfy the demands of his overlord, the French king); the French invasion of Flanders that followed, which prompted some of the Ghenters to call for Edward III to declare himself king of France in 1328; the death penalty imposed on Robert of Artois in 1334, which seemed an unwarranted extension of royal judicial authority and alarmed the lords of northern France; the renewal of English overlordship in Scotland in 1333, which revived the Franco-Scottish alliance and ensured the continuation of war in the north until Edward III took a different tack in the later 1340s.

Clashes of jurisdiction were thus central to the causation of the Hundred Years War, and they were also part and parcel of its unfolding. The war began in 1337 with the French confiscation of the Plantagenet fiefs of Gascony and Ponthieu, because Edward III was harbouring the king's traitor and felon, Robert of Artois; it moved rapidly to Edward's assumption of an imperial vicariate, which gave him formal authority in the Low Countries, and to his assertion of a claim to the crown of France in 1340. The latter was accompanied by propaganda that suggested that Edward would interpret the rights of that office in a manner much closer to what northern French nobles recognised as good custom: in other words, he was intervening – not necessarily cynically – in existing debates over the French king's jurisdiction. The war continued, from 1342, with the exploitation of the Breton succession dispute by the two contending overlords, and with attempts by Edward and his northern French allies to inflame Norman concerns over high royal taxation and the accumulating threat to their liberties. In the 1350s, the military war was accompanied by a complicated struggle for the reform of the realm, in which the (partly) pro-Plantagenet faction headed by Charles of Navarre was more than just an aristocratic network: it also gained support and credibility from its view of how far the king's rights extended and what control the realm and its representatives should exercise over his actions. By this point, the debate over the proper scope of royal authority was becoming a more purely French affair, but jurisdictional questions remained integral to the Anglo-French conflict for decades to come: the choice of Plantagenet or Valois overlordship, and the fact that that choice existed, shaped the options of many powers across the great terrains between the Rhine and the Pyrenees. The opportunities presented by this conflict of jurisdiction, and not only to the chief protagonists, help to explain why it proved so enduring.

Many other major wars were similarly concerned with jurisdiction – the great town wars in Germany in the 1370s and 1380s, the conflicts over the growth of the Swiss Confederation, the war between Ludwig of Bavaria and John XXII, and the massive conflicts for control of northern and southern Italy between papal agents and allies and their various opponents. As we have seen, these wars were conducted in dialogue with a mass of much smaller and more localised quarrels of a similar kind, involving churches, towns and lords. The archbishop of Rouen, for example, found that during the 1360s he was able to expand the authority of his courts to the detriment of the king's: his close links with Charles of Navarre, and the chaos reigning in much of Normandy, made royal resistance impossible. By the 1370s, however, the tide had turned and the crown was strong enough to have the archbishop arraigned before the *Parlement* for his offences against the royal *bailli*, and orders were issued for the seizure of his temporalities until the king should be satisfied by a large fine. This was not quite the end of the story, however. The archbishop resisted, appealing to his other overlord, Pope Gregory XI. The result was a compromise solution: translation to the see of Auch, west of Toulouse, where the archbishop – perhaps buoyed up by the deviant allegiances of the far south-west – opted to defy the Clementist position of the French Church in the Great Schism, and ended his days as a cardinal in Rome. As in the conflict between Philip IV and Boniface VIII, pope and prelates could find each other unreliable allies, but the possibility of invoking alternative authorities could provoke bold action in what was effectively a three-cornered struggle.

In multi-centred Italy, meanwhile, the interplay of different jurisdictions was all the more complicated. The anti-imperial city of Bologna, for instance, saw a closer alliance with the Papacy as the best means of protecting itself from Frederick II's reassertion of imperial power, though it is worth noting that the city's move into the Guelf alliance was principally contrived by its substantial *popolo*, which exploited factional divisions among the ruling nobility of the commune to achieve this end and to advance its own claims. Later in the thirteenth century, it was the Papacy and the Este lords of Ferrara who posed the greatest threat to Bolognese independence. The commune, for its part, responded by aligning itself closely with the papal vicar of the Romagna, while the Este built up a party in the city and sought to obtain control by exploiting its divisions to secure appointment as *podestà* for one of their supporters. In the event, it was another noble faction, the Pepoli, that succeeded in securing a loose lordship over the city in the 1310s. This family was initially hostile to papal influence, and was one of a number of Romagnol tyrants who flourished in the disturbed circumstances that followed Henry VII's invasion. They were not strong enough to withstand the massive papal armies that reimposed authority on the region in the 1320s, however, and in 1327 the city was subjected to full papal lordship for the first time. Under these circumstances, the commune was greatly modified, and the *popolo* suppressed; John XXII even considered transferring his seat from Avignon to Bologna in 1332. But the city was reluctant to accept such complete lordship, and it exploited the turmoil created by John of Bohemia's invasion to ally itself with the now antipapal Este and regain a kind of freedom in 1334. This freedom was quickly exploited by the Pepoli, and the Papacy cut its losses by awarding them a number of vicarial powers in the later 1330s. Bologna had lost its independence amid the universal, regional and civic conflicts in which it had been forcibly engaged, but it preserved some freedom of action through an independent signory in loose alliance with the Papacy, which, in turn, was able by these means to maintain something of its assumed right over the Emilian town. This solution was, in fact, to endure for another thirty years, since the Milanese takeover in 1349–50 was only achievable with the preservation of some local liberty and the payment of large sums to the Papacy. Only from 1360 was the Papacy able to revive its full lordship of the town, but even then the War of the Eight Saints provided an opportunity for rebellion in 1376, and the ensuing Schism left papal control of Bologna in tatters, though the local legate, Baldassare Cossa, soon to be John XXIII (and no doubt for that reason), was able to build up an effective power base in Emilia after 1403. In this lengthy example, then, we can see that jurisdiction was maintained (and lost) partly by armed force and partly by the interactions of groups, whether parties, dynasties or other networks, but it was not meaningless: it existed in frameworks of rules and powers, frameworks which could be rejected if they denied local customs and freedoms too completely. It was the equal availability of alternative structures of power and government that enabled every player in this game – the Pope, his agents, the Bolognese *popolo* and nobility, the Este and so on – to respond so flexibly to the vagaries of fortune.

Jurisdictional conflict, then, was spread across all political levels, and not infrequently conflicts at different levels intersected, as in the above examples, or in others not discussed – the interaction of London conflicts with the troubles of Richard II's reign, for instance; the links between the town wars of southern Germany and the difficulties of Wenceslas with the Electors and the Bohemian magnates; the three-cornered struggle over territory, justice and taxation revenue between the Castilian municipalities, the nobles and the divided monarchy in the reign of Ferdinand IV (1295–1312); or the dialogue between the succession war in Brittany, the larger Anglo-French conflict, and the struggles of Breton dukes with lords and bishops for control of their duchy. Nor were jurisdictional disputes confined to the west and centre of Europe, from which most of the above examples have been drawn. The detail of conflicts in the north and east is harder to reconstruct from the historiography, but it is clear that many of the tensions and compromises between the kings of Scandinavia, Bohemia, Poland and Hungary, on the one hand, and the powerful nobilities of these regions, on the other, concerned the desire of the latter to preserve their freedoms and assets, and of the former to exert greater influence, through experiments with land tenure, or taxation, or the assertion of military obligation, or the forced resumption of royal lands and regalities. This is very clear in the resistance to Magnus Eriksson in Sweden, to Valdemar IV in Denmark and to Casimir III in Greater Poland; it is also apparent in the leagues of magnates, lesser nobles (*szlachta*) and towns that sprung up in Poland during the 1370s and 1380s to negotiate new constitutional settlements with the Angevins and the Jagiellonians respectively. As we have seen, the tendency was for the immunities of magnates to be preserved and increased in these kingdoms, but the interests of lesser nobles – nominally equal in status to the great magnates – in avoiding subjugation, and in preserving such rights as they could realise through local tribunals, such as the Hungarian county magistracy or the *sejmiki* developed in fifteenth-century

Poland, left open the possibility of jurisdictional disputes and secured for the crown a means of influence.

Conflicts of political community

The activities, even the innovations, of governments were not always unacceptable, of course. The growth of jurisdiction, regulation, taxation, troop-raising and representation that occurred in so many parts of Europe would not have been possible if subjects of various kinds had not been willing to accept these new institutions. More than this, indeed, pressure from subjects was a powerful stimulus for governmental growth. As we have seen, royal and papal jurisdiction tended to grow because litigants wanted to use it: other authorities had to take positive action to forestall its gravitational force, if they wanted to preserve their own courts and customs. Legislation expanded in response to the petitions and complaints of the people, and so, less directly perhaps, did central and local administrations. Even the levying of taxes might follow public demand, as in the French example of the 1340s, 1350s and 1360s, in which representatives agreed to far heavier taxation in order to improve urban defences, pay off the Companies, restore the coinage and meet the terms of the king's ransom. Clearly enough, there were trade-offs in all these instances, and every agreement arose from a complex balance of interests, since neither the government nor the people was a simple, united group. But co-operation was evidently possible, even normal at times, and there was a tendency for extensions of government to foster one another – for example, the English Parliament and its associated tax system came in on the back of the king's effective monopoly of secular jurisdiction, while the claims of French and Castilian kings to universal military service rested partly on their confirmations of the rights of municipalities. We have seen that, by the end of the century, in many kingdoms and some principalities and towns, a strong sense of common political identity had developed, afforded by recognised constitutional norms and shared historical myths. This phenomenon is a demonstration that governmental growth could have integrative effects, and it is also one of the resources from which a higher degree of political co-ordination was achieved in the following century. Almost every fourteenth-century polity experienced several decades of unity and power, as all or most of its constituent forces pulled together around an effective ruler or regime: these laid down precedents for the future and helped to counteract the fissiparous tendency of other developments.

Even so, a glance at the narratives in the first part of this chapter makes it clear that governmental activity also provoked conflict, even when it came from authorities whose sway was normally accepted. Government was a powerful source of political education, and it created new media of authority and resistance, the use of which could have divisive, even chaotic, results. The second general cause of fourteenth-century conflicts, therefore, lay in the reaction of subordinates to the performance of those who governed them. Resentful populations did not necessarily declare independence when confronted with the innovative burdens of fourteenth-century government, but they did take steps to register displeasure, to negotiate reductions in new demands or to revise them so that they suited local or sectional interests. These actions shaded into the contests of jurisdiction that we have just been discussing: after all, a common way governments offended was by asserting unaccustomed rights – by exceeding their jurisdiction, in other words. But what marks out this second group of conflicts is the acceptance on the part of protestors that they constituted (or were part of) a community that was in some way under the authority of the government in question, or at least shared its territory, a community to which that government had obligations. The leagues which arose in late thirteenth-century Castile and Aragon, or early fourteenth-century France and Denmark, for instance, explicitly acknowledged the authority of the kingdom in each case, but they sought both to enshrine certain rights and liberties and to modify the rule of the king. In a parallel way, the gatherings of knights and towns that met in Brandenburg in 1280, in Austria in 1281, in Lower Bavaria in 1311 or in Liège in 1316 challenged and restrained the activity of the princes, but they also accepted membership of a *Land* and the framework of mutual rights and obligations that this implied. Equally, the *popoli* of Italian towns, and the guilds and other organisations that challenged communes and other urban regimes from the mid- or late thirteenth century onwards, were generally content to work within the confines of a common municipal authority: they simply wanted to correct its abuses or to take part in its deliberations. All of these organisations had some potential for autonomy, and in deep crisis or in circumstances of external conflict, they might pull away – as urban interest-groups in Italy were drawn into the larger networks of Guelfs and Ghibellines, for example, or as the rebel cities of Rouen and Paris considered alliance with Ghent in the troubles of 1380–2 – but more typically they worked for reforms or improvements within the jurisdictions they usually recognised (and even in these two cases, the parties did not go outside the superior jurisdictions of the kingdoms of France and 'Italy' respectively).

These 'conflicts of political community' consequently had some integrative effects: they helped to identify shared political space and to affirm the overall authority of governments, even as they sought to challenge their activities. The results of these conflicts typically took integration further, as rulers and regimes accepted legal frameworks and upheld liberties, or agreed to work with representative and consultative institutions, or adopted various kinds of power-sharing, or modified the incidence of taxation and military obligation, so that these were less obnoxious to the leading interests among their subordinates. In these ways, the political units of Europe became more complex and more richly textured as their governments expanded. The character of domestic political conflict consequently changed, but it is important to realise that neither its incidence nor its severity was reduced: the growth of government, and of conflict over government, did not only produce new means of political integration, it also produced new means of resistance, including some that helped to coordinate power at lower political levels. First of all, these processes strengthened the media of protest. It was easier to organise assemblies, for instance, when these had become a familiar part of the dealings between ruler and people. We have already seen how the French Leagues of 1314–15 built partly on the national assemblies of 1302–3 and 1304, and on the local assemblies which Philip IV's taxes had brought into being; in a like way, the Estates General of the 1340s and 1350s built on the more tentative consultative exploits of the 1310s and 1320s, gradually increasing in frequency and boldness until the improved government of the 1360s removed the need for them. Similarly, great public covenants, such as the Hungarian Golden Bull of 1222, or the Aragonese *privilegio general* of 1283, served as totems and models in later conflicts, the Hungarian nobles demanding the confirmation of the former in 1351, and the Aragonese estates extending the terms of their *privilegio* in 1287 and reviving the *Unión* which had obtained it in the crisis of 1347–8. It was not only confrontations that laid down precedents of this kind: the public initiatives of kings and other rulers could have the same result. For example, the efforts of King Rudolf I to restore the imperial fisc through diets at Nuremberg in 1274 and 1281 affirmed the role of Electors and princes in guarding the goods of the Empire and in initiating *reformatio imperii* (imperial reform): it thus helped to lay the foundations for future reformist and dissident action, by the Electors especially, including the imperial depositions of 1298 and 1400.[33] While all these episodes had the consolidating effect of making it clear that lords and other estates were part of the kingdom in each case, they also inscribed traditions of collective and representative action that would ensure that, whenever reform became necessary in the future, a portion of the political elite would always be willing to take action to achieve it. As the governments of kingdoms, principalities and towns invested in structures of consultation and representation, then, they also affirmed structures and traditions of protest.

Meanwhile, both the development of government and its associated politics helped to create and advertise a set of political expectations among the governed. Many of the claims of regimes were based on their provision of justice and defence, and as the agencies related to those claims expanded, governments came under increasingly articulate pressure to deliver. Processes of protest and negotiation created a series of assumptions, against which the performance of government could be measured. It came to be axiomatic that kings, lords, aldermen and officers of all sorts should keep the laws and maintain order; that they should deliver equal justice; that they should levy taxes at accustomed rates and for accustomed purposes; that extraordinary levies should only be made in extraordinary circumstances; that the public fisc should be properly maintained to cover the expenses of government without burdening the people; that rulers should possess the cardinal virtues of prudence, justice, temperance and fortitude; that they should take counsel from the good and wise, should reform abuses and redress the grievances of their subjects; and so on. This grid of expectations, varying from place to place and embellished with the more localised demands, helps to explain the crises and conflicts that broke out when governments failed to rule effectively. Often, this was the result of flaws in the ruler. Children, bastards, madmen, invalids, dotards, females, usurpers, doubtful claimants or − in communal systems − councils that did not effectively represent the balance of power within the district: these were the typical kinds of inadequate

---

[33] Quotation from J. Leuschner, *Germany in the Late Middle Ages*, trans. S. MacCormack (Amsterdam, 1980), p. 96.

ruler, mostly placed in power by hardening laws of succession or election, but unable to do the job properly when they got there. In some cases, their inability was physical; in others, it was political – the mere fact that they were not the only source of legitimate authority was what weakened the position of usurpers, women and teenagers, for instance: opposite them stood other claimants, or husbands, or sisters, or regents.

As governments did more for their subjects, moreover, so expectations spread and deepened, and the consequences of misrule grew more and more serious. Not only did it spark reaction, it also caused division, as some of those at the centre of power – grandees, leading officers or churchmen, members of the royal family – aligned themselves with the criticisms made by leagues, estates or other groups representing the political community. The coupling of inadequate leadership with mounting expectations is clearly a factor in many fourteenth-century political convulsions: those of the reigns of Ferdinand IV and Peter I of Castile, for instance, or those in England under Edward II or Richard II, or in Scotland under Robert III, in France under Charles VI, or in the Empire under Wenceslas. Less obviously, it was a factor in other confrontations – in cases when rulers were doing well under difficult circumstances, for instance, but nonetheless failing to preserve order, or keep the laws, or manage their finances (as in the France of John II, for example, or in the England of the 1330s, or – in a different way – in Greater Poland under Casimir III and in Bohemia under Wenceslas IV: these last two kings were too harsh and/or intrusive for local conditions; Casimir was able to crush the resulting opposition with few ill effects, but Wenceslas was not). Crises of misrule also occurred in communal regimes – as in Venice in 1310 and 1355, when subversive activity followed defeats for the Republic in wars against Ferrara and Genoa respectively, or in Ghent in 1338, when the powerful and excluded weavers' guild rebelled against a regime that had allowed a prolonged embargo on English wool. And they occurred in the Church: in many ways, this was the root cause of the Schism of 1378, which was sparked by the offences of Urban VI against the expectations of the cardinals, but also reflected the more general reaction of church leaders to widespread dissatisfaction with the curial tax burden. The spread of government and the raising of political expectations were thus fertile sources of fourteenth-century political conflict.

A third way in which the growth of government produced means and causes of resistance lay in the way that it generated structures and resources which smaller powers could use to consolidate their influence or jurisdiction locally. Examples include centrally licensed armies; taxation districts and/or taxation-sharing; networks of office; outright grants of local authority, like French *apanages*, Castilian *mercedes* or German *Pfände*. Naturally enough, princes, lords, towns and churches already possessed local rights, powers and networks, and they were often using the new political technologies of the era to strengthen them, but the tendency of larger governments, especially kingdoms, to share the results of their innovations with these more localised regimes provided further reinforcement to that strengthening. It is clear, and long-acknowledged, that the expanded structures of the French state were an important factor in the creation of many of the *états princiers* of the later fourteenth and fifteenth centuries – great fiefs like Brittany and Gascony had long existed, and were developing independently (though they were able to copy the frameworks of metropolitan France as well), but new or recreated principalities, such as the duchies of Bourbon, Berry, Burgundy and Orleans, depended heavily on the absorption of royal administrative and fiscal structures. A similar point might be made about the *bonnes villes*, towns on which the crown relied to act as governmental and fiscal centres, and for which it provided various privileges in return: royal favour strengthened the governments of these towns, increased their fiscal autonomy and gave them a more prominent position in the polity; these benefits enabled them to form independent networks in 1358 and to challenge royal fiscal policy sharply and successfully in 1379–82, and on other occasions. Similar examples could be supplied from many other places – Scandinavian *len/län*, the *honores* and palatinates granted to Hungarian nobles, the wardenships of the English Marches towards Scotland, and the lieutenancies and other offices given to Anglo-Irish lords at points in the fourteenth century and more consistently in the fifteenth. These concessions, as we have seen, have often been regarded as an unwise and somewhat gutless mortgaging of regnal assets, but the reality is more complicated. For one thing, it was generally new or increased governmental power that was being shared, and, for another, the royal or central element in these consortia was not meaningless: although the crown's agencies could be used against it in periods of misrule, it was hard for the holders of delegated royal power to break away completely, as the events of the fifteenth century were to show.

All these legacies of governmental growth emerge in one particular form of communal protest for which the fourteenth century is famous: popular revolts. Whatever part was played in their causation by social and economic tensions, or by the anti-sectarian preaching of the friars, the appearance of these risings was also due to the widening reach of government and the spread of political and governmental discourse. It has long been recognised that taxation was a cause of popular insurrection, and among the various means of government this probably was the one that most consistently and directly affected the lower orders across the continent. Many of the major risings of the century are related to new or excessive impositions: the *Pastoureaux* of 1320–1 to royal manipulation of Jewish debts; the Flemish revolt of 1323–8 to the revival of the 'transport' tax with the succession of a pro-French count (Louis of Nevers, 1322–46); the *Jacquerie* of 1358 to the increased taxation of the 1340s and 1350s; the *Tuchinat* of the 1360s and 1380s to the levies of the duke of Berry in the Languedoc; the English Peasants' Revolt to the renewed taxation of the 1370s and the poll taxes of 1377–81; the pogroms in Castile to the high taxation of the 1370s and 1380s. But it is less commonly recognised that tax was not only a provocation: it carried with it a series of expectations and principles which themselves were influential in the stimulation of these revolts. In the case of the *Jacquerie*, for instance, anger at the nobility was partly related to awareness of their tax exemption: peasants paid taxes to the king so that the lords of the realm would defend them in arms, but, as Edward III's armies roved around the Paris Basin in the wake of Poitiers, it was all too clear that the nobles had failed in this essential task. In England, meanwhile, the rebels believed that they were being taxed unfairly because a coven of traitors around the king was siphoning off his assets and revenues; like the *Jacques*, or the *Tuchins*, they knew the principles of taxation and were taking responsibility for the common defence upon themselves. Nor was taxation the only governmental development that stimulated popular action. Military organisation was also central: the militias and coastguards established in England were an important means through which the rebellion of 1381 was organised, just as the militarisation of French villages was a factor in the *Jacquerie* and the *Tuchinat*. Other administrative structures were equally important: the offices of the count of Flanders, for instance, provided an essential means by which the rebels of the 1320s, 1340s and 1380s were able to establish control of the countryside. Developments in law and justice were often a spur to action: in fourteenth-century England, mass use of the legal system spread its values of equality before the law through-out a highly unequal society, sharpening the sense of injustice among those less able to influence its procedures; equally, there are signs that, from the 1380s, Catalan *remences* (unfree peasants) were beginning to use legal principles to contest the *mals usos* that had been imposed on them a century before. In a similar way, the extension of representa-tion to elite guilds in a number of Italian, Flemish and German cities was a clear stimulus to the rebellious activities of worker-organisations, such as the weavers' guild in Ghent or the *Ciompi* of Florence, or – for that matter – the partly humble supporters of John of Northampton's attempt to wrest power from the aldermen of London in the 1380s. The development of political and governmental structures was thus a powerful stimulus to popular political action. It is striking that several of the popular revolts of this period were either regnal or provincial in scope – as in Flanders or the Languedoc – or focused on regnal centres like London and Paris. Not only does this reflect the impact of governmental forms and ideas, it also draws attention to the close links between popular political action and the politics of more elite groups. Could the Peasants' Revolt have hap-pened without the Good Parliament of 1376 and its aftershocks? Was not the *Jacquerie* linked to the meetings of the Estates General between 1355 and 1358, and the rebellion of Etienne Marcel in Paris? The connections between the Flemish revolt and the vexed politics of urban faction, comital power and French royal interference are all too clear. Conflicts of political community, then, could involve a very broad cross-section of society in the more intensively governed parts of the continent.

Popular political action was often directed at other groups in society besides the ruler: indeed, these risings were often emphatically loyalist, and their targets were typically sectional groups who could be presented as divisive or inappropriately powerful – evil councillors or courtiers, heavy-handed officers, magnates and prelates, Jews and other minorities whose networks were regarded with suspicion. This reminds us that the communities that evolved in dialogue with governmental development and its associated political consciousness were complex and diverse. While rulers had to manage a range of interest groups, each of which might require its own distinctive kind of treatment, they also had to meet public demands which ignored these complexities. This introduced a further range of difficulties for the governments of the period. The courtly entertainments and grants of pensions, lands or office that were desirable for managing great princes and lords were often unpalatable to taxpayers; and so, of course, was high military spending, and associated measures such as loans or tax-farming, which almost always generated suspicion from representatives and popular critics. Equally, the gap between the pretensions of judicial systems and the necessary toleration of lordship and its devices – feuding and private war, retaining and influence – could also produce protests from subjects who were less well connected, or less able to protect themselves. During periods when governmental demands, fiscal pressure and the state of order were generally tolerable, these tensions were unproblematic. But in periods of high taxation, judicial assertion, disorder or military threat, or when the ruler did not command the confidence of the dominant powers, the differences between how governments actually ruled and how they were supposed to rule were damaging and divisive. Kings and other regimes might be able to escape their difficulties by introducing reforms, but reforms were not cost-free – there were usually good reasons not to withdraw lucrative taxes, nor to default on loans, punish miscreants or eject key councillors – and the governments of the period typically dug their heels in, as Edward III did in 1340, or Charles of France in 1357–9, or Peter of Castile in 1354. Under these circumstances, the tendency was for divisions to break out across political society, as some of the elite sided with the critics of the government. Public pressure combined with pre-existing divisions to encourage prominent magnates, prelates and oligarchs to lend their support to popular protests, as the count of Urgel joined with the *Uniones* of Aragon, or as Richard II's relatives headed public and parliamentary moves against him in 1387–8, or as Salvestro de' Medici was willing to side with the populists in the priorate of 1378 which led to the rising of the *Ciompi*. Rulers had supporters too, of course, and they could face down their opponents – more often than not, in fact – but large-scale domestic divisions could be very serious and long-lasting in the general situation of shaky jurisdiction and recurrent warfare. For one thing, half-healed conflicts easily revived when circumstances changed – as the towns and lords that Peter the Cruel had overcome in the mid-1350s turned against him in the 1360s, for example, when his invasion of Aragon provoked an international counter-attack. For another, internal conflicts frequently involved external intervention, as participants in the long civil wars in Flanders, Scotland, France, Castile and Naples attracted support from neighbouring rulers with jurisdictional and other interests in these territories.

Drawing all this together, then, it is clear that the growth of government, and of associated notions of community, were major factors in the copious political conflict of the fourteenth century. While both processes could enable rulers and regimes to control larger spaces, to penetrate other jurisdictions more effectively and thus to begin to forge the variegated polities that emerged more firmly in the fifteenth century, they also generated conflicts and divisions, and, in the resulting chaos, the gains of central governments might be reversed and the influence of other jurisdictions and formations increased. Governmental growth, therefore, was an ambivalent process, and, under such circumstances, one might ask why it continued. One answer lies in the models of authority discussed in the previous chapter: these were a stimulus to almost all power-holders and their advisers, and it is not surprising that attempts to implement them were pushed so hard, especially during the high tide of juridical thinking in the century or so straddling 1300. But certain kinds of institutional and administrative development arose in response to domestic political reaction: the establishment of representative institutions, for instance, or the sharing of expanded jurisdiction, fiscality and office-holding with local powers. Put crudely, then, just as government was a cause of politics, so politics was a cause of government. In larger units, such as kingdoms, the texture of political life unquestionably changed over the century, even if the activities of government remained as contested as before. Where, earlier in the century, reactions were more likely to involve leagues of powerful subjects, gathering to protect their liberties and reject royal intrusions, we have seen that the picture later in the century – at least in the West – was more complex. Reaction was more likely to come from representative assemblies (and typically, in the first place, from lesser nobles and towns, rather than magnates); it was likely to involve some acceptance of royal impositions, albeit with a desire to renegotiate their terms; it often focused on the management of a royal/public fisc which hardly existed earlier on; it might involve the common people; and it might focus on the inner workings, or personnel, of the king's government, showing the way in which subaltern groups had become educated in the processes of administration and concerned to improve its direction. By the middle decades of the century, many subjects were beginning to benefit from the operations of larger governments, and they increasingly wished to maintain these, even if they also wished to correct abuses or shape the distribution of burdens. A somewhat similar trajectory can be detected in other units – the more kingdom-like principalities and lordships, the larger towns (which, by mid-century, usually included some sort of representation for middling interests besides the commune or *signoria*), and even the universal Church, where the constitutionalist activities of the cardinals in a time of mounting clerical dissatisfaction with the 'beneficial system' parallels experiments with councils in secular kingdoms. In many northern and eastern kingdoms, however, and even to a point in the Empire, the situation was different. Here, leagues of magnates or towns, seeking charters to protect their liberties, remained the dominant form of political response to government throughout the century. The comparatively limited juridical and fiscal penetration of eastern and northern kings removed some of the strongest pressures towards common action, and, broadly speaking, it was sectional groups, seeking to defend sectional interests, that wielded the language of regnal community in these places. But even in these regions, later in the century, there were moves which show that lesser powers in these kingdoms wished to establish a more formal, collective and public dialogue with royal government: haltingly, from the 1350s in Hungary and from the 1380s in Poland, not just magnates, but also representatives of lesser nobles and sometimes towns, began to meet with kings and royal agents, laying the foundations for the diets of the following century.

By and large, the growth of government has been underestimated as a cause of conflict by historians of Europe. It is generally accepted that taxation produced tensions, especially among the common people, and the 'particularism' of towns and magnates is widely recognised as an obstacle to royal power (and commonly condemned), but the major causes of conflict have typically been seen as large-scale and more or less external to political life. Most emphasis has been given to the effects of socioeconomic crisis, the impact of war and the influence of a putatively general culture of disorder and violence. Objections to these interpretations have been raised above, and it should be clear by now that there are other ways of approaching the turbulent politics of the period. But there is a fourth interpretative tendency in the literature that may deserve a little more attention here. When individual political episodes are under examination, the historians of this period often stress the particular, contingent, even fortuitous aspects of causation – accidents of heredity, flaws of personality, sudden deaths, the outcome of battles – rather than more structural or systemic causes.

On one level, this is entirely justifiable. It is hard not to feel that certain accidents of heredity had determinative results: the failure of the French royal line in 1316 and 1328, for instance, or the premature deaths of the sons of Louis the Great of Hungary, which opened the way for succession disputes in Poland and Hungary and terminated the twelve-year-old union of the crowns. Other freak events could be just as important: the Black Death, for instance, had a series of direct and significant political effects, halting the English war effort in France at the height of Edward III's success after the Crécy-Calais campaign; rescuing Peter IV of Aragon from the *Unión* of Valencia; and sweeping away both Alfonso XI and an Anglo-Castilian marriage alliance, among other examples. At the same time, however, it seems important to remember that chance and contingency were far from being the only causes of these various events; we should recognise that they stemmed from processes of calculation and common frameworks that have structural features. After all, there is nothing especially surprising about the Anglo-French marriage that created the English title to the throne of France, and the Black Death did not prevent the resumption of activities that it had temporarily stalled: the English resumed their campaigns in the 1350s, with just as much success; Peter IV was already making headway against the *Unión* of Aragon before his victory in Valencia; Anglo-Castilian alliances and marriages came in the 1360s and 1370s, instead of the 1340s. It is also clear that contingencies themselves fall into patterns that reveal structures. That royal minorities, for example, caused such problems in the fourteenth century tells us something about the hardening of succession rules and the widening scope of royal power. That they were more damaging in Castile or Hungary than in Sweden or Scotland tells us something about the relative political coherence of these kingdoms. Conversely, if we compare the way in which minority was handled in Castile early in the century, with the ways in which it was handled in England and France in the 1370s and 1380s (or in Castile itself in the first decade of the fifteenth century), it is clear how much more bureaucratic, and how much more integrated, these polities had become in the intervening decades. In interpreting the course of political development across the century, therefore, it is certainly important to recognise what the major contingencies were, and to allow them their full significance in shaping a complex pattern of development; but it is also crucial to generalise, to recognise that contingencies were not altogether random, and to remember that, because contemporaries knew both the strength and the vulnerabilities of the various power structures around them, the political norms of the period were partly adapted to them.

Resolution

Much of the discussion so far has centred on the nature and causes of conflict, and that seems appropriate, given the frequently disturbed nature of fourteenth-century political life, but it is also important to explore the routes by which a tolerable level of peace and co-operation was established. Broadly speaking, there seem to have been two main ways in which the potentially clashing jurisdictions of Europe resolved their differences. The first was the negotiation of treaties, charters or other agreements between powers that essentially wished to exclude each other, or at least to determine their common boundaries. The most straightforward examples of these are treaties between contending rulers, such as the Treaty of Caltabelotta (1302), in which the island of Sicily was conceded to the Aragonese cadet Frederick (d.1337), in return for his abandonment of claims to rule the mainland part of the *Regno*; or the Treaty of Brétigny-Calais (1360), in which an enlarged Aquitaine was granted to Edward III, in return for renunciation of his claims to the French throne; or the Union of Kalmar (1397) and its associated treaties, in which arrangements were made for the rule of Denmark, Norway and Sweden under the shared kingship of Eric of Pomerania. Besides these, however, we might equally include many of the more solemn and formal agreements made between kings and the inhabitants of their realms, on the grounds that these typically involved the restriction of royal government. Sometimes, as in the case of the *privilegio general* of Aragon, these agreements verged on the complete exclusion of royal influence; more commonly, like the French charters of 1315–16 or the statute of Koszyce in 1374, they established clear limits to royal claims and protected other jurisdictions. The constitutions of self-governing cities might be seen in a similar light: as we have seen, guilds, neighbourhood organisations, lords and *consorterie*, parties and *popoli* were, in some sense, autonomous institutions, agreeing to share power on a declared basis. On the whole, formal treaties and agree-ments of this kind did not tend to last, and the more independent the signatories, the shorter the duration typically was. Sicily and Naples were at war again twelve years after Caltabelotta, while Brétigny – which, tellingly, was never formally concluded by either side – lasted only nine years; Kalmar lasted longer, it is true (it was renegotiated in 1438), but this may owe something to its relatively loose terms. Meanwhile, national and provincial charters were fairly rapidly re-negotiated or modified in practice, even if outright confrontations – such as those in Aragon in the 1340s – were rare. Urban constitutions, on the other hand, tended to settle down for quite long periods of time, once a working compromise was found, but it is worth noting that that of Florence changed three or four times between 1293 and the more enduring arrangements of 1382. The reason for the generally temporary nature of treaty-type settlements is clear: the parties were merely suspending the pursuit of rights, claims or interests which they intended to resume when circumstances changed; they did not really accept these compromises as foundations for a common future. Where formal arrangements of this kind did endure, as in some of the fundamental laws that began to develop in this period (such as the imperial Golden Bull of 1356, or the treaties that held the Swiss Confederation together), it is usually a sign of mutual acceptance of a shared political space.

This leads neatly on to the second type of resolution, in which the hegemony of one power over another was recognised – formally or tacitly – in return for some kind of compromise (which itself could be formal or tacit). These settlements were not necessarily very different from treaties, and they could certainly be fragile: lesser or greater parties often sought to reshape the terms of their relationship as circumstances changed, and where subordinate powers were reason-ably coherent or autonomous, they might move towards secession or threaten it, as did Sicily, Gascony, Béarn, Brittany, Wales and various Irish lordships, for instance, or the towns of northern Germany, Tuscany or the Po Valley. At the same time, as in the rough distinc-tion drawn above between jurisdictional disputes and conflicts of political community, there was a tendency for these settlements to reflect the general acceptance by the parties of some kind of hierarchy and common identity. Sometimes rapidly in the wake of victories, sometimes over a longer time, kings, princes and communes drew in lords, churches, provinces, towns and other bodies and networks.

They used a mixture of formal media, such as representative assemblies, and relatively informal ones, ranging from negotiation and counsel, to the sharing of appointments to office, revenue, territory and other assets. Some of the resulting polities were relatively centralised, others were relatively federal, their constituent parts preserving larger areas of freedom within a regnal framework. Some were more stable than others, both in terms of the range of territories and powers accepting membership over time, and in terms of the general state of political order. Often the initiative for integration or association came from above, but we have noted that this kind of activity was not limited to top-level powers: not only did vassal lords, bishops and chartered towns often use a parallel range of devices in their own regions, they might also colonise the structures of superior authorities, as did the cities of Flanders and Brabant, or the urban–noble alliances of *Hoeken* and *Kabeljauwen* in Holland, or the princes of France, Naples and Castile. Either way, however, these moves helped to consolidate larger territories and to develop more complex political communities.

Many kings, princes and self-governing cities increased their purchase on the smaller powers of their *mouvances*. This was especially marked in the case of the Church, where, as we have noted, the spread of papal provisions typically advanced the ecclesiastical influence of kings and princes, while the growth of regnal jurisdiction, together with the reluctance of the post-Bonifacian Papacy to get into confrontations over secular power, reduced the scope for clerical independence. It was also noticeable in the case of lords and towns: the expansion of jurisdiction, representation and consultation at the regnal level, together with the concession of shares in taxation, office, courtly networks and military activity, all helped to harness urban and rural power to the rule of larger authorities. Even so, it is important to recognise that these developments were mostly still at a relatively early stage in the fourteenth century, and varied widely in their intensity and stability. Across most of the continent, and especially in the Empire and Italy, the relations between kings, lords, towns and churches remained highly variable, and even in comparatively settled places like the intensely governed kingdom of England or the lightly governed kingdom of Scotland, they could be full of bitterness, or subject to dislocation. Governmental innovations could shake up the most complaisant territories, and so, of course, could the major convulsions of the period – not just plagues, famines and wars, but also heretical movements like that of Wyclif, popular revolts and the Great Schism in the Church. Typically, the results of such shocks were ambivalent, producing some results that worked in favour of regnal co-ordination and others that worked against. While there were signs of a trend towards more integrated and complex polities, therefore, the process was a halting one, full of checks and reverses, some of them prolonged.

It should be clear, by now, why fourteenth-century political settlements were mostly rather shaky. For one thing, they were brokered between powers whose rights and interests frequently clashed, sometimes fundamentally. For another, they depended as much on informal compromises as on formal ones, and this usually meant a further dependence on the personal skills of rulers or on the maintenance of interpersonal relations; these were bound to come under strain, and to face frequent interruption and revision as leading participants failed or died. Even when all the powers in a given area succeeded in working out durable patterns of association, these were vulnerable to the sheer difficulty of ruling fourteenth-century states, with their broad social range, their protean administrative structures, their unfixed borders and their vulnerability to events. Taking all this into account, it is not hard to see why the politics of the period were so full of fluctuation, and why it is so difficult to draw out clear trends from the jumbled course of events. All the same, there was perhaps a drift towards the consolidation of norms and expectations in many areas, even if this did not extend to the establishment of outright obedience and clear boundaries. We have seen that there were few independent and self-governing towns by the end of the century – outside a few examples in Germany and Italy, 'city states' were either 'territorial states', members of town leagues or estates, or prominent subjects of kings and princes. The regnal framework was becoming more meaningful for most churchmen, even if one last remarkable attempt to challenge it would be made in the era of the Councils after 1400. The kingdoms and principalities of the fourteenth century may have kept falling apart, or changing hands, or forming novel unions, but there was coming to be something ineradicable about many of them by the end of the century. In 1300, Edward I of England thought he could be High King of the British Isles (and perhaps of the Plantagenet domains in France); Philip IV meant to rule a French kingdom in which Flanders, Gascony and Languedoc were fully obedient, and in which the Rhône, and maybe the Rhine, were the natural borders;

a little later, Henry VII and Ludwig attempted to restore the Empire, while Alfonso XI dreamed of ruling a neo-Roman *Hispania*, in which the future of the crowns of Portugal and Aragon-Catalonia was rather uncertain. These fantasy kingdoms proved unachievable, but they were by no means unthinkable. By the second half of the fourteenth century, however, such radical territorial revision was less plausible: even the grant of an enlarged Aquitaine to Edward III proved too much. While the distribution of territory remained fluid towards the imperial centre of Europe, and while the balance of power and authority was ever-changing almost everywhere, some boundaries were beginning to harden and, in some places, multiple political units were coming more often and more lastingly into phase.

4

THE FIFTEENTH CENTURY

———————— • ————————

The kinds of politics explored in the previous chapter – disputes involving overlapping jurisdictions, conflicts over government – continued unabated into the first half of the fifteenth century. Indeed, this period contained some of the most vivid examples of each, dominated as it was by the prolonged struggle for reform and control of the universal Church that took place in and around the Councils of Pisa, Constance and Basle. Why this conflict was so central to the politics of the first half of the century is a matter to be discussed below, but its fading in the middle decades is one of the reasons for breaking the narrative of events in about 1450. In the second half of the century, jurisdictional conflicts became less common. There were certainly plenty of wars, and conflicting rights played a part in causing and justifying them, but almost everywhere political boundaries began to settle and become less permeable, while authority came to be more concentrated at the regnal level. This did not mean an end to conflict – the distribution of right and power within these more defined polities went on being contested; and these contests were not always contained within regnal boundaries, as we shall see – but the political actors of the second half of the century generally acknowledged the primacy of the regnal political order; the bulk of politics turned on the relations between authoritative centres and the representatives of provinces and communities; and it is not surprising that the tendency of the period was towards the enhancement of central government and the improvement of its means of rule. Wars continued – indeed they grew in scale and intensity as the century went by – but they are

2　Europe in 1500

more easily differentiated from domestic conflicts, even if they could have a profound effect on the internal politics of states.

A break around 1450 is not by any means a novel idea. The year 1453, for instance, has been seen as a turning point since the fifteenth century itself. It witnessed the fall of Constantinople to the Ottoman Turks, an event of such contemporary significance that it features in most of the chronicles of the period, however local their concerns. Because Gibbon made it the final episode in his *Decline and Fall of the Roman Empire*, and because it was rapidly followed by the development of printing with movable type in 1455, it was once regarded by historians as inaugurating the High Renaissance and the birth of modern times. And these were not the only epoch-defining events of these years. Also in 1453, a French victory at the battle of Castillon, near Bordeaux, is supposed to have brought an end to the Hundred Years War between England and France. In fact, both Anglo-French warfare and internal French conflict were to continue for some decades, but it is hard to deny that the political boundaries of France were rendered more stable by the expulsion of the English from Normandy and Gascony, or that the political alignments of western Europe began to shift in the wake of these events. On a similar note, the following year, 1454, brought the Peace of Lodi between Venice and Milan, who were soon joined by Florence. This was followed, in 1455, by the formation of the 'Italian League', which – though born in Venetian reactions to the fall of Constantinople – tacitly acknowledged the division of Italy among its pre-eminent territorial states and ushered in four decades of relative peace in the peninsula. Rather than being especially formative themselves, these 1450s episodes reflect the gradual consolidation of fairly large regnal or regional polities, a process with roots running throughout the period covered in this book, but one which becomes most readily apparent in the second half of the century.

These features of fifteenth-century politics mean differences in the organisation of this chapter. The narrative sections are significantly longer, and more of the task of characterising and explaining political developments is carried out within them. This is for three main reasons. First, and most important, the politics of the fifteenth century were deeply and self-consciously interwoven with processes of political and constitutional growth: although it is possible to generalise about the structural developments of the period – and some generalisations will be offered in the final section of this chapter – it is impossible to do justice either to the events or to the institutions and practices of the period without discussing them together. While European polities continued to have much in common and to interact copiously with one another, they were increasingly preoccupied with the definition and development of their own particular political and constitutional traditions, and – for all the parallels among these processes – it seems helpful to depict them on a country-by-country basis. A second reason is that the politics of the first half of the century, in particular, were extremely dense and complicated, as an explicit concern with the institutions of government and their rights and wrongs combined with a jurisdictional situation that was still frequently unclear. This complexity makes more detailed discussion necessary, especially as the way in which lower-level powers, such as churches, towns and lords, interacted with high-level processes, such as the 'Conciliar movement', or the Hundred Years War, or 'imperial reform', plays an important part in explaining the advance of regnal polities in the course of the century. A third and final reason for the greater length of the following narratives is that the fifteenth century is better documented than the fourteenth, and the historiography is richer. These factors too argue for a fuller account, though it is worth noting that narratives of the fifteenth century as a whole remain unusual. The presence of that great dividing line, the 'Renaissance', in our period means that textbooks often start or end within the century, leaving its 'medieval' headwaters strangely cut off from its 'early modern' outflow.

THE COURSE OF EVENTS

C.1400–C.1450

The Councils, the Church and the Papacy

The 'Conciliar movement', as it is often called, arose from two main impulses: first, the growing desire, on the part of churchmen and secular rulers alike, to find a way of resolving the Great Schism in the Papacy; and second, the pressure for 'reform', which was a constant undercurrent in the Church, but had reached a kind of crescendo by the beginning of the fifteenth century. While the convocation of a general council was, to some extent, the obvious solution to both problems, it was also something of a last resort. Since the conflicts of the early fourteenth century, in which a council at Vienne had been

forced on the Papacy, and doctrines proposing constitutional government for the Church had been aired, councils had been regarded as
threatening to papal authority. Popes, therefore, were unwilling to
summon them, and it was not clear that anyone else had the right to
do so. In the context of schism, moreover, there was no pope capable
of summoning a council that could represent the whole Church, and
lay rulers were unwilling to support a venture that could result in
the condemnation of the pontiff to whom they had given allegiance.
Any council would thus need a novel basis of authority and the
juridical means to impose withdrawal on both the popes. The solution
that emerged during the first decade or so of the century lay in the
enunciation of a series of fundamental principles: that the common
good of the Church was higher than anything else, that churchmen
acting collectively for that common good were consequently able
to assemble as a council, and that a council so assembled held its
authority directly from Christ and was, at least in certain respects,
higher than the Papacy. These principles, contained in the writings of
the Parisian masters, Conrad of Gelnhausen (*c.*1320–*c.*1390), Henry of
Langenstein (1325–97), Jean Gerson (1363–1429) and Pierre d'Ailly
(1352–1420), and enacted in the famous decree of 1415, *Haec Sancta*
(This Holy…), were the foundation for both the achievements and
the problems of the Conciliar period, providing the conceptual basis
for the deposition of the schismatic popes, for the election of a new
one, and for ongoing conflict over the direction of the Church. While
there were conciliarist thinkers, and while many churchmen had
come, by the first decade of the fifteenth century, to believe that a
council provided the best means of solving their problems, the real
motor of the 'Conciliar movement' was *Haec Sancta*. Strengthened by
the 1417 decree *Frequens*, which established the regular intervals at
which councils must take place, it created a world in which there was
a real authority above the Papacy to which anyone capable of mobi-
lising opinion could appeal. That authority would have awesome
powers to make new law for the common good of Christendom,
and it was under no single leadership, besides that of Christ. So it was
that a logical, in some ways conventional, solution to the predicament
of the Church contained within it the seeds of radical action and
further schism.

  The other source of radicalism was the pressure for reform. In part,
this was a moral and theological concern: the Church was always felt
to be in need of reform, but the spread of religious education and the

mounting scandal of the Schism made that need seem all the more pressing by the early fifteenth century. The perception that heresy was growing was also a factor. The fraternal critiques of the early fourteenth century, with their denunciations of the Papacy and their challenge to ecclesiastical worldliness, had been revived and taken onward in the powerful assaults of the prominent Oxford theologian John Wyclif (d.1384). While Wyclif himself had been silenced in the early 1380s, and his following within the English Church had been contained over the following decade or two, his writings circulated widely, and in Bohemia, linked to England by a marriage alliance (1382–94), they found a sympathetic reception from a circle of influential preachers led by the rector of Prague University, Jan Hus (c.1370–1415). Heresy, then, was apparently on the march, and it was clear to many churchmen that 'reform in head and members' – a more spiritual, disciplined and educated clergy, from the papal Curia to the parishes – would be essential to its defeat.

At the same time, however, calls for reform arose from more straightforwardly political tensions over the distribution of power and resources within the Church. The 'beneficial system' developed by the Papacy since the later thirteenth century was a particular focus of criticism. While papal provisions offered some benefits to prelates, academics and rulers, the taxation and lobbying that accompanied them were widely resented. This resentment grew during the Schism, as the benefits diminished, because provisions were more easily defied, and as the burdens mounted, especially in France and Aragon, where the collectories of Avignon continued to function and the embattled popes revived direct taxation to support themselves. By the 1390s, as we have seen, the French church was ready to abandon its allegiance to Pope Benedict XIII, and the three councils that met at Paris in 1395–8 began to formulate a new model in which the king would replace the Pope as protector of ecclesiastical liberty, free canonical election would replace the majority of papal provisions, and beneficial taxation would cease. These 'Gallican liberties' provided an ideal to which other clerics might aspire, and thus helped to animate the wider reform movement, but they were not without disadvantages for the Church. For one, royal protection came at a price: as early as 1398, the French crown requested that the tenths historically paid to the Papacy should now be paid directly to itself. For another, the provisions system proved harder to dismantle than reformers had expected: there was pressure from university men to maintain it, since it

provided their wherewithal, and copious disagreement over the conflicting rights of electors and patrons in most major benefices. Within
a few years, French ecclesiastical leaders were willing to contemplate
renewed submission to Benedict (1403–4), and the next few decades
saw them trying to find a suitable compromise between the Scylla of
papal control and the Charybdis of Gallican liberties and royal intervention. In these ways, the French experience anticipated the predicament faced by the rest of the international Church in the era of the
Councils: the interests of cardinals, metropolitans, other bishops,
scholars, the religious orders and the various kinds of lay power cut
across one another; everyone could agree on the desirability of
reform, but even identifying satisfactory improvements, let alone
imposing them, was a very difficult business. In that predicament lay
the seeds of division within the Councils and a central reason for the
(qualified) victory eventually won by the Papacy.

The period of the Councils began, as we have seen, in a rebellion of
exasperated cardinals. Proposals for a general assembly convoked by a
joint delegation from the two obediences had emerged from Paris by
1406; once the newly elected Roman Pope, Gregory XII (1406–15),
refused to resign, as he had promised, and as it became clear that
negotiations between the pontiffs were destined to fail, the majority of
the cardinals – eight Roman and seven Avignonese – met with French
representatives at Pisa and summoned a council to meet there in
March 1409. Delegates from France, England, Milan, Florence,
Bologna, the deposed Emperor Wenceslas IV and a number of
other principalities in Italy and Germany proceeded to announce
the deposition of the two existing popes and the election of a third,
Alexander V (1409–10); at the same time, they deferred discussion of
reform to a further council, to meet a few years later. Unfortunately,
Pisa did not succeed in destroying either Benedict or Gregory: the
former retained the support of Aragon, Castile and Scotland; the latter
retained the support of the Emperor, Rupert of the Palatinate (1400–
10), Ladislas of Naples and a few other Italian and German powers.
While pressure from reformers and the advice of jurists was important
in shaping these decisions, it is clear that the political interests of lay
leaders had a significant role to play in them: the crown of Aragon was
reluctant to relinquish its own native pope, whose support might be
invaluable in securing Sicily; Rupert and Ladislas both relied on the
Roman Papacy for legitimation; and many of the Italian powers
supported the Pisan Pope as a counterweight to Ladislas, who had

occupied Rome in 1407. In 1410, Alexander died and was succeeded by his most powerful local supporter, Baldassare Cossa, cardinal-legate of Bologna, who became John XXIII (1410–15). Backed by Florence and the duke of Anjou, John took on Ladislas, defeating him at Roccasecca and regaining control of Rome in 1411. He also appointed a number of progressive cardinals, the conciliar theorists Pierre d'Ailly, Guillaume Fillastre and Francesco Zabarella among them, and convened a council at Rome to discuss reforms. But this promising start to the Pisan Papacy was not fulfilled: Ladislas reoccupied Rome in 1413; John was forced to flee, and turned to the new Emperor, Sigismund of Luxemburg, king of Hungary, for aid. This was the configuration that led to the Council of Constance. Not only was it clear that a second council would be necessary to resolve the persisting Schism, its convocation promised to advance the interests of both John and Sigismund. The former might expect to be confirmed in his position, and the latter, who had secured his throne with some difficulty following a double election in 1411, was looking for the vindication that a restoration of ecclesiastical unity would bring.

If John XXIII had hoped to dominate the Council of Constance through the support of Italian bishops, he was to be disappointed. The cardinals pressed for the inclusion of university masters, doctors and the representatives of princes among those entitled to vote, and an English proposal for voting by nations ensured that any papal bloc would be a minority. The non-Italian nations – 'German', 'French' and 'English' – favoured the simultaneous abdication of all three popes, believing that this was the best way of re-establishing the papal office on a properly universal basis and also of ensuring that reforms could be introduced without papal resistance. While Gregory XII accepted his fate, John fled and tried to reconvene a council under his own direction at nearby Schaffhausen. This act hardened the council's resolve: in April 1415, it issued *Haec Sancta*, with its firm statement of conciliar supremacy in matters of faith, schism and reform; the following month it tried and deposed Pope John. It took another two years to detach the supporters of Benedict XIII (deposed 1417), and during this time the council achieved little of note, besides the burning of Jan Hus (1415) and the issue of a decree condemning the notion of tyrannicide. In 1417, with a fifth, 'Spanish', nation present, discussion turned to the question of whether to give priority to devising reforms or electing a new pope. A fudge resulted, in which a small number of reforms were agreed in October 1417 – by far the most important being the decree *Frequens* – and a conclave arranged soon after. That the new Pope, Martin V (1417–31), was a cardinal of the Colonna family suggests that there was support for the revival of a strong, Rome-based Papacy. Martin proceeded to sidestep the council by agreeing concordats separately with the various nations (1418). These involved the reduction of provisions, tenths and beneficial taxation, and promised better representation in the Curia through the appointment of more non-Italian cardinals. In a sense, therefore, the prelates of Europe got the reforms they most wanted: the Schism was ended; the burden of papal taxation was significantly reduced; a stand had been taken against heresy; and there was some discussion of common ecclesiastical abuses plus a commitment to further reform at future councils. To this extent, Constance was a success. Whether the council had done much for clerical liberty or unity is another matter. In several cases – France and Castile in particular – kings began to wield powers that had formerly been exercised by popes, Charles VII going so far as to impose three tenths on the French Church during the council itself (even the Emperor obtained one in 1418). While the Schism had blown open the fragile compromises that the pre-1378 Papacy had established with lay and ecclesiastical powers alike, Constance had not created new ones. The future structure of the Church, the balance of clerical liberty, papal (and now conciliar) authority, and lay stewardship remained wide open.

Although Martin V succeeded to revenues only a third the size of those enjoyed by the Papacy before the Schism, his pontificate was remarkably successful. Colonna power brought him Rome in 1420, and, by granting vicariates to the leading lords, he was able to restore control of most of the Papal States by the middle of the following decade: only Bologna, lost with the fall of John XXIII, eluded him. By 1426–7, his income had grown by half, mainly because of the contribution made by these territories; he thus laid the foundations of the so-called 'Renaissance Papacy', in which princely power in central Italy was the main ingredient. Within the Church, he raised crusades against the Hussites, opened talks with the Orthodox Greeks, and pressed for the restoration of papal prerogatives across Europe (obtaining the submission of Valois France in 1425, for example); but he also took care to operate within the law and according to the new conciliarist norms. The first council appointed under *Frequens* was allowed to assemble at Pavia in 1423, but Martin did not attend, and when few others did either, he transferred it to Siena and dissolved it in 1424. Under its aegis, a series of reforms to the clergy were considered – most of them proposing stricter adherence to established rules – but French pressure for further restriction of papal beneficial and fiscal rights was successfully diverted, and negotiations begun with Alfonso of Aragon eventually terminated the Avignonese Papacy (1429). Even so, there were weaknesses as well as strengths in Martin's position. For one thing, the conciliar framework remained: while the papal right to summon and dissolve councils had been tacitly accepted, *Frequens* remained in force, and the termination of the Council of Pavia-Siena was accompanied by agreement to a further council to meet at Basle seven years later. For another, the revival of an Italian Papacy meant the revival of factional struggles within the Curia. On Martin's death, the Orsini cardinals and their allies secured the election of a pope hostile to the Colonna, Eugenius IV (1431–47). The result was violent conflict in the Papal States, and in 1434 the Papacy was once again driven out of Rome, to spend nine years in Tuscany.

The Council of Basle (1431–49) opened soon after Eugenius' election, and was immediately embroiled in a constitutional conflict with the new Pope, when a cardinal who had missed the conclave appealed to its superior authority to quash the result. Eugenius countered by trying to dissolve the council, unwisely insisting on the papal plenitude of power and provoking the reissue of *Haec Sancta* (1432) in response. Basle moved to suspend the Pope for contempt, proceeded to take up the government of the Church and to set up four commissions – on reform, faith, peace and 'common matters' – to carry out its work. It was able to deal so confidently with Eugenius for a number of reasons. First of all, it was extremely well attended, larger even than Constance. Second, it enjoyed the firm backing of the Emperor, the prelates of central Europe and even the legate sent to open it, Cardinal Cesarini: these men had all been engaged in fighting the Hussite heretics during the 1420s; they had come to see negotiation as the only route to peace and regarded a council as the ideal vehicle. Finally, the demand for reform was unabated among the clergy, and the organisation of the council – equal voting rights for all who swore to obey its decrees, the intermingling of nations in the various commissions – looked more likely to deliver it. By the end of 1432, fifteen of Eugenius' twenty-one cardinals were supporting Basle against him, while the canonist Nicholas of Cusa wrote a major treatise,

De Concordantia Catholica (On Catholic Concordance, 1433), arguing that justice required both Pope and Emperor to rule in tandem with councils of their subjects. Under such co-ordinated pressure, the Pope was finally obliged to accept the legitimacy of the council and its right to consider 'reform in head and members' in the bull *Dudum Sacrum* (Recently, the Holy..., 1433). The ensuing years saw the council acting authoritatively and successfully on a host of fronts: it maintained negotiations with the Hussites, which culminated in the Compacts of Prague in 1436; it brought a measure of peace to France, with the Congress of Arras in 1435; and it enacted sweeping reforms – the withdrawal of most benefices from papal provision in 1433 and 1436, and the abolition of annates in 1435. These last measures, accompanied by orders to Eugenius to enforce the council's decrees and threats to reform the Curia, precipitated a fresh crisis. The Pope could not possibly accept such a direct assault on his rights and revenues, and, in a tract known as the *Libellus Apologeticus* (Defensive Pamphlet, 1436), appealed to lay rulers for support, denouncing the council's claim to independent authority and citing the general threat posed by democratic bodies of this kind. The following year, he formally transferred the council to Ferrara, in anticipation of a meeting with representatives of the Byzantine Church; Basle, which had been trying to arrange a similar meeting with the Greeks under its own direction, responded by declaring *Haec Sancta* an article of faith and denying the papal right to transfer the council without its agreement. It began new proceedings against Eugenius, which culminated, in 1439, in his formal deposition and the election of the retired duke of Savoy as Pope Felix V (1439–49); the Pope's response was to excommunicate those still at Basle and depose them from their offices.

   These dramatic events faced both ecclesiastical and lay powers with a dilemma. During 1436–7, all but one of the cardinals returned to Eugenius: the threat of renewed schism, alarm at the direction of conciliar policy, a sense that the assault on papal revenues was going too far, and positive enthusiasm for the proposed reunion of the eastern and western churches were probably the main reasons. Several lay rulers withdrew their delegations, uncertain of the council's status and probably exhausted by its long duration. Many bishops, on the other hand, wished to uphold the reforms of Basle, and this helps to explain the declarations of neutrality which emerged from Valois France, the Empire and Castile, in 1438–9: the rulers of these territories continued to deal with Basle rather than Ferrara/Florence, and they enacted its measures on provisions and taxation, but they did not accept its claims to supremacy, and they maintained contact with the embattled Pope.[1] In each case, these moves enabled kings and princes to pose as the defenders of ecclesiastical liberties while extending their own jurisdiction over the churches in their domains: they were thus another decisive step in the general move towards national, or regnal, churches. The king of England, already the effective steward of his Church, had nothing to gain from encouraging clerical liberty and gave firm support to Eugenius; the duke of Burgundy followed suit, perhaps in the hope of influencing papal appointments in the expanding sphere of his territories. Poland, Aragon and Milan, on the other hand, all supported Basle, the last two in pursuit of antipapal territorial interests in the *Regno* and the Papal States respectively, but the Polish position (and perhaps the Aragonese) was shaped by local ecclesiastical pressure and general support for measures to protect liberties.

Europe had thus returned to schism, but it was a very different kind of schism from that of 1378. The reforms of the 1430s, so widely taken up, neutralised the power of the Papacy and the council alike. Support for Basle was notably shaky. Attendance dwindled after Eugenius' bull of excommunication, and this made conciliar claims to derive authority from representing the Church problematic, at least outside the Empire. Eugenius, on the other hand, began to prosper. His council, transferred to Florence in 1439, witnessed the formal reunion of the Greek and Latin Churches under a limited papal leadership. Since this act was immediately disowned by the bulk of the Orthodox establishment (as well as by some canonists), its significance may be questioned, but it helped to stimulate confidence in the Papacy, and may have played a part in the torrent of canonical justification for the papal supremacy that flowed from the reunited Curia between the bull *Moyses Vir* (Moses, the man…, 1439) and the *Summa de Ecclesia* produced by Cardinal Juan de Torquemada in 1448–9. While *Moyses* condemned the schismatic and heretical behaviour of the remaining delegates at Basle, Torquemada's treatise offered a thoroughgoing defence of papal monarchy as the source of

---

[1] The French document was known as the Pragmatic Sanction of Bourges (1438). The Germans declared neutrality at Frankfurt in 1438, and accepted a number of Baslean reforms in the Acceptation of Mainz (1439).

authority and unity in the Church, a condemnation of *Frequens* and a firm statement that none of the pretensions of conciliarists were grounded in the faith. More tangibly, Eugenius' abandonment of the Angevin cause in Naples permitted a *rapprochement* with the victorious Alfonso V (1442–3) and enabled the Pope to return to Rome. A few years later, in 1447, Bishop Olésnicki of Cracow brought Poland back to the papal obedience, in return for a cardinal's hat and the dominance of the Polish Church that it implicitly conferred. In the same year, Emperor Frederick III (1440–93) ejected the rump of the council from Basle; following a council of German princes, he sealed the Concordat of Vienna with the new Pope, Nicholas V (1448–55), in 1448. This document, which effectively gave Frederick rights of nomination over the sees of his Austrian lands, and conferred similar rights on other princes when they came to ratify it, cut across the conciliarist and reformist emphasis of the Acceptation of Mainz, and provoked decades of grumbling from the German Church.

The council finally dissolved itself at Lausanne in 1449, and Felix V resigned. While the conciliar ideal retained support in the Empire, and also at Paris, and canonical support for councils as a solution to emergencies within the Church remained strong, the 'Conciliar movement' was effectively over. The Pope had emerged as the only plausible leader of the universal Catholic Church; pontiffs from Nicholas V onwards were able to ignore *Frequens*; and Pius II (1458–64) faced virtually no resistance when he forbade appeals to future councils in the bull *Execrabilis* (1460). Antony Black has remarked on the way that the Councils of Pisa, Constance and Basle demonstrated 'the late-medieval talent for constitutional adaptation and creation'.[2] This is surely right, and the Councils gave both a positive and a negative example to contemporaries, first by encouraging parallel constitutional experiments in the Empire and elsewhere, and second, in the later years of Basle, by helping to create the circumstances in which articulate defences of monarchical authority might be made. Whatever its ideological victories, however, there is no question that the papal monarchy over the Church was weakened by the Conciliar period, and especially by the long period of tension and schism with Basle. While Martin V had

---

[2] A. Black, *Council and Commune: The Conciliar Movement and the Fifteenth-Century Heritage* (London, 1979), p. 3.

enjoyed some success in regaining control of both provisions and beneficial taxation, this was rapidly eroded during the 1430s and 1440s, and, during the second half of the century, especially from the 1470s, the Papacy surrendered most of its remaining rights of appointment and taxation to the princes of Europe – only in central and southern Italy did it firmly defend them. The 'Conciliar movement' thus had the ironic and partly unintended result of promoting the development of regnal churches under princely control, though it is important to remember that these had been in formation for some time, and that papal influence over them had always involved negotiation with local powers. Meanwhile, papal control over central Italy was generally strengthened in this period, and the revenues of the Papal States became a more important element in papal finances (though the reign of Eugenius is an exception in both respects); but that tells us more about the advance of territorial power in the later middle ages, a phenomenon occurring across Italy and elsewhere at the same time.

The Empire

The history of the Empire in this period was not only interwoven with that of the Councils, it also parallelled it. Not only did the century begin in schism – since the deposition of Wenceslas and election of Rupert of the Palatinate were supported by only half the Electors – it was also characterised by frequent meetings of the imperial diet, especially between 1439 and 1446, and by a strong emphasis on reform. Like the cardinals, the Electors were frequently ready to work together, independently of the monarch, as representatives of the Empire; they raised armies and summoned diets, introduced reformist schemes and even ruled collectively as a committee of regency (*Kurverein*) for brief periods in 1394, 1399, 1424 and 1438; they deposed Wenceslas and threatened to do the same to Sigismund in 1422, if he did not come and attend to the affairs of the Empire. These parallels are not particularly surprising: the leaders of the Holy Roman Empire were bound to take a special interest in the reform of the Latin Church, and reform in one sphere was bound to stimulate similar activity in the other. The *Reformatio Sigismundi*, for example, a widely circulated tract of 1439, declared the purpose of the Councils to include 'a proper reformation of spiritual and secular affairs', and mingled Baslean and even Hussite proposals for reform of the Church with social criticisms and demands for the restoration of imperial authority.[3] But imperial reform was also rooted in local traditions, most notably the role that the Electors, and secondarily other princes, had come to play in protecting the goods and rights of the Empire and in delivering its consent to the laws and acts of the Emperor. In common with ecclesiastical reform, one of its guiding principles was the returning of institutions and practices to what they ought to have been, but where the Councils were generally concerned to reduce the pressure of papal government, imperial reformers wished to revive imperial authority. The reforms proposed by Nicholas of Cusa, for example, included annual councils of the Empire for the transaction of common business and the making of laws; the creation of twelve or more provincial appeal courts, under imperial control, to ensure the enforcement of peace, law and justice; the resumption of the imperial fisc; the establishment of a common treasury; and the introduction of general taxation to support an army for defence and policing.

Not surprisingly, these initiatives appealed to the Emperor as well as the Electors, and proposals along these lines were discussed at the frequent diets of the period. There were some tangible results. Perhaps the most striking developments were the experiments with taxation and military obligation, which took place against the background of the Hussite raids of the 1420s. In 1422, a system of military quotas was drawn up – the *Matrikel* – and tax burdens apportioned accordingly. The revenues of the tax were disappointing, and a lot of the money went not to the Emperor but to the various princely and urban authorities that collected it, but the principle of common obligations was established, and, rather as in the France of the 1340s, this first initiative was a basis for later development. Meanwhile, schemes for a number of panels to maintain *Landfrieden* and provide arbitrative justice under imperial supervision were discussed in 1415 and 1417, 1434, 1437, 1438 and 1442. Once again, little came of these discussions, and there was usually disagreement about the composition and location of the panels, but the idea of imperial co-ordination of justice was firmly established, and, once again, bore fruit later in the century. No emperor was able to make much headway in restoring the old imperial fisc, and indeed the last bits of territory were pledged away by the end of the 1430s, but Sigismund and his successors were able to police and protect their remaining fiscal and judicial rights, collecting

[3] A translation appears in G. Strauss, *Manifestations of Discontent in Germany on the Eve of the Reformation* (Bloomington, IN, 1971), 3–31; quotation from p. 6.

information on obligations, such as the list of urban tax liabilities in 1418, levying sizeable fines for infringements through the office of the *procurator fiscalis*, maintaining the power to dispose of major fiefs, and enjoying some success with the application of the imperial ban (most notably against Frederick, count of Tyrol, when he aided Pope John XXIII in 1415; a parallel initiative against Philip of Burgundy failed in 1434). However far these early reform initiatives fell short of the fantasies of their exponents, they strengthened the conceptual and even institutional infrastructure of the Reich.

The achievements and limitations of imperial reform throw a revealing light on the realities of political organisation in the Empire. As in the Church, reform was a structure, available for exploitation by interest groups. One strong source of support for it was the four western Electors, whose territories were comparatively scattered: lacking the means of regional co-ordination, they generally aligned themselves with the strengthening of imperial influence. They were particularly concerned by the eastern power base and eastern focus of the Luxemburg and Habsburg emperors, and, although they sometimes fell out among themselves, they generally wished to establish strong imperial institutions in the West under their own direction. The eastern Electors, the other princes and many of the towns had a more equivocal attitude to reform. The electors of Brandenburg and Saxony were generally allies of the Emperor in this period; their territories were comparatively extensive, and their orientation towards the east and north; they were not particularly interested in the collective rule of the Empire. Most other princes had no wish to be directed by the Electors, and their attendance at diets was patchy in the first half of the century. Their activity was focused on dynastic management and the projection of authority in the region of their lands; apart from unusual crises like the Hussite wars of the 1420s, or the great town war of 1449–52, it was only their dealings with the Emperor that drew them into politics at the imperial level.

Even so, there seems to have been a genuine and widespread concern with the state of order in the Empire – perhaps especially across Swabia and Franconia, the old imperial heartlands, where political boundaries were least fixed and where the gathering strength of some regional principalities, notably the (Upper) Palatinate, the Swiss Confederation and the county of Württemberg, threatened the independence of other princes, towns, religious houses and lesser nobles. These regions looked naturally towards the monarch, and

Peter Moraw has termed them *königsnah* (near to the king), but even here, no party wished to surrender any of its own liberties, and nor could the Empire – which was believed to exist for their protection – reasonably ask them to do so.[4] Towns might be ready to accept some tax obligations to the Emperor, and they had some interest in imperial protection, but they were not about to forfeit control of their own financial resources; nor were they willing to subject themselves to judicial panels or *Landfrieden* when these might turn out to be a means of imperial or princely interference. Instead, many Swabian towns joined with knights and disgruntled princes in the League of Marbach in 1405, to resist the tax demands of King Rupert; in 1441, they formed a purely urban league to defend their trade routes (and, later in the decade, their independence) from local princes. Those lesser nobles who were direct vassals of the emperor followed a similar course, forming the 'Swabian Society of the Shield of St George' against the Swiss in 1408, for example, and receiving recognition from Sigismund as 'imperial knights' in 1422. Sigismund's action reminds us that the emperors might be just as interested in winning the support of local networks as in promoting legal and institutional reforms; in 1415, interestingly, against the tenor of the Golden Bull, he had offered recognition to urban leagues, provided they accepted the presidency of an imperial agent. Imperial support for reform was therefore variable, and it is worth noting that the emperors were absent from many of the diets of the period, dealing with them by proxy. They were consistently unwilling to accept reforms that could limit their own freedoms and prerogatives – so that Frederick, for example, gave plans to establish a *Reichsregiment*, or governing council of Emperor and Electors, short shrift in 1455 – and they had other fish to fry, in Bohemia, Hungary, Austria and elsewhere, besides the business of the Empire.

This emerges very clearly when we look at what happened in the first half of the fifteenth century. Rupert's only success during his short reign was to afforce the territory of the Palatinate and to extend its *mouvance* into Alsace. His attempt to invade Italy, to conquer Milan and secure coronation from the Roman Pope ended in ignominious withdrawal from Pavia in 1402. He spent much of the rest of his reign in vain attempts to raise taxation to repay his debts, while the bulk of

---

[4] P. Moraw, *Von offener Verfassung zu gestalteter Verdichtung: Das Reich im späten Mittelalter 1250 bis 1490* (Berlin, 1985), pp. 175ff.

electoral and princely opinion steadily deserted both him and the Roman Papacy. Rupert's successor, Sigismund, enjoyed much greater success in wielding the powers of the Empire, notwithstanding his many other commitments. He did not even enter Germany until 1414, and spent much of the next two decades abroad – ruling his kingdom of Hungary; campaigning in Bohemia or against Venice; negotiating with the English, French and Spanish during the era of Constance; and securing coronation in Milan and Rome in 1431–4. Although his absences provoked tensions with the Electors (and prompted Sigismund himself to threaten resignation in 1429 at the lack of assistance he was getting), an effective network of his supporters pulled the kingdom together and engaged it in a long struggle to contain the Hussites (1420–34), which suited Sigismund's interests. Most of the Emperor's major supporters in this venture were the princes in the front line of Hussite raiding – the margraves of Meissen, on whom he bestowed Saxony and its electorate in 1423; the dukes of Bavaria and Austria; and the towns and knights of Franconia. But Sigismund's skilful patronage also played a part in winning him support: Albert of Austria, for example, was given Moravia, along with Sigismund's daughter and heiress, in 1422; the Emperor enlisted the Swiss through his struggle against the count of Tyrol in 1415; and his grant of Brandenburg to his retainer Frederick of Hohenzollern gave him a mainly reliable lieutenant and electoral ally (while the two men were briefly at odds over Poland in the early 1420s, it was the Emperor who had the upper hand).

Imperial influence seems to have weakened in the mid- to late 1430s, however. The Electors took the lead in dealing with the schism provoked by Basle, and Albert II (1438–9) was too absorbed by the task of winning his kingdoms of Hungary and Bohemia to have any impact on the Empire during his short reign. Frederick III began quite promisingly, taking steps to negotiate a settlement in the Church and discussing reform plans at diets in 1442 and 1444. But from that year onwards, he was continuously absent for twenty-seven years, most of it taken up with attempts to secure and maintain control of the various territories of Austria. While he established a separate chancery for the Empire in 1442 and left behind capable lieutenants, the 1440s and 1450s saw a succession of serious conflicts in the south of the kingdom, most notably a French invasion in support of Zurich's rebellion against the Swiss (1443–5), and a second great town war, pitching Nuremberg and the Swabian towns against the attempt of Albert

'Achilles' of Brandenburg to restore the duchy of Franconia (1449–52). Under these circumstances, and feeling provoked by the collapse of Basle, the absence of Frederick and his double-dealing with the Papacy, the western Electors revived the reform initiative, the arch-bishop of Mainz explicitly arguing that Church reform and imperial reform should be linked, and the new Count Palatine, Frederick I (1451–70), calling for the Emperor's deposition in 1455. But the Emperor simply refused to co-operate, and divisions among the Electors meant that their schemes petered out. By 1458, the Count Palatine, backed by Hesse, Württemberg and the rising Wittelsbach duke of Bavaria-Landshut, was at war in Swabia and the Rhineland with the archbishop of Mainz, Albert Achilles and the Elector of Saxony. While this lengthy and sprawling conflict of major princes led to further calls for Frederick's resignation, and helped to produce an extraordinary scheme for an international league, proposed by the king of Bohemia in 1462, it demonstrated the lack of unity in the Empire at this time, and the impossibility of more co-ordinated rule.

Drawing this together, it is clear that too much should not be made of the supposed 'dualism' of the Empire – a distinction between the rights and interests of the Emperor on the one hand, and those of the Empire, represented by its estates, especially the Electors, on the other. For one thing, the estates were frequently unwilling to line up behind the Electors, and, for another, the emperors could win extensive support by dealing informally and individually with the various powers and interest groups of the Empire. There certainly was a persisting dynamic in favour of reform, and it tended to promote legal and institutional frameworks under the direction of representative bodies, but the emperors were not consistently at odds with these initiatives; rather, they adopted the same attitude of partial co-operation as all the other estates. Only in the later 1450s and 1460s did the links between the Emperor and the Empire show signs of breaking, but once Frederick had overcome a uniquely challenging situation in Austria, his involvement in imperial affairs resumed. Finally, it may be worth emphasising the wrongness – at least for this period – of the old view that the Electors sought to choose emperors who would be weak and unable to challenge the rights of the estates. Not only are there few signs that any Emperor wished to challenge these rights, but each of the three emperors elected after Rupert – Sigismund of Luxemburg (1411–37), and the two Habsburgs, Albert V of Austria (1438–9) and Frederick of Styria (1440–93) – was the strongest figure in the dominant imperial family.[5] In many ways, the negotiations over imperial reform were not so very different from the kinds of dialogue that existed between other kings and the estates of their kingdoms: collective action was a means of power for rulers and subjects alike, but they also had other means of achieving their interests and were not to be pinned down by constitutional innovations.

Bohemia and the Hussite revolution

Perhaps the most dramatic example of early fifteenth-century constitutional experimentation was provided by the kingdom of Bohemia. The interaction of Wyclifite heresy with Czech pietistic tradition, and the complicated relationship between the king, the nobility, the Church and the towns, produced a revolutionary convulsion that horrified European opinion and reshaped the Bohemian polity for decades. The immediate origins of the Hussite crisis lay in Wenceslas' decision to align himself with the plans for a general council in 1408, in the hope of overturning his deposition from the Empire, which the Roman Pope had sanctioned in 1403. By the decree of Kutná Hora in 1409, the Czech masters and their leader, Jan Hus, were placed in charge of Prague University and thus enabled to preach freely against the Papacy, and against the tenure of property and authority by the clergy more generally. When the archbishop of Prague excommunicated Hus in 1410, the king deposed him from his see, appointed a new archbishop and began to take the possessions of the diocese into his own hands. Thwarted by the rapidly changing situation in both Papacy and Empire, Wenceslas seems to have thought better of this kind of radicalism, and moved to restrain Hus and his supporters in 1412, but the situation was moving out of his hands. Over the next two years, Hus gained the protection of the nobility, and Hussite preachers attracted widespread support for the reformation of the Church. When Constance executed Hus in 1415, placed another interdict on Bohemia and condemned the spreading practice of utraquism,[6] the

---

[5] The divided election of 1410 is an exception, in which the majority of the Electors chose Jöst of Moravia, instead of Sigismund, but that partly reflects the machinations of the discarded Wenceslas. On Jöst's suspicious death in early 1411, the two Luxemburg brothers came quickly to terms, and Sigismund's election was assured.

[6] This was the taking of both bread and wine by the laity during communion. Conventional Catholic practice was to restrict the laity to bread alone, and communion in both kinds, with its implication of equality between the priesthood and the laity, had become the keynote of Hussite allegiance by the end of 1414.

situation escalated: leagues of Hussite and Catholic nobles formed; lords of both confessions began to exercise more direct control of ecclesiastical appointments and property; attacks were made on the lands of the pro-Constance bishop of Litomysl; and, as preachers of all kinds roamed freely, radical sentiments spread across the country. An attempt by Wenceslas to resume control of Prague in 1419 provoked a rebellion of the city ('Defenestration of Prague') and the establishment of religious communities in the mountains, named after the biblical sites of Tabor and Horeb. When the king died shortly afterwards, the magnates moved from supervising the Church to seizing its assets and those of the crown: a third or more of Bohemia's cultivable land thus changed hands in five years between 1419 and 1424, and, in the resulting chaos, large numbers of peasants left their holdings to join the communities ('brotherhoods') in the hills. While the magnates and the Prague council were willing to contemplate a settlement with Wenceslas' heir, Emperor Sigismund, his rejection of Hussite beliefs at the Diet of Breslau (1420), and a victory of the radical Taborites over the royalist nobles at Sudoměř, ruled this out. Instead, Church and Empire embarked on a series of crusades against the Hussites (1420–31), which both united the Bohemians and shifted the balance of power away from the more tractable magnates and towards the now-militarised brotherhoods, under their skilful captain Jan Žižka (d.1424). At the Diet of Čáslav in 1421, Sigismund was deposed, his throne was offered to the ruler of Lithuania, Vytautas, and a regency council comprising Hussite magnates, the city of Prague, other towns and the brotherhoods (and from 1424 other commons) was established. Over the next decade and a half, this body, assisted by intermittent diets, was the formal government of Bohemia, though its practical influence was limited – power on the ground being alternately contested and shared between Hussite and Catholic nobles and the brotherhoods. The German crusades produced short periods of relative unity among the Hussites, and provoked counter-attacks from 1427 to 1431, in which Czech armies raided the neighbouring territories of Germany, Austria, Silesia and Poland, but when the pace of foreign intervention slackened, the magnates gradually regained control of Bohemia and opened negotiations with Sigismund and the Council of Basle from 1433. With the defeat of the brotherhoods at Lipany in 1434, the way was open for a settlement, and Sigismund, having agreed to tolerate utraquism, but insisting on the restoration of episcopal authority, was admitted to his kingdom in 1436.

The revolution was thus at an end. In one sense, it had revealed just how slender were the threads that held the Bohemian polity together. When the king turned against the Church, he undermined the main prop for royal authority in the kingdom; leagues of magnates intervened to save the 'land', just as they had done in the 1310s, 1390s and 1400s. But power did not simply fall into the hands of the magnates either. The disruptions arising from the unmanaged transfer of ecclesiastical and royal property combined with the militarising effects of foreign invasion and the egalitarian values of Hussite Christianity to create circumstances in which groups of ordinary people could assert themselves. In the political situation of the 1420s, in particular, it was necessary for the nobility to negotiate with towns and brotherhoods as well as with each other. As contemporaries noted, this produced a kind of anarchy, composed of informal agreements between localised zones of authority, rather than an effective popular or national government. No less than the Council of Basle or the structures devised in the early period of imperial reform, the Bohemian diet was unable to govern its kingdom, and the Hussite experiment played a prominent part in exposing the dangers of ecclesiastical and political reform. Much as the magnates recovered authority in the 1430s, they could not rebuild the old balances between royal, ecclesiastical and noble power. Too much land was in too many pairs of hands, and the new weakness of the crown was fortuitously prolonged: first, by the deaths of Sigismund (1437) and his heir, Albert of Austria (1439); and then by the succession of Albert's baby son, Ladislas Posthumous (1440–57), who was in the custody of the new Emperor Frederick III. In 1439, even the *zemský soud* was wound up, and in 1440 the diet acknowledged that juridical and governmental power lay with the dozen or so *landfridy* or *kraje* – peacekeeping districts, each dominated by a rough alliance of magnates and the representatives of other estates. Bohemia thus became a federation of more-or-less sovereign, semi-constitutional lordships, although the persisting tension between Catholics, oriented towards Austria, and Hussites, dominating the east of the country, enabled some co-ordination. By 1444, the Hussite baron George of Poděbrady was the master of a union of five eastern *kraje*, and from this base he launched a war for control of the kingdom, gaining Prague in 1448. Between 1451 and 1453, Frederick III, the Bohemian diet, and finally Ladislas himself recognised George as governor. Following Ladislas' death, he was elected king by the diet, and ruled Bohemia for another thirteen years (1458–71).

The unions of Krewo and Kalmar

The same themes of constitutional experimentation and consolidation were apparent in the kingdoms to the north and east of the Empire. The previous century had ended in the formation of two great unions – between Poland and Lithuania, at Krewo in 1385, and (on a different basis) between Norway, Sweden and Denmark, at Kalmar in 1397 – as well as a series of dynastic liaisons between the great families of east-central Europe: the Luxemburgs, Habsburgs, Angevins, Piasts and Gediminids.[7] Both developments meant tensions between foreign rulers and subjects whose sense of their indigenous political traditions was rapidly sharpened. The unions raised new challenges for political leaders to solve, while the dynastic mingling of east-central Europe encouraged the transplantation of constitutional techniques and customs across the region. While the period is often seen as one of mounting 'constitutionalism', especially in Poland and Scandinavia, it furnishes plenty of examples of effective, and even penetrative, kingship. What was really at work, in all these kingdoms and also in the Hanseatic network and the Prussian *Ordensstaat*, was a process of political integration and definition, conducted against a background of recurrent dynastic and military crisis. As elsewhere, this process was conducted in dialogue with similar ones in Church and Empire.

The union of Poland and Lithuania had three major consequences for the former kingdom. First of all, it drew the Poles back towards war with the Teutonic Knights, an enterprise with more appeal to the magnates of Greater Poland, which bordered the *Ordensstaat*, than to those of Lesser Poland, centred on Cracow and more interested in harmonious relations with the powers of the Empire. Lithuania had been the main target of the Order's expansion, and victim of the *reisen* which continued into the 1390s and beyond; in 1398, she had been forced to surrender her coastal homeland of Žemaitija, and the grand duke, Vytautas (1392–1430), was eager to win it back. His cousin, King Władisław II (1386–1434), seems to have been just as enthusiastic, lending support to a league of Prussian nobles from 1397 and increasing economic pressure on the Baltic ports by cutting links to Cracow and favouring their neighbours. War broke out in 1409, with

---

[7] The rulers of Bohemia, Austria, Hungary, Poland (up to 1370) and Lithuania, respectively.

a rising in Žemaitija, and the Poles and Lithuanians won a spectacular victory at Grunwald/Tannenberg in 1410, in which the Grand Master was killed and many knights captured. The Treaty of Thorn (1411) left the Polish boundary more or less unchanged, but a large ransom was to be paid, Žemaitija was returned, and the *Ordensstaat* subsided into internal conflict as the disgruntled inhabitants faced new tax demands from their defeated masters. Victory was followed by a confirmation of the union, at Horodło in 1413, in which Polish magnates secured a nominal vote in the selection of the grand duke, and Lithuanian nobles received some of the liberties enjoyed by their Polish counterparts. The exchange of influence between the two polities was thus a mutual one, and even though Lithuania flirted with independence on several occasions in the 1420s and 1430s, it remained attached to Poland; secure in the west, meanwhile, Vytautas was able to extend his influence over the princes of Belarus and even in Moscow.

As the account above suggests, however, a second change to Polish politics was that the Jagiellonian crown was more inclined towards Greater Poland than its Piast predecessors. This was a significant reason for the decades of tension with the Lesser Polish establishment, which was centred in the royal council, influential in the magnate-dominated *Sejm* (diet), and led from the 1420s by Zbigniew Olésnicki, bishop of Cracow. Władisław found himself having to confirm the noble and ecclesiastical liberties agreed in 1374, 1382 and 1386 on numerous occasions. His vulnerability to the *Sejm*, which met virtually annually in the first half of the century, was greatly increased by the third major consequence of the Polish-Lithuanian union: the ambiguous position of the Jagiellonian dynasty. While Władisław was functionally king of Poland, he was formally no more than *dominus et tutor regni* (lord and guardian of the kingdom), and the deaths of the Piast queen, Jadwiga, in 1399, and of her daughter (also Jadwiga) in 1431, produced crises of legitimacy in which the *dominus* was forced to seek confirmation and re-election by the Polish magnates. The same thing happened in the 1420s when he sought recognition for his sons by his fourth wife, a Lithuanian princess: frequent diets and demands for the confirmation, even extension, of liberties, to which the king was forced to accede. When Władisław died in 1434, Olésnicki was able to stage an election, and even though the new king, Władisław III (1434–44), was his father's son, he was accepted only in return for a confirmation of liberties. As he was a child, moreover, a regency council was set up, in which Olésnicki was again dominant, and the association between the Lesser Poland elite, the defence of noble liberties and the prominence of the *Sejm* was affirmed.

The ensuing two decades were full of conflict, as Olésnicki strove, mainly successfully, to retain control of the royal administration and its traditional network of supporters in Lesser Poland, which he cultivated with grants of office and estates. Faced with a clerical leader, albeit one fiercely antipapal at this stage, Olésnicki's opponents embraced Hussitism, at least nominally, and a Hussite League for 'the good order of the state' emerged from Greater Poland and Kuiavia in 1438, to be defeated in battle in 1439. With noble support, Władisław was elected king of Hungary in 1440, and went there to rule in person, thus prolonging the rule of the bishop and *Sejm*. On his death at Varna in 1444, the *Sejm* offered the crown to his younger brother, Casimir, who had joined a rebellion in Lithuania, and had become its grand duke in 1440. Casimir took the unusual step of rejecting the invitation, with its associated demands for the confirmation of liberties, and instead began to win support for his coronation from the provincial assemblies (*sejmiki*) of eastern and northern Poland. These assemblies, first noticeable in the 1380s, tended to represent the lesser nobility, or *szlachta*, and their members had been prominent in the 1430s opposition to Olésnicki as they sought a greater role for themselves in the direction of affairs. Casimir's ingenious policy divided the bishop's supporters and secured him the crown (as Casimir IV, 1447–92). Eight years of tension followed, in which the king, based at Vilnius, and backed by a coalition of Lithuania, Greater Poland, the archbishop of Gniezno, the *sejmiki* and the towns, held out against demands for a charter of liberties, while Olésnicki held sway in Lesser Poland and tried to move the *Sejm* to threaten deposition. In the end, the seeds of a realignment in Polish politics came from Prussia, where resistance to the Knights had been growing steadily throughout the 1430s and 1440s. In 1454, a league of Prussian towns and nobles, formed in 1440, sought Casimir's help. The king declared Prussia to be part of the crown of Poland and embarked on the 'Thirteen Year War' with the *Ordenstaat* (1454–66). While this drew him into further negotiations with the *sejmiki*, and concessions to the *szlachta* over their right to be consulted on military service and legislation (Statute of Nieszawa, 1454), it also allowed him to press the Church for money and generally to regain control of his kingdom.

Looking back, then, it had been partly a matter of accident that Poland had moved towards electoral monarchy and conciliar government – the result of recurring dynastic failure between 1370 and the 1440s. But it was also a consequence of the shifting focus of the monarchy from Lesser to Greater Poland, and, in the longer term, of the growth of political infrastructure. While Poland's rulers would henceforth have to deal with new constitutional forms – a *Sejm* representing the magnates, with an upper house beginning to think of itself as a Senate; provincial *sejmiki* representing the lesser nobles – these were not necessarily unco-operative, nor were they set in stone, and Casimir IV would show how powerful the monarchy could be.

If the Union of Krewo broadly strengthened the Polish crown, the same cannot really be said of the effect of the Union of Kalmar on royal authority in Scandinavia. For the Danes and the anti-Mecklenburg magnates in Sweden, who were the real powers in the region, the union had offered the prospect of protecting the liberties and customs of churches, nobles and provinces. These were solemnly guaranteed in the coronation charters agreed between Eric of Pomerania and the councils of the three constituent kingdoms, and were confirmed at Kalmar in 1397. At the same time, however, it is clear that Queen Margaret and (from 1400) King Eric aimed at a more direct form of royal rule, based in Denmark but employing the royal right, acknowledged in the charters, to appoint to castles and other *län/len* throughout the three kingdoms. By this means, and through the influence over the Church that came from good relations with the Roman Papacy, Margaret and Eric were able to resume crown lands and levy taxation using networks of supporters endowed from royal holdings. The *Danehof* and the councils of Sweden and Norway were allowed to wither, and the symbolically important post of *drost/drots/drottsete* (steward) went unfilled in each realm, so that there was no real check on the power of the crown. Eric embarked on a vigorous pursuit of Danish interests, discarding his aunt's prudent alliance with the Hansards and imposing tolls on traffic through the Danish Sound (1426 onwards), signing a treaty with Poland (1417), and starting a long war of conquest in Schleswig in 1410. But in this last initiative, which involved a decade of intense conflict with the Hansards and the count of Holstein (1426–35), he overreached himself. Tensions rose over the appointment of Germans and Danes to royal castles and *len* in Sweden, and when these were exacerbated by heavy war taxation and a symbolic dispute over the see of Uppsala in 1432, in which royal will was pitched against free canonical election, the country rose in rebellion. In 1434, a squire, Engelbert Engelbrektson, emerged as the leader of a mixed popular and freeholder revolt, organised through the local assemblies (*things*) and supported by the *riksråd* in 1435. Similar risings broke out in Finland (1438), where Swedish magnates were the major landowners, in Denmark (1434) and in Norway (1436). Eric was forced to make peace in the Schleswig war, and to allow discussions between the councils of Denmark and Sweden in which the terms of the union were renegotiated. The settlement which emerged in a second treaty of Kalmar in 1438 placed the council and officers (steward, chancellor) of each realm in charge of its own affairs. There was still to be a royal element in the revised union – the king would retain his rights over castles and *len*, and was ordered to circulate through his realms according to a fixed rotation – but, in future, the monarchy was to be elected by the estates of each realm, and there was no guarantee that the individual kingdoms would choose the same ruler.

Against a background of royal insufficiency, embryonic representation and acute concern for the protection of liberties, the new union opened the way to a period of conciliar rule in Scandinavia. Eric withdrew to his castle of Visborg in Gotland and was duly deposed by Sweden and Denmark in 1439 (Norway remained loyal, but only in return for the re-establishment of an independent chancery and stewardship in the kingdom, measures which effectively allowed it to govern itself). While Sweden was ruled by its aristocratic marshal,[8] Karl Knutsson, and his supporters in the *riksråd*, Denmark invited Eric's nephew, Christopher of Bavaria, to act as regent, offering him the crown in 1440. Sweden followed suit in 1441, handing Finland and Öland over to Knutsson, and Norway did the same in 1442. Christopher's brief reign is regarded as 'the heyday of council constitutionalism': Sweden and Norway were ruled by their councils, and the archbishop of Lund dominated the Danish council, backed by a Church loyal to Basle and freed from royal influence; the king moved back and forth between Stockholm and Copenhagen and seems only to have been able to assert himself in foreign affairs, where he pursued policies more sympathetic to Lübeck than the Norwegians, in particular, wished.[9] Christopher's death without issue in 1448 produced a

---

[8] This office was coming to replace the old post of *drots*, or steward, in importance.
[9] Quotation from K. Helle, ed., *The Cambridge History of Scandinavia I: Prehistory to 1520* (Cambridge, 2003), p. 694.

lasting division in the union when Denmark and Norway elected Christian of Oldenburg, the nephew of Duke Adolf of Schleswig, as king (in 1448 and 1449, respectively), while Sweden chose Karl Knutsson. War broke out, as both the Swedes and the Danes attempted to regain control of the long-disputed territory of Gotland, where Eric of Pomerania stoked competition by selling his rights to one side and then the other. Christian I (1448/9–81) had gained control of the island by 1449, but war with Sweden continued off and on until 1456. Its disruptive effects on the trading and mining interests around Stockholm, together with Knutsson's attempt to fund himself by resuming church land, created a movement against him, and he was driven out in 1456. The regents appointed by the *riksråd* offered Christian the throne in 1457, but he was not to keep it for long. By the 1450s, the struggle to redefine the union along conciliar lines had become a conflict over whether or not the manifestly Danish-centred crown would be able to rule Sweden as it increasingly ruled Norway, where the stewardship lapsed and conciliar power dwindled. Swedish political society was divided between those who gained more from association with Denmark and those who preferred the Baltic orientation of Knutsson and his heirs. Factional divisions among the magnates, the frameworks of ecclesiastical and national liberties, the sensitivity of the population to excessive taxation and the widespread desire for stability (which no ruler seemed able to satisfy) lent further complication to the kingdom's politics.

Much as Poland, Sweden and Denmark experienced serious internal divisions during this period, the constitutional frameworks of these kingdoms were clearly strengthened (it is less easy to make that claim for Norway). While the conciliar experiments demonstrate how much remained to be settled in the relationship between king and realm in each country, the conflicts of the period tended to force recognition of the centrality of that relationship in political life. For the other two powers of the Baltic region, the Hanseatic League and the Teutonic Knights, the situation was less promising. In the latter case, this was partly a matter of the dynastic union of the Order's principal victims, Poland and Lithuania, but the threat was intensified by the ambivalent position of the major towns and by the internal tensions that the growth of government in the *Ordensstaat* had unavoidably provoked. Danzig, Thorn and other towns were linked to the Hansa as well as being subjects of the Order; this fact, together with their wealth, their frequent meetings and the ways in which their economic interests commonly diverged from the political interests of the Knights, made them a potentially challenging group. Meanwhile, the new judicial structures developed in the 1320s and 1330s set up districts and structures through which Prussian knights and tenants could represent themselves. With the coming of taxation in the later fourteenth century, and with trade disrupted by worsening relations with Poland-Lithuania, the Knights began to face criticism from meetings of estates. Tensions grew after the defeat of 1410, intensified in 1432–5 (with assemblies in both Prussia and Livonia), and issued forth in a Prussian League in 1440. This was the body that precipitated the war of 1454–66, in which western Prussia was lost to the Polish crown, and the rest of the Order's holdings reduced to vassalage. Perhaps the *Ordensstaat* was too precarious a mixture of different structures and allegiances – German barons, mercantile towns, Prussian knights and tenants, and a network of bishops under the hostile archbishop of Riga – to withstand the pressure of a more united and sophisticated kingdom in Poland; its growing pains were too easily exploited by its unfriendly and increasingly co-ordinated neighbour. It is ironic that western Prussia achieved greater consolidation under Polish rule in the 1460s and 1470s, when an alliance of leading towns and royalist magnates was able to contain the estates movement and exclude the lesser nobility from influence.

The Hanseatic League faced somewhat similar difficulties. Its capacity to harness and unite the towns of the Baltic and North Sea was unrivalled while it possessed the only navy of any consequence in the region, and while the surrounding kingdoms and lordships were either disorganised or focused elsewhere. But by the fifteenth century, neither condition was true any longer, and the consequence was another set of damaging interactions between internal tension and external pressure. The Hanseatic towns were no less vulnerable than other German cities to the tensions between patricians and guilds, and Lübeck, Wismar, Rostock and Hamburg were all forced to accept councils representing a wider cross-section of the political community in the years after 1405. In Lübeck, this developed into a damaging eight-year schism, 1408–16, in which two councils claimed authority and negotiated with outsiders. Once the patricians were back in control, Lübeck attempted to strengthen the terms of the League. The diet of 1418 agreed measures to intervene against guild uprisings in any member city; it also established a framework for common diplomacy and defence, with leadership bestowed on the Wendish towns and costs apportioned to each member. The latter agreement remained mostly a dead letter, but the former was widely resented, and weakened allegiances in many of the cities. Between the 1420s and the 1460s, moreover, the interests of the different groups of Hansa towns diverged: while Lübeck and the Wendish towns sought to exclude Dutch and English competition and were happy to blockade the Sound and divert traffic through the Elbe–Trave canal, the towns of Livonia, Prussia, Cologne and the Zuider Zee were more interested in free trade. The eastern cities increasingly looked to Poland or the see of Riga to promote their interests, and this was partly why the Livonians were able to take over the Novgorod Kontor after 1422. Meanwhile, Cologne became increasingly unhappy with the League and even joined England in her war against the Hansards (1468–74); the towns of Brandenburg were pulled out of the League by the margrave from about 1450; and Stettin, in Pomerania, was more or less detached in 1428. Hansard privileges were eroded in Norway and the Low Countries, and the 1441 Treaty of Copenhagen conceded free entry to the Baltic to Dutch shipping, so that by the end of the century more than two-thirds of ships passing through the Sound were not Hanseatic but Dutch. While the Peace of Utrecht (1474) saw Hansard privileges in England restored and Cologne forced into submission, the League was no longer the dominant power that it had been, and – apart from Lübeck and the other Wendish cities – its members seem to have given more priority to other authorities and associations.

France

The politics of the kingdom of France in the first half of the fifteenth century show some similarities with those of the Church and Empire and the kingdoms of central and northern Europe. Here too there was pressure for reform, there was schism and vacuum about the throne, and there was a period of frequent assemblies. But notwithstanding the fantasies of Paris University, or of the *Cabochiens* who rose up in Paris in 1413, there was no real attempt to promote conciliar government, and the predominant forms of power in France remained royal and princely. The outcome of the conflicts that engulfed France in the declining years of Charles VI was unpredictable, but it was certain that some sort of kingdom would remain, and not altogether surprising that the royal machine, with its remarkable mixture of formality and flexibility, survived the grave challenges of the 1410s and 1420s.

By 1400, tensions had begun to emerge between the leading princes at the head of Charles VI's government, especially the king's brother, the duke of Orleans (d.1407), and his uncle, Philip the Bold, duke of Burgundy (d.1404). With territorial interests in Aquitaine and Italy, Orleans favoured war with the usurper king of England, Henry IV (1399–1413), together with restoration of the Avignon allegiance; Burgundy, on the other hand, as ruler of Flanders and Artois, preferred peace with England and supported Parisian moves towards a settlement of the Schism. Both dukes drew large pensions from the crown, which in turn meant regular taxation and rising discontent from the French population. At the same time, these princes and others – Berry, Bourbon, Brittany and Armagnac among them – were taking advantage of the absence of royal direction to extend their claims over royal taxes and to exclude or suborn royal officers in the sphere of their estates. The independence and localised power won by these means helps to explain the ambivalent behaviour of the princes in the following decades. Influence at the centre remained important, however: not only to secure pensions and protect usurpations of royal assets from legal assault, but also because of a burgeoning public debate, centred in Paris, over the state of the realm. The king's prolonged illness, coupled with the crisis in the Church, in which Paris was taking a leading role, generated public discussion of reform. This was picked up by the dukes of Burgundy, both Philip and his son, John the Fearless (1404–19), who began in 1402 to enunciate something not dissimilar from the 'Navarrais' doctrines of the previous century – lower taxation, more lawful and consultative rule, and reform of the royal administration – while Orleans defended the superior claims and rights of the crown. What tipped this cleavage into crisis was the death of Duke Philip in 1404, which gave Orleans unchallenged dominance of the royal machine; the Burgundian pensions were cancelled, and, in 1405, John the Fearless circulated reform schemes to Paris University and the leading towns. Receiving an obdurate response from Orleans, Burgundy had him murdered in 1407, and entered Paris, justifying his shocking action as tyrannicide. The next few years saw Burgundy increase his influence over Paris and the royal government, allying with the queen and securing the wardship of the young dauphin, Louis, duke of Guyenne (d.1415). He was opposed by a network of princes led by the young duke of Orleans and the count of Armagnac, but was able to prevail against them until a meeting of the Estates General of Languedoïl in 1413 stirred up such reformist fervour that its 258-clause reform ordinance sparked a popular rising in Paris which led, in turn, to the flight of Burgundy and the elevation of the dauphin. The so-called 'Armagnacs' returned to power, but were quickly catapulted into war with the aggressive new king of England, Henry V (1413–22). Burgundy stood by, as Henry's armies won an extraordinary victory at Agincourt (1415) and proceeded to conquer Normandy (1416–19). In 1418, with Guyenne and a second dauphin dead, and only the fifteen-year-old Charles left to represent the main royal line (Charles VII, 1422–61), Burgundy re-entered Paris, killing Armagnac and attempting to win public support by cancelling *aides* throughout the kingdom (though not in his own domains). Dauphin Charles left the capital to establish a regency based at Poitiers and Bourges,[10] while the Queen and Burgundy opened negotiations with England. In 1419, a last-ditch attempt to arrange peace between the dauphin and the Paris establishment ended in disaster when the duke of Burgundy was murdered by Charles' men at Montereau. This was the background to the remarkable Treaty of Troyes (1420), in which Dauphin Charles was excluded from the French succession, and the right to succeed Charles VI was bestowed on Henry V and his progeny, provided that they maintained the rights of the kingdom of France and made war on the regime at Bourges until the realm should be reunited again.

From 1420, then, there were two kingdoms in France: one centred on Bourges and the royal estates in Poitou, Berry, Auvergne and the south; the other centred on Paris and Normandy and afforced by armies from England. Each side was supported by fluctuating coalitions of interest, complicated by the progress of English arms and by the absence of some of the most important princes – Bourbon and Orleans imprisoned in England, Anjou in the kingdom of Naples. The Parisian kingdom had the allegiance of the dukes of Brittany and Burgundy, the latter – Philip the Good (1419–67) – initially an enthusiastic ally, but increasingly disenchanted, as the regency of France went first to Henry V (1420–2) and then, on the death of Charles VI, to John, duke of Bedford, elder uncle of the new king, the infant Henry VI (1422–61, 1470–1). Excluded from direct influence in Paris, but with his French interests secured by Troyes, Burgundy embarked on a programme of expansion in the Low Countries, building on the network of alliances and marriages developed under

---

[10] The *parlement* was in Poitiers, the court and *chambre de comptes* at Bourges.

his predecessors. In 1425, he went to war against English and Bavarian interlopers to secure the heiress of Hainault, Holland and Zealand, Jacqueline, who made over her estates to him in 1428. In 1421, he bought the county of Namur, and in 1430 he seized the duchy of Brabant on the expiry of its Valois cadet line. By 1432, Philip was master of all the richest territories of the Low Countries. Because he trampled on imperial prerogatives and allies, he faced some resistance from Sigismund in the 1430s, and he had to fight to gain his final acquisition, Luxemburg, between 1441 and 1451, but he had assembled a substantial principality, which produced enough revenue and political support to make him less concerned with French affairs. The English tried to win Burgundy back with an offer of regency in 1430, but while this led to his capture of Joan of Arc at Compiègne, he was already moving towards a settlement with Charles VII. This came at the Congress of Arras, in 1435, and brought French concessions which helped to secure the Burgundian territories in Picardy and in Burgundy itself. A brief period of Franco-Burgundian military action followed in 1436, in which Paris and the Île-de-France were regained for King Charles, and Calais was unsuccessfully besieged, but there were limits to how far a Low Countries prince could carry his subjects against the English. English raids in Flanders helped to stimulate a rebellion in Bruges (1436–8), and in 1438, Duke Philip signed a treaty with Henry VI which remained in force throughout his life.

The French military victories of 1436 could not have been predicted in the 1420s. After Troyes, the English and Burgundians secured the Seine and the Île-de-France, and a defeat at Baugé in 1421 did not halt them. After Henry V's death, the regent Bedford continued the conquest, securing the borders of Normandy with victories at Verneuil and Crevant (1424), overrunning the county of Maine, and preventing the defection of Brittany in 1427. While these victories helped to drive the house of Anjou and the Breton captain (and claimant) Arthur de Richemont further into the arms of Charles VII, they did little to secure the king's position: Charles was threatened by plots against his person in 1428 and 1432; his allies, Richemont and La Trémoïlle, fought each other in Poitou; and the duke of Orleans tried to interest other princes in a negotiated settlement which would reduce the Valois to princely status under the English king. Two factors saved Charles' position. One was the political and financial support he obtained from the southern half of the French kingdom: he summoned the Estates General of the

Languedoc almost annually in the 1420s, and while its generosity was rarely matched by actual payments from towns and provinces, this regular dialogue helped to establish Charles' legitimacy, and began to deliver real money by the end of the decade. The second factor was the military and diplomatic disaster which enveloped the English when, in 1428, they tried to capture Orleans, prior to a direct attack on the kingdom of Bourges. Not only did this lead to a string of notable defeats at the hands of Richemont and Joan of Arc (at Orleans itself, and Patay and Jargeau, all in 1429), it undermined English credibility with the princes, and enabled Charles VII to secure Rheims and obtain a coronation at the ancient centre of French kingship. While Henry VI's government was able to secure a parallel coronation for the English king in Paris in 1431, there was a growing commitment to Valois recovery across much of the rest of France. The Norman estates had ceased to pay taxation, and the duchy was rocked by revolt in 1435, but Charles was now able to assemble estates from both Languedoïl and Languedoc, to raise both *aides* and *tailles*, increasingly without needing consent, and to draw the duke of Burgundy back towards him. Back in Paris from 1436, he was the real king of France, and even the English began to acknowledge it.

It took another fifteen years before Charles could recapture Normandy, however. In part, this was because of the surprisingly stubborn defence which the English were able to mount in the duchy: French defeats at Avranches and Dieppe in 1439–40, and sizeable English raids in 1441 and 1443 suggested that the time for a frontal assault was not yet ripe. But a more profound reason is that the domestic politics of the kingdom of France seem to have taken priority over the war. A corollary of Charles' frequent assemblies, which continued up to 1439, was the prominence given to the traditional concerns of the estates: the removal of freelance soldiery (often called *écorcheurs* – flayers – in this period); the restoration of royal lands and rights; and controls on taxation. In 1436, in return for three years' worth of *aides*, Charles agreed to a resumption of all royal grants made since 1418; in 1439, he issued the famous *ordonnance* proclaiming that only the king was entitled to raise troops and taxes. These measures, which directly threatened the lands, militias and fiscal powers of the princes, provoked strong resistance: a major rising of leading princes and the teenage dauphin, in the so-called 'Praguerie' of 1440; a second league of princes in 1442; and, in the same year, a move towards the English on the part of the count of Armagnac and the Albret family, the leading magnates of Gascony. But, backed by the towns and the Gallican Church, Charles and his military captains moved decisively against his princely opponents and bought them off with concessions, while regaining many of the jurisdictions and fiscal powers they had acquired since the beginning of the century. From 1439, the king was able to levy the *taille* on a permanent and annual basis, negotiating its rate upwards in the early 1440s with the agreement of the towns. Between 1445 and 1448, moreover, he used a truce with the English to solve the *écorcheur* problem and gain control of the kingdom's military forces by establishing a tax-funded standing army of 12,000 men under royally appointed captains. By 1449, he was ready to move against the English and seized the opportunity presented by their attempts to regain the allegiance of the duke of Brittany. In less than a quarter of the time it had taken Henry V to conquer it, Charles overran Normandy in 1449–50, winning its towns and castles with a mixture of artillery and bribery. In 1450–1, he also conquered English Gascony, extinguishing the last resistance from Bordeaux in the battle of Castillon in July 1453. In thirty years, this rather unpromising-looking king had healed the civil war that had begun in his childhood and ended the Hundred Years War; he had well earned his soubriquet of '*le trèsvictorieux*'.

Britain and Ireland

The wars in France and their associated strains came equally to dominate the politics of England in the first half of the fifteenth century, but the fluctuating quality of royal government was also a central factor in affairs. However unpopular Richard II had been, his deposition in favour of the duke of Lancaster, Henry IV, had a number of disruptive effects. The usurper faced a series of opportunistic attacks and revolts within his first year, the most serious of which was a rising in North Wales in 1400, in which a descendant of the Welsh royal house, Owain Glyndŵr, aped the actions of King Henry and declared himself prince of Wales. Over the next eight years, the king was forced to send army after army into Wales, as the rising spread across the principality, and Owain established a parliament and a university and called upon the French and Scots for aid. The costs of the conflict, exacerbated by Henry's need to endow a new nobility and maintain a substantial retinue, meant a series of difficult parliaments between 1401 and 1406, which imposed councils on the king and demanded cuts in non-military expenditure. Some of the king's leading lieutenants – notably the earl of Northumberland and his son, Hotspur, who had inflicted a major defeat on the Scots at Homildon Hill in 1402 – began to waver in their allegiance to the usurper, Hotspur joining with Welsh and English rebels to confront the king in battle at Shrewsbury in 1403, while Northumberland joined forces with a popular rising in Yorkshire in 1405. Backed by his sons, his retinue, the majority of the magnates and a large cross-section of county and urban opinion, however, Henry was able to prevail: the rebellions failed; Wales was more or less under control by 1408; and a stroke of luck brought the capture of the king of Scots, James I (1406–37), as he made his way to France. Although Henry himself sank into illness from 1406, the succession was secure and his ministers and allies were able to govern fairly effectively under the leadership of his eldest son. By the last years of the reign, it was possible to contemplate intervention in France, and English expeditions left in support of Burgundy in 1411 and Armagnac in 1412.

The accession of the twenty-six-year-old Henry V in 1413 set the seal on the Lancastrian achievement: a vigorous young king, proven in the wars in Wales and experienced in government, would be able to complete the restoration of authority and pursue the royal rights in France. Henry's spectacular victory at Agincourt and conquest of Normandy were balanced and facilitated by skilful leadership of the English political community: the king restored order with a judicial tour of the Midlands in 1414; he was able to raise so much taxation without complaint because he managed his large patrimony with care and economy; he used the war as a means of probation and restoration for the sons of nobles and gentlemen who had risen against his father. He thus created a fund of goodwill and common feeling which helps to explain the success with which both war and government were prosecuted after his early death in 1422. Even so, the problems that faced the regime of the nine-month-old Henry VI were formidable. It is not clear that the Treaty of Troyes, with its heavy demands on Anglo-Norman resources, was quite the settlement that Henry had wanted, but he needed peace in 1420 and this was all that was on offer. The addition of another whole realm to the crown of England alarmed Parliament, and, having secured a statement that Henry's English subjects would not be subject to his kingdom of France, MPs used it to avoid granting taxes for most of the 1420s. The burden of the war thus fell mainly on Normandy, which strained the fragile loyalties of the newly conquered province and limited what could be done against the Valois. Meanwhile, it was impossible for the regent, Bedford, to control affairs in England while he was based in Rouen and Paris, and, although the council which governed during Henry VI's minority was reasonably united, it could not run the fiscal and governmental machinery with the vigour of an adult king. The regime became steadily more indebted, and, in the absence of a clear line of command, it was difficult to prevent damaging divisions over policy, such as the duke of Gloucester's support for Jacqueline of Hainault, which alienated Burgundy in 1425, or the earl of Salisbury's insistence on the Orleans campaign, which had such disastrous consequences. Unfortunately, as Henry VI reached the age of majority, it became clear that no direction could be expected from him. Beyond founding colleges at Eton and Cambridge, the king seems to have done very little, and the result was a prolongation of the minority council well into the 1440s. Headed by the duke of Suffolk, the leading magnates did what they could to maintain the war effort, and sought a satisfactory peace via negotiations in 1435, 1439 and 1444, but tax revenues dwindled and it became impossible both to pay the garrisons and to maintain the confidence of England's friends and allies in Normandy, Brittany and Gascony. Last-ditch efforts to win over the house of Anjou (1444–8) and to secure Brittany (1449) failed ignominiously, and the government was barely able to mount a defence when the end came in 1449–50. The loss of Normandy, the bankruptcy of the government and the widespread perception that both were due to the evil rule of the men about the king led to a parliamentary assault on Suffolk's regime and, in the summer of 1450, a huge popular rising which occupied London and murdered several of the king's advisers. When the duke of York took up the commons' demand for reform in the autumn of that year, England embarked on a confrontation strikingly similar to the one that had engulfed France five decades earlier.

    More than in the fourteenth century, the fifteenth-century phase of the Hundred Years War reduced English pressure on the rest of the British Isles. After Henry IV's opportunistic attack on Scotland in 1400, there were very few English invasions of that country, and none that reached beyond the Borders until the 1540s: indeed, it was the Scots who went to war, trying (with some success) to regain the border fortresses of Roxburgh and Berwick, in 1436, 1455–7 and 1460–1, but even their efforts were sporadic. English financial and military resources were at fuller stretch than they had been in the

1350s and 1360s, and the wardens of the Northern Marches and lieutenants of Ireland were given minimal support. For Ireland, this meant a further period of adaptation, in which the lieutenancy was frequently given to Anglo-Irish magnates, whose informal modes of rule were increasingly at odds with the expectations of the Dublin establishment and the English-leaning towns. Much of the period from the 1410s to the 1440s was dominated by a feud between the earls of Ormond and the Dublin-based Talbots, the former aiming to incorporate and manage the Gaelic Irish forces around them, the latter attempting a more formal kind of rule, but without the necessary financial and military means. While the grant of the lieutenancy to a powerful prince of the royal blood, Richard of York, seemed to presage a change of policy in 1447, it was short-lived: York briefly took the submissions of a host of Gaelic lords in 1449–50, but received no money from the English exchequer, and was soon back on the mainland and absorbed in political conflict. His return to Ireland, in flight from his Lancastrian enemies in 1459–60, coincided with a recognition by the settlements around Dublin that they were effectively on their own. The Parliament of Drogheda in 1460 issued a famous statement that 'the land of Ireland is and at all times has been corporate of itself', and was not subject to English laws unless these were endorsed locally.[11] Like the institutions proposed for Wales by Owain Glyndŵr, this was a sign of the way in which constitutional advancement complicated colonial power structures, particularly when contact between settlers and the metropole became attenuated. While the Ireland of the Pale around Dublin was on the way to articulating its political and cultural distinctness from England, it was also increasingly distinct from the complicated mixture of Anglo-Irish lordship and Gaelic clan structures which surrounded it. Things were not to change greatly in the second half of the century: although the claims of 1460 were swiftly reversed, and the Irish parliament was formally subjugated to the English one in 'Poynings' Law' of 1495, the crown effectively ceded power to the earls of Kildare from the later 1470s onwards, and they used it to establish informal hegemony over most of the island by the end of the century.

In Scotland, meanwhile, the reigns of James I (1406–37) and James II (1437–60) saw a return to assertive kingship after the weak rule of Robert II and Robert III, and a long period of relative calm during the

---

[11] A.J. Otway-Ruthven, *A History of Medieval Ireland* (London, 1968), p. 387.

governorships of the duke of Albany and his son (1402–24). Rather as in Charles VII's France, James I's efforts to rebuild royal authority centred on a revival of dialogue with the estates – the Scottish parliament met more than once a year during his adult reign and those of his two successors – coupled with attempts to strengthen the resources of the crown and to extend its claims. James' demands for taxation, indulged in 1424–5, were rejected by later parliaments; his inquiries into the fate of royal lands, which led to a series of confiscations, created alarm, particularly as, contrary to custom, he had retained in his hands most of the earldoms that had escheated to the crown since the beginning of his reign. When the king embarked on a series of attempts to extract 'benevolences' – forced gifts – from his leading subjects, the patience of the Scots was exhausted, and, following an unsuccessful assault on the English-held fortress of Roxburgh, he was murdered by men linked to his uncle, the earl of Atholl, in 1437. This produced another round of executions and escheats, so that when James II came of age, in 1449, he held most of the ancient earldoms in his own hands: apart from the great regional power of the lords of the Isles, which stretched across the Highlands from the 1430s and could not effectively be challenged until the 1470s, there was only one sizeable lordship left outside the royal family – that of the Douglases, who controlled much of the Southern Uplands and had dominated the later stages of the king's minority. Following a series of slights on royal authority, James hacked the eighth earl to death in 1452, and made war on the rest of the family, emerging victorious in 1455. Under the terms of an 'Act of Annexation', the Douglas lands were joined to the crown estate, not to be alienated without parliamentary assent. In fact, James II would go on to endow his family and some other supporters with earldoms, but the map of landed power in Scotland was permanently changed. Henceforth, lords generally held smaller and less concentrated territories under a crown whose patrimony, including customs and some judicial rights, was the basis of its revenues; a service nobility – the 'lords of parliament' – emerged from the 1440s; and 'bonds of manrent' appeared, as less comprehensively powerful and less established magnates sought new ways of sealing ties of lordship and service.

This new balance of power continued, with only slight complications, for the rest of the century. Presented with a range of opportunities by the civil wars in England and France, James III (1460–88) attempted a more ambitious foreign policy, but was roundly put in his place by the lords in the parliament of 1473. He continued to press hard on his fiscal and judicial rights, alienated leading magnates, and was ambushed and murdered in 1488. This correction of an errant monarch seems to have had few after-effects. The next king, James IV (1488–1513), was both more active and more tactful: by roving across the kingdom and intervening in disputes, he was able to advance royal justice (and to enjoy the associated revenues) without forfeiting aristocratic confidence. In 1493, he completed the destruction of the Macdonald lordship of the Isles, which had begun in the 1470s. This brought the Highlands back within the royal orbit, and, while the management of this vast and fragmented zone was entrusted to the lieutenancies of old-style provincial earls – the Gordons of Huntly in the east, and the Campbells of Argyll in the west – these great magnates were loyal to the crown for decades to come. James IV's retreat from holding parliaments after 1495 suggests that, in a relatively decentralised kingdom with little taxation to speak of, the estates were important mainly for the negotiation of change; a ruler who maintained the status quo and consulted informally could do without them. By 1500, therefore, the Scottish polity was more extensive, more textured and more integrated than it had been in 1400; while its low-pressure kingship was relatively unusual in western Europe, it was not so very different from the monarchies of the North and East.

Portugal, Aragon and Castile

The Iberian peninsula experienced many of the same political and constitutional pressures as other parts of Europe, but its three kingdoms followed divergent paths, the politics of Aragon being more characteristic of east-central Europe, in that the kings of the period clashed with relatively solid liberties protected by collective action, and those of Castile being more like those of France, where influence over a penetrative monarchy was essential for the holders of power in the provinces. Portugal, meanwhile, was different again: less governmentally developed than either Aragon or Castile, its politics in the fifteenth century were shaped by inward consolidation and outward expansion. In his long reign, John I (1385–1433), assisted by his son as regent and successor (Edward, regent from 1410s, ruler 1433–8), was able to use frequent meetings of the *Cortes* to institute regular taxation and to establish royal jurisdiction over noble and clerical lands and rights, in the *Lei*

Mental[12] of 1434 and the *concordata* of 1427. Peace with Castile, confirmed in 1411, enabled the revival of war against the Muslims, and the glorious, if expensive, capture of Ceuta in 1415. Thereafter, Portuguese royal policy wavered between conducting warfare in Morocco, supporting exploration in the Atlantic, where Madeira and the Azores were discovered between 1419 and 1432, and developing commerce along the African coast. Alfonso V (1438–81), who began to rule after a long minority in 1448, was more interested in war – first in Morocco, and later in Castile – but, although this tended to mean the reconfirmation of former privileges to the Church and the nobility, Prince Henry 'the Navigator' (d.1460) and the merchants of the flourishing towns of Oporto and Lisbon were sufficiently wealthy and independent to sponsor their own voyages of discovery and to develop trade. From 1475, these were given further impetus by Prince John, who, as John II (1481–95), eagerly encouraged the voyages of da Gama and Cabral, negotiated a division of Atlantic interests with Spain in the Treaty of Tordesillas (1494), and won back control of the magnates with a short, bloody and very successful civil war (1481–4).

The failure of the Aragonese royal line in 1410, and the ensuing succession of a Trastámaran prince, Ferdinand of Antequera (1412–16), crystallised and exacerbated tensions that had developed in the domains of the crown of Aragon over the second half of the previous century. Late in Peter IV's reign, and under John I (1387–96), attempts were made by the kings to claw back some of the rights and political leverage which they had lost to the nobility, the *Cortes* and the Catalan *diputació* amid the wars and financial strains of mid-century. Peter sponsored a revision of the government of Barcelona in 1386, intending to break the stranglehold of the oligarchs. Similarly, in 1388, John began to challenge the *mals usos* (evil customs) by which Catalan peasants were made subject to their lords, and created a new estate of lesser knights in the *Corts* of 1388–9: both moves sought to broaden the political community as a means of reasserting the authority of the count-king over the alliance of nobles and leading townsmen that dominated the fiscal, representative and judicial agencies of Catalonia. These moves were thwarted, and the popular rising of 1391, which was as much against the nobles and oligarchs as it was against the Jews, demonstrated some of the consequences. John's successor, Martin I

---

[12] I.e. a law that was based on the king's thoughts, or what he had in mind.

(1396–1410), managed a tactful compromise between the resumption of royal lands, which was necessary to balance the books, and the protection of privilege through consultation of the *Corts* and *Cortes*. The succession of a ruler with interests in Castile, however, reversed Martin's achievements. In order to raise money and gain agreement on resumption, Ferdinand was forced to allow the *diputació* to become the full-time protector of Catalan laws and liberties; it soon developed into a parallel government for Catalonia, reducing the king, as he protested, to the status of a 'proctor', or delegate. Similar deputations of the *Cortes*, albeit with less-sweeping powers, were established in Aragon in 1412 and Valencia in 1419. Under Alfonso V, 'the Magnanimous' (1416–58), the situation in Catalonia became even more polarised: the *Corts* refused aid from the very beginning of the reign, and embarked instead on a series of reformist demands, including the right to appoint the king's councillors and the establishment of independent justices. Alfonso, on the other hand, decided in 1420 to pursue the royal claim to Naples and spent the large majority of his reign campaigning – and then, from 1442, ruling – in the *Regno*. His financial demands and long absences bred resentment among the leaders of Aragonese society, not least because the king's wars entailed conflict with Genoa, which disrupted the trade of both Barcelona and Valencia. Alfonso had little patience with Aragonese demands. Around 1439, he established a council to help govern his various realms, and although it included representatives from the Spanish territories, it was based in Naples and increasingly dominated by Neapolitans. More seriously, he followed fourteenth-century precedent by offering to sell the abolition of the *mals usos* to the peasantry from 1448, and by encouraging challenges to the government of Barcelona on the part of the broadly based '*Busca*' party, finally placing them in power in 1452. The result of these moves was near-turmoil in Catalonia by the end of the decade: the oligarchical '*Biga*', now firmly hostile to the Castilian monarchy, resumed control of the capital in 1460; meanwhile, in the countryside of Old Catalonia, the lords bought off the king's concession in 1456, leaving the peasantry furious and organised. The seeds of the civil war of the 1460s were well and truly sown.

In Castile, the increasingly complex relationship of king, magnates and municipalities was disturbed by three factors. The first was the marked decline in Christian attitudes to the Jews, who played such a central role in the royal financial system. The terrible pogrom of 1391 was followed in the 1410s by legislation barring Jews from municipal and royal office and a series of preaching campaigns aiming at their conversion. One result of this was the creation of an extensive class of '*conversos*', former Jews who retained all their royal and financial connections, but now, as Christians, were entitled to hold office, both at court and in the cities. With the connivance of the crown, especially in the 1420s and 1430s, *conversos* established dominant positions in Seville, Burgos, Segovia, Toledo, Cordoba and other leading towns, and this, in turn, made the *Cortes* more amenable to royal tax demands and less representative of wider opinion. While the crown limited the number of towns represented in the *Cortes*, gained control of the appointment of representatives and excluded urban deputies from the king's council, it was unable to increase revenues beyond the 1430s, and its policy bred resentment from excluded interests, helping to create a constituency hostile to, and suspicious of, the *conversos* which would shape the politics of the 1460s and after. At the same time, the delicate power-play of princely aristocrats and urban oligarchs, in which the former steadily extended their influence over taxation and jurisdiction in dialogue with the latter, was disturbed by these manoeuvres. Where magnates were excluded, they tended to react, and this not only helped to feed the civil war of 1438–45, but also prompted royal concessions, which eroded both the crown's revenues and its jurisdiction from about 1440 onwards.

A second factor was the weakness of the king, John II (1406–54), who, like Henry VI of England, came to the throne as a small baby and seems to have grown up a nonentity. While his minority was reasonably calm, thanks to the effective stewardship of the queen mother and Ferdinand of Antequera – the latter reviving the *Reconquista* and seizing the great Granadan fortress which gave him his soubriquet – the king was allowed to come of age at the first possible opportunity (1419). He was promptly seized by his cousin Henry, the Grand Master of Santiago, at Tordesillas in 1420, and then rescued by a court faction headed by Álvaro de Luna, which retained control of him for most of the next thirty years. Like the duke of Suffolk in England, Luna was recognised as the king's leading *privado*, his closest counsellor, chief minister and principal representative. While this position came almost to be institutionalised in Spain and elsewhere, it was a novelty for one man to hold such power in Luna's time, and the *privado* was consequently engaged in a continual struggle to retain control. He did this partly by engaging in legitimising projects like making war on Granada, which he did in 1431 and 1445, but it was also one reason for the extensive *mercedes* to which he helped himself – not least the right to collect *tercias*[13] in many towns, which was extended to other lords after his fall – and it also explains his move against the powerful Manrique family in 1437, which led to the seven-year war, in which he was twice exiled from court (1439, 1441) and nearly overturned.

The third major influence on Castilian politics in the first half of the century was the so-called '*infantes de Aragón*'. In circumstances remarkably similar to those of the 1350s, John II's government had to cope with the extensive power wielded by a group of brothers closely linked to the royal family. These were the sons of Ferdinand of Antequera, endowed by him during his regency – in particular, Alfonso, who became king of Aragon in 1416; John, who became king of Navarre in 1429; Henry, who was Master of Santiago, and holder of several countships – and his daughter Mary, who was married to King John. Whether Ferdinand had built them up to strengthen the Castilian crown, or to be capable of succeeding if John died in childhood, or yet to benefit Aragon, is not clear, but they acted as a powerful and disruptive pressure group, uniting the rest of the Castilian nobility against them when Henry seized the king in 1420, or when John and Alfonso invaded in 1429, but helping to deepen its divisions in 1438–45.

These divisions were about more than magnate faction: they arose above all from the inadequacy of John II and from the rule of Luna which was its unsatisfactory solution. The ambivalence of the rebels, who included towns as well as nobles, is striking, but their calls for the king to rule in person (1440) and/or for a small council to rule him (1442), and their pressure for a law against magnates seizing revenues (also 1442), were not necessarily contradicted by their willingness to league against John, to capture him (1441) and even to supplant him altogether, when John of Navarre took up the rule of the realm in 1443–5. While the anarchy of these years certainly meant extensive usurpation of royal assets by the magnates, especially the infantes, this – rather as in contemporary Hungary, or in France in the 1410s and 1420s – was as much a response to the absence of central authority as a smash-and-grab assault on the resources of the crown. Even so, it quickly became clear that authority could only be rebuilt from the

---

[13] The royal third of ecclesiastical tithes.

top, and when the heir, Prince Henry (Henry IV, 1454–74), switched sides, to support Luna and his allies, from 1443, the writing was on the wall for the rebels. In 1445, they were defeated at Olmedo, where *Infante* Henry was killed and John of Navarre driven out. Rule returned to Luna, but on a more circumscribed footing than before, with Prince Henry and his allies, among whom the marquis of Villena was the most prominent, taking a share in power. Tensions persisted – the *Cortes* of 1447 wanted a resumption of royal assets, the coinage was debased, the king of Navarre invaded in 1448–9 and there was serious trouble in Toledo in 1449 – but there was no real means of restoring the situation while John II lived. In 1453, as part of a coup involving magnates and courtiers, Luna was charged with treason and executed, a shocking move which recalled the days of Peter the Cruel and helps to explain some of the troubles which broke out after Henry IV's accession the following year.

Italy

In northern Italy, the late fourteenth-century trend towards the development of 'territorial states' was continued and accentuated in the first few decades after 1400. For Venice and Florence, this was partly a response to the activities of Giangaleazzo Visconti in the 1390s. His aggressive expansion across the Po Basin, and even into Tuscany, prompted other cities and lords to seek protection, either by expanding their own spheres of influence, or by accepting the rule of a more powerful neighbour; his acquisition from the emperor of the title of duke of Milan in 1395, with its associated rights over fief-holders and its implication of public authority, was an inspiration to competitors, such as the rulers of Savoy (dukes from 1416) and Mantua (marquises from 1433). When the Milanese dominion collapsed, in 1402, this was a further stimulus to expansion: in 1404–5, Venice seized Vicenza and Verona, and then turned on Padua to stop it from filling the vacuum of Visconti power (she went on to take Brescia in 1426 and Bergamo in 1428); Florence, whose implicit leadership of Tuscany had almost collapsed under Visconti pressure, acquired Pisa in 1406; and Ferrara regained Parma and Reggio in 1409. But Milan was by no means the sole cause of regional expansion. Venice also strengthened her control of the Dalmatian hinterland: she bought the rights of Ladislas of Durazzo/Naples to Dalmatia in 1409, which meant a renewal of war against Hungary, and she conquered Friuli in 1420. The purchase of Livorno by Florence, in

1421, looks like an attempt to complete the commercial domination of Tuscany, though her determined attempt to acquire Lucca and Siena from 1429 may reflect their adherence to Milan in the 1390s. To some extent, therefore, this kind of state-making was an act of policy – one hotly debated in both Venice and Florence in the 1420s – but it was also part and parcel of a more general consolidation of authority, shared in by other Italian powers, such as the Papacy or, on a smaller scale, Ferrara and Mantua, and, as we have seen, characteristic of principalities and kingdoms across contemporary Europe. In every case, outward expansion was matched by internal political development, and the governments of Milan, Florence and the Papacy all grew in robustness in this period. It was under Filippo Maria Visconti, who restored Milanese control of western Lombardy during the 1410s and gained Genoa in 1421, that a more durable and effective system of government was created for the territories beyond the city; he, not Giangaleazzo, was the first to police the feudal rights of the duchy effectively and to create lasting bonds with the neighbouring towns. Meanwhile, the Albizzi (in the 1420s) and, more strikingly and completely, the Medici (from 1434) stabilised the Florentine oligarchy and created the political means to renovate the tax system and sustain the large-scale wars that dominated the 1420s, 1430s and 1440s. Even Venice, whose government was already so extensive and effective, experienced new developments in this period – in the arrangements for the government of the '*Terra Ferma*' (i.e. the new mainland possessions), in the election of a youthful doge, Francesco Foscari, who was allowed to reign for thirty-four years (1423–57), and, not insignificantly, in the redesignation of the regime as '*dominio o signoria*' instead of '*comune*', in 1423.

These developments were not yet matched in the *Regno*, where instability continued (though some of the great principalities, such as that of the Balzo-Orsini, focused on Taranto, may bear comparison with northern territorial states). Ladislas' interventions in northern Italy were aimed at defeating his Angevin opponents, but he had won no convincing victory by his death, and the war between the Durazzeschi and the Angevins continued into the reign of his sister, Joanna II (1414–35), complicated, as we have seen, by the interventions of the Aragonese claimant, Alfonso V, after 1420. In 1423, the Queen switched to support Louis III of Anjou (d.1434), initiating two decades of struggle between Alfonso and Louis and his son, René (d.1480), culminating in the Aragonese king's six-year war of conquest (1436–42). Only in the 1440s was it finally possible to restore the influence of the Neapolitan kingdom over the barons and princes of the south, and from that decade, the *Regno* began to resemble the other polities of the peninsula, and of the continent more generally.

The rise of territorial states made for new patterns in the larger play of Italian politics. Instead of a protracted struggle between great alliances focused on the Papacy and Empire respectively, there was a succession of conflicts based on fluctuating associations between the four great powers of the north and centre, the contending parties in Naples, and the great mercenary companies. These last, it must be admitted, were a considerable check to the development of territorial states in the first half of the fifteenth century. As in the thirteenth century, but not the fourteenth, most of them were now Italian; they were hired on longer contracts, and given fiefs and estates, and were thus able to wield more continuous power both within the regimes that employed them and over their own dependants. The greatest of them, the Sforza company, was a decisive force in many of the wars of the period, retarding the progress of Alfonso V in Naples in the early 1420s, sustaining Milan against Venice and Florence later in the decade (and Venice against Milan in 1438–41), undermining the Papal State from its base in the March of Ancona in the 1430s and 1440s, and finally, in the person of Francesco Sforza, becoming duke of Milan in 1450. Equally, the power wielded in the kingdom of Naples and across central Italy by families close to the Papacy, such as the Colonna and the Orsini, meant that the conflict of Guelf and Ghibelline networks was not altogether dead, even if some of the participants had changed side (Milan siding with the Papacy, Colonna and Angevins in the 1420s, for example, against the Aragonese and the Orsini prince of Taranto). Even so, the main lines of conflict in the north, between the death of Ladislas in 1414 and the peace of Lodi forty years later, were between Venice and Florence, on the one hand, and Milan on the other. The Papacy switched from a Milanese association under Martin V, to side with Venice and Florence under Eugenius IV; it switched back again when Alfonso V's alliance with Milan, developed in the wake of his capture by the Genoese at Ponza in 1435, enabled him to prevail in Naples (1442). The last twist in the alliance system came in the years around 1450: under Cosimo de' Medici, Florence ended her alliance with Venice in 1449 and supported Francesco Sforza against the Ambrosian republic (1447–50) which had sprung up in Milan following the death of Filippo Maria

Visconti; Venice, fearful of losing her gains in eastern Lombardy, allied with Alfonso, who – perhaps motivated by dreams of reuniting Italy under a reborn Empire – embarked on a series of unsuccessful campaigns in Tuscany (1447–8, 1452–4).

At this stage, however, as the Italian powers neared deadlock and exhaustion, a series of external events helped to produce a settlement. The fall of Constantinople, in 1453, strengthened the concern of Venice to protect her interests in the eastern Mediterranean; the refusal of Frederick III, in 1452, to recognise Sforza as duke of Milan inclined the latter towards peace with Venice (Lodi, 1454); and the revival of the Angevin cause in Naples, supported in 1453 by a French army, dampened Alfonso's aggression. The *Lega Italica* (Italian League), sealed in 1455 under the aegis of the Papacy, acknowledged the primacy of Milan, Florence, Venice and the *Regno*: they were the signatories, while the other Italian lords and cities appear only as *amici, collegati, aderenti* and *raccomandati* of the big four *potentiae* (powers). The four were not to fight or seek alliances separately, and they were to maintain a common army and use it to protect the peace and security of Italy. These high ideals were not, in practice, to be achieved, but the second half of the fifteenth century was to be significantly different from the first: the *condottieri* were effectively subsumed within the framework of the states (not least by a sequence of gruesome executions and murders), and the conflicts of the great powers were mostly short-lived and rarely ranged them against each other. In fact, the first significant exception to this development proved the wisdom of the Lodi settlement and encouraged adherence to it. The Valencian Pope Calixtus III (1455–8) perversely chose to support the Angevins against Alfonso and his heir Ferrante (1458–94). This produced almost a decade of mayhem in the Papal States and the *Regno*, until the combined efforts of Pius II, Florence, Milan and Ferrante brought about a settlement in 1463. The second exception, the so-called Pazzi war of 1478–84, had more lasting consequences and will be discussed below.

Hungary and the Balkans

The kingdom of Hungary experienced many of the developments common to the rest of Europe in the first half of the fifteenth century, but its political and constitutional affairs were also affected by a factor which it shared only with the other Christian regimes of the Balkans: the pressure of war against the Ottomans, who soon recovered from the disaster at Ankara in 1402 and were raiding northwards again by the 1410s. While the historiography tends to emphasise the growth of 'constitutionalism' and the decline of royal power and resources, developments in Hungary conformed substantially to a common European model: royal agency was only neutralised for the two decades following Sigismund's death in 1437, and even then only partly, and in the context of inadequate royal leadership. Meanwhile, constitutional development was perfectly compatible with effective kingship, as well as being a response to crisis; and the Ottoman war may explain more of the political and constitutional curiosities of the period than the traditional historiography allows.

Sigismund's rule of Hungary centred on a powerful network of magnate supporters – many of them in his twenty-two-member Order of the Dragon, established in 1408 – together with military retainers and expert councillors. He reassembled as much of the old royal domain as was now realistic, and kept it in royal hands, staffing its castles with retainers, and (after the 1390s) dispensing offices, rather than *honores*, to loyal magnates. His powerful position vis-à-vis the popes and councils of the period enabled him to establish a remarkable dominance of the Hungarian Church, seizing the estates of the bishops for the duration of his reign, mulcting grants of benefices, and securing recognition of the royal right to govern the Church and appoint its ministers from Constance in 1417. Partly out of a desire to restore the balance between the magnates and the lesser nobles, which had been a source of tension since the 1350s, and partly seeing the fiscal and military resources of the latter as the key to Hungary's defence, Sigismund strengthened the jurisdiction of the counties and, in the 1430s, opened up a dialogue with them over taxation and defence. Sigismund's plan was for military obligations to be defined and organised more effectively, so that a nominated group of fifty banderial lords would be supported by a county-based system for levying men at arms and a peasant militia. The first diet since 1397, meeting at Pozsony (now Bratislava) in 1435, agreed to the militia element of this scheme while reiterating the responsibility of the king, and the right of the barons and their *banderia* forces, to conduct the kingdom's defence; representatives of the counties voted a tax to support the costs of defence, and accepted the principle – first mooted in 1397 – that they came with full authority to bind their districts to whatever they agreed. These initiatives were the springboard for the demands made by the diets of the later 1430s, but it is important to realise that military pressure, peasant revolt and a vacuum on the throne were the central reasons for the assertiveness of the lesser nobility in the period after Sigismund's death.

From 1413–14, Sigismund and his lieutenants were obliged to deal with the Ottoman revival in the Balkans. The king had used the lull in Turkish power to re-establish Hungarian influence over the states along the southern and eastern borders: the rulers of Wallachia and Serbia became Sigismund's clients in 1395 and 1403 respectively, and were given lands in Hungary and Transylvania; Bosnia, which was more hostile to the Catholics, was overrun by his troops between 1404 and 1411. Meanwhile, to defend these gains, a line of fortresses was established in the south between 1419 and 1429; their garrisons were costing perhaps 300,000 florins by 1430, way beyond the capacity of royal revenues, and another reason for the diets of the ensuing decade. The 1410s and 1420s saw a certain amount of raiding and fighting across the Balkans and southern Hungary, but these defences more or less held: Serbia accepted Ottoman suzerainty after the death of its ruler, Stephen Lazarević, in 1427, and Bosnia did the same in 1436, but Wallachia was still in the hands of the Hungarian client Vlad 'Dracul', father of the famous impaler, at Sigismund's death.

The demise of Sigismund proved to be a turning point. Albert of Austria (1437–9) quickly gained acceptance as king, but he faced pressure from the Church and lesser nobles to reverse his predecessor's 'innovations and harmful customs', while Sigismund's magnate supporters sought to subject the new ruler to their counsel. Albert's departure for Bohemia in 1438 prompted the Ottomans to attack, and the Hungarians to redouble their pressure on the monarch: at the Diet of Buda in 1439, he accepted conciliar authority, which produced a rash of grants to magnates from the royal domain. Before we condemn this dismemberment of the Hungarian crown, however, we should note that the Turks had raided Transylvania in 1438 and reoccupied Serbia in 1439, both without royal response; the magnates, doubtless long unpaid, and now unled, must have felt entitled to the assets necessary for the kingdom's defence. The situation worsened when Albert died. Belgrade was attacked in the spring of 1440, and, as a diet met and elected Władisław III of Poland king (1440–4), Albert's posthumous son, Ladislas V (1440–57) was born, and was promptly crowned by a group of Sigismund's closest magnate allies. Although Ladislas was swiftly moved to Austria for his own safety, the next two years witnessed a bitter civil war between the supporters of the two kings, in which Władisław and his leading captain, John Hunyadi, gained control of all but the north of the kingdom and launched attacks on the Ottomans across the border. This boldness encouraged support for a crusade, which the Papacy had been promoting since the reunion of the churches in 1439, and, through papal mediation, the civil war was briefly suspended in 1443–4 for action against the Ottomans; but the disastrous defeat at Varna in 1444, in which Władisław was killed, meant a resumption of internal conflict. It was healed through negotiations in a succession of diets, meeting annually from 1445 and attended by towns and lesser nobles as well as magnates. These assemblies established a governing council, featuring representatives of each side in the war, and appointed Hunyadi, who had won extensive domains in the south and east, to act as regent alongside it from 1446. The law courts were reopened and most of the grants and confiscations made since 1440 cancelled; a measure of peace returned to the kingdom, and, following another huge defeat at the hands of the Ottomans (second battle of Kosovo, 1448), negotiations were opened with Frederick III for the return of King Ladislas. This was agreed in 1453, and the government of the kingdom was consequently remodelled along more traditional lines, with Hunyadi downgraded to the post of captain-general, but the diet continuing to meet annually, providing consent to legislative acts, restoring Sigismund's militia scheme and voting extraordinary taxation from 1454. Hunyadi continued to control a substantial amount of royal property and revenue, which Ladislas, backed by the captain's enemies, attempted to regain; but, with Ottoman activity reviving again in the wake of the conquest of Constantinople, little could be done, and a united Hungarian army marched to lift the siege of Belgrade in 1456. On Hunyadi's death in the same year, King Ladislas saw his opportunity to regain the family's lands and moved against the captain's heir, also called Ladislas. The ensuing struggle, in which both Ladislas Hunyadi and the royalist count of Cilli were murdered, might have returned the kingdom to civil war, were it not for the sudden death of the king in 1457. The Hunyadi dynasty was now the only power capable of ruling Hungary, and the diet consequently chose the eldest remaining son, Matthias (Matthias Corvinus, 1458–90), as king.

To the south, finally, the rhythm of events was very much set by the Ottomans. The disaster of Ankara (1402) produced more than two decades of dynastic conflict within the ruling house, and obliged successive sultans to spend time and resources in the reconquest of Anatolia, but this did not leave the Christian powers of the Balkans altogether free to do as they pleased. Muslim client rulers and marcher lords (*udj beys*) remained in power across much of the region, and Süleyman (1402–11) rapidly regained control of them, dominating Rumelia and restoring influence over Serbia for a time in 1409. Thessalonica returned to Byzantine rule in 1403, but pressure on the remaining imperial territories was not abated for long: Constantinople was briefly besieged in 1411, and, as soon as Murad II (1421–44, 1446–51) was secure on the throne, he returned to the Balkans, investing Thessalonica in 1422 (it fell in 1430) and overrunning Serbia, Epirus and Albania between 1427 and 1435. The death of Sigismund prompted Murad to intervene in Hungary: he regained Serbia in 1438–9 and raided into the kingdom in 1440. This fifteen-year period of conquest formed the background to the negotiations at Florence between John VIII Palaeologus (1425–48) and Pope Eugenius, and to the crusading initiative that followed; but while the latter succeeded in halting the Ottoman advance for most of the 1440s (the disaster at Varna notwithstanding), and even reversed their conquests in Albania and parts of Greece, the 'union of the churches' seems to have been the final straw for Byzantine political unity: the Orthodox clergy and their supporters mostly opposed the settlement and rejected the emperor. 'Better the turban of the Turk than the tiara of the Latin' was the view of Grand Duke Luke Notaras in 1453, and this attitude may help to explain the ease with which first Constantinople and then Morea (1460) were absorbed into the Ottoman domains once Mehmed II (1444–6, 1451–81) had secured Anatolia and protected the northern frontiers by a series of treaties.[14]

c.1450–c.1500

By the second half of the fifteenth century, the onward progress of political differentiation had produced a series of increasingly stable and self-contained polities, whose internal and external dealings were more clearly separate from one another, even if the mutual influence of these remained very considerable. While this meant many localised developments, it is possible to group the individual narratives around three main themes: the large-scale and sometimes prolonged civil

---

[14] Quotation from *NCMH* VII, ed. Christopher Allmand (Cambridge, 1998), p. 782.

wars that swept through most of the western kingdoms between the 1450s and the 1480s; the noticeable emergence of stronger and better co-ordinated regimes from about the 1460s – many of them monarchical in nature, though several preserving an integral role for estates; and the major wars that broke out in the Balkans in the 1450s, in the Low Countries and the Rhineland from the 1470s, and in Granada and Italy in the 1490s.

Civil wars

In mid-century, the kingdoms of England, France, Castile and Aragon were all affected by prolonged sequences of civil disturbance, punctuated by periods of all-out civil war. In England, the so-called Wars of the Roses began in the 1450s and lasted, with interruptions, into the 1480s and 1490s. In France, the '*Guerre du Bien Public*' (war of the public good) was less protracted, with the main confrontations concentrated in the mid-1460s, but tensions persisted into the later 1470s, and were paralleled by a second sequence of disorders surrounding the '*Guerre Folle*' (mad war) of the 1480s. Castile experienced a decade of war and disorder between 1465 and 1475, and Catalonia was deeply divided and at war with its king between 1462 and 1472. While the 'new monarchies' that arose out of these convulsions have often been treated comparatively, the wars themselves have not been, although the historiography features some common themes. Older works tend to posit an inherent and growing opposition between the interests of centralising kings, on the one hand, and particularist magnates, or princes, on the other. More recent works – especially on England and Spain – are more inclined to recognise the interdependence of aristocratic power and royal government: many of them explain the mid-century breakdowns in personal, or interpersonal terms, invoking incompetent kings or overmighty magnates; others emphasise the role of economic or fiscal problems that pitted the leading nobles against their rulers. Only a handful of accounts emphasise the public dimension of these conflicts or consider the ways in which they arose from the developing structures of later medieval polities, and almost none notes the fact that they occurred at the same time.

In a way, the lack of a comparative treatment is surprising, because these wars share a number of common causes, common forms and common outcomes, most of them rooted in the ways that European polities had evolved over the previous couple of centuries. Economic problems were certainly an important part of the background to fifteenth-century civil wars: there was a growing crisis in the supply of silver and gold from the 1430s, and much of Europe was consequently plunged into slump between *c*.1445 and *c*.1465. But a more fundamental factor was the complicated and delicate relationship that had developed in each of these kingdoms between royal government, public opinion (and its various representatives) and the leading powers of the realm – princes, nobles, towns and, more fleetingly, popular armies. In each case, this relationship depended on effective royal coordination and a reasonable balance between the interests of sectional groups and the publicly recognised common interests of the realm. In this period, in all four kingdoms, that balance was upset, and the real difficulty facing contemporary politicians – kings, magnates and popular leaders alike – was that it was both extremely important and extremely difficult to restore it once it was lost. Herein lie the reasons why these conflicts were so prolonged, or at least recurrent, and why they were so all-embracing.

The causes of conflict in each kingdom were roughly similar, and contained three main ingredients. The first was public dissatisfaction – resentment, on the part of the people of town and countryside, of high, or unduly persisting, taxation, disorder and injustice, and/or the erosion of rights, privileges and customs. This dissatisfaction was highly vocal, captured in manifestoes and petitions, and presented by poets and popular rebels, by the *diputats* of Catalonia and the delegates of municipalities and shires at *Cortes*, parliaments and estates, or by magnates, acting – like York or Warwick, or Carrillo and Villena, or Charles the Bold, or Louis of Orleans – for the common weal, *cosa pública* or *bien public*. A second ingredient was the disgruntlement and unease of leading magnates, both on their own account (because they had enemies about the king or elsewhere within the realm, or because they felt insecure in their possessions) and on account of the dissatisfaction abroad within the realm, to which they were obliged by their position in society to respond. While the historiography has emphasised the former set of concerns, the latter were just as pressing for most magnates: even great princes with remote and coherent domains, like the dukes of Brittany and Burgundy, or the Guzmán dukes of Medina Sidonia who ruled over much of Andalusia, could not avoid entanglement in the affairs of the kingdom – their fiscal and commercial interests, their allies and satellites, invariably drew them in. A third element was the inability of many of the kings of the period to provide the kind of independent, authoritative and representative leadership that was required. In some cases, notably that of Henry VI of England, the inability was largely personal. In most cases, it was circumstantial – the result of a problematic inheritance, or dynastic uncertainty, or conflicting demands, or often some combination of these. It is a striking feature of the wars of the 1460s that they were a second stage of conflicts or divisions that had begun earlier – in England and Aragon in the 1450s, in Castile in the 1430s and 1440s, in France in the struggle of Burgundians and Armagnacs in the opening decades of the century. These had produced only fragile settlements – the uncertain victory of one faction over another, redistributions of power which had not yet settled down, animosities among the leading families – so that Edward IV of England (1461–70, 1471–83), John II of Aragon (1458–79), Henry IV of Castile (1454–74) and even Louis XI of France (1461–83) came to the throne as insecure rulers in conditions of some instability. That three of them were slow to produce heirs compounded their difficulties, especially as leading princes of the blood and heirs presumptive were, in every realm, willing to side with their critics and opponents. Their insecurities also led them to rule in ways that went against contemporary ideals, with negative results – they were unduly partisan and/or unduly generous with grants from the royal fisc; they levied charges of treason against their opponents and thus created a climate of insecurity; or they were too ready to forgive those who opposed them, frustrating their supporters and eroding the bonds of obedience. It is clear, then, that attempts by kings, magnates and people to resolve the problems of government that had sparked these conflicts tended only to produce further conflicts – the product of weakened and/or threatening rulers, dangerous and vulnerable magnates, lack of political trust, and lingering public disaffection. Moreover, since these troubles broke out in adjoining realms – in the case of England and France, realms that had long been at war with each other – they also tended to involve foreign interference, a far from negligible factor that worsened the predicament (but also increased the opportunities) of rulers and subjects alike. While the cycle could be broken, there were false starts in France, England and Castile, and, as the conflicts in the last two kingdoms lengthened and deepened, they lost clarity, with kings, pretenders, magnates and towns hedging their bets, switching sides with disconcerting rapidity, joining together to make settlements and then abandoning them, drifting away into local feuds and/or semi-independence. The causes and processes of these civil wars, then, were interwoven: the problem of the common weal – which was real as well as rhetorical – did not go away, and many of the efforts to resolve it produced further grievance and instability.

If we turn to the outcomes of these civil wars, we find that these too were similar. First of all, the wars strengthened the sense of the realm as the primary political forum, and emphasised that its common good was the primary political goal; the copious public discussion the wars provoked, and the attempts of regimes and their opponents to legitimise themselves with reference to history and myth, also intensified national self-consciousness. The sprawling impact of these conflicts made it clear that trouble with the king was trouble for everyone, and they thus had an integrative effect. Rulers and subjects may have found it difficult to resolve their difficulties, but they recognised that they had a common stake in resolving them, and, in the longer term, this was a sentiment on which more robust regimes could be based. In a similar way, the dispersal of regnal assets – whether jurisdictional or fiscal, or both – eventually inspired support for royal schemes of resuming them, partly so that royal allies (and former enemies) could benefit from the grants that they had been given, but also, surely, because of general recognition that, without some independent means and central co-ordination, royal government could not function and disorder would continue. By varied routes – inheritance and confiscation in England and France, resumption in England and Castile, negotiation in Castile and Aragon, and war itself everywhere – the kings of the 1470s and 1480s regained much of what their predecessors had lost, and, in most cases, rather more than that. The crowns of the later fifteenth century typically controlled more land and more jurisdiction directly; their fiscal and military rights were generally more complete, even though the overall burden of taxation – in France and England, at least – was lower by the 1480s and 1490s than it had been for much of the hundred years before the civil war. With royal resumptions went the reform of royal institutions: improvements to councils and law courts, the redesigning of local and national offices, new arrangements for consultation. Many of these developments had got underway earlier in the century, and had sometimes contributed to the tensions producing civil war, but they were fulfilled, and mostly with less controversy, in the aftermath of the conflicts. Unauthorised public action was more clearly delegitimised – it became more difficult to justify assaults on the crown, even in the name of the common or public good – and criticism, even representation, began to acquire the taint of rebellion and conspiracy. Of course, there were still means for important interests to gain access to royal attention – kings would have been unable to rule otherwise – but these means were more likely to involve the king's court and his councils, and less likely to involve the action of representative estates, such as the Castilian *Cortes*, which ceased to meet between 1483 and 1497, or the Estates General of France, which met just twice after 1450, both times in moments of political crisis: 1468 and 1484. The view expressed by Louis XI's former servants in 1484, that 'it is *lèse-majesté* to talk of assembling Estates', captures the mood well, and even the English Parliament, which remained an important political institution, became a more technocratic body, in which negotiation between ruler and community involved less public confrontation and more mediation and management by royal networks.[15] Finally, in France, England and, to a lesser extent, Aragon, there were important changes to the position of the leading magnates – reductions in the number of princes, and unrelenting pressure on independent territorial influence. Some of these changes were partially reversed later on, and, it is now realised, were scarcely attempted in the Castile of Ferdinand and Isabella (though even there the crown reasserted some of its former control over the municipalities); but royal co-ordination of territorial power advanced almost everywhere, making these kingdoms more coherent and less like a series of compromises between different layers of authority.

Some of these political and governmental developments will be discussed at more length in the final section of the chapter, but, here, let us briefly survey the events of the wars and their outcomes in each of the four kingdoms, starting with England, where the crisis was most protracted and intractable. Trouble had started in the final decade of the reign of Henry VI, in the wake of the loss of Normandy, the fall of Suffolk and the rebellion of Jack Cade, all of which had struck in 1450. Richard, duke of York (d.1460), the leading magnate of the realm, and holder of a claim to the throne which could be presented as technically superior to that of the ruling house of Lancaster, led a series of protests against Henry VI's government, which sharpened into

---

[15] Quotation from P.S. Lewis, 'The Failure of the French Medieval Estates', *Essays in Later Medieval French History* (London, 1985), ch. 8, p. 109.

armed conflict against his supporters at St Albans in 1455. A real tension over the need both to advance the common weal and to protect royal authority became enmeshed both with a factional struggle between groups of magnates and with a dynastic cleavage, opened up by York when he claimed the throne in 1460, and confirmed when his son, Edward IV, gained the throne in 1461 without capturing or destroying Henry VI or his son Edward of Lancaster (1453–71). Edward, rich with land, from his own estates and those seized from Lancastrian magnates, initially attempted to rule in the way the reformers of the 1450s had proposed, with less taxation, better justice and a more effective prosecution of the king's rights in France, but the experiment proved impossible. The new king found himself having to fight a long and expensive war on the northern border, where the regency of James III (1460–88) supported the Lancastrians (1461–4), and, despite raising several taxes, was unable to campaign in France as he had wished. His pursuit of an alliance with the new duke of Burgundy, Charles the Bold (1467–77), combined with financial difficulties and the political problems raised by his attempt to create a new landed establishment in the wake of the wars of 1459–64, produced risings against him in 1469–70, led by the earl of Warwick (d.1471) and supported by Louis XI of France and the remaining Lancastrians, who briefly regained the throne in 1470–1. With the support of his allies, of London and the Burgundian connection, and because he offered a better long-term chance of political order than the regime that had supplanted him, Edward won back his throne at the battles of Barnet and Tewkesbury (1471) and proceeded to rule with great success until his early death in 1483. His young son briefly succeeded him, as Edward V, but a twelve-year-old was in no position to govern the insecure Yorkist establishment, and the throne was seized by its greatest landowner and military captain, Richard, duke of Gloucester (Richard III, 1483–5). Richard too was soon overthrown: the rest of the Yorkists joined forces with the remaining Lancastrians and some French support, to deliver a victory at Bosworth (1485) for Henry Tudor, earl of Richmond (Henry VII, 1485–1509), whose weak Lancastrian blood claim had been strengthened by a promise to marry Edward IV's daughter. Like Edward (after 1471) and Richard before him, Henry retained the much-expanded estates of the crown in his own hands and used them to sustain an extensive network of gentry servants instead of trying to create a new nobility. He pursued a vigorous campaign of restoring royal rights, facing down the resulting opposition with a mixture of determination and good fortune. Attempts to unseat him through pretenders failed in 1487 and 1497–9, despite the backing, at one time or another, of most of England's neighbours, including the semi-independent network of the earls of Kildare that had taken control of Ireland during the civil wars. Although the spectre of civil war hung over England well into the sixteenth century, and popular ferment remained a prominent way of responding to royal failures vis-à-vis the common weal, the capacity of the crown to manage the various powers beneath it was restored, and even somewhat extended, by 1500.

In Castile, the crisis was no less deep, but was rather shorter than that in England. At the beginning of his reign, Henry IV faced a divided and uneasy nobility, with large amounts of royal jurisdiction and resources in its several hands. Like Edward IV, his response was a sensible one: to pardon those excluded under his father; to confirm the bulk of earlier royal grants; to establish new supporters; to attempt resumption of the fisc wherever possible; and to revive traditional rights over neighbouring powers, which led, in this last case, to three years of war against Granada, 1455–8, and ultimately to the capture of Gibraltar in 1462. While the king conceded the right to collect *servicios* on their lands to the nobility in 1455 (and thus surrendered a third of nominal tax incomes at a stroke), he took other steps to protect the *realengo*, appointing *corregidores* in many towns, reviving the *hermandades* and joining them together under royal agents, tightening municipal control of the *alcabalas* in 1462 and promoting urban economic interests. These steps caused some controversy, but, in many ways, Henry put up a good performance in the first decade of his rule. What brought him down was an unfortunate confluence of circumstances, in which the key ingredients were the king's dynastic weakness (no direct heir until 1462, and then only a baby girl; two half-siblings – the children Alfonso and Isabella, offspring of John II's second marriage); an expensive and inconclusive war with Aragon-Navarre (1461–3); and the instability produced by the overweening power of the marquis of Villena, Henry's principal ally and lieutenant in the last decade of his father's reign. Fearing that the king was about to move against him, and resentful at Henry's promotion of his close ally, the new count of Ledesma, to the grand mastership of Santiago, Villena joined forces with Archbishop Carrillo of Toledo, sometime leader of the Castilian delegation at the Council of Basle, to raise a league in the name of the *cosa pública* and the young *infantes* in 1464.

Playing heavily on anti-*converso* feeling, and alleging all manner of perversions against the king, their manifestoes nonetheless captured a wide range of popular and municipal grievances and culminated in a massive programme, the *Sentencia de Medina del Campo* (1465), which proposed to subject the king to the rule of a magnate council and a freely elected *Cortes* with full control of taxation. Henry rejected this unworkable scheme and raised troops; his opponents responded by deposing him in effigy ('Farce of Ávila', 1465), making Alfonso king, and embarking on three years of warfare. In this conflict, Henry and his allies gradually prevailed, winning over the towns, and, when Alfonso died in 1468, forcing the dissident magnates to terms; but the resulting agreement – in which Henry rejected his daughter, Juana, in favour of Isabella (1474–1504) – soon unravelled when the new heiress showed her independence by betraying her stepbrother and marrying Ferdinand of Aragon (1469). The last few years of the reign were marked by the gradual desertion of Henry's allies, either to the party of Ferdinand and Isabella, or to that of Juana, who was supported by Alfonso V of Portugal with an invading army in 1475–6. Henry's pacific instincts and his inability to provide a clear line of succession were central causes of his undoing; his decision, in 1469, to confirm grants to the nobility in preference to restoring the fisc cost him the sympathy of the towns, and helps to explain the drift of support towards Ferdinand and Isabella as the most convincing defenders of the *realengo* in the longer term.

Having defeated the Portuguese at Toro in 1476 and gained the tacit support of most of the magnates, these two, in their turn, faced the now-familiar predicament of how to rule Castile when the crown's assets were so extensively redistributed. Their solution was not, in fact, so very different from Henry IV's. They too sought the goodwill of almost all the major magnate houses, confirming the bulk of *mercedes* (especially those granted before 1464), while resuming enough control of revenue to ensure that confirmed *juros* were duly paid. At the same time, they confirmed the union of the *hermandades* (*Santa Hermandad*, 1476–98), extending its powers so that it became a prominent means of taxation, representation and armed force during its twenty-year existence. They also secured the grand masterships of the military orders by the 1490s; and they regained control of many royal towns, partly by generalising the system of *corregidores*, partly by confirming local magnates in office, and partly by outlawing *bandos* and creating more regular procedures for election. They placed a council of experts in charge of policy and grants (*Consejo Real*, 1480), and ensured that all the magnates were equally excluded from its deliberations. At the same time, they maintained good relations with their titled subjects, leading them into a glorious war to complete the *Reconquista* with a ten-year invasion of Granada (1482–92). Finally – and this was their most original policy – they decisively broke with the Jewish and *converso* networks that had controlled royal finances before the war: the latter were policed by the notorious Inquisition, established in 1478, while the former were expelled from Spain in 1492. This striking departure from the traditions of the Castilian monarchy had become possible, even logical, because of the disintegration of the old financial structures, the rapid intensification of anti-Semitic feeling, and the development of new media for governing the towns and managing taxation. The other policies of the 'Catholic Monarchs', as they were known from 1494, were mostly more traditional, but they worked because the succession was secure (until 1497), the threat from Aragon and Portugal was neutralised, and the crown had regained enough political and fiscal assets to offer independent leadership. Ferdinand and Isabella ruled well, but they did not transform Castile, nor unify Spain, and the queen's death in 1504 produced a crisis which took Ferdinand and the Castilian political community two years, and some good fortune, to master.

The civil war in Aragon was both more predictable and more straightforward than the conflict in Castile. It was clearly brewing before the death of Alfonso V, and it broke out soon after the shaky succession of his younger brother, John II (1458–79). John's insecurity stemmed from his uncertain tenure of the throne of Navarre, where his eldest son, Charles of Viana (d.1461), had been the rightful king since 1441. Fearing that Charles was intriguing to regain his lost kingdom, John arrested him in 1460, provoking a rising in Catalonia and an invasion from Castile. This impossible situation drove the king to accept the *Capitulacion* of Vilafranca (1461), which placed Catalonia more completely than ever under the government of the *diputació*, with Charles as lieutenant; but the prince's sudden death and John's opportunistic dealings with the Catalan peasantry in 1461–2 meant that the settlement was shortlived. In 1462, the *diputats* offered the county of Barcelona to Henry IV, whose armies thus returned; the *remences* rose up in protest at the king's failure to deliver on a promise to suspend the *mals usos*; and John II invaded Catalonia in alliance with the French, to whom he surrendered the border territories of

Roussillon and Cerdagne. Over the next ten years, the king, aided by the Valencians, some armies of *remença* peasants and elements hostile to the pactist elite in Catalonia, struggled to regain control of the deviant province, while the *Biga* rulers of Barcelona, the *diputats*, many Catalan nobles and a succession of foreign lieutenants fought them off (Aragon-proper remained aloof, and Louis XI helped each side in turn). The marriage of John's heir, Ferdinand II (1479–1516), to Isabella of Castile improved John's prospects, and in 1472, with the fall of Barcelona, the war was ended. While the king forgave many of the surviving nobles and confirmed most of the pre-1461 liberties of Catalonia, the situation remained tense: the *remences* lost their liberties again in 1474–5, attempts to regain Roussillon and Cerdagne failed, and feuding broke out in both Valencia and Aragon. Ferdinand thus inherited an uneasy situation, but his own deft rule, the gradual accommodation of the three home provinces to a system of viceroys and absentee kings, and the overall relaxation of fiscal pressure (as the new king relied on Castilian revenues), combined to make settlement possible. In the *Observança* that followed the *Corts* of 1480–1, Ferdinand enshrined Catalan liberties in statute law; he also managed a tactful expansion of the city governments, and, judging that the time was right, successfully freed the *remença* peasants in the *Sentencia de Guadalupe* of 1486. Regaining Roussillon and Cerdagne by treaty in 1493, infiltrating Navarre, and conquering Naples from the French in 1504, he had reassembled all the conquests of Aragon-Catalonia under the effective rule of a Castile-based council of regents (Council of Aragon, 1494).

The final set of wars took place in France. Because they were by no means as bad as the conflicts of the Hundred Years War period, and because they disrupt historiographical notions of unstoppable progress towards absolutism, the troubles of the 1460s, 1470s and 1480s have been rather neglected by historians, but they were closely comparable to the disturbances in the other kingdoms we have considered, and could easily have turned out worse for the crown than they did. The last decade of Charles VII's reign was not as untroubled as the scale of the king's victory might lead one to expect. Relations between the king and the princes became, if anything, more uneasy, as Charles went to war against the count of Armagnac (1455), arraigned the duke of Alençon for treason (1458), threatened the rights accorded to the duke of Burgundy in the Treaty of Arras, and seized the Dauphiné as part of an obscure but lengthy struggle with his son and heir (1456–9).

Meanwhile, the persisting tax burden provoked reaction in Normandy and elsewhere, and so did the nationwide inquiries into local customs that began in 1454. Louis XI's first actions as king – removing and punishing the ministers of his father, restoring his victims and cancelling the Pragmatic Sanction of Bourges in favour of a new papal concordat – may have been a response to burgeoning unrest, but they had an instantly destabilising effect: encouraging popular expectations of an end to taxation, which were swiftly disappointed; alienating some of the Caroline establishment and the Church; and provoking popular complaint. Since the king accompanied these gestures with moves against the liberties and interests of Burgundy, Brittany, Orleans and Anjou, he soon found himself the object of a princely *Ligue du Bien Public*, which called for a regency under his brother, Charles of France, a restoration of magnate counsel and office-holding, lower taxes and other reforms. The king raised the royal army that his father had created in 1445, but was unable to defeat Charles the Bold (duke of Burgundy, 1467–77) in battle at Montlhéry, near Paris, in 1465. Faced with the converging forces of Burgundy, Berry, Brittany and Anjou, and signs of disaffection in Normandy and Paris, the king was forced to negotiate a treaty at Conflans (1465), in which he accepted the creation of a reform commission, promised to summon a meeting of the estates, and granted titles and offices to the dissenting princes. In the event, Louis went on to regain the support of notables by broadening his council, restoring the Pragmatic Sanction (on the advice of the *Parlement*), and making an *ordonnance* giving officers security in their posts; he was thus able to break up the coalition against him, and to turn the Estates General of Tours (1468) to his advantage. Even so, he could not secure the goodwill of his two most powerful subjects, the dukes of Brittany and Burgundy, and, from 1468, these two were in regular contact with Edward IV of England, in the hope of arranging a joint invasion.

By the early 1470s, Burgundy was pushing for full independence from the kingdom of France, and England was able to send a large army to Picardy in 1475. The unease of Brittany, the distraction of Burgundy (also at war in Lorraine and the Rhineland) and the willingness of the impecunious Edward IV to accept a large financial settlement from Louis XI, saved the French king from the most serious incursion since the 1410s. Once the English were removed, Louis went for his enemies, binding Brittany to obedience in 1475, trying and executing the count of St Pol (1475) and the duke of

Nemours (1477), forging an alliance with the duke of Lorraine, the Swiss and the Rhinelanders against Burgundy, and overrunning the duchy, together with Franche-Comté, Picardy and Artois, when Duke Charles died at the battle of Nancy in 1477. The last years of the reign were spent in a bitter war against the new duke of Burgundy, Maximilian Habsburg, son of the Emperor, in which Louis more or less retained his conquests (1477–82). The king had silenced opposition within the kingdom: the political conflict over reform, in which a wide range of interests were involved, had become a war with the leading provincial magnates, in which Louis had just enough fiscal and military resources to prevail. He had also gained some important additions to the royal *domaine* – the estates of Armagnac (1473) and Anjou (1481), both by default of heirs. But he had not resolved the structural tensions in the French kingdom, as the events that followed his death were to reveal.

Soon after the accession of the thirteen-year-old Charles VIII (1483–98), the king's closest male relative, Louis, duke of Orleans, demanded the regency, and secured the backing of most of the major princes, including not only the erstwhile opponents of Louis XI, but also men like Alain d'Albret, and the prince of Orange, who had received his favour. These men forced the assembly of an Estates General, which again met at Tours (1484) and, when it denied Orleans' request, rose up in the name of the *bien public*. The regime around the king, dominated by the king's sister and her husband, Pierre de Beaujeu, won public support by cutting the *taille* by more than half and subjecting its future grants to estates control (a concession it was able to withdraw after 1486); it faced down Orleans in 1485, and went confidently to war against him and the duke of Brittany in 1487–8, defeating both dukes and their foreign allies, forcing the latter to accept vassal status and conquering his duchy in the wake of his death (1489–90). The new duchess of Brittany, Anne, was forced to abandon the marriage to Maximilian which her father had hastily arranged, and was betrothed instead to the young king, with the result that Brittany joined the royal *domaine* in 1498. In 1491, Charles VIII came of age, and proceeded to release Orleans from prison, to make peace with his neighbours and, in 1494, to go to war in Italy, in pursuit of the old Angevin claim to Naples. The victories of Charles VII, the harshness of Louis XI and the *adresse* of the Beaujeus and Charles VIII had effectively destroyed the swelling principalities of the mid- to late fifteenth century. A powerful duchy of Bourbon remained, but, unlike the great provincial lordships of Aquitaine, Brittany, Burgundy and the far south-west, its potential for independent action was limited by its position. The links forged by the crown with the middle-ranking nobility enabled it to rule a more extensive kingdom without needing to depend on princes: these men were the key holders of captaincies in the army, of regional lieutenancies, governorships and *bailliages*, and they made up the bulk of the notables retained by the king as councillors and *gens du roi*. Reductions in the tax burden (though it was creeping up again by 1500) and a more relaxed attitude to local jurisdictions eased relations with the mass of the inhabitants. France had avoided the twin extremes of administrative tyranny and what Bernard Chevalier neatly calls 'princely polyarchy'.[16]

Consolidation through dialogue

Many, indeed most, other polities underwent less convulsive processes of consolidation in this period. While these were not devoid of confrontation, negotiation, whether formal or informal, is a more prominent characteristic. Older historiography tends to characterise both the dynamics of this period and their outcomes as 'dualistic' – especially in relation to the Empire and the kingdoms of east-central and northern Europe. In each case, proto-absolutist 'new monarchs' (sometimes cunningly allied with towns and lesser nobles) are supposed to have been pitted against magnate-led estates, who were aiming to restrict royal innovations and protect entrenched liberties. In many kingdoms – Bohemia, Poland, Hungary, in some respects Scotland – the second half of the century thus seems to involve the rise and fall of monarchical assertion, while in others – the Empire, Denmark, Sweden – the struggle of opposed interests is too evenly matched, and the result is a kind of deadlock, or anarchy. But while confrontation could certainly occur in these countries, and while they often possessed strong traditions of collective action in securing noble liberty or territorial immunity, it is coming to be recognised that this older picture is too preoccupied with conflict, and with constitutional conflict at that. As in the first half of the century, estates opposition was rarely united for long and was at its most obdurate in circumstances of royal inadequacy or absence. Meanwhile, since the demands of the estates tended to promote the integrity of the

---

[16] *NCMH* VII, p. 409.

kingdom, co-operation usually offered something to the ruler, even if, in practice, it was difficult for representatives to bind those they stood for. What looks like a series of set-piece battles in diets or parliaments might thus be reinterpreted, as they have been by historians of the fourteenth-century West, as a kind of dialogue (indeed, this is just what historians of Poland, Hungary and Bohemia are beginning to do). In practice, then, movements on behalf of 'the Empire' or 'the land' or 'the crown' tended, in this period, to strengthen the polities of Europe, not to drive wedges between kings and subjects. These trends were afforced by other processes of negotiation and compromise, typically more informal and expressed through media of grace and the management of networks, which, as in the West, came to be more effectively deployed towards the end of the century.

These processes of consolidation are apparent in most of the polities we have been concerned with – empires, kingdoms, principalities and the few remaining city states – and it was part and parcel of that development that the differences between these power structures faded in the second half of the century. That is one reason why the period is often seen as one of rising princes or monarchies: the regnal polity was the characteristic political format, even if it is crucial to recognise that it was the work of many elements in political society besides the monarch. It is also a reason for many of the internal conflicts of the period, as the potential contradictions between princely and urban jurisdictions and the developing regnal structures above them were more sharply exposed. In what follows, we shall begin by looking at the two western empires, then the kingdoms, and finally the principalities and other territorial states.

By the 1490s, the Empire was coming to be known by the revealing name of 'Holy Roman Empire of the German Nation'. While the Emperors Frederick III and Maximilian retained many interests outside the German lands and the ideal of universal monarchy persisted (to be given new meaning in the reign of Maximilian's successor, Charles V (1519–56), who combined his grandfather's holdings in Austria, Burgundy and the Low Countries with the kingdoms of Spain and Naples, the duchy of Milan and the new American territories), the mounting concern of German powers with the internal welfare and institutions of the *Reich* in the last three decades of the century emphasised and strengthened its regnal and national features. While various fiscal and judicial initiatives were discussed in the 1460s, the first significant moves towards the implementation of reform schemes came in the 1470s. Following a Turkish raid into Styria, Frederick returned to Germany for the Diet of Ratisbon in 1471 and presented a request for general taxation to fight the Turks. A scheme was agreed (and another in 1474), though little actual money resulted, but a second imperial initiative – the removal of the Emperor's chamber court (*Kammergericht*) from the royal household, and its establishment as a judicial resort for those affected by violence – was put into effect, and flourished for several years under the archbishop of Mainz. Frederick stayed in the Reich to rebuff the demands of Charles the Bold for a crown (1473) and to co-ordinate resistance to his aggressions in Lorraine and at Neuss; somewhat paradoxically, he also secured a marriage for his son to Charles' daughter, Mary, which resulted in Maximilian's succession to the Burgundian domains in 1477. With the invasion of Austria by the king of Hungary, Matthias Corvinus (1458–90), Frederick returned to the *Erblände*, and it was thus Maximilian, elected king of the Romans in 1486, who conducted debates with the frequent diets of the 1480s and 1490s. The principal aim of the king was to secure financial help with as little damage to his prerogatives as possible. That of the reformers, led for much of this period by Berthold, archbishop of Mainz, was to secure effective judicial, defensive and decision-making institutions for the Empire, conceding that taxation might be necessary, but seeking to ensure that it would be properly levied and spent on the defence and administration of the German lands, and not simply exploited by the Emperor for whatever schemes he might wish to pursue. A decade of debate at well-attended meetings encouraged rapid development in the forms and procedures of the diet itself (known as the *Reichstag* from 1495), and broke down the resistance of both Maximilian and the various estates to the development of common policy and common institutions. Its upshot, in the *Reichstag* at Worms in 1495, was fourfold: the establishment of a permanent *Reichslandfriede*, banning feuds and upheld by ten peace-keeping 'circles' (*Kreise*) from 1512; the revival, under estates authority, of the fixed chamber court, or *Reichskammergericht*, at Frankfurt (now given jurisdiction over the princes and entitled to hear appeals from their subjects); an agreement to annual *Reichstage*; and the introduction of regular annual taxation, in the form of the Common Penny. Inevitably, there was some backtracking from these agreements in the following years. While Austria was subject to all of them, Maximilian tended to ignore restraints upon him as

Emperor, and was briefly forced to accept the rule of a *Reichsregiment*, or governing council, in 1500–1. The Common Penny raised less than it should have done, and petered out after just four years, and the diets did not meet annually. But the trend of events was running the reformers' way: *Reichstage* ended in joint declarations of what had been agreed from 1497, the chamber court grew into a robust institution, and the *Matrikel* tax, first attempted in the 1420s, became a regular source of revenue from 1521. These formal steps towards integration were matched, and perhaps underpinned, by more informal moves. From about 1470 onwards, with his return from Austria, Frederick III began to change the complexion of his court, recruiting almost half its members from outside the *Erblände*, and this pattern continued under Maximilian, whose court was more conveniently situated in the Tyrol in any case, and included Burgundians and Dutch alongside Austrians and Germans. The continuity of the succession, the acquisition of the Burgundian lands in 1477, and the reassembly of the Habsburg lands (including those in Swabia) from 1493 made the emperor more convincing as a pan-German figure. He also gained considerably from the fulfilment of one of Sigismund's schemes: in 1488, a Swabian League was founded under imperial leadership. From 1492, this organisation included princes as well as towns, and by 1500 it had a constitution and fiscal, judicial, military and administrative frameworks. For several decades it was an effective means of enforcing imperial authority on the powers of the south, curtailing the expansionist moves of the duke of Bavaria-Landshut in 1492 and destroying the duke of Württemberg in 1519. It was not always triumphant, however: in a telling episode, the League went to war against the Swiss Confederation in 1499, to enforce a judgement of the *Reichskammergericht* and to protect the Tyrol; a Swiss victory at Dornach brought the war to an end, and opened the way to full independence from imperial jurisdiction for the Confederation's members.

The Empire, then, was in many ways strengthened as a kingdom in the later fifteenth century, and Maximilian was consequently able to draw upon more than the resources of the *Erblände* to support his wars in Italy. What of the other Roman empire in this period – that of the Papacy? As a political institution, the universal Church or papal empire had very largely ceased to exist in the wake of the Conciliar period. Much as the popes retained vestigial rights to some appointments, and more significant influence over the orders of regular clergy, the secular church hierarchies were organised more or less on regnal lines, increasingly subject to the jurisdiction (or at least supervision) of the lay judicial order in each territory, and heavily influenced by the prevailing political structures of the surrounding territory. The Papacy itself, meanwhile, was becoming a powerful Italian principate. From the pontificate of Pius II onwards (1458–64), its control of the Papal States generally advanced: the *signori* were more effectively contained, even eradicated; several cities came directly under cameral control, and while vicariates became longer (almost like fiefs, in some cases), they were more closely policed, and vicars who did not pay over the papal *census* (tax), or uphold papal rights, were challenged and sometimes ejected. Papal incomes rose from about the same time – partly from the alum mines at Tolfa, but also from the proceeds of taxes on the cities and the introduction of venal offices;[17] by 1480, Sixtus IV (1471–84) was drawing revenues comparable to those of the 1370s, albeit that two-thirds of the money now came from central Italy. This Italian focus was reflected in the make-up of the College of Cardinals: its membership, which grew from the 1450s, now went beyond the old Roman families, but mainly to include representatives from the other leading powers of the peninsula. Against this background, dynasties linked to individual popes – the della Rovere of Genoa, dominant in the 1470s and 1480s under Sixtus IV and Innocent VIII (1484–92), and the Borgias of Aragon, who came in with Calixtus III and regained the tiara in 1492 (Alexander VI, 1492–1503) – filled the spiritual and temporal offices of the Papal States and, in pursuit of their interests, encouraged aggressive engagement in the conflicts of Italy. It is striking that all three of the wars that broke the peace of Lodi arose from papal schemes. This sometimes meant the reversal of papal achievements – by the end of Sixtus' reign, for instance, the Papal States were in disarray, and Bologna and Perugia were moving into the orbit of Milan and Florence, respectively – but it also undermined the other powers of Italy, and one can readily see why Machiavelli blamed the Holy See for the subsequent misfortunes of the peninsula.

Notwithstanding these developments, the international role of the Papacy did not vanish overnight. In some ways, indeed, contact

---

[17] These were offices granted to papal creditors, who were allowed to collect the profits from them. They were not quite sinecures, even so: while the papal staff grew very considerably in this period, so did the business before them.

between the papal Curia and the mass of European Christians increased, as the sale of indulgences and granting of dispensations multiplied, and the frequency of jubilees was doubled again, to take place every twenty-five years.[18] The Papacy continued to be the centre of a major and well-developed diplomatic network, and it used it not only to forward its Italian interests, but also to promote crusades and to protect what remained of its universal jurisdiction. Notwithstanding the efforts of Pius II, whose Council of Mantua (1459) was devoted to gathering support for a crusade, papal initiatives were mainly thwarted after Varna: the defence of Christendom became the work of frontline Catholic powers, Hungary, Venice, Poland-Lithuania and Castile, with the papal role restricted mainly to granting their kings fiscal and juridical rights which were in danger of being usurped anyway. But papal concessions over the rights and assets of national churches could not yet be taken for granted: Henry IV of Castile's attempt to place the Spanish military orders directly under the crown in the 1450s was, for example, blocked by the refusal of a papal bull, prompting the king to secure the mastership of Santiago for Ledesma, with the explosive results described above; only in 1493 was this privilege granted to the Catholic monarchs, who also depended on papal consent for the establishment of their Inquisition (1478), and for their large share in crusade taxation. The Papacy also remained the natural choice for international arbitration – as in the Treaty of Tordesillas (1494), which divided the New World between Spain and Portugal – and the spectre of conciliarism continued to be invoked by rulers, or, more occasionally, by cardinals or the University of Paris, as a means of attacking papal policy. Even so, it is not without significance that the one real return to the ecclesiastical politics of the early fifteenth century – the convocation by rebel cardinals of a council at Pisa in 1511, initially with the backing of the emperor and the king of France – was substantially provoked by the politics of Italy, not those of the international Church. The Papacy was unquestionably strengthened in the later fifteenth century, both as an Italian prince and as a spiritual authority over the European laity, but its role as the head of an ecclesiastical empire was very greatly reduced.

---

[18] Those taking a pilgrimage to Rome in a jubilee year could win special remission of sins, in return for suitable offerings.

For the kingdoms of Hungary, Poland and Bohemia, meanwhile, these were years of stabilisation, as the relationship between king and estates was gradually settled and effective means of representing the latter were established. All three kingdoms were recovering from civil wars and disorders – lightest in Poland in the 1420s and 1430s, heaviest in Bohemia between the 1410s and the 1440s, but appreciable in Hungary too in the 1440s and 1450s. These internal conflicts were not unlike those in the West that we have just been discussing, but they occurred earlier and, with the exception of the Hussite wars, were less all-embracing and arguably less traumatic. Even so, their impact needs to be borne in mind when considering the weaknesses and the strengths of the three warlord kings of the 1450s and 1460s – Casimir IV of Poland, George of Bohemia and Matthias of Hungary: while they were all duly elected, electoral monarchy was a new custom in these kingdoms, and, in functional terms, these men were more or less usurpers, like Edward IV of England or Isabella of Castile. That George and Matthias had no royal blood in their veins – not unlike Henry VII in that respect – only increased their vulnerability, but it did not stop them restoring the rights of the crown or negotiating the proper extent of those rights with their subjects.

In Poland, as we have seen, Casimir soon regained control of the government following the death of Olésnicki in 1455. The *Sejm* receded from view for about forty years, while the king established his own network of councillors, magnate allies and compliant bishops, concentrating offices in reliable hands and drawing on the political and financial benefits of the victorious war in Prussia and the continuing dialogue with the *sejmiki* – now meeting in two groups – to support his regime. Although the upper house of the *Sejm* began to call itself by the name of 'Senate', the king was able to express the view in 1480 that there were no born counsellors in Poland, and he would take advice from whom he pleased. Casimir kept Lithuania on a tight rein, refusing to concede a lieutenant, but extending Polish noble privileges to the boyars. He seems to have intended to establish a network of Jagiellonian princes across eastern Europe, backing the attempt of his eldest son to obtain the thrones of Bohemia (Vladislav II, 1471–1516) and Hungary (Ulászló II, 1490–1516), while designating his second son, John Albert, heir to Poland (1492–1501), and his third, Alexander, grand duke of Lithuania (1492–1506). These last successions went smoothly, but both sons had to face challenging external conditions. Muscovy, which had been on the back foot for most of the first half of the fifteenth century, recovered its energies under Grand Prince Ivan III, who overran the various lordships of north-eastern Rus' and then proceeded to attack and conquer the trading cities of Novgorod (1471–8) and Tver' (1485), both of which had enjoyed Lithuanian protection. By 1500, the grand duke was engaged in all-out war against the grand prince, in an attempt to protect his lands across the River Dnieper. Meanwhile, to the south, the Polish/Hungarian client state of Moldavia was subjugated by the Ottomans in 1484, leading first Casimir and then John Albert towards intervention, which finally came in a disastrous expedition of 1497. The atmosphere of mounting military pressure affected the internal politics of Poland, and the 1490s saw the return of the *Sejm*, meeting from 1493 alongside the *sejmiki*, which formally became its lower house, following a precedent of 1453. When Alexander succeeded his brother as king of Poland (1501–6), in the wake of the Moldavian débâcle, he faced a strong reaction from the magnates, and was forced to surrender control of the government to the Senate in 1501–2, but, having made peace with Muscovy in 1503, the king was able to restore the situation. In 1505, a diet attended by town representatives as well as magnates and *szlachta*, passed the decree *Nihil Novi*, which bound the king to the consent of both houses of the *Sejm* for any legislation or taxation, fixed the offices of the realm and served as a basic constitution for much of the sixteenth century. While it prevented the freewheeling rule of Casimir's reign, *Nihil Novi* was by no means a restraint on royal power; it merely ensured that royal policy would be consonant with the common interests of the greater and lesser nobility of Poland. The experimental consultation of the towns, however, was to be short-lived: in a move closely paralleled in Hungary and, to a lesser extent, Bohemia, the new constitution excluded them from the diet.

The politics of Hungary in this period are strikingly similar to those in Poland, save only that Matthias was able to draw on the military and fiscal traditions of the Hungarian crown to create a much more substantial army, which was for some decades the terror of central Europe. Matthias had to spend the first six years of his reign fighting to secure his coronation, but from 1464 he was in full control of the kingdom; he overhauled the treasury, cancelled exemptions on existing taxes, promoted his allies to available offices and *honores*, and, in the regular diets of the 1460s and 1470s, induced the county representatives to vote the heavy taxes necessary to support a permanent mercenary army of 20,000 men. This army, ostensibly created to fight the Turks, was actually used against another papal enemy, the Hussite king of Bohemia, George of Poděbrady, against whom Matthias crusaded from 1468. Bought off by George's successor, Vladislav, with Moravia, Lusatia and Silesia, Matthias turned on Austria in 1477, partly in revenge for Frederick III's support of the archbishop of Esztergom, who had rebelled against him in 1471, but also as a means of sustaining the massive army, whose cost outstripped even the inflated taxation of the period. He had conquered the bulk of the Habsburg territories by 1485 and turned his attention to domestic affairs, reforming the high court by replacing magnate stewards with trained jurists, and issuing a national law-code, the *Decretum Maius*, in 1486. While Matthias' dazzling rule had provided many benefits for his subjects and supporters, its costs were considerable, and after his death in 1490 there was a predictable reaction against his brand of royal single-mindedness. Matthias' illegitimate son was not elected king, and a four-way contest for the throne was resolved in favour of Vladislav Jagiellon, the king of Bohemia, who agreed to suspend the uncustomary taxes of his predecessor; the 'Black Army' that Matthias had created was consequently disbanded in 1492. Because the diet met frequently during the ensuing decade, and sought to exert control over the royal treasury and the king's choice of councillors, the 1490s have often been seen as a period of 'baronial reaction', but normalisation might be a better description. The assemblies voted taxes; and a sizeable army, together with the means to fund it, was recreated in a series of military reforms agreed and enacted between 1498 and 1500. Because this army was to be jointly controlled by king and magnates, it was more politically sustainable, and it gave the diet a meaningful basis for negotiation with succeeding rulers and for financial support in the longer term. The diet developed as an institution too: the principle that extraordinary taxation required agreement was firmly established in 1493, and the insistence of 1490 that all nobles should be entitled to attend was abandoned in favour of representation by the magnates, while lesser nobles were consulted through the more realistic avenue of the counties where their influence over local office steadily increased.

In Bohemia, there were rather more disturbances, as one might expect in the wake of a revolution like that of the 1410s and 1420s, but the trend of events was substantially similar. The Hussite king, George of Poděbrady, who had fought his way to the throne, continued to have to fight – first of all against the Catholic towns of Moravia, which resisted his election, and then, from 1465, against a league of Catholic nobles, who received papal backing in 1466 and promptly elected Matthias Corvinus king. To defend himself, George summoned regular meetings of the diet, including representatives of the towns and lesser nobles alongside the magnates. He walked a tightrope between these last two groups, restoring the land-court, which had been the cynosure of magnate power, as early as 1451, and allowing the magnates to buy out their tenants from 1467, but also – like Wenceslas – attempting to fill as many judicial and military offices as possible with allies among the lesser nobles, and ennobling townsmen as a further source of support. It may be that these antics helped to stimulate the league of 1465 against him, and it is significant that, while George was able to raise an extensive national militia from loyal nobles and towns in 1470, he was unable to resist the huge army of Matthias. When George died suddenly in 1471, his son was passed over in favour of the teenage son of the king of Poland, Vladislav, a relative of Vytautas, to whom the Hussites had offered the throne in the 1420s, but also a Catholic and thus likely to be the bringer of peace. In fact, the Papacy declared for Matthias, and the Polish prince was only able to win Bohemia by the humiliating treaty of 1479, which released all but the core territory to Hungary and placed the king under a council whose membership was partly determined by the diet. The next few years were very difficult, as Vladislav wavered in the commitment he had given to uphold the Compacts of Prague, and consequently faced trouble in the localities and a Hussite revolt in the capital in 1483. In 1485, however, peace was restored between the two confessional camps, and the king won the support of the magnates by agreeing to exclude representatives of the towns and lesser nobles from future diets. Over the next decade or so, the rule of the magnates was generally affirmed: the land-court was removed from royal influence, the council was filled with barons, and the 'Land Ordinance' of 1500, which the king accepted as a general statement of public law, confirmed the marginalisation of the towns and the first steps towards the re-enserfment of the peasantry. The magnates did not have it all their own way, however. In the frequent diets of the period – 190 between 1471 and 1526 – the lesser nobles continued to be represented in a separate house, while the city communes, having rejected the Land Ordinance and formed a 'Union of Towns', fought their way back to representation in the diet in 1508, and achieved recognition of their jurisdictions and other liberties in 1517. While Bohemia remained a relatively decentralised kingdom, with considerable amounts of jurisdiction remaining in the *kraje* or in individual towns, the overall rule of a council of magnates with a diet representing the major secular estates was a realistic outcome to a century which had seen the haemorrhaging of royal and ecclesiastical rights and resources, while the other classes and powers of Bohemia won freedoms for themselves. It was also a reasonable and workable reaction to royal absenteeism, which became ingrained after Vladislav's accession to the throne of Hungary in 1490.

In Scandinavia, dialogue between ruler and estates was less central to the consolidation that Denmark, at least, experienced in the second half of the century. The countries of the Union of Kalmar had weak traditions of collective constitutional action: there was ecclesiastical conciliarism, there were leagues and alliances of magnates, and there were popular revolts, but the whole tendency of political action, and of institutions such as the councils of the realms, was to preserve individual liberties, not to open up negotiation between ruler and subjects. While the period witnessed the advance of royal power in Denmark – and also over Norway, which was fast becoming a Danish colonial satellite, rather as Finland was to Sweden – this was achieved more at the expense of aristocratic and ecclesiastical power than through negotiation with it, though, especially under Christian of Oldenburg (1448–81), the king pursued policies that appealed to the majority of nobles, and took scrupulous care to consult the *rigsråd* over war and taxation. Even so, from the 1470s, the king – first Christian, and then his son Hans (1481–1513) – was able to expand his chancery, which gave him an administrative edge over the Danish *rigsråd*, and to gain more control over his finances and the allocation of castles and fiefs. Thanks to agreements with the Papacy in the 1450s and 1470s, he was able to influence the major ecclesiastical appointments in Denmark and Norway, and, in the wake of a dispute with the powerful Axelsson dynasty beginning in the late 1460s, he was able to infiltrate his supporters into the *rigsråd* itself. The successes of the two Oldenburg kings can be measured in the grievances expressed by Danish representatives in the *håndfaestnings* of 1483 and 1513, and, more darkly, in the noble uprising that engulfed Denmark in 1523: clearly, the advancement of royal power was not fully accepted, though the complications of war with Sweden and of the Reformation had roles to play in this revolt.

In Norway, rule belonged nominally to the *riksråd* – and this body was indeed generally able to manage justice and to conduct an independent trade policy. In practice, however, it was the Denmark-based king who ruled, partly through his chancery at Copenhagen, and partly through the three Danish magnates who held Norway's most important castles; his right to control the royal lands in the kingdom, without regard to the *riksråd*, was even acknowledged in the 1483 *håndfaestning*. While Norwegian independence was not forgotten, and the kingdom revolted in 1501 and 1524, its suppression by Denmark in 1536 was clearly based on fifteenth-century foundations. The nut that the Danish kings could not crack, of course, was Sweden, which they fought to control for most of the 1450s and 1460s, and again from 1497, gaining only brief success in 1457–64, 1497–1501 and 1520–1. It was not that they lacked supporters there: several great magnate factions promoted the Danish cause – the Oxenstierna and Vasa between the 1430s and the 1460s, and the Axelsønner in the 1450s and 1460s; even the Swedish *riksråd* became increasingly sympathetic to union from the 1480s. The trouble was that some groups were implacably hostile to foreign rule (notably the common people and the merchants and burghers of Stockholm), while the kingdom was too fragmented for the unionists to prevail. This last factor also created problems for Karl Knutsson, who returned to Sweden in 1464–5, and his successor and nephew, the regent (*riksföreståndare*) Sten Sture, who ruled between 1470 and 1497. Although Sten Sture won a tremendous victory over the Danes and their Swedish allies, at Brunkenberg in 1471, obtained recognition as de facto king from the Church and *riksråd* in 1474, and had some success in distributing fiefs to his own supporters, his attempts to exercise independent authority were increasingly resented by opponents in the council. His downfall came in the 1490s, when dealings with Lübeck, which enabled the export of Swedish copper to Germany, provoked the Danes to ally with Ivan III of Muscovy, who promptly closed Novgorod to Baltic trade and raided Finland in 1494. In the resulting chaos, the *riksråd* broke with the regent, and Hans invaded, securing the throne for four years. While it was not long before Sten Sture returned, he and his supporters were unable to secure control. A long sequence of wars, skirmishes and treaties ensued before, in the course of the 1520s, Gustav Vasa (Gustav I, 1523–60) succeeded in the task that had eluded every ruler since Magnus Eriksson, and established a lasting and effective monarchy in Sweden.

It was not only kingdoms that experienced consolidation in this period; principalities – 'princely states', as French historians in particular have called them – were generally growing in coherence and continuity. Perhaps the most spectacular example was the Valois duchy of Burgundy, where the period of conquest in the 1420s and 1430s gave way to several decades of strengthening rule and co-ordination among the disparate provinces. Among the earliest means through which this was achieved were curial and informal. One was the ducal court, which provided a common point of contact for the elites of the Burgundian domains, and was an important means of preserving links with the nobility of the two Burgundies when the dukes became more settled in Flanders and Brabant, as they did from the 1450s. A second was Philip the Good's order of chivalry, the *Toison d'Or*, founded in 1430, and a valuable way of binding the leading lords in faithful service. Other informal means of power were important too: through good relations with the Papacy, assiduously cultivated from the 1430s onwards, the dukes were generally able to control the appointments to surrounding bishoprics; they influenced municipal elections and filled the governing councils of the provinces with their placemen; they also granted pensions to the lords and urban leaders of both subject and adjacent territories, and the mass of contiguous territory they possessed in the Low Countries gradually convinced the elites of the region that they had more to gain from co-operation with the dukes than from resistance. It is striking that the urban risings of the Valois period – Bruges in 1436–8, Ghent in 1449–53 and 1467–8, Liège in 1465–8 – were not supported by the patriciates of these towns, and were firmly repressed by the dukes, who followed up their action with legislation to strengthen oligarchical control in the cities while advancing the jurisdiction of the ducal councils. By the 1460s and 1470s, with the union a generation old and the international situation worsening, it was possible to contemplate more radical extensions of ducal government. The estates of the northern provinces were meeting together as Estates General by 1464, and they granted Charles the Bold six years' worth of taxes in 1473 (a similar initiative in the southern territories was less enduring, though it made a similar grant). In 1468, the duke secured full juridical independence for his western lordships from the kingdom of France, and in 1473 he set up a *parlement* at Mechelen to provide appellate justice to all his domains. By a series of ordinances in 1471–3, he established a standing army, on the French model, and set up a central financial office to ensure its payment. Also in 1473, he began negotiations with the Emperor for a royal title – preferably (if unrealistically) king of the Romans, but failing that, king of Burgundy or of Frisia. Frederick temporised, but the demand is a telling one: the duke was looking not only for honour and grandeur, but for the juridical identity that would protect the continuity and sovereignty of his duchy, now that it had the accoutrements of every other kingdom of the period. In the event, that was not to be: Charles' death in battle at Nancy in 1477 led to the rapid dismemberment of his principality, and even the Low Countries provinces, which held together under his daughter Mary and her husband Maximilian of Habsburg, demanded the reversal of the 1470s innovations in their 'Grand Privilege' of 1477. Charles may have attempted too much too quickly, but the basic unity of the territories assembled from the 1380s was assured, and even the institutions of the 1470s reappeared once the Habsburgs were secure.

Developments in Burgundy were not unique among French, or indeed German, principalities. Among the former, the duchy of Brittany reached the height of its power in the mid- to late fifteenth century. As a coherent bloc at the western extremity of the French kingdom, it had developed many state-like institutions at an early stage – roughly in step with the French crown, in fact (and it is striking to note that royal taxation, levied in the Burgundian lands until the civil war of the early fifteenth century, was not raised from Brittany for almost two hundred years after Philip IV). The duke obtained a papal concordat as early as 1411, and was claiming the benefit of *lèse-majesté* by 1420; he introduced military ordinances like those of Charles VII as early as 1450, and was using a royal crown, with fleurons, by the end of that decade.[19] Quite clearly, Brittany was a small kingdom in all but name, and other princely territories within the French orbit were approaching this status in the middle and later fifteenth century – the duchy of Bourbon, the counties of Armagnac and Foix-Béarn, for example: all of them were acquiring greater administrative solidarity, even if the political picture, as we shall see, is more nuanced. In the Empire too, princely territories were, in general, acquiring greater solidity and durability in this period. There were certainly some counter-examples – the duchy of Brunswick, in the north of the

---

[19] Fleurons – flowers – differentiated the Breton crown from the simple circlets normally worn by dukes, and symbolised kingly rule of the various estates in the duke's territories.

Reich, lost its coherence, as a series of dynastic settlements partitioned the family territories, and the towns drew together under the umbrella of the Hanseatic League – but most other substantial principalities prospered in this period. The strong tradition of partible inheritance continued to pose problems, notwithstanding the formal adherence of many princely families and estates to the principle of impartibility imposed upon the Electors in the Golden Bull. This meant the subdivision of the Austrian territories into two from 1365, and into three between 1411 and 1463; of Bavaria into four between 1392 and 1445; and of Saxony into two or more for most of the fourteenth and fifteenth centuries. Even so, the estates of these *Länder* often continued to work together or in tandem, holding Saxony together between 1428 and 1445, for example, or bringing about the reunion of Bavaria under Duke Albert IV in 1504–5. While attempts by estates to outlaw partition and/or alienations of princely land tended to fail, they were increasingly able to push for solutions which preserved the integrity and viability of core territories, so that, for example, the nobles of the Rhine Palatinate were happy to back the succession of the adult Frederick I over his infant nephew in 1452, provided that he promised to remain unmarried and to adopt the child as his son. Under such co-operative circumstances, it is not surprising that, during the second half of the century, estates began to meet in dialogue with the ruler, as *Landtage* (provincial assemblies), and to vote taxation with more willingness than previously. By the later years of the century, several princes were able to levy direct taxes every five or ten years, raising very sizeable sums – the typical take from Lower Bavaria being around 100,000 florins from the 1460s onwards, more than half the likely income of the Common Penny of 1495. Princely governments increased in rigour and organisation too: the dukes of Saxony established permanent residences from the 1450s, enabling them to create more elaborate conciliar and administrative cadres; in the 1460s and 1470s, they began to recruit trained jurists to their service, showing their intention to organise and strengthen their jurisdiction; the landgraves of Hesse introduced superior courts for their domains from the 1450s, bringing these together in a *Hofgericht* at Marburg in 1500. Systems of *Pfandschaft* were refined, with new contracts increasingly issued under the 'Newer Statute', which left proprietary right with the grantor, so that this ingenious method of raising money and staking out territory began to look more like the farming of office and less like the mortgaging of property. As they signed up to the Concordat of

Vienna, meanwhile, princes acquired the patronage of churches in their domains – Frederick III was even able to induce the Papacy to create three new bishoprics in the 1460s to assist his control in Austria. In a like way, several princes took steps to bring the towns of their domains under princely control: this happened from the 1440s in Brandenburg, in the 1420s and 1490s in Pomerania, and – notoriously – in 1462 in Mainz, where the archbishop's artillery smashed the city and its commune was permanently repressed. Not all the consolidations of this period centred on princely intervention, however. In Austria, the pattern of development was towards the establishment of collegial regimes under the control of provincial diets, first in Styria and Carniola, then in the Tyrol, and finally in Upper and Lower Austria themselves. These regimes, which became firmer from the 1490s onwards, offered fiscal and political support to the prince – in this case, the Emperor – and were willing to work together for the collective interests of the House of Austria, but they protected their distinctness, and Maximilian retreated from plans to impose a common government on Austria in 1514. This was also the pattern in the Swiss Confederation – not a principality at all, of course, but a more cohesive federation of territories as the century wore on: while the governments of individual provinces (*Orte*) became more oligarchical in nature, and developed systems of taxation and military obligation, the Confederation acquired a representative assembly, in the form of the *Tagsatzung* from 1415, and tightened its bonds in the Compact of Stans, which included arrangements for peacekeeping, in 1481.

This tale of princely growth, which might equally be extended to Italy (discussed below), or to Ireland, or Castile, or arguably Hungary, needs to be balanced by a recognition of the limitations facing principalities in this period. First of all, the greater solidity of princely territories provoked anxiety and opposition from surrounding powers, both larger ones, like kings and emperors, and smaller ones, such as lords and towns. In France, the kings of the fifteenth century and their officers maintained near-continual pressure on the jurisdictions and other rights exercised by the princes. The royal *baillis* of Montferrand, positioned just to the south of the Bourbonnais, harried the dukes of Bourbon even in the danger years of the 1420s, and intensified their efforts from the 1460s onwards; both Charles VII and Louis XI exploited royal 'enclaves' in the duchy of Burgundy – religious houses, French-leaning sees, even towns like Tournai, which were ready to play one lord off against the other – to undermine the political authority of the Valois dukes; they paid pensions out of the vast royal tax incomes to leading councillors of the dukes of Brittany and Burgundy, and gave major offices in the kingdom to leading lords, such as the constables du Guesclin, Clisson and Richemont and the admiral Coëtivy – Bretons all. These initiatives could certainly fail – many were the times when kings had to call off the *gens du roi* and confirm princely liberties; and, as the war of Burgundians and Armagnacs revealed, the interpenetration of royal and princely networks could pull the kingdom apart instead of undermining the princes – but they preserved the notion of a superior royal structure, and reminded those in the *mouvance* of the princes that there was a greater lord to whom they might be able to appeal. In fact, the age in which the leading French principalities came closest to independence – itself, perhaps, a rather desperate move prompted by royal pressure – was also the age in which they failed. While the fall of Charles the Bold has several explanations, the unremitting hostility of Louis XI, and his prompt invasion of the French-speaking lands of the duchy on the duke's death in 1477, was certainly one of them. Royal hostility may have been even more central in the collapse of the duchy of Brittany in 1487–90: outright confrontation with the crown destroyed the unity of the Breton political elite and helps to explain the failure of the duchy's impressive military defences.

A major factor in the demise of these French principalities and many others was a failure of adult male heirs. We have seen that this was also problematic for kingdoms, but by the fifteenth century these were juridically and institutionally robust enough to survive as political entities, whatever strains arose from minorities, elections or succession disputes. Principalities, on the other hand, tended to collapse under such circumstances, especially in France, where the crown was eager to exploit its rights over the descent of *apanages*. Default of male heirs brought the end of the house of Anjou in 1481 and almost destroyed Orleans after 1465;[20] it contributed to the fall of Burgundy, since Mary could not legally inherit her father's *apanages*, and to that of Brittany, whose heiress was forcibly married to Charles VIII. In Italy too, the succession was a serious problem, helping to explain the fluctuating borders of Milan in the fourteenth and

---

[20] Following the death of Duke Charles in 1465, Louis XI used his powers as guardian to marry the heir, Louis, to his disabled, and apparently barren, daughter Jeanne, in 1476.

fifteenth centuries (and the brief emergence of an 'Ambrosian republic' on the expiry of the Visconti line in 1447), and causing serious
instability in Florence when the two great Medicean princes, Cosimo
(d.1434) and Lorenzo (d.1492) were succeeded by young and
unpromising heirs. Although there are counter-examples – notably
Savoy and Ferrara, which successfully negotiated a number of dynastic
mishaps – it is clear that principalities typically lacked the juridical
status and/or permanence of authority to overcome interruptions in
the ruling dynasty, particularly when they were surrounded by
powerful overlords or hostile neighbours. This helps to explain the
princes' search for formal dignities such as crowns, duchies and counties, though even these could be unavailing without long usage.

The great exception to this picture of dynastic vulnerability is the
Empire, where, as we have seen, long experience of partible inheritance
and the (qualified) interest of lesser powers – estates – in maintaining the
ancient territories over which the princely families ruled combined to
produce ways of keeping provinces together. One reason why this was
possible was the relative lack of pressure from above, even if the reforms
of the 1490s set limits to princely jurisdiction. In the German lands, the
main threat to the principalities came from those towns and nobles
whose liberties they threatened, and who might league together against
them. One of the most dramatic examples of this tendency was the
League of Constance, formed in 1474 by Basle, Strasbourg, the Swiss
and the towns of Alsace against Charles the Bold, following his aggressive interventions along the western borders of the Empire: while the
encouragement that this League received from Louis XI was certainly
welcome, it is worth remembering that it was imperial troops that
destroyed Charles and his army in the battles of Murten, Grandson
and Nancy. The same general impulse informed the Swabian League,
which prevented the establishment of any overarching power below
the Empire in Swabia, and the League of Franconian knighthood,
formed in 1495–6 by the nobles of the region, in response to the
Common Penny: the League wished to be a taxable unit in itself,
fearing that taxation via local princes would entail subjection and
destroy the historic freedom of this heartland of the Empire. Even the
representative devices of princes themselves could cause them problems, as, for example, the Estates General that Philip the Good had
created for the Low Countries met to promote the defence of individual provincial and urban liberties in 1477, and contributed to the
divisions and conflicts of Philip the Fair's minority (1482–93).

In all, therefore, princely consolidation was often an ambivalent process: it drew on the goodwill of surrounding powers, but it was also vulnerable to their hostility, especially when customary relationships – with either larger or smaller powers – became too distorted. Few principalities were powerful enough to deal with concerted action by the towns, lords and princes of their regions, and none of them could face down the growing military might of the leading monarchies, especially France and Spain. This emerging truth was to be borne out over and over again in the major wars that marked the last quarter of the century.

The new warfare
From about the middle of the fifteenth century, the practice of warfare began to change. One element in this was that artillery, first widely used in the 1370s, was now becoming a practicable battlefield weapon, while developments in shot and firing-rate meant that, in sieges, cannon were increasingly devastating. For a period of roughly fifty years, covering the second half of the century, almost no fortification was safe from attack by an army with the latest artillery, and the use of cannon in battles gravely undermined the advantages of the defender and made set-piece confrontations much more attractive to attacking armies. These developments, apparent in the fall of Rouen in 1449 (where the captain surrendered rather than face inevitable destruction), at Castillon in 1453, and – most famously of all – at Constantinople in the same year, encouraged aggression on the part of the best-equipped armies, and help to explain the diplomatic moves of Europe's powers, both great and small. A second influence on the conduct of war was the move towards larger, more organised and more permanent armies. Improvements in discipline and technique, in which the Swiss were particularly prominent, made large infantry armies attractive again in the later fifteenth century. But cavalry also remained very important and, from around the 1420s, 1430s and 1440s, a number of European rulers, led by the major Italian states and the kings of Hungary and France, but anticipated by the Ottomans and possibly influenced by the standing Lancastrian army in Normandy, began to establish permanent forces of men-at-arms and foot soldiers. Together with expenditure on artillery (and increasingly on navies), permanent forces were ruinously expensive, but, by the 1460s and 1470s, other regimes that could raise the necessary taxation – Brittany, Burgundy, Castile – were following suit, and

the result was that a cluster of kingdoms and principalities were able to raise substantial forces rapidly and under a high degree of central control. Discipline, training and other hallmarks of professionalisation also advanced, so that, while aristocratic participation remained crucial to warfare for some time to come, the major armies of Europe were more experienced, better co-ordinated and more easily directed by the ruler. These armies required regular exercise in order to maintain control of them and to justify the taxation raised to support them; their existence was thus a stimulus to military expansion and escalation. So it was that a top tier of military powers emerged in the last quarter of the century: France, Spain, Hungary, Venice, Burgundy (in the 1470s) and the Swiss Confederation. Together with the Ottomans, who had been active at this level from at least the 1420s, they introduced a culture of permanent, large-scale warfare in the regions where their interests overlapped. Lesser powers, such as England, Scotland or the Empire, Denmark, Sweden and the Hansards, Poland, the Papacy, Florence, Milan and Naples, invested in some of the accoutrements of the new warfare, and certainly continued to engage each other, or even to fight the states of the front rank (typically in alliance with others, or during periods of internal disorder – in France, especially), but their diplomatic options were increasingly circumscribed by their relative inferiority. Not only was there consolidation in the internal politics of European countries in this period, therefore, there was also the emergence of a recognisable order of military powers, a concert of states.

There were, broadly speaking, four major zones of conflict in the last quarter of the fifteenth century. The first two have already been touched upon, and can be dealt with fairly briefly: the conquest of Granada, by Ferdinand and Isabella, between 1482 and 1492; and the sequence of wars in the Rhineland and Low Countries that began in the reign of Charles the Bold. The Granadan war was, in many ways, an obvious choice for Ferdinand and Isabella, once the threat from Portugal had been repelled and the realm reduced to some measure of order; yet it is important not to miss the fact that their war was not a sequence of glorious sallies into the Muslim kingdom, but a thoroughgoing attempt at conquest, a move which would have been unthinkable without modern artillery and the fiscal and political capacity to mount annual campaigns over ten years. Many elements of the war were conventional enough – the prominent role of magnates and their retinues besides the royal forces, the *guardas reales* and *Santa Hermandad* (indeed, the conflict arguably began on the initiative of the marquis of Cadiz, not that of the Catholic Monarchs); the part played, as in Brittany at the same time, by bribery and division within the enemy camp – but not only was the triumphant completion of the *Reconquista* an event of massive significance for Spanish political culture, it also signalled the definitive emergence of a co-ordinated military power which the Trastámaras and their Habsburg heirs would go on to develop in the 1490s, and then to employ in Italy, America and the Low Countries. The wars conducted by Charles the Bold, in Guelders, Lorraine, Alsace and Switzerland between 1473 and 1477, have a slightly different significance. First of all, they are a good illustration of the expansionary tendency of the military reforms of the period: Charles may have improved his army in response to the threatening situation in France, but he deployed it in pursuit of ambitions in the Empire. Second, they demonstrate the new prominence of battles: Charles and his opponents positively sought confrontation, and one result was the utter destruction of the Burgundian army in the bloody fights at Murten and Nancy. Third, while relations between the Burgundian domains and the powers of the Empire returned to a more peaceful footing after 1477, conflicts and tensions with France continued, and this was to shape the experience of the Habsburg Netherlands for the next few decades. While French armies were defeated at Guinegate in 1479, and treaties were signed at Arras in 1482 and Senlis in 1493 – the second of which returned Franche-Comté and Artois to the Habsburgs – French influence over the outlying satellites of the Low Countries was significantly increased (for decades in the case of Guelders, which returned to independence in 1492). This contributed, in turn, to the difficult relations between the leading cities of Flanders, the other provinces of the region, the estates and the would-be Habsburg overlord. Not until Duke Philip the Fair came of age in 1493 did unity return to the Low Countries, and although a decade of stabilisation was to follow, his death in 1506 ushered in another period of external pressure and internal tension.

A third major theatre of conflict was the former Byzantine region of the Balkans, the Black Sea and the eastern Mediterranean. Here, as before, the Ottomans were the main aggressors, and, in particular, Mehmed II (1451–81), whose entire reign was consumed with warfare, much of it orientated towards the west, though there was a lull of sorts while the sultan dealt with the threat from Uzun Hasan, ruler of the Akkoyunlu Empire to the east of his domains. This period saw the Ottomans moving towards a more direct control of their territories: client rulers were replaced by a network of provincial and district governors, the former linked to the sultan's household and imperial council, the latter often the converted descendants of local lords, including the marcher lords of Rumelia. Not just Constantinople, but Serbia (1458), Bosnia (1463), Hercegovina (1463–6), Morea (1458–60, 1470), most of Albania (1466–7) and a succession of Genoese and Venetian possessions along the Black Sea and Aegean coasts were conquered during this period and placed under direct Ottoman administration. The submission of Wallachia (1462) and Moldavia (1475, 1484) was renewed, Hungary was kept in check, and a long war against Venice, over her Greek and Ionian territories (1463–79), ended in near-total defeat for the *Serenissima* and led to a brief foray into Italy (Otranto, 1480–1), which only Mehmed's death brought to an end. Rhodes alone eluded the sultan, despite a vigorous assault in 1480. Ottoman aggression, as elsewhere, was fed by the development of a permanent army, and by institutions designed to support its activities. Even so, Bayezid II (1481–1512) found it both possible and necessary to retrench: continual war had meant excessive taxation of the peasantry and interference with customary property rights, and the new sultan was keen to make peace and consolidate his gains. This did not prevent sporadic conflicts in the 1480s and 1490s, but, despite Charles VIII's grand talk of a crusade, and notwithstanding one or two raids into Dalmatia and Friuli, and even into Poland (1498), the peace broadly held, and after 1503 the Ottomans turned their attention towards the east and south for another two decades.

Finally, and perhaps most famously, there is the sequence of wars which began to affect Italy from the French invasion of 1494. Although, as we have seen, these originated partly in the dynastic good fortune and military policy of the French crown, they were also the outcome of returning instability in the Italian political order. During the second half of the fifteenth century, the major polities of the peninsula experienced the same political trends as everywhere else. On the one hand, the governments of the leading 'territorial states' moved to consolidate their newly extended domains, and so did the Aragonese rulers of the south, who enjoyed remarkable success in rebuilding royal power in the *Regno*. As we have seen, this initiative inclined the various rulers towards the establishment of peace across the peninsula as a whole, which produced the treaty of Lodi and the

Italian League. At the same time, there were plenty across Italy whose interests ran counter to peace and consolidation: excluded factions, such as the pro-Angevin nobles in Naples, or the Pazzi in Florence; powerful families like the Orsini, Colonna, della Rovere and Borgia, with interests across the peninsula, but no substantial principality; and, more equivocally, subject towns and nobles, who had much to gain from the relative security created by the major powers and the comparatively peaceable conditions upheld by the League, but who might chafe at the erosion of their liberties. Some regimes managed this difficult situation better than others. In Savoy, for example, regular meetings of the estates between the 1450s and the 1490s helped to hold the duchy together, protecting both ducal rights and the common interests of the territories either side of the Alps: the weakness of the ducal family may have helped to strike a balance between authority, collectivity and more localised interests. In Naples, meanwhile, Alfonso the Magnanimous had done much to restore royal control, removing the magnates from the central administration, rebuilding the tax system and regaining some of the lost royal patrimony. He was able to do this partly because of his overwhelming military victory, but also because he was willing to strike a balance with the magnates, confirming their jurisdiction over their own tenants and thus leaving them the substance of territorial power. His successor, Ferrante, intervened more confidently in the politics of landed society than his father had done, seizing the lands of rebels, retaining great fiefs like Taranto in royal hands when the holders died, and allowing the sale of fiefs, so that the aristocracy became more diverse and began to include men close to the new dynasty. Ferrante's efforts helped to cause revolt in 1485–6, but he successfully strengthened the links between the royal court, the city of Naples and the leading territorial families, laying the foundations for the more centralised rule of the Habsburgs in the following century. In the northern republics, meanwhile, oligarchical power generally became more defined: Cosimo and then Lorenzo de' Medici introduced new councils to Florence – the One Hundred of 1458, the Seventy of 1480 – thus formalising the dominance of the Medicean network; while in Venice, the Ten took over foreign policy from the Senate, and the *Collegio* came to dominate domestic matters, so that a smaller number of officers were more continuously entrusted with the direction of affairs. Finally, in Milan, Galeazzo Maria Sforza (1466–76) spent lavishly on his court, which, as in Burgundy, was an important means of drawing the nobility of the region around him; he also seems to have been trying to sidestep the influence of the semi-formal *consiglio segreto* (privy council). Although the Sforza introduced an elaborate structure for the government of their duchy, they do not seem to have succeeded in meshing together the ducal network and the elites of the subject cities, Milan among them, and this was to prove fatal during the French invasion of 1499–1500.

There are signs that, by the later 1470s, disaffection with Italy's princely governments and exasperation with the post-Lodi order had become widespread. In 1476, Galeazzo Maria Sforza was assassinated, and, two years later, Lorenzo de' Medici narrowly escaped the same fate. Pope Sixtus IV raised war against Florence in 1478–9 and encouraged Venice against Ferrara in 1482–4. It looked for a time as if Italy was returning to the patterns of the earlier part of the century, but Ferrante of Naples, shocked by the Ottoman occupation of Otranto in 1480–1, was able to impose a peace. In 1485–6, it was Ferrante's turn to face revolt, as a party of noblemen rose up against his relatively high taxation and his son's repressive measures. They received papal backing, but, despite Cardinal della Rovere's best efforts, the French refused to intervene and the revolt was suppressed. The peace held for the rest of the 1480s and beyond, but, in 1494, when Charles VIII decided to pursue the Angevin claims in Naples, the Italian League – and all of the major Italian states but Venice – were in total disarray: Ludovico Sforza, the usurper of Milan since 1479, had joined the della Rovere in persuading France to intervene; Florence, shaky after the death of Lorenzo, was on the point of throwing out the Medici and restoring a republic (1494); the Borgia pope, Alexander VI, was insecure in Rome and uncertain how to respond to the sudden Angevin revival. These were among the reasons why Charles was able to march down Italy and into Naples within a matter of months in 1494–5, but the huge size of his army, and his fast-moving artillery – which kept pace with his troops and blew great holes in the defences of the *Regno* – were also important factors in his dramatic success. Although Ferrante's grandson, Ferrandino, quickly regained the Neapolitan throne once the French had withdrawn (1496), Charles VIII's intervention had decisively undermined the wobbling regimes of the peninsula. Shorn of Pisa, which Charles liberated in 1494, Florence's new republic began in humiliation and was faced by a long and expensive war to regain its lost position in Tuscany. When Louis XII pursued the Orleanist claim to Milan in 1499, the duchy, saddled with the expense of buying back Genoa (where the French had reasserted their rights in 1494), put up little resistance, and Ludovico was forced to flee. Louis continued down to Naples, which he overran in 1500–1. Although the French king was once again soon ejected, it was not by the Neapolitans, but by Ferdinand the Catholic, who conquered the kingdom from the south and returned it to Spanish rule in 1503–4. Naples would remain in Spanish hands for a long time to come, but France retained an extensive network of interests and allies in the peninsula, and the fragmented situation in the north invited further intervention from these two great powers. Thus was the stage set for the 'Italian wars' that dominated the first half of the sixteenth century and reduced the region's 'territorial states' to the status of French and Spanish satellites.

CO-ORDINATION AND CONSOLIDATION: THE REGNAL POLITY

It will be clear from the account of fifteenth-century politics in the preceding pages that this period was one of advancing political co-ordination and consolidation. In older literature, these processes are typically captured by accounts of the rise of 'renaissance princes', or 'new monarchs', whose putatively centralising policies began to prevail in the second half of the century. Buoyed up by enhanced revenues and large standing armies, these rulers are supposed to have triumphed over particularist nobles and/or towns, to have evaded representative institutions, and to have opened the way to the 'modern' nation states of the sixteenth century and later. More recently, however, much of this picture has come to be questioned. First of all, it is becoming clear that the comparatively confused politics of the first half of the century contributed to the growth of stability: the 'recovery' of the 1450s, 1460s or 1470s is really the product of longer-term processes, including the constitutional experimentation and conflict characteristic of the later fourteenth and early fifteenth centuries. Second, it is now customary to emphasise the *de*centralised nature of most of the 'new monarchies', and to note that in Spain, France and Scotland (even in England, in many respects), royal regimes continued to rely heavily on the co-operation of the nobility. Against the familiar image of ever-rising taxation, it is recognised that the tax revenues enjoyed by Charles VIII and Louis XII were a good deal lower than those of Louis XI or Charles V, that the incomes of Henry VII were less than those of Henry V, and that Ferdinand and Isabella barely raised sums comparable to those of the later fourteenth century once the devaluation of Castilian money is taken into account. There certainly were larger, better-equipped and more permanent armies in a number of leading kingdoms, but these were not commonly used to enforce the royal will on dissenting subjects, and, when they were, they did not always prove effective (Louis XI's failure to defeat his opponents at Montlhéry in 1465 is perhaps the most striking example). Meanwhile, it has become clear that the western monarchies and principalities on which the traditional picture is based were not the only successful powers of the period. The remarkable republic of Venice; the northern, central and eastern kingdoms, with their evolving representative and electoral traditions; confederations like those of Switzerland and the Low Countries (or, in effect, the territories of the House of Austria): all these grew in internal coherence during the period, and were frequently capable of imposing themselves beyond their borders. In short, it is clear that, while the emergence of comparatively stable and bounded, large and medium-sized polities is undeniably a feature of the later fifteenth century, we need to think more flexibly about its causes. Here, the emphasis is on the gradual consolidation of authority at the regnal level, a process involving the more effective co-ordination of lesser powers and of representative forces and institutions. The forceful activity of rulers, and their enhanced powers, played a part in that process, but it was very far from being the whole of it (and was indeed partly a product of it). The 'making of polities', which is the underlying theme of this book, did indeed reach a kind of fruition in this period, but that outcome is not quite the one commonly supposed. While the main aim of this final section of the chapter is to trace and explain the political and constitutional achievement of the fifteenth century, therefore, it will be necessary to begin by saying what that achievement was.

It may help to start by defining some of the terms I have chosen to use. By 'consolidation', I mean the increasing definition of political boundaries. This was less a case of the literal determination of territorial bounds, many of which had been laid down centuries before, and plenty of which were contested, than the drawing of sharper distinctions between domestic politics and foreign affairs, and the establishment of relatively firm and well-known distributions of power and authority within each polity. The increased separation of internal politics from external war and diplomacy enhanced the

centripetal tendency of fifteenth-century polities and helped to stabilise politics by ensuring that conflicts would be more confined
within the regnal borders: as we have seen, the civil wars of the
mid-fifteenth century generally involved much less cross-border
intervention than those of the fourteenth. Consolidation was also
taking place in the political and constitutional traditions of each polity.
Not everything was nailed down, of course – there was plenty of
constitutional adaptation between 1500 and the eighteenth-century
revolutions – but, during the course of the fifteenth century, most
European countries had evolved a series of agreed, recorded and
celebrated institutions and practices – constitutional identities which
they recognised as distinctive to themselves (and which were, indeed,
increasingly distinctive) and which were an important and self-
conscious influence on future political and governmental behaviour.

'Co-ordination' is a closely related phenomenon. In this period,
most kingdoms and other large or medium-sized polities proved more
consistently able to command the allegiance of the smaller and lesser
political units within their territories, and to draw them together in
common initiatives directed from the centre. It was not new for
towns, princes, nobles, churches and representative estates to
acknowledge the leadership of surrounding rulers, nor to work
together under them, but in this period their subject status generally
became more obvious and undeniable, they experienced more consistent intervention and regulation, and their political strategies were
more completely focused on advancing and defending interests
within an acknowledged polity rather than on playing off one jurisdiction against another. There were limits to this development, as we
shall see, but it was very widespread and central to the developing
texture of the polities of the period, which had to be able to compre-
hend and provide for a considerable diversity of activities, interests and
varieties of power. The choice of 'co-ordination' also serves to remind
us that these subordinate political units retained political agency: the
polities of this period were better able to co-opt them partly because
they were readier and better able to cater to their interests and needs.
This, in turn, draws attention to the fact that the stronger polities of
the later fifteenth century were forged as much from below, or from
within, as they were from above: mechanisms of representation and
dialogue, means of upholding order and distributing social and political goods were just as important as the new tools of authority in
creating the more integrated states of the period.

Two other terms of art that have been used here and throughout this book are 'regnal' and 'polity'. 'Regnal' – Susan Reynolds' helpful coinage, as we have seen[21] – is here taken to mean pertaining to a realm, in the sense of a sizeable territory under a single government. It is a better word than 'national' for the polities that were solidifying in the fifteenth century because not all of those polities claimed to possess a distinct ethnic character, though they all tended to claim historical authorisation for themselves and to celebrate their distinctive constitutional traditions. It is a better word than 'royal' because not all of these polities were monarchies, and even when they were, they might draw as much (or more) of their political and ideological substance from notions and traditions of collective participation and political community as they did from the rights and powers of the ruler. By 'the regnal level', I mean the level of government claiming more-or-less sovereign authority over the territory. In most European countries, this was a monarch, but, in many cases, the monarch was conceived as an officer of the crown, realm or land, and, almost everywhere, his or her government was believed to include a representative element, whether formal or informal. This is worth emphasising, because, if we take the criteria of sovereignty identified by Hendrik Spruyt – 'territorial exclusivity', or 'internal hierarchy and external autonomy'[22] – it is clear that there is little to choose between a country like Bohemia, where the king was elected and the constitutional developments of the decades around 1500 vested effective authority in the magnate-dominated council, the land-court and the diet, and one like France, where the king was untrammelled by representative institutions and more or less unconfined by law. Both of these were increasingly consolidated realms in which local powers were coming to be co-ordinated under the general sway of central governments.

Finally, the word 'polity': this, of course, is a term that can be applied to any political community, and it has been an argument of this book that, particularly in the early part of our period, the political potential of jurisdictions smaller or larger than the kingdom needs to be fully acknowledged. By the later part of the fifteenth century, however, regnal polities had differentiated themselves from other

---

[21] See above, pp. 30, 69.
[22] H. Spruyt, *The Sovereign State and its Competitors. An Analysis of System Change* (Princeton, 1994), p. 3.

political forms, in having the fullest kind of political community combined with the most complete level of authority. In considering the 'making of polities', then, this book has been tracing the development of region- or kingdom-sized regnal territories, ruled by more-or-less sovereign rulers and containing a diversity of smaller powers which more or less accepted their subjection. The choice of the word 'polity' rather than 'state', which might seem to do just as well for this kind of political community, lies first in the emphasis that 'polity' gives to negotiation between government and people, second in its implication of mutual action, and third in its freedom from the baggage associated with the rise of the modern state. It is the case, however, that the 'polities' which I see gaining in stability and definition during this period have much in common with the 'states' discussed in other literature.

By the end of the fifteenth century, then, a series of comparatively solid, stable, bounded, regnal polities had come into being across much of Europe. There were certainly places where this was less true – large parts of the Empire, or the upland territories of Ireland and Scotland, the Pyrenees, Alps and southern Balkans, the more loosely structured spaces on the frontiers of Lithuania and Muscovy – but even in these areas, constitutional norms were generally more established than they had been, and managed complexity was advancing at the expense of fluidity. It is also important to acknowledge that the solidity and stability of a given polity is a different thing from its political health or its military robustness: most of the countries of 1500 were to suffer bouts of military defeat, political convulsion and dynastic upheaval during the century to come; their alliances were to be broken up and re-formed, and they were to find themselves associated and divided in unexpected ways because of the vagaries of dynastic policy or confessional allegiance. But much as 'composite monarchies' were a prominent feature of the European political scene in the sixteenth century, their constituent parts have a meaningful and partly independent existence.[23] Those parts were, in many cases, the polities of 1500 whose development we have been exploring in the earlier section of this chapter. In what follows, we shall look at the three main groups of factors that explain the trend towards regnal consolidation and co-ordination in the

---

[23] J.H. Elliott, 'A Europe of Composite Monarchies', *Past and Present*, 137 (Nov. 1992), 48–71.

period: the influence of political culture; developments in government; and the practice of politics itself.

Political culture

The fifteenth century was a period of unprecedented richness in political culture. Even more than in the fourteenth century, learned writers and thinkers were turning their skills towards the predicaments of political life as it was actually lived by the members of more diverse and multifaceted political communities; they wrote for councillors and members of the widening public, as well as for princes, prelates and fellow cognoscenti; they were as likely to write in the vernacular as in Latin, and an increasing number had acquired their learning in the course of political and administrative careers, as much or more than as a result of study in faculties of theology and law. The academic world was itself becoming a larger and more diverse place. Thanks mainly to the activity of princely founders, there were twice as many universities in 1500 as there had been in 1400, with the result that the overwhelming prestige of Paris or Oxford, Bologna or Orleans, was gradually diluted. At the same time, other centres of learning – the London Inns of Court, the 'academies' of Florence or Rome, the chanceries and courts of princes, networks of private scholars, supporters of the observance movement or the *devotio moderna*, and even the new kinds of grammar schools developing across the continent – came to be just as important in shaping thought and setting intellectual trends. The diversification of learning, together with the growing sense on the part of politicians that they needed to communicate with a broad cross-section of society in order to justify public action or to guide public behaviour, intensified the political, persuasive and public orientation of scholarship in this period. These priorities influenced the shape of academic thought: it was so that 'educated men, adorned with knowledge and virtue, might at length serve the *res publica* and provide it with wholesome counsel' that the count of Provence founded the University of Aix in 1413, for instance.[24] But, more importantly for us, the same priorities helped to shape the political world, sharpening the quality of political debate and introducing new complexity and ambition in the making of policy.

[24] Quoted in J. Verger, *Men of Learning in Europe at the End of the Middle Ages*, trans. L. Neal and S. Rendall (Notre Dame, IN, 2000), p. 101 and n. 35 (my translation).

A prominent factor in these developments was the spreading interest in the *studia humanitatis* – that is, the study and emulation of the literature, rhetoric and scholarship of classical Rome and Greece – which grew in strength and refinement during the course of the century until it had assumed a position of near-dominance almost everywhere by the early 1500s. *Romanitas*, as we have seen, was nothing new, but the precision with which its cultivation was attempted, particularly in Italy, seems to have increased sharply with every generation from Petrarch onwards, fed by the rediscovery of lost classical texts, which Petrarch inspired, Boccaccio continued, and early fifteenth-century humanists, notably Poggio Bracciolini, took further. By this time, there was a growing interest in Greek writing – notably the works of Plato, which had only been selectively or indirectly grasped in the medieval West before the fifteenth century – and there was also a swelling neoclassical literature, among which some works, such as Leonardo Bruni's *Laudatio Florentinae Urbis* (eulogy of the town of Florence), Lorenzo Valla's treatise on rhetoric, the *Elegantiae*, or the writings of Enea Silvio Piccolomini (later Pope Pius II), enjoyed a status approaching that of the ancient authors themselves. While humanist scholars were a varied group, their concern with the recovery and communication of ancient texts meant a particular engagement in the dissemination of their discoveries. Equally, their interest in cultivating *eloquentia* – the art of conveying truth in an attractive and persuasive manner – made it natural for humanists to seek to write well, to publish their findings and to stimulate a culture of learned public discussion. These biases, in turn, secured them places in the courts and chanceries of cities and princes across the continent, and, at the same time, encouraged the denizens of such institutions to seek classical learning and refinement for themselves. Humanists were interested in anything that caught the attention of the ancients, but their impact on the discussion of politics was especially marked. Politics had been a central concern of many of the most widely appreciated classical writers, and this naturally led their latter-day admirers into discussion of political questions: stylised treatises on the best kind of polity or the nature of true nobility typically included topical references, and, by the generation of Erasmus, Machiavelli and Sir Thomas More, humanists were writing fully developed analytical works on contemporary political problems, informed by a mixture of experience, observation and classical example.[25] Equally, the classical forms of discourse that humanists commonly revived – letters, memoirs, speeches, dialogues and topical treatises – mingled political reflection and persuasion in accessible ways. Although there was an influential cult of Stoic withdrawal and Platonic contemplation in the circle of Ficino at Florence in the second half of the fifteenth century, most humanists in most places embraced the Ciceronian ideal of active life in the service of *res publica*: that is, the civic life and the common good of the political community. Many of them did this in the manner of Sallust – by writing and speaking more than by becoming statesmen themselves – but, in any event, they succeeded in canvassing a richer notion of politics which involved learning, debate, persuasion and public communication, as well as the more familiar ingredients of judgement, fortitude, service, loyalty and so on.

At the same time, it is important to realise that what the humanists were doing intersected with, and built upon, attitudes and practices that were already well developed in fourteenth- and fifteenth-century culture; fifteenth-century scholars read classical texts in a new way, but they were not the first to read them, nor to perceive their utility. We have already seen that fourteenth-century juristic thought was typically concerned with real-world problems, and that many Aristotelians were already focused on the mass communication of scholarly knowledge. Older receptions of the more accessible works of Roman writers, especially Cicero, Seneca, Ovid, Livy and Valerius Maximus, had made European readers familiar with classical mores and examples; it had already been understood that Latin was the vernacular of the Romans, and that the *translatio studii* (transfer of learning), which had already occurred between Greece and Rome, could now be repeated between Rome and the modern nations. Stories from Sallust, translations of Virgil, Plautus and Terence were circulating in France in the first decade of the fifteenth century, and are likely to have played their part in the culture of the Armagnac-Burgundian wars, just as the works of Caesar, Sallust and Cicero influenced discussion of the English Wars of the Roses a few decades later. Influential works of vernacular political comment, such as Alain Chartier's *Quadrilogue Invectif* (1422), in which 'France' debates with

---

[25] For instance, Erasmus' *Education of a Christian Prince* (1516), More's *Utopia* (1515) and Machiavelli's *Prince* (c.1513) and *Discourses on Livy* (1513×17).

the three estates, or Sir John Fortescue's *Governance of England* (*c.*1470), which considered how the king might restore his authority through financial and institutional reforms, certainly owed something to humanistic example, but they also drew on older traditions of analysis and comment. As we shall see, the scholastic debates, vernacular literature and public discussion that had accompanied regnal political development since the fourteenth century were just as important as classical letters in shaping the highly developed political culture of the later fifteenth century. The aim in the rest of this section will be to explore what these various intellectual and cultural developments contributed to the consolidation of regnal polities which is the overall theme of the chapter. In both their content and their forms, the works of the learned had an important role to play.

As far as the content of fifteenth-century political thought is concerned, it is possible to identify four broad strands, three of them very roughly associated with successive political trends, and the fourth – the celebration of national history and identity – a persisting, if expanding, feature, as it had also been in the fourteenth century. In the first third of the century, there was a strong emphasis on the constitutional or communitarian nature of authority. To some extent, this was related to the crisis in the Church, and the Conciliar solution which gained ground from around the 1390s: for Jean Gerson, for example, the predicaments of 'Church' and 'State' were very similar; it was natural to argue, as he did in 1405, that the king should be bound to the views of his councillors, and there are many links between the conciliarism of the University of Paris and the communitarian and reformist policies promoted by the Burgundians in the first two decades of the century. The emphasis of conciliarists on the universally representative nature of the Councils as the source of their legitimacy may well have contributed to such democratic statements as the 'Klatory principle', enunciated by the Hussites in 1424, that the people could govern themselves if the authorities were remiss; and it may be possible to discern the theories of the Baslean theologian, John of Segovia (1386–1458), in the view of a Polish jurist of 1507 that, while the king was above all men, he was below society as a whole. But the widespread emphasis on the responsibilities of rulers; the presentation of their dignities – notably the crown, in England, Hungary and France – as symbolising the collectivity of their subjects, including the very lowest; and the understanding of the realm as an organism composed of interlocking estates, each (including the king) with duties to the others, was derived from a host of other sources, such as fraternal sermons, mirrors for princes, the products of royal chanceries and the political debates of representative assemblies. A typical work like Christine de Pizan's *Book of the Body Politic* (1404) amalgamated material drawn from authorities like Aristotle, Cicero, Giles of Rome and John of Salisbury with the experience of French political life. Its division of the realm into king, nobles and 'commons' (including the clergy) has nothing in common with conciliar theory, and differs from traditional models of the three estates, but the broad emphasis of the work is much the same: while knights and commons must play their social roles and be obedient, kings must defend them and judge them fairly, they must keep to the law, should listen to wise counsel and prize the good of their subjects, however humble, above all else. Its message has more in common with the civic humanist writings of early fifteenth-century Florence than one might expect, provided that we allow for the differences between a monarchy and an Italian popular commune, and for the special utility of Roman republicanism in supporting the aims and identity of the latter: Salutati and Bruni were celebrating a polity in which virtuous citizens worked for the *res populi*, the concerns of the people; their aims, like Christine's, or Nicholas of Cusa's in his *Catholic Concordance*, or Thomas Hoccleve's in his *Regement of Princes* (1411), were to reconcile authority and community.

As the account of politics above makes clear, conciliarist and communitarian ideas were often employed in political confrontations. They were readily embraced and deployed by popular insurrections like Jack Cade's rebellion of 1450, or estates movements, like those in Hungary in the 1430s and 1440s, and their prominence helps to explain their use by the dissenting magnates of the mid-century civil wars. Even so, because these principles and discourses emphasised the common interest of the realm or republic, and associated the ruler and his government with the various interest groups and estates within the realm, they unquestionably contributed to the definition of political space, and to the consolidation of regnal polities. In Valois Burgundy, for example, the argument that '*le commun bien de la chose publique*' (the common good of the republic) was threatened by Louis XI and defended by the duke was a prominent element in the attempts of Charles the Bold to legitimise his sovereignty.[26] By the later fifteenth century, indeed,

---

[26] Guillaume Hugonet in 1473, quoted by A. Vanderjagt, '*Qui sa vertu anoblist': The Concepts of Noblesse and Chose Publique in Burgundian Political Thought* (Groningen, 1981), p. 55.

references to the '*res publica*', '*chose publique*', 'common weal' or, in a different idiom, to the '*police*' or 'policie' of the realm, were becoming commonplace, so that, by this time, a concern with the health of the political and governmental order was becoming as prominent as a concern for the common good of the subjects. In part, this small but important transition in meaning, towards a modern conception of 'the state', must have been due to the swelling influence of classical and neoclassical republicanism; but it also reflects the growth of government and the expansion of discourse about government that had been such marked features of the previous two centuries. Whatever its debt to the universalist perspectives of ecclesiastical conciliarists, therefore, communitarian writing tended to affirm the regnal polity, with its varied social content, as the natural political space. In city states, it is true, it emphasised the head-city, not the 'territorial state', but so did the literature of republican and imperial Rome: the celebration of the city, its polity and its history was compatible with maintaining the integrity of a federation like Florentine Tuscany, or the Venetian *Terra Ferma*.

Communitarian themes remained strong in many parts of the continent for much of the century, but from about the 1430s onwards, a more authoritarian and hierarchical strand is perceptible in a lot of European political writing, especially in the West. Once again, this was closely related to the turn of political events – in the Church, and in many realms. We have already seen that Pope Eugenius tried to persuade the kings of Europe that a direct connection existed between the conciliarist revolt at Basle, and the troubles they faced with their own subjects, and many contemporaries, scandalised by the events in Bohemia, were ready to draw their own parallels between these and communitarian risings closer to home: the name 'Praguerie', given to the Burgundian-style rising of French princes in 1440, neatly captures this line of thinking. The writings of both papalists and secular commentators in the middle years of the century developed newly sophisticated defences for monarchical authority (even if the former insisted that the papal monarchy was a distinctive and superior form). This was not, of course, a novel reflex: earlier crises, such as the troubles of the Papacy in the later thirteenth century, or the problems faced by fourteenth-century kings, had produced works reflecting on the need for effective authority. What was striking about fifteenth-century writing in this tradition was that it typically embraced the communitarian sympathies of earlier works, while explaining that their aims could not be achieved without obedience to the king, or government, and without due ordering within society. Interestingly, as J.H. Burns has noted, this kind of writing was not incompatible with a recognition of fundamental laws, especially in France; it might even go so far as to subject the king to his high court of *Parlement*, as in a statement of 1489.[27] But this kind of restriction, also found in Fortescue's writings, only affected the person of the king (and that only in limited ways); it placed his office and its key administrators high above the rest of political society, and certainly did not extend to placing the king below councils of lords or representative estates.

Besides the ecclesiastically focused works of Torquemada and Nicholas of Cusa, some of the best examples in this authoritarian tradition are English, perhaps in reaction to the particular strength of communitarian tradition in that kingdom, and to the difficulty of containing the 'community' in a country which did not differentiate the nobles from the rest as sharply as many others. The major works of Fortescue (*c.*1468–75) and the tract 'Somnium Vigilantis' (1459) linked the restoration of royal authority very closely to the aims of defenders of the common weal; many texts of this period, including Fortescue's, also enunciated a more stratified picture of society: the common people, more clearly defined as a lower-class group, were to stay in their place at the bottom of society. English writing was by no means unique in either respect: there are plenty of continental works with similar themes – those of Christine and Chartier, already mentioned, or the sermons and treatises of Jean-Juvenal des Ursins (though he favoured consultation of the estates for taxation); or the *Suma de la política* of Rodrigo Sánchez de Arévalo (1455), which depicted the Castilian realm as a *corpus mysticum*, ruled by the king, with the aid of counsellors and judges, for the benefit of the people (no nobles, strikingly); or the third section of Nicholas's *Catholic Concordance*, which argued for a restoration of the powers of the Emperor in the interests of the German people. Ideas like these were also widely canvassed in more ephemeral sources – public sermons, proclamations, manifestoes and speeches – which celebrated the association of ruler and public good, and also drew attention to the anarchic and self-interested tendency of the appeals of magnates and popular rebels to the common welfare. Charles VII's success at this kind of

---

[27] J.H. Burns, *Lordship, Kingship and Empire: The Idea of Monarchy, 1400–1525* (Oxford, 1992), pp. 58, 157–8.

propaganda has coloured interpretations of the noble leagues of 1440 and 1442 ever since, and the similar efforts of English and Castilian rulers help to explain the ambivalence with which the rebels of the 1450s and 1460s have historically been regarded. While this kind of writing and thinking typically emphasised royal power, it once again associated the rule of the king with the wellbeing of the regnal polity. Its discouragement of political pluralism – not king in dialogue with estates, but king and ministers ruling society according to the laws – must also have had a consolidating effect, denying representative legitimacy to the lesser political units of the realm, and reminding them that unlicensed public action could only produce anarchy. Here, the influence of neoclassicism may have had a particular significance. Whether the writings of Greeks and Romans were republican or imperial in temper, they tended to propose a polity very different from the regnal or provincial communities characteristic of thirteenth- and fourteenth-century political theory: the world of emperor, consuls, senate and plebs did not contain obvious political roles for either the Church, or lesser towns, or territorial magnates (especially as, in most kingdoms – though, tellingly, not in Poland – the place of senators was taken by councillors and ministers of modest birth).

A third kind of political literature and sensibility, which developed quite markedly in the last third of the century, might be described as scientific or technocratic. This was the burgeoning interest in political comparison and inductive analysis of political activity which flowered in the works of Machiavelli, but is already perceptible in the *relazioni* (reports) of Italian and other diplomats, in the memoirs of Commynes (1488–98), in the tracts of Fortescue and, later, Claude de Seyssel, and in many other works. Commynes, for instance, mused on the inevitability of division, listing countless examples from across Europe and claiming that they were a rough-and-ready means through which God corrected the sinfulness of greedy rulers (since their councillors refused to challenge them); he noted that, while the English won battles, the French were superior negotiators and tended to win treaties; and he warned against interviews between princes, supplying a rationale for his view as well as examples of the disastrous results. Comparative perspectives might also be directly employed in politics: Konrad Schott, for example, an agent of the Count Palatine, wrote to the princes of the Nuremberg region around 1498, warning them that the city was like Venice, a greedy republic seeking to suppress local lords through the use of its commercial wealth; Warwick the Kingmaker and the commons of 1469 drew comparisons between the councillors of Edward IV and those of Edward II, Richard II and Henry VI, who had brought about the depositions of these kings. Once again, this kind of 'realism', as it has been called,[28] was not unprecedented – the records of Florentine *pratiche* (advisory meetings), which stretch back to the 1340s, the treatises of Bartolus, and some of the *consilia* of fourteenth-century jurists clearly tend in this direction – but a combination of factors, including the experience of the Church Councils, in which representatives of different countries had to exchange political ideas, the spread of diplomats, and the comparative impulse unleashed by the emulation of Roman models, meant that this approach to politics became more widespread in the later fifteenth century. It brought with it a new sense of politics, less as a species of moral philosophy, and more as a kind of art or science, in which the leading practitioners were less kings, princes and lords than councillors and courtiers. Where the adjective '*politicus*' had carried connotations of representativeness – and still did in the works of Fortescue – it and its cognates were increasingly used to refer to the constitutional order (as in Seyssel's notion of '*police*', or the English chancellor, Bishop Russell's reference of 1483 to 'the policie in Christen Remes'). By the early sixteenth century, 'politic' was coming to be used in its modern sense of politically prudent, and notions of 'policy' as a deliberate course of action designed to achieve some object had developed. From being principally concerned with the provision of defence and justice, kings and their councils were increasingly expected to deliberate on political problems, anticipating dangers and taking steps to avoid them, developing policy and using the arts of propaganda (a term developed in the later sixteenth century) to promote it. In a characteristic example, which captures this atmosphere, the Spanish ambassador to England, Pedro de Ayala, remarked that Henry VII 'would like to govern England in the French fashion, but he cannot'.[29] Meanwhile, the Franconian knighthood, threatened by the Common Penny and restrictions on feuding at the diet of 1495,

---

[28] By, for example, A. B. Ferguson, in *The Articulate Citizen and the English Renaissance* (Durham, NC, 1965), p. xiv. The assumption that these people were seeing more clearly than their predecessors rather than thinking in different ways deserves further thought.

[29] Quoted by S. B. Chrimes, *Henry VII* (London, 1972), p. 300.

insisted that 'they would not let themselves be put on a level with the French [nobility] who once were also free'.[30] By the end of the century, political comparison and analysis were so widespread that historians sometimes talk of the emergence of a new language of politics in this period. Both the presence and the content of this language helped to define the political sphere, and, once again, to encourage the sense that the political sphere that really mattered was the regnal one, and that the enterprise of politics was best carried out in its major centres.

Aspects of the culture we have been discussing may have been stronger in the centre, south and west of the continent than they were towards the east and north. The humanist Pannonius described his native country of Hungary as a 'barbaric land' in 1458, while Piccolomini observed rather snootily in the 1440s that it was no use inquiring 'about Plato among the Hungarians', but this is the kind of thing that mid-century humanists said of anywhere beyond the Roman core of Europe, and, in any case, Hungarian humanism was shortly to receive a great boost from the cultural investments of Matthias Corvinus. Bohemian Hussite intellectuals were initially hostile to Latinity, which they associated with the Catholic Church, but there are signs that – thinly explored as it is in modern western historiography – Bohemia possessed a lively and educated vernacular public culture for much of the century. In Poland, meanwhile, Cracow played host to a circle of humanists, centring on the Italian Callimachus, while the habit of referring to the *Sejm* as the 'Senate' suggests a certain neoclassical consciousness, and the wide circulation of lives of Bishop Olésnicki attests to a literate interest among the nobility in the historic defence of their liberties. The cultural gap between 'East' and 'West' may thus be rather narrower than was once imagined, or indeed non-existent: the state of the historiography makes it hard to be sure. The position may be different further north, however: it does look as if some of the trends in public writing and public debate discussed above made relatively little headway in Scandinavia until the early sixteenth century.

One phenomenon found almost everywhere in the fifteenth century, however, is the writing of national history, and – since we know that some of these histories were widely owned – this must have had a

---

[30] Quoted by H. Zmora, *State and Nobility in Early Modern Germany. The Knightly Feud in Franconia, 1440–1567* (Cambridge, 1997), p. 129.

profound influence on consciousness of the regnal polity in at least some parts of its territory. In France, for example, the *Grandes Chroniques*, which associated the destiny of the kingdom with that of the ruling house of Capet/Valois, were translated from the later thirteenth century and these translations circulated widely in manuscript from the 1380s. Fifteenth-century historical writing was orientated towards offering readers a brief recapitulation – as in Noel de Fribois' *Abrégé de Croniques* (*c.*1459) or Robert Gaguin's printed *Compendium* (1495) – or to celebrating the legendary origins of the French people (and their Salic law), as in the 1492 *Annales* of Nicolas Gilles. In England, the most influential historical works were probably the Brut Chronicles, which told of the Trojan origins of the kingdom, and narrated its British, Saxon and English history with a strong monarchical, but also communitarian, tinge: dozens of English-language version survive from the fifteenth century. In Scotland, the *Scotichronicon* of Walter Bower (late 1440s) seems to have been widely read, as were the two great vernacular epics, Barbour's *Bruce* (1370s) and Blind Harry's *Wallace* (1470s), both of which looked back to the Wars of Independence and the heroic defence of the country's freedom by both king and people. Great national histories and people's chronicles were produced elsewhere too: Bruni's *History of the Florentine People* (1415–44), which centred on the city's tradition of defending liberty; Jan Długosz's *Annales seu Cronici Incliti Regni Polonie* (1455×80), which linked the history of the realm with that of the Church, promoting the latter as the defender of both crown and people; the highly patriotic *Chronica Hungarorum*, written by the judge and nobleman, János Thuróczy, and printed in 1488; Viktorin Kornel's *Nine Books on the Laws, Courts and Land Registers of Bohemia* (1499); and a Latin history of Sweden, *Chronica Regni Gothorum*, which was written towards 1470 and celebrated Swedish political traditions while presenting Uppsala as a new Jerusalem.

As that last example suggests, chronicles and histories could also have an urban setting – those of Augsburg, Nuremberg and Lübeck are well known, as are those of London – but these typically recorded and celebrated the affairs of the *regnum* as well as those of the city (and in some of these cases, *regnum* and city were the same, of course). This was the era in which the court of Corvinus perpetrated the notion that the Hungarian people were descended from the Huns, and that their ruler was a second Attila; it was when the folk tales of William Tell and other popular heroes were first woven into a mythical account of the origins of Switzerland, in the White book of Sarnen (*c.*1470); and it was when Edward IV and Henry VII presented themselves as fulfilling Merlin's prophecy by restoring the line of British kings. Across Europe, then, national stories were becoming more defined and embellished, were dignified with refreshed Latinity, or were more widely and efficiently circulated – often all three. While this development must have responded to political developments, and commercial ones, such as the growth of the book trade and the spread of printing, it also helped to further them and to strengthen the national and regnal paradigm in which political life was increasingly exclusively conducted.

It will be clear from much of the above that the forms in which ideas circulated played an important role in establishing their significance and shaping their impact. In the fifteenth century, the sense of a 'public', and therefore of a '*res publica*', was strengthened by the manifold links between published works, public speech, the content of posted bills and manifestoes and the growing readership for works of public edification. By the end of the fourteenth century, as we have seen, fine writers were already showing an interest in depicting the broad sweep of society, including its political values and arrangements, and this was strength-ened in the vernacular histories, chronicles and moral writings of the fifteenth century. Works as various as the anonymous English tracts 'Richard the Redeless' and 'Mum and the Sothsegger', Michel Pintoin's *Chronique* of events in Paris under Charles VI and the *Reformatio Sigismundi* showed a marked awareness of, and interest in, the content of public and popular opinion, and they did not always draw a dis-tinction between the two. A host of translations, handbooks, primers, dictionaries and compilations, written by people whom Jacques Verger calls 'intermediary intellectuals', provided a bridge between the works of the learned and the tastes of the people.[31] Chronicles, annals and commonplace books, compiled and exchanged by the elites of large towns like London, Paris and Florence, included copies of bills, poems and proclamations circulated by rebels and by the authorities, and the influence of these, blended with learning, is clear in the more devel-oped works, memoirs and treatises of the *penseurs-fonctionnaires* – 'civil-servant thinkers' – who were the typical theorists of the period.[32] There

---

[31] Verger, *Men of Learning*, pp. 125–37.
[32] This neat phrase appears in J. Dumolyn, 'Justice, Equity and the Common Good: The State Ideology of the Councillors of the Burgundian Dukes', in D'A.J.D. Boulton and J.R. Veenstra, eds., *The Ideology of Burgundy* (Leiden, 2006), 1–20.

was already a well-developed trade in books in most urban centres by the first half of the century, and this was substantially extended by the development of printing from the 1440s (Strasbourg) and 1450s (Mainz) onwards. Presses were established in Rome and Cologne by 1465, in Venice and through much of southern Germany by 1469, in Paris in 1470, and in Bohemia, the Low Countries and England within a few years of that, reaching Copenhagen and Stockholm by the 1480s. By 1500, in the German lands alone, there were around 200 presses: printing was thus a technology that proliferated rapidly, transforming the culture of written exchange. The political impact of the spread of printing is not easy to characterise, even so. In some ways, it greatly increased the diversity of public knowledge: printers produced for a variety of markets and in a variety of forms and languages, from vernacular handbills, through working texts for scholars, to fancy illustrated works for the entertainment of ladies and gentlemen; foreign books moved across borders in greater numbers and with greater ease than ever before, ensuring that the Latinate readership was as international as ever in the later years of the century. But in some respects, the printing trade helped to canalise and define regnal and regional cultures: it helped to extend and stabilise the vernacular in many European countries (though the activities of chanceries, especially in the fifteenth century, also played a part in those developments); and it could strengthen the sense of national history and national literature by publishing well-known vernacular works and presenting them as the reading matter of every cultivated person. In all these ways, printing set the seal on a long period of growth in public communication, a period which, by 1500, had bestowed on every polity a rich cultural definition.

Developments in government

The fifteenth century saw less spectacular innovation and expansion in the institutions and practices of government than the fourteenth century had done, but it was the scene of important developments nonetheless. By and large, these developments increased the effectiveness and acceptability of regnal governments: they did not simply advance central power, they also modified its operations in ways that elicited more consistent support and co-operation from other elements in each polity. As in the previous chapter, we shall take them in turn, beginning with jurisdiction.

In 1400, the distribution of jurisdiction was a great deal clearer in some parts of Europe than in others. The tendency of the ensuing century was to extend the areas of clarity and hierarchy, so that even regions of overlapping jurisdiction, such as the Low Countries, or the German lands, or places where jurisdiction was highly dispersed, such as Naples or France, or places where it was very informal, such as Ireland or parts of Scotland, developed better co-ordinated systems. In many cases, this was because of easier access to central courts: in the Burgundian Netherlands, for example, the jurisdiction of the ducal officers and councils which presided over each province was steadily advanced at the expense of the municipalities and nobles from the first half of the century, and while the supreme court of the duke at first elicited suspicion and was little used, it was firmly established by the 1440s and had acquired an effective appellate jurisdiction by the 1520s. Similarly, in France and Castile, royal justice was made more easily available, both by expansion of central agencies such as the *Parlement*, *Châtelet* and *requêtes* in France, and the *audiencia* and *Consejo Real* in Castile, and by the establishment of high courts in the provinces, with *parlements* emerging in Bordeaux, Rouen, Dijon, Grenoble, Aix-en-Provence and Rennes, as the great fiefs and principalities returned to the crown, and *audiencias* established by the Catholic kings at Santiago, Seville and Granada to join the original one at Valladolid. Alfonso of Naples revived royal jurisdiction in the *Regno* through the flexible means of the royal council, which began to receive appeals and petitions in 1449: while this threatened to erode the feudal jurisdiction of the magnates, which Alfonso had confirmed in 1443, he was able to strike a balance between their rights and his, and so to restore the sense of a regnal framework to a pretty anarchic territory. Even in England, with its historically centralised system, this period saw the institution of new local resorts – the councils of Wales and the North (and, for a time under Henry VII, that of the Queen Mother, in the East Midlands), dispensing authoritative and equitable justice to some of the wildest parts of the realm. But it was not always royal courts which triumphed. In Bohemia, Catalonia and Poland, the authority of land-courts came gradually to be accepted by the crown, so that, instead of competing systems of royal and seigneurial, municipal or communal justice, clearer boundaries were established. Equally, the kings of England, Scotland or, for that matter, Hungary, were ready to leave jurisdiction in the hands of palatine lords and clan leaders, such as the Fitzgeralds, the Gordons, the Campbells and the *voivodes* of Transylvania, where this was the most effective means of keeping the peace. In these instances, of course, there was a kind of continuity with older compromises and informalities, but these dynasties were drawn more closely into the orbit of royal power than their predecessors had been, and could be reined in, albeit with some difficulty, when they strayed too far from royal policy. In other areas where feuding had been conventional, such as the Empire and the less remote parts of Scotland, steps were taken to restrain it, whether through new courts like the *Reichskammergericht* and the various high courts developed by the leading princes, or through direct royal action.

At the same time, the procedures of central jurisdictions were frequently improved in this period. The provision of discretionary justice was increasingly removed from the direct judgement of the king and his courtiers, to be dispensed instead by legal experts in less political circumstances: the resulting courts of the council, or chancery, or 'requests', or royal audience, or 'personal presence', as it was known in Hungary, continued to offer all the advantages of equity, authority and speed, but they won the confidence of litigants with enhanced record-keeping and somewhat greater fairness and predictability. Of course, the users of discretionary or equitable courts wanted justice to go their way, regardless of the strengths or weaknesses of their case, and there were limits to how systematic and apolitical these kinds of courts could usefully be, but this was an age of rising legal consciousness, and a more subtle politics of influence and legal chicanery was coming to be preferable to more arbitrary forms of judgement. Part of this rising legal consciousness was the spreading of codification across the continent. In 1409 and 1415, the commune of Florence made two redactions of its statutes, and embarked on a new campaign of enforcing existing regulations. The laws of Catalonia were catalogued in 1413 and those of Aragon a few years later. In 1420–2, the law-code of Casimir III, which had been a somewhat controversial exercise of royal fiat when it appeared in the 1360s, was reissued, together with more recent statutes, such as those of Koszyce and Czerwinsk, as the *Digesta* of the laws of Poland. The *Landlaw* of Sweden was reissued and extended in 1442 and 1474, and a '*decretum maius*' fixed the order of the Hungarian courts in 1435, while a national code, the *Tripartitum*, was produced in 1514 (and the same impulse lay behind the

Bohemian Land Ordinance of 1500).[33] As we have seen, Charles VII appointed the codification of French customary law by an ordinance of 1454, and, by the end of the century, his successors were once again beginning to amend and correct provincial custom, this time by legislation rather than judicial action. In England, and no doubt elsewhere, private ownership of statute collections grew over the course of the century (facilitated, from the 1480s, by the practice of printing them). While codes of Roman and canon law had, of course, existed for a long time before this, and had generated a copious literature for practitioners – manuals, glosses, commentaries and the like – the extension of these habits and practices to the laws of kings (or kingdoms), princes, provinces and towns from the later fourteenth century onwards must have helped to strengthen the sense of living within legally defined spaces. Equally, that the act of codification tended to involve definition of the juridical and legislative hierarchy meant that the priority of sovereign jurisdictions was reinforced and advertised by this kind of activity. By the end of the century, therefore, most Europeans lived in more fully developed and fully described jurisdictions, with a more structured range of courts, and a knowable set of laws which they came to associate with their national history and constitutional fabric.

In many countries, armed forces were brought more fully under regnal control, as we have seen.[34] Armies generally included more professional troops, they were better disciplined, their pay was more typically disbursed from the centre, rather than being supplied through fiefs or shares in local taxation, and both recruitment and command were more extensively supervised by government officers. Not all countries had permanent standing armies on the French or Venetian model, even so: in England, Poland and post-1490 Hungary, for example, men at arms had to be raised from the aristocracy each time there was a war, and, in practice, this had to be negotiated through dialogue with representative estates. But even in these cases, the central co-ordination of military power was tending to increase. The development of the *sejmiki* from the 1430s and 1440s onwards enabled the Polish kings to deal directly with the *szlachta* who formed the bulk of their armies, and to raise the taxation that enabled their payment. In

---

[33] The *Tripartitum* was printed in 1517, but not approved by the diet, which wished to preserve the freedom to negotiate law and custom.

[34] Above, pp. 370–1.

Hungary, meanwhile, where the experiments of Sigismund and Matthias with national tax-funded armies were ultimately thwarted by the magnates, who wished to retain control over their followers, the crown and the diet regained the upper hand by the end of the 1490s: banderial lords had to accept registration and to undertake to supply large forces in order to claim royal revenues; they received their money from taxation raised through the diet, and not from grants of castles and *honores*, and so came to resemble military contractors more than territorial princes. Similarly, in England, while magnate retinues remained the mainstay of the army, the lords recruited their troops under royal licence from the 1480s onward, infantry forces were raised through county militias, and the royal court and household were the most prominent element in the forces raised in 1475 and 1492. Even in Spain, where the military aristocracy of Castile had steadily increased its control over royal taxes under the Trastámara kings, the reigns of Ferdinand and Isabella brought changes: the 1480 Act of Resumption enabled the crown to restore control over military payments, and, while resumed bonds on royal taxes had to be rapidly redistributed, royal officers had regained administrative oversight. Castile and its army remained highly aristocratic, but a permanent royal guard was created, and a partly separate network of urban militias was raised, first through the *Santa Hermandad*, and later through a national system of military obligation, created in the 1496 ordinance of Valladolid. Once again, enhanced co-ordination proves to be a better way of describing governmental development than increased control. Even in France, the *compagnies d'ordonnance* were made up of noblemen with independent and local interests to set alongside their royal duties. Over time, their tenure of their offices became more secure, their links with other captains less official and more personal. Two princely constables at odds with the kings of France had leaders of *compagnies* in their personal retinues – the count of St Pol under Louis XI, and the duke of Bourbon under Francis I. But it is equally important to note that, in the confrontations of 1475 and 1523 (unlike 1465), it was the princes who were deserted by their servants, not the kings. In France, as elsewhere, the institutions and mechanisms developed in the fifteenth century decisively increased and regularised the royal element in the management of armed force, while the growth of military training and tradition, the circulation of ordinances and commissions, the spread of manuals and memoirs all contributed to a growing association between the army and the national polity.

The pattern of fiscal development in fifteenth-century Europe, on the other hand, is more complicated and variable. As ever, the level of taxation was set principally by the degree of military pressure on each government, and the extent of its purchase on the territories under its sway; consequently, there is no pattern of steadily rising revenues, as there is for so many regimes in the fourteenth century. However, this rather open-ended statement conceals an important development: namely, that general public taxation itself had, by the fifteenth century, become very widespread and regular enough in most places to be a familiar phenomenon. The kingdoms of Poland and Hungary, the *Ordensstaat*, Austria, Bavaria, Brandenburg, Saxony, several other principalities and even the Empire itself all began to experience formal and recurring direct taxation between the middle years of the century and its end, with the result that one of the most insistent reminders of membership of a large political community was extended to the subjects of most of central and eastern Europe, just as it had spread across the West in the previous century. Regular royal taxation was revived in Sicily and Naples from the reign of Alfonso the Magnanimous, and in the Papal States from the 1420s (or, more lastingly, the 1450s). Even Bohemia, so long resistant to royal action outside the demesne, and torn apart for most of the century, seems to have experienced fairly regular taxation during the period of frequent diets that began in the 1490s.

We have seen that taxes tended to produce particular kinds of political reaction: popular revolts in response to excessive or novel demands, since the peasantry and urban communities bore the brunt of almost all taxation in the period; debates between rulers and estates, in which the responsibility of the former to preserve and manage the patrimony before imposing burdens on the subjects was a common theme. Revolts occurred mainly in places where direct taxation had rarely been levied before, or only at a low level, as in Sweden in 1434–6, in Hungary in 1436–7, in Transylvania in 1467 or in the see of Salzburg and Switzerland in the later decades of the century (most other German principalities where levies increased seem to have avoided trouble by keeping the frequency low and/or imposing taxes indirectly). In 1489 and 1497, there were also risings in England, where the tax burden was much lighter than before in the second half of the century, but here a central cause was innovation in both the form and the pattern of taxation. Fiscal debates were a feature of all the polities which had introduced substantial taxation over the previous hundred years or so: as we have seen, they were an element in the programme of Church reform, in the governing councils imposed on Henry IV of England and in the detailed provisions of the *Cabochien* ordinance of 1413, whose clauses were devoted to the elimination of waste and corruption in royal government, and the resumption of royal resources. These measures built on fourteenth-century precedents, but they were more detailed, more systematic and more efficacious: the financial burdens on the Church were ultimately reduced and restructured; Henry IV's councils managed royal finances for much of his reign, and, especially between 1406 and 1410, restored fiscal order, won public confidence and opened the way to the heavier taxation of the ensuing decade. The *Cabochien* ordinance, it is true, was a dead letter as France plunged into civil war, but it probably helped to inspire and justify the resumption which Charles VII enacted in 1418. Almost everywhere, kings were enjoined by the representatives of taxpayers to restore and husband their patrimonial rights and assets. It was a policy that they greeted with some ambivalence, not wishing to forfeit rights to taxation by accepting the principle that the king should 'live of his own', and uneasy at the potential disturbance to relations with the nobility, the principal holders of assets regarded as belonging to the crown.[35] Following periods of political crisis, however, in which the crown's assets had become so dispersed among warring magnates that the restoration of order looked impossible without it, resumption could appeal to a sufficient cross-section of political opinion for it to be a viable policy: this was the position in Hungary and France in the 1440s and 1450s, for instance, in England in the 1460s or Castile in 1480. Inevitably, proceedings of this kind were full of political compromises – there was no resuming the royal lands of the Hunyadi, for instance, and the pensions of the French princes, explicitly threatened by Charles VII in 1440 and 1442, remained in their hands – but they tended to confirm royal prerogatives and to advance fiscal thinking. This was especially the case in countries where taxes had come to be part of the king's customary rights – as in Castile, where the *realengo* was really a series of

---

[35] The quotation is from the English King Edward IV, but the phrase itself, as well as the notion behind it, appears in several European languages. See, for example, J. Krynen, *Idéal du prince et pouvoir royal en France à la fin du moyen âge* (Paris, 1981), p. 192 and R. Bonney, ed., *Economic Systems and State Finance* (Oxford, 1995), p. 112 (Sweden).

towns and taxes, or in France, where the novelties of John II and Charles V could be treated as customary by Charles VII and relatively quickly reconstructed. In practice, however, the widespread discussion of the ruler's patrimonial or fiscal claims tended everywhere to advance the sense of a *res publica* at the regnal level, and to enable kings and princes to exploit their patrimonial resources with greater public agreement, and to levy consensual taxation whenever those resources proved insufficient.

While there were innovations in some quarters, the fifteenth century thus saw a high degree of settlement in fiscal structures. There were places where taxation grew, notably in Venice and the Netherlands, or remained at a high level, as in France and Castile, but this was mostly achieved with a notable lack of friction. In Venice, this was perhaps because of the remarkable alignment of the Republic's policies with the interests of its leading subjects – the real hikes came from the 1460s to fund an unavoidable war with the Ottomans – but the fact that some of the additional burden was imposed on the helpless rural subjects of the *Terra Ferma* must have helped. In France, the extremely high taxation of Louis XI did cause strains, and must explain some of the tensions of the reign (even if those tensions were also its cause), but when taxes fell back to the level of 1461 and remained there from the 1480s to the 1520s, the burden on subjects was a fifth less than it had been in the 1370s. The position in Castile was rather similar, with Ferdinand and Isabella drawing revenues comparable to the highest levels of the fourteenth century by 1504, but from a population and economy which had significantly increased in size. Only in the Netherlands did high taxation, which persisted beyond the 1470s until the mid-1490s, produce the sort of reaction more typical of the fourteenth century, with Flanders in rebellion for most of the decade 1482–92. But, in explaining this resistance, we need to remember that it was only from the 1460s that the Low Countries had been subjected to such levels of generalised extraction and co-ordination; until the 1420s, these had been separate principalities, with mostly weak princes whose policies were above all shaped by the interests of powerful cities. Across much of the rest of the continent, rulers struck acceptable compromises with representative estates, scaled back tax demands to tolerable levels, relied more heavily on indirect taxes than direct ones, and exploited their prerogatives in the manner recommended by parliamentarians. The involvement of estates in royal and princely fiscality – almost everywhere, in fact – allowed for a degree of elasticity.

Later fifteenth-century rulers were not, as used to be thought, caught in an 'antiquated strait-jacket of endowed monarchy': they retained the means to negotiate changes in fiscal structures wherever they maintained dialogue with their subjects.[36]

The conventional view of representative institutions in the fifteenth century is that they declined, but this is highly misleading. Most parts of the continent experienced considerable growth in representation, especially at the regnal level. This is most marked in the centre, east and north of the continent – in Scotland, Bohemia and the Empire from the 1420s, in Prussia, Livonia, Poland, Scandinavia and Hungary from the 1430s, and in several German principalities, where separate or independent estates organisations were drawn together under the prince in what were called *Landtage* – but there are examples elsewhere too: Neapolitan parliaments were revived under Alfonso and Ferrante, for instance, meeting eight times between 1443 and 1458 alone. Not all these innovations lasted: in 'Royal Prussia' after the Polish conquest of the 1460s, for instance, an elite of military magnates was able to suppress the representation of both the towns and the lesser nobility; the power of the Danish *rigsråd*, which represented the prelates and magnates more than any other groups, was eroded from the 1470s onwards. Not all assemblies had the formal or real power to carry their constituents with them – in Sweden, for instance, provincial structures typically had more binding effect – but most of them gained in legitimacy and institutional solidity as the century progressed. They could be powerful vehicles of dissent, as in the high-tax western kingdoms of the fourteenth century, but they were by no means anarchic: they co-ordinated that dissent at a national level, and even the radical proposals of the Hungarian estates in the 1440s, or those of the Bohemians in the late 1490s, were clearly geared towards making the government of the kingdom possible and effective.

Turning to the West, estates organisations continued to play a much more important role in the political fabric of most countries than the literature tends to suggest. In the crown of Aragon, for instance, they remained central to the government of all the realms in the federation, even under Ferdinand the Catholic; in the Low Countries, the new Estates General of the 1460s preserved its

---

[36] The quotation is from J. R. Lander, *Conflict and Stability in Fifteenth-Century England* (London, 1969), p. 113.

influence even during the difficult period of the 1480s; and in England, while parliaments became less frequent, they lasted much longer and remained crucial for negotiating taxes, fiscal reforms and political problems, and for providing legislative solutions to the complaints of individuals and groups and matters of general public concern. It is really only in France and Castile that representation can be shown to have declined – in the second half of the century, in particular – and even there the picture is very mixed. In both countries, the capacity of estates to consent to taxation has been taken as central to their political efficacy, and the fact that the *alcabala* could be levied without consent from *c.*1400, while after 1440, Charles VII did not need to consult the Estates General of Languedoïl or Languedoc to raise *tailles* and *aides* (even many local and provincial estates ceased to be necessary for this purpose after about 1460), is thus supposed to have produced decline. Meetings of the Estates General were certainly few and far between after Charles VII's reconquest – in Languedoïl, which covered most of France, it met only twice, in 1468 and 1484; while in Castile, as we have seen, the *Cortes* barely met between 1480 and 1498, the number of towns represented in it shrank, the nobility ceased to attend and, from as early as 1430, the crown was feeing and appointing the *procuradores*. Even so, there is more to this than meets the eye. The Estates General had never met frequently in France: that it did so at moments of acute political tension, in the 1460s and 1480s, just as in the 1340s and 1350s, is testimony to a continuing sense that, in a crisis, the realm required direct representation beside the king. Regional estates continued to operate, and to have some influence over taxation, in those parts of France where they had been most vigorous, such as Normandy and Languedoc, and in areas newly annexed to the crown, such as Burgundy and Provence. In Castile, meanwhile, it was the most important towns that continued to be represented in the *Cortes*, and their political and fiscal support remained essential (especially when the experiment of the *Santa Hermandad* – which also represented urban power, of course – was wound up). The *Cortes* would, moreover, play a central role in the resistance that led to the major revolt of the *comuneros* (townsmen) in 1521, so its political teeth were as sharp as ever in circumstances where the royal will diverged from municipal interests. The ideal of representation, and to some extent the familiar institutions that provided for it, thus retained influence in both these kingdoms. And they might have been more influential still had not other media of representation and accommodation been maintained and developed. Many of these were informal, and are discussed below. Others, such as the machinery for handling petitions, have been mentioned above. Worth mentioning here are the development of a vast *conseil du roi* in France, whose membership (462 under Louis XI alone) seems to have extended to include very many of the middling nobility who were becoming so important in the royal administration and army from the 1450s onwards. Most of these men rarely came into contact with the king, and were more like retainers than councillors, but there seems little doubt that the great network to which they belonged was an important means of representing aristocratic and provincial opinion, just as Louis XI's assiduous dialogue with the leaders of the various *bonnes villes* enabled both the representation of urban interests and the continuing incorporation of the towns in the royal polity. In Castile, meanwhile, the juntas of the *Hermandad*, the magnates and even royal officers like *corregidores* and *gubernadores*, who held their posts for long periods of time, were means of communication between the crown and its constituents. These smoother means of rule, for which parallels can also be found in England and elsewhere, may even have enhanced the representation of local interests, because they accomplished dialogue without the more confrontational techniques and crude reformism typical of formal assemblies. In short, all across Europe – and rather as one might expect – representation remained a crucial facet of political life. While it is certainly worthwhile to note the differences between areas in which relatively informal mechanisms were replacing assemblies and those in which assemblies remained frequent, it is important not to miss the fact that evolving (often improving) media of dialogue between rulers and subjects were an important element in the increasing co-ordination of regnal polities.

The fifteenth century was a period of continuing administrative growth, especially at the regnal level, where it was particularly celebrated, but also in towns and principalities. As far as central governments were concerned, perhaps the most striking development was the rise of more specialised and expert councils. In Castile, for example, there were councils to oversee the various territories, plus the Inquisition (from 1483) and the military orders (from 1495). There was a supervisory council placed above these, dominated by legally trained advisers and (after 1480) excluding the great magnates; and – besides secretarial judicial and financial bodies – there was also the *cámera de Castilla*, developed by Ferdinand and Isabella to provide more systematic and efficient management of royal grace. This distribution of roles and activities partly reflects the growth of the scope of royal government in Castile, as elsewhere, but the creation of small, expert councils to look after areas of administration is also significant: while these bodies were essentially subservient to royal will, and were thus qualitatively different from the councils of magnates recurrently imposed on earlier rulers of Castile (or of the Empire, or England, or more rarely France), they were expected to develop policy as well as to administrate, and were trusted to handle at least some decision-making independently. Similar bodies developed in most of the western kingdoms, amid a similar extension of the deliberative aspects of government. With less elaboration, 'privy councils' of this kind also appeared around the kings of Hungary, Poland and the Empire.[37] In northern Italy, complex conciliar structures already existed, but the acquisition of territorial states usually meant further development, so that the Florentine administration was overhauled between the 1380s and the 1420s, while the Venetians introduced new '*savi*' for the *Terra Ferma* in 1421, and divided the records of the Senate into '*Terra*' and '*Mar*' (sea, including overseas possessions) from 1440. Everywhere, rulers continued to consult their most powerful subjects, but the mixed councils of magnates and administrators, which had been a recurring feature of political life for a hundred years after *c.*1350, tended to recede from mid-century, at least in the more integrated kingdoms of the West and South. In Bohemia and Scandinavia, and more intermittently in Poland and the Empire, 'regnal' councils of magnates, electors and great officers persisted, to uphold liberties, or to ensure that royal government coincided with the will of the estates.

One reason why more 'policy' was required in the regimes of the later fifteenth century was their growing investment in diplomatic relations with their neighbours. A series of powers, beginning with the Papacy, and then, in the age of the *Lega Italica*, the secular Italian states, and finally, by the end of the century, France and Spain, established permanent ambassadors at the courts of their most important partners and rivals. This significantly increased the flow of

---

[37] Maximilian's *Reichshofrat* of 1498 was partly a riposte to the *Reichsregiment* proposed by the reformers in 1495 and later: while the membership of his council was determined by him, the *Reichsregiment* was to be shaped and dominated by the Electors.

political information passing through the governments of Europe, stimulated political comparison and reflection, and encouraged rulers not only to police their foreign relations, but to pursue more ambitious diplomatic initiatives. But diplomacy was not the only stimulus to conciliar development: fiscal administration was enhanced in many countries – Alfonso V and Matthias Corvinus entirely overhauled the systems of accounting and revenue collection in Naples and Hungary respectively, for instance; while the expansion of centralised equity jurisdiction, and the increasing use of legislation, called for juristic learning. Lawyers and other middling-born but well-educated men were thus prominent in these councils by the end of the century: the so-called *letrados* of Henry IV and the Catholic Monarchs; men like Pieter Bladelin and Guillaume Hugonet in Valois Burgundy, or Reginald Bray, Richard Empson and Edmund Dudley in Henry VII's England. In many ways, these were simply the laicised successors of the learned clerks who had served in the chanceries and treasuries of the high middle ages, but their increased numbers, their increasingly humanistic education, and the expectation that they would develop initiatives, as well as resolving legal and administrative problems, introduced a different tenor into government. These expanded conciliar elites could, in their own way, act independently towards the kings of the later part of the century, drawing on their knowledge of an increasingly substantial and complex administration to shape, even to block, royal policy. They could plot, as they seem to have done against Galeazzo Maria Sforza, in 1476; they might form factions with allies in the court, as did the councillors of Henry VIII of England (1509–47), or they might form powerful groups around their departments, as did the *parlementaires* under Francis I; but the growth, even the normalisation, of this kind of politics is testimony to how large and important the administrative entourage of Europe's kings had become. That development, in turn, was another factor helping to draw political activity towards the regnal level: to advance or protect one's interests within the realm, it was increasingly important to have representation or presence at the royal centre.

Local government remained, as it had always been, a compromise between regnal authority and local power, but, in many countries, the tendency of the period was towards a more effective and stable balance of the two elements. Some governments were more aggressive in their prosecution of their territorial rights than others, but two broad trends are perceptible: one is a withdrawal from the practice of conceding great fiefs or *apanages*, wherever this was feasible; the other is a tendency to tolerate local liberties and authorities, while ensuring that their place within the overall regnal structure was more clearly defined or articulated. As we have seen, many fifteenth-century kings engaged in efforts to resume or expand the royal demesne, whether by pressing inheritance rights, instituting legal proceedings, confiscating the territories of rebels, or, in the case of usurpers, like Matthias Corvinus, or collateral heirs, like Louis XII, bringing large estates with them to the throne. In the early part of the century, and later too in some places – Poland, for instance, or Castile, even under the Catholic Monarchs – these gains were rapidly recirculated to leading royal allies, partly to reward loyalty and partly to enable effective rule in the periphery. From about mid-century, however, kings were more likely to retain great estates in their own hands – as in England or Naples – or to break them up, stripping them of any significant jurisdiction, and granting them out in portions to nobles of lesser or middling rank, as in France or Hungary. The passing of territorial magnates and princes inevitably created difficulties in areas that were accustomed to their rule, and kings responded in a variety of ways. One solution, attempted in England and France, was to expand the scope of royal retaining to forge more extensive links between the crown and the lesser or (in France) middling nobility. Another, found in these kingdoms and also in Scotland under James IV, was to provide more attentive and flexible means of royal justice, replacing the mediating role of magnates with direct intervention by the crown. Efforts were made in England and Spain, and even in the Empire and France, to police the localities in a more determined way, keeping down the level of violence, feuding and vigilante justice, so that lesser landowners had less need to turn to magnates for protection. A third solution, characteristic of France, was to create powerful regional officers in areas used to princely rule: between 1450 and 1520, ten *gouvernements* were created, drawing together the royal officers of large regions under powerful *lieutenants-généraux*, drawn mainly from the same class of middle-ranking nobles that underpinned the new order of Louis XI and his sixteenth-century successors. The *corregidores* of Castile in many ways fulfilled a similar role (in a polity where magnates continued to flourish):[38] whatever their local connections,

---

[38] *Corregidores* were municipal officers, but Castile's municipalities, as we have seen, were the major centres of jurisdiction, wealth and power, bestowing influence over whole provinces. See above, p. 213.

which were often considerable, these officers, like the *lieutenants*, owed their positions, and their entitlement to pensions or *juros*, to the crown; it might not be easy, or desirable, for the king to remove them, but equally it made sense for them to behave in ways that would maintain royal goodwill. These great territorial offices were not particularly novel – England had had wardens of the Northern Marches and lieutenants of Ireland since at least the early fourteenth century; Castilian *adelantados* (the provincial equivalents of *corregidores*) go back further still. Nor were they peculiar to monarchies – the Burgundian dukes ruled Holland and Zealand, two long-united provinces which they rarely visited, through a *stadholder* and council from 1428;[39] Venice and Florence managed their territorial states through a network of *rettori* (rectors) presiding over communes that typically retained much of their old jurisdictions and customs. It would not do to present these offices as the sinews of a new impersonal state: informal power remained central to their efficacy – *stadholders* had places in the ducal court, for example, and, from the 1430s, Florentine *rettori* were normally Medicean clients; nor was there a total retreat on the part of kings from the endowment and employment of princely lines – Edward IV created a palatinate of Cumberland for his powerful brother, Richard of Gloucester, for instance; Louis XI bestowed a substantial *apanage* in Guyenne on his brother Charles, and his successors made life-grants of *gouvernements* to royal cadets and other princes. But notwithstanding all these caveats, the patterns of local office as they developed in the later fifteenth century typically involved royal government more formally and consistently in the rule of the provinces than before. There were certainly less-integrated polities – German principalities, Sweden, Poland, Bohemia, for example – and, in these, local offices frequently retained a more feudal character (or gained that character, as in Poland, where the *starosties* became associated with the major landowners of the provinces), but even in these countries, these decentralised arrangements were protected by regnal governments and formed a recognised part of the constitutional order.

What, finally, of the part played by the courts of rulers in the consolidation of fifteenth-century polities? In general, the fifteenth

---

[39] The name '*stadholder*' was only used from 1448: M. Damen, 'The Nerve Centre of Political Networks?... The Integration of Holland and Zealand into the Burgundian State, 1425–1477', in S. Gunn and A. Janse, eds., *The Court as a Stage* (Woodbridge, 2006), 70–84.

century witnessed a continuation of fourteenth-century trends. Courts grew bigger, grander, more ceremonious. Those attached to the duke of Guelders' court rose from around 40 in 1342 to 100 (160, including the duchess' entourage) in 1390, and between 550 and 600 by the mid-fifteenth century; the Burgundian domestic establishment was almost three times this size in the later years of Philip the Good's reign, while the court of Milan was using half the duke's very considerable revenues by the 1470s, and Galeazzo Maria added a hundred extra courtiers in one single grand ceremony at Christmas 1474. Investment in furnishings, books and manuscripts, paintings and tapestries, clothing and festivities grew steadily during the century, so that while it remained common for rulers to move quite freely in the summer months with smaller followings, their winter courts became less manoeuvrable, and the courtly 'season' was typically restricted to a small number of large and richly decorated palaces. Buda, where the Corvina library may have contained 2,000 volumes by the 1490s; Brussels, which tripled in size between 1300 and 1464, under ducal patronage; Innsbruck, where the Emperor Maximilian held court, close to the silver mines of his county of Tyrol: these were among the new capitals of the century, created by a mixture of royal choice, increasing sedentariness, and the influx of lords and ministers who bought themselves fine houses close to the centre of power. In these ways, then, the pattern of development helped to differentiate a smaller number of especially prestigious courts from the rest, identifying the real heads of state, and encouraging lesser powers to act as satellites around the sun of princely power, increasing the grandeur of the ruler and the drawing power of the regnal establishment.

Other trends continued too. Court life became more ritualised, with ceremonies on what were called 'days of estate' increasingly emphasising the distance, or sacrality, of the ruler, as in the public audiences introduced by Charles the Bold. The physical organisation of courts became more complex, with access to the king or prince more tightly controlled, as the numbers in the court expanded, and particular elites of noblemen, gentlemen or ministers were marked out as particular intimates, entitled to enter the most private spaces – the 'privy chamber', as it was known in England from the 1490s. Yet courts were far from private places. One reason for their swelling size was the continuing desire of rulers to attach local and international notables to their service: retainers and servants *à terme*; leading noblemen; travelling scholars, artists and musicians; diplomats and their entourages were among the denizens of the leading courts and helped to make them the distinctive centres that they were. Towards 1500, the princely courts of Bavaria and Württemberg were drawing in the unattached nobles of Swabia, for instance, as those of Brandenburg-Anspach and Bavaria again were attracting those of Franconia. Increasingly, historians see courts as pluralistic places. Much as they magnified the ruler, and much as their governing ordinances became ever more detailed and complex, the courts of the later fifteenth century were only loosely controlled: they became places of intrigue and advancement for a host of great men – ministers and nobles who built up clienteles by being able to secure access to the ruler, or by having the power to appoint to offices in the household or administration. These royal centres were large and complex places, then, in which the ruler's ultimate authority was shared and somewhat manipulated by his leading servants, but if that state of affairs raises doubts about the completeness of monarchical power at the end of the fifteenth century, it confirms the general picture of advancing political co-ordination at the regnal level. The courts of the great powers – republican Venice and Florence or papal Rome as much as the secular monarchies – became the main full-time forums for political activity, sucking in everyone who counted and emphasising the provincial subordination of everywhere else.

Many of the governmental developments discussed above were duplicated by cities, both self-governing and subordinate, and also by princes and lords, but this simultaneous constitutional and institutional growth no longer produced the kinds of jurisdictional conflict it once had. Some of the reasons for this have already been discussed; others are discussed below, but important and obvious factors were the superior size of the regnal administrative estate, the growing coherence of its operations and its strong sense of its own sovereignty. It would certainly be wrong to overstate the strength of late fifteenth-century government, and it is important to recognise that areas of significant contestation or extreme informality persisted – in the Empire, in many highland areas, in parts of Scandinavia, especially Sweden, in parts of the Balkans and on the Steppes – but the growth of government is always a relative phenomenon, and the ways in which government grew in the fifteenth century advanced the co-ordination of political space beyond the levels achieved in the fourteenth century, and did so in a political world greatly more sophisticated and extensive than that of the thirteenth century.

The practice of politics

The trends and dynamics of fifteenth-century politics themselves played a part in the consolidation of regnal polities, focusing attention at the regnal level and contributing to the disintegration of both larger and smaller units as viable alternatives to regnal authority. This has already been implicit in the discussion of political events above, so here the treatment will be restricted to the broad conclusions that can be drawn. Whether we look at politics at the international or universal level, the regnal or national level, or the sub-regnal level, the tendency is the same: towards the affirmation of comparatively stable, bounded, national/regnal polities.

As we have seen, the politics of the first half of the century were dominated by conflicts within the universal Church. The omnipresence of papal power and the interaction between the various different, but overlapping, structures within and around the Church – the College of Cardinals, the universities, the Papal States, the religious orders, the national hierarchies, the tenants of church lands, and the various lay patrons and advocates with interests in ecclesiastical property – meant that these conflicts involved everybody. The addition of a widespread pressure for reform, both spiritual and secular, made this conflict even more all-consuming, particularly given two factors: the widely shared belief that councils representing the universal collectivity of the people should be part of the solution; and the inevitable disagreements over how to reconcile these councils with other authorities and the liberties they protected. Between roughly the 1390s and the 1440s, therefore, much of Europe was consumed in a common struggle to resolve common difficulties. These difficulties played out differently in different regions or political units, of course – 'reform' meant different things in revolutionary Bohemia, or in the German lands of the Empire, or in the France of Burgundians and Armagnacs; the relations of rulers and councils in Poland and Hungary were different from those between aldermen and councils in London or Lübeck, and different again from those between ecclesiastical collectivities and their superior officers – but there is a sense in which the politics of the continent in this period were more than usually interconnected, and not only thematically. Even so, it has long been clear that the outcome of the Conciliar period was the affirmation of secular, and in fact regnal, authority over the churches of Europe, and it can be argued that the upshot of conciliar or communitarian struggles in secular polities was much the same: the advance of the regnal framework of power. In the ecclesiastical conflict, part of the reason for this outcome lay in the evolved dynamics of royal, papal and hierarchical relations. As we have seen, in the fourteenth century especially, the Papacy tended to co-operate with the secular rulers of defined regions and realms in making ecclesiastical appointments and governing the assets of the Church; it is not surprising that the restoration of the Papacy involved the enhancement of royal and princely power over churches. But secular rulers did not only extend their influence by deals with the Papacy; they had also joined forces with their leading churchmen in the Schism, and they did so in its resolution, and in the subsequent pursuit of reform. Advised by primates and university men – sometimes, as in Poland, under their control – kings and princes conducted negotiations with the popes and Councils, sent representatives and concluded treaties, all of these initiatives affirming the regnal structure as the natural forum for ecclesiastical politics. The nations of Constance may not have been the actual nations of Europe, but they provided a natural umbrella for the assertion of national ecclesiastical interests, and the concordats of 1418 were a model both for the numerous detailed treaties between the Papacy and secular rulers that followed, and for the declarations of neutrality (or compliance) that issued forth from kingdoms and principalities during the period of Basle.

Meanwhile, the transfer of ecclesiastical conciliarism to the secular sphere – most marked perhaps in the Empire, though almost everywhere it formed a strand in the evolution of indigenous structures of representation and counsel – also gave priority to the regnal order. For one thing, the realm gained additional status as the *universitas* which ought to be represented, but, more importantly, for the 'making of polities', participation in conciliar and representative initiatives habituated its inhabitants to working together, or at least to using communitarian devices and principles to achieve their ends. Not only did subaltern powers, such as the towns of Bohemia, Hungary and, more occasionally, Poland, gain a voice by these means, they might also be drawn away from particularistic strategies, or from alliances which threatened the integrity of the realm (as the Hanseatic towns of Prussia drew away from the League to join local knights in negotiations with the *Ordensstaat*, for instance, or as the ruling elites of Ghent, Bruges and Ypres began to see the duke of Burgundy's Council of Flanders as a more satisfactory means of realising their interests than the individual municipalities to which they belonged). Almost everywhere, the conciliar experiments of the early fifteenth century produced conflict – holders of rights and liberties were unwilling to see these challenged by supposedly representative bodies; there were disagreements over which powers should be represented and how much; and the administrative and political flimsiness of most leagues, estates and parliaments meant that they were rarely able to hold together for long, or to enforce what they agreed. But these conflicts tended to involve a wide cross-section of political society in each case, and to focus its attention on the welfare and the organisation of a realm to which all in common belonged. At the same time, the inability of most councils, whether ecclesiastical or secular, to deliver real government to their constituents meant that subjects of all kinds continued to work with rulers. Representative councils could demonstrate dissatisfaction and they could legislate (often by extracting formal public concessions), but apart from one or two examples – such as the *diputació* of Catalonia, which was ruling a territory not much larger than, or very different from, a city state – they could not provide the increasingly detailed and multifaceted governance that most subjects had become used to. Experiments with conciliar rule were thus short-lived, and their beneficiaries, in most cases, were the kings and princes of Europe, who exploited the principles enunciated by councils, and the structures they created, to provide more extensive and legitimate government. In this way, even the failings of councils tended to advance the regnal polity.

General Councils were not the only supranational factors in fifteenth-century politics, of course: wars and the machinations of the most powerful dynasties were also important dynamics, as they had been in the fourteenth century. In the thirteenth century, and to some extent in the fourteenth, these had often had a significant effect on political boundaries, creating new associations and structures and dissolving old ones. But the elasticity of the political map was generally reducing over time, and although some protean spaces remained – parts of the Empire, Ireland, Russia, the territories of the Byzantine/Ottoman world – by the fifteenth century, neither wars nor dynasticism had much impact on the integrity of political territories; indeed, both processes tended to affirm regnal solidarities, not to corrode them. While the great wars of the fifteenth century often featured the conquest of one power's territory by another, this rarely involved the eradication of the previous political framework: the

Castilian annexation of the kingdom of Granada following the war of 1482–92 is almost the only example outside the Balkans, and even there a distinctive structure of government was in place for some years before the revolt of the Alpujarras (1499) inclined the crown towards the removal of the Muslim population, and the imposition of more typically Castilian norms.[40] In most other wars, conquering parties protected the bulk of the liberties, customs and integrity of the territories they acquired, as the English did in Normandy (1419–49) and, more surprisingly, perhaps, in the kingdom of France (1420–36), or as Matthias Corvinus did with his conquests in Bohemia and Austria. Where conquests endured, subject territories were gradually absorbed, it is true, especially when they were much smaller than the conquering power: the duchy of Guyenne may have retained a high court after 1453, for example – may even have been recreated as an *apanage* for Charles of France between 1469 and 1472 – but its political and tenurial geography was changed, its independence greatly reduced, and its ties with the rest of France significantly increased. Equally, it was quite common for towns to lose their subject territories and/or many of their political rights when they were conquered, though the Venetians, and to a lesser extent the Florentines and Burgundians, saw benefits in preserving these, and so did the kings of England and France, at least in the short term. But if the smaller polities of Europe were vulnerable to incorporation, the larger ones were not, and this too reinforced the solidification of authority at the regnal level. The Treaty of Troyes, by which the Plantagenet crown finally secured the succession to the crown of France, is a prime example: Henry V was bound to preserve the integrity of the French kingdom and to rule France according to its established laws and customs. This he and his successors largely did, to the detriment of their relations with the dukes of Burgundy and Brittany (although Normandy remained a rather special case). Since the English Parliament extracted a concession that the affairs of England should never be subject to the king's new crown of France, and used this to withhold taxes for most of the 1420s, it is clear that Henry V's conquest did little to erase the distinctness of the two polities: it

---

[40] A similar case could be made for the Polish conquest of 'Royal Prussia'. The liberties of the territory were supposed to be preserved in the treaty of 1466, but, in practice, the lesser nobles were subjugated and the territory regranted to Polish warlords, who ruled in association with the larger towns.

disturbed the affairs of both kingdoms, and certainly affected the balance of monarchy and 'princely polyarchy' in France, but it did not create a merger, a true 'dual monarchy'.[41] Moreover, the Hundred Years War in the fifteenth century was much more clearly a war of English and French than it had been in the fourteenth, notwithstanding the substantial involvement of Burgundians, Bretons and especially Gascons on either side. This national dimension was a further sign of the times: no doubt wars had always involved the casting of opponents as aliens, but the wars of the fifteenth century were typically accompanied by more elaborate and substantial outpourings of nationalistic apologetic; they were presented as wars of peoples and nations as much as wars of princes, and it is not surprising that the century has commonly been seen in terms of 'shaping the nation' or as witnessing the 'birth of the nation'.[42]

The resistant qualities of Europe's emerging polities are even more noticeable in the dynastic context. The great international dynasties of the fifteenth century – the Jagiellonians, the Habsburgs, the Luxemburgs, the Valois, the Trastámaras and the house of Pomerania – ruled over loose conglomerates of self-governing territories, with only a limited capacity to transfer resources from one of their domains to another. While their informal influence could be considerable, and most of these rulers brought networks of foreign allies to help them govern their dynastic (or sometimes electoral) acquisitions, their formal powers were usually tightly circumscribed, and, by and large, they either ruled in dialogue with nationalistic estates and their representatives or faced conflicts with leading subjects who stood up for the liberties of the realm, crown or nation. Only in the Low Countries was a real and lasting union forged out of disparate territories – the Spain of Ferdinand and Isabella was no more than a federation of distinct and independent states, and so it remained under their Habsburg successors – but it has been argued that the cities and provinces of the Netherlands were moving together before the Burgundian period, and for a variety of economic and political reasons

---

[41] For 'princely polyarchy', see B. Chevalier, 'The Recovery of France, 1450–1520', *NCMH* VII, ch. 19(b). 'Dual monarchy' is the common term for the joint kingship of England and France, established in 1420.

[42] G. L. Harriss, *Shaping the Nation: England, c.1360–1461* (Oxford, 2005); C. Beaune, *Naissance de la nation France* (Paris, 1985). The English translation of the latter work, by S. R. Huston and F. L. Cheyette, is entitled *The Birth of an Ideology* (Berkeley, 1991).

which drove the dynastic agenda more than they arose from it. Meanwhile, dynastic partitions were also increasingly resisted. This had long been the case in kingdoms, but, as we have seen, the subdivision of German *Länder* was also being challenged and restricted by their estates. It is important to recognise that groups of knights, towns and churchmen could not effectively prevent great princes from subdividing both landed assets and territorial jurisdiction, but they could often regulate these practices, or smooth over the resulting difficulties.

If international politics tended to develop and affirm the regnal polity, so – not surprisingly – did the politics of realms themselves. As we have noted, the adequacy of central government was usually the issue on which the politics of fifteenth-century kingdoms, principalities and city states turned, and this politics was typically played out in ways that linked that government to the inhabitants of each realm. In part, this was a matter of discourse and debate. We have seen that, by now, politics took place in societies with a well-developed public life, and appeals to publicly accepted principle were both commonplace and effective in building alliances between representatives of all kinds and their constituencies. The content of these appeals emphasised the interdependence of the regnal government and the various interests and social groups under its sway. In most cases, they took the right of the king or prince or city to rule every part of its domain for granted and concentrated on the delinquent way in which the task of rule was being carried out. Typically, as we have noted, complaints focused on the wastage of the fisc or on the iniquity of the ruler's councillors. While the solutions to these problems could damage the individual ruler – breaking up the informal networks around him, threatening his customary freedoms – they did not damage the claims of central authority: on the contrary, they advanced them. Whatever the private or sectional interests of fifteenth-century politicians, and these were various, the fact that they often presented a public case, focusing on the faults of government and the needs of the *res publica*, or *bien public*, or *chose publicque*, or common weal, or *cosa pública*, or the good of the crown, or land, or commune and people, or city or Empire, must have reinforced the priority of the realm in the political imagination of subjects.

These linkages between central government, the health of the realm, and the interests of individuals and sections were not only imaginary or discursive, however, they were also made real in political practice, especially in kingdoms. A lot of fifteenth-century political activity was representative in nature, and representative initiatives typically had far-reaching effects, linking the ruler and his agents with the affairs of the localities. Representative assemblies often entailed elections; they meant the participation of elites, the production of petitions by collectivities, the circulation of news; they were typically followed by the publication of statutes, the levying of taxes and, more infrequently, the introduction of governmental novelties, such as new officers, new regulations, new inquiries or commissions and so on. More informal kinds of representation and collective action – popular uprisings, the raising of a retinue or an army, the circulation of manifestoes – were even more involving, whether one wished to join in, on either side, or not. While historians have tended to treat popular, municipal and aristocratic politics separately, it is immediately clear from most of the political confrontations of the fifteenth century that they were interwoven: partly because of the increased penetration of central power, the iniquities and shortcomings of government were the concern of almost everybody. Equally, local politics was increasingly likely to involve some kind of central intervention, and while royal officers were able to take action partly on the basis of private power and local influence, their connection to the centre was always a significant factor: it would shape the ways they operated and indicate how they might be countered; it could determine their allies and influence their chances of success. The fifteenth-century practice of politics thus typically affirmed the connections that were supposed to exist between government and people.

Meanwhile, both the experience and the dynamics of national political confrontation tended to strengthen the reliance of subjects on the centre – again, especially in kingdoms. Confrontations generated disorder, and provoked calls for better justice; they threatened division and anarchy, and thus created support for the enhancement of central resources or central authority. In most kingdoms, the outcome of civil wars, or even lesser political convulsions, was the strengthening of royal authority, even if that authority was also often regularised and/or shared with representative estates. It is less easy to find the same dynamic in principalities, if only because these were less likely to survive internal political convulsions – at least where there was any alternative authority – but the role of the estates of Saxony in trying to prevent, contain and then settle the war between contending heirs to the duchy in the 1440s and 1450s provides one example, and the support given by the estates of the Palatinate to Elector Frederick I provides another. In some kingdoms, notably Sweden, but also, to a lesser extent or at some times, Bohemia, Poland, Denmark and the Empire, internal discord followed a different pattern: in these polities, princes, lords and other smaller powers and collectivities – such as towns, or districts like the *kraje* or the *things* – were not consistently willing to accept the authority of regnal institutions, whether these represented estates or kings. As we have seen, this invites qualification of the traditional view that these polities possessed 'dualistic' systems, in which royal structures were counterbalanced by others representing the estates: while these frameworks certainly existed at a formal level, the binding power of either was limited, and, in most of these countries, kings proved quite adept at drawing their semi-independent subjects around them. At the same time, this kind of resistance also invites some qualification of this chapter's emphasis on consolidation and co-ordination: while the inhabitants of all these kingdoms recognised the link between the regnal structure and the defence of their liberties, and were consequently willing to fight foreign enemies, or to work together for various common purposes, their acceptance of central government might be very limited. Even so, most of these kingdoms were considerably more cohesive than they had been in the thirteenth century, and those that were not – Bohemia, perhaps? Denmark? – were much more governmentally sophisticated.

If we turn, finally, towards the politics of smaller units, we find that these were developing in ways that assisted their integration into the larger kingdoms and principalities around them. Sometimes, this was the result of positive engagement. Broadly speaking, as we have seen, regnal media of representation expanded during the period, especially if informal dialogues – such as those between the French crown and the *bonnes villes*, or between many other rulers and the aristocrats, clergy and leading merchants associated with their courts – are included. But even formal representative institutions expanded their reach in some parts of the continent. Imperial cities began to attend the *Reichstage* from the 1470s, for example, and this may explain why there are fewer town leagues later in the century; in Hungary, Poland and Bohemia, lesser nobles and leading towns achieved fairly regular representation in diets and *sejmiki* for the first time in the fifteenth century. As rulers strengthened their jurisdictions, fostered trade and/ or provided means of common agreement, dialogue with them offered better ways of realising the interests of towns and lesser lords than older techniques such as feuding, leaguing, making bilateral treaties and/or retreating behind the walls. As consultation and representation became more frequent and regular, moreover, smaller units became habituated to their routines, and their leading figures were more likely to find places in royal networks of office or patronage. Meanwhile, attempts to go it alone were more likely to run into problems in this period, as we have seen. Towns which tried to uphold their independence were more likely to face prolonged wars with princes who, particularly in the later part of the century, were better able to break down their resistance: the fates of Mainz in 1462, or Liège in 1468, are well known, but these were not unique examples. A Venice, a Florence or a Nuremberg may have been able to survive, but two of these three cities lay at the centre of sizeable states, and the third had powerful allies and supporters. Even cities as rich and powerful as Milan or Genoa were conquered in this period, the latter (by agreement) several times: small wonder that most of them threw in their lot with nearby kings or princes.

In a similar way, most princes, magnates and lords were either drawn or driven into compliance with the regnal structures around them. This was less the case in Italy and the German lands, of course – though it is telling that both of these regions witnessed more central co-ordination, via the Italian League and the various initiatives of imperial reform, than they had done – but it was marked in France, Scotland and England, and noticeable in Denmark, Hungary and Poland. Influence over churches, connections with towns and lesser nobles, spreading networks of patronage, office and jurisdiction, all enabled kings to interfere in principalities and lordships, ever more consistently and even in remote parts of their realms. This, in turn, complicated the allegiances of princely subjects. When princes and magnates stood up to the king, therefore, they often found that satellite towns and lords – sometimes their own councillors and retainers – refused to support them. They increasingly found it necessary to negotiate their interests in alliance with other magnates, and frequently with other political groups, but, as French princes and English magnates found, these were not propitious circumstances in which to defend their personal or sectional claims: sooner or later, the crown was likely to win the argument that its own superior authority was the best guarantee of the common good and the peace of the realm, and that disorderly magnates, holding great chunks of the fisc, were part of the problem, not the solution.

Finally, the internal development of subordinate principalities and towns tended to assist co-ordination at the regnal level. In part, it did so negatively: excessive bureaucratic or jurisdictional assertion on the part of princes provoked conflicts with superiors and underlings in which, as we have seen, the crown was likely to be the winner. In a similar way, the trend towards more oligarchical government in fifteenth-century cities, which made perfect sense in the light of their increasing governmental responsibilities, often provoked reaction from the members of guilds and councils whose status was downgraded, and this, in turn, provoked royal intervention, as at Freiburg under Emperor Maximilian, or, in a sense, at Bruges and Ghent under Philip the Good. On the other hand, these developments could make a positive contribution to the consolidation of regnal polities. As the French crown took over the '*états princiers*', for instance, it acquired administratively developed provinces used to working together around regional centres: if this made for a cellular, rather than unitary, basis for the French state, it certainly helped with the process of absorption. Meanwhile, the rise of narrower oligarchies in urban governments seems to have marched in step with the forging of more consistent and meaningful relationships between urban leaders and the courts and councils of kings and princes. All in all, regimes that in the thirteenth- and even the fourteenth-century world would have found themselves frequently at odds, were increasingly finding their places in a roughly ordered hierarchy. There was, of course, no end to the confrontation of local and national interests, or of provincial and municipal privilege and national demands, but these were at least recognised to form part of a common politics. The great growth in later medieval government and the simultaneous advance of political life combined, at length, to produce more co-ordinated and complex polities by the end of our period.

5

CONCLUSION

·

The main argument of this book has been that a meaningful, and positive, trajectory can be detected in the complex and often turbulent politics of fourteenth- and fifteenth-century Europe. It is a trajectory which stretches across the whole period and across the whole continent, and it takes the form of a continuous process of governmental and political growth. It was full of conflict, because neither the growth of institutions nor the advancement of political culture produces order in itself, but these later medieval conflicts should not necessarily be seen in a negative light: they themselves contributed to the political and governmental outcomes of the period, and should be seen in the same rational light as the other convulsions and confrontations that mark the great pathways of historical development.

The book has also argued for a particular way of understanding politics – as a phenomenon dominated by structures more than by individuals or collective solidarities, whether the latter are nations (as they often are in the historiography of this period), or estates, or classes. This is not to say that individuals were unimportant, nor to insist that solidarities never existed, but simply to recognise that the options, identities and actions of these familiar groups of political actors were deeply and obviously conditioned by the prevailing institutional, ideological, discursive and communicatory frameworks of their time. Over time, as will now be clear, the prevailing structures changed. The period between *c.*1200 and *c.*1350 was particularly dominated by notions and techniques of jurisdiction, afforced by the development of governmental literacy, the keeping of records and the making of laws. In this fertile period, many of the struggles of the later middle ages were born, because these developments enabled a wide range of powers to claim certain kinds of autonomy and authority for themselves, and to legitimise their actions with reference to shared legal and political theory. From the later thirteenth century and during the fourteenth century, meanwhile, both the range of governmental activities and the media of communication expanded, so that the exercise of authority acquired a less purely juridical character and discourses of good governance were more widely spread within society. So it was that, against a background of jurisdictional conflict, enlarged and complicated by the new intrusions and resources of governments, protests over the quality of rule became a prominent feature of politics, as smaller powers that had accepted a measure of subordination to larger ones acted to protect their interests, both sectional and common. This kind of domestic political conflict, prominent between about the mid-fourteenth and mid-fifteenth centuries, could have an integrative effect in polities like kingdoms, which were becoming less vulnerable to jurisdictional challenge, but for the Church, and for some principalities and city states, it could be devastating, as protesters decided they were better off with other sources of authority. Even so, by the fifteenth century, the rights asserted by governments were becoming more familiar, and more effective mechanisms of consultation and delegation had grown up to make them acceptable. The regnal paradigm had gained ground against other forms and levels of association, and in many places, frameworks of authority, power and allegiance came more closely into alignment. By the end of the century, a sense of the constitution, an interest in the wellbeing of the political order (*res publica*) as well as that of the people (*bonum commune*), and an expectation of 'policy' on the part of rulers and their expert councillors prevailed across much of Europe; domestic discords became more manageable, and the differentiation between war and civil disturbance became sharper. Over time, therefore, the interactions of government, community and ideology – or rather of the people who deployed these various structures – produced a distinctive pattern of developing conflict and developing resolution.

In emphasising the political achievement of the later middle ages, it is important not to overstate it, nor to imply that some sort of end point had been reached in 1500. The polities of the later fifteenth century were to face new challenges in the decades that followed, and they continued, of course, to develop and change: this book ends when it does not because some sort of completeness had been attained, nor yet because the major dynamics of medieval politics had run their course, but rather because it has to end somewhere, and because one of its main aims has been to reconsider older interpretations of the fourteenth and fifteenth centuries. We must remember that, at the beginning of the sixteenth century, there were still more than 500 separate self-governing political units in Europe: if the twenty or thirty 'regnal polities' had acquired considerable solidity and hegemony, their authority was not complete. It is also clear that these polities varied greatly in size, form and power: while they had various qualities in common, and those have been emphasised in this account in order to illustrate a broad pattern of development, there is no intention to deny their differences. At the same time, it is also clear that some of the more familiar distinctions drawn between different parts of the continent deserve to be questioned. While some eastern and northern kingdoms were less intensively governed than most of their western neighbours, for instance, they were not necessarily less integrated, and they possessed the same kind of constitutional definition and self-consciousness at the end of the period; their semi-electoral kingships were not so very different from that of England in the Wars of the Roses, and the political dynamics of Hungary, say, were similar to those of Castile, or even France, while Poland and the Scandinavian countries have much in common with Scotland. The Empire may have had a kind of uniqueness in being a type of regnal polity that contained a number of other regnal polities within it, and its sheer size continued to make it unusual, but Poland-Lithuania was bigger still, while France and Aragon-Castile were not far behind, and these kingdoms and federations also contained a mixture of semi-autonomous subkingdoms, cities, principalities and networks. No two places were the same, but nor were they as incomparable as an older historiography, centring on nation states, tended to suggest.

One thing this book does have in common with older historiography — that of the nineteenth century, in fact — is an emphasis on politics. Its argument is not that political outcomes arose exclusively from political causes (including political culture and ideology and political and governmental forms and institutions within that definition); nor is it that political causes were always of central importance. Rather, it has aimed to show that, in the words of Fernand Braudel, quoted in the first chapter, 'politics and institutions can themselves contribute to the understanding of politics and institutions'; some of the things we tend to think of as having socioeconomic causes, or as arising from some sort of collapse of collective morality, could have had roots in the development of political and governmental forms.[1] While this may appear to reflect an Anglo-Saxon bias in favour of 'internal' or 'domestic' politics, as against a German emphasis on the politics of war and international relations, it is actually a different kind of argument. The assumption here has been that 'internal' and 'external' politics can only be fully distinguished from each other when sovereign states, or something like them, exist. In most of the period covered by this book, therefore, war is simply a continuum of politics and government, and the same values and technologies that animated the latter animated the former. Of course, the superior military power of the biggest players could dictate the political experience of surrounding territories, but not only is this part and parcel of what has often been considered the internal politics of states – as towns, churches and princes accepted some kind of submission to the more effective kings and emperors of the period – but it is also important to realise that it was only in the later fifteenth century that overwhelming force could be applied widely enough, and for long enough, to trump more political processes of negotiation and accommodation. There was something truly disproportionate about the armies deployed by the Ottomans in south-eastern Europe, or by Spain in Granada, or (to a lesser extent) by France and Spain in Italy, but even in these cases, political avenues remained open and important to many of the powers of the region. The Ottomans, for example, were willing to work with Balkan princes and their networks, or with the privileged governments of trading towns; the small states of Italy and other peninsular networks retained some freedom of action during the wars that followed 1494, not least by playing French, Spanish, papal and imperial interests off against each other. Politics must take its place alongside demography and commerce, warfare and religion, in explaining why things happen, but it fully merits that place – just as it is partly the product of these other things, so it also helps to structure them.

The political life of the later middle ages has been difficult for historians to capture. To a large extent, of course, this is due to the presuppositions that have been brought to its study: the narratives of

---

[1] Above, p. 39.

growth, decline and recovery have a lot to answer for. But it is also the result of other factors. One is the growth (and persisting limitations) of the documentation: besides the inventiveness of devotional and literary writing, and the spread of correspondences, the main yield of the period is a huge multiplication in the formulaic records of government, furnishing copious evidence of crime and disorder and an impression of stagnation, dullness and unmanageability. Another factor is a legacy of the period's long marginalisation from the major foci of western historiography, which favoured the high middle ages, on the one hand, and the era of renaissance and reformation, on the other: this means that the major critical and technical vocabularies were established for the study of these periods and not ours, and that it is correspondingly difficult to express the complicated mixture of overlapping jurisdictions, public–private tensions and interactions, polyvocality and authoritarianism that is so characteristic of the period. A third factor is that it is easier to narrate innovations than it is to characterise their subsequent implementation and evolution: while it is obvious that the fourteenth and fifteenth centuries were years of political and governmental growth, it is also easy to see why this has not been more remarked – the embryonic forms and/or underlying ideas that informed later medieval institutions are already perceptible in the classic sources of the twelfth and thirteenth centuries; small wonder that historians have mostly recoiled from a period which only seemed to show the dreary, or muddled, or violent realisation and contestation of what had once (on the drawing boards of Rome, Paris and Bologna) looked clear and inspired.

But it should be clear by now not only that the period has its own political logic, that the actions of its inhabitants were as rational as those in other times, but that it has things to teach us about the nature of political life. One important lesson is that the ideas and tools of governments and other cultural centres are quickly picked up and deployed by subjects and neighbours and used creatively in pursuit of their own interests. Government thus produces resistance and subversion, even as it accumulates power and provides benefits; it advances subaltern groups of all kinds as well as its own agents; and the results of governmental growth are complex and diverse, rather than simple and orderly. A second lesson is that political integration or coordination arises from below, as well as from above: it cannot be imposed by authorities, however powerful; it is always the product of some kind of negotiation between interest groups, including the various governments with a stake in each territory. This reminds us that subject groups have a certain interest in working with one another and with those that claim to rule them, even if they also have an interest in maintaining media of resistance, advice and consent. It also means that what can appear to be erosions or enhancements of central power are really elements in a more complex pattern of negotiation, in which the limitation, restructuring and even the extension of government might be driven from anywhere and everywhere in political society. The polities that emerged from the fourteenth and fifteenth centuries had stronger centres, more complex administrations and clearer boundaries, but they had all these things because of pressure from below as well as design from above, and because of processes of conflict as well as the exercise of authority. The politics of later medieval Europe were the products of rapid governmental and cultural expansion in a society which may well have been contracting physically, but was not at all in crisis; this was an age of 'growth', of 'making', just as much as any other in human history.

BIBLIOGRAPHICAL NOTES

———————— • ————————

These bibliographical notes are mainly intended to enable English-language readers to follow up points made in the text. They are arranged chapter by chapter, excluding Chapter 1, because it already contains a fully footnoted discussion of the more general literature on later medieval Europe. The final section features some of the foreign-language works which I have found most useful: it is intended less as guidance to the reader than as proper acknowledgement of my scholarly debts.

2 EUROPE IN 1300: THE POLITICAL INHERITANCE

General

The obvious starting point for thirteenth-century European history is *The New Cambridge Medieval History* (henceforth *NCMH*) V, c.*1198–c.1300*, ed. D. Abulafia (Cambridge, 1999): like other volumes in this series, it contains a mixture of thematic essays and country-by-country surveys, as well as extensive bibliographies of primary and secondary sources. Major interpretative works throwing light on the forms and workings of power and government in the thirteenth century include S. Reynolds, *Kingdoms and Communities in Western Europe, c.900–1300*, 2nd edn (Oxford, 1997) and also her 'Medieval *origines gentium* and the Community of the Realm', *History*, 68 (1983), 375–90; R. Bartlett, *The Making of Europe: Conquest, Colonization and Cultural Change, 950–1350* (London, 1993); R.R. Davies, *Domination and Conquest: The Experience of Ireland, Scotland and Wales, 1100–1300* (Cambridge, 1990); R.I. Moore, *The Formation of a Persecuting Society* (Oxford, 1987); J. Heers, *Parties and Political Life in the Medieval West*, trans. D. Nicholas

(Amsterdam, 1977); B. Weiler, 'Politics', in D. Power, ed., *The Central Middle Ages* (Oxford, 2006), ch. 3.

The Papacy and the Church

Perhaps the most useful general treatments of the politics of the Papacy and universal Church are R.W. Southern, *Western Society and the Church in the Middle Ages* (London, 1970), F. Oakley, *The Western Church in the Later Middle Ages* (Ithaca, NY, 1979) and C. Morris, *The Papal Monarchy: The Western Church from 1050 to 1250* (Oxford, 1989); but W. Ullmann, *A Short History of the Papacy in the Middle Ages* (London, 1972; reissued with introduction by G. Garnett, 2003) remains valuable and thought-provoking, while B. Tierney, *The Crisis of Church and State 1050–1300* (Toronto, 1988) prints many of the documents in which papal and imperial theories were hammered out. A. Padoa-Schioppa, 'Hierarchy and Jurisdiction: Models in Medieval Canon Law', in Padoa-Schioppa, ed., *Legislation and Justice*, European Science Foundation, Origins of the Modern State in Europe series (Oxford, 1997), ch. 1, is an excellent, short account of the rise of papal jurisdiction, while G. Barraclough, *Papal Provisions* (Oxford, 1935) remains indispensable for that subject, and B. Tierney, *Foundations of the Conciliar Theory*, rev. edn (Leiden, 1998) discusses some of the strands of resistance to papal supremacy. J. Sayers, *Innocent III* (Harlow, 1994), T.S.R. Boase, *Boniface VIII* (London, 1933), J.A. Watt, 'The Papacy', *NCMH* V, ch. 5, N. Housley, *The Italian Crusades* (Oxford, 1982) and J. Dunbabin, *Charles I of Anjou* (Harlow, 1998) provide especially helpful accounts of papal policy and of the major pontificates of the century. J. Riley-Smith, *The Crusades: A Short History* (London, 1987) offers a wide-ranging introduction to the crusades, including taxation and the military orders.

The Holy Roman Empire

A helpful introduction to the idea of the Empire appears in B. Arnold, *Medieval Germany, 500–1300: A Political Interpretation* (Basingstoke, 1997), pt II; but see also R.L. Benson, 'Political *Renovatio*: Two Models from Roman Authority' in Benson and G. Constable, eds., *Renaissance and Renewal in the Twelfth Century* (Oxford, 1982), 339–86 and L.E. Scales, '*Germen Militiae*: War and German Identity in the Later Middle Ages', *Past and Present*, 180 (Aug. 2003), 41–82. D. Abulafia, *Frederick II: A Medieval Emperor* (Oxford, 1988) is particularly helpful for the Italian dimension of the thirteenth-century Empire, though there is useful material in the papal section above and also in J. Larner, *Italy in the Age of Dante and Petrarch, 1216–1380* (London, 1980), chs. 2–3. On the Empire in

Germany, T. Reuter, 'The Medieval German *Sonderweg*? The Empire and its Rulers in the High Middle Ages', in A. Duggan, ed., *Kings and Kingship in Medieval Europe* (London, 1993), 179–211, is inspirational, while B. Arnold, *Princes and Territories in Medieval Germany* (Cambridge, 1991) gives a real sense of the texture of power. M. Toch provides a very good introduction to political life in the German lands in 'Welfs, Hohenstaufen and Habsburgs', *NCMH* V, ch. 14(a), and J. Gillingham, 'Elective Kingship and the Unity of Medieval Germany', *German History*, 9 (1991), 124–35 sounds an important revisionist note. Otto Brunner's foundational work, *Land and Lordship: Structures of Governance in Medieval Austria*, ed. and trans. H. Kaminsky and J. van Horn Melton from the 1965 edn (Philadelphia, 1992) remains extremely valuable and thought-provoking (and see B. Arnold, 'Structures of Medieval Governance and the Thought-World of Otto Brunner (1898–1982)', *Reading Medieval Studies*, 20 (1994), 3–12, for a critique).

Kingdoms, lords and principalities

Apart from the general treatments listed above, many of the main sources for this discussion are the same as those for Chapter 3, below. Besides those, I found the following works especially helpful on individual kingdoms and principalities prior to 1300: J. Dunbabin, *France in the Making, 843–1180*, 2nd edn (Oxford, 2000); E.A.R. Brown, *Politics and Institutions in Capetian France* (Aldershot, 1991); J.R. Strayer, *The Reign of Philip the Fair* (Princeton, 1980); and J.F. Benton and T.N. Bisson, eds., *Medieval Statecraft and the Perspectives of History* (Princeton, 1971); R. Bartlett, 'The Impact of Royal Government in the French Ardennes: The Evidence of the 1247 *Enquête*', *Journal of Medieval History*, 7 (1981), 83–96; Abulafia, *Frederick II*; Dunbabin, *Charles of Anjou* (Sicily); J.C. Holt, *Magna Carta*, 2nd edn (Cambridge, 1992); G.L. Harriss, *King, Parliament and Public Finance in England to 1369* (Oxford, 1975); R.R. Davies, *The First English Empire* (Oxford, 2000); P. Freedman, *The Origins of Peasant Servitude in Medieval Catalonia* (Cambridge, 1991); S. Barton, *The Aristocracy in Twelfth-Century León and Castile* (Cambridge, 1997); J.F. O'Callaghan, *The Learned King. The Reign of Alfonso X of Castile* (Philadelphia, 1993); L. Wolverton, *Hastening Towards Prague. Power and Society in the Medieval Czech Lands* (Philadelphia, 2001); K. Krofta, 'Bohemia to the Extinction of the Přemyslids', *Cambridge Medieval History* (henceforth *CMH*) VI, ed. J.R. Tanner, C.W. Prévité-Orton and Z.N. Brooke (Cambridge, 1929), ch. 13; P. Gorecki, *Economy, Society and Lordship in Medieval Poland, 1100–1250* (New York, 1992); G. Tabacco, *The Struggle for Power in Medieval Italy* (Cambridge, 1989).

On the impact of learned law and governmental literacy, M.T. Clanchy, *From Memory to Written Record*, 2nd edn (Oxford, 1993) remains fundamental, but see also his 'Remembering the Past and the Good Old Law', *History*, 55 (1970), 165–76. The best short introduction to Roman law is P. Stein, *Roman Law in European History* (Cambridge, 1999), and to canon law, J. Brundage, *Medieval Canon Law* (Harlow, 1995), while M. Bellomo, *The Common Legal Past of Europe, 1000–1800*, trans. L.G. Cochrane (Washington DC, 1995), B. Tierney, *Religion, Law and the Growth of Constitutional Thought, 1150–1650* (Cambridge, 1982) and M. Ryan, 'Rulers and Justice, 1200–1500', in P. Linehan and J. Nelson, eds., *The Medieval World* (London, 2001), ch. 29, are useful for their spread and applications. A. Harding, *Medieval Law and the Foundations of the State* (Oxford, 2002) is informative and thought-provoking.

Communes and leagues

Reynolds, *Kingdoms and Communities*, ch. 6, offers an excellent introduction to municipal politics and government, while D. Nicholas, *The Growth of the Medieval City* (Harlow, 1997) provides a wealth of examples, and Heers, *Parties and Political Life* provides an incomparable portrait of urban political life. Some of the best work on the early history of communes focuses on Italy, and I found E. Coleman, 'Cities and Communes', in D. Abulafia, ed., *Italy in the Central Middle Ages* (Oxford, 2004), ch. 1, Tabacco, *Struggle for Power* and P. Jones' massive volume on *The Italian City State* (Oxford, 1997) particularly helpful. For other countries, the following were among the most useful: S. Reynolds, *Introduction to Medieval English Towns* (Oxford, 1977); Dunbabin, *France*, ch. 11(b); P. Dollinger, *The German Hansa* (London, 1970); S. Bensch, *Barcelona and its Rulers, 1096–1291* (Cambridge, 1995); T.F. Ruiz, 'The Transformation of the Castilian Municipalities: Burgos, 1248–1350', *Past and Present*, 77 (Nov. 1977), 3–32; D. Nicholas, *Medieval Flanders* (London, 1992); R.A. Rotz, 'German Towns', in J.R. Strayer *et al.*, eds., *The Dictionary of the Middle Ages* (New York, 1985), vol. V, 457–71. Besides some brief comment in Heers, *Parties and Political Life*, there seems to be little comparative work on leagues, but *Landfrieden* and other German unions are quite well covered in Arnold, *Princes and Territories*, while A. Mackay, *Spain in the Middle Ages* (London, 1977) has a few things to say about *hermandades*.

Ideas and discourses

Among the major works on this subject, J. Canning, *A History of Medieval Political Thought, 300–1450*, 2nd edn (London, 2005) is a short, clear guide, especially good for the ideas of jurists and canonists, though it is thin on the fifteenth century; J.B. Morrall, *Political Thought in Medieval Times* (London, 1958) is wonderfully lucid and suggestive, and especially good for thirteenth-century theology; A.J. Black, *Political Thought in Europe, 1250–1450* (Cambridge, 1992) is another fairly short treatment and impressively wide-ranging; *The Cambridge History of Medieval Political Thought, c.350–c.1450*, ed. J.H. Burns (Cambridge, 1988) is encyclopaedic and authoritative, with notably good essays by Canning (on law, and on twelfth- to thirteenth-century thought in general), Watt (on spiritual and temporal powers) and Dunbabin (on government).

As far as particular themes are concerned, many theological and juristic ideas are explored in the sources listed above under 'The Papacy and the Church' and 'Kingdoms, laws and principalities', but see also Magnus Ryan's Carlyle Lectures, given at Oxford in 2004 under the title, 'The legal framework of political thinking 1150–1600', and soon to be published; M. Lambert, *Medieval Heresy*, 2nd edn (Oxford, 1992); R.W. Southern, 'The Changing Role of Universities in Medieval Europe', *Historical Research*, 60 (1987), 133–46; H.A. Oberman, 'Fourteenth-Century Religious Thought: A Premature Profile', *Speculum*, 53 (1978), 80–93; R.E. Lerner, 'Medieval Prophecy and Religious Dissent', *Past and Present*, 72 (Aug. 1976), 3–24; and S. Ozment, 'Mysticism, Nominalism and Dissent', in C. Trinkaus and H.A. Oberman, eds., *The Pursuit of Holiness in Late Medieval and Renaissance Religion* (Leiden, 1974), 67–92. M.S. Kempshall, *The Common Good in Late Medieval Political Thought* (Oxford, 1999) explores the handling of Aristotle and Augustine in the scholastic thought of *c.*1250–*c.*1320 through the lens of this central concept; M. Viroli, *From Politics to Reason of State* (Cambridge, 1992) contains a very useful survey of discussion of the virtues and of notions of politics across the middle ages. For medieval national identity, I found the ideas of Susan Reynolds particularly useful, notably in her 'Medieval *origines gentium*' and *Kingdoms and Communities*, and also those of Rees Davies, perhaps especially his presidential lectures, in *Transactions of the Royal Historical Society* (henceforth *TRHS*), 6th series, 4–7 (1994–7); but see also A. Smith, *National Identity* (Harmonsworth, 1991), chs. 1–3; J.R. Llobera, *The God of Modernity* (Oxford, 1994), pt 1 and L. Scales and O. Zimmer, eds., *Power and the Nation in European History* (Cambridge, 2005). The major introduction to orders and estates is G. Duby, *The Three Orders*, trans. A. Goldhammer (Chicago, 1980), but see also J.H. Denton, ed., *Orders and Hierarchies in Late Medieval and Renaissance Europe* (Basingstoke, 1999). For chivalry, the best way in remains M. Keen, *Chivalry* (New Haven, CT 1984). N. Cohn's brilliant book, *Europe's Inner Demons*, rev. edn (London, 1993) provides insights on fears of conspiracy, though it doesn't explain their flowering in the decades around 1300; for that, see Moore, *Formation of a Persecuting Society*, D. Nirenberg, *Communities of Violence* (Princeton, 1996) and M. Barber, *The Trial of the Templars* (Cambridge, 1978), esp. ch. 7. Miri Rubin's essay, 'Europe Remade: Purity and Danger in Late Medieval Europe', *TRHS*, 6th series, 11 (2001), 101–24, highlights the wide range of divergent voices and sources of spiritual and intellectual authority in later medieval Europe: it is an inspiration for my understanding of the overall cultural and political atmosphere.

For some of the more important thinkers of the period and their works, see A.P. D'Entrèves, *Aquinas: Selected Political Writings*, trans. J.G. Dawson (Oxford, 1959); C.F. Briggs, *Giles of Rome's* De Regimine Principum (Cambridge, 1999); Ptolemy of Lucca, *On the Government of Rulers/* De Regimine Principum, ed. and trans. J.M. Blythe (Philadelphia, 1997); Marsilius of Padua, *The Defender of the Peace*, ed. and trans. A.S. Brett (Cambridge, 2005); G. Garnett, *Marsilius of Padua and 'the Truth of History'* (Oxford, 2006); C. Fasolt, *Council and Hierarchy* (Cambridge, 1991) (on William Durand); Dante, *Monarchy*, ed. and trans. P. Shaw (Cambridge, 1996); Vegetius, *Epitome of Military Science*, ed. and trans. N.P. Milner, 2nd edn (Liverpool, 1996); C. Allmand, 'The *De re Militari* in the Middle Ages and the Renaissance', in C. Saunders *et al.*, eds., *Writing War* (Cambridge 2004); and S. Bagge, *The Political Thought of the King's Mirror* (Odense, 1987).

Communication

Most of my perceptions and illustrations of the nature of communication in the period are drawn from useful essays in *NCMH* V and VI or from works cited in the section above; but some works I found especially helpful were D. D'Avray, *The Preaching of the Friars* (Oxford, 1985); J. Coleman, 'Some Relations Between the Study of Aristotle's Rhetoric, Ethics and Politics in Late Thirteenth- and Early Fourteenth-Century University Arts Courses and the Justification of Contemporary Civic Activities', in J. Canning and O.G. Oexle, eds., *Political Thought and the Realities of Power in the Middle Ages* (Göttingen, 1998), 127–57; C.F. Briggs, 'Teaching Philosophy at School and Court', in F. Somerset and N. Watson, eds., *The Vulgar Tongue: Medieval and Post-Medieval Vernacularity* (Philadelphia, 2003), 99–111; and 'Literacy, Reading and Writing in the Medieval West', *Journal of Medieval History*, 26 (2000), 397–420.

Networks

Central to my understanding of networks has been the work of three historians: C. Carpenter, especially *Locality and Polity: A Study of*

Warwickshire Landed Society, 1401–1499 (Cambridge, 1992) and 'Gentry and Community in Medieval England', *Journal of British Studies*, 33 (1994), 340–80; J. Heers, *Parties and Political Life* and *Family Clans in the Middle Ages*, trans. B. Herbert (Amsterdam, 1977); and P. S. Lewis, *Later Medieval France: The Polity* (London, 1968), in his *Essays in Later Medieval French History* (London, 1985), and more recently in 'Reflections on the Role of Royal Clientèles in the Construction of the French Monarchy', in N. Bulst, ed., *L'État ou le roi* (Paris, 1996), 51–67. Many of the examples are taken from works cited in the politics sections below.

3 THE FOURTEENTH CENTURY

Besides the essays in *NCMH* V and VI, and other overview works listed above, I drew my material for this chapter and the next from a mixture of works on the political and constitutional history of individual territories and more general and comparative treatments of institutional or constitutional, ideological and cultural developments.

Individual states, regions, countries

For the Papacy in the fourteenth century, several older works remain very useful, in particular, B. Smalley, 'Church and State, 1300–77: Theory and Fact', in J. Hale, R. Highfield and B. Smalley, eds., *Europe in the Late Middle Ages* (London, 1965), ch. 1; G. Mollat, *The Popes at Avignon, 1305–1378*, trans. J. Love (London, 1949); and Y. Renouard, *The Avignon Papacy*, trans. D. L. T. Bethell (London, 1970); P. Zutshi, 'The Avignon Papacy', *NCMH* VI, ch. 19, gives a neat picture of today's understanding. Among individual popes, Boniface VIII is well covered by Boase, while D. Wood, *Clement VI* (Cambridge, 1989) provides a valuable treatment of one of the worldlier Avignon popes; there is no modern full-length treatment of the important reign of John XXII in English, which is a pity. For the Schism, W. Ullmann, *The Origins of the Great Schism* (London, 1948) provides an essential starting point, while, among other treatments, H. Kaminksy's essay, 'The Great Schism', *NCMH* VI, ed. Michael Jones (Cambridge, 2000), ch. 20, offers a recent and lively overview.

The politics of northern Italy in the period are hard to grasp as a whole, though J. Law, 'The Italian North' and L. Green, 'Florence and the Republican Tradition', in *NCMH* VI, chs. 15(a) and (b), are helpful, as is Larner, *Italy in the Age of Dante*, and, for the role of the Papacy in particular, S. Dale, '*Contra damnationis filios*: The Visconti in Fourteenth-Century Papal Diplomacy', *Journal of Medieval History*, 33 (2007), 1–32. For the south,

D. Abulafia, *The Western Mediterranean Kingdoms, 1200–1500* (Harlow, 1997) provides a valuable contextualised treatment. J.M. Najemy, ed., *Italy in the Age of the Renaissance* (Oxford, 2004) offers an up-to-date introduction to fourteenth- and fifteenth-century Italy, though its thematic arrangement means that it is more useful for structures and patterns than political dynamics. Among the many monographic studies of Italian states, I found the following particularly useful: T. Dean, *Land and Power in Late Medieval Ferrara* (Cambridge, 1988); G. Brucker, *Florentine Politics and Society, 1343–1378* (Princeton, 1962); W.M. Bowsky, *A Medieval Italian Commune: Siena under the Nine, 1287–1355* (Berkeley, 1981); B.G. Kohl, *Padua under the Carrara, 1318–1405* (Baltimore, 1998); F.C. Lane, *Venice – A Maritime Republic* (Baltimore, 1973); S.A. Epstein, *Genoa and the Genoese* (Chapel Hill, 1996); S. Kelly, *The New Solomon: Robert of Naples (1309–1343) and Fourteenth-Century Kingship* (Leiden, 2003); and, on the Papal States, P. Partner, *The Lands of St Peter* (London, 1972). A meaty new treatment of Florence is J.M. Najemy, *A History of Florence, 1200–1575* (Oxford, 2006). J. Martin and D. Romano, eds., *Venice Reconsidered* (2000) offers insights on the newer historiography of Venice. Milan still awaits a full-length modern treatment in English; good introductions to the Visconti lordship at Milan can be found in Tabacco, *Struggle for Power*, ch. 6, and D. Hay and J. Law, *Italy in the Age of the Renaissance, 1380–1530* (Harlow, 1989), 236–44.

For French political life in the later middle ages, Lewis, *Later Medieval France* is still the most perceptive and interesting overview in English, but D. Potter, ed., *France in the Later Middle Ages* (Oxford, 2002) offers a series of valuable, up-to-date essays on various themes by many of today's leading Anglophone historians of France, and M.C.E. Jones, 'The Last Capetians and Early Valois Kings, 1314–1364', *NCMH* VI, ch. 14(b) is extremely good. For the course of events, E.M. Hallam and J. Everard, *Capetian France, 987–1328*, 2nd edn (Harlow, 2001) is useful, and can be extended via the works of Strayer, cited above, R.W. Kaeuper, *War, Justice and Public Order. England and France in the Late Middle Ages* (Oxford, 1988) and J.H. Henneman, *Royal Taxation in Fourteenth-Century France: The Development of War Financing, 1322–56* (Princeton, 1971) and *Royal Taxation in Fourteenth-Century France: The Captivity and Ransom of John II, 1356–1370* (Philadelphia, 1976). Unfortunately, little of the crucial work of Bernard Guenée, Raymond Cazelles and Françoise Autrand has yet found its way into English (though Autrand's chapter in *NCMH* VI – 'France under Charles V and Charles VI', ch. 14(b) – offers an epitome of her views), but some insights on the texture of French politics in the fourteenth century can be gained from the following works in English: N. Wright, *Knights and Peasants: The Hundred Years War in the French Countryside* (Woodbridge, 1998); C. Small, 'Appeals from the Duchy of Burgundy to the *Parlement* of Paris in the Early Fourteenth Century', *Mediaeval Studies*, 39 (1977), 350–68; J.B. Henneman, 'The Military Class and the French Monarchy in the Late Middle Ages', *American Historical Review*, 83 (1978), 946–65; E.A.R. Brown, 'Reform and Resistance to Royal Authority in Fourteenth-Century France: The Leagues of 1314–1315', in Brown, *Politics and Institutions in Capetian France*; J.B. Henneman, *Olivier de Clisson and Political Society in France under Charles V and Charles VI* (Philadelphia, 1996). For the French regions, see J. Le Patourel, 'The King and the Princes in Fourteenth-Century France', in Hale *et al.*, eds., *Europe in the Late Middle Ages*, ch. 5; M. Jones, 'The Duchy of Brittany in the Middle Ages', in Jones *The Creation of Brittany* (London, 1988), ch. 1; R. Vaughan, *Philip the Bold* (London, 1962, reissued by Boydell, 2002); P. Contamine, 'The Norman "Nation" and the French "Nation" in the Fourteenth and Fifteenth Centuries', in D. Bates and A. Curry, eds., *England and Normandy in the Middle Ages* (London, 1994), ch. 16; G. Bois, *The Crisis of Feudalism. Economy and Society in Eastern Normandy, c. 1300–1550* (Cambridge, 1984); M. Vale, *The Origins of the Hundred Years War* (Aquitaine) (Oxford, 1990); G. Pépin, 'Towards a New Assessment of the Black Prince's Principality of Aquitaine: A Study of the Last Years (1369–1372)', *Nottingham Mediaeval Studies*, 50 (2006), 59–114.

The Hundred Years War is best approached through A. Curry, *The Hundred Years War*, 2nd edn (Basingstoke, 2003) and C.T. Allmand, *The Hundred Years War* (Cambridge, 1989), with some newer insights in the essays of C. Taylor and C.J. Rogers in J.S. Bothwell, ed., *The Age of Edward III* (York, 2001) and also in C.J. Rogers, *War, Cruel and Sharp. English Strategy under Edward III, 1327–1360* (Woodbridge, 2000). For a starting point on the history of England in the fourteenth century, G.L. Harriss, *Shaping the Nation: England, 1360–1461* (Oxford, 2005) is the leading work, and the same author's *King, Parliament and Public Finance in Medieval England to 1369* (Oxford, 1975) has useful material on the earlier part of the century (for which, see also M.C. Prestwich, *Plantagenet England*, Oxford, 2005). For Scotland, M. Brown, *The Wars of Scotland, 1214–1371* (Edinburgh, 2004) supplements and updates A. Grant, *Independence and Nationhood* (Edinburgh, 1984); Grant's essay, 'Fourteenth-century Scotland', in *NCMH* VI, ch. 13(d) is extremely good. For Wales and Ireland, the essays by A.D. Carr and R. Frame in *NCMH* VI, chs. 13(c) and (e), are very useful, while R.R. Davies, *The Age of Conquest: Wales 1063–1415* (Oxford, 1991), R. Frame, *Ireland and Britain, 1170–1450* (London, 1998) and *The Political Development of the British Isles, 1100–1400* (Oxford, 1990), and A. Cosgrove, ed., *A New History of Ireland II: Medieval Ireland, 1169–1534* (Oxford, 1993), take things further.

The Low Countries are fairly thinly covered in English writing for the pre-Burgundian period, though the article by W. Prevenier in *NCMH* VI, ch. 17 is a useful overview. W. Te Brake, *A Plague of Insurrection* (Philadelphia, 1993) ranges more broadly than the Flemish revolt of the 1320s on which it centres; D. Nicholas, *Medieval Flanders* (Harlow, 1992) contains some valuable material; S. Boffa, *Warfare in Medieval Brabant, 1356–1406* (Woodbridge, 2004) surveys Brabantine political organisation as well as warfare; R. Vaughan, *Valois Burgundy* (London, 1975) digests the author's four studies of the Valois dukes, while W. Blockmans and W. Prevenier, *The Promised Lands: The Low Countries under Burgundian Rule, 1369–1530*, trans. E. Fackelman (Philadelphia, 1999) relates state formation to economic and cultural developments. Two wide-ranging essays from the collection *Regions and Landscapes*, ed. P. Ainsworth and T. Scott (Oxford, 2000) throw light on patterns of state formation in the region: G. Croenen, 'Regions, Principalities and Regional Identity in the Low Countries', 139–53 and P. Stabel, 'Urbanisation and its Consequences: The Urban Region in Late Medieval Flanders', 177–203.

The major modern treatment of later medieval Germany, written by Peter Moraw in 1985, has regrettably not been translated into English (see below), though a rough sense of his ideas can be gained from his essay 'Cities and Citizenry as Factors of State Formation in the Roman-German Empire of the Late Middle Ages', in C. Tilly and W.P. Blockmans, eds., *Cities and the Rise of States in Europe, A.D. 1000 to 1800* (Boulder, 1994), while M. Toch, in *NCMH* V, ch. 14(a) gives an up-to-date picture of the thirteenth-century background, and P. Herde and I. Hlavacek, in *NCMH* VI, chs. 16(a) and (b) provide details of events from the 1290s to the 1340s and a breezy interpretation of 1346–1400, respectively. F.R.H. Du Boulay, *Germany in the Later Middle Ages* (London, 1983) remains a useful textbook, though it only gets going at 1350, while H.S. Offler, 'Aspects of Government in the Late Medieval Empire', in Hale *et al.*, eds., *Europe in the Late Middle Ages*, ch. 7, is full of insight, albeit reliant on perspectives in older German literature that are now questioned. J. Leuschner, *Germany in the Late Middle Ages*, trans. S. MacCormack (Amsterdam, 1980), though sketchy and also dated, contains some good insights. On individual emperors, there is not much that is recent and in English, but see W.M. Bowsky, *Henry VII in Italy* (Lincoln, NE, 1960); H.S. Offler, 'The Last Struggle of Empire and Papacy', *Transactions of the Royal Historical Society*, 5th series, 6 (1956), 21–47 (Ludwig); and B. Jarrett, *Emperor Charles IV* (New York, 1935), which contains a translation of the

Emperor's memoir. For the German regions, Brunner, Land *and Lordship*, is a stimulating starting point on Austria and on local politics and state formation generally; J. Bérenger, *A History of the Habsburg Empire, 1273–1700*, trans. C. A. Simpson (London, 1994) is straightforward, but quite useful on the Austrian lands; H. J. Cohn, *The Government of the Rhine Palatinate in the Fifteenth Century* (Oxford, 1965) is very perceptive and has a little on the fourteenth century; F. L. Carsten, *The Origins of Prussia* (Oxford, 1954) has material of value on the north-east; and P. Dollinger, *The German Hansa*, ed. and trans. D. S. Ault and S. H. Steinberg (London, 1970), is an excellent treatment of the Hanseatic League.

The politics of the Iberian kingdoms in the fourteenth century are getting more accessible to the Anglophone reader than those of the Empire. A. Mackay, *Spain in the Middle Ages* (London, 1977) still offers the best overview, but there are also J. N. Hillgarth, *The Spanish Kingdoms, 1250–1516*, 2 vols. (Oxford, 1976–8), T. N. Bisson, *The Medieval Crown of Aragon: A Short History* (Oxford, 1986) and Abulafia, *Western Mediterranean Kingdoms* (again for the crown of Aragon). A new book, T. F. Ruiz, *Spain's Centuries of Crisis: 1300–1474* (Oxford, 2007) takes the 'crisis' approach which I have rejected, but it offers useful brief narratives of each reign in Castile and Aragon. *NCMH* VI is essential, especially P. Linehan's essay on Castile, Navarre and Portugal (ch. 18(b)). C. Estow, *Pedro the Cruel of Castile, 1350–1369* (Leiden, 1995) is extremely helpful for this important reign, and for political society in fourteenth-century Castile more generally. Other useful works for fourteenth-century Spanish politics include: T. F. Ruiz, 'The Transformation of the Castilian Municipalities: Burgos, 1248–1350', *Past and Present*, 77 (Nov. 1977), 3–32; P. Rycraft, 'The Role of the Catalan Corts in the Later Middle Ages', *English Historical Review*, 89 (1974), 241–69 (which anticipates today's historiography in seeing the Catalan count-kings and the *Corts* as partners rather than opponents); D. J. Kagay, 'A Government Besieged by Conflict: The Parliament of Monzón (1362–1363) as Military Financier', in Kagay and L. J. A. Villalon, eds., *The Hundred Years War: A Wider Focus* (Leiden, 2005), 117–50 (offers more on fiscal and representative relations in Aragon-Catalonia); P. Linehan, *History and the Historians of Medieval Spain* (Oxford, 1993) (especially good on the modern historiography, and on Alfonso XI); L. J. A. Villalon, '*Deudo* and the Roots of Feudal Violence in Late Medieval Castile', in P. J. Kagay and Villalon, eds., *The Final Argument. The Impact of Violence on Society in Medieval and Early Modern Europe* (Woodbridge, 1998), 55–72.

For east-central Europe, the historiography is now beginning to expand, though obtaining more detail of political life beyond the very good essays by

S.C. Rowell ('Baltic Europe') and C. Michaud ('The Kingdoms of Central Europe in the Fourteenth Century') in *NCMH* VI, chs. 21–2, is not easy – especially for Bohemia, Poland and the *Ordensstaat*. J.W. Sedlar, *East-Central Europe in the Middle Ages, 1000–1500* (Seattle and London, 1994), offers a decent and reasonably up-to-date overview of the whole region. On Bohemia, M. Teich, ed., *Bohemia in History* (Cambridge, 1998), is quite useful, and also L.E. Scales, 'At the Margins of Community: Germans in pre-Hussite Bohemia', *TRHS*, 6th series, 9 (1999), 327–52; J.M. Klassen, *The Nobility and the Making of the Hussite Revolution* (New York, 1978) gives a good impression of Bohemian political society and governmental structures in the fourteenth century. On Poland, N. Davies, *God's Playground: A History of Poland I. The Origins to 1795* (Oxford, 1981; rev. edn 2005) remains a valuable starting point, but is thin for the fourteenth and fifteenth centuries, while P.W. Knoll, *The Rise of the Polish Monarchy* (Chicago and London, 1972) goes into more detail on 1320–70, but concentrates on foreign affairs rather than domestic politics. O. Halecki, *Jadwiga of Anjou and the Rise of East-Central Europe* (New York, 1991) handles the 1380s and 1390s in a similar way, though the same author's essays in W.F. Reddaway *et al.*, eds., *The Cambridge History of Poland (to 1696)* (Cambridge, 1950) provide helpful insights on domestic politics. The study of Hungarian political developments is greatly aided by two excellent modern books: P. Engel, *The Realm of St Stephen: A History of Medieval Hungary*, trans. T. Pálosfalvi and ed. A. Ayton (London, 2005), and M. Rady, *Nobility, Land and Service in Medieval Hungary* (Basingstoke, 2000). E. Fügedi, 'The Aristocracy in Medieval Hungary. Theses', trans. J.M. Bak, in Fügedi, *Kings, Bishops, Nobles and Burghers in Medieval Hungary* (London, 1986), ch. 4, is also valuable. L. Péter, 'The Holy Crown of Hungary, Visible and Invisible', *Slavonic and East European Review*, 81 (2003), 421–510, usefully challenges traditional views on the idealisation of the crown of the realm (but replaces them with others, not altogether convincingly).

For the rest of Europe, I have relied on a narrow range of sources. *NCMH* VI has been essential: Kollmann on Russia (ch. 23), Laiou on Byzantium (ch. 24) and Kunt on the Ottomans (ch. 26) are particularly good. For northern Europe, K. Helle, ed., *The Cambridge History of Scandinavia, I: Prehistory to 1520* (Cambridge, 2003) is indispensable. For the Balkans, J.V.A. Fine, *The Late Medieval Balkans* (Ann Arbor, 1987) is highly detailed, but useful. R.O. Crummey, *The Formation of Muscovy, 1304–1613* (London, 1987) is a good, accessible account. For the Ottomans, C. Imber, *The Ottoman Empire* (Basingstoke, 2002) is very clear and helpful.

Governmental developments

On law and justice, the European Science Foundation (henceforth ESF) volume in *The Origins of the Modern State in Europe* series, *Legislation and Justice*, ed. A. Padoa-Schioppa (Oxford, 1997) is a very useful collection of essays, most of them dealing with the situation in different countries in our period. My account is pieced together from essays in this book, together with material on individual countries listed above and one or two foreign works, notably Guenée's superb study of the *bailliage* of Senlis, the Krynen/ Rigaudière collection and an essay on the formation of Toledan lordships in the Rucquoi collection on Spain (all below). Among other sources, F.R.H. Du Boulay, 'Law Enforcement in Medieval Germany', *History*, 63 (1978), 345–55 and A. Musson and W.M. Ormrod, *The Evolution of English Justice: Law, Politics and Society in the Fourteenth Century* (Basingstoke, 1999) were helpful.

P. Contamine, ed., *War and the Competition between States* (Oxford, 2000), for the ESF, makes a patchy but interesting introduction (M.N. Covini's essay on military structures in Italy between the thirteenth and sixteenth centuries is particularly good), while Contamine's single-authored volume, *War in the Middle Ages*, trans. M.C.E. Jones (Oxford, 1984) and J.F. Verbruggen, *The Art of Warfare in Western Europe during the Middle Ages*, trans. S. Willard and S.C.M. Southern (Amsterdam, 1977) are more helpful and comprehensive. M. Keen, ed., *Medieval Warfare* (Oxford, 1999) contains recent essays by N. Housley and C. Rogers. M. Mallett, *Mercenaries and their Masters: Warfare in Renaissance Italy* (London, 1974) and K. Fowler, *Medieval Mercenaries I: The Great Companies* (Oxford 2001) are insightful on fourteenth-century mercenary armies. Details on military structures in other countries have been compiled from material in works cited above.

While R. Bonney, ed., *Economic Systems and State Finance* (Oxford, 1995), for the ESF, contains valuable essays by Ormrod (on Western European monarchies) and Poulsen (Scandinavia), the same editor's companion volume, *The Rise of the Fiscal State in Europe, c.1200–1815* (Oxford, 1999), is much more useful to the general reader, offering a series of very good country-by-country surveys on the fiscal systems of the major western monarchies, together with the Empire, the Papacy, Venice, Russia and (from the fifteenth century) Poland.

The ESF volume bearing on representation – P. Blickle, ed., *Resistance, Representation and Community* (Oxford, 1997) – is not terribly helpful as an overview, though it contains some interesting material (notably on relations between state structures and the lower orders, especially in Scandinavia, on the varying strength of communes and on the relationship between princes and towns in the Low Countries). A clever institutional survey is W.P. Blockmans, 'A Typology of Representative Institutions in Late Medieval Europe', *Journal of Medieval History*, 4 (1978), 189–215. Older works, such as A.R. Myers, *Parliaments and Estates in Europe* (London, 1975) and A. Marongiu, *Medieval Parliaments*, trans. S.J. Woolf (London, 1968), retain much of value, while volumes 35 and 36 of *Anciens Pays et Assemblées d'États: Gouvernés et Gouvernants* (1965–6) contain important essays on representative institutions in individual kingdoms, some of which (e.g. Hungary, Scandinavia) are in English. Once again, I drew on the national and regional studies listed above, though the following additional items were very useful: Harriss, *King, Parliament and Public Finance*; P.S. Lewis, 'The Failure of the French Medieval Estates', *Past and Present*, 23 (Nov. 1962), 3–24; K. Górski, 'The Origins of the Polish Sejm', *Slavonic and East European Review*, 44 (1966), 122–38 and also his article on east European estates in the foreign-language section, below.

The discussion of administration and officers is mainly put together from materials in the previous section, though B. Guenée, *States and Rulers in Later Medieval Europe*, trans. J. Vale (Oxford, 1985), ch. 7, offers a good broad interpretation, while T. Ertman's interesting book, *Birth of the Leviathan. Building States and Regimes in Medieval and Early Modern Europe* (Cambridge, 1997) erects a grand theory of state formation on patterns of office and local government. There are some suggestive general essays in W. Reinhard, ed., *Power Elites and State Building* (Oxford, 1996), for the ESF, which looks at mediators of state power between 1200 and 1800, both formal and informal. Some specific case studies, not mentioned above, are by Mattéoni, Wojciechowski and Menjot in the Rucquoi collection, all listed in the foreign works section below, and also J. Dumolyn, 'Nobles, Patricians and Officers: The Making of a Regional Political Elite in Late Medieval Flanders', *Journal of Social History*, 40 (2006), 431–52.

Among informal structures, courts and households are relatively thinly covered for the fourteenth century, though Malcolm Vale's study of the courts of north-western Europe 1270–1380 has made a big difference: *The Princely Court* (Oxford, 2000). Other particularly useful works for this period include M. van Landingham, *Transforming the State: King, Court and Political Culture in the Realms of Aragon (1213–1387)* (Leiden, 2002); C. Given-Wilson, *The Royal Household and the King's Affinity* (New Haven and London, 1986); G. Nijsten, *In the Shadow of Burgundy: The Court of Guelders in the Late Middle Ages* (Cambridge, 2003). On retaining, there is important material in Dean, *Land and Power*, and see also P.S. Lewis, 'Decayed and Non-Feudalism in

Late Medieval France', *Bulletin of the Institute of Historical Research*, 37 (1964), 157–84, and M. Jones and S.K. Walker, eds., 'Private Indentures for Life Service in Peace and War, 1278–1476', *Camden Miscellany* XXXII, Camden Society, 5th series, 3 (London, 1994), 1–190. The works of Heers, above, provide a good overview of networks, and G. Lind, 'Great Friends and Small Friends: Clientelism and the Power Elite', in Reinhard, ed., *Power Elites*, 123–47, is an interesting general essay, though it underplays the public element in politics. *Pfandschaft* is helpfully discussed in H. Zmora, 'Princely State-Making and the "Crisis of the Aristocracy" in Late Medieval Germany', *Past and Present*, 153 (Nov. 1996), 37–63. As far as I know, there is no general/comparative treatment of royal and princely granting practices in this period – not even in England, home of 'patronage' history – but we could certainly do with one.

For political thinking and writing, many of the sources are the same as those listed under 'Kingdoms, lords and principalities' and 'Ideas and discourses', above, or in the lists for individual countries. Particularly significant and/or additional items include: J. Dunbabin, 'Government', in *Cambridge History of Medieval Political Thought*, ed. Burns, ch. 16; E.A.R. Brown, 'Laity, Laicisation and Philip the Fair of France', in P. Stafford *et al.*, eds., *Law, Laity and Solidarities: Essays in Honour of Susan Reynolds* (Manchester, 2001), 200–17; M. Ryan, 'Bartolus of Sassoferrato and Free Cities', *TRHS*, 6th series, 10 (2000), 65–89; J. Coleman, 'The Science of Politics and Late Medieval Academic Debate', in R. Copeland, ed., *Criticism and Dissent in the Middle Ages* (Cambridge, 1996), ch. 6; and N. Havely's chapter on the vernacular in *NCMH* VI, ch. 12. Among translated texts, Philippe de Mézières' *Songe du Vieil Pélerin*, ed. G.W. Coopland, 2 vols. (Cambridge, 1969), Walter de Milemete's *Tractatus de nobilitatibus…* in C.J. Nederman, *Political Thought in Early Fourteenth-Century England* (Tempe, AZ, 2002) and *Francesc Eiximenis: An Anthology*, trans. R.D. Hughes and ed. D. Guixeras and X. Renedo (London, 2008), are particularly revealing of the public intellectual culture of the fourteenth century.

Political developments

Much of the material for this section is drawn from the sources discussed in the two sections above. For some stimulating general ideas on the relationship between government and political community, however, see Reynolds, *Kingdoms and Communities*; G.L. Harriss, 'Political Society and the Growth of Government in Late Medieval England', *Past and Present*, 138 (Feb. 1993), 28–57; C. Carpenter, *The Wars of the Roses* (Cambridge, 1997), ch. 2; and the works of J.-Ph. Genet, including 'Which State Rises?', *Historical Research*, 65 (1992), 119–33.

Among the various kinds of political conflict witnessed in the fourteenth century, popular revolts receive attention in a cluster of important works, now led by two books by S.K. Cohn: *Lust for Liberty: The Politics of Social Revolt in Medieval Europe, 1200–1425* (Cambridge, MA, 2006), which offers an original and interesting interpretation, and *Popular Protest in Late Medieval Europe* (Manchester, 2004), an annotated collection of translated sources. Valuable studies of individual revolts include Nirenberg, *Communities of Violence*, ch. 2 (for the Pastoureaux, 1320–1); W. TeBrake's excellent treatment of the Flemish revolt of the 1320s, *A Plague of Insurrection* (Philadelphia, 1993); R Cazelles, 'The Jacquerie' and S.K. Cohn, 'Florentine Insurrections, 1342–1385, in Comparative Perspective', in R.H. Hilton and T.H. Aston, eds., *The English Rising of 1381* (Cambridge, 1984), chs. 4 and 6, respectively; Freedman, *Origins of Peasant Servitude in Catalonia*; Wright, *Knights and Peasants*; R. Hilton, *Bond Men Made Free* (London, 1973) (which focuses on the English revolt of 1381, but contains some European comparisons); J. Dumolyn and J. Haemers, 'Patterns of Urban Rebellion in Medieval Flanders', *Journal of Medieval History*, 31 (2005), 369–93; P. Wolff, 'The 1391 Pogrom in Spain: Social Crisis or Not?', *Past and Present*, 50 (Feb. 1971), 4–18. D. Nicholas, *The Later Medieval City, 1300–1500* (Harlow, 1997), ch. 4, contains many brief accounts of later medieval urban revolts.

4 THE FIFTEENTH CENTURY

Much of the material for this chapter comes from items already listed above – especially works on individual territories, listed under Chapter 3, and on political thought, under Chapters 2 and 3. A general source for fifteenth-century European history is, of course, *NCMH* VII, ed. C.T. Allmand (Cambridge, 1998), which contains excellent bibliographies as well as up-to-date essays by leading specialists.

Individual states, regions, countries

Probably the most useful general work on the fifteenth-century Papacy is J.A.F. Thomson, *Popes and Princes, 1417–1517* (London, 1980). For the ecclesiastical politics of the Conciliar era, C.M.D. Crowder, *Unity, Heresy and Reform, 1378–1460* (London, 1977) is probably the most useful broad treatment, together with the chapters by J.-Ph. Genet ('Politics: Theory and Practice') and A.J. Black ('Popes and Councils') in *NCMH* VII, ed. Christopher Allmand (Cambridge, 1998) (chs. 1 and 3); Black's essay in

Burns, *Cambridge History of Medieval Political Thought*, ch. 17.II, is a helpful introduction to the conceptual dimension. Other valuable material on the Conciliar period includes P.H. Stump, 'The Reform of Papal Taxation at the Council of Constance (1414–18)', *Speculum*, 64 (1989), 69–105; P. Partner, *The Papal State under Martin V* (London, 1958); and A. Black, *Council and Commune* (London, 1979). For the relationship between the Papacy and 'national' churches during the course of the century, see P.E. Tillinghast, 'An Aborted Reformation: Germans and the Papacy in the Mid-Fifteenth Century', *Journal of Medieval History*, 2 (1976), 57–79; D. Hay, *The Church in Italy in the Fifteenth Century* (Cambridge, 1977), ch. 3; Lewis, *Later Medieval France*, ch. 4; J.W. Stieber, *Pope Eugenius IV, the Council of Basle and the Secular and Ecclesiastical Authorities in the Empire* (Leiden, 1978); and N. Nowakowska, *Church, State and Dynasty in Renaissance Poland* (Aldershot, 2007), ch. 1. The Papal States are well covered in A. Ryder's essay in *NCMH* VII, ch. 23(b), together with Partner, *Lands of St Peter* and 'The "Budget" of the Roman Church in the Renaissance Period', in E.F. Jacob, ed., *Italian Renaissance Studies* (London, 1960), 256–78. P. Jones, *The Malatesta of Rimini and the Papal State* (Cambridge, 1974) brilliantly conveys the texture of politics in middle Italy.

For the Empire, there is a really excellent essay by T. Scott, 'Germany and the Empire', in *NCMH* VII, ch. 17; his book, *Society and Economy in Germany, 1300–1600* (Basingstoke, 2002), also contains important and refreshing insights on politics. On imperial reform, F. Hartung's elderly but thorough essay (written in 1913) remains extremely helpful, even if we would now tend to see negotiation between emperor and estates where he saw conflict: 'Imperial Reform, 1485–95: Its Course and its Character', in G. Strauss, ed., *Pre-Reformation Germany* (London, 1972), 73–135; K.S. Bader's 1954 essay on the reform movement in the same volume (136–61) is also useful, though German readers will want to look at P. Moraw, *Von offener Verfassung zu gestalteter Verdichtung* (Berlin, 1985) and H. Angermeier, *Die Reichsreform, 1410–1555* (Munich, 1984) for more recent opinions; H. Cohn, 'The Electors and Imperial Rule at the End of the Fifteenth Century', in B. Weiler and S. MacLean, eds., *Representations of Power in Medieval Germany, 800–1500* (Turnhout, 2006), 295–318, takes a fresh approach by looking at visual representations of Electors, Emperors and Empire. Two important treatments of imperial fiscality are the chapter by E. Isenmann in Bonney, ed., *Rise of the Fiscal State* and S. Rowan, 'Imperial Taxes and German Politics in the Fifteenth Century: An Outline', *Central European History*, 13 (1980), 203–17. On the political life of individual regions or principalities, two works stand out: Cohn, *Government of the Rhine*

Palatinate, and H. Zmora's rich and intelligent study of order, justice and power in Franconia, *c.*1450–*c.*1550: *State and Nobility in Early Modern Germany* (Cambridge, 1997). Also useful are S. Rowan, 'Germany: Imperial Knights', in *Dictionary of the Middle Ages*, vol. 5, 497–8; T.F. Sea, 'The Swabian League and Government in the Holy Roman Empire of the Early Sixteenth Century', in J.G. Rowe, ed., *Aspects of Late Medieval Government and Society* (Toronto, 1986), 247–76; T.A. Brady, *Turning Swiss: Cities and Empire, 1450–1550* (Cambridge, 1985), and also his essay 'The Common Man and the Lost Austria in the West', in E.I. Kouri and T. Scott, eds., *Politics and Society in Reformation Europe* (Basingstoke, 1987), ch. 7 (together with R. Sablonier's overview essay on the Swiss Confederation in *NCMH* VII, ch. 25). There are brief portraits of individual fifteenth-century emperors in Du Boulay, *Germany in the Later Middle Ages*; the only full-length treatment in English is G. Benecke, *Maximilian I* (London, 1982).

Coverage of Bohemia in the Hussite period is predictably strong, though even here there is relatively little on political structures. J. Klassen's essay, 'Hus, the Hussites and Bohemia', in *NCMH* VII, ch. 18 is a helpful introduction, which gives good attention to the Bohemian polity (as does his book on *The Nobility and the Making of the Hussite Revolution*), while T.A. Fudge, *The Magnificent Ride: The First Reformation in Hussite Bohemia* (Aldershot, 1998) is a recent general work. H. Kaminsky, *A History of the Hussite Revolution* (Berkeley, 1967) gives a thorough treatment up to 1424, and F.M. Bartos, *The Hussite Revolution, 1424–37*, ed. and trans. J. Klassen (New York, 1986) covers the rest of the revolutionary period. F.H. Heyman, *George of Bohemia: King of Heretics* (Princeton, 1965) is useful on the second half of the century, as is the chapter by Macek in Teich, ed., *Bohemia in History*, and also W. Eberhard, 'The Political System and the Intellectual Traditions of the Bohemian *Ständestaat* from the Thirteenth to the Sixteenth Century', in R.J.W. Evans and T.V. Thomas, eds., *Crown, Church and Estates: Central European Politics in the Sixteenth and Seventeenth Centuries* (London, 1991), 23–47.

Poland-Lithuania is even more thinly covered in English in the fifteenth century than in the fourteenth, but A. Gieysztor's essay in *NCMH* VII, ch. 28 is a decent introduction, and Nowakowska, *Church, State and Dynasty in Renaissance Poland*, ch. 1, gives an excellent overview. For Hungary, the situation is better, thanks to Pál Engel, Martyn Rady and János Bak (Bak's essay, 'Hungary: Crown and Estates', in *NCMH* VII, ch. 27, takes a traditional line, but is clear and helpful). M. Rady, 'Rethinking Jagiełło Hungary (1490–1526)', *Central Europe*, 3 (2005), is an attractive revisionist essay which I have followed in the text. For Scandinavia, the Hansards and the Teutonic

Knights, I used the same sources as for Chapter 3, with the addition of the chapter by T. Riis, 'The States of Scandinavia, *c.*1390–*c.*1536', in *NCMH* VII, ch. 26.

Fifteenth-century France is well treated in several of the items listed for Chapter 3, especially Lewis, *Later Medieval France*, Lewis, *Essays*, and Potter, ed., *France in the Later Middle Ages*. There are useful general essays by M. Vale and B. Chevalier in *NCMH* VII, chs. 19(a) and (b). In Anglophone writing, the most neglected period is the first couple of decades of the century, on which R. Vaughan, *John the Fearless*, 2nd edn (London, 1979) provides a helpful and textured narrative (F. Autrand, *Charles VI* (Paris, 1986) and B. Guenée's two works, *Un meutre, une société: l'assassinat du Duc d'Orléans, 23 novembre 1407* (Paris, 1992) and *L'opinion publique*, below, offer more for French readers). For the war, and for Charles VII's reign, M.G.A. Vale, *Charles VII* (London, 1974) is indispensable, while R.G. Little, *The Parlement of Poitiers: War, Government and Politics in France, 1418–1436* (London, 1984) offers a revealing view of politics and government in the 'royaume de Bourges'. For the rest of the century, P.S. Lewis, ed. *The Recovery of France* (London, 1971) contains much of value (above all, perhaps, Richard's essay on royal enclaves in the duchy of Burgundy), while D. Potter, *A History of France, 1460–1560* (Basingstoke, 1995) is a useful, somewhat institutional, survey. Details of Louis XI's reign are perhaps most easily obtained from the essay by Petit-Dutaillis in the old *CMH*, VIII, ed., C.W. Prévité-Orton and Z.N. Brooke (Cambridge, 1936), ch. 8, while Krynen's Francophone essay on the 'War of the Public Weal', below, is unmatched by anything comparable in English (there is, equally, no sensitive treatment of the 'Praguerie' of 1440 to set alongside Favreau's essay below). The cultivation of French national feeling is explored by C. Beaune, *The Birth of an Ideology*, trans. S.R. Huston and ed. F.L. Cheyette (Berkeley, 1991), while M. Wolfe, *The Fiscal System of Renaissance France* (New Haven, 1972) remains useful for the decline and reconstruction of royal fiscality during the century. An excellent recent essay on structures of clientage is G. Prosser, '"Decayed Feudalism" and "Royal Clienteles: Royal Office and Magnate Service in the Fifteenth Century', in C. Allmand, ed., *War, Government and Power in Late Medieval France* (Liverpool, 2000), 175–89.

The Low Countries are well covered by Blockmans and Prevenier, *Promised Lands*, and in the works of Richard Vaughan: *Valois Burgundy* and *John the Fearless*, and *Philip the Good* (London, 1970) and *Charles the Bold* (London, 1973) (note that these last two works were reprinted in paperback by Alan Sutton in 2002, with valuable prefaces by Graeme Small and Werner Paravicini, respectively). The essays of C.A.J. Armstrong, collected in

England, France and Burgundy in the Fifteenth Century (London, 1983), are still useful. G. Small, 'Centre and Periphery in Late Medieval France: Tournai, 1384–1477', in Allmand, ed., *War, Government and Power in France*, 145–74, throws a revealing light on the pressures to which the western territories of the Burgundian sphere were subject. The relationship between the Burgundian court, the nobility and the cities is a major theme of research in this period. For some insights, see Dumolyn, 'Nobles, Patricians and Officers'; A. Brown, 'Bruges and the Burgundian Theatre State: Charles the Bold and Our Lady of the Snow', *History*, 84 (1999), 573–89; and the essays by A. Janse, M. Damen and P. Stabel in A. Janse and S.J. Gunn, eds., *The Court as a Stage: England and the Low Countries in the Later Middle Ages* (Woodbridge, 2006), chs. 3, 5 and 7.

For England, Harriss, *Shaping the Nation*, can be extended by C. Carpenter, *The Wars of the Roses* (Cambridge, 1997) and S.J. Gunn, *Early Tudor Government, 1485–1558* (Basingstoke, 1995). For Scotland in the later fifteenth century, J. Wormald, *Court, Kirk and Community* (Edinburgh, 1981) and *Lords and Men in Scotland* (Edinburgh, 1985), and R. Tanner, *The Late Medieval Scottish Parliament* (East Linton, 2001) are essential reading. M. Brown's spiky article, 'Scotland Tamed? Kings and Magnates in Late Medieval Scotland: A Review of Recent Work', *Innes Review*, 45 (1994), 120–46, is also rewarding. Grant, *Independence and Nationhood*, covers the earlier part of the century, while J. Wormald, 'Scotland: 1406–1513', *NCMH* VII, ch. 22(b), offers a broad overview. For Wales, see R.R. Davies, *The Revolt of Owain Glyn Dŵr* (Oxford, 1995) and G. Williams, *Renewal and Reformation: Wales, c.1415–1642* (Oxford, 1987). For Ireland, A. Cosgrove's essay in *NCMH* VII, ch. 22(a), and his *Medieval Ireland*, are helpful.

Iberia is better covered in English for the fifteenth century than the fourteenth. The essays by A. Mackay (Castile), M. Del Treppo (Aragon) and A. De Sousa (Portugal) in *NCMH* VII, chs. 24(a–c) are good, up-to-date overviews. John II's long and important reign is perhaps the most thinly treated part of the century, but there is a useful essay by J. Torres Fontes on Ferdinand of Antequera in *Spain in the Fifteenth Century*, ed. R. Highfield (London, 1972), ch. 4, and also N. Round's biography of Luna, *The Greatest Man Uncrowned* (London, 1986). For the middle years of the century, W.D. Phillips, *Enrique IV and the Crisis of Fifteenth-Century Castile* (Cambridge, MA, 1978), is indispensable, while A. Ryder, *Alfonso the Magnanimous* (Oxford, 1990) is helpful for Aragon, and his *The Wreck of Catalonia* (Oxford, 2007) offers a new treatment of the civil war of the 1460s. For Ferdinand and Isabella, J. Edwards, *The Spain of the Catholic Monarchs, 1474–1520* (Oxford,

2000) is now the most useful treatment. It is hard to gain a clear under-standing of Iberian political structures, but, besides items cited under Chapter 3, above, and French and Spanish material listed below, the follow-ing items throw light on the realities of power in the peninsula: J.R.L. Highfield, 'The Catholic Kings and the Titled Nobility of Castile', in Hale *et al.*, eds., *Europe in the Late Middle Ages*, ch. 12; S. Haliczer, *The Comuneros of Castile* (Madison, 1981); I. Del Val Valdivieso, 'The Urban Oligarchy's Affairs in the Government of Castilian Towns in the Late Middle Ages', in M. Boone and P. Stabel, eds., *Shaping Urban Identity in Late Medieval Europe* (Leuven, 2000), 255–67; H. Nader, *The Mendoza Family in the Spanish Renaissance, 1350 to 1550* (New Brunswick, NJ, 1979); A. Mackay, 'The Hispanic-Converso Predicament', *TRHS*, 5th series, 35 (1985), 159–79, 'Popular Movements and Pogroms in Fifteenth-Century Castile', *Past and Present*, 55 (May 1972), 33–67, and also his *Money, Prices and Politics in Fifteenth-Century Castile* (London, 1981); J.H. Edwards, 'Religious Belief and Social Conformity: The "Converso" Problem in Late-Medieval Córdoba', *TRHS*, 5th series, 31 (1981), 115–28.

Among treatments of Italy, Hay and Law, *Italy in the Age of the Renaissance* really comes into its own for the fifteenth century; Najemy, ed., *Italy in the Age of the Renaissance* is also useful, and there are fine essays by M. Mallett and A. Ryder on northern and southern Italy respectively in *NCMH* VII, chs. 23 (a) and (b). J. Kirshner, ed., *The Origins of the State in Italy, 1300–1600* (Chicago, 1995) contains an excellent short introduction on the Italian historiography of state growth by Kirshner, together with an outstanding essay on 'The "Private", the "Public" and the State', by Giorgio Chittolini (34–61) and a very good treatment of Florentine politics and public finance in and before the Medicean era by Anthony Molho (97–135). A fresh approach, from an ideological perspective, but with much to say about the role of pan-peninsular connections in fifteenth-century politics is S. Ferente, 'Guelphs! Factions, Liberty and Sovereignty: Inquiries about the Quattrocento', *History of Political Thought*, 28 (2007), 571–98. Among older works, D.M. Bueno de Mesquita, 'The Place of Despotism in Italian Politics', in Hale *et al.*, eds., *Europe in the Late Middle Ages*, ch. 10, and P.J. Jones, 'Communes and Despots: The City State in Late-Medieval Italy', *TRHS*, 5th series, 15 (1965), 71–96, remain useful and stimulating. Among treatments of individ-ual 'territorial states', W.J. Connell and A. Zorzi, eds., *Florentine Tuscany* (Cambridge, 2000) is a good collection of essays, with a helpful introduction; there is also G. Pinto, '"Honour" and "Profit": Landed Property and Trade in Medieval Siena', in T. Dean and C. Wickham, eds., *City and Countryside in Late Medieval and Renaissance Italy* (London, 1990), 81–91; J. Law, 'The

Venetian Mainland State in the Fifteenth Century', *TRHS*, 6th series, 2 (1992), 153–74; Jones, *Malatesta of Rimini*; and E. Sakellariou, 'Institutional and Social Continuities in the Kingdom of Naples between 1443 and 1528', in D. Abulafia, ed., *The French Descent into Renaissance Italy* (Aldershot, 1995), 327–53 (a certain amount can also be learned about Milan from Chittolini's essay in the same volume: 'Milan in the Face of the Italian Wars (1494–1535)', 391–404). The internal politics of Venice and Florence are very extensively treated in Anglophone writing. On the former, I found R. Finlay, *Politics in Renaissance Venice* (London, 1980) particularly helpful; on the latter, Najemy, *History of Florence*, J.R. Hale, *Florence and the Medici* (London, 1977) and P.C. Clarke, *The Soderini and the Medici. Power and Patronage in Fifteenth-Century Florence* (Oxford, 1991). Abulafia, *French Descent into Renaissance Italy* is a good way in to the crisis of 1494 and its various contexts and consequences, and see also Alison Brown's chapter in Najemy, ed., *Italy in the Age of Renaissance*, ch. 12.

For the Ottomans, the Balkans and Russia, I relied on the same sources as for Chapter 3, above, supplemented by *NCMH* VII, chs. 29–32.

Political culture

Fifteenth-century thought lacks a rounded overview, but the intellectual atmosphere of the period is nicely captured in J. Verger, *Men of Learning in Europe at the End of the Middle Ages*, trans. L. Neal and S. Rendall (Notre Dame, 2000), and see also the same author's essay on schools and universities in *NCMH* VII, ch. 11, together with J.-Ph. Genet's chapter on political theory and practice in the same volume (ch. 1). A.B. Ferguson, *The Articulate Citizen and the English Renaissance* (Durham, NC, 1965), though elderly, puts its finger on a prominent aspect of fifteenth-century public culture, while J.L. Watts, 'The Pressure of the Public on Later Medieval Politics', in L. Clark and C. Carpenter, eds., *The Fifteenth Century* (Woodbridge, 2004), vol. IV, 159–80, is an attempt to think about some of its political implications in an English context. Other work which looks at the political impact of the concepts of the period includes Krynen, *Empire du Roi*, below; J. Dumolyn, 'Justice, Equity and the Common Good: The State Ideology of the Councillors of the Burgundian Dukes', in D.A.J.D. Boulton and J.R. Veenstra, eds., *The Ideology of Burgundy* (Leiden, 2006), 1–20; A. Vanderjagt, *'Qui sa Vertu Anoblist': The Concepts of Noblesse and Chose Publicque in Burgundian Political Thought* (Groningen, 1981); J. Najemy, 'The Dialogue of Power in Florentine Politics', in A. Molho *et al.*, eds., *City States in Classical Antiquity and Medieval Italy* (Stuttgart, 1991), 269–88; J.L. Watts, 'Ideas,

Principles and Politics', in A.J. Pollard, ed., *The Wars of the Roses* (Basingstoke, 1995), ch. 6.

Humanism is well introduced by R. Black in *NCMH* VII, ch. 12. The literature on this subject is massive, but, among works which are helpful for understanding its political impact, see A. Goodman and A. Mackay, *The Impact of Humanism on Western Europe* (London, 1990); R. Porter and M. Teich, eds., *The Renaissance in National Context* (Cambridge, 1992); B. Bradshaw, 'Transalpine Humanism', in J.H. Burns, ed., *Cambridge History of Political Thought, 1450–1700* (Cambridge, 1991), ch. 4; Q. Skinner, *The Foundations of Modern Political Thought*, 2 vols. (Cambridge, 1978), vol. I. J.H. Hankins' controversial essay, 'The "Baron Thesis" after Forty Years and Some Recent Studies of Leonardo Bruni', *Journal of the History of Ideas*, 56 (1995), 309–38, surveys the historiography of Florentine 'civic humanism' from a sceptical perspective. For humanism in central Europe, see H.B. Segel, *Renaissance Culture in Poland: The Rise of Humanism, 1470–1543* (Ithaca, NY, 1989) and M. Tanner, *The Raven King: Matthias Corvinus and the Fate of his Lost Library* (New Haven, CT, 2008).

For conciliarism and its ramifications, see the various works of A.J. Black, listed above in the Papacy and Councils section under 'Individual states, regions, countries', and J. Quillet, 'Community, Counsel and Representation', in Burns, ed., *Cambridge History of Medieval Political Thought*, ch. 17.I. A well-contextualised treatment of Gerson is B.P. McGuire, *Jean Gerson and the Last Medieval Reformation* (Philadelphia, 2005), and, for Christine de Pizan, see S.J. Dudash, 'Christine de Pizan and the "menu peuple"', *Speculum*, 78 (2003), 788–831. For the monarchical trend of the mid-century, J.H. Burns, *Lordship, Kingship and Empire: The Idea of Monarchy, 1400–1525* (Oxford, 1992) is extremely helpful, while A.J. Black, *Monarchy and Community* (Cambridge, 1970) explores one of its origins in the Conciliar debates of the 1430s. The technocratic tendency of later fifteenth-century thinking is reflected in J.H. Hexter, 'Claude de Seyssel and Normal Politics in the Age of Machiavelli', in C.S. Singleton, ed., *Art, Science and History in the Renaissance* (Baltimore, 1967), 389–415, and also in Blanchard's book (in French) on Commynes. The changing understanding of the political is explored in Viroli, *From Politics to Reason of State*, and more specifically in N. Rubinstein, 'The History of the Word "Politicus" in Early-Modern Europe', in A. Pagden, ed., *The Languages of Political Theory in Early-Modern Europe* (Cambridge, 1987), ch. 2.

The material on historiography in the text is mainly taken from works on individual countries: there is no English-language overview of fifteenth-century historical writing, though the topic is broached in Guenée, *States and Rulers*, pp. 58ff (see also his bibliography), while E. Cochrane, *Historians and Historiography in the Italian Renaissance* (Chicago, 1981) gives a broad treatment of Italian historical writing, and G. Small, *George Chastelain and the Shaping of Valois Burgundy* (Woodbridge, 1997) is an important study of the context and impact of one major historian. French readers can learn more from J.-Ph. Genet, ed., *L'histoire et ses nouveaux publics dans l'Europe médiévale (XIIIe–XVe siècles)* (Paris, 1997); see also R. Stein, *Politik en Historiografie* (Leuven, 1994), which looks at fifteenth-century Brabantine historiography and contains a French résumé. A new collection of essays, mainly in French and German, on urban historiography in the later middle ages is H. Brand *et al.*, eds., *Memoria, Communitas, Civitas. Mémoire et conscience urbaines en occident à la fin du moyen âge* (Ostfildern, 2003). For printing, see E. L. Eisenstein, *The Printing Revolution in Early Modern Europe*, 2nd edn (Cambridge, 2005), and (for details) S. Füssel, *Gutenberg and the Impact of Printing*, trans. D. Martin (Aldershot, 2003).

Some indicative ideological texts, available in modern English translation, are Leonardo Bruni, *History of the Florentine People*, ed. J. Hankins and D.J.W. Bradley, 3 vols. (Cambridge, MA, 2001–7); Christine de Pizan, *The Book of the Body Politic*, ed. K.L. Forhan (Cambridge, 1994); Nicholas of Cusa, *The Catholic Concordance*, ed. P.E. Sigmund (Cambridge, 1991); Sir John Fortescue, *On the Laws and Governance of England*, ed. S. Lockwood (Cambridge, 1997); Philippe de Commynes, *Memoirs*, ed. M.C.E. Jones (Harmondsworth, 1972); Claude de Seyssel, *The Monarchy of France*, trans. J.H. Hexter (New Haven, CT, 1981). Cicero, *On Duties*, ed. M.T. Griffin and E.M. Atkins (Cambridge, 1991) is a useful text for later fifteenth-century attitudes and assumptions.

Developments in government

Much of the material for this section comes from the sources listed above, either in the sections on individual states, or in the section on 'Governmental developments' for Chapter 3. The main additional reading is on the fifteenth-century court, for which see the excellent collections edited by R.G. Asch and A.M. Birke, *Princes, Patronage and the Nobility: The Court at the Beginning of the Modern Age* (London, 1991), and D. Starkey, *The English Court* (London, 1987).

The practice of politics

Again, much of the content of this section is derived from sources listed above. Two particular themes on which there is some additional material, however, are the relationships of royal/princely governments with nobles, on the one hand, and with cities, on the other. An excellent wide-ranging treatment of the former set of relationships is H. Zmora, *Monarchy, Aristocracy and the State in Europe, 1300–1800* (London, 2001), chs. 1–4. On the latter theme, C. Tilly and W.P. Blockmans, eds., *Cities and the Rise of States in Europe* (Boulder, 1994) is very useful, especially the overview essays by the two editors. Both themes are well covered, especially from French, Breton and Burgundian examples, in J.R.L. Highfield and R.M. Jeffs, eds., *The Crown and Local Communities in England and France in the Fifteenth Century* (Gloucester, 1981).

SELECT WORKS IN FOREIGN LANGUAGES

Anciens Pays et Assemblées d'États: Gouvernés et Gouvernants, 35 and 36 (1965–6), special issue on later medieval representative institutions.

F. Autrand, *Charles V, le Sage* (Paris, 1995).

J. Blanchard, *Commynes, L'Européen: l'invention du politique* (Paris, 1996).

M.-Th. Caron, *Noblesse et pouvoir royal en France, XIIIe–XVe siècle* (Paris, 1994).

R. Cazelles, 'Jean II le Bon: quel homme? Quel roi?', *Revue Historique*, 251 (1974), 5–26.

'Le parti navarrais jusqu'à la mort d'Étienne Marcel', *Bulletin Philologique et Historique*, 1 (1960), 839–69.

'La réglementation royale de la guerre privée de Saint Louis à Charles V et la précarité des ordonnances', *Revue Historique de Droit Français et Étranger*, 4th series, 38 (1960), 530–48.

La société politique et la crise de royauté sous Philippe de Valois (Paris, 1958).

Société politique, noblesse et couronne sous Jean le Bon et Charles V (Geneva, 1982).

V. Challet, 'Au miroir du Tuchinat: relations sociales et réseaux de solidarité dans les communautés languedociennes à la fin du XIVe siècle', *Cahiers de Recherches Médiévales*, 10 (2003), 71–86.

P. Contamine, 'De la puissance aux privilèges: doléances de la noblesse française envers la monarchie aux XIVe et XVe siècles', in Contamine, ed., *La noblesse au moyen âge, XIe–XVe siècles* (Paris, 1976), 235–57.

A. Coville, *L'ordonnance cabochienne* (Paris, 1891).

A. Demurger, 'Guerre civile et changements du personnel administratif dans le royaume de France de 1400 à 1418: l'exemple des baillis et sénéchaux', *Francia*, 6 (1978), 151–298.

J. Dumolyn, 'Les réseaux politiques locaux en Flandre sous la domination bourguignonne: les exemples de Gand et de Lille', *Revue du Nord*, 88 (2006), 309–29.

J. Favier, *Les finances pontificales à l'époque du Grand Schisme d'Occident, 1378–1409* (Paris, 1966).

R. Favreau, 'La Praguerie en Poitou', *Bibliothèque de l'École des Chartes*, 129 (1971), 277–301.

C. Gauvard, *Crime, état et société en France à la fin du moyen âge*, 2 vols. (Paris, 1991).

J.-Ph. Genet, 'Culture et communication politique dans l'état européen de la fin du moyen âge', in S. Berstein and P. Milza, eds., *Axes et méthodes de l'histoire politique* (Paris, 1998), 273–90.

'Droit et histoire en Angleterre: la préhistoire de la révolution historique', *Annales de Bretagne*, 87 (1980), 319–66.

'L'État moderne: un modèle opératoire', in Genet, ed., *L'État moderne: genèse* (Paris, 1990), 261–81.

La genèse de l'État moderne: culture et société politique en Angleterre (Paris, 2003).

La mutation de l'éducation et de la culture médiévales, 2 vols. (Paris, 1999).

M.-C. Gerbet, *La noblesse dans le royaume de Castille* (Paris, 1979).

K. Górski, 'Les débuts de la représentation de la *communitas nobilium* dans les assemblées d'états de l'Est européen', *Anciens Pays et Assemblées d'États*, 47 (1968), 37–55.

B. Guenée, 'État et espace dans la France du bas moyen âge', *Annales ESC*, 23 (1968), 744–58.

'État et nation en France au moyen âge', *Revue Historique*, 237 (1967), 17–30.

L'opinion publique à la fin du moyen âge, d'après la chronique de Charles VI du religieux de Saint-Denis (Paris, 2002).

Tribunaux et gens de justice dans le bailliage de Senlis à la fin du moyen âge (Paris, 1963).

Institución Miló i Fontanals, *Pere il Cerimoniós i la seva Epoca* (Barcelona, 1989).

A. Jamme, 'Renverser le pape. Droits, complots et conceptions politiques aux origines du Grand Schisme d'Occident', in F. Foronda *et al.*, eds., *Coups d'état à la fin du moyen âge?* (Madrid, 2005), 433–82.

J. Krynen, *L'empire du roi: idées et croyances politiques en France, XIIIe–XVe siècles* (Paris, 1993).

'La rébellion du bien publique (1465)', in M. T. Fögen, ed., *Ordnung und Aufruhr im Mittelalter* (Frankfurt, 1995), 81–97.

and A. Rigaudière, eds., *Droits savants et pratiques françaises du pouvoir (XIe–XVe siècles)* (Bordeaux, 1992); essays by Hilaire (on appeals), Rigaudière (on a fourteenth-century handbook) and Krynen (on quarrels between lawyers and theologians) are particularly useful.

Y. Lacaze, 'Philippe le Bon et l'empire: bilan d'un règne', *Francia*, 9 (1981), 133–75, and 10 (1982), 167–227.

M. A. Ladero Quesada, ed. *En la España medieval V. Estudios en memoria del profesor D. Claudio Sánchez-Albornoz*, 2 vols. (Madrid, 1986); essays by Navarrete ('Fiscalidad regia y poder municipal en Burgos'), 481–99, and Ladero Quesada ('Corona y ciudades en la Castilla del siglo XV'), 551–74.

E. Lalou, 'Les révoltes contre le pouvoir à la fin du XIIIe et au début du XIVe siècle', in *Violence et contestation au moyen âge*, Actes du 114e Congrès National des Sociétés Savantes (Paris, 1990), 159–83.

I. Lazzarini, *L'Italia degli stati territoriali: secoli XIII–XV* (Rome/Bari, 2003).

A. Leguai, *Les ducs de Bourbon pendant la crise monarchique du XVe siècle* (Paris, 1962).

'Les états princiers en France à la fin du moyen âge', *Annali della Fondazione Italiana per la Storia Amministrativa*, 4 (1967), 133–57.

'Les révoltes rurales dans le royaume de France du milieu de XIVe siècle à la fin du XVe siècle', *Le Moyen Âge*, 88 (1982), 49–76.

A. Marchandisse and J.-L. Kupper, eds., *A l'ombre du pouvoir. Les entourages princiers au moyen âge* (Geneva, 2003), especially conclusion and essay by M. Boone on Flanders.

O. Mattéoni, 'Office, pouvoir ducal et société politique dans la Principauté Bourbonnaise à la fin du moyen âge', in Musée Anne de Beaujeu, Moulins, *Le Duché de Bourbon des origines au connétable* (St-Pourçain-sur-Sioule, 2001).

P. Moraw, *Von offener Verfassung zu gestalteter Verdichtung: Das Reich im späten Mittelalter 1250 bis 1490* (Berlin, 1985).

C. Péneau, 'Separare regem a regimine regni: "Coups d'état" et l'expression de la loi dans la Suède de XIVe et XVe siècles', in F. Foronda *et al.*, eds., *Coups d'état à la fin du moyen âge?* (Madrid, 2005), 51–71.

E. Perroy, 'La fiscalité royale en Beaujolais', *Le moyen âge*, 38 (1928), 5–47.

A. Rucquoi, ed., *Realidad e imágenes del poder. España a fines de la edad media* (Valladolid, 1989).

Z. Wojciechowski, *L'État polonais au moyen âge* (Paris, 1949).

P. Wolff, *Automne du moyen âge ou printemps des temps nouveaux?* (Paris, 1986).

INDEX

———————————— • ————————————

Most popes, kings and other leading rulers, together with many thinkers, are listed under
their first names, which are generally Anglicised unless there is no obvious English equivalent.
Rulers who are less well known as individuals are listed under their principal territories, as in
'Bourbon, dukes of'. Place names are Anglicised where possible. The regnal dates for Holy
Roman Emperors cover the time they were kings of the Romans (i.e. rulers of the German
lands) and not simply the period following coronation in Rome. Note that not all kings of the
Romans were crowned Emperors, though they had much the same powers and interests as
those who were.